INSIDE
THE
BROTHERHOOD

By the same author
Crime Inc.

Martin Short

INSIDE
THE
BROTHERHOOD

Further secrets
of the Freemasons

GRAFTON BOOKS
A Division of the Collins Publishing Group

LONDON GLASGOW
TORONTO SYDNEY AUCKLAND

Grafton Books
A Division of the Collins Publishing Group
8 Grafton Street, London WIX 3LA

Published by Grafton Books 1989

British Library Cataloguing in Publication Data

Short, Martin
Inside the brotherhood: further secrets
of the Freemasons.
1. Freemasonry
I. Title

366'.1

ISBN 0-246-13020-2

Photoset by Deltatype Ltd, Ellesmere Port
Printed in Great Britain by
William Collins Sons & Co. Ltd, Glasgow

CONTENTS

ACKNOWLEDGEMENTS

First I thank those many men and women who have supplied me with information on Freemasonry but who have asked me not to name them. Most of the men are Freemasons themselves. In essence this book is their story. I am merely a conduit for the expression of their hopes, fears and anxieties. They are my primary sources. If any more wish to come forward in the future, I promise total confidentiality.

I also thank all those Masons and non-Masons, public figures and private citizens, whom I have been able to name and whose stories I tell chapter by chapter. Further thanks go to hundreds of other folk who have courteously replied to my letters or talked to me on the telephone. A book like this can be written only with the direct assistance of literally thousands of people.

I express my gratitude to those many reporters whose stories in Britain's local and national press have enabled me to assemble a vast mosaic of information about Masonic activities in all parts of the country. In this respect Durrant's Press Cuttings agency has provided an invaluable service. Fellow journalists to whom I owe direct thanks include Mary Beith, Andy Bell, Liam Clarke, Andrew Jennings, Paul Lashmar, Graham McLagan, Alex Marunchak, Mike Unger and the *1 in 12* Publications Collective of Bradford.

Other people who have greatly assisted (from diverse quarters) include Carol Andrews, Anne Archer, Harvey Brown, Blaize Compton, Dr Peter Fenwick, Tony Frewin, Chris Hudson, Vernon Jamieson, Bruce Kitchen, Leonard Knight, Gerard Moate, David Pidcock, Mark Radford, Cyril Ruskin, Francesco Siniscalchi and Deborah Woollard.

Thanks also to my agent Andrew Hewson, to long-suffering editor Janet Law, and to Richard Johnson and the staff of Grafton Books.

In several chapters I have relied heavily on other people's books. I express my particular indebtedness to the work of Walton Hannah

(*Darkness Visible* and *Christian By Degrees*, Augustine Publishing), Sir Kenneth Newman and Albert Laugharne (*The Principles of Policing*, Metropolitan Police), Peter Tompkins (*The Magic of Obelisks*, Harper & Row), John Stalker (*Stalker*, published by Harrap), and Andrew Arden (the *Final Report* of his Inquiry into the London Borough of Hackney).

I acknowledge the Masonic learning I have derived from *AQC* (the Transactions of Quatuor Coronati Lodge) and *Masonic Square* (Ian Allan/Lewis Masonic). I also pay tribute to Commander Michael Higham, Grand Secretary of the United Grand Lodge of England, for his painstaking replies to my detailed written inquiries. I doubt if he will treasure this book but I hope he will accept that I have written it in a spirit of fairness and with integrity. Had we made each other's acquaintance over anything other than Freemasonry we might have got on well.

Finally I thank my wife for her inordinate patience. 'Masonic widows', whose husbands are out on 'Masonics' five nights a week, might sympathize with a wife whose spouse has spent almost every night *in* for the past three years studying the brotherhood's literature. This is not often a source of humour nor is its wisdom easily communicated to someone who is not equally deeply immersed. To help me make up, would any publisher now commission me to write a book on *Great Holiday Hotels of the World*? All research expenses paid for two, of course!

FOREWORD

> It is an obvious truth, that the privileges of Masonry have long been prostituted for unworthy considerations, and hence their good effects have been less conspicuous.

These words were written more than two hundred years ago by William Preston, one of Freemasonry's greatest teachers. In 1772 he could see his beloved brotherhood sinking into a 'general odium, or at least a careless indifference'.[1] Today Freemasonry has an even worse public image than in Preston's day but does it deserve it? In this book I try to weigh all its good effects against the cost of its enduring prostitution.

Inside the Brotherhood has its origins in the pioneering work of Stephen Knight who died in July 1985 aged thirty-three, just eighteen months after the publication of his bestselling, controversial and much-disputed exposé of Freemasonry, *The Brotherhood*.

Had he lived, Stephen would have written his own sequel. Instead I stepped, almost literally, into a dead man's shoes. I tracked down many of his sources and read hundreds of letters sent in response to his book but which he never pursued because of illness. More than three years after his death, fanmail still pours in for him from all over the world.

Like Stephen I have had to feel my way through the fog of obfuscation, ignorance and malice that engulfs Freemasonry. I have had to identify and dismiss the tales of *agents provocateurs*, as well as the paranoid ravings of fantasists and 'nutters'. Twenty years' tramping round the lower depths as an investigative reporter was some training, but no other subject in my experience is so infested with traps laid by deceivers, both unwitting and deliberate. The task was made no easier by the outpourings of Freemasonry's current public relations campaign, which raises far more questions than it answers.

Much of the difficulty stems from a surfeit of published information.

No other 'secret' or closed society has been so voluminously documented by its enemies or its own members. By 1926 one researcher had logged 54,000 books and articles on every aspect of the brotherhood.[2] 'If there is one secret in Masonry, it is that there are no secrets.'[3] Since then hundreds more books have spumed in a tidal wave of Masonic scribbling. Little of this makes sense to the uninitiated, as I discovered while trying to write a book which non-Masons would understand but which Masons would find neither naïve nor shallow.

During three years' research I have had to find and then decipher hundreds of books on Freemasonry. Many were deliberately encoded. Many more seem to have been written on the assumption that the reader is already an expert in Christian theology, Judaism, archaeology, Egyptology, ancient Near Eastern languages and religions, Druidism, anthropology, the Knights Templar, the occult, the Kabbala, Rosicrucianism, Theosophy, witchcraft, devil-worship and Freemasonry itself. Angels would fear to tread anywhere near most of these *arcana*. Don't shoot the reporter. He is doing his best. Or, as Chaucer said (after Hippocrates),

The Life so short, the Craft so long to learn.

The questions raised about Freemasonry by today's 'profane' outsider are much the same as they were 250 years ago when the first 'exposures' were published. Why do as many as half a million men in the British Isles, and another 5 million around the world, spend at least four and as many as 100 nights a year pursuing its mysteries? Why do so many husbands joyfully don an apron at the lodge when they would not be seen dead in one at home? What compels males of almost every social class to dress up in white gloves, chains and jewels, to utter bloodcurdling oaths, and to enact ritual murder and resurrection? What seeming religiosity attracts these fellows inside a Masonic 'Temple' when most of them rarely (if ever) show up in church? Are their ceremonies of God – and if so, which God? Or are they of the devil?

There are no easy answers, for the lodge is all things to all Masons. It can be a place of good fellowship and 'brotherly love' but may be riddled with malice and ill-will. It can be dedicated to charity and benign mutual aid or exploited for career advancement and financial gain. It may help outsiders or work against them. It can be a serious drain on the resources of one Mason but a source of great profit for another. A brother can pursue his 'Craft' selflessly or for crooked and corrupt ends of any kind.

Freemasonry is a club where old men are treated with a respect they no longer receive from the world at large, and where younger men can make friends from all walks of life. Some Masons enjoy performing the historical playlets in the rituals, just as they might enjoy amateur dramatics. Others may discover a religious experience, even a religion in itself. One man may find rational and philosophical wisdom, another may discover the mysteries of the occult.

Other men find the ritual tedious but enjoy the bonhomie of the all-male eating and drinking sessions when the ceremonies are over. They may recapture the camaraderie they used to know in the armed forces. The lodge can be an excuse to get away from 'the wife', but the wife too may get fun out of 'Ladies' Nights' when she meets her husband's colleagues and their wives. Freemasonry claims to support family life, yet some women say it has destroyed their marriages.

Freemasonry can spiritually enrich a lifetime. It can also be a staggeringly boring waste of time, and many men quit as soon as they find a diplomatic excuse.

Freemasonry can be a conservative, reactionary force in politics or a cover for revolution, from left or right.

In general, Masons are no better or worse beings than non-Masons. Their virtue is no greater than anyone else's, though their rituals tell them it is. Likewise their tendency to evil is not as great as some detractors have claimed. Yet because Freemasonry claims above all to be a 'system of morality' it lays itself open to justifiable attack when well-publicized events show members acting corruptly. These reinforce suspicions widely held among non-Masons about incidents they have observed but never fathomed: crimes condoned or unpunished; favours granted or withheld; the inept promoted, the able destroyed; the offending parent awarded custody; the corrupt deal which costs the company, the ratepayer or the taxpayer a fortune. Whenever such events cannot be explained otherwise, they are often blamed on the Masons.

Today, a coalition of forces has caused a crisis of confidence in the premier institution of world Freemasonry, the United Grand Lodge of England (UGLE). Mounting hostility from churches, journalists, politicians and the public has forced it to take the throat-cutting, tongue-tearing and disembowelling oaths out of the mouths of 'hoodwinked' initiates, yet it dare not remove them altogether from the rituals for fear of outraging the Masonic faithful. Even fraternal 'Charity' has caused a most uncharitable and un-brotherly row. In 1986 a bitter dispute over the Royal Masonic Hospital took the 'Unity' out of the UGLE and threatened to cause the biggest schism in English Freemasonry for two hundred years.

Despite these troubles, Grand Lodge claims that applications to join are flowing in. In 1955 it issued more than 20,000 certificates to new Master

Masons, in 1987 just than 14,144, yet every year some forty new lodges are formed and today's recruits are allegedly joining at a younger age than previous generations. This contradicts a general sense that Masonry is losing public respect but, if true, only proves again that all publicity is good publicity. Perhaps the high society gossip, Horace Walpole, was right in 1743 when he wrote that the Freemasons were 'in so low repute' that 'nothing but a persecution could bring them into vogue again'.[4]

In this book I try to show why Freemasons are again in 'so low repute', why they are 'persecuted' and why – in spite of everything – their Craft may yet be in 'vogue'. I try to explain not just their weird rituals and bloodcurdling oaths, their mythical heroes and fabricated history, but also how many combine against the public good. Such activities are never acknowledged by Grand Lodge, which insists that Masons (with the odd exception) are guided by the principles of Brotherly Love, Relief and Truth. Yet an increasing section of the public seems to think Masons are guided by greed and self-interest, and constitute nothing less than England's 'Mafia'.[5]

This might be unjust, but the Mafia tag sticks because lodges rarely punish brethren who break the criminal law of the land. In the past thirty years (until September 1988) Grand Lodge has expelled only seven Masons for criminal acts, even though many more have been convicted of spectacular crimes (see Chapter 18). Social pressures make it difficult for an honest Mason to complain about criminal or immoral conduct by his brothers. Indeed it is he, not the wrongdoers, who faces ostracism and even exclusion from his lodge. He will probably opt for the less courageous route of quietly withdrawing from Freemasonry, embittered at what he sees as the sham, humbug and hypocrisy whereby serious abuses go unpunished (see Chapter 36).

Inside the Brotherhood is a tribute to many thousands of Masons who feel that Freemasonry as a body does not practise what it preaches, and that its principles are now more honoured in the breach than in the observance. Such men have contributed much of the information in this book, often with heart-searching and at great personal risk. If their brethren accept the findings which I now present, they may be able to cleanse the Craft before it falls into greater disunity and even lower repute.

The crisis, within Freemasonry and without, has been bubbling for decades but Stephen Knight brought it to the boil. *The Brotherhood* was sensationally reviewed and achieved huge sales. It also put individual Masons on the defensive. When their families and friends read the book (or heard about it) they demanded answers. Rank-and-file brethren looked to their Grand Lodge leaders for guidance, but for fifty years Freemasons' Hall had maintained a stony silence against outside criticism. Now a new generation of Masonic officers saw that this was no way to deal with the public or the media in the 1980s.

In the Introduction I show how this policy was reversed. On *The Brotherhood* itself, Grand Lodge took two years to deliver its verdict: 'A supposedly serious and impartial study of Freemasonry which is marred by gross error, hearsay, innuendo, supposition and a conspiracy theory.'[6]

Knight's book certainly contained mistakes, but Grand Lodge seems unable to admit that he got anything right. In fact, he touched on so many truths about Freemasonry that he became the focus of much hatred in Masonic circles. For that reason I feel the Introduction must deal with the extraordinary rumours about his premature death, as well as look at the opprobrium heaped on anyone who has criticized or investigated Freemasonry.

The Brotherhood also brought Freemasonry's enemies to the boil, so that Grand Lodge's biggest task today is to convince an increasingly cynical public that the Craft is neither a standing conspiracy nor a secret society, nor even a 'society with secrets',[7] but a harmless private club which benefits the entire community by inculcating lofty moral and spiritual values in its members.

Inside the Brotherhood explores the truth of that proposition. Part One investigates Masonic ritual: its disputed origins, the myth of its 'secrets', its current (cosmetic?) reconstruction, its religious and occult elements and its psycho-sexual symbolism. Freemasonry's rapidly worsening relations with the Protestant churches are also chronicled, as are the Vatican's bizarre twists and turns since the 1970s. Part Two tries to solve the riddle of how many Masons there are in the British Isles, reveals what kind of men they are (by class and occupation), offers some observations on why they join, and lays out one high-ranking Mason's view of the brotherhood's real but covert aims.

Part Three – a book in itself – exposes Freemasonry's role in Britain's police forces, its part in the notorious Woollard and Stalker 'affairs', and its use as a nexus for crooked detectives and leading figures in organized crime. Part Four uncovers the Craft's power and often corrupt influence in many other areas of British life: the law, local government, education, the medical profession, the City of London, business, the armed forces, the Home Civil Service, the Foreign Office, the secret services and even the Houses of Parliament. It shows how Freemasonry breaks people's careers, and sometimes breaks people as well. It reveals hitherto concealed aspects of Italy's P2 imbroglio, and demonstrates clear links between P2 and English Freemasonry which Grand Lodge has always denied.

Part Five looks into the Craft's much-vaunted commitment to charity.

It also probes some scandalous internal financial doings. It charts the 'Apron War' over the future of the Royal Masonic Hospital and tells the tragic story of one Mason who has convinced himself that he was destroyed by a Masonic conspiracy. It also shows the shattering impact which Freemasonry can have on marriage and the family. A final chapter suggests some overdue reforms to deal with this remarkable but far too often corrosive and contaminating fraternity.

I make no apology to the brethren for openly discussing their ritual 'secrets'. These have been 'exposed' many times before. I justify revealing their rows and splits not only on grounds of public interest, but also because Masonic scholars have never been shy about exposing the troubles of other people's secret societies.

Many staunch brethren will find *Inside the Brotherhood* unpalatable. The Freemasonry I portray may bear no resemblance to the cheery gatherings which they attend, year in year out, with no thought of material gain or career advancement, deriving above all 'fun' and 'sheer enjoyment':[8] 'Happy have we met, happy have we been, happy may we part, and happy meet again',[9] as one Masonic saying goes. I am also well aware of a line by one fringe-Mason, the poet W. B. Yeats:

Tread softly, because you tread on my dreams.

I only ask Masons who may be upset by my findings to consider the crushed dreams of my many Masonic witnesses, including this man who (as Chapter 38 reveals) believes he was ruined by the acts of his brother Masons:

In Freemasonry today the three great principles on which our movement rests – Brotherly Love, Relief and Truth – have been replaced by Envy, Hypocrisy and Lies. A Freemason's word of honour, which was once regarded as sacrosanct and something to be relied upon, now has no moral worth whatsoever.

I leave all my readers, Masons and non-Masons, to judge whether this claim is true.

THE BROTHERHOOD AND
ITS AFTERMATH

In today's world the organisation which does not communicate effectively ceases to exist.

Thus spake the public relations firm hired by the United Grand Lodge of England to counter the torrent of hostile publicity provoked by *The Brotherhood*. Yet to the aristocrats who rule the world's premier Masonic institution the very idea of 'communication', let alone PR, was alien and repellent. They could argue, with good reason, that Freemasonry had flourished for more than 250 years largely because of its secrecy, its mystery, its *lack* of communication.

The idea also conflicted with the 'Antient Charges' taught to all Masons: 'to be cautious' so that not even 'the most penetrating stranger' can find out 'what is not proper to be intimated', to 'divert a discourse and manage it prudently for the honour of the worshipful fraternity' – in short, to fulfil the motto on the Grand Lodge crest: '*Aude, vide, tace*' (Hear, see, and be silent).

Most Masons would not have accepted that a PR firm was needed to repair Freemasonry's image, so very few were told. Only the handful of lords, honourables and full-time officials who govern Grand Lodge were allowed to see the confidential report prepared by Profile Public Relations in September 1985, which chided the fraternity for its self-defeating clandestinity:

> For years Masons have considered their very membership to be confidential and have been unsure how far to go when asked about the Craft even by close friends and members of their own family. This despite the fact that the enquirer could probably obtain more information about the Craft than most Masons know by a visit to their local public library.

The report advocated a revolutionary programme of publicity brochures, audio-visual presentations, television interview training sessions and 'media survival kits'. All this followed on from a view expressed by the Duke of Kent in his capacity as Grand Master – titular head of all orthodox Masons in England and Wales – when he addressed the officers of Grand Lodge at their investiture on 25 April 1984.

Brethren, you will be aware that the Craft has recently been the subject of another 'exposure', this time by an author who seems to make it a speciality to attack Freemasonry [a reference to Stephen Knight]. Many of his arguments are on the basis that because some Freemasons may have misused the Craft, the Craft itself is corrupt, and that because we are staunchly private, our privacy is sinister. At the same time, fresh impetus seems to have been given to renewed expositions attempting to show why Freemasonry is incompatible with Christianity and it is even reported that local authorities are debating whether membership of the Craft is compatible with local government.

Our response was, in the traditional manner, to be largely unresponsive. This may have temporarily dampened the delight which the media seem to take in Mason-bashing – and it is remarkable how resolute but courteous refusal to comment dampens debate – but I am beginning to wonder whether our stonewalling attitude is necessarily the best for the interests of the Craft. Giving little or no information may stifle immediate interest, but it does nothing to discourage malicious speculation or to dispel unnecessary suspicion. I believe that we shall need to give the matter close attention before very long.

The Duke said he was 'not advocating a reversal of our traditional attitude and still less an active Public Relations campaign', yet that is what now occurred. Within a year Grand Lodge's spokesmen were popping up on radio or television almost every week, displaying instant media skills. Reporters had packs of glossy brochures thrust on them at Masonic press conferences. Non-Masons, women and children were invited to tour London's Freemasons' Hall. They were even allowed to penetrate the portals of the Grand Temple itself.

The climax of this new policy came on 4 July 1986 when the Duke opened a permanent exhibition at Freemason's Hall, telling the official history of the English Craft. On show were portraits of kings and princes who were Masons, an ornate Masonic throne, a Grand Master's apron, the symbolic tools of Freemasonry, jewels, regalia and silverware,

Masonic theatrical bills and proof of the brotherhood's charitable work. There was also a cavalcade of famous Masons: painters, writers, actors, composers, scientists, soldiers, statesmen and priests. Any visitor would have been impressed by worthies ranging from Hogarth to Kipling, from Scott of the Antarctic to Peter Sellers.

Masonic Square magazine claimed the exhibition was 'probably the most important step taken in the lifetime of Freemasonry today'.[1] Yet it seems to have been devised to beguile non-Masons into believing that at last the Craft was revealing its innermost secrets, so long hidden from the 'Profane' (the term Masons use to describe the rest of us). A gullible outsider might now have thought there was nothing left to hide. *Masonic Square*'s correspondent knew better. He assured the brethren that the 'genuine secrets of Freemasonry' were not on view as they could be found only 'in the hearts and minds of those who are obedient to its precepts'.

'Now you see the secrets, now you don't!', chuckled one visiting Mason in relief as he realized this was a false dawn. All the Craft's offensive artefacts had been kept from the public gaze. There was no tyler's sword to fend off intruders. There was no hoodwink to blindfold initiates, no poniard or dagger to thrust against their breasts, and no rope or cable-tow to loop round their necks, all symbols of the traditional fate awaiting any Mason who betrays the brotherhood. There was no human skull as used in the Knights Templar ritual, and no 'Sacred and Mysterious Name' of God, composed (according to the Royal Arch 'Mystical Lecture') of the names of three pre-Christian deities, some with satanistic overtones.

The same is true of a PR videotape entitled *The Freemasons* which went on public sale in May 1988. To a stately theme from Mozart (himself a Mason) the Grand Lodge flag fluttered in the wind before the viewer was treated to testimonials on the joys of being a Mason. Brothers old and young, public school and working class, white and black, talked of good citizenship, morality, fellowship and charity. Masonry is not a secret society, said one enthusiast, it is just that Masons do not reveal their 'compelling and memorable' rituals because this would spoil the fun for those coming after. One African Mason told how he enjoyed making new friends and exchanging cards, and a Welshman said Masonry gave him the fellowship he used to get from playing rugby and 'being with the boys'. The film showed Masonry's good works for the aged, sick, orphaned and widowed, and its gifts to non-Masonic causes. Yet as it answered none of the nasty things being said about the brotherhood, one newspaper branded it the first of a new genre, the 'Video Nicely'.[2] Another said: 'Freemasonry was once a closed book. These days it is a closed video.'[3]

The day after Grand Lodge gave its video a press launch, another film on Freemasonry was shown, in the Channel Four television series 'Dispatches'. This was an independent production,[4] but it was made with Grand Lodge's co-operation and featured many prominent brethren, clad in aprons and clutching swords. However, because the programme contained a few mildly critical voices, Grand Lodge felt moved to complain. This was an over-reaction, for Masonry's greatest critics were convinced the show was a recruiting film, not a hatchet job.

Masonic chiefs were probably upset because the film undermined their pretence of revealing all while in fact revealing nothing. One wickedly funny sequence showed brethren walking brusquely into Freemasons' Hall, then freezing in front of the camera positioned inside. They looked like astonished rabbits caught in the glare of a car's headlights. The programme's pictures and commentary both stressed that, whenever the brethren marched into a temple to perform their rituals, the doors clanked shut leaving the camera crew outside. 'Profane', non-Masonic viewers might have guessed they were being 'hoodwinked' yet again. In contrast, Masons may have muttered the words of near-contempt which oozes from many a traditional Masonic song.

> The world is in pain, Our secrets to gain,
> And still let them wonder and gaze on;
> They ne'er can divine, The Word or the Sign
> Of a Free and an Accepted Mason

This verse from 'The Entered Apprentice's Song', published in 1723,[5] is still sung at lodges following a Mason's initiation. It remains a challenge to non-Masons to expose the brotherhood's secrets, yet when non-Masons take up the challenge, some brethren complain that this is just like Hitler's attacks on the Jews. Ever since Ludendorff, Hitler and Goebbels lumped Jews and Masons together in one 'rootless cosmopolitan' plot, it has been fashionable to claim that anti-Masonry and anti-Semitism are the same thing. In April 1988, Richard Cobb, former Professor of Modern History at Oxford, complained in *The Times*:

> Why do people go on so about the poor old Masons, about them being in the police and so on? It is a strange twist of history, nearly 50 years after they were proscribed by Vichy's anti-Masonic and anti-Jewish legislation of 1940. Then it was the German Nazis, the French *maurassiens* and the French Catholic hierarchy who were in the habit of referring darkly to a Judaeo-Masonic conspiracy. . . .
> I have always thought of Masons as harmless people who make a

point of looking after their own: good Masonic schools and hospitals. Now, for some reason, it has become fashionable to vilify these victims of fascism and clericalism in the 1930s and 1940s. I hope someone stands up for them. No-one did in France in the summer of 1940.[6]

This liberal defence of Freemasonry appeals to all men of goodwill, for it is indisputable that those enemies of reason – Mussolini, Hitler and the Vichyites – each tried to crush Freemasonry, that Masons died in the concentration camps just for being Masons, and that many of the Jews who died were also Masons. Yet this does not earn Freemasonry a 'free pass' from criticism for all time. It does not mean that one must never mention the *Affaire des Fiches* of the early 1900s, in which Masons discriminated against Catholic non-Masonic officers in the French army and excluded them from high rank. Nor does it mean that current allegations against British Masons – in the police or elsewhere – should not be investigated to see if they contain any truth. So long as they are blandly dismissed by whichever reasonable man happens to be Home Secretary, anti-Masonic fear and loathing will fester and grow.

This does no one any good, least of all the Freemasons. If the price of liberty is eternal vigilance, that vigilance must be applied not by oppressing those who make allegations against Freemasonry, but by investigating the allegations. These may turn out to be the fantasies of unhinged personalities, but that is only to be expected. Secret societies (even 'pretend' secret societies) bring such hatred on themselves. If you form a private club and then imply that its members know the secret of the philosopher's stone or the names of tomorrow's winning horses – or secrets so secret that you cannot say what they are *about*, let alone what they are – you are in effect inviting outsiders to try and smash your door down. If you then turn round and say (as Masons today seem to be saying), 'Ah well, we don't really have any secrets after all', why should anyone believe you? In short, Freemasonry and paranoia were made for each other; they deserve each other. But now it is not just anti-Masons who are paranoid. Many Masons have become paranoid about everyone else, to the point where 'witch-hunt' springs from their lips far more often than Boaz, Jachin or even JAHBULON!

The debate about Freemasonry today is not a cleaned-up version of Hitler's Judaeo-Masonic conspiracy theory, and yet one of Britain's foremost columnists, Bernard Levin of *The Times*, has twice misguidedly blasted his readers along these lines. In April 1988 he was so upset by articles in *The Independent* supporting an anti-Masonic policeman named Brian Woollard, that he reworked an argument he had first expressed four years earlier when attacking Stephen Knight.[7] In both pieces he quoted recent anti-Masonic allegations but in place of the word 'Mason' he inserted the word 'Jew'. He did this to convince readers that anti-Masonry and anti-Semitism are equally irrational, offensive and dangerous – indeed, that they are identical.

> First, throughout the centuries since Freemasonry came into existence, the Masons have been welded inseparably to the Jews as their co-agents in evil; I know of no anti-semitic movement that has not embraced anti-Masonry as well. Second, such campaigns are identical to anti-semitic ones in [that] they cannot be refuted, because if any Jew/Mason can prove beyond doubt that he has never done anything wrong, the accuser can always – and *does* always – retreat to the logically impregnable position of saying, 'Well, you're innocent, but the other Jews/Masons aren't.' Third, when such campaigns rely, as they must, on tittle-tattle, the very repetition of hoary charges gives them a credence, so that the tittle-tattle gradually becomes apparently substantial.

Fourth, says Levin, the 'evil principle' of condemning whole groups of people (be they Jews, Catholics or Masons) for the wrongdoing of one of their number 'has been, throughout the ages, one of the very greatest stains on human history'.

Levin is wide of the mark at every stage of this onslaught. If all anti-Semitic movements in his ken have embraced anti-Masonry, that does not mean all anti-Masonic movements embrace anti-Semitism. In my researches I have spoken to hundreds of 'anti-Masons'. I can think of only two who were also anti-Semitic. Neither figures in this book. Some of the most virulent anti-Masons I have met are Masons themselves. Several others are Jews.

Anti-Masonic 'campaigns' *can* be refuted: by showing that Masonry has nothing to hide, by demonstrating that allegations against it are not supported by evidence, and by proving that the Craft is as pure as the white lambskin of an initiate's apron. Incidentally, in my experience anti-Masons do not tell Masons, 'You're innocent, but the other Masons aren't'; they are more likely to say, 'Why don't you get rid of your bent brothers? If you don't keep your fraternity clean, you must share the blame.'

If it turns out, however, that many allegations are supported by evidence, an anti-Masonic campaign might be justified. Current hostility towards the Craft does not rely on 'tittle-tattle'. It is based on hard evidence, much of it provided by Masons. This is the case with Brian

Woollard, the former policeman whose downfall Levin seems to mock. Throughout this book I have concentrated on evidence, not tittle-tattle. Some sources have asked that I do not name them. They have documentary proof for their claims, but they also believe in Masonic vengeance.

Condemning groups of people on grounds of race or religion is inexcusable be they Jews, Catholics, Muslims, blacks, whites, Arabs or anyone else. It is also wrong to condemn nationalities for the policies of their leaders: Americans because of Vietnam, Russians over Afghanistan, Britons or Argentinians over the Falklands, or Germans for the Third Reich. Yet collective guilt for the Holocaust *is* still being inflicted on Germans, and indeed on all European Christendom, however just or unjust that may be.

Of course, Masonry is not a nation, a race or (so Masons now tell us) a religion. It is an organization of men of many races and religions, who voluntarily swear mutual aid and to guard each other's secrets. Each self-governing Constitution in Masonry such as the Grand Lodge of England has its own strict rules, inquiry systems, punishments and courts of appeal. Because Masonry claims to be a system of morality, any Grand Lodge bears some responsibility for its members' offences, whether they commit them as Masons or as citizens of the wider community. It has the power to expel offenders, but if it rarely exercises this power – however strong the evidence or numerous the 'criminals' – outsiders have every right to condemn the institution as a whole.

This is no 'evil principle', nor is it 'one of the very greatest stains on human history'. It is the application of the time-honoured legal principle that a corporation or association may be held responsible for the actions of its employees or members. This has nothing to do with anti-Semitism. As Mr Victor Epstein told *The Times* in a letter responding to Bernard Levin's 1984 attack on Stephen Knight, 'to be a mason is optional; to be a Jew is not'.[8]

Perhaps Mr Levin's perception of Freemasonry would be different if he knew that, long before the rise of Hitler, the leading Masonic orders in Gemany were themselves anti-Semitic.

For generations Germany's three biggest Grand Lodges (the 'old Prussian') claimed to be Christian orders and refused to accept Jews. They thus ignored Masonry's first Antient Charge, that no man was excluded 'provided he believe in the glorious architect of heaven and earth and practise the sacred duties of morality'. In contrast, six smaller Grand Lodges (known as 'Humanitarian') allowed Jews to join. As soon as Hitler came to power in 1933 the Humanitarians closed down, but even the Prussian Grand Lodges were forced to dissolve in 1935 despite protesting they had nothing to do with Jews. One even tried to transform itself into a 'German Christian Order of Templars' but this did not impress the Nazi Party which shut it down anyway.[9]

It seems likely that most of Germany's 80,000 Masons – Jews and Gentiles – opposed Hitler and National Socialism, but some wished to join the Nazi Party. The party would not admit them unless they quit the Craft. In 1933 Walther Hörstmann of the Selene Lodge in Luneberg wrote his brethren a letter of resignation in which he praised National Socialism. He explained that he had totally renounced the Masonic spirit and said: 'I do not wish to be considered a second-class citizen because I belong to a suspect organization.'[10]

Hörstmann survived World War II to become transport director for the town of Celle. He also had the nerve to rejoin Freemasonry and reached the high rank of Senator in Germany's new supreme Masonic authority, the United Grand Lodges. This seems to have operated no screening system to prevent it becoming a bolt-hole for old Nazis. Hörstmann was forced to resign in the 1960s but only after a concerted campaign by men who had remained loyal to Freemasonry throughout the Nazi era.

These men were even more outraged by the Masonic career of Dr Heinz Rüggeberg who became Grand Master of the United Grand Lodges in 1967. During the war Rüggeberg had been an ardent Nazi and served as a judge in occupied Poland. While making an inspection of a concentration camp he was recognized by two prisoners who had been Masons with him in the Rhineland before 1933. They gave him the Masonic sign of grief and distress but he did not respond. Miraculously, they survived the war and swore the truth of this story under Masonic oath in 1959.

In the 1950s when Brother Rüggeberg was a senior judge, he joined a lodge in Lörrach-Schopfheim which one Swiss Mason described as 'a refuge for many ex-Nazis'. The town was the birthplace of Hermann Strübe, the 'poet laureate of Nazism'. On Strübe's eightieth birthday, the future Grand Master organized a public festival in Strübe's honour. When a young Mason called Bäuerle complained about neo-Nazism in the lodge, Rüggeberg had him banned not only from the Lörrach lodge but even from Bäuerle's own 'mother' lodge.

In 1974 another Nazi became Grand Master of Germany's United Grand Lodges. In 1933 George C. Frommholz had resigned from his lodge to join the Nazi Party. Within a year he was a Truppführer in the SS, as surviving Nazi records prove. Frommholz's later SS career is unclear, but there is no reliable evidence to show he quit the party before Hitler died and the war was lost.

In 1949 Frommholz resurfaced in Freemasonry, but the lodge he joined also contained members of the American Army of Occupation who denounced him as a Nazi and had him expelled. Imagine the surprise of one of these Americans, Major Harvey Brown, when, passing through Berlin in 1962, he learned by chance that Frommholz had become Venerable Master of a Lodge named 'Zum Todtenkopf und Phönix' ('Death's Head and Phoenix'). Brown was appalled. The Death's Head was the symbol of Frommholz's old regiment: the SS or the 'Death's Head Brigade'.

Brown protested against Frommholz's new Masonic career, but this time it was not the SS man who was forced out. In 1974 the United Grand Lodges of Germany demanded Harvey Brown's expulsion from a Berlin Lodge which he had helped found: 'Zum Spiegel der Wahrheit' ('Mirror of Truth'). The stated reason was that Brown also belonged to an 'irregular' Masonic body known as the Universal League of Freemasons, but he knew his real sin was challenging the irresistible Masonic career of a Nazi. Despite expulsion Brown still attends the 'Mirror of Truth' Lodge at least once a year, even though he is now almost ninety and has to fly in from Texas.[11]

While Grand Master of all the Fatherland's Masons, Frommholz was also ultimate Master of eleven English lodges in Germany whose members are mostly officers and civilians in the British Army of the Rhine. The one-time SS Truppführer must have enjoyed 'commanding' so many British soldiers. No doubt he also enjoyed the official visit he paid to the Grand Lodge of Israel. 'Hiding his SS epaulettes under his Masonic apron',[12] he pulled the remarkable stroke of attending a lodge named after Leo Müffelmann, a German Jewish Mason who survived the concentration camps only to die after the war of wounds inflicted by his Nazi torturers.

If at least two Nazis have reached the supreme office in postwar German Freemasonry, the brotherhood may have been infiltrated by many more one-time goose-steppers. How piquant that some of Hitler's followers should have found refuge in a fraternity which he tried to destroy. To point this out might be 'anti-Masonic', but not even Bernard Levin could brand it anything like 'anti-Semitic'.

Today, as for the past 250 years, Freemasonry's most effective adversaries are not anti-Semites but disgruntled Masons, radical pamphleteers and devout Christians. The earliest known exposure was *Masonry Dissected*, published in 1730 by 'Samuel Prichard' who claimed to be a Mason. Fuller revelations came in the 1820s with works by Richard Carlile in England and William Morgan in America. In 1952 the Revd Walton Hannah wrote the definitive exposé of Masonic ritual: *Darkness Visible*.[13]

We know nothing of Prichard's fate but the others suffered troubled lives. Carlile spent nine years in prison for publishing a stream of dissenting and revolutionary books. Morgan (himself probably a Mason) was kidnapped by avenging brethren who were later convicted of the crime and jailed. Morgan was never seen again. He was probably murdered.[14] Hannah was ostracized by the Church of England for attacking Freemasonry and its strength among the bishops. He entered the Roman Catholic Church and died in exile in Canada.

The latest in this courageous line was Stephen Knight.

The Death of Stephen Knight

> Knight's light went out very quickly, and justice was seen to be done, since he caused a lot of distress to many wonderful people, notwithstanding the fact that he has put thousands more on the dole. Hopefully the same thing will happen to you, if as suspected you write aduterated [sic] rubbish.

Stephen Knight's light did go out very quickly. He died in July 1985, just eighteen months after *The Brotherhood* was published. An aggressive brain tumour had destroyed him in one excruciating year. He was only thirty-three.

When I took on the task of writing this sequel to *The Brotherhood*, I asked Freemasons and non-Masons, through personal column advertisements and letters to newspapers, to send me any views or information on the 'Craft'. In March 1987 I received an anonymous reply containing the above remarks. The writer claimed to be a Freemason, 'a member of nearly 20 Lodges'. Nothing in his 900-word diatribe indicated this was a lie. And nothing revealed any of that much-trumpeted Masonic virtue, Brotherly Love.

The Freemason's glee in Stephen's premature death was matched by his offensive tone all round. What Knight had written about the Craft was 'utter cock'.

> I see you are writing a sequel to 'the Brotherhood', and quite honestly I do not blame you, because Stephen Knight made an awfull [sic] lot of money out of writing Bull Shit, so you should be able to do the same. . . . If you write the truth regarding Freemasonry, I feel quite sure you are well aware that you would not sell any books at all. It is only sensational garbage that sells books, and just goes to show how far we have sunk into the cesspit of imorality [sic].

Far more worrying than the letter-writer's implied threats ('Hopefully the same thing will happen to you') was his belief that Stephen had been sentenced to death by Masonic 'justice', a view held by other people who have written to me, including many Masons. Some have told me that in their lodges this is the accepted truth. One Mason claimed the proof lay in Stephen's age when he died. It signified the thirty-three degrees of the Rose Croix, an elect 'Christian' Masonic order which he had attacked in *The Brotherhood*. Thirty-three was also Christ's age when he 'died', a death which Masons re-enact in the Rose Croix's 31st degree.

Another brother confided he had learned of the 'murder' over dinner at his Masonic Temple. He was told Knight had been killed either by human hand (with a slow poison) or by the intervention of the Great Architect of the Universe – better known to non-Masons as Almighty God. Around the 'Festive Board' the first theory was greeted with silence, the second with applause.

These notions are worthless as evidence about Knight's death, but they say something about the Masons who express them. They need to believe in a 'justice' that avenges the Craft with bolts of Masonic lightning. Most Masons are revolted by this idea, but some have told me they fear wayward colleagues might have punished Stephen for his 'crimes'. Such an act would have been 'unmasonic' but the perpetrators might have thought it served Masonic interests: 'Just as Henry II said of Thomas à Becket, "Who will rid me of this turbulent priest?", some fellows might have got it into their heads to polish off young Knight.'

I have lost count of the brethren who have mused over Stephen's death before cautioning me to 'watch out' or 'take care'. One man, whose evidence sent a fellow Mason to jail, told me of his fears during that trial and the extreme precautions he had taken to stay alive. He advised me to do the same.

All this may have been childish nonsense concocted to put me off writing my book. Perhaps the idea was to tease, like those jolly jests about having my 'tongue torn out' and 'throat cut across', being disembowelled like Jack the Ripper's victims or hanged from Blackfriars Bridge like Roberto Calvi in 1982 (see Chapter 33). Joking apart, there is a seeming tradition of Masonic murder inflicted on folk such as Mozart, Morgan and Calvi who are judged to have damaged the Craft. Knight clearly fell into that category.

The belief that he was murdered is also widespread among non-Masons. I first encountered it when I bought a tattered copy of Knight's 1976 book *Jack the Ripper: the Final Solution* in a London street market. The stall-holder spontaneously told me the author had been 'finished off' by Masons outraged by both *Jack the Ripper* and *The Brotherhood*. When I asked how he knew, he just winked. I had said nothing to the man about writing a sequel to *The Brotherhood*. If I had, he would probably have walked to the nearby flower-stall and ordered a wreath in my name.

Of all the 'advice' I have received, the most disturbing came from a doctor who is himself a Mason. 'My friend, don't ever have an operation in this country. Go abroad. Heaven help you if you fall into their hands over here.' Was he a fantasist, a hoaxer or an *agent provocateur*? At the time I felt I had no need to worry because there seemed no doubt that Stephen had died from natural causes, albeit of a most unpleasant kind.

I had heard that his troubles began in 1977 when he had an epileptic fit. He had a brain-scan which was interpreted as revealing a 'cerebral infarct', a small dead area of the brain which might have been caused many years earlier when he had been accidentally hit with a cricket bat. This condition is not necessarily dangerous, but it might have been the cause of the epilepsy. In the next three years Stephen suffered more epileptic attacks until they were striking every six weeks.

He had been told to have another scan but he did not have £100 to pay for it. However, in 1980 he spotted a newspaper advertisement for guinea-pigs to help with a BBC television 'Horizon' programme on epilepsy. He volunteered and was tested on a new brain-scan machine which revealed a cerebral tumour: a malignant cancer which, if untreated, would certainly kill him. 'Horizon' captured this awful moment on film. With Stephen's full accord his fight for survival now became the programme's main theme. He promptly underwent a biopsy (an operation) which removed 70 per cent of the tumour. He was told the rest could be treated with radiation and he had a good chance of full recovery. The epilepsy ceased, Stephen took this to mean the illness was over, and got on with the rest of his life. When I met him in 1981 he was recovering well physically and was in good mental form.

The Brotherhood was published in 1984, but by then epilepsy had returned. Within six months the tumour also recurred but this time it was much more aggressive. With X-ray treatment and chemotherapy it was regressed, but at this point Stephen decided to drop chemotherapy in favour of 'alternative', non-medical therapies. His specialist told him he thought this was unwise but the patient's wish prevailed. A few months later another test showed that the tumour was out of control. Stephen was now walking with difficulty. His speech became hesitant and his ability to muster thoughts was seriously impaired. He tried to live life to the full but in Scotland in July 1985 Stephen died. He is survived by his young daughter.

'Knight's light went out very quickly, and justice was seen to be done.' If my anonymous Masonic correspondent believes this 'justice' was achieved by Act of God, then the Great Architect is a cruel and sadistic master. If, on the other hand, he believes it was perpetrated by earthly avengers, might he be right? Could the tumour, or the epilepsy which was its harbinger, have been caused by human intervention?

The only reason Stephen's epilepsy had ever been attributed to a blow by a cricket bat was because that was the only thing he could think of when asked about bumps on the head. However, his first confirmed epileptic attack occurred in bizarre circumstances: in Australia while he was giving a public lecture on his book *Jack the Ripper: the Final Solution*.

This seems an odd occasion for epilepsy first to manifest itself in someone used to public speaking. Conspiracy theorists might wonder if the attack had been induced by ionizing- or X-rays, or electro-magnetic rays (laser-beams) aimed from the audience at Stephen's head. One Mason wrote to me claiming Stephen could have been implanted with a radioactive source or a slow-release capsule containing a cancer- inducing poison. In recent years some nations' security services are supposed to have used such techniques to destroy their enemies. Remember the minute metal sphere, filled with poison and injected by umbrella-tip into Georgi Markov, a dissident Bulgarian exile who died in London in 1978.[15] Conspiracy theorists might make more of this notion if they were aware of the strength of Freemasonry in Britain's armed forces and security services (see Chapters 31 and 33).

All this sounds far-fetched. Surely no Mason, however mad, would go to such lengths to disable a mere author? Yet Stephen's Jack the Ripper theory was no less extraordinary. I summarize his own account.

In *Jack the Ripper: the Final Solution* I demonstrate how the murders of five prostitutes in the East End of London in 1888 were perpetrated not by one person working alone but by three men operating together for a specific purpose. Four of the five women shared a dangerous secret. They had to be silenced because they had learned first-hand of a secret which the British government had been striving to maintain for nearly four years. Prince Edward, grandson of Queen Victoria and Heir Presumptive to the throne, had illegally married and fathered a child by a Roman Catholic commoner.

The Prince's wife had been bundled off to a lunatic asylum by Sir William Gull, the Queen's Physician, who was a Freemason. He concluded that the only safe way to silence the women was to execute them, as traitors to the nation. They would be mutilated according to the penalties laid out in masonic ritual, hence the ritualised and specifically masonic nature of the injuries inflicted on the Ripper victims.

The importance of the murders was not so much in the tragedies of the five women, but in what followed: an official cover-up of immense proportions that confirmed Freemasonry was the unseen power behind throne and government alike. The man responsible was Sir Charles Warren, Commissioner of the Metropolitan Police and one of the country's most eminent Freemasons. He impeded the investigation, caused endless confusion and delays, and personally destroyed the only clue the Ripper ever left. This was a scrawled chalk message on a wall near the site of the fourth murder. According to a careful copy made by a constable who was at the scene early (then concealed in the Scotland Yard case files for nearly 90 years before I gained access), the message read:

> The Juwes are
> The Men That
> will not
> be blamed
> for nothing

The moment he was told, Warren rushed to the place before the message could be photographed and *washed it away*. He had realised that the writing on the wall was a *masonic* message, telling the world, 'The *Freemasons* are the men that will not be blamed for nothing.'[16]

In quoting Stephen's theory I am not endorsing it, any more than I back the theories of those *ripperologists* who greeted his with derision. True or not, the idea that the Ripper murders were part of a Masonic conspiracy is so offensive to Freemasonry, and has brought it into such worldwide disrepute, that an over-zealous brother might have vowed to inflict something far worse than epilepsy on its originator. It certainly induced apoplexy in many Masons![17] If the first attack did happen in Australia, that would not have surprised one man who wrote to a British MP in 1984 about his own experience in that country: 'The Masonic hold on Australia is far worse than here – no Lodge, no business.'[18]

But steady. Conspiracy theories – like dogs, armies and politicians – are best kept under control. I am assured by medical experts that ionizing rays could only induce brain cancer if the victim was given several 'treatments'. These would also cause marked side-effects, such as violent sickness and complete loss of hair. None of these happened when Stephen first suffered epilepsy. Proton beams and radium treatment could cause brain cancer, but only with the use of a large piece of equipment. They would also cause skin burns, as in radiation sickness. Similarly, electro-magnetic rays would visibly affect the skin and scalp before they afflicted the brain. Stephen suffered no skin burns.

Certainly Stephen could have been injected with a cancer-inducing agent or carcinogen (as in the Markov case), but the cancer would probably have arisen in another part of the body, not the brain. The same applies to a carcinogen secreted in someone's food or drink. Nor, I understand, is it odd that Stephen was first struck with epilepsy when speaking in public. His was 'a classic left-frontal pole tumour'. In other words it occurred in that part of the brain which is greatly pressured during public lectures and speeches. Overall, there seems little room for doubt that Stephen Knight's brain cancer was anything other than natural.[19] The tumour's progress, histology, its response to X-ray and chemotherapy treatment were all normal. However, I have not had the time to pursue a fundamental question: can a natural brain cancer be induced by unnatural means which cause no visible side-effects, cannot be noticed at the time, and are impossible to detect during later tests and examinations?

Murder and vengeance form the centrepiece of some of Freemasonry's most emotive rituals,[20] so it is hardly surprising that one recurring feature of anti-Masonry is the claim that Masons really do go around killing people to protect their secrets and avenge injuries to their reputation. The evidence varies in strength but has rarely been tested in court. However, one recent incident justifies concern. In the American state of Washington, a preacher named Edward Decker runs a mission called 'Free the Masons Ministries'. In a little book, *The Question of Freemasonry*, which has sold 250,000 copies, he argues that the doctrines of Freemasonry set it apart from Christianity: 'I know this will cause offence to many Masons, and for that I am truly sorry. But I would rather that the Mason be offended at me and be restored to true fellowship with Jesus Christ than to remain silent any longer.'

In March 1986 Decker was touring Scotland giving lectures on Masonry and Mormonism when he was struck down by a severe illness. As he explained in a letter to me, he was lucky to recover.

We had gone to Inverness to speak and have our message videotaped for TV distribution. We arrived about midday on 24 March. Our host was a bit nervous for he didn't know two fellows who were waiting for me. They claimed to be from another town and had heard that I would be there and wanted to go to lunch with us. Since our host was busy, we opted for the lunch and went downtown to a pizza shop. During the meal one of them motioned to my empty coke glass and jumped up to bring a refill. He didn't offer to fill anyone else's glass.

Within the hour I was having great stomach pains, diarrhoea and trying to be polite and not vomit. I spent the rest of the day in convulsive reaction and did not think I'd be able to get up long enough to speak. However, I did complete the speaking at the YMCA, and went immediately back to being ill. I was convinced I had food poisoning and tried to 'tough it out'. I spent the next several days eating absolutely nothing and became ill even if I nibbled on a piece of toast.

I left Scotland and flew to Northern Ireland, still very sick and now having tingling in the extremities, convulsive body, leg and arm twitching and terrible intestinal pains. I could barely manage a cup of tea. I was so sick I could barely stand. With the help of my Irish host I got my bags and flew to London. I laid sick all night in an airport hotel and was on a plane to the States at 6 next morning.

My wife picked me up [at Seattle airport] where we immediately called my doctor who reported my symptoms to the Poison Control Center at the University of Washington. They immediately diagnosed acute arsenic poisoning and called a prescription into our pharmacy by the time we went home.

The main thrust was to ease the intestinal pain. I was told much of the digestive capillary system was damaged. After a few weeks I began to calm down and could hold down simple foods. Then my hands and elbows began to boil over. The backs of my hands were a terrible mess and I went to Dr Russell Caldwell, a skin specialist. He said my body was trying to remove the arsenic, and gave me salve to ease the pain and blistering. This ran through the rest of my body and finally came out in my scalp and hair. My hair began to smell like urine. It didn't help win friends, but my dog sure followed me around a lot more. I had to use perfume, for the sake of my family.

Three months after the original poisoning almost every carryover was gone, but in late July I became ill from an infection brought on by my weakened condition and I lay sick through September. Sounds like a fun time!

We did not pursue it back in Inverness. Our friends there would only be in personal jeopardy should they testify. We have since received a number of threats from Masons who so identified themselves. In one case, a man was arrested after a death threat. In the last several large meetings we had to evacuate the buildings because of bomb threats.

It all comes with the territory, and is not something to really panic about. The worst thing that could happen is that I am killed.

However, to be out of this body is to be with my Lord, so I don't react too seriously to the danger. If I did, I'd choose another line of work.

Even if Decker *had* reported the poisoning as soon as it was diagnosed, the Inverness police would have found it difficult to gather forensic evidence or identify the poisoners. On this tour Decker was lecturing against Freemasonry, but he is also known for publicly speaking out against Mormonism. Thus we may never know if the arsenic was administered in the name of the Great Architect to whom Freemasons pray, or in the cause of the Latter Day Saints – unless, of course, the perpetrator is 'restored to true fellowship with Jesus Christ' and confesses all.

There is no evidence to link Decker's poisoning with Stephen Knight's death, but other people's reactions to these tragedies show how Freemasonry's image as a death-dealing conspiracy recurs with each generation. Consumed by mutual fear and loathing, extremist Masons and anti-Masons both seize on such events to claim the brotherhood acts like Murder Incorporated. Why should the interested bystander quarrel with their consensus?

In recent times no individual has had more masonic opprobrium heaped upon him than Stephen Knight. The irritation he caused may be sensed from a semi-official response, *The Craft*, written by John Hamill, Librarian and Curator at Freemasons' Hall in London. Acknowledging *The Brotherhood* as the probable catalyst for recent attacks, he claimed it was 'mediocre': 'a supposedly long-researched, serious and impartial study of Freemasonry but containing many factual errors, a great deal of third-hand rumour and speculation, and gross exaggerations.'

In fact, Stephen made very modest claims. In his prologue he explained *The Brotherhood* was 'a factual report, researched intensively over a relatively short period, but because I was working without the benefit of a secretary or researchers the report does contain gaps'.

Mr Hamill's attack was part of a long campaign. In 1985 he complained to the Church of England newspaper about an article which had described *The Brotherhood* as 'carefully researched'. Listing some of the book's 'errors' he seized on a line saying that Sir Winston Churchill had become a Freemason in 1903. Hamill stated that Churchill resigned from his Lodge within ten years and then had no further contact with Freemasonry.

This is true, but Knight had stated only that Churchill became a Mason in 1903. If not referring to his resignation was an error then Hamill's employer, Grand Lodge, is equally culpable. In its exhibition at Freemasons' Hall, and in the accompanying brochure, Sir Winston is listed among Freemasonry's most famous members. Nothing is said about his resignation.

In 1986 Grand Lodge itself went on the official offensive in its evidence to the Church of England inquiry into Freemasonry and Christianity.[21] Before listing fourteen 'major errors' in *The Brotherhood*, Grand Lodge provided this potted biography:

Stephen Knight was a freelance journalist working mainly for local newspapers in Hampstead. He was a devotee of the Sri Rajneesh Bagwan cult. His first book *Jack the Ripper: the Final Solution* claimed the Ripper murders were a masonic plot to conceal the illicit marriage of the Duke of Clarence and a London prostitute. Central to his thesis was his claim that the main protagonists in his story were all Freemasons, despite his having been informed by Grand Lodge Library Staff that of the names he provided only the Commissioner of the Metropolitan Police [Sir Charles Warren] had been a Freemason.

Grand Lodge committed three errors in this paragraph alone:

1. Knight never worked for local newspapers in Hampstead.

2. He was a follower of Bhagwan Shree Rajneesh for a mere two years, starting in July 1983. This was after he had completed most of his work on *The Brotherhood* and *seven years* after the publication of *Jack the Ripper*. Before his death he was received back into the Church of England.

3. According to Knight, the Duke of Clarence married a chaste shop assistant, not a prostitute.

Knight did claim that six of the main protagonists were Masons: Gull, Warren, Deputy Commissioner Anderson, Prime Minister Lord Salisbury, the Duke of Clarence and the Prince of Wales. According to John Hamill, three of these (Gull, Anderson and Salisbury) were not Masons.[22] If so, Knight's theory is seriously flawed, indeed Hamill considers his entire Ripper book 'a scurrilous piece of sensational journalism masquerading as historical research'.

There are errors in *Jack the Ripper* and *The Brotherhood* but who can first cast a stone? All writers make mistakes, including those with brain cancer, but because Freemasonry is in many respects a 'secret society' and has always concealed its inner workings, any book about it is bound to contain errors. In contrast, Grand Lodge has little excuse for its slipshod summary of Stephen's life which, unlike the Craft, was an 'open book'.

One last point about my anonymous death-threat Mason. Looking through hundreds of letters which Stephen received after *The Brotherhood*, I came across one written by the same man. This too is anonymous but the type, lay-out, spelling mistakes and style of argument match the letter which I received. The writer lives in the Midlands, and belongs to many Masonic orders, including the Rose Croix. He is a businessman, possibly a contractor or a salesman, and he likes his golf. In his letter to Stephen he was just as splenetic as he was to me:

> You have been responsible for the persecution of many of our members, who have lost their jobs because of your book. This has caused great hardship to their wives and children, and writers like you ought to know better. I do not know if [sic] anyone who has committed suicide yet, but if they do it will be you and you alone who has murdered these unfortunate people . . .
>
> Sorry no name, but this could effect [sic] promotion in the order and as you may have gathered I am a keen student.

PART ONE

Ritual or Religion?

one

RITUAL POISON

Freemasons are not different kinds of people. They have simply found a different pastime.

Grand Secretary Michael Higham to the press, 5 May 1988

Let us imagine for one moment that somebody, somewhere, is creating a movement, identical to that of the Freemasons, inclusive of all the beliefs, traditions and rituals. Let us put it to the test by presenting it for study to a panel of educated men – theologians, scientists, philosophers. What would be their reactions? They would laugh and ridicule the project, just as they have done with recent attempts at creating new religions. But somehow because the Freemasons boast of a long tradition, that tradition seems to make it right and credible.

An anonymous Freemason in *Whichever Way*, the story of why he left the brotherhood, *c.* 1980

There are two main traditions in Freemasonry: one genuine and one false. More than 250 years ago the genuine tradition – a claim to be descended from the stonemasons of medieval times – was perverted by the false one of fanciful rituals, newly-coined legends and bloodcurdling oaths. In succeeding centuries the false tradition itself became hallowed by custom, so that today few Freemasons can sort fact from fantasy, truth from fiction, tradition from travesty.

But what *is* Freemasonry?

Freemasonry is a peculiar system of Morality, veiled in Allegory, and illustrated by Symbols.

This brain-numbing definition[1] is likely to be the first shot fired by a

Freemason at any curious outsider. It will almost certainly 'divert the discourse' (as laid down in the Craft's Antient Charges). Better still, it might end conversation altogether.

A cynic would agree that Freemasonry is 'peculiar', in the word's usual present-day meaning – odd, weird, perverted – but a Mason would point out that 'peculiar' is used in an archaic sense: special, particular, private. The 'allegory' is to be found in stories recounting the fraternity's presumed origins, but do they contain any historical truth?

The fundamental allegory lies in Freemasonry's claim to be descended from the fraternal groupings of 'free-stone' masons of the Middle Ages. Today's brethren wax poetic over these craftsmen because they built the Gothic cathedrals that rank among Europe's greatest architectural glories. Consider 'the supreme excellence of their workmanship', says a clergyman who is now one of England's highest-ranking Freemasons. 'They were not working for men, they were working for God, and only the best was good enough.'[2] In recent years England's Masonic Grand Charity has given grants to many cathedral restoration funds, 'to mark Freemasonry's links with its operative forebears'.[3] Some brethren become so misty-eyed over these buildings that they seem to regard them as monuments not so much to God and his only begotten son Jesus Christ as to Freemasonry itself.[4]

In fact, the Gothic cathedrals were mostly built between A.D. 1100 and 1400, 300 years before some gentlemen calling themselves the 'Antient Fraternity of Free and Accepted Masons' formed the Grand Lodge of England in 1717. There was a kind of truth in these Free Masons' claim to be the heirs of the cathedral-builders, but during the 1600s and early 1700s that truth had withered as almost everything they had inherited from their 'forebears' was taken apart and reconstructed. One such thing was the 'Lodge'.

The stonemasons of medieval times probably spent their entire working lives on a few big sites: a cathedral, some churches and maybe a secular building such as a castle. On each site some kind of hut or 'lodge' would be erected where masons could shelter in bad weather, store tools, organize work rotas and even sleep or 'lodge'. Cathedrals might take a hundred years to build, so the lodges took on a near-permanent form. Through them the stonemasons seem to have developed a system of mutual aid, and at times exercised great economic power. After the Black Death of 1348–9, which killed as many as 1.5 million people in Britain, there was such a shortage of stonemasons that the survivors were able to bargain high wages through annual assemblies. By 1425 the assemblies had become so powerful that they

were outlawed by Parliament and anyone attending them risked imprisonment.

Through their 'lodges' the stonemasons protected themselves against a
harsh and unforgiving world. They safeguarded their own jobs, and
maintained work standards, through a controlled rank structure of three
degrees: apprentice, fellow craft and master mason. They also laid down
rules governing relations between masons and with the world at large.
Like the city guilds of the day, they seem to have given charity to
members on hard times.

If this is how stonemasons ran their lodges, the modern equivalent is
not the private society of Freemasonry and *its* lodges but the trade unions
with their branches and chapels, or 'locals' in America, at or near the
workplace.

If the 'lodge' is little more than a word which modern Masons have
borrowed from the old stonemasons, there are other features common to
both groups of men, notably a passion for secrecy. Within their lodges
the stonemasons probably 'worked' rituals in which initiates swore not to
reveal the skills and trade secrets of their craft. To block infiltration by
unskilled outsiders they may also have devised a secret code of
passwords, handshakes and other signs of recognition. If so, it was these
elements which ensured that the lodges, in quite another form, would far
outlast the men who had set them up.

The stonemasons were economically vulnerable because they did most
of their work for one supremely rich patron, the Christian Church. At
that time there was only one Church in the West, headed by the Pope of
Rome. If any secular prince were to puff up his chest and break with
Rome, the stonemasons would be among the first to suffer. Building
cathedrals may have been the supreme skill of that or any other age, but
most of the builders would be redundant overnight if the Church no
longer had the assets or income to pay for new cathedrals, abbeys or
parish churches.

In 1534 the unthinkable happened. Henry VIII broke with Rome,
denied the authority of the Pope, became an Anglican and threw England
into the Reformation. In a few years he seized the Church's wealth,
dissolved and dispossessed the monasteries and brought ecclesiastical
building to a halt. Suddenly the number of stonemasons far exceeded
demand. Just like twentieth-century trade unionists in dying or changing
industries (miners, printers, seamen), they lost their bargaining power.
Their lodges decayed and their assets, if any, were looted by the State. In
1545 Henry desperately needed money 'for the maintenance of the
present wars'. This gave him an excuse to confiscate the assets of all
'fraternities, brotherhoods and guilds'.[5] These were Catholic insti-

tutions, so their assets were considered fair game. By 1600 most fraternities had disappeared along with their records, which is why the true history of the stonemasons' lodges is anybody's guess.

A few lodges survived, but only by throwing membership open to men who had never worked stone in their lives, such as merchants, landed gentlemen and aristocrats. Soon these 'speculative' masons, as they came to be called, far outnumbered the 'operative' or working masons who had let them join. The earliest surviving complete membership roll of any lodge is for Aberdeen in 1670.[6] Of forty-nine master and fellow craft members only ten were working masons. Another fifteen were artisans: carpenters, slaters, glaziers, wigmakers, a smith, an armourer, a hookmaker and a cardmaker. All the rest would now be called middle class: nine merchants, three clergymen, three gentlemen, two surgeons, a collector of customs, a lawyer, a professor of mathematics and four noblemen, of whom three were earls. Quite a slate for a town of only 8,000 souls!

Such folk were not only attracted by the quaint customs of this workmen's self-defence organization; they also had the money to revive it. Within decades a Trojan Horse filled with landowners and merchants had appropriated an originally Catholic labour union and turned it into a predominantly Protestant gentlemen's club. The name 'lodge' was retained, but rather as the façade of an old building is preserved to maintain a historic appearance. Behind it the old structure has been demolished and a new one is rising in its place.

The first recorded initiation of a 'speculative' Freemason in an English lodge was in 1646 when Elias Ashmole, the antiquary, astrologer and alchemist, joined a lodge in Warrington which had not a single working mason in it.[7] By the late seventeenth century, so many gentlemen – including a lot more antiquaries, astrologers and alchemists – were intrigued by the brotherhood and its developing rituals that new lodges were being created to satisfy the craze to join. By this time lodges were also claiming to be schools of moral instruction, which is where·the image of the stonemason painstakingly learning his craft came in handy. Each working tool – the square, compasses, level, plumbline, gauge, gavel, chisel – became the symbol of some process in man's moral and spiritual perfection. After his initiation, the 'Entered Apprentice' is told he is like a rough stone or Ashlar, 'in his infant or primitive state'. He is then meticulously hewn into a Perfect Ashlar, 'a fit member of civilized society', presumably through the arts of Freemasonry.[8]

However, this high moralizing fell on some deaf ears. Many eighteenth-century Masons used their lodges only as social clubs, indulging in 'the dissipations of luxury and intemperance'.[9] If this had been Freemasonry's only charm it would have soon died out, like many other drink-sodden fraternities of the day. There had to be another incentive to attend. The Craft's claim to be a 'moral' society gave it some appeal, although one cannot believe that eighteenth-century man was keen to have morality stuffed down his throat at the lodge mid-week when on Sundays he endured fire and brimstone in church. He may have been more attracted by a realization that this honourable façade could provide cover for less honourable activities: not moral but malign, not social but self-serving. In Aberdeen, for instance, the lodge's social mix would have made it one of the best places to learn what was going on in local business, in politics and in almost every Aberdonian's private life. Although lodges might claim to inculcate Masonry's 'peculiar system of morality', they could easily become cells of intrigue, self-advancement and corruption.

Such potential exists in lodges to this day. Indeed, the rituals at each degree legitimize a certain malevolence towards outsiders. Masons often argue that these elements merely echo the medieval ceremonies on which Freemasonry is based. Yet, as less strident Masonic historians admit, the rituals worked today were not devised until the early 1700s.[10] For instance, the stonemasons never uttered the sadistic oaths or 'obligations' traditionally sworn by candidates as they enter modern Masonry's three 'Craft' degrees. All the evidence indicates that these were invented by Freemasonry's eighteenth-century masters who found the genuine oaths too tame for their purposes.

In Masonry's first degree the initiate, candidate or would-be Apprentice, swears he will never reveal any of the Craft's secrets or mysteries. He further promises not to write down those secrets in any form or to 'cause or suffer it to be done by others if in my power to prevent it, on anything movable or immovable, under the canopy of Heaven . . .'

Throughout the formal history of English Freemasonry, until 1986, the blindfolded, bare-breasted and noosed candidate has had to place his hand on the open Bible and 'solemnly swear' to observe these vows:

under no less a penalty . . . than that of having my throat cut across, my tongue torn out by the root, and buried in the sand of the sea at low water mark, or a cable's length from the shore, where the tide regularly ebbs and flows twice in twenty-four hours, or the more effective punishment of being branded as a wilfully perjured individual, void of all moral worth, and totally unfit to be received into this worshipful Lodge, or any other warranted Lodge or society of men, who prize honour and virtue above the external advantages

of rank and fortune. So help me God and keep me steadfast in this
my Great and Solemn Obligation of an Entered Apprentice Mason.

Similarly, in the second degree, that of Fellow Craft Mason, for over
250 years the candidate has faced the penalty of 'having my left breast laid
open, my heart torn therefrom, and given to the ravenous birds of the air,
or devouring beasts of the field as a prey'.

Likewise, the would-be Master Mason who dares to divulge the secrets
of the third degree has risked 'being severed in two, my bowels burnt to
ashes, and those ashes scattered over the face of the earth and wafted by
the four winds of heaven, that no trace of remembrance of so vile a wretch
may longer be found among men, particularly Master Masons.'

In 1964 Grand Lodge allowed candidates to swear all these oaths only
'ever bearing in mind the traditional penalty' rather than 'under no less a
penalty'. This was to make it clear that none of these grotesque ways of
killing would really be inflicted, but many lodges stubbornly kept to the
original version, as if the penalties were real after all.[11] When the Italian
banker Freemason Roberto Calvi was found hanging from London's
Blackfriars Bridge in 1982, Masons and non-Masons alike wondered if
death 'where the tide ebbs and flows' might still be the punishment
inflicted on Masonic traitors (see Chapter 33). Alternatively, if the
penalties are just symbolic, what do they really stand for? A fate worth
avoiding, it seems, for most Masons keep their vow of silence even when
they drop out of the brotherhood. Some even stick to it when publicly
condemning Freemasonry on religious grounds.

One Anglican clergyman, Andy Arbuthnot, recently published a
pamphlet advising Christians they should not be Masons.[12] A footnote
reads: 'The author was at one time a Freemason and therefore took the
oath of secrecy. No information is however disclosed above, which is not
freely available to the public.' This implies that even Revd Arbuthnot still
feels bound by his Masonic 'Obligations'. Grand Lodge justifies the
anomaly that these bind a Mason to keep secrets even before he knows
what they are, by saying he is in a similar position to someone who signs
the Official Secrets Act.[13]

The truth is that when a man leaves Freemasonry (by resigning, by not
paying his dues or by being excluded or expelled for some other offence)
he is not released from his oaths; there is no mechanism for unswearing
them. When a man says, 'I used to be a Mason but I'm not any more', he is
deluding himself. The oaths allow no going back. He might go to a
Commissioner for Oaths and try to unswear them, but I know of no one
who has ever done so, nor would his brothers be likely to recognize the
move.

In 1986, after more than twenty years' internal debate and public ridicule, Grand Lodge resolved that all these penalties should be removed from the oaths and inserted in another part of the ritual where they would be spoken only by the lodge Master. Some critics of Freemasonry feel it matters not who utters such grotesque threats but that they are uttered at all. The candidate no longer swears them but instead the Master addresses them directly to him as the new boy under instruction in each degree. He will hear them many more times during his Masonic career so he knows he will be branded 'a wilfully perjured individual, void of all moral worth', if he ever reveals Freemasonry's secrets. When he becomes Master of a lodge, as many thousands do, it will be his turn to intimidate some novice with the same threats.

England's ever-affable Grand Secretary, Commander Higham RN, brushes the oaths aside as nothing more than the nonsense rhymes of the school playground: 'cross my heart and hope to die, cut my throat if I tell a lie.'[14] To him, initiation is 'the first phase of humiliation, to cut the candidate down to size, like a naval recruit being sent away to find red oil for the port lamp'.[15] The sceptic might wonder whether a blindfold over the eyes, a noose round the neck and a dagger to the heart can be so lightly dismissed. And if the oaths and rituals *are* only childlike traditions – mere words in a 'fun' one-act play[16] – is everything else void of meaning, including the brotherhood's moral precepts? Is the entire affair a charade?

Besides, what is 'traditional' about the penalties? They were not inherited from the cathedral-builders, for sure. Anyone who joins Freemasonry to honour those men should hesitate before mouthing any part of the oaths, for they have no historical validity. We know this because, miraculously, some stonemasons' rulebooks have survived. Masonic historians call these documents the 'Gothic Constitutions', although only the two oldest were written while Gothic cathedrals were still being built. They show that stonemasons' oaths were straight-forward and the penalties plain: anyone who disobeyed the rules was simply thrown out of the lodge. The earliest constitution talks of imprisoning masons who disobey the masons' assembly, but such assemblies never had civil authority so they could never legally have jailed anyone. In any event, the traditional rituals were pretty dull stuff: nothing worth building a fraternity round, and certainly nothing about throats being cut, bodies cut in two, bowels burnt to ashes, or hearts ripped out and fed to ravenous birds.

The most significant constitution seems to be the 'Grand Lodge Manuscript' (so called only because it now belongs to the Grand Lodge of England). Written in 1583, it lists many rules or 'charges'. For instance, the mason's oath had to be sworn on the Bible but it was perfunctory and contains no penalty: 'These charges that we have no rehearsed unto yu all and all others that belong to Masons, ye shall keepe, so healpe you God and your hallydom [holy judgment], and by this booke in yor hande unto yr power. Amen, so be it.'

Another manuscript, written in 1686, 'Buchanan',[17] is hotter on words but still threatens no penalty: 'These charges that you have received you shall well and truly keepe not disclosing the secrecy of our Lodge, to man, woman nor child; sticke nor stone; thing moveable, nor immoveable, soe God Helpe, and his holy Doome, Amen.'

In short, the throat-cutting, tongue-tearing and bowel-burning bunkum recited by every lodge Master today is a sadistic farrago concocted by the scribes of Grand Lodge Masonry in the early 1700s. It was never uttered by the men who built the cathedrals. On the contrary, the Masonic oaths are a slander on the craftsmen of medieval England perpetrated hundreds of years later.

Praiseworthy elements in Freemasonry, however, do stem from precepts laid down in the 'Gothic Constitutions'. Today these live on in the Antient Charges read to each Master before he is installed (appointed) 'in the chair'. They are also printed in the Book of Constitutions handed to each Mason on initiation.[18]

When a man applies to join any lodge under the United Grand Lodge of England he must declare on a registration form 'I do not expect or anticipate any pecuniary benefit as a consequence of my being a member of the Craft.'[19] In Freemasonry's first degree the candidate must say that he offers himself for initiation 'uninfluenced by mercenary or other unworthy motive'. Masons cite these commitments to rebut claims that they are 'only in it for what they can get'. Whether they take such protestations any more seriously than the penalties is explored later in this book, but one Mason who certainly ignored them was one of the most significant figures in the fraternity's history.

Dr James Anderson was born in Aberdeen in about 1680. After becoming a minister in the Church of Scotland, he made his way to London. In 1721 he started rewriting Freemasonry's Constitutions 'in a new and better method'. He claimed he was asked to do this by the new Grand Lodge of England (founded in 1717 when four lodges came together under one authority), but he may have suggested it himself. Leading Masonic historians have admitted that he 'was commercially as well as masonically motivated'.[20] He retained personal copyright in the Constitutions and later talked Grand Lodge into discouraging Masons from buying what he claimed was a 'pyrated' edition.

Anderson not only exploited Masonry for the money; he wrote into his Constitutions the principle of Masonic preferment which has inspired anti-Masonic paranoia and conspiracy theories ever since. If a 'strange brother' (meaning, a stranger who is a Mason) 'is in want you must relieve him if you can, or else direct him how he may be relieved. You must employ him some days, or else recommend him to be employed.' Anderson continues: 'you are not charged to do beyond your ability; only to prefer a poor brother that is a good man before any other poor people in the same circumstances.'

Anderson based his efforts on the 'Gothic Constitutions' in Grand Lodge's possession at the time. These nowhere told stonemasons to favour a brother mason over anyone else, but they were asked to give work to 'strange fellows' (masons from elsewhere). Anderson took this principle – honourable enough when confined to one medieval trade – and broadened it into a standing order to all 'speculative' Freemasons to favour each other over non-Masons. Thus did the Craft's best-known scriptwriter twist the rules of the cathedral builders into a binding code of preferment, partiality and mutual aid.

Anderson goes on to state that a Mason must cultivate 'brotherly love, the foundation and copestone, the cement and glory of this antient fraternity, avoiding all wrangling and quarrelling, all slander and backbiting, nor permitting others to slander any honest brother but defending his character and doing him all good offices, as far as is consistent with your honour and safety, and no farther.'

This appears to mean that while a Mason's duty to a brother is limited so as not to damage his own interests, it is boundless in every other respect. Also, in obliging Masons to defend a brother's interests, Anderson puts no limits on the damage or slander they may inflict on non-Masons.

In his first 'Antient Charge' – 'Concerning GOD and RELIGION' – he portrays Freemasonry as the 'union between good men and true, and the happy means of conciliating friendship amongst those who must otherwise have remained at a perpetual distance'. A Mason is one who 'practises the sacred duties of morality'. Masons unite 'with the virtuous of every persuasion in the firm and pleasing bond of fraternal love'. They are 'taught to view the errors of mankind with compassion and to strive, by the purity of their own conduct, to demonstrate the superior excellence of the faith they may confess'.

The young Anderson had learned Masonry from his father, a member of the Aberdeen Lodge whose 1670 roll has miraculously survived. This lists James Anderson (the Elder) as a 'Glazier and Mason and Clerk to our Honourable Lodge'. As clerk, Anderson wrote out the lodge's Constitution, which has also survived. This lays down the fearful penalty to be inflicted on any brother who refuses to pay a fine imposed by the lodge. If he dares go to a civil judge for justice, the Lodge Master and the other brethren

> will go to that judge he complains to and will make him a perjured man, and never any more hereafter to be received in our Lodge, nor have any part nor portion in our charity nor mortified money, nor none of his offspring although they may be needful, nor get any more employment with any of our number, nor from any other far nor near, in so far as we can hinder.

The brethren could only have made their colleague 'a perjured man' by all standing up in court to swear that *he* was a liar. The other punishments awaiting their victim would have been enough to put him out of work for life, especially in a small closed community like seventeenth-century Aberdeen. Surrounded by this wall of hostility, he and his family would have to leave the town for ever – or starve.

The Aberdeen Constitution reveals a society motivated less by 'sacred duties of morality' than by retribution. Here was no 'union between good men and true' but a gang ready to destroy any member who sought a fair hearing elsewhere. These folk are driven not by 'purity of conduct', 'compassion' for the 'errors of mankind' or the 'pleasing bond of fraternal love'; for them relief and truth are restricted to a very small circle, beyond which it is acceptable to tell co-ordinated lies to achieve the economic ruin of others.

When James Anderson Jnr wrote his English Constitutions he shrewdly did not express the lust for vengeance manifested by his brethren in Aberdeen. Yet, simultaneously, in Freemasonry's rituals, vengeance was sanctified with the insertion of a new legend which would transform the Brotherhood's entire outlook on the world. This was the Bible story of Solomon's Temple, travestied by the most emotive of Masonic fairytales: the 'murder' of the Temple 'architect', Hiram Abiff.

According to the Book of Kings, Solomon had already built his temple in Jerusalem when he sent for a man called Hiram to come from the city of Tyre to complete the decorations. He was neither a mason nor an architect but a worker in brass. The Book of Chronicles mentions such a man, but says he arrived in Jerusalem *before* the temple was built. He too was an ornamental metal-worker, not an architect or mason. One verse says he was skilled 'in stone' but the context shows his skill lay in decoration, not construction.

How did Hiram turn up in Masonic ritual in about the 1720s when he had never before rated a mention, even in the quasi-Biblical legends beloved by Medieval masons? Their 'Gothic Constitutions' had contained grandiose tales of the Creation, the Flood, Babylon, Nineveh, the Hebrews, Ancient Egypt and Greece. They spoke of England in the Dark Ages, of St Alban and the Saxon King Athelstan. The purpose of all these stories was to inflate the role played by builders throughout the ages. Everybody who had ever been *anybody* must have been a mason.

Even so, these Constitutions gave only brief accounts of the building of Solomon's Temple and made no reference to Hiram the metal-worker. Some refer to Hiram, King of Tyre, a different man who is also revered in Freemasonry for helping Solomon build the Temple by supplying cedarwood from Lebanon. This raises another issue. The Bible says the Temple was built mainly of wood and was a modest erection: just thirty feet wide and ninety feet long, no bigger than a modern-day synagogue or church hall. If it needed an architect he would not have been a stonemason. Yet when eighteenth-century Freemasons got hold of the story, they inflated Solomon's Temple into a gigantic stone palace, 'resembling a 10-acre college campus'.[21] They gave Hiram equally imaginative proportions. First he acquires a surname: 'Abiff'. Then Anderson hails him as 'the most accomplished Mason upon Earth'. Then he claims 'this divinely inspired workman' erected the temple himself.

The 'Hiramic legend' reaches its fully inflated form in Freemasonry's third degree ritual, where Hiram is described as the Temple's 'principal architect'. The Fellow Craft seeking to become a Master Mason must personify Hiram and then be 'murdered'. Just as there is no Biblical or historical evidence that Hiram was an architect or a mason, so neither the Bible nor the 'Gothic Constitutions' say the architect – whoever he was – was slain. The story seems to have been devised in the early 1700s, by Anderson or other brethren, to give much-needed drama to the third degree. Without it the ritual would be very dull indeed.

Instead, the third degree tells how three Fellow Craft Masons tried to force Hiram to betray the secrets of a Master Mason. Armed with stonemason's tools, they warned him 'death would be the consequence of a refusal'. He retorted that he would rather suffer death than betray this sacred trust. 'This answer not proving satisfactory', the ruffians bludgeoned him to death.

Playing Hiram, the candidate appears bare-armed, bare-breasted, bare-kneed and shod in slippers. When it comes to the murder he is struck down, with gestures not blows, and laid back into a grave. In some lodges this is represented by a sheet depicting an open grave surrounded by skulls and cross-bones. In others a floor trap opens to reveal a grave-shaped cavity. In a few lodges 'Hiram' is laid in a real coffin. To heighten the sense of doom an organist plays funereal music, such as the Dead March from Saul, and a clock strikes twelve, the noonday hour when

Hiram was allegedly slain. In the seaside town of Ilfracombe in Devon, there is a Temple where necrophilia goes deeper still.

> Immediately in front of the Master's pedestal is a deep grave that goes down to the basement. At the bottom is a decayed coffin and a skeleton. At the appropriate stage of a third degree ceremony, the candidate is taken to the edge of the grave and a blue coloured light is switched on to illuminate the emblems of mortality.[22]

One day a visiting Mason who was a police surgeon shocked the local brethren by saying, 'You have a woman down there.' A human skeleton was acceptable to them but a woman was not, as they are not allowed in Lodge meetings alive or dead. I am assured, however, that the brethren are not looking for a male replacement. In Spilsby, Lincolnshire, another female skeleton is knowingly used

> in a dramatic way when the candidate is lowered into a trap below the level of the temple floor. After he is raised and the emblems are pointed out to him, it appears to him that he was laying alongside the skeleton. It is interesting that this lodge meets on the Friday on or before Full Moon, no doubt so that they can see their way home.[23]

In the Masonic myth Hiram Abiff dies. In the ritual his stand-in is resurrected, but only after the Lodge Master has applied the Master Mason's handshake to the cadaver. He then 'raises' the candidate to the third degree and invests him with his Masonic apron.

The Master now tells how Hiram's disappearance threw the workmen into confusion. King Solomon ordered a search, the body was found 'indecently interred' and reburied 'with all respect and reverence'. Meanwhile, another search party had caught the killers on the road to Joppa (the modern Jaffa). Unable to escape, they confessed and were taken back to Jerusalem where 'King Solomon sentenced them to that death the heinousness of their crime so amply merited'.

In some versions of the ritual, the Master explains that the murderers (Jubela, Jubelo and Jubelum) were so overcome with remorse that each exclaimed how he wished to die. Jubela wanted his throat cut across and his tongue torn out, Jubelo wanted his left breast torn open and his heart fed to vultures while Jubelum fancied having his body severed, his bowels burnt to ashes and scattered before the four winds of heaven. Solomon, ready to oblige, 'ordered them to be executed agreeably to the several imprecations of their own mouths'. Ever since, their utterances have been recalled by Freemasons in the penalties ordained in each of the three degrees.

This entire saga is an eighteenth-century invention. Just like the penalties, the fantasy of Hiram's murder is a slander on medieval masons who, ignorant and unlettered as they must have been, were less prone to bogus history than the Georgian gentlemen who hijacked their tradition.

Hiram's murder is in the rituals because, without such a martyrdom, Freemasonry would have no ritual climax. The Master now resurrects the candidate, first by applying the Master Mason's handshake, next by placing his right foot, knee and breast against the candidate, whom other lodge officers slowly raise. Finally the Master lays his left hand over the candidate's back. He then explains these gestures as the 'Five Points of Fellowship':

> Hand to hand I greet you as a brother; foot to foot I will support you in all your undertakings; knee to knee, the posture of my daily supplications shall remind me of your wants; breast to breast, your lawful secrets when entrusted to me as such I will keep as my own; and hand over back, I will support your character in your absence as in your presence.

This is the most emotive expression of mutual aid in Freemasonry. It comes after a solemn, even frightening, enactment of murder which sometimes brings the candidate to tears. After going through this experience in front of as many as fifty 'brothers', the new Master Mason might justifiably feel he owes them an over-riding loyalty.

If Masons in eighteenth-century England had not been obliged to act out Hiram Abiff's 'murder' – or mouth the bloodcurdling oaths – they might have lightly betrayed their fraternal secrets. Without the freshly-minted myth of Solomon's architect, the ritualists could not have enriched the Craft with the word 'Temple' or invoked its many religious and mystical properties. Indeed the brotherhood might have died out in decades, for who could imagine kings and princes patronizing a club where everybody aped the plain trade-union customs of a crowd of journeyman building workers? Instead, transformed with the ceremonies, symbols, finery and regalia of a new magical order, Freemasonry became a dynamic movement which in less than 150 years would spread throughout the world.

Today, some Freemasons feel that, by taking the blood out of the 'Obligations', Grand Lodge has diminished the Craft's appeal. They are appalled that newcomers no longer swear the penalties, and they resent

Grand Lodge's high-handed approach. One affronted Mason told me
that the changes were never formally put to his lodge.

> We never discussed them and nor did any other lodge, as far as I
> know. We were suddenly told they were happening, and that was
> that! The penalties gave the rituals their edge, their tension and
> magic. Now they are as exciting as watching paint dry. Grand
> Lodge cares more for outsiders' ridicule than our concern.

In October 1986, a rebel Masonic publication, *Third Rising*, damned
the changes as an act of cowardice and emasculation forced through only
at a meeting packed with seekers after Grand Rank (Freemasonry's
elaborate system of promotions and awards).

> The penalties form a vital part in the process by representing the
> enormity and seriousness of our sacrifice and of our Masonic
> endeavour to rebuild the Temple. To bring our Creator's light,
> through our actions at all levels, into our fallen world and thereby
> bring Peace to the whole earth. It is an enormous task – but one
> which we are sworn to serve.[24]

Grand Secretary Higham riposted that:

> the decision was on a free vote, by a very large majority, in an
> unusually well attended Grand Lodge comprising, as usual, Grand
> Officers, and the Wardens, Masters and Past Masters of private
> Lodges. It is masonically improper for any Freemason to question
> that decision and unseemly for it to be done in a way which casts
> aspersion on the integrity of others.[25]

'Apron War' was now well and truly joined. The rebels counter-
blasted that moving the penalties was masonically illegal, according to
one Antient Charge which every Lodge Master promises to enforce:
'You admit that it is not in the power of any Man or Body of Men to make
innovation in the Body of Masonry.' Grand Lodge's Board of General
Purposes (its inner government of some forty-seven members) promptly
dug out a document of 1723 which showed the Charge had originally
ended with the phrase, 'without the consent first obtained of the Grand
Lodge'. In December 1986 they stuck that phrase back in the Charge, in
the vain hope that it might silence the Ritual fundamentalists.[26]

Over the centuries, but particularly in recent years, the penalties must
have repelled more Masons from the Craft than they have attracted. In

1979 even the Duke of Kent confessed to his own 'definite sensation of repugnance' over the penalties, and 'the distasteful aspect of calling upon God to witness an Oath which is scarcely practical and certainly barbarous'. Grand Lodge admitted that, if enforced, they would also involve 'a serious criminal offence'.[27] Several, surely! (Kidnapping, grievous bodily harm, torture, mutilation, breaches of the Clean Air Acts – unauthorized bowel-burning and ash-wafting in public – as well as murder and conspiracy.) In the first degree ritual all this must have 'come as a surprise and a shock' to the novice who had just been told that there is nothing in Freemasonry which is 'incompatible with your civil, moral or religious duties'!

In April 1986 the Duke of Kent told Grand Lodge that any future change over the penalties would 'be of our making, and not because people outside Freemasonry have suggested it'. Yet only four weeks later, when the change was accepted, the Board of General Purposes admitted the penalties had to go partly because they gave 'ready material for attack by our enemies and detractors'.[28]

Freemasonry's detractors had far more than a little throat-cutting to complain about. Not content with dreaming up foul oaths and the fantasy of Hiram Abiff, the brotherhood's eighteenth-century founders made a third and even more revolutionary change: they stripped the rituals of Jesus Christ.

two

WHATEVER HAPPENED
TO JESUS?

Ye dull stupid mortals, give o'er your conjectures,
Since Freemasonry's secrets ye ne'er can obtain

Eighteenth-century Masonic song[1]

Among the 'dull stupid mortals' who are not Masons are most of
Britain's Christians. From time to time individual Protestant clergymen
– armed with a few 'secrets' – have attacked the Craft, but their
denominations maintained a formal silence until the 1980s when one
church after another expressed doctrinal revulsion against the fraternity.

It is remarkable that this issue, at this time, should have united 'auld
enemies' who have disagreed on almost everything else for 400 years.
Scotland has seethed with religious discord since the Reformation took
hold in 1560. In the history of Christianity few tribes have loathed each
other more than Scots Catholics and Presbyterians, among them the Free
Church of Scotland. Yet recently the 'Wee Frees' have come round to the
'Papist' view of Freemasonry: total opposition. Today the brotherhood
stands condemned by *both* churches.

The faithful who enrol in Masonic associations are in a state of grave
sin and may not receive Holy Communion.

Declaration by the Vatican, November 1983

The Masonic Order is a work of darkness. The further people are led
into it the more they learn of its idolatrous, heathenish nature.

Revd Hugh Cartwright addressing the General Assembly
of the Free Church of Scotland, May 1986

Reverend Cartwright did not fulminate in vain. The Free Church's elders, massed in Edinburgh, resolved overwhelmingly that 'active membership of Freemasonry is incompatible with membership or office of the Christian Church'. They asked Masons in the kirk to renounce the Craft or face disciplinary action, in effect threatening excommunication just like Bishops of Rome have been doing to their flock since 1738 (see Chapter 8).

Few Masons could be discomfited by the onslaught of so small a church, yet the 15,000 Wee Frees, most living in the remote Highlands, were torch-bearers for a conflagration of hell-fire anti-Masonry. Not to be outdone, the Free Presbyterians (the Free Church's more Puritanical rivals) condemned Masonry as 'anti-Christian and of the works of darkness'.[2] Even the Church of Scotland – the biggest church north of the border – dared to set up an inquiry into the compatibility of the Craft and Christianity, despite the fact that most Scottish Masons belong to the Church and despite threats from some of its ministers who are Masons. One prophesied that the investigation would be an instant recipe for losing members.[3] 'Who do we take on next?' said another, 'the innocent ladies who take yoga classes?'[4]

Whatever the Church eventually decides, Scotland's Grand Lodge will probably hold on to its 100,000 brethren. Indeed, its Grand Master Marcus Humphrey claims membership is increasing by 5 per cent a year.[5] Ironically, many Scots join the Craft to escape the gloom of Presbyterian worship, according to Dr David Steel (a former Moderator of the Church of Scotland and father of the recent Liberal Party leader):

The Church in Scotland, I think largely through the Puritan influence of the eighteenth century, has become somewhat barren of imagery, somewhat suspicious of ritual . . . I think myself that this subconsciously is one of the attractions of Freemasonry to men in Scotland. They find in it this richness of symbol and imagery, which articulates deep feelings which they may have, not in any rational sense, but in an imaginative way.[6]

Dr Steel has no problems reconciling his Freemasonry with his Christian beliefs but what outrages other churchmen, in Scotland, England and elsewhere, is that nowhere in the Craft's ritual or rulebook does Christ or Christianity get a mention. This would not matter if the fraternity were a golf club, a trade union or any other society dedicated to social, material or political ends, but many Christians find it repellent in a movement which purports to have moral, spiritual and religious goals. The repulsion might not arise if the Freemasons had retained the

Christian beliefs of the stonemasons which they always expressed in their ceremonies.

> The might of the Father of Heaven and the wisdom of the glorious Son through the grace and the goodness of the holy ghost that is three persons and one God, be with us at our beginning and give us grace so to govern us here in our living that we may come to his bliss that never shall have ending. Amen.

This prayer comes from the third oldest Constitution, the so-called 'Grand Lodge' manuscript. Like almost all medieval rulebooks it is thoroughly Christian, which is only to be expected since the stonemasons worked mainly on Christian buildings in a wholly Catholic nation. 'The established church was the bedrock for the predecessors of modern Freemasonry.'[7] Yet when Dr Anderson drew up his Constitutions in the 1720s he decided Freemasonry was better off without the Holy Trinity.

In his first Antient Charge, 'Concerning GOD and RELIGION', Anderson condemns both atheism and irreligion. He states that in 'ancient Times' masons were obliged to follow the religion of their own country, but then announces: "'tis now thought more expedient only to oblige them to that religion in which all Men agree, leaving their particular Opinions to themselves.' Here Anderson is dismissing as ancient even some stone-masons' rulebooks written during his own lifetime.[8] He was cooking history to fit his private opinions or the dictates of Grand Lodge. Either way, the deception comes ill from a Presbyterian doctor of divinity. He also decided that the religion in which all men agreed was belief in a Supreme Being. It was allegedly for this reason that Jesus was struck out: to eliminate all cause for sectarian bickering. Henceforth, every kind of Christian, even Catholics, could unite in Masonry. So could Deists and Jews.

There could have been another reason for the change. At the heart of almost all major rites and religions there is a legend of a lost leader, a dying god. Few faiths with a human element (as opposed to plain sun-worship, for example) allow their central figure to die peacefully in bed. Ritual demands a martyr, but now that Freemasonry had its own martyr in the newly-minted character of Hiram Abiff, it no longer needed Christ crucified. Freemasonry is a rite, but is it a religion?

Throughout the eighteenth century, Masonic ritual retained a few Christian traces from the New Testament, but by 1816 even these had been removed.[9] The ritual remains de-Christianized today, leaving each Mason to interpret the Supreme Being in his own way: as the God of the Christians or the God of Jews, Muslims or Buddhists. A Mason need not go to church or belong to any organized faith. He need only profess belief in a single universal force. Grand Secretary Michael Higham says a Mason's God 'must be a good one',[10] but there seems to be nothing in the rituals to stop him worshipping a God that is good *and* evil, or even *wholly* evil. A Mason may believe God and Satan are one, or that God *is* Satan.

A candidate has only to say he puts his trust in God, whom the rituals call the 'Great Architect' or the 'Grand Geometrician', and he is welcome in Freemasonry. Since all *discussion* of religion is banned, 'masonry is the centre of union between good men and true, and the happy means of conciliating friendship amongst those who must otherwise have remained at a perpetual distance.'

When Anderson wrote these sentiments[11] they would have held considerable appeal to men of reason. For 200 years Europe had been torn apart by brutal wars fought in the name of God. The British Isles had been wracked repeatedly by Popish plots, real and imagined. In 1685 a war was fought to depose the Catholic King James II and replace him with a Protestant, William of Orange. In 1715, only eight years before Anderson went into print, the Jacobites had rebelled with the aim of putting James II's son on the throne. It was a time when the spectre of vengeful Catholics stringing up Anglicans and dissenters was never far from England's imagination.

In such a climate there was probably a need for a humanistic fraternity based on religious tolerance. From its formal beginnings this is what 'speculative' Freemasonry claimed to be. It may have been as good as its word: in 1729 one of England's first Grand Masters was a Catholic, Thomas Howard, 8th Duke of Norfolk. Equally remarkable was the admission of Jews when they were excluded from most other organizations. Indeed, it seems that Christian elements in the ritual were removed in deference to Jewish sensitivities. At that time probably the only Muslims in Britain were a few Turkish merchants, but in today's multi-racial society, as a leading Masonic clergyman recently asked, 'If the Craft had to be de-Christianized for the sake of our Jewish brethren, ought it perhaps to be "de-Judaized" for Muslim adherents, and even "de-scripturized" for the Hindu seeker?'[12]

Many non-Masonic Christians believe that de-Christianized Masonry contains huge theological errors. It has certainly had idiotic side-effects. For example, the patron saints of the stonemasons were the 'Quatuor Coronati' or Four Crowned Martyrs. Confusingly their legend starts with five Christian stonecutters being put to death in Rome in A.D. 298 for refusing to sculpt the image of a pagan God. When the statue was completed by other hands, four more masons were beaten to death for refusing to offer it incense. In the 1700s the Freemasons who expunged

Christ kept the Crowned Martyrs as their patron saints, 'the first legendary Masons to feel the brunt of hatred for noble principles'.[13] Yet if the Martyrs had practised the 'tolerance' of modern Freemasons, they would have respected other men's gods and sculpted the statue. They would even have offered incense, for as Anderson said, 'in ancient Times Masons were charged' to observe every country's prevailing religion, '*whatever it was*'. Christians may rightly revere the Crowned Martyrs, but by Masonic lights they were bigoted fools.

To this day Masons claim tolerance is one of their strengths, saying the Craft can work only on the basis of multi-faith goodwill. 'It is sad,' says the Duke of Kent, 'in these days of ecumenism and, in some quarters, tolerance, that it should be considered a criticism of Freemasonry that it is not specifically Christian.'[14] One brother put it more bluntly to me: 'Anti-Masonic priests are hypocrites. We've been practising true Christian-style understanding for three centuries. The churches yap on for decades about coming together, but they achieve nothing.'

In 1985 Grand Secretary Higham took to a City of London pulpit to deliver a lunch-time talk entitled, 'Freemasonry – from Craft to Tolerance'. He was breezy and informal but stood firm against Christian anti-Masonry. He pointed out that he was a Christian and a sidesman at his local Anglican church, and said Masonic ritual omits Christ only so men of different faiths may come together without compromise.

Many Christians feel that Masons have reached common ground only by creating their own religion: a kind of spiritual Esperanto. Higham said there is no such religion. Freemasonry encourages morality but only 'at ground level, religion takes it upwards'. The same year Grand Lodge issued a leaflet[15] stating that Freemasonry is not a religion or a substitute for religion. Members must believe in a Supreme Being, but there is no separate Masonic God. A Mason's God is the God of the religion he professes. Freemasonry lacks a religion's basic elements. 'It has no theological doctrine, and by forbidding religious discussion at its meetings, it will not allow a Masonic theological doctrine to develop.' It offers no sacraments, nor does it claim to lead to salvation by secret knowledge or any other means. As for Freemasonry's secrets, these are concerned not with salvation, but 'modes of recognition'.

All this conflicts with the kind of view expressed by many prominent Masons earlier this century, when they had no worry about public opinion and could proclaim their beliefs with impunity in Masonic books and journals, and even courts of law. Thus in 1903 the Grand Lodge of New York presented this statement when successfully defending itself against a claim of unfair expulsion brought by a wayward brother.

The precepts contained in the 'Landmarks and the Charges of a Freemason' formulate a creed so thoroughly religious in character that it may well be compared with the formally expressed doctrine of many a denominational church. The Masonic fraternity may, therefore, be quite properly regarded as a religious society.[16]

In 1914 the first edition appeared of one of American Freemasonry's best-selling books: *The Builders* by a Baptist minister named Joseph Fort Newton. This has been acclaimed as 'the most notable writing of the century' and is still on sale in Masonic bookshops on both sides of the Atlantic.[17] To Newton, 'Masonry is not *a* religion, but it is Religion, a worship in which all good men may unite, that each may share the faith of all'.[18]

Instead of criticizing Masonry, let us thank God for one altar where no man is asked to surrender his liberty of thought and become an indistinguishable atom in a mass of sectarian agglomeration . . . High above all dogmas that divide, all bigotries that blind, all bitterness that beclouds, will be the simple words of the one eternal religion – the Fatherhood of God, the moral law, the golden rule and the hope of a life everlasting![19]

In the 1920s J. S. M. Ward wrote books linking Freemasonry with cults and religions from all ages, countries and cultures: 'I consider Freemasonry is a sufficiently organized school of mysticism to be entitled to be called a religion . . . I boldly aver that Freemasonry is a religion.'[20]

Ward's staunch ally, Sir John Cockburn, Grand Deacon of England and Deputy Grand Master of Australia, dismissed the row between Masonry and religion as 'merely a war of words', and yet: 'If the title of a religion be denied to Freemasonry, it may well claim the higher ground of being a federation of religions. It is a form of worship in which all religions unite.'[21]

In 1924 an eminent British Masonic scholar, W. L. Wilmshurst, wrote that Freemasonry is not a religion, but promptly followed this with Masonic double-speak: 'A brother may legitimately say, if he wishes – and many do say – "Masonry is my religion" but he is not justified in classifying and holding it out to other people as a religion.'[22]

This seems to be telling Masons that they may embrace Freemasonry as a religion, but should not let outsiders in on the secret. In 1952 another Anglican minister, using the pseudonym Vindex, defined Freemasonry as a super-religion: 'There has always been an inherent longing to penetrate deeper, to achieve a more profound personal communion with nature, with reality and with God than was possible through official state religions.' Masonry satisfies this longing: 'Good men and true literally by the thousand seek out the Craft every year, attracted to it by some magnetism that seems almost the supernatural workings of the Holy Spirit.'[23]

In 1954 no less an authority than a Grand Chaplain of Grand Lodge addressed the question: is Freemasonry a religion?

> I firmly believe that it is. The tests of any religion lie (1) in its belief in Almighty God and the Obligation to serve Him; (2) on the performance of duties to God and Man based on the divine law found in a divine revelation (the Bible); (3) [in its possessing] a system of faith and worship.
>
>   Freemasonry conforms to all of these, and those who have met within its sacred precincts have experienced that inspiration which comes from being nearer to God. It may not be a complete religion since it does not attempt to minister to women and children, and because it is highly selective, but it is nonetheless a religion.[24]

Grand Chaplain is one of the highest offices in English Freemasonry. It is filled each year by a man of religion chosen to personify the movement's spirituality. This man's views can hardly have been perverse, nor were they disowned at the time by his brother in 'cloth' and 'apron': Geoffrey Fisher, Archbishop of Canterbury.

Today, Masonic researchers say most of these writers were over-enthusiastic crackpots whose scholarship is now discredited. Grand Librarian John Hamill tellingly entitled a recent lecture 'The Sins Of Our Masonic Fathers'.[25] In it he claims that some of the authors quoted above 'had a complete misconception as to the nature and purpose of Freemasonry', but 'what our critics do is to use these misguided interpretations to bolster their case against the Craft'.

Hamill may be right but, if so, practically all the Masonic writers, historians and sages of the past 100 years shared the same misconception and certainly spread it around. Together their books sold in hundreds of thousands. Many are still being reprinted and sold through Masonic bookshops. It is difficult to know whom to believe: the dead Masons who claim Freemasonry is a religion or the living who claim it is not. Who knows? In fifty or a hundred years' time, a new crusade of Masonic writers may be preaching once again that Freemasonry is the universal religion to save all mankind.

The current claim that Freemasonry is no such thing is the only publicly acceptable defence to attacks on the Craft from Christians of many persuasions. Thirty years ago Masons were so entrenched in the Protestant hierarchies that they never seemed to have asked themselves whether Freemasonry conflicted with Christian doctrine. A mere priest who dared ask, such as Walton Hannah, found himself out in the cold. Today, when (it seems) no serving Anglican bishop is a Mason, the cult has fewer friends in high places. An evangelical revival and the rise of the charismatic 'Born Again' brigade have reduced Masonic clergymen to a tiny minority. This is not the time for any Mason to claim Freemasonry is a religion, even if he thinks it is.

In 1984 England's highest Masonic authority, the Duke of Kent, told his brethren to curb their tongues: 'It will certainly help if the phrase "Freemasonry is my religion" is never uttered again. I cannot think of any words more likely to give a false impression of the Craft.'[26] Yet the phrase is still being uttered. Masons have admitted to me that they feel Freemasonry is a religion: it does demand belief, it has dogma, it does offer sacraments, and it even promises a kind of salvation: when a Mason dies he goes to the 'Grand Lodge Above', which may mean the Christian Heaven but sounds more like a Masonic Valhalla.

Masons are well-prepared for a Masonic after-life by their training on earth. They meet in 'temples' which have 'altars'. When a new lodge is founded it must be 'consecrated'. The rituals have a spiritual, even holy, atmosphere whipped up by hymns and prayers offered by 'chaplains'. One Mason's wife tells me that after lodge meetings her husband comes home glowing, not from alcohol but from something resembling a religious climax. Reverend 'Vindex' achieved similar satisfaction: 'To witness a Third Degree Ceremony for me, as a Christian Priest, is to relive Good Friday.'[27] For him a ritual built on the fairytale of Hiram Abiff's death became a deep religious experience. Most religions are built on fairy- or folk-tales, of course, but if Masons choose to point this out, they may only be acknowledging that Freemasonry too is a religion.

Masons could even be given Masonic funerals, elaborate ones,[28] but in 1962 Grand Lodge decreed that the 'final obsequies of any human being, Mason or not, are complete in themselves' and do not call for any Masonic prayers at the religious service or the graveside. This ban came after incidents such as that engulfing the Bishop of Southwark, Mervyn Stockwood, in 1959. The relatives of a Mason had asked to hold a Masonic funeral in a local church.

> I carefully studied the proposed service and I found that the words 'Jesus Christ' were omitted from the prayers and the word 'Architect' substituted. Worse still, the cross was to be removed from the altar and an additional non-Christian ceremony was to take

place at the graveside. I informed the vicar that while people must be free to bury their dead in their own way, I thought that in this case it would be better for the service to take place in a Masonic temple. A bishop, when he is consecrated, promises to banish strange doctrines; therefore I could not allow the doctrine of the divinity of Christ to be treated as peripheral. Moreover every church was dedicated in the name of the Holy Trinity and not in the name of the Architect.

This line I took stirred up a hornets' nest. I was warned that I had offended important benefactors and that the diocese would suffer financially. It may have done so.[29]

This issue was to break a long-standing friendship between Stockwood and Geoffrey Fisher, the former Anglican Primate. Stockwood felt Freemasonry was divisive: Anglican bishops were themselves supposed to be a brotherhood, but here was 'a secret society which demanded an absolute loyalty. It was calculated to divide us into two groups and could lead to conflict.' The conflict broke in the press in 1967, with Stockwood saying, 'A Christian has no need to go beyond the Church. His loyalty to Christ and his church is paramount. The fact that Lord Fisher is a Freemason proves nothing. His successor at Canterbury will have no truck with it.'[30] Privately, Fisher defended the Craft with revealing candour: 'The ritual is glorified nonsense based on a legend of sort. Why not? We all *like* that kind of play-acting if it is in a friendly atmosphere and even more if it poses as a secret!'[31]

Some Masons admit they have no religion: not Freemasonry or anything else. They have no belief in God, do not go to church, and know little of religion beyond their dim memories of instruction at school. One former Mason told me he resigned from his lodge when he lost his belief in God. His colleagues urged him to stay. They said they did not believe either, but if people resigned on such flimsy grounds the lodge would soon lose all its members.

This reflects ill on a fraternity which, in the Duke of Kent's words, is 'an ally of religion and is firmly rooted in religious belief', yet it reflects the hypocrisy with which the Craft used to be run at the highest levels. In 1956 Grand Lodge tried to get rates relief on Freemasons' Hall on the grounds that Freemasonry's main objects were 'the advancement of religion'. The High Court turned this down because Freemasonry provided no religious instruction, no programme for the persuasion of unbelievers, no supervision to ensure that its members remained constant in their various religions, no holding of services and no pastoral or missionary work of any kind. Indeed, the judges found that a Mason did not have to practise any religion whatsoever.

Grand Lodge fought this case just to avoid paying taxes, but to do so it had to perform some nifty verbal tricks. In court it claimed that Freemasonry is dedicated to advancing religion, but outside it was saying the Craft has no dogma and bans religious discussion. This must be a nonsense. How can Freemasonry 'advance' religion, and educate its members in spirituality, if they are not allowed to discuss the meaning of the ritual's religious elements?

The ban is itself the assertion of a pyramid of dogma in the ritual, which must be incomprehensible to many of its performers precisely because they are not allowed to discuss its meaning. What actor could rehearse a religious play without asking the meaning of the lines? Yet each Mason, it seems, must fumble his own way through the ritual's labyrinth of ideas from all manner of primitive and mystical cults, some pre-dating even Judaism.

On the other hand, if Freemasonry really does have no dogma or doctrine, then Grand Lodge has no right to claim Freemasonry is *not* a religion, and surely Masons can believe what they like. If some want to believe it is a religion, then – for them – that is what it is. The constitutional position is clearly explained by Alphonse Cerza, an American Masonic historian who (until his death in 1987) belonged to the elite London research lodge, Quatuor Coronati.

Freemasonry has no 'official' voice as that term is used by some churches . . . the word 'free' in Freemasonry means exactly what it says and that each member is free to speak his mind. If a Mason has an active imagination and wants to interpret the symbols and lessons for himself, that is his privilege . . .

Freemasonry being non-sectarian in religious matters and non-political, no officer or group of Masons has authority to speak for the Craft; when they speak of such matters they are expressing their individual opinions only.[32]

This means that all the Grand Lodge of England's utterances on religion, including its glossy pamphlets, are neither official nor binding. They are not 'Holy Writ', merely opinions put forward by the hierarchy to arm the Craft against present-day Christian concern. The phrases 'PR job' and 'cosmetic exercise' spring to mind.

The irony is that, to preserve its religious 'universality' and 'tolerance', Freemasonry has martyred at least one Christian. In 1853 William Tucker was dismissed as Grand Master of Dorset, allegedly for showing up at Provincial Grand Lodge wearing the robes of another Masonic order: the 'Christian' Rose Croix, in which he was a Sovereign Grand Inspector

General of the 33rd degree. His supporters (a minority in Grand Lodge) claimed his sacking was 'harsh and unwise, and entirely unwarranted by the reasons assigned to it'. His real offence seems to have been repeatedly proclaiming the Craft was 'universally Christian' and Trinitarian: 'Christianity is our basis, our groundwork; and to every right-thinking and well-intentioned Mason, it constitutes the true secret of Free-masonry.' Such views undermined the removal of Christ from the rituals which had been completed forty years earlier. With Tucker discredited, the last hopes of a re-Christianized Craft were destroyed. Tucker died only eighteen months later, still distressed by his Masonic humiliation.

When this story was examined by Masonry's Quatuor Coronati research lodge in 1969[33] one member, a Dr Vacher, observed that Tucker's 'exaggerated Christianity was no doubt part of his normal make-up, yet his final aberration could only be accounted for by mental disturbance. It would not, for example, have surprised me if he had died of General Paralysis of the Insane, or a Cerebral Tumour.' As it happens, Tucker's death certificate says he died of Pulmonary Phthisis, a wasting lung disease. Some Christians – not least the four crowned martyrs – might be outraged by the very idea of a condition such as 'exaggerated Christianity', but to accuse a man of insanity just for wearing the wrong robe to a Masonic meeting seems harsh, even when the accuser is a Mason.

three

CLOTH AND APRON,
CROSS AND SQUARE

It is absolutely useless for a Frenchman to try to understand English
Masonry unless he realizes that the Crown, the Anglican Church,
and the United Grand Lodge of England are one God in three
persons.[1]

In the early 1950s, when those words were written, King George VI was a
dedicated Mason. In earlier years two of his brothers (the Duke of
Windsor and the late Duke of Kent) had been ardent members of the
Craft. Today in contrast we have a Queen who cannot be a Mason, and a
consort who joined his father-in-law's lodge in 1953 but has rarely if ever
donned an apron since. None of their three sons is in the Craft or is likely
to join.

   In 1953 the Archbishop of Canterbury and sixteen other Church of
England bishops were 'on the square'. Now, it seems, no Mason wears an
English mitre. This drift from Freemasonry has been going on for
decades but it became obvious only in 1984 when *The Brotherhood*
emboldened Anglicans to criticize the Craft. They were astonished to
find their hierarchy in general agreement. The ground was prepared by
the Methodists, whose 1985 Conference considered a report voicing
these main objections:

   Masonic secrecy is 'destructive of fellowship' whereas the Christian
   community is open to all.
     Candidates swear not to discose the secrets of Freemasonry
   before they know what they are, but Christians should not enter
   'into rituals and obligations whose content is unknown and whose
   implications are shrouded in secrecy'.
     Masons pray to a 'Supreme Being' to allow men of different faiths
   to come together, but the worship is so watered down as to be

'unsatisfactory in any religious tradition'. Christians must be concerned that in the minds of some Masons the Supreme Being is not the God of Christians and that prayers are never offered in Christ's name.

In its rituals Masonry seems to offer salvation through secret knowledge. The Royal Arch ritual implies that rediscovering Masonry's lost secrets may help a Mason obtain eternal life. In contrast Christianity offers salvation through knowledge 'freely available to all'.

In some rituals the candidate is told he is making a journey from darkness into light. This can only be interpreted as spiritual enlightenment, but in Christianity this can be achieved only through Christ. In the third degree the candidate is put to a symbolic death from which he is raised by Masonic ritual. In Christianity the same passage from death to life is achieved through Baptism. Masonry thus performs ceremonies which are 'equivalent to essential parts of Christian practice and offer alternatives to important elements of Christian faith'.

Freemasonry claims not to be a religion, the report concluded, but its rituals contain religious practices and carry religious overtones. The Christian who becomes a Mason may compromise his beliefs and his allegiance to Christ, perhaps without realizing it: 'Consequently Methodists should not become Freemasons.' The committee acknowledged the many sincere Methodist Masons 'whose commitment to Christ is unquestionable' and who see no conflict in their dual membership, but to allay suspicion, they should declare they are Masons or, even better, quit Masonry altogether.

Conference not only adopted this report; it banned lodges from meeting on Methodist premises. All Masonic services now had to accord with Methodist public worship. Henceforth no service could proceed without mention of Christ.

Methodist Masons were appalled. The church's newspaper, the *Methodist Recorder*, rarely vibrates with controversy but now its letters column was bombarded by Masons who felt bereft and stigmatized. Many stressed the Craft's charity and good works. Some contrasted the warm friendship they had found in Masonic lodges with the frosty reception on offer from some Methodist congregations. A Mason's wife protested her husband's devotion to Christ and Methodism, but lamented that this anti-Masonic drive might force them both out of the church.

One minister who is also a Mason told them not to be defeatist. 'Try not to feel hurt,' said Revd Frank Thewlis, 'don't give way to those who seem determined to turn Methodism into an exclusive minor sect.' He ridiculed Conference by reminding readers of its past votes: *for* total abstinence from alcohol, *against* charity lotteries because they were a form of gambling. Other resolutions had decided homosexuality was not a sin and that doctors ought to be allowed to put teenage girls on the Pill without their parents' knowledge. If Methodists were required to agree with all these votes, said Thewlis, 95 per cent would have to resign. Most ignored them, so Freemasons did not have to quit either. They should stand and fight.

Then someone remembered a memorial stained-glass window in Wesley's Chapel, Methodism's mother-church in London. It was paid for by Masons to honour Methodists killed in World War I and is decorated with the square-and-compass and a Masonic Star of David. It shows Jesus embracing a dying soldier, whose right leg is bared to the knee as if he is an apprentice Mason. One wag wrote to the *Recorder* suggesting it should be boarded up until 'Light' was restored to the theologians.

Methodism has had a 'love-hate' relationship with Masonry for over 200 years. The Church's founder, John Wesley, was strongly opposed: 'What an amazing banter upon all mankind is Freemasonry! And what a secret it is which so many concur to keep! From what motive? Through fear or shame to own it?' However, John's nephew, the composer Samuel Wesley, was a Mason and became Grand Organist. In 1917 Methodist Masons set up their own lodge in London and called it Epworth, after John's birthplace. Other Epworth Lodges were founded in Manchester and Liverpool, with six more in Ireland and Australia.

With so strong a tradition, 6,000 Methodist Masons set up their own association to fight the 1985 Conference decision, but one year later their petitions were dismissed. Their secretary Ronald Harris lamented: 'We have been judged and found wanting without being given a hearing.' He vowed they would overturn the policy in future years, but they have not yet succeeded.

There are only 500,000 Methodists in Britain, but the decisions of this most senior congregation in world Methodism are heeded in many countries, including America, where 13.6 million Methodists outnumber Anglican Episcopalians by nearly five to one. The Grand Lodge of England had been ill-prepared for the Methodist onslaught, but it could ignore all Nonconformist yelps so long as they did not start the dogs barking in the Anglican Church. Too late! The anti-Masonic plague was spreading like rabies.

In February 1985 the Church of England General Synod voted to investigate the 'compatibility or otherwise of Freemasonry and Christianity'. Laymen and priests expressed concern about Masonic 'light', the oaths, the failure to distinguish between religions, the apparent offer of salvation through secret knowledge, and whether Masons believe they can get into Heaven through good works rather than faith in Christ. A working group was set up to consider these charges and many more brought by Christian thinkers in recent books.[2] By my reckoning the brotherhood stands accused of practising at least ten heresies. They make tough reading:

Syncretism – Different religions are equally valid, or may be treated as equal, or fused. Illogical compromises are committed in the attempt to reconcile different systems of belief or notions of God which are incompatible.

Polytheism – A Mason may believe in only one God but Freemasonry welcomes all Masons' Gods in the same Pantheon.

Dualism – Masonic and Christian perceptions of God are in conflict. No Christian can subscribe to both 'without suffering spiritual schizophrenia'.[3]

Socinianism – God the Father is elevated at the expense of God the Son.

Pelagianism – Man is not cursed with original sin, but may achieve perfection on earth and Heaven through good works, not faith. Christians believe man is corrupt and can only be redeemed through Christ.

Rationalism – Terms like Supreme Architect and Great Geometrician imply God merely built the world and does not intervene in its affairs. Christians believe God asserts his will on Earth through Christ.

Gnosticism – Salvation can be attained through secret knowledge.

Manicheanism – God is not all good, but both good and bad.

Idolatry – Some parts of the ritual may break the Second Commandment not to make graven images or bow down to them.

Satanism – Devil worship.

Wrong-footed by the Methodists, Grand Lodge was not going to be caught out by the Anglicans. It got in first with specially printed evidence, later assembled in a fifty-page booklet,[4] attacking all the usual anti-Masonic charges. It dismissed the Methodist committee's report as 'hurried and ill-researched' and littered with errors. This was not surprising, said Grand Lodge, since all its members were non-Masons.

The Anglican group tried to get off to a better start. Among its seven members were two Masons. One was England's highest priest-cum-

Mason: Peter Moore, Dean of St Albans. It also included two women, whose enthusiasm for an all-male society might have been understandably modest.[5] Despite only five meetings and a very tight budget, by 1987 they completed a report: *Freemasonry and Christianity, are they Compatible?*

This challenged Grand Lodge's claim that Masonry is *private* rather than secret, and its only secrets are the 'signs, grips and words used in proof of membership'. Not so, said the group. The rituals themselves frequently define secrecy far more widely, to cover not just the Order's secrets but every individual Mason's 'lawful secrets' too.[6]

On Freemasonry as a religion, the group were 'at one in rejecting the assertion that the rituals contain no element of worship'. They cited prayers offered to an Almighty God in all the rituals, which echo 'familiar Christian prayers and phrases denuded of their normal Christian reference'.[7]

In its evidence Grand Lodge had claimed that, 'prayers in a masonic context are not acts of worship but the simple asking for a blessing at the beginning of work and returning thanks at its successful conclusion.' Yet the group could not understand how, in the ordinary meaning of words, 'prayer' can be distinguished from 'worship'. Was Grand Lodge not guilty of 'a Humpty-Dumpty use of language'?[8]

And just whose God is this Great Architect or Grand Geometrician? Grand Lodge says that these names simply allow men of different faiths to join in prayer, but there is no separate Masonic God: a Mason's God is the God of his own professed religion.[9] This was far too woolly for the Anglican investigators. To them Craft Masonry is typical eighteenth-century Deism. Two hundred years on, must not this 'represent a slur or slight on Christianity'?[10] Some group members thought it must, and agreed with these points sent in by other Christians.

> If the unique claims of Christianity are to be taken seriously how can a man claiming to be a Christian belong to a Deist organisation in which there is a free and easy acceptance of any religion – Hindu, Sikh, Muslim, Jew et al. – whose God(s) are their own and wholly alien to the God of the New Testament?

> Has the Christian not a clear and overwhelming responsibility continually to witness to the higher claims of Christianity?

The entire group, Masons and non-Masons, felt that parts of the ritual of the Royal Arch (another order, discussed in the next chapter) must be considered blasphemous. Otherwise they divided on predictable lines.

The reflections of the Working Group itself reveal understandable differences of opinion between those who are Freemasons and those who are not. Whilst the former fully agree that there are clear difficulties to be faced by Christians who are Freemasons, the latter are of the mind that the Report points to a number of very fundamental reasons to question the compatibility of Freemasonry with Christianity.[11]

When the findings leaked out, Grand Lodge was outraged. It had asked to be allowed to comment before publication and to bring evidence to refute any 'alleged incompatibilities', yet this offer was spurned. It had supplied stacks of evidence and 'replied to all questions with candour; it is a pity that the candour was not reciprocated'.[12]

Grand Lodge rejected all the report's findings, by asserting that Freemasonry contains no heresies, blasphemies or elements of religion. It *does* deal in morality and encourages its members to live a better life, and it certainly has a spiritual basis. Thus it cannot be a danger to Christianity, but rather 'its very useful companion'.

In June 1987 Grand Lodge distributed a hurried counterblast to all Synod members as they assembled to discuss the report at York. This may have done the trick. The report was backed by 394 votes to fifty-two and commended for further discussion, but Masons claimed they had won the debate.[13] There would be no 'sleazy heresy hunt, based on unsubstantial evidence', as one priest put it, and no witch-hunt either. Even if some Masonic ceremonies might be blasphemous in parts, that does not mean Masons are blasphemers.

This was getting too serious, felt the Archbishop of Durham, Dr John Habgood. In his speech he took the benign view that Freemasonry was 'a fairly harmless eccentricity'. While 'no doubt there are cases of people being unheathily absorbed in what is by any standards a rather odd society', words like heresy and blasphemy were inappropriate. Free-masonry was not his kind of eccentricity – he would have difficulty 'worshipping an architect' – but he could see that 'men get a certain pleasure out of doing things which they wouldn't do in front of their wives. These are all harmless pleasures. And if people enjoy it, why shouldn't they?'

Habgood felt that Masons brought much of their troubles on themselves by their aura of secrecy: 'however trivial the actual secrets . . . if something looks like a conspiracy, then people will treat it as one, whatever the disclaimers.' He said the atmosphere of conspiracy and secrecy was so infectious that when he was sent a copy of the report, he very nearly ate it.

The Anglicans had looked only at the religious aspects of Freemasonry. It had not been their job to investigate allegations about Masonic mutual aid, career preferment or corruption. Yet Habgood did say that people in public roles 'are well advised to be cautious. It is possible to give the impression of being one of a clique while in fact behaving entirely honourably. Hence I am glad that most modern Bishops have avoided the Craft.'

Masons might have found some of the Archbishop's remarks blunt or contemptuous, but he had coated the pill with so much sugar that Grand Lodge reprinted his speech in full and distributed it to all brethren. Meantime, one non-Masonic vicar in Wales turned the argument on its head in a letter to the *Church Times*.[14]

Perhaps the Masonic Order could carry out an investigation into the Church. They will doubtless find, among the endless hypocrisy, the occasional blasphemy and considerable self-seeking.

four

JAHBULON – THE SACRED
WORD TO KEEP

If a spiritual or religious secret is worth knowing, it is worth sharing with the whole world.

An Anglican priest who used to be a Mason

The 'secret' of Masonry is completely indefinable . . . it can only be obtained by those who come of their own free will and accord, properly prepared and humbly soliciting. And the knowledge that this humility has been shared by everyone else in the room is the cement which binds Masons. The 'secret' is the shared experience . . . Trying to explain the joys of Masonry to an outsider is rather like trying to describe the joys of motherhood to a spinster: Masonry, like motherhood, has to be experienced before it can be understood.

Canon Richard Tydeman[1]

Beyond Craft Freemasonry lie many fanciful orders, each with its own arcane jargon and grandiose titles. Canon Tydeman, for example, is a Past Grand Scribe Nehemiah of the Supreme Grand Chapter of Royal Arch Masons of England. He is also Grand Prior (33rd degree) of the Rose Croix, Grand Sovereign of the Red Cross of Constantine, and a Knight Commander of the Great Priory of Malta. Even a man of the Canon's dedication, energy and charm must have found it difficult to fit all this Masoning in with his former duties as a Church of England vicar. Just buying all the gear must surely have consumed much of his meagre clergyman's stipend.

To join any of these orders, a Mason must already have reached the third degree in the Craft, but if he goes no further he is no other Mason's

inferior. His Master Mason's ritual tells him he knows all the funda-
mental secrets. Even the Rose Croix, some of whose 30,000 members in
England and Wales soar to the 33rd degree, claims no ascendancy over the
Craft.[2]

Only one order makes that claim: the Holy Royal Arch, Freemasonry's
self-styled 'Supreme Degree'. Safe within its 'Chapters', the Royal Arch
dismisses the Craft's third degree as incomplete and its secrets as sham.
There are some 150,000 Royal Arch 'Companions' in England and
Wales, which means only one Mason in every three or four joins the
order.[3] All the rest are unaware that their tongues might have been torn
out and throats cut across just for betraying 'secrets' which are bogus,
even by Masonic standards.

'Darkness is for those without,' says the Royal Arch ritual.[4] Thus,
the Craft's hoodwinked masses are not only excluded from Masonic
light; they also suffer increasing public hostility over a secret they are not
even allowed to share: the 'Grand Omnific Royal Arch Word',
JAHBULON.

The Methodist inquiry found that 'the most serious objection' for a
Christian in all Freemasonry

> lies in the Royal Arch ritual which reveals the Supreme Being's true
> name as JAHBULON. Clearly each of this word's three syllables
> conform to the name of a divinity in a particular religion. The whole
> word is thus an example of syncretism, an attempt to unite different
> religions in one, which Christians cannot accept.[5]

This view also permeated other Christian denominations, including
the Church of England. In October 1987 the Reading *Evening Post*
published an article by Canon Brian Brindley in which he described
JAHBULON as 'an unholy compound of the Hebrew name of God,
Jehovah, with the heathen names for Baal and Osiris'.[6] Springing to
JAHBULON's defence was Grand Secretary Higham who doubles as 'Grand
Scribe Ezra' of Royal Arch. The jobs go together at Freemasons' Hall,
London, where 'Ezra' Higham speaks for some 180,000 'Companions' in
2,836 'Chapters' in England and Wales. He now scribed that the Canon
had got it wrong.

> The tri-syllable word in the Royal Arch is a word and not a name of
> God. It is not an attempt to combine the names of gods of differing
> religions, nor does it have any reference to Pagan gods. Attempts to
> relate its second and third syllables to Baal and Osiris are simply
> semantic games played by uninformed critics of Freemasonry.[7]

Few *Post* readers could have made sense of this – not least because Mr
Higham, like all Royal Arch Companions, has sworn never to divulge
the word he was defending. If he ever 'dares to pronounce' JAH-BUL-ON
outside Royal Arch circles (it is pronounced YAHBULON, by the way) the
good Commander risks having his 'head cut off' and, according to some
versions of the ritual, his 'brains exposed to the burning rays of the sun'.[8]

If this was not a big enough impediment to free speech, Higham was
labouring under a more practical disability: he was misrepresenting the
Royal Arch ritual. This tells how the Jews were freed from captivity in
Babylon in the sixth century B.C., and how they returned to Jerusalem to
rebuild King Solomon's Temple. The aspiring candidate is given a shovel
to dig the foundations but during excavations another worker discovers a
vault from the original Temple. This contains a gold plate inscribed with
two words: JEHOVAH, described as the 'Sacred and Mysterious Name of
the True and Living God Most High'; and JAHBULON. The candidate is
told these are Masonry's 'long-lost secrets', which Hiram Abiff died for
rather than betray 500 years before. Helping to rediscover them wins the
candidate 'exaltation' to the rank of Companion. Only then is he told that
all the secrets he learned in the first three degrees are 'substituted secrets',
adopted 'until time or circumstances should restore the genuine'.[9] Thus
Masonry's 'Supreme Degree' drops the bombshell that all the hocus-
pocus in the Craft is counterfeit.

To enact this rediscovery, the top of the Royal Arch 'altar' is adorned
with a plate not of gold but of brass. This is inscribed with a circle on
which is written JE-HO-VAH, split into three syllables. Within the circle is a
triangle. On each side of the triangle is written JAH-BUL-ON, also split in
three. In England this ritual is performed in dozens of variations or
'workings', but most include a 'Mystical Lecture' which all Companions
must drink in.[10]

> In times of antiquity, names of God and symbols of divinity were
> always enclosed in triangular figures. In the days of Pythagoras, the
> triangle was considered the most sacred of emblems . . . The
> Egyptians termed it the sacred number, or number of perfection,
> and so highly was it prized by the ancients, that it became amongst
> them an object of worship. They gave it the sacred name of God . . .
> This sacred Delta is usually enclosed with a square and circle,
> thereby expressing its vivifying influence, extending its ramification
> through all created nature; for these reasons it has ever been
> considered the Great All, the *Summum Bonum*.
> The word on the triangle is that Sacred and Mysterious Name you
> have just solemnly engaged yourself never to pronounce.

This leaves little room for doubt that, contrary to Mr Higham's assertion, JAHBULON *is* a name of God and not just a word. Indeed, it seems to be the 'Sacred and Mysterious Name' of God. It is certainly not the Sacred and Mysterious Name of a man, dog, pig or rat. The lecture continues.

It is a compound word, and the combination forms the word JAH-BUL-ON. It is in four languages, Chaldee, Hebrew, Syriac, and Egyptian. JAH is the Chaldee name of God, signifying 'His essence and majesty incomprehensible'. It is also a Hebrew word signifying, 'I am and shall be', thereby expressing the actual, future, and eternal existence of the Most High. BUL is a Syriac word denoting Lord, or Powerful, it is in itself a compound word, being formed from the preposition Beth, in or on, and Ul, Heaven or on High. ON is an Egyptian word signifying Father of all, thereby expressing the Omnipotence of the Father of All, as in that well-known prayer, Our Father, which art in Heaven. The various significations of the word may thus be collected: I am and shall be; Lord in Heaven or on High.

This demolishes Higham's claim that JAHBULON is '*not* an attempt to combine the names of gods of differing religions, nor does it have any reference to Pagan gods'. The Mystical Lecture clearly asserts just that. In ancient times the Chaldeans, Syrians and Egyptians all worshipped pagan gods, to whom their alleged words meaning 'God', 'Lord on High' and 'Father of All' must be understood to refer.

What of Higham's last swipe: against the 'semantic games' played by those 'uninformed critics of Freemasonry' who attempt to relate BUL and ON to Baal and Osiris? Clearly the Church of England Working Group fall into this category, for they were perturbed by the meaning of both JAHBULON and three Hebrew letters A, B and L – Aleph, Beth and Lamed – set at the triangle's corners. The Mystical Lecture explains these letters may be juggled to spell the divine incantations: AB BAL (meaning Father Lord), AL BAL (Word Lord), and LAB BAL (Spirit Lord).

The group said the obvious result is to emphasize BAL, which they clearly felt was simply another spelling of Baal,

the name of a Semitic deity bitterly opposed by Elijah and the later Hebrew prophets; to associate this name in any way with that of Jehovah would have deeply shocked them. It is also a result which gives colour to the view that, in fact, the name on the triangle, far from being a means of describing God, is a syncretistic name for

God made out of the name of Yahweh, Baal and Osiris (the Egyptian fertility God).[11]

The unanimity with which the group condemned JAHBULON was all the more damning because two of its members were Masons (though not Royal Arch). The group concluded: 'JAHBULON (whether it is a name or a description) . . . must be considered blasphemous: in Christian theology the name of God (Yahweh/Jehovah) must not be taken in vain, nor can it be replaced by an amalgam of names of Pagan deities.'

When Grand Lodge read this onslaught, it claimed that BAL was not the same as Baal: 'Royal Arch masons would be as shocked as the Working Group if they thought their ritual associated Baal with the name of God. It is also worth pointing out that the second word on the triangle is not BAL.'[12]

However, as recently as November 1984 these oh-so-shockable folk *had* been told that BUL was a deliberately disguised form of Baal. The messenger was the Revd Francis Heydon, Third Grand Principal of the Royal Arch addressing its ruling council, the Supreme Grand Chapter.[13]

Now that Freemasonry was attracting an 'unusual amount of interest', Heydon said it was time to restate the origins of JAHBULON – a word which even among his fellow Grand Companions he dared not utter. In 1836, a committee formed to compose the Royal Arch ritual had tried to imagine how the three original Grand Masters – King Solomon, King Hiram of Tyre and Hiram Abiff – might each have uttered the name of God in his own language. The committee decided King Solomon would have used the Hebrew name JAH, and King Hiram the Syrian name Ba'al or Bel, but it 'preferred not to use this form, which is all too well-known in a most unacceptable context', so they substituted BUL.

Hiram Abiff posed another problem for, according to Heydon, he 'was a Kenite, of the tribes that lived on the shores of the Red Sea, in part of the Egyptian Empire'. Thus the committee had to find an *Egyptian* word for God, and thought they had found one in Genesis, Chapter 41, which says Joseph's father-in-law was 'Potipherah, priest of ON'.[14]

Heydon's speech was promptly distributed to every Chapter by the indefatigable Commander Higham, who simultaneously instructed Royal Arch members to tell non-Masons ('if the subject arises in private conversation') that 'no part of the second name has any reference to Baal'. The Companions only had to turn the letter over to see Heydon had said just the opposite: BUL meant Ba'al.

If anyone was playing 'semantic games' now, it was Higham. Ba'al and Baal (and indeed Bal) are the same word. Including or omitting the apostrophe does not change its meaning. The Oxford English Dictionary confirms Baal is synonymous with the Hebrew Ba'al. Both mean 'the Chief Male Deity of the Phoenician and Canaanitish nation, hence false god'. Baalism and Baal worship mean idolatry, a usage which the OED quotes for the very decade when the Royal Arch ritual was drawn up.[15] Now whether you think the Phoenicians and Canaanites worshipped idols depends on your religion and your knowledge of these ancient peoples. The Jews condemned Ba'al largely because he was the God of their enemies, but in the fiery religious climate of the 1830s, the Royal Arch ritualists knew that most of their contemporaries – and indeed most Masons – would have interpreted Baal/Ba'al only in the most hostile sense. To them he was the Devil – a very odd bed-fellow for JAH!

Baal had to be disguised, perhaps because the Royal Arch ritualists were devising exactly what Freemasonry's critics now claim: a syncretistic extravanganza uniting three different gods – and conflicting religions – in JAHBULON as the one 'Sacred and Mysterious Name of God'. All in Freemasonry's Supreme Degree!

Although Revd Heydon's speech was distributed only to members of the Royal Arch, it soon leaked out to the 'profane', as Canon Richard Tydeman revealed in 1985 when he gave Grand Chapter a different view of 'the words in the triangle'.[16]

> Recent attacks on Freemasonry have shown up all too clearly that the Royal Arch is one of our most vulnerable fronts, and the thing that our critics have seized upon as proof of our evil intentions is the composite word or words on the triangle in the very centre of every Chapter.
>
> Unfortunately we are not giving the right impression at all. Only the other day I was accosted by a vociferous churchwarden. 'How can you,' he said, 'how can *you*, a minister of religion, take part in ceremonies which invoke heathen gods by name?', and as evidence for his accusations, he brandished before me, not a copy of Stephen Knight's book, but a copy of . . . the address by the Revd Francis Heydon.

Tydeman would not say Heydon's explanations were *wrong*, but they were

> definitely unwise in the present climate. As the Apostle Paul once remarked, 'All things are lawful unto me, but all things are not expedient' – and it is most certainly not expedient to lay ourselves open to charges of idolatry or syncretism at a time when churches are seriously examining our beliefs and doctrines.

Tydeman claimed JAHBULON ('the words on the triangle') was a wholly
Hebrew concoction, meaning 'The True and Living God – the Most
High – The Almighty'. It was not three names of God – or three gods
joined together – but three qualities of a single deity. Tydeman said the
Methodist committee believed JAHBULON *was* the Royal Arch name for
God because many ritual 'workings' say just that. This 'brings us into
disrepute with the world outside, and will cause an increase in the
misgiving which already exists among our own members.' Tydeman
urged change.

Four months later Grand Chapter heard yet another theory. Relying on
notes that have survived since 1836, Colin Dyer said JAHBULON does
represent the name of God in different languages, but was originally
meant to be used as 'a secret word – a test word if you like – for a Royal
Arch mason', never 'a new name for God'.[17]

This seems to reduce JAHBULON to the level of those sham passwords of
the Craft degrees: Boaz, Shibboleth, Jachin, Tubal-Cain, Machaben and
Machbinna – very poor company for the 'Sacred and Mysterious Name
of God'. Dyer may be right, but how strange that all these cosy
explanations for JAHBULON are being dug up just when the Christian
churches are on the attack. Freemasonry desperately needs to 'clean up its
act', hence the 'expedient' rush to rid the Royal Arch of any hint of
paganism.

If outsiders feel the attempts to dump Ba'al are unconvincing, they
may be even less impressed by the battle over JAHBULON's last syllable.
Revd Heydon claimed the 1836 committee made a big mistake over ON.

> They did not know that On was the name of a city, and thought in
> their ignorance of Egyptology that it was an Egyptian name of God,
> hence they put it into the mouth of Hiram Abiff. However, On
> cannot be identified with the name of any Egyptian deity.

Canon Tydeman demolished this theory by quoting the Scriptures.
Hiram's mother 'was a widow of one of the northernmost tribes of Israel,
as far from Egypt as you could get, and his late father had been a man of
Tyre, which was even further away, so although Hiram could have
spoken both Hebrew and Syriac, he certainly would not have addressed
God in Egyptian'.

Tydeman is correct. Both Bible references to the man Masons call
Hiram Abiff show he was unlikely to have spoken Egyptian. Of course,
the 1836 team *might* have thought he did, decided he would have called
God ON, and therefore smacked ON on the triangle.

Higham stoutly claims JAHBULON contains no reference to 'any

Egyptian deity',[18] but both the Royal Arch Mystical Lecture and Revd Heydon claim an Egyptian deity is exactly what ON was intended to mean. If the 1836 team got it wrong, that is because they knew even less about Egyptology than about the Bible. But could they really have been so ignorant – these leaders of an order so rich, even today, in Anglican priests? Could they ever have believed Hiram Abiff was an Egyptian? His Biblical entries say only that he was 'Hiram out of Tyre . . . a widow's son of the tribe of Naphtali and his father was a man of Tyre' (1 Kings, 7: 13–14), and 'the son of a woman of the daughters of Dan' whose father was 'a man of Tyre' (2 Chronicles, 2: 14). Even if these verses refer to the same man (which is doubtful because of the confusion over the mother), Hiram was clearly not Egyptian. Nor could any member of the 1836 committee have thought he was.

But *could* they have been wrong about Joseph's father-in-law, Potipherah? He is mentioned just three times in the Bible, always baldly as 'Priest of On'. 'On' appears nowhere else, so there is nothing in the Bible to indicate it was a place. So if the Royal Arch men of 1836 really thought On was the Egyptian name of God, do they have a good excuse for doing so?

No, they do not. By the 1830s both Bible scholars and Egyptologists were well aware that 'On' was a place. Indeed, by then it was one of the touristic sites of Egypt, albeit under another name. As early as 1743 the celebrated traveller Richard Pococke had described Heliopolis, near Cairo, as 'On of the Scriptures, famous for the worship of the Sun'. These remarks appeared in his bestselling book, *A Description of the East and Some Other Countries*, without which no gentleman's library was complete.[19] In the 1820s Napoleon's team of savants published their *Description de l'Egypte*.[20] They too identified Heliopolis with Potipherah the Priest. When the German Richard Lepsius visited the site in the 1840s he also described it as the Biblical On where Joseph married Potipherah's daughter.[21]

In 1836, therefore, at least some members of the Royal Arch team must have known On was Heliopolis. They certainly dabbled in Biblical and Near Eastern studies, for their ritual claims knowledge of all sorts of ancient cults and mysteries: Egyptian, Hebrew and Greek. Only if the committee was composed entirely of charlatans would ON have appeared in JAHBULON as God's name uttered by an Egyptian-speaking Hiram Abiff. It is far more likely that ON is a hidden signpost to the city which, for thousands of years, was the centre of Egypt's most powerful cult – a place which the conquering Greeks called Heliopolis precisely because it was the 'City of the Sun'.[22]

At On–Heliopolis the Sun was worshipped through the cult of the Sun

God Re or Ra. When Osiris became Egypt's most popular God, his cult was grafted on to Ra's and practised in On's temples. Of course, such paganism would have appalled the devout Christians of the 1830s, so the Royal Arch ritualists knew they could not reveal – even to Master Masons – that ON meant Heliopolis without causing problems as serious as if they had owned up to Baal. This may be why they performed yet another cover-up by defining ON as Father of All.

Some readers may feel that branding Masonry with such deviousness is anti-Masonry gone mad, but its own principles declare that it will go to any lengths to conceal Masonic truth. First it is founded on concealment (if its secrets are secrets no more, that is no thanks to United Grand Lodge). All Masons are taught to 'be cautious in your words and carriage, that the most penetrating stranger shall not be able to discover what is not proper to be intimated'.[23] Secondly, its signs, grips and symbols are rarely what they seem, as any Mason joining the Royal Arch discovers when the secrets of the lower degrees are revealed as Masonic fool's gold. Thirdly, concealment Egyptian-style is the first art a Mason learns.

First degree initiates are meant to study a 'Tracing Board', an amateurish picture filled with images, such as the compass-and-square, a cross, three pillars, the Moon and the Sun. The Ritual offers an 'Explanation' of these images as symbols of either the 'Deity whom we serve', the virtues of Freemasonry or the moral qualities expected of a good Freemason. The Explanation opens by declaring:

> The usages and customs among Freemasons have ever borne a near affinity to those of the ancient Egyptians. Their philosophers, unwilling to expose their mysteries to vulgar eyes, couched their systems of learning and polity under signs and hieroglyphical figures which were communicated to their chief priests or Magi alone, who were bound by solemn oath to conceal them.[24]

This leaves no room for doubt that Freemasonry is an arcane mystery, with Gnostic pretensions, modelled on Ancient Egyptian religions. When the Church of England group quoted this teaching in their 1987 report, Grand Lodge moved the goalposts twice: it claimed this Explanation is no longer 'worked' in the first degree ceremony, and then dismissed it as nonsense: 'Its introduction is fairly typical of once fashionable attempts to create a more ancient history for Freemasonry. "Affinity" should not be taken literally. The Masonic scholars who claimed Egyptian, etc, origins for Freemasonry are now discredited.'[25]

It is now clear that as soon as any investigators (churchmen *or* journalists) focus on sinister aspects of Masonic ritual/teaching/history,

Grand Lodge claims they are no longer performed/taught/endorsed by Freemasons. The brotherhood's bosses are not just moving the goalposts: they are throwing the baby out with the bathwater. Forced to disclaim so many basic elements, they only seem prepared to stand by their claim to be descended from the medieval stonemasons. As we have seen in earlier chapters, even this is a slander on the stonemasons. In terms of ritual, modern Masons may owe more to Ancient Egyptians than to England's cathedral-builders, something they can scarcely admit today.

But who are these 'discredited' Masonic scholars? Presumably they include Freemasonry's founding fathers: Anderson and his unknown brethren who drew up the Craft rituals in the eighteenth century. Also condemned are nineteenth-century writers like Mackey, Gould and Pike, all of whom said the myth of Hiram Abiff was based on the legend of the Egyptian God Osiris. It has to be said that the eccentric Albert Pike (the most influential man in the history of American Freemasonry) made his claim in an attack worthy of today's Church of England:

> No man or body of men can make me accept as a sacred word, as a symbol of the infinite and eternal Godhead, a mongrel word, whose name has been for more than two thousand years an appelation of the Devil. No word has any business in the Royal Arch degree that makes the name of a heathen deity one of the names of the true God.[26]

Among twentieth-century Masonic historians J. S. M. Ward is definitely unclean. His book *Freemasonry and the Ancient Gods*[27] conjoins Assyrian, Indian, Chinese, African, South American and even Australian Aboriginal rituals in a grand tapestry, designed to prove Freemasonry is the last guardian of a magic embracing all races and stretching back to the origins of man. Ward is a dazzling juggler of ill-digested learning, yet he draws convincing parallels between the legends of Hiram Abiff, Osiris and the Phoenician god Adonis.

In 1986 Grand Lodge foresaw the Anglican group might cite Ward to prove Freemasonry was incompatible with Christianity, so it rubbished him in advance as a 'poor historian' and an 'idiosyncratic interpreter' of ritual. Yet to this day his books are prominently displayed in bookshops such as Lewis's, Britain's biggest and official Masonic publisher, in all but name. Lewis still publishes Ward's three handbooks to the Craft degrees. When Sir John Stubbs, past Grand Secretary, wrote his autobiography, it was Lewis who published it in 1985. If Grand Lodge damns Ward as a poor historian, how odd that his books appear alongside Grand Lodge's own publications on Lewis's shelves.

Three other books on Lewis's current list are by Manley Hall, an American Mason who was still going strong in the 1970s. He also believes the fraternity is descended from Ancient Egypt. In *The Lost Keys of Freemasonry* he claims 'almost undeniable' evidence that the Mysteries of Ra and Osiris are Masonry's primary sources and progenitors. The *Book of the Dead* is likewise a 'treasure house of Masonic lore': 'If the identity of the Osirian and Hiramic myths be accepted, then the *Book of the Dead* is the open sesame of symbolic Masonry, revealing a hidden beauty beneath the rituals, an unsuspected splendor in the symbols, and a divine purpose actuating the whole of Masonic procedure.'[28]

Despite these claims, Freemasonry probably has no *lineal* descent from Ancient Egypt. There is no historical continuity linking Ra, Osiris, Heliopolis or the *Book of the Dead* with the secret society which grew up in seventeenth-century Britain. Hiram Abiff and Osiris may have much in common, but the murdered god or prophet is central to many of the world's cults and religions. In this sense Freemasonry may owe as much to the Druids, Essenes and the Ancient Greeks and Romans – all of whom have had enthusiastic backing from Freemasonry's broad lunatic fringe – as to the priests of On.[29]

Trying to discover if modern Freemasonry has ancient origins is a tortuous, futile and self-defeating exercise which appears to have driven several Masonic historians crazy.[30] It is far more important to understand what the fraternity's seventeenth- and eighteenth-century begetters were trying to achieve. They claimed a historical connection with the Ancient Hebrews which was fantasy, but they were genuinely attempting to invoke the power of Hebrew philosophy and of the Kabbala, a system of magic developed by Jews in medieval times. A century later Masonic ritualists had become besotted with Egypt and other Near Eastern cultures. They tried to bend history, archaelogy and Egyptology to fit an obsession that Freemasonry was the key to man's ancient wisdom and to his glorious future.

So what did the Royal Arch team really want JAHBULON to mean in 1836? We must weigh their Mystical Lecture explanation against redefinitions by today's Royal Arch defenders, always bearing in mind the trickery and sleight-of-hand which Freemasonry admits to practising – even against its own members. Thus we still have JAH, the Chaldee name of God; BUL, the Syriac word for Lord but admitted by some to be Ba'al in disguise; and ON, the City of the Sun. So if JAHBULON means anything, it probably means 'God, the Lord of On', or possibly 'He Who is the Lord of On'. Whether that god is the Sun God Ra or Osiris the God of the Dead depends on which period of Egyptian history takes your fancy.

The Royal Arch ritual is thus performed on two levels. There is a playlet in which the Companions act the Jews' return from Babylon and the rebuilding of the Temple. Then there is the magical incantation of a made-up word which has nothing to do with the God of the Jews, but a lot to do with the pagan cults of Ba'al, Ra and Osiris. As such, it seems inconceivable that this word can be acceptable to Christians of any persuasion — or to Jews or to Muslims.

MASONIC LIGHT,
RESURRECTION AND GNOSIS

As Grand Lodge prepared evidence for the Church of England inquiry into Freemasonry in 1986, it feared the inquirers would be greatly influenced by the late Walton Hannah, whose 1950s books *Darkness Visible* and *Christian by Degrees* are still the most incisive and clinical debunking of Masonic ritual from a Christian point of view.[1]

England's Masonic bosses therefore sought to devalue the message of his books with a few sniping comments, just as it had with Stephen Knight.[2] It stated that in 1947 Hannah was an Anglican priest with 'sufficient private means' to give up his job as a priest to research 'the evils of Freemasonry' – as if having private means was the main factor in his decision. It then said that in 1956 he renounced Anglicanism and became a Roman Catholic priest. It did not say this was partly because the Church of England had refused to act against 'the evils of Freemasonry' – including the power wielded within its own ranks by Masons such as the Archbishop of Canterbury, sixteen bishops and more than 500 priests.[3]

I have already explored most of the objections raised by Hannah and others (to the penalties; to Freemasonry as worship; to its syncretism; to its amalgam of paganism, pre-Christian mysticism and non-Christian religions). Here I look at three more allegations which Hannah and other Christians have made, but which Grand Lodge fiercely rejects.

1. Freemasonry imparts spiritual light.
2. The Third Degree is a resurrection rite.
3. Freemasonry is a gnostic sect.

1. LIGHT. In the first degree ritual the would-be Mason is blindfolded with a hoodwink and described as a 'poor candidate in a state of darkness'. He is then asked, 'What in your present situation is the predominant wish of your heart?' He replies 'Light' and his hoodwink is removed. Grand Lodge claims this light means only material light: 'nowhere is it stated or

implied that the Candidate enters in a state of spiritual darkness and is then raised to spiritual light.'[4]

Concerned Christians, of course, believe only Jesus can bring spiritual light so, faced with their attacks, Grand Lodge had to make this defence. Yet many Masonic writers, including Albert Mackey, say the entire system of 'intrusting' secrets begins with the communication of light, 'one of the most important symbols in the whole science of masonic symbolism'.

> When the candidate makes a demand for light, it is not merely for that material light which is to remove a physical darkness; that is only the outward form, which conceals the inward symbolism. He craves an intellectual illumination which will dispel the darkness of mental and moral ignorance, and bring to his view, as an eye-witness, the sublime truths of religion, philosophy and science, which it is the great design of Freemasonry to teach . . . *Light*, therefore, becomes synonymous with truth and knowledge, and *darkness* with falsehood and ignorance.[5]

Darkness reminds the candidate of his ignorance and evil nature, whereas light symbolizes Masonic truth and knowledge. Darkness also symbolizes death. When the candidate is granted light he learns 'the lesson of regeneration or resurrection'.

There is hardly a Masonic writer who does not interpret Masonic light as spiritual enlightenment, rather than candlepower or electricity. Indeed, as Worshipful Brother Robert Burns well knew, Freemasons used to call themselves the 'Sons of Light':

> Oft have I met your social band,
> And spent the cheerful, festive night;
> Oft, honoured with supreme command,
> Presided o'er the sons of light.[6]

Grand Lodge may say Burns and Mackey got it all wrong but the views of a modern Masonic sage, George Draffen of Newington, are harder to dismiss. This eminent Scots Mason, who died in 1986, was 'revered throughout the Masonic world' for his knowledge of Masonic history and ritual.[7] In the Grand Lodge of Scotland's 1986 Yearbook[8] Draffen explained the symbolism of the hoodwink by reminding us that

all life begins in the dark. Nature has ordained that even the tiniest seed must rest in the dark before fruiting to full stature . . . In all animals, including primates, conception and fertilisation take place in the darkness of the womb. It is thus that the hoodwink reminds the candidate that he is undergoing a birth process.

Draffen then explains that the cable-tow or rope round the candidate's neck is 'a symbolical umbilical cord uniting his pre-initiation life and which is, of course, removed at the conclusion of the Obligation [oath-swearing], symbolising the completion of the birth and new life.'

If this intra-uterine explanation does not make sense to you non-Masons, remember Canon Tydeman's advice: 'Trying to explain the joys of masonry to an outsider is rather like trying to describe the joys of motherhood to a spinster: Masonry, like motherhood, has to be experienced before it can be understood.'[9] Motherhood? Birth? Whatever next?

Despite Grand Lodge denials, there can be little doubt that light means spiritual and moral illumination. As soon as the blindfold is off, the candidate is told about the brotherhood's three great emblematical lights: 'the Volume of Sacred Law . . . to govern our faith, the Square to regulate our actions, and the Compasses to keep us in due bounds with all mankind, particularly our brethren in Freemasonry.'[10]

Christians'may feel they can see the light of their 'VSL' (the Bible) without Freemasonry's aid, and without the help of its three 'lesser lights': the Sun, Moon and Lodge Master.

The Freemason who seeks the Royal Arch degree is again 'hood-winked' before being allowed to 'participate in the light of our mysteries'. At one point he goes on his knees and gropes around for a scroll on the floor. Because he is still blindfolded he cannot read what it says.

Let that want of light remind you that man by nature is the child of ignorance and error, and would ever have remained in a state of darkness, had it not pleased the Almighty to call him to light and immortality by the revelations of His Holy Will and Word. Rise, wrench forth the Key-stone, and prepare to receive the light of the Holy Word.[11]

The Holy Word, of course, turns out to be the 'Sacred and Mysterious Name of God' – JAHBULON – which most Christians would regard as a word of darkness, not light.

2. RESURRECTION. In the third degree ritual the candidate acts the part of Hiram Abiff. He is symbolically slain, then brought to life again. Grand

Lodge denies this is a resurrection rite in any sense, yet many Masonic writers claim it is. In *Who was Hiram Abiff?* J. S. M. Ward traced the Hiramic legend back to many Near Eastern gods who died to be born again. He explores myths of death and resurrection from all parts of the world, but plumps for Adonis as the true model for Hiram Abiff. Grand Lodge regards Ward as discredited,[12] but Mackey is less easily dismissed:

> Take, for instance, the Hiramic legend of the third degree. Of what importance is it to the disciple of Masonry whether it be true or false? All he wants to know is its internal significance; and when he learns that it is intended to illustrate the doctrine of the immortality of the soul, he is content with that interpretation.[13]

If, despite what Grand Lodge is now saying, Freemasonry does have a doctrine dealing with the soul's immortality, and illustrated by a resurrection rite, this would disturb Christians who hold that only belief in Christ's resurrection can bring immortality.

3. GNOSTICISM: 'the system or principles professed by the Gnostics', says the Oxford English Dictionary which defines the Gnostics as 'certain heretical sects among the early Christians who claimed to have superior knowledge of things spiritual, and interpreted the sacred writings by a mystic philosophy'. Walton Hannah defined Gnosticism as 'a theosophical philosophy [which] professed to reveal to an inner elite of initiates esoteric teachings concealed from the many'.[14]

The 1986 Church of England team objected to the Royal Arch ritual because of its 'gnostic' claims that 'further "revelation" beyond that found in Christ is necessary or possible'.[15] Grand Lodge retorted by defining Gnosticism as 'relating to special knowledge' and then said 'Freemasonry claims no special knowledge'.[16]

This again is nonsense. Through myriad orders and degrees Freemasonry unveils to an ever more elite group a seemingly endless progression of spiritual mysteries: from darkness to light, from death to resurrection, from the first degree password Boaz to the incantation of JAHBULON and beyond. Meanwhile, behind Freemasonry's 'surface-rituals and doctrine', says the Masonic writer W. L. Wilmshurst, the Brethren may research and discover a '*Gnosis* or Wisdom-teaching as old as the world'.[17]

At this point we should look again at Canon Tydeman's explanation of the Masonic secret, which Grand Lodge felt would help its case with the Church of England:[18]

The 'secret' of Masonry is completely indefinable and will always be inexplicable to the uninstructed outside world because it can only be obtained by those who come of their own free will and accord, properly prepared and humbly soliciting. And the knowledge that this humility has been shared by everyone else in the room is the cement which binds Masons. The 'secret' is the shared experience and the presence of even one non-Mason who has not shared that experience would be enough to lose that cement completely.

This seems remarkably like the Gnostic heresy. This would be no sin in a non-Christian but is not the kind of thing one expects to hear from a Church of England minister!

Colin Dyer is one of today's most respected Masonic interpreters. In his book *Symbolism and Craft Freemasonry* he quotes many sources to show that the Craft's eighteenth-century revisers consciously reshaped it to resemble Gnostic-style groups such as Pythagoreans, Essenians, Cabbalists and Druids. None of these was Christian but all offered *Gnosis* – which the OED defines as 'a special knowledge of spiritual mysteries'. In the eighteenth century Europe was in intellectual ferment. Many people, not just Masons, were seeking Gnostic secrets. Yet only Freemasonry succeeded in welding this kind of 'knowledge' into a spiritual system which would be embraced by large numbers of nominal Christians.

Christian churches are not concerned about sects who claim Gnostic insights into *other* religions. What upsets them about Freemasonry is that it deals in ideas about faith, redemption and immortality which they believe ought only to be pursued through Christ. And if Masons, by luck or judgement, really have discovered anything worth knowing, it surely is un-Christian – and a Gnostic crime – for them not to tell all humanity, instead of chanting it to each other within their temples.

Beyond the non-Christian Craft and Royal Arch degrees are the self-styled 'Christian Orders' including the Knights Templar, the Red Cross of Constantine and the Rose Croix. The 1986 Anglican inquiry did not explore their rituals, but in the 1950s Walton Hannah dissected them with his usual tenacity. No words of mine can improve on his analysis of the ritual which enables Rose Croix Masons of the 18th degree to vault straight to the 31st. For Hannah it was 'certainly Gnostic'.[19]

The obligation pledges fidelity to the 'secrets of any mysteries of this Order,' and the various emblems, principally the rose and the cross, are called 'symbols of hidden Truths known only to the perfect Mason' . . . The Princes Rose Croix are bidden to 'treasure up the sacred doctrines of the Order in the secret repository' of their hearts.

The emphasis seems to be on the initiate's impersonation of Christ in achieving his own salvation through enlightenment . . . The initiate gives his age as 33, whatever it may be in reality. He travels for 33 days in seven concentric circles representing the seven periods of the world's existence. He passes through the blackness of death to his resurrection in the Red Room, and ascends the ladder to glory and perfection. He hears the Resurrection in the Closing ceremony described as 'the hour of a perfect Mason'. This seems a little sinister, but far less so than the description of Our Lord's triumphant redemptive death on the Cross as a 'dire calamity for Masonry' – a phrase which carries the unfortunate suggestion that the defeat of Satan is being mourned. But, in any case, why a calamity for Masonry in particular, unless Masonry represents an inner circle of illuminati, more particularly concerned than the rest of mankind? How absurd it would sound to call the Crucifixion a dire calamity for the Mother's Union or the Church of England Men's Society!

Yet even now the 31st degree Freemason has another degree to go before he becomes a 'Sublime Prince of the Royal Secret'.

The Anglican report did not mention Hannah's brilliant dissection of the Rose Croix, which got off lightly. In contrast, Grand Lodge felt that its spurned evidence should have been 'accepted as authoritative' because it is 'likely to be more expert' in interpreting rituals than other people.[20] Its expertise was not in doubt, only its honesty. It may have administrative authority over the Craft but it has no authority over how Masons should interpret their rituals. Any Mason's view is as valid as any other's precisely because Grand Lodge claims there is no dogma and no Vatican-style seat of infallible power, as we saw on page 53.

Grand Lodge ruefully observes that Walton Hannah is quoted so often because he wrote commentaries on ritual 'which Freemasons will not do'.[21] This is nonsense. Many more Masons have written commentaries than non-Masons. Hundreds of books have been published explaining Freemasonry's rituals and symbols. Without them most Masons would have no idea what their ceremonies mean. For a hundred years research lodges have published thousands of articles to increase understanding. In 1888 the Quatuor Coronati Lodge published its first volume of papers on subjects such as:

An Early Version of the Hiramic Legend
Freemasonry and Hermeticism
The Orientation of Temples

Links between Ancient and Modern Freemasonry
The Religion of Freemasonry Illuminated by the Kabbalah
English Freemasonry Before the Era of Grand Lodges
Two New Versions of the Old Charges.

The lodge has since heard lectures on the Worship of Death, the Noose Symbol, the Tau Cross, the Masonic Apron, the Tracing Board, the Rosicrucians and Freemasonry, Death and the Freemason, Pillars in the Porch of Solomon's Temple, Gnostic Sects and Their Influence on Freemasonry, the Evolution of Masonic Ritual, the Templar Legends in Freemasonry, Freemasonry and the Essenes, Freemasonry and the Cult of Mithras, the Mason Word, Masonic Initiation Aboard Ship, the Obligation and its Place in the Ritual, Solomon and his Temple in the Masonic Tradition, Rituals of the Royal Arch, the Masonic Penalties, the Change from Christianity to Deism in Freemasonry, 600 Years of Craft Ritual, the Passing the Chair Ceremony, etc., etc.[22]

In all this verbiage, in books, and week by week in Lodges of Instruction all over the world, Masons have always commented on the rituals. Hannah is quoted so often only because he makes some sense of the many Masonic theologies which have developed, despite the ban on religious discussion.

In 1754 a book was published called *The Free Mason Examin'd*.[23] This bestseller revealed that the rituals of Freemasonry were really based on the building of the Tower of Babel. It may have been a spoof, but when it comes to sorting out the truth about Freemasons and religion from their own writings, the Tower of Babel seems wholly appropriate:

And the Lord said . . . let us go down, and there confound their language, that they may not understand one another's speech.

six

OBELISKS AND EGYPT

Today Freemasons may deny that any part of their cult hearkens back to the pagan gods of the Nile. Yet in Freemasons' Hall, Dublin, home of the world's second oldest Grand Lodge, the Holy Royal Arch Room contains two large sphinxes and other sculptures aping Ancient Egypt. In Philadelphia USA the Masonic Temple boasts 'the finest specimen of Egyptian decoration outside Egypt'.[1] Even London's Great Eastern Hotel at Liverpool Street station has a magnificent Egyptian Temple for lodges to rent for their ritual nights out.

The most blatant symbols of Freemasonry's obsession with Egypt are not hidden in its temples. They stand on public view in the centre of London, Paris, New York and Washington. How they came to be erected shows both the immense power of Freemasons in the nineteenth century and their love affair with the most evocative symbol of all Egyptian religion: the obelisk.[2]

Why the obelisk? To early Egyptians it was the shape sacred to the Sun God Re or Ra; the creator of humanity, the source of all heat and light, the being on whom man was totally dependent. By the fifth dynasty Re had become so popular he was elevated to the role of state deity. His main centre of worship was On–Heliopolis where the first kings erected primitive obelisks, rough-hewn and truncated, but tipped off by the pyramidion shape which distinguishes obelisks from other monumental columns. These prototype obelisks were known as 'benben' stones.

> The spirit of the Sun-god was supposed to enter the stones at certain periods, and on these occasions human sacrifices were offered to it. The victims were probably prisoners of war who had been captured alive, and foreigners, and when these failed, the priests must have drawn upon the native population.[3]

At On–Heliopolis king after king erected benbens in Re's honour, so that by 1300 B.C. the city was full of obelisks: some decorated with gold to resemble the sun's rays, others with inscriptions glorifying Re's daily passage through the skies, or hailing earthly occasions such as victories, feasts and jubilees.

The pharaohs of later dynasties switched their obelisk-erecting affections to Osiris: God of the earth, vegetation and the Nile flood that gave life to all Egypt; God of rebirth; God also of the Underworld, the Last Judgement and Life after Death. As this cult became ever more popular, the priests at Heliopolis shrewdly grafted it on to Re-worship by claiming Osiris was Re's grandson.[4] This ensured that Heliopolis remained the greatest religious centre in Egypt and the entire Mediterranean region. Even the Roman author Pliny knew of this city where kings 'entered into a kind of rivalry in forming elongated blocks of stone, known as *obelisks*, and consecrated them to the divinity of the *Sun*'.[5]

The Egyptians found Osiris particularly attractive because of the bittersweet myth of his life, death and reincarnation. This has been told many times in many ways, but Masonic historians have tended to agree on a version that satisfies their ritual needs.[6]

Osiris was a King of Egypt who married his sister Isis. His brother, Set, wished to usurp the throne and so plotted his death. He tricked Osiris into climbing in a golden chest. As soon as he was inside, Set nailed down the lid and flung the chest into the Nile. It was carried off to Byblos in Syria where it came to rest against a small tamarisk or acacia tree, with the dead Osiris still inside.

Isis found out what Set had done to Osiris, so she set off to find her husband. A vision led her to Byblos, where she recovered his body and took it back to Egypt. Alas! Set stole it and tore it into fourteen pieces, which he scattered through Egypt to prevent Osiris coming to life again.

Isis recovered all but one of the pieces and gave Osiris a fit burial. Their son, Horus, avenged him by slaying Set. Another son, Anubis, resurrected Osiris with the lion grip. Having triumphed over the grave, Osiris now reigns as King and Judge of the so-called dead.

The piece of Osiris which Isis never recovered was the penis, which Set had cruelly thrown into the Nile where it was eaten by fish. Everresourceful, Isis 'manufactured an artificial organ around which the Egyptians established a cult and festival'.[7] From this it is a small step to the conclusion that the benben or obelisk was itself a phallic symbol. Whether of Osiris, Re or of fertility in general, it was a symbol of fatherhood: 'the rock that begot.'[8]

To Freemasons groping for mystic enlightenment in the 1800s the obelisk was the only architectural symbol of Osiris still in existence. And if, as some Masonic historians claim, Hiram Abiff is really Osiris reborn, there could be no greater proof of Masonic ascendancy in the modern world than Egyptian obelisks thrust by Masons into the heart of the West's greatest cities. These would also symbolize Boaz and Jachin, the twin pillars which Masons claim were built in front of Solomon's Temple, in 'imitation of two obelisks at the entrance of Egyptian temples'.[9] These are mentioned even in the *Book of the Dead*, the texts which every well-heeled Ancient Egyptian had placed in his tomb to make sure he was resurrected in the Kingdom of Osiris: 'Two pillars at the gateway to his house were Set and Horus.'[10]

Obelisk mania had already engulfed Freemasonry by the time Napoleon Bonaparte set sail for Egypt in 1798. Whether Napoleon was a Mason is fiercely disputed but his four brothers certainly were. He was also encircled by Masonic advisers who convinced him Egypt held the original secrets of history, philosophy and (of course) Freemasonry. Masons figured among the 150 scholars who joined the Emperor on his triumphant Nile progress, pillaging pyramids, temples and tombs all in the name of learning. They instantly realized that the Rosetta Stone (unearthed by French soldiers) might unlock the lost language of Egypt. To decipher its hieroglyphs took many years and the genius of Champollion, yet even he needed the help of an obelisk bearing Cleopatra's cartouche, which was removed for shipment to England in 1818 by a Masonic adventurer: Giovanni Batista Belzoni.[11]

Belzoni was a mountebank archaeologist who opened up the temple of Abu Simbel and the second pyramid at Giza. He began his Masonic career in Cairo, appropriately, in the Lodge of the Pyramids and then joined lodges in Cambridge and Norwich. He died in 1825, searching for Timbuctoo or the source of the Niger, but not before doing Freemasonry an inestimable service by claiming to have discovered an ancient Masonic temple in Thebes. He claimed its wall paintings showed Osiris being initiated into Freemasonry, pursuing its 'sublime mysteries', and – clad in a distinctive Masonic apron – awarding another Mason a higher degree.[12]

After Belzoni died his wife Sarah transcribed his notes, including this declaration: 'Let the Masonic brethren search, and they will find, that the Egyptian Masonic Key will unlock the hitherto unrevealed mysteries of Egyptian wisdom.'

Sarah had been left destitute by her husband's death, but the United Grand Lodge of England gave her the substantial sum of £50 to help bear the 'irreparable loss which she, as well as the lovers of science and literature' had sustained.[13] No matter that his 'Masonic temple' proved to be the tomb of Pharaoh Seti I and that all he (or Sarah) had written was bunkum, Masons felt they owed much to Belzoni. His Masonic 'discoveries' sent packs of them off to Egypt in search of any obelisk they could plunder.

Paris was the first major city to groan under the weight of this Masonic fad. In 1830 the Viceroy of Egypt, Mohammed Ali, gave France's King Charles X a magnificent obelisk, but the French themselves had to remove it from Luxor where it had stood for 3,500 years. As the 92-ft prize weighed 246 tons this was no easy task. Before it could be achieved, a Masonic conspiracy had deposed Charles and replaced him with King Louis-Philippe. Among the conspirators was Louis Thiers who was Minister of Public Works by the time the obelisk had been floated down the Nile and up the Seine. When it was erected five years later in the Place de la Concorde, Thiers was Prime Minister. Thirty-five years later in 1871 he became France's first President.

At this time an obelisk which Mohammed Ali had awarded England back in 1819 was still prostrate in Alexandria, where it had fallen centuries before. It was not until 1875 that an eminent Mason, General Sir James Alexander, resolved to ship 'Cleopatra's Needle' to London. This now occurred, but only because another Mason, Dr Erasmus Wilson, agreed to put up £20,000 to ship and erect it. The two engineers who planned its transportation, Dixon and Stephenson, were also Masons. In 1877 the obelisk was encased in an iron cylinder, christened Cleopatra, and towed out from Alexandria. The voyage was a catastrophe. During a storm in the Bay of Biscay the Cleopatra broke loose. Six men drowned. The obelisk did not sink but was recovered and eventually towed to England. At last on 13 September 1878 it was erected alongside the Thames on Victoria Embankment – a less glorious site than Parliament Square, which some worthies had suggested but which had been ruled out because of the damage which the obelisk's 186 tons might do to underground gas and sewer pipes. For his massive expenditure Erasmus Wilson received a knighthood.

Various items were encased in the obelisk's new pedestal: a box of hairpins, a portrait of Queen Victoria, a shilling razor and chapter 3 verse 16 of the Gospel of St John in 215 languages: 'For God so loved the world, that he gave his only begotten Son, that whosoever believeth in him should not perish, but have everlasting life.' As this was buried out of sight, posterity might find the inscriptions on the obelisk more eloquent. These spoke of the Sun God Ra, of Horus and of Osiris: another God's son whose death gave believers everlasting life.

The news that English Masons had succeeded in erecting Cleopatra's Needle encouraged American Masons to ship its twin across the Atlantic. Both had stood at Heliopolis until the Roman Emperor Augustus moved them to Alexandria around 22 B.C. to adorn a new palace, but whereas England's needle had toppled centuries ago, the 'American' obelisk was still standing. It had been given to America in 1877, but two years passed before a benefactor was found to pay for its shipment and erection, and a sailor-cum-engineer volunteered to attempt the task. The prime mover was a New York editor named William Hulbert, the benefactor (to the tune of $75,000) was William J. Vanderbilt, and the sailor was a Lt-Cmdr Henry Gorringe. All were Freemasons.

Gorringe needed even greater spunk than his British counterparts. The obelisk's removal provoked bitter local objections. Lowering, then loading its 220 tons on board ship were delicate and dangerous tasks. Then the ship had to survive a near mutiny and severe storms before sailing into New York in July 1880. A site was finally agreed – in Central Park near the Metropolitan Museum – and a ceremony to fit the occasion was arranged for 9 October.

This was a brazenly Masonic affair. Nine thousand Freemasons marched with bands through the streets to Greywacke Knoll where Jesse Anthony, the Grand Master of New York Masons, laid the 7-ton cornerstone. After extolling Egypt as the birthplace of science, astronomy, literature and art, he told his enthralled audience that Masons needed to revise their thinking on the origins of their order: 'There can be no question but that in the secret societies of Egypt are to be found some elements now embraced in the principles or symbolism of Masonry.'

It took another four months to drag the obelisk from its landing stage to its 50-ton pedestal, also shipped from Alexandria. When it was finally erected in January 1881, the tune of Martin Luther's hymn 'Ein' Feste Burg' was sung with specially written words, whose significance no Mason could miss:

> Great God, to Whom since time began,
> The world has prayed and striven;
> Maker of stars, and earth, and man –
> To thee our praise is given!
> Here by this ancient Sign
> Of Thine own Light Divine,
> We lift to Thee our eyes,
> Thou Dweller of the skies –
> Hear us, O God in Heaven!

For some Masonic enterprises, an orginal Egyptian benben was not good enough. Since 1848 an obelisk had been going up in Washington DC to honour America's founding President, George Washington, who had been a Freemason. His funeral in 1799 had been conducted according to Masonic rites. The coffin had been draped with a Masonic apron given by a brother revolutionary and Mason, the Marquis de Lafayette, and the many Masons present each cast a sprig of acacia, to symbolize both Osiris' resurrection and Washington's own imminent resurrection in the realm where Osiris presides.[14]

The cornerstone for the Washington monument was a 10-ton slab of marble given by a Freemason. Unlike its Egyptian forebears this obelisk would be made not from a single stone but from marble blocks weighing 81,000 tons. The Civil War halted construction, so it was not until 1884 that the obelisk reached its full 555 feet and was topped off by an aluminium capstone with due Masonic pomp. On 21 February 1885 – Washington's birthday – the monument was dedicated in another dose of fraternal self-congratulation. One prominent brother spoke of Masons now as builders of human society. Their stones were living men, 'their minds enlightened with divine love, their hearts radiant with discovering the joy of pure love, their souls cherishing – like the ancient Egyptian worshippers of Osiris – the hope of immortality'.

The nineteenth century saw a forest of obelisks sprout in cities all over the Masonic world. Even a small town like Comber in Ireland acquired one, unveiled in 1844 before the banners of thirty-five lodges in Irish Freemasonry's largest public gathering. Yet not all obelisks are Masonic symbols. Rome has eleven, mostly brought from Egypt by ancient Emperors with delusions of grandeur. After re-erecting Caligula's obelisk in St Peter's Square in 1586 Pope Sixtus V exorcized it, consecrated it and surmounted it with a Holy Cross. Many British war memorials built after World War I are obelisk-shaped, but they are usually adorned with a saying from the New Testament or a sculpture of Christ on the Cross. There is a clear difference in meaning and intent between these Christianized forms and the pagan monuments which Masons erected in London, New York and Washington 100 years ago.

Christians may be offended by Masonry's obsession with things Egyptian, although agnostics may feel the afterlife offered by Osiris is more attractive than the Christian prospectus of Purgatory, Heaven or Hell. Either way, 'profane' students suspect that today's Masonic spokesmen are denying the brotherhood's past embrace with the gods of the Nile just to keep present-day Christians at bay. In Australia they are not so coy. In 1978 a new Masonic Royal Arch temple was built in Petersham, New South Wales. The Mayor and other town dignitaries came to the opening, and admired the painstaking care with which an Egyptian room had been transferred from the old temple. Around the walls was a mural of paintings taken from the *Book of the Dead*, including images of Osiris 'the god of light and the god of the quick and the dead'.[15]

One Royal Arch Mason told me his fraternity's love affair with obelisks was nothing more than a 'bunch of pricks in search of needles', but can dabbling in ancient cults be so easily dismissed? Despite the bluster, might any part of Freemasonry go beyond sun-worship or the commemoration of ancient Gods into the realms of devil-worship?

seven

SORCERY, SEX, SATAN
AND SKULLS

I became a Freemason in 1970, but even as I was going through the first degree ritual I had misgivings. It felt odd swearing that horrific oath on the Bible while a sharp compass point was thrust hard against my naked left breast. It felt odder still to be told to seal that oath by kissing the Bible, and then have my face thrust into the compass and square as they lay cradled on its open pages. It was only later that I realized the compasses and square were arranged in the shape of the *vesica piscis* and the whole ceremony had sexual overtones.

Despite my unease I passed through the three Craft degrees in just three meetings. During the third degree ritual the Deacons laid me on the floor and wrapped me in a shroud: a black sheet with white skulls and crossbones embroidered on it. They told me to stay as still as if I were dead, until they lifted me to my feet and the Lodge Master applied the Master Mason's grip.

As I lay there I suddenly felt the overpowering presence of evil. I had never consciously thought about evil before, let alone felt it, but now my brain was pounding. I felt a piercing pain in my skull, like the worst headache you can ever imagine. Even so, I went through with the ceremony and became a Master Mason.

This story may sound like the ramblings of a man obsessed by occult fantasies, someone who probably cannot hold down a decent job. In fact, the speaker is a leading City of London financier. Over lunch in the heart of the Square Mile, he explained how he had been through a deeply disturbing experience.

The stabbing headache kept coming back – not only on Lodge nights but *every* night for more than ten years. I suffered the worst attacks in my bedroom of all places, so I got into the compulsive habit of laying out a pair of socks in the form of a cross on the floor beside my bed before I could get to sleep. I don't know if my wife ever noticed this. I suppose I was trying to repel evil, though I never reasoned it out that way at the time.

I attended my Masonic lodge for seven years, and then resigned. Later I realized this period coincided exactly with years when I was suffering constant illness: glandular fever, chronic pharyngitis, spontaneous haemorrhaging and malignant skin cancer. I might have induced these conditions myself, I suppose, but the skin cancer went far beyond most people's psychosomatic powers. By now I was constantly swallowing Valium and sleeping pills. I was also afflicted with acute trigeminal neuralgia: a facial paralysis, rather like what you feel from a dental injection but it doesn't go away. Also a dental injection prevents pain, but this was causing it: so much that sometimes I screamed out in agony.

By 1980 I was near to suicide. One Sunday, when I was very low indeed, I went to my parish church and felt compelled to take Communion. When I got to the rail I begged for forgiveness and asked to be fed with the bread of life. I don't remember taking the sacraments, but when I got home my family says my face was shining. Several months later I realized, that was the very same day I suddenly stopped taking all those pills.

It sounds corny, I know, but I had 'found God'. I became a committed Christian and spoke to groups all over the country but I was still in torment, as I realized during a meeting in Peterborough. The Chairman volunteered me to pray for any people present who were in distress. Someone came forward desperate for help, but I had no experience of this kind of work. I tried to extend my arms in support but my elbows were locked rigid. I felt terrible. I got out of the hall as soon as I could. I knew there was something seriously wrong with me, so I prayed for help.

I told a friend who introduced me to a Pentecostal minister. He said he felt I was treasuring some things which, in the eyes of God, formed a spiritual bondage with an illicit past. He did not identify the objects, but he said the source of the evil was in my bedroom: on top of the wardrobe and in the dressing table. These were the exact places where I kept my Masonic regalia and ritual books. When I got home I took them straight round to my vicar. He said the only thing to do was to destroy them, so we threw them on a bonfire.

That night I stopped arranging my socks in the shape of a cross! I knew at last the oppressive curse had been broken. Thinking back to the Masonic ceremony when I had first sensed overpowering evil, I realize I may have been particularly susceptible to such feelings. Perhaps I'm psychic whereas most other Freemasons – good men, I am sure – simply don't respond to such vibrations. Whatever the explanation, I would not wish on anyone the distress which that Masonic rigmarole caused me for so many years.

I quote this testimony at length because it is typical of many 'confessions' I have heard in the past three years, usually from 'Born-again' or 'Charismatic' Christians. Under the noses of the main denominations, a fundamentalist revival has been taking place. This is not good news for some sections of the Anglican hierarchy. It is bad news for Freemasonry. David Vaughan, an Ipswich businessman, says 'in Freemasonry Satan affects the wife as well as the husband' by making it difficult for couples to pray together. Since Jesus led him out, he and his wife have prayed together: 'I sold all my regalia and burned the rituals and certificates. Ever since then I have always advised "Freed Masons" to burn the lot!'[1]

Vaughan belongs to a group calling itself the Full Gospel Business Men's Fellowship. I went to one of its meetings in Oxfordshire one torrential night. In the unlikely surroundings of an ex-servicemen's club – all booze, fags and darts – some sixty sober Christian folk shared a meal and heard a surveyor named John Walker tell of his flight from the Mason cult. 'I believe it is of the devil,' he said, 'it has a satanic origin', and then he went through the full slate of Christian objections. He recalled how he once went to a Masonic Knights Templar meeting which five Anglican clergymen also attended. While everyone else was dressed as Crusaders, the priests were clad in surplice, cassock and biretta, as if to show Christian support for the rituals. 'Many Masons are fine men,' said Walker, 'but they are held in spiritual bondage.'

When Walker renounced Masonry he was afraid of losing business, because 'being involved in Freemasonry is a useful adjunct to your career'. He was very worried about the reaction of one Mason architect who gave him a lot of surveying work. When Walker told him, 'Jesus means more than Freemasonry' the architect replied, 'John, you're a fool!' Walker thought the man would never employ him again, but 'we're still working for him. God has protected us. Jesus is the Lord of my business and my life.'

Walker told me that sometimes at these meetings people openly renounce Freemasonry and declare for Jesus. No such thing happened this evening. There were many 'Hallelujahs!' and much speaking-in-tongues, until one woman came forward to give herself to Christ. She was embraced by healers, laid back on the floor in a swoon and then resurrected. It all seemed a bit like Freemasonry's third degree.

Neutral observers might feel that Born-Again Christians attacking Freemasonry is like the pot calling the kettle black, but there is evidence to justify concern over the psychic/psychiatric impact which the rituals might have on susceptible personalities. The Church of England Group was convinced by submissions it had received (from sources other than mine) that 'the dramatic effect of the rituals has had a "psychic" effect'. Some Christians found them 'positively evil', including one ex-Mason whose letter was quoted in the Anglican report.[2]

> For a long time, even after my conversion, I defended Masonry, and maintained that I was able to reconcile its philosophy and precepts – supposedly based on teaching morality and charity – with Christianity.
>
> But in His time and in His own gentle way, the Holy Spirit began to show me how blind I had been, and how effectively the enemy can use his weapons of subtlety and rationality in the blinding process. It was to the point of having my eyes fully open, and my heart sufficiently convicted of the evils attaching to masonry and the powerful bondage it imposes. It was one of the hardest things I have ever had to do – getting rid of my regalia, Masonic literature and all the outward trappings of this evil craft. But this was not enough – the Holy Spirit showed that another step had to be taken in order to completely release me from the bondage I was in, and that was to approach a brother in Christ who would pray for my release. This he did with the laying on of hands.
>
> What a beautiful sense of lightness and freedom I experienced when that oppression was lifted!

For obvious reasons the report did not name this man, but Dr Michael Clift of Gloucester has given me permission to quote from a long note which he wrote about Freemasonry in his family. Dr Clift, who was born in 1928, is a 'Lewis' (the name Masons use to describe the son of a Mason) and a 'Martin' (a Mason's brother), but from an early age he found Freemasonry repellent in every way. This was partly because of the way his father lived it.

> My father was dedicated to Freemasonry, and made sure this was borne in upon all of us. It took priority over everything else. Paradoxically he made regular and nauseating references to his Masonic status while yet tantalizing us with its secrecy. His Masonic

friends were all of similar types, pompous and covert, and I
supposed them all to be similar to him in the matter of honesty. But
yet he would say, 'I am an upright man, I am a Freemason'.

It has to be said that many of the reasons why Michael Clift hated his
father had nothing to do with Freemasonry. Indeed, if the son is correct,
the father manifested few qualities which Freemasonry claims to
cultivate.

He was a truly appalling creature, arrogant, shabby, sly, vindictive,
cruel, cowardly and a bully. He delighted in humiliating people,
especially my sister and me. He would break confidences and break
his word, yet he would say, 'My word is my bond. I am a
Freemason'. The worst thing to me is that I cannot in any way
defend or admire him – and I know how this makes me appear now –
but I just couldn't, for this would be gross dishonesty. He was the
worst human being I have ever met; the only difference between him
and the great ogres of history (like Ivan the Terrible) is that he didn't
have the same extent of power.

To explain Michael's relationship with his father would take a book in
itself. Rightly or wrongly, he felt his father favoured his other son, Tony,
who was twelve years older. Even so, Michael developed a strong
affection for Tony, a 'good brother: straightforward, logical with a keen
scientific mind'. Tony became a dentist. When he came home from
World War II, his father persuaded him to join the Craft.

Within three years of his initiation my brother was becoming a
stranger to me. His logical and scientific mind was now giving way
to occult influence and crankiness of the more extreme kind. He
began going regularly to seances, and he developed an interest in
flying saucers. The book *Flying Saucers Have Landed* was to him all
believable, even to the extent of 'Venusians' having learned English,
and having taken the author up in their machine and around the
moon where a city was to be seen! Tony not only took this as Gospel
but even refused to unbelieve it when the Apollo series proved him
wrong. In 1950, when I was a medical student, he told me that he
thought that drinking one's own urine could be a cure-all – even for
cancer. I was flabbergasted and told him so. Blandly he asked if I had
tried it. As I had not, he said, with what authority could I speak?
     At the time I did not think of any connection with Freemasonry.
Indeed I knew so little of what went on in Lodges that I didn't even

realize there was a quasi-religious side to it, and I did not know about the astrological, geometrical, and hieroglyphical mumbo-jumbo with which the whole thing is riddled. But now I realize that my brother's decline from a man with a fine, scientific brain into a hulk filled with nonsense and superstition can only have been precipitated by his obsessive enthusiasm for Freemasonry.

Tony Clift became one of Gloucester's most eminent Masons. He was master of his Lodge and joined Gloucestershire's Installed Masters Lodge. He was in Chapter, the Mark Masons and the Royal Ark Mariners. He also reached the 30th degree of the Rose Croix and basked in the title of Grand Elected Knight Kadosh, Knight of the Black and White Eagle.

When he died in 1980, Michael arranged a memorial service through Tony's brother Mason, Archdeacon Walter Wardle, who supplied Gloucester Cathedral free of charge. Michael only found out later that Tony had not put any money aside in his will to repay a large but undocumented loan from Michael twenty years earlier. This further disillusioned Michael about Freemasonry's much-vaunted principles of Brotherly Love, Relief and Truth.

> Apart from its obvious use in bringing personal benefits, Free-masonry is really a potty enterprise and not worth any attention at all, so to ignore it is the best thing. What a pity that those who are harmed by it, or excluded from advancement by it, cannot do likewise. And yet I must say that, however naive the individual Mason might be, the movement as a whole is a development of cunning. All they do, all they say, all they stand for, has been deliberately conceived in the first place by the most intelligently deceitful minds of long ago, and kept alive by similar ones today. One might describe it as 'the Craft of the Crafty'.

Dr Clift has been deeply scarred by a series of appalling family relationships, by emotional deprivation as a child and by a deep sense of betrayal as an adult. His hatred of Freemasonry has to be seen in that light. Yet he also struck me as a man of outstanding intelligence, able to detach himself from his own troubles and arrive at a view of Freemasonry which is by no means improbable.

From such personal testaments two strands emerge: the psychic and psychiatric distress which Freemasonry can cause in certain personalities; and the idea that, somewhere in all this, the devil is making himself manifest.

The devilish side of the argument ties in with the Baal/Ba'al interpretation of JAHBULON. Those who believe BUL really is the devil in disguise would not be at all surprised if the devil takes possession of Masons and uses them for his own ends. Those who believe in neither the devil nor God may find this hard to swallow, but of course they would find all Freemasonry indigestible! Believers might want to know if any other references to the devil may be found anywhere else in its rituals or literature, or indeed in the lives of any Masons.

Yes, say some anti-Masons, citing the writings of America's most celebrated Mason, Albert Pike. This bizarre soldier, adventurer and poet was 'Grand Commander, Sovereign Pontiff' of Scottish Rite Freemasonry in the southern and western United States from 1859 to 1891. His most famous work, *Morals and Dogma*, is a weird jumble of learning: ill-digested, often incoherent, yet – like *Finnegans Wake* – a work of nigh-impenetrable genius.

On 14 July 1889 Pike allegedly issued these instructions to twenty-three Scottish Rite Supreme Councils throughout the world:

> That which we must say to the crowd is – we worship a God, but it is the God that one adores without superstition. To you, Sovereign Grand Inspectors General, we say this, that you may repeat it to the Brethren of the 32nd, 31st and 30th degrees – the Masonic Religion should be, by all of us initiates of the high degrees, maintained in the purity of the Luciferian Doctrine.
>
> If Lucifer were not God would Adonay (The God of the Christians) whose deeds prove his cruelty, perfidy and hatred of man, barbarism and repulsion for science, would Adonay and his priests, calumniate him?
>
> Yes Lucifer is God, and unfortunately Adonay is also god. For the eternal law is that there is no light without shade, no beauty without ugliness, no white without black, for the absolute can only exist as two gods: darkness being necessary for light to serve as its foil as the pedestal is necessary to the statue and the brake to the locomotive.
>
> Thus the doctrine of Satanism is a heresy; and the true and pure philosophical religion is the belief in Lucifer, the equal of Adonay; but Lucifer, God of Light and God of Good is struggling for humanity against Adonay, the God of Darkness and Evil.

There are problems with this quotation: its meaning is not immediately clear and its authenticity is in doubt. It was first attributed to Pike in 1894 by a French authoress who detested Freemasonry, yet no original text seems to exist. Genuine or not, England's Grand Lodge dismisses it by pointing out Pike must have been eighty at the time and 'may also have been dotty'.[3]

Yet the quote sounds authentic. Its pyrotechnic language and bombastic poesy recalls Pike's earlier writings, and the message is not so different from that of *Morals and Dogma*. If genuine, it indicates there is a Satanic – or Luciferian – strain in American Masonry. Pike seems to be saying there are two gods in the universe locked in an eternal struggle for ascendancy. He says Satanism is heresy because it infers Lucifer is evil and the God of the Christians is good. On the contrary, says Pike: the Christian God is evil whereas Lucifer is good.

Yet even if the quote is genuine and Pike was a Satanist, his writings and rituals have no place in English Masonry's version of America's Scottish Rite, the Rose Croix.[4] Even if it did, the Rose Croix has no authority over the vast majority of English Masons who do not belong to it. To prove Satanism is part of mainstream Freemasonry, any 'prosecutor' has to prove direct links between Satanist groups and the Grand Lodge of England.

'The cornerstone of all modern occultism' is how one present-day Masonic author describes the notorious Order of the Golden Dawn.[5] Although this group is alleged to have petered out sixty years ago, its influence on twentieth-century literature, art and music – including rock – has been immense. It still has an extraordinary fascination for students of ritual magic, both in and out of Freemasonry.

Freemasons were prominent throughout the Golden Dawn's bitter, bitchy history. It was founded in 1887 by a Freemason, William Wynn Westcott, who claimed to have deciphered a coded alchemical manuscript containing initiation rituals of a secret German occult order, 'Die Goldene Dämmerung'. It seems clear from some published accounts that Westcott probably forged the manuscript and invented a lady named Anna Sprengel in Nuremberg as the order's only living practitioner. She authorized Westcott to found a new branch in England and to write her signature on all necessary documents. Even more obligingly, she died in 1890 leaving him to develop the Golden Dawn along any lines that took his occult fancy.

Westcott already had experience of concocting magical rituals. Back in 1865 he had helped found a wholly Masonic order, the Societas Rosicruciana in Anglia, modelled on a mystical German fraternity of the Middle Ages which had itself been inspired by the magic of the Kabbala and Ancient Egypt. Today the 'Soc Ros', as it is known in Masonic circles, has 'colleges' all over England. One in Brighton bears the name William Wynn Westcott in his honour.[6] When creating the Golden Dawn ritual Westcott may have plagiarized the 'Soc Ros' ritual on the grounds that the two orders shared the same occult inspiration. I am only guessing, for I have been unable to acquire the 'Soc Ros' ritual. Certainly the Golden Dawn had close physical links with Freemasonry. For many years it held meetings and performed rituals in the London headquarters of the thoroughly respectable Mark Masons.

Westcott drenched the Golden Dawn in Rosicrucianism but what gave the order wider appeal was opening membership to non-Masons and even women. Its groups were called Temples and Westcott gave them names such as Isis-Urania, Osiris, Horus and Amen-Ra. The order was plagued by scandal and power struggles. In 1891 Westcott lost control to another Freemason-Magician named MacGregor Mathers. Six years later Westcott quit the order to keep his job as a coroner. The legal authorities had discovered his predilection for magic and threatened to sack him. Of course, they had no objections to his occult activities within Freemasonry!

MacGregor Mathers refined Westcott's ritual with the aid of another member, the poet W. B. Yeats, but in 1900 Mathers was ousted because of his tyrannical rule. In 1903 power was seized by A. E. Waite, yet another Freemason and the author of an acclaimed Masonic encylco-paedia. So many coups and so much hatred make it difficult not to view all these men as forgers, con-men and back-stabbers. Clearly, any enlightenment which Golden Dawn members gained from the Kabbala, alchemy, hermetism and theosophy could not overcome grubby human ambition. Some prominent writers and artists were among its 400 members, but most were nonentities indulging in hocus-pocus beyond their comprehension which might seriously have damaged their mental health.

The rituals of the Golden Dawn may not have been devil-worship but they strayed dangerously close to what Christian counsellors today would call possession or witchcraft. Each Golden Dawn Temple was presided over by a 'Hierophant' who represented the Rising Sun and who invoked the elements of earth, air, fire and water. All neophytes had to be 'purified' by water, then 'consecrated' by fire. The penalty for revealing the order's secrets was to suffer

> a hostile current of will set in motion by the Divine Guardians of the Order, living in the light of their perfect justice, who can, as tradition and experience affirm, strike the breaker of the mystical obligation with death or palsy, or overwhelm him with misfortunes. They journey as upon the winds. They strike where no man strikes; they slay where no sword slays.[7]

At the Old Bailey in 1901 two Golden Dawn associates, Mr and Mrs

Horos (not Horus!), were tried for rape. They were jailed for fifteen and seven years respectively, but only after it was revealed that they had used the Golden Dawn initiation ceremony to beguile their juvenile victims. The Solicitor-General read out huge chunks of Mathers' revised ritual including being 'slain or paralysed without visible weapon, as if blasted by the lightning flash'. He branded the entire ritual 'most blasphemous' but did not point out that large passages had been lifted from Craft Freemasonry.

The Golden Dawn was Freemasonry with the occult lid off. It resurrected those magical elements in the seventeenth-century cauldron of ideas which had given birth to Freemasonry. In 1987 a conference was held in London to mark the centenary of the Golden Dawn's 'conception'. It was organized by the Hermetic Research Trust whose trustees include the Marquess of Northampton, a prominent Royal Arch Freemason. Deservedly prominent in the proceedings were three experts on the Golden Dawn who are also Masons. I am assured that their interest in this 'fringe Masonry' is purely academic!

The 'GD' itself petered out years ago. Its most notorious member was a declared satanist: Aleister Crowley. Some people have characterized this self-styled 'Beast 666' as the devil himself. He died – in mortal form at least – in 1947 but at the height of 1960s flower-power he was resurrected as one of the main influences on the tragi-comical hippie drug guru, Professor Timothy Leary. Crowley was also among that pantheon of cult figures portrayed on the cover of the Beatles LP, 'Sgt Pepper's Lonely Hearts Club Band'.

He was already trying to make contact with the devil in 1898 when he first tasted the 'Magick' of the Golden Dawn. By 1900 he was MacGregor Mathers' staunchest ally, but they later fell out when Crowley dared to publish Mathers' secret rituals. Crowley was soon bored with the Golden Dawn and was always seeking fresh stimulants to gratify his hunger for the occult. These included initiation into regular Freemasonry in the Anglo-Saxon Lodge of Paris, or so he claimed in his Confessions.[8] He also claimed he became Master of 'one of the oldest and most eminent Lodges in London'. There seems to be no record of this event at Freemasons' Hall, so either Crowley lied or the records have gone astray.

In 1912 he became the British head of the Ordo Templi Orientis (OTO), a neo-Masonic order of German origin, which he re-created with a progression of magic rituals offering 'a rational basis for universal brotherhood and for universal religion'. Crowley was thus seeking much the same goals as Freemasonry but he hoped the OTO would have greater success. Indeed, he claimed he was reconstituting Freemasonry, which in practice was 'either vain pretence, tomfoolery, an excuse for drunken rowdiness, or a sinister association for political intrigues and commercial pirates'. Nevertheless, he felt his association with Freemasonry was 'destined to be more fertile than almost any other study, and that in a way despite itself'.[9]

Crowley's views on the devil were astonishingly similar to those attributed to the giant American Freemason, Albert Pike. In his *Magick* Crowley wrote,

> 'The Devil' is, historically, the God of any people that one personally dislikes . . . This serpent, SATAN, is not the enemy of Man, but HE who made Gods of our race, knowing Good and Evil. He is . . . Life and Love . . . he is Light, and his Zodiacal image is Capricornus, the leaping goat whose attribute is Liberty . . . the Godhead which, if it becomes manifest in man, makes him Aegipan, the All.[10]

Somewhere in the potion of Kabbalistic magic and occultism which hepled to create Freemasonry, the idea seems to exist that God is indeed Satan–Lucifer–the Devil. Quoting a few lines from a 500-page book is no way to explore the complexities of Crowley's argument, nor is this the place to test clinically whether he was any less 'dotty' (to use Grand Lodge's term) than Albert Pike. Grand Lodge might dimiss Crowley as a charlatan – certainly in his claims to have belonged to an English Lodge – but he was directly linked with Grand Lodge through a man who was one of England's leading Masonic scholars: John Yarker.

Yarker admitted Crowley as a 33rd degree Freemason in his own version of the Rose Croix or Ancient and Accepted Rite. He ran this institution from Manchester, much to the fury of England's orthodox Rose Croix which expelled him in 1870. However, United Grand Lodge never expelled Yarker from *Craft* Freemasonry. He was still giving lectures to its premier research lodge, Quatuor Coronati, forty-two years later.[11]

Yarker also inducted Crowley into the 95th and 90th degrees of his combined Memphis–Misraim Order. This lives on today in the person of Desmond Bourke. Few if any of his suburban London neighbours know he is the 97th degree Grand Hierophant of Sovereign Imperium of the Mysteries. Bourke was 'installed' in this office in 1964 alongside the mysterious 'David Sard', yet only Sard's elevation was reported in *Pentagram*, the Witchcraft Research Association magazine for occult enthusiasts.[12]

When I asked Mr Bourke about Memphis–Misraim he said he held his authority through John Yarker who had himself acquired it from the

order's leaders in France. Two other groups in England lay claim to
Yarker's M–M inheritance but only one is active. Bourke assured me
neither he nor the order was into devil-worship. Indeed, he has been
more active as a Druid: heading the Universal Druidic Order, the Ancient
and Archaeological Order of Druids, the Ancient Order of Druids
Hermetists and the Order of the Holy Wisdom. In 1966 he authorized the
foundation of another Druidic outfit known as the Golden Section
Order.

These credits are relevant only because Bourke is also an eminent
Freemason. In September 1984 *Masonic Square* reported that Worshipful
Bro. Desmond Bourke was President of the Arcadian Masonic Study
Circle, which would be holding a series of meetings in Freemasons' Hall,
London.[13] Bourke later told me he was no longer president but was still a
member. He said the circle's lectures and discussions covered various
Masonic subjects. 'Including Memphis–Misraim?', I inquired. He
replied: 'We might do a rehearsal of its rituals at Grand Lodge.' The
rituals of Memphis–Misraim have never been published, but they are
probably another attempt at re-creating the cults of ancient Egypt. The
Order's immediate forebear, the France-based Rite of Memphis, gave its
lodges names such as Osiris and Heliopolis.[14] Perhaps the Arcadian
Circle has been re-creating Heliopolis in Great Queen Street.

The Masonic obsession with Ancient Egypt and Greece, with the
Kabbala, Mithras, the Essenians and the Druids, may never have had
much to do with devil-worship. It may be more like the obsession of an
adopted child desperately seeking its true parents and identity. Either
way, the Freemason's love of the occult has not yet featured in Grand
Lodge's PR handouts or its videos. It might be a good selling point. One
life insurance salesman told me that he joined Freemasonry because he
was a ritual magician. I naively asked him if he was a member of the
Magic Circle. 'Not that kind of magic,' he sneered, 'I mean the Kabbala.'
I did not ask if he sold after-life insurance as well.

The works of Albert Pike and Aleister Crowley show that men
preoccupied with paganism, the devil and the occult are attracted to
Masonry, if only (as in Crowley's case) on the way to somewhere else. It
is also true that Crowley's appetite for mystical satisfaction was matched
by his insatiable sexual hunger. Occult symbols are often also sexual
symbols, and in these Freemasonry abounds. What about that *vesica piscis*
which my city financier felt was formed by the square-and-compasses on
the open Bible?

In Latin *vesica piscis* means 'bladder of fish', although it might also mean
'a bladder which, when filled with wind, would be in the form of a fish'.[15]
In architecture it means a pointed oval shape, whose sides are formed by

the intersection of two equal circles which pass through each other's centres. It was frequently used by medieval artists to enclose religious portraits.

For obvious reasons this lozenge shape came to symbolize a woman or womankind. In medieval heraldry it became an acute diamond. At least one Masonic historian, J. S. M. Ward,[16] says that in Freemasonry 'the lozenge is easily represented by the square and compass', into which the financier's nose was so abruptly thrust. In Masonic ceremonies the square-and-compass's femininity is complemented by the masculine tools, the level and gavel. The level has the shape of a tau cross. The gavel is like a hammer. Ward again explains that alongside the square and compass in the Masonic lodge 'lies the gavel or tau, and so the cross and the *vesica piscis* are brought together in conjunction with the third great light in Masonry [the Bible], at the very moment when the Candidate takes his Oath'.

Ward explains that the candidate makes his first step in Freemasonry through these symbols: 'obligated *in* the *vesica piscis*' and 'ruled *by* the Tau cross'. Out of this he concludes that the newcomer 'thereby publicly declares his intention of trampling underfoot those primitive and animal passions which war against the soul'. Thus he is reminded that,

> as he must enter this material world through the *vesica piscis*, so he must enter the life of initiation by the same road, and only after he has done so can he see the Light . . . This *vesica piscis* is the female or preservative principle of God, without which we could not exist for a single day, nor without it could we hope to be preserved from the powers of darkness and evil which threaten us on our spiritual journey.

In *The Entered Apprentice's Handbook* Ward writes that the Master of the lodge 'represents the male aspect of the deity, as is shown by the tau crosses, called levels, on his apron, and by his use of the gavel, which represents the same emblem. The Tau Cross is, of course, a phallic symbol and stands for the male and creative aspect in Man.'

The symbols on Masonic aprons extend this male–female interplay, says Ward. All full lodge members display the *vesica piscis* on their aprons in the form of roses 'to remind them that their duty is passive, to obey the commands of the Worshipful Master who, to remind us of his masculine function, wears the three taus in place of the three rosettes'.

Ward was aware that his arguments might be thought 'far-fetched', but he is not alone in interpreting Masonic symbols in sexual terms.

Take another symbol, the point within a circle. The first degree 'Explanation' says that in all regular lodges 'there is a point within a circle round which Brethren cannot err'. During the rituals a Mason walks round this circle, touching on various items including the Bible: 'while a Mason keeps himself thus circumscribed he cannot err'.[17]

In attempting to clarify this less-than-obvious explanation, Masonic authors have stated that the point in a circle may refer to a Freemason's duty to be 'good Men and true' within the boundary line of duty to God. A Mason may be seen as the 'point' or centre, and the circle as the world. A more mystical theory is that man is insignificant, a mere point without length or breadth. In contrast, the circle is perfection, without beginning or end, infinite and eternal, Almighty God.[18]

Albert Mackey, the Masonic encyclopaedist, says the explanation about a Mason's duty is 'trite and meagre'. He then claims that, both in ancient times and in modern Freemasonry, the point in a circle is a 'sacred hieroglyphic' standing for worship of the phallus, a 'sculptured representation of the *membrum virile* or male organ of generation'. This was 'a peculiar modification of sun-worship' said to have originated in Egypt with our old friend, Osiris.

Remember that, in the legend, Isis recovers all the parts of her husband's body, which Set had cut up, 'except the organs of generation' which had been eaten by Nile fish. According to some versions, Isis then made an artificial penis, either of wood or beeswax, transplanted it on to the reassembled body of her husband and impregnated herself with it. The result of this remarkable act was their son Horus, who must have set about killing Set with a double dose of vengeance. The story is remarkable not only for recording two medical 'firsts' (the first successful penis transplant and the only act of necrophilia ever to have produced a child); it also helps explain the popularity of the obelisk among Ancient Egyptians and Victorian Freemasons.[19]

According to Mackey, the phallus is the point, whereas the circle represents the 'female generative principle' – the Greek *Cteis* – 'a circular and concave pedestal . . . on which the Phallus or column rested'. So the point in the circle is 'the union of the Phallus and Cteis, or the Lingam and Yoni [in India] in one compound figure, as an object of adoration'.

After a Cook's Tour of many more pagan deities, Mackey tells us that in a Masonic lodge the Master and the wardens are the Point within the Circle. They symbolize the Sun, as does the Point. The Circle, meantime, symbolizes the Universe 'invigorated and fertilized by his generative rays'. Mackey does not explain whether the circle also symbolizes society at large, invigorated and fertilized by Freemasons. That would be an apt metaphor for the way non-Masons feel, after falling victim to a 'Masonic conspiracy'. However, they usually express their sense of penetration in coarser terms.

Not to be outdone, J. S. M. Ward states that in the 'Christian' Masonic order known as the Rose Croix, the 'cross' and the 'rose' are again 'only another name for the phallus and the *vesica piscis*'. He then depicts the symbols united as ⊕ and ♀ . Ward then announces that 'thus the cross of suffering has become united with the phallic cross', before finding more examples of the *vesica piscis* embedded in various Masonic jewels.

Ward may have been as mad as a hatter, but his approach to Masonic symbolism is shared not only by Mackey but by the modern Masonic seer George Draffen who asserted in 1986[20] that the 'hoodwink' or blindfold in the first degree ritual reminds the candidate that he is 'undergoing a birth process', just as 'conception and fertilisation take place in the darkness of the womb'. Even the cable-tow round his neck is 'a symbolical umbilical cord' which, when cut, symbolizes 'birth and new life'.

The Masonic obsession with birth and women's organs has an even odder aspect. In 1933 W. L. Wilmshurst delivered a lecture to the Leeds research lodge, Living Stones (no. 4957), of which he was the founding Master. His subject was the new Freemasons' Hall in London, then known as the Peace Memorial Temple. He explained that it was 'deeply and designedly symbolic', and launched into this eulogy:

> Every Masonic lodge is impliedly . . . a secret place of birth, and is known to those initiated in it as the 'Mother' from whom they received their Masonic life. It is fitting, therefore, that the inmost sanctuary of the Mother Grand Lodge of the world-wide Craft should be so located as to be a symbolic place of birth and be in

The Grand Temple within Freemasons' Hall, London:
a symbolic womb, according to the Masonic
author W. L. Wilmshurst

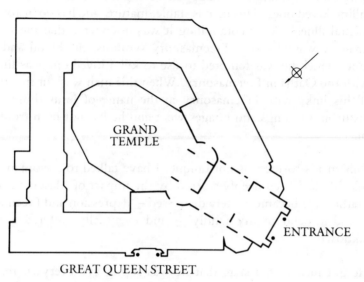

GRAND
TEMPLE

ENTRANCE

GREAT QUEEN STREET

structural correspondence with the human female organism. The Grand Temple is literally a symbolic womb, centrally placed within, but isolated from, the body of the edifice. In this respect it follows the oldest known symbolic place of Initiation, the Great Pyramid, whose central chamber of rebirth and resurrection is similarly constructed and with the same mystical intention.

Sigmund Freud was not a Mason, but Freemasonry would have given him unlimited opportunities to enhance even his perceptions of repressed sexuality. It seems some 6 million men alive today have been conceived and incubated in a Masonic womb, then 'born again' through 'mother lodges' consisting entirely of men. No wonder they do not let women join!

Today's Masonic spokesmen may argue that such interpretations are totally discredited – even though they all come from reputable Masonic sources. But they do not explain how Masonic symbols, oaths and rituals can so prey on a Freemason's brain that he feels compelled to commit the most appalling acts, even against his own family. The Church of England report prints part of a letter from a Church of England minister which illustrates the problem.

A young man in his early forties confided in me recently about obscene sexual images that he was having during his times of spiritual communion, as well as disturbing feelings about blood and killing loved ones. This man is stable, mature, and has no history of mental illness. After counselling it was discovered that the sexual imagery was linked to Freemasonry symbols, the blood and the knife which he was tempted to use to kill a loved one was linked with the Oaths in Freemasonry. When this man was cut free from all his links with Freemasonry in the name of Jesus those very disturbing feelings and images went and he has not been troubled since.

This man's torment is not unique. I have talked to a woman whose family life had been deeply scarred by the impact of Masonic ritual on her father. He became acutely depressed – 'depression and Freemasonry go hand-in-hand in my family' – and eventually suffered a mental breakdown.

He got into such a state that he was seeing evil everywhere. He thought something terrible was going to happen, so he tried to kill us all. Someone called the police and they arrived just in time. My father was put in a mental home. He's out now. He doesn't have anything to do with Freemasonry these days, but I don't know what he thinks about it. I daren't ask in case I spark off the old trouble all over again.

Anything can be read into Freemasonry. Everything has been – mostly by Masons. Yet when men suffer severe psychiatric illness as a result of Masonic symbolism, the Freudian slips of some Masonic authors and the neo-pagan interpretations of others cannot all be dismissed as wrong. There are elements in Freemasonry which bring out the worst in some men. Whether they are 'possessed' by evil spirits or just mentally destabilized by occult mumbo-jumbo, they are a danger to society and themselves. Does Freemasonry deny all responsibility for their actions?

There is a Masonic motto – *Lux e tenebris* – light out of darkness. There is, of course, another bringer of light: the Morning Star. It is odd that the phrase 'bright morning star' is the only allegedly Christian reference left in the Craft Rituals. When the two warring Grand Lodges in England – the Moderns and the Ancients – were united in 1816, the rituals were revised to exclude all Christian elements. Somehow the 'bright morning star' was left in, even though it is said to be derived from the last page of the New Testament: 'I Jesus . . . am the root and the offspring of David, and the bright and morning star' (Revelation, 22:16).

It seems inconceivable that the men who revised the rituals could have accidentally retained a phrase whose derivation and meaning was so obviously Christian, when they scrupulously deleted almost every other New Testament phrase. It has survived, even though it still distresses Jewish brethren, such as the outstanding Masonic scholar Harry Carr: 'As a Christian reference this passage must cause embarrassment to brethren who are not of that faith.'[21]

Might it have another, non-Christian, interpretation which has been overlooked? As it happens, there is another bringer of light who is also known as the 'morning star': Lucifer. Once common as a poetic name for the planet Venus, Lucifer was the rebel Archangel who fell from Heaven as he tried to dethrone God: 'How art thou fallen from heaven, O Lucifer, son of the morning!' (Isaiah, 14:12). But Lucifer had a great career ahead of him, for he went on to become Satan or the devil – at least, that is how Biblical interpreters saw him.

Is it possible that the Morning Star remained in the rituals, not by mistake, but as a deliberate but cryptic Masonic reference to Lucifer, Satan, the devil? If so, this would invert the meaning of a crucial section of the third degree ritual:

> Let me now beg you to observe that the light of a Master Mason is darkness visible, serving only to express that gloom which rests on the prospect of futurity . . . Be careful to perform your allotted task while it is yet day; continue to listen to the voice of Nature, which bears witness, that in this perishable frame resides a vital and immortal principle, which inspires a holy confidence that the Lord of Life will enable us to trample the King of Terror beneath our feet, and lift our eyes to that bright Morning Star, whose rising brings peace and salvation to the faithful and obedient of the human race.

To the men who drew up this ritual in 1816, who was the Lord of Life and who the King of Terror? Could God be Lucifer, and Lucifer God? Might they be sitting in each other's seats? Are Masons today inadvertently worshipping the devil instead of a benign God?

Nonsense, a member of the Masonic Knights Templar (or Great Priory of Malta) might say, for in that 'Christian' ritual the Bright Morning Star is applied to he 'whose rising brought peace and salvation to mankind'. In this order, the 'Novice' must be 'the faithful soldier until death' of the great 'Captain of Salvation'. But what kind of Christianity do the Knights Templar pursue: meek and mild or murderous? We get some idea when the Novice swears to keep the secrets of the Order and to

faithfully defend and maintain the holy Christian faith . . . under no
less a penalty than loss of life, by having my head struck off and
placed on the point of a pinnacle or spire, my skull sawn asunder,
and my brains exposed to the scorching rays of the sun, as a warning
to all infidels and traitors. So help me Christ.

The novice is 'invested' with a white tunic, adorned with a plain red
Latin cross, stretching to his knees. He dons a mock-medieval belt,
breastplate, spurs and helmet, takes hold of a shield and is girded with a
sword. He is then told to draw his sword 'in defence of the Holy Christian
faith' before setting off on seven years' warfare. The secret sign of a
'Crusader' is a cross made with the sword. The secret word is GOLGOTHA.
Having achieved this labour in a few minutes by walking seven times
round the room, he must undergo one year of penance and mortification.
He is given a skull and a taper and told to walk slowly round the room
again, keeping his eyes fixed on those two 'emblems of life and
mortality'. He then swears: 'May the spirit which once inhabited this
skull rise up and testify against me, if ever I wilfully violate my obligation
of a Knight Templar.' To complete the oath, he must 'Seal it with your
lips seven times on the skull'.

After being told to 'abstain from fleshly lusts', the novice is made a
Knight of the Temple and the Holy Sepulchre 'in the name of the Holy,
Blessed and Glorious Trinity'. He is given a ribbon, cross and star, and
then garbed in a crusader's white mantle, the 'symbol of the Christian's
Faith and Hope', and told the Order's Grand Word, EMMANUEL.[22]

This ritual fills me with ignoble thoughts. There are some 13,000
Masonic Knights in England and Wales, including Commander Michael
Higham. They must all be Master Masons of the good old Craft which, as
Grand Lodge tells us, took Christ out of its rituals 'to enable men of
different faiths to join in prayer (to God as each sees Him)'.[23] Yet here
such men enter an order which is not only exclusively Christian: it is
bigoted, militant and commemorates the Crusaders who pillaged and
slaughtered their way round the Eastern Mediterranean for centuries.
When the ritual talks of 'infidels' it means Muslims: people who are
allegedly welcome in Freemasonry, 'which is open to men of all religious
faiths'. Perhaps British Muslim Masons (a few exist, I understand) should
form themselves into the Knights of Saladin, in order to revere a Muslim
leader with more humanity that any Crusader king.

There are times when the whole of Freemasonry seems like an
overgrown schoolboy's morbid fantasy, with war-games thrown in. It
all reeks of Just William and his gang, although William would probably
have steered clear of the whole affair, as a typically adult charade. The

bathos of the Knights Templar, and indeed all Freemasonry, is captured in one tiny old newspaper story:

A human skull found at Marple Bridge, Cheshire, has turned out to be a ceremonial relic used by Dukinfield Masonic Lodge. It was thrown out in a pub spring-cleaning.[24]

eight

ST PETER'S SQUARED

If they were not doing evil they would not have so great a hatred of
the light.

Ever since 1738 when Clement XII issued his bull *In Eminenti* against the
'depraved and perverted' societies of Freemasons, the Roman Catholic
Church has been condemning Freemasonry as if it were the child of the
devil. Ironically, it was only in recent years, as Protestant churches were
at last plucking up courage to round on the brotherhood, that the Vatican
softened its opposition and seemed almost to welcome its centuries-old
enemy beneath the canopy of St Peter's itself.

In Eminenti – the first of more than twenty bulls against Freemasonry –
was issued partly on doctrinal grounds but also because, in the 1730s, the
Papacy felt its temporal power was being subverted by a lodge in
Florence. The lodge, set up by Englishmen, was being used by English
agents as a cell for intrigue and espionage. As I explain in Chapter 33, the
agents' target was the Stuart Pretender, James III, who was holding court
in the Holy City, but the lodge also contained Italian free thinkers who
mocked the Papacy. On both these grounds Clement railed against
societies called 'Liberi Muratori' or 'Freemasons' for the 'great mischiefs'
they did to the 'temporal tranquility of the State':

> Since we are taught by the divine word to watch, like a faithful
> servant, night and day, lest this sort of men break as thieves into the
> house, and like foxes endeavour to root up the vineyard . . . we do
> condemn and prohibit the same societies . . .

The Pope commended that no members of 'the faithful in Christ',
whatever their status, laymen or clergy, should join Masonic societies, or
give Masons shelter, help them meet, 'afford them counsel, help or

favour', assist them to recruit, or 'in any manner aid and promote them'. Those who did would suffer the penalty of excommunication 'without any other declaration; from which no one can obtain the benefit of absolution from any other but us . . . except at the point of death'.

Enforcing the new law fell to the Holy Inquisition which promptly jailed an Italian member of the Florence lodge. The lodge closed but some of its members still conspired against Rome. For the next 100 years Freemasonry grew throughout Italy as a cover for nationalist revolutionary activity. According to one Masonic writer, from the middle of the nineteenth century 'the salient point of Italian politics was war against Catholicism directly led by the lodges'.[1] By 1848 Pius IX and the Papal States were overwhelmed by the movement for Italian unification. The papal prime minister was assassinated, an act which the revolution's leader, the Freemason Giuseppe Mazzini, deemed 'necessary and just'. Rome rebelled, Pius fled, and Mazzini set up a Roman Republic. It did not last. In 1850 the French put Pius back on the Roman throne, but the secret societies had signalled the end of his territorial power. Twenty years later Italian unity was achieved, largely through the efforts of three Masons: the revolutionary Mazzini, the soldier Garibaldi and the statesman Cavour. By 1870 these men had destroyed the Pope's earthly dominion. Rome was made the capital of an independent secular nation state and the Papacy was reduced to 108 acres around St Peter's. In his tortured thirty-two-year reign Pius IX issued six bulls attacking Masonry but the definitive condemnation came in 1884 with *Humanum Genus*, in which Leo XIII lamented that the pontiff was falsely

> deprived of temporal power, the stronghold of his rights and of his freedom; he was next reduced to an iniquitous condition, unbearable for its numberless burdens until it has come to this, that the sectarians may openly say what they had already in secret devised for a long time, namely, that the very spiritual power of the Pope ought to be taken away and the divine institution of the Roman Pontificate ought to disappear from the world.

Leo endorsed the view that the Freemasons' 'real supreme aim' is 'to persecute Christianity with untamed hatred, and they will never rest until they see cast to the ground all religious institutions established by the Pope'. Masons insinuate themselves 'into the hearts of Princes' in order to exploit them as 'accomplices to overcome Christianity'. Then they resolve 'to shake the foundations of the thrones, and persecute, calumniate or banish those sovereigns who refuse to rule as they desire'. The Masons deceive the people too into believing that 'the Church is the

cause of the iniquitous servitude and misery in which they are suffering'
but, 'It would be more according to civil wisdom and more necessary to
universal welfare that Princes and Peoples, instead of joining the
Freemasons against the Church, should unite with the Church to resist
the Freemasons' attacks.'

Leo confirmed all existing penalties against Catholic Masons,
including excommunication. He made no exception for members of the
self-styled 'regular' Freemasonry of Britain, the Empire and the USA,
even though this might claim to support Church and State. Leo lumped it
together with the priest-hating continental variety which had made the
Pope a beggar. He could do no other, for Mazzini – past Grand Master of
Italy's Grand Orient – had been supported in his revolutionary
endeavours by Protestant politicians in Freemasonry's birthplace,
England. The Vatican had already achieved token revenge by causing a
crisis in England's Grand Lodge. In 1874 its Grand Master, the Marquess
of Ripon, had turned Catholic. To comply with the papal ban he resigned
as Grand Master. Grand Lodge turned this crisis into a triumph by
replacing Ripon with the Prince of Wales.

For the next 100 years 'regular' Masons divided into those who felt
that, if only the Papacy could be persuaded they did not plot against it, the
historic conflict could be ended; and those who made unrelenting attacks
on the Church and did plot against it – notably America's Scottish Rite
Masons.[2] Neither viewpoint prevailed because of a third, inert force: the
majority of Masons who had no great animosity to the Vatican but who
cared not what it thought, said or did. On the Catholic side there was no
great impetus for 'peace' either, because few Catholics (outside South
America) wanted to become Masons. It was not until the 1960s that
'peace' appeared to be a possibility.

The turning-point was the papacy of John XXIII. In 1962 his second
Vatican Council promoted a new climate of religious tolerance and raised
hopes of a coming together of all churches and faiths. It called for a
dialogue with all 'men of goodwill' who showed a readiness to talk with
the Church.[3] Leading Masons felt this must include them because their
order was built on a similar concept of religious tolerance. Rome noted
the Craft's claim to 'gather together, beyond the limits of the various
religions and world views, men of goodwill on the basis of humanistic
values comprehensible and acceptable to everyone'.[4] It was also told that
Masonry's moral values encourage men to embrace their own religions
even more strongly, so that Catholics who are Masons become even
better Catholics.

In the decade after Vatican II, Catholic leaders in several countries were
solicited by Freemasons. In 1968 a prominent English Mason named

Harry Carr persuaded the Cardinal Archbishop of Westminster to propose a softer line on Freemasonry to the Vatican. Cardinal Heenan was sympathetic because of the sad tale of one of his parishioners. In his autobiography[5] he told of his visits to a Yeoman of the Guard (a Beefeater at the Tower of London) who was 'over seventy with a well-trimmed white beard'. The man always attended Sunday Mass and 'prayed with great recollection', but never took Communion. 'There was only one black mark in the Yeoman's record. He had not received the sacraments within living memory. His children knew the reason. In the army he had become a Freemason in the belief that this would further his career.'

Heenan felt it was 'probably only a matter of time' before the general ban on Masonry would be lifted, but not even he dared ask the Vatican to allow the Yeoman to take Communion while he was still a Mason. Instead the Cardinal urged the Beefeater to quit the Craft, but he never did because he 'was under the almost certainly false impression that he would have to cease to be a Yeoman if he resigned from his masonic lodge'.

As it happens, the Yeoman's 'impression' was almost certainly correct for the Craft is strong in the army, the Territorials and in many quasi-military organizations.[6] At that time it may have held sway among Beefeaters. Ignoring such worldly obstacles, Heenan embraced Carr's view that 'regular' Masons had never plotted against the Church and accepted the need to draw a 'sharp line' between English-style Free-masonry and the 'atheistic or anti-Christian Grand Orient type'. In his own book Carr says he urged Heenan to urge Rome that it could use the English model to distinguish between good and bad Freemasonry. He added: 'What we really need is an intermediary, to convince your authorities.' Heenan replied: 'I am your intermediary.'[7]

The Cardinal then took up the cause of 'regular' Freemasonry with Pope Paul VI. By 1971 he was able to report some progress. He told Carr of the recent case of a London Protestant who had married a Catholic woman. He now wished to become a Catholic but did not want to give up Freemasonry. Heenan sought guidance from the Holy See and was told the husband could become a Catholic 'without restriction'. This meant he could remain a Mason and take Communion. He entered the faith and even persuaded one of his Masonic brothers to follow his example.

Similar Church–Mason canoodling was going on in France, where Freemasonry has an even stronger anti-clerical tradition than in Italy. The French Revolution was largely inspired by Masonic notions and by Masons such as Diderot, Voltaire and Lafayette. French history thereafter is littered with Masonic onslaughts on Catholics and Catholicism. By 1948, however, the main French order, the Grand Orient, had a small 'regular' rival: the Grande Loge Nationale Française. This GLNF had the backing of regular grand lodges abroad, including those of England, Ireland and Scotland. By the 1960s a French non-Mason named Alec Mellor had written several books on Masonic–Church relations.[8] A convinced Catholic, Mellor was also convinced that the GLNF was no enemy of the Church. In 1969 he informed the Archbishop of Paris that he intended to become a Mason. Presumably the Archbishop raised no objections for Mellor was duly proposed by the GLNF's Grand Master, Ernest van Hecke, and initiated. In 1971 van Hecke pressed Pope Paul to end the ban on regular Masonry.

For years the leaders of Italy's largest Masonic order had also been lobbying the Vatican but, as their 'Grand Orient' bore the same name as the notorious French order, the Papacy could hardly be expected to lift its ban. In 1972, however, they at last won recognition from the United Grand Lodge of England, as I explain in Chapter 33. Now they could tell Pope Paul their Grand Orient was 'regular' and had nothing to do with the anti-clerical French. Elsewhere in Europe and in the USA Masons were making similar conciliatory noises, until suddenly they all seemed to win the exemption they had long sought. In 1974 Cardinal Seper, Prefect of the Sacred Congregation for the Doctrine of the Faith (the old 'Holy Office' or Inquisition), reinterpreted Canon 2335 in the Code of Canon Law which had stood since 1917. This said:

> Those who enrol in the masonic sect or in other associations of the same kind which plot against the Church or against the legitimate civil authorities, by this very fact incur excommunication, absolution from which is reserved to the Holy See.[9]

Regular Masons had long claimed this should never have been applied to them because their orders had never plotted against Church or State. In contrast, anti-Masonic churchmen claimed it banned Catholics from *all* forms of Freemasonry, whether they plotted *or not*. The lack of a comma in the original Latin text made no difference. Fifty-seven years later Cardinal Seper declared that 'the opinion of those authors who hold that the aforesaid Canon 2335 refers only to Catholics who enrol in associations which actually plot against the Church may be safely taught and applied'.

Catholic Bishops in England and Wales promptly spread the word:

> Times change . . . Canon 2335 no longer automatically bars a Catholic from membership of Masonic groups . . . And so a Catholic who joins the Freemasons is excommunicated only if the

policy and actions of the Freemasons in his area are known to be hostile to the Church.[10]

In England Harry Carr claimed the 'sad story which began in 1738 is now happily ended'.[11] The Frenchman Alec Mellor said that henceforth in specific cases it is 'compatible to be a Roman Catholic and a Freemason. The historic conflict . . . is now over.'[12] Many Catholics in England, France, Italy, America and other countries felt free to join the Craft. In 1976 Terence Cardinal Cooke addressed 3,000 Masons at a Masonic Dedication Breakfast in New York.

> I lament that in bygone days in many places, due to some extent to a failure to communicate, there was at times an estrangement between your ancestors and some clerics, of all faiths . . . Whatever happened in the past should not stand between us and the future. Your invitation to me is a joyful event on the road of friendship between the Masons and the Catholics of America.[13]

Cooke and everyone else in this star-crossed love-affair were in for a shock. In 1981 the Sacred Congregation issued a statement saying the 1974 letter had made no change. Excommunication still applied. Peter Hebblethwaite, a former Jesuit turned writer on Vatican affairs, commented sarcastically: 'Rome knows best. No change. We are back to square one.' William Whalen, America's leading Catholic critic of Freemasonry, responded: 'Square one is exactly where the Catholic Church should stand on this question. Liberals as well as conservative Catholics should applaud this clarification. This is no time to encourage RCs to join one of the most racist and sexist institutions in American society.'[14]

Confusion returned in January 1983 when the Church promulgated its new Code of Canon Law. Out went the anti-Masonic Canon 2335. In came Canon 1374 which made no mention of Masonry but forbade membership of all societies which conspire against the Church. The irrepressible Masonic convert Alec Mellor proclaimed, 'excommunication has disappeared as far as Freemasonry is concerned': this new law 'relieves the conscience of the many Catholics who are already members of the Craft and it can only be welcomed by non-Catholics'. The rejoicing was premature. In November 1983 the Sacred Congregation's new Prefect, Cardinal Ratzinger, issued a counterblast approved and ordered by Pope John Paul II. 'Masonic associations' were not now mentioned in Canon Law but that made no difference.

The Church's negative judgement in regard to Masonic associations remains unchanged since their principles have always been considered irreconcilable with the doctrine of the Church and therefore membership in them remains forbidden. The faithful who enrol in masonic associations are in a state of grave sin and may not receive Holy Communion.

In March 1985 the Vatican newspaper, *L'Osservatore Romano*, published an article showing that all those cosy chats between folk like Harry Carr and Cardinal Heenan had missed the central issue. What mattered was not which lot of Masons plotted against the Church but whether Freemasonry's 'philosophical ideas and moral conceptions' could ever be reconciled with the fundamentals of Christian faith. Even a century before, when the Papacy had just been territorially destroyed by Masons, its opposition had been primarily doctrinal. In *Humanum Genus* Leo XIII condemned the brotherhood's 'rationalistic naturalism'. Elsewhere, he said: 'Christianity and Freemasonry are essentially irreconcilable, so that enrolment in one means separation from the other.'

L'Osservatore Romano expressed in its Latin way most of the objections later raised by Britain's Protestant churches.

Above all it must be remembered that the community of 'Freemasons' and its moral obligations are presented as a progressive system of symbols of an extremely binding nature. The rigid rule of secrecy which prevails there further strengthens the weight of the interaction of signs and ideas. For the members, this climate of secrecy entails above all the risk of becoming an instrument of strategies unknown to them.

Freemasonry's 'relativism', its failure to differentiate between right and wrong paths to God, reducing all religions to facets of 'a broader and elusive truth', is unacceptable. A Catholic cannot

live his relation with God in a two-fold mode . . . dividing it into a supraconfessional humanitarian form and an interior Christian form. He cannot cultivate relations of two types with God, nor express his relation with the Creator through symbolic forms of two types . . . On the one hand, a Catholic Christian cannot at the same time share in the full communion of Christian brotherhood and, on the other, look upon his Christian brother, from the Masonic perspective, as an 'outsider'.

The Sacred Congregation felt Freemasonry's notion that there are many paths to God leads to 'the opinion that truth cannot be known', which is an essential element in the 'general crisis' of our era. The newspaper was too coy to state that 'Truth' to the Vatican means Christianity as defined by the Vatican, but it did say 'only Jesus Christ is the Teacher of Truth, and only in him can Christians find the light and the strength to live according to God's plan, working for the true good of their brethren'. That Masonic orders may have different attitudes to the Church is irrelevant. The threat to Christianity lies in the principles they have in common.

After fifteen years of flirting with Freemasonry, the Church had come back to where it had stood before Vatican II, and before that for more than 200 years. Yet from 1974 an unknown number of Catholics had joined the Craft. The Vatican has still not made clear where they now stand. Should they follow a 1911 decree which instructed Catholic Masons to move into 'passive membership', abstaining from all participation and 'communion' with Freemasonry, or quit altogether if they can so do without causing themselves or their family 'serious harm'?[15] Without express guidance, Catholics already active in Freemasonry will probably stay active. They may find 'grave sin' more fun than Holy Communion.

The dalliance is over, but crucial questions still need to be answered. Why did the kissing stop in 1981? And how had it ever begun? Was it just Vatican II which caused the Church to drop its centuries-old hostility or was some other force at work?

A 'topside' interpretation might claim the kissing had to stop as soon as Germany's bishops produced a devastating statement on six years of discussion with their Masonic countrymen. In 1980 they reported: 'It is impossible to belong to the Catholic Church and to Freemasonry at the same time.' For all the Craft's humanitarian and charitable aspects, and its stand against 'materialistic ideology', it still denies the 'objective validity of revealed truth'. Being a Mason 'is to question the fundamental principles of Christian life'. The bishops slated Freemasonry for its many 'isms': indifferentism, relativism, subjectivism, deism. To the Mason 'all religions are competitive attempts to express the ultimate unattainable truth about God'. This 'undermines the faith of a Catholic' whose Church – despite Vatican II – still lays claim to absolute truth.

The bishops' statement was published ten months before the Vatican made its 1981 declaration that Catholic Masons still faced excommunication, but everything they said was as plain as a Swiss Guard's pikestaff. Anyone with the slightest awareness of Catholic dogma and Masonic 'tolerance' would already have known the two cults could never be reconciled without intellectual dishonesty. It is likely, therefore, that the volte-face had nothing to do with the German bishops but everything to do with the scandal of Propaganda Massonica Due, the 'regular' Masonic Lodge otherwise known as P2.

I tell the inside Masonic story of P2 in Chapter 33. Here I point out that this plot to subvert the entire Italian nation first penetrated St Peter's in the 1960s, soon after Vatican II. It was only on the eve of the P2 scandal that the Sacred Congregation published its 1981 'no-change' statement. P2's shocking 'state within a state' membership lists were discovered one month later, but magistrates had already been investigating P2's Grand Master Licio Gelli for two years and knew how deeply he and his Masonic cronies had subverted the Vatican in the eighteen years since Paul VI had become Pope.

Now the Vatican suddenly realized Freemasonry was still a perfect vehicle for conspiracies against Church and State. 'Times change,' the English bishops had said in 1974. They failed to say that Freemasonry remains the same. The P2 scandal was 1738 and 1848 all over again. 'Men of goodwill' in Britain, France and Italy would bluster that P2 had nothing to do with 'regular' Freemasonry, but this was a lie and those who uttered it were either fools or knaves. P2 was a recognized part of the 'regular' Grand Orient of Italy – itself recognized by the Grand Lodge of England in 1972 – and three successive Italian Grand Masters were up to their necks in the conspiracy.

Even back in 1974 the Vatican should have had more sense than to pussyfoot with Italy's Grand Orient. The names of its lodges alone showed this leopard had not changed its spots. Sixteen were named after Garibaldi, twelve after Mazzini, four after Cavour, and another forty after various victims of papal persecution or debunkers of dogma such as Galileo, Voltaire and Charles Darwin. To anyone concerned with mankind's intellectual advance such people are worthy of acclaim, but to popes and cardinals they reek of heresy and subversion. Another ten lodges were called '20th September' – the date in 1870 when Italian unification had been proclaimed and the Papal States were killed off.

This makes the 1974 soft line even more extraordinary, but by then elements within the Vatican were in league with three notorious Masons – Michele Sindona, Roberto Calvi and Licio Gelli – who make the nineteenth-century trio of Mazzini, Garibaldi and Cavour look like St Francis of Assisi. At least *their* war on Rome was patriotic and openly declared. In contrast, Italy's most notorious modern Masons insinuated themselves into the Vatican's inner circles and then almost bankrupted it. They achieved this by working hand-in-Masonic-glove with cardinals and archbishops at the heart of the papal *curia* or court.

As early as 1976 a group calling itself the International Committee of Defence of Catholic Tradition named many powerful Vatican priests as Masons. The claims were denied, of course, for even Cardinal Seper's 1974 declaration had not changed the rule forbidding priests from becoming Masons. At the time few Catholics would have believed the list because it came from a group more extreme than even Archbishop Lefebvre, which was bent on discrediting the Vatican by any means. In retrospect, however, if this group was lying, it is remarkable how it named several men deeply implicated in the P2 scandal nearly five years later. They included Monsignor Pasquale Macchi (Paul VI's private secretary), Cardinal Casaroli (Vatican foreign minister), Cardinal Ugo Poletti (Vicar of Rome) and the most powerful papal official of all, Secretary of State Cardinal Villot. He had allegedly become a Mason in 1966.

In *The Brotherhood* Stephen Knight said it was 'widely believed' that Villot had pressured Cardinal Seper to issue his 1974 declaration exonerating 'regular' Freemasonry. If so, this may tie in with Villot's earlier role in smoothing the way for the first rogue lay Mason to penetrate the Vatican. In his alarming, best-selling book, *In God's Name*, David Yallop argues that the death of Pope John Paul I in 1978, just thirty-three days after his election, was a case of murder. Yallop names Villot as a suspect because he felt threatened both by the doctrinal reforms and the personnel changes which John Paul I had in mind. After John Paul's death, however, Villot kept his job as Vatican 'Prime Minister' until his own death in 1979.

Villot had control of the Vatican Treasury, the Administration of the Patrimony of the Holy See, known as APSA. Yallop claims he bears some responsibility for bringing Michele Sindona – the swindling banker, Mafia money-launderer and future convicted murderer – into contact with the Vatican's own bank, L'Istituto per le Opere di Religione (IOR). In 1971 Sindona introduced his partner-in-bank-crime, Roberto Calvi, to the head of IOR, Bishop Paul Marcinkus. Calvi soon built a special relationship between IOR and his own bank, Ambrosiano. IOR became a major shareholder in Banco Ambrosiano, and nominally ran many of its subsidiaries in shady offshore tax-havens. When Ambrosiano collapsed in 1982, it went down with £800 million of other people's money. This put the Vatican in deep trouble. It lost a lot of its own money but was also liable for much of Ambrosiano's other debts. IOR later paid creditors £164 million but claimed this was done out of moral obligation not as an admission of guilt. In 1987 Italian authorities issued a warrant for the arrest of the now Archbishop Marcinkus on charges of bank fraud. It later gave up the attempt, mainly because Vatican officials enjoy diplomatic protection in Italy.

The Church's flirtation with fast-lane fraudsters left it foundering for cash to pay its priests. Even more embarrassing, the fraudsters Calvi and Sindona were both Masons in the notorious P2 Lodge, of which the long-standing fascist, Licio Gelli, was Master. Through the 1960s and 1970s Gelli was himself a regular visitor to the Vatican. He had audiences with Pope Paul VI and was the confidant of cardinals and archbishops. His right-hand man in P2, a lawyer and businessman named Umberto Ortolani, had been a Vatican power-broker even longer. David Yallop says that, soon after John XXIII's death in 1963, Ortolani hosted a secret meeting at his villa near Rome. His guests were senior cardinals with the power to swing the election of the new pope. At Ortolani's home they vowed to support the future Paul VI. After his election, Paul showered Ortolani with many Vatican awards, including the honoured rank of 'Gentleman of Holiness'.

The pro-Paul lobby was allegedly motivated by the need to maintain Vatican II's 'liberal' momentum. Its most ruthless exploiters were, of course, the Freemasons. No sooner had Paul VI ascended the papal chair than Sindona followed him into the Vatican. The two men had come to know each other in Milan where the banker had his headquarters and where Paul had been plain Archbishop Montini until he became Pope.

By the time Paul died in 1978 Sindona, Calvi and their P2 cronies had achieved near complete control of the Vatican's investments and brought the Church to the edge of financial ruin. If Yallop is right, such men had much to fear from Paul's successor, John Paul I, who planned to cast the money-changers out of the temple (or rather to stick them back in the *Masonic* temple whence they came). After his death they maintained their position for two more years until the P2 scandal broke. Their reign in the Vatican coincided exactly with the Church's 1974–81 Masonic love-affair. During these years the Vatican sought peace with 'men of goodwill' while 'regular' Masons of extremely ill will were destroying it morally as well as financially. By 1985, however, it seemed all the Masonic termites had been fumigated from St Peter's as the Vatican regained the courage of its own dogmas. Even their one-time sponsor, Archbishop Marcinkus, seems to have been allowed to remain on its staff only to spare him from the painful process of Italian law.

Yet . . . Times change. In February 1987 Michel Baroin, France's most powerful Mason, died in a plane crash in Cameroon. Paris fell into near official mourning for Baroin was also director-general of a huge mutual savings fund with 2.4 million subscribers. A former police chief and town mayor, he had risen to such influence that his friend President François Mitterrand had chosen him to head the committee planning the bicentenary celebrations of the French Revolution. Baroin was also an intimate of Prime Minister Jacques Chirac. He said Baroin 'was a friend for more than thirty years. We have lost a great humanist, a man who played a pre-eminent role in the French economy.' Some commentators even spoke of him as a future president. One reverential obituary ended: 'In a country where tolerance has never been one of the cardinal virtues, the example of Michel Baroin will be cruelly missed.'

For all his virtues, many Catholics were shocked to learn that the Cardinal Archbishop of Paris had authorized a church funeral for this past Grand Master of the traditionally priest-hating Grand Orient. On 12 February 1987 the service was duly performed (with Premier Chirac in attendance) and Baroin was buried in a Christian cemetery. This controversial decision was defended by Father Michel Riquet, a respected Jesuit, in the columns of Le Figaro. He recalled how, in his youth, Freemasons used to try every trick to stop a priest administering the last rites to a dying brother. Even a Mason could get a Catholic funeral if he made a death-bed conversion.

Riquet then recited the many wounds inflicted by Grand Orient Masons on the Church in France. For instance, they had destroyed its control over education and achieved the separation of Church and State. Yet all that mattered now was Baroin's attitude to the Church at the moment he died. Riquet claimed Baroin had never been an enemy of the Church, in which he was both baptized and married. He had also baptized his three children who all received a Christian education. Therefore, 'in his heart, if not in practice, he had always remained a Christian'.

How could one refuse a Catholic funeral to someone whose sudden and brutal death had prevented him from expressing his last wishes, but which were known to be ever more those of his Catholic youth and marriage? How could a Christian not rejoice that, whereas in the past Freemasons used to revel in refusing a religious funeral, today a Grand Master of the Grand Orient wished in his heart to be accompanied to his final resting place by the prayers of the Church?

Riquet seemed to be hinting at a reverse take-over. Freemasonry had not pulled a trick on the Church. The Church had merely reclaimed one of its own. Yet surely Baroin was still a Mason when he died, so is he now in Heaven, Hell or the Grand Lodge above? Would the answer be different if the Vatican really is full of closet Masons? Or is God Himself 'on the square'?

PART TWO

Who are the Masons?

FIGURING THE FACTS

If I were here as an official spokesman, I would be representing between a quarter and a half a million Freemasons of the English Constitution.

If England's Freemasons have any official spokesman it is the man who made these remarks: Grand Secretary Michael Higham, in effect the chief executive of the United Grand Lodge and its 'Prime Minister'.[1] Sometimes it seems as if the brotherhood's biggest secret – one which not even the Grand Secretary may be trusted with – is how many brothers there are. When as sharp and precise a man as Commander Higham RN has no idea if there are 250,000 or 500,000 men in his navy, what hope has any outsider of calculating their strength?

Higham's vagueness is all the more perplexing because Grand Lodge keeps a record of every Master Mason. First it issues a certificate to each brother who attains the third degree. Then each active Mason pays annual dues to his lodge secretary. Then every secretary (one for each of some 7,600 lodges in England and Wales) sends details of all paid-up members every year to none other than Grand Secretary Higham. It would seem a simple task for someone in his office to add up these figures and arrive at a total, but apparently not.

The confusion is caused partly by Freemasonry's high death rate – due to old age not ritual slaughter! Masons are dying off faster than Grand Lodge updates its records. If the age profile of one London lodge is typical, many more brothers will soon depart for the 'Grand Lodge Above' (the Masons' name for Heaven). In 1986 the Borough of Hackney Lodge had some eighty-one members: six were aged over eighty, fifteen more were over seventy and a further twenty-four were over sixty. Only eight members were under forty.

Some of the yearbooks issued by Freemasonry's English provinces give exact details of every lodge's membership. These confirm the high death rate. Lodges tend to have about eighty members. On average two die every year. Another two resign because they have moved elsewhere, have lost interest, cannot afford the fees or are too old to turn up. Yet, overall, Masonic membership may be increasing. Resignations are usually matched by Masons joining from other lodges, and deaths are outnumbered by initiations. In 1988 Grand Secretary Higham said that the average age of initiates was now younger than it has been for decades. Until recently two or three English lodges were going out of existence every year because they had too few members. Most of these were based in inner city areas with a falling white population. Now even lodges which have been on the verge of closing have men queueing to join.[2]

Lodges are still shutting down abroad, where 800 have 'warrants' from the Grand Lodge of England. The losses have been greatest in Islamic countries where the Craft is now banned (and Masonic Temples were always called the House of the Devil),[3] and in Argentina where – since the 1982 Falklands War – joining a British secret society can hardly be the wisest career move. Some English lodges in Buenos Aires have survived, including one bearing the same name as the ship sunk so controversially by the Royal Navy with the loss of 368 lives. General Belgrano was not only a great Argentine patriot; he was also a staunch Mason, although even he might have turned in his grave at the thought of an English navy commander in charge at Freemasons' Hall.

Every year some forty new lodges are formed in England and Wales, mostly in outer suburbs, new towns and other areas with a growing population and some prosperity. As soon as a new community grows up a group of Masons will form a new lodge around it. That is how Masons who had moved to South Woodham Ferrers recently founded one, even though the Essex town had been built on farmland only a few years earlier. Sometimes a common sporting interest provides the focus. In 1981 the British Sub-Aqua Lodge was 'consecrated', although I am assured that all their rituals are performed above water. More often it is work that brings brethren together, as later chapters disclose.

I estimate that some 15,000 paid-up Masons in England and Wales are dying every year, while another 15,000 men are joining. In 1987 Grand Lodge issued 14,144 certificates, rather fewer than 1985 (16,126), 1975 (18,309) or 1955 (20,362). However, all estimates of the movement's total strength are confounded because thousands of Masons belong to two lodges, and hundreds subscribe to three or more. If 7,600 lodges averaged eighty members there would appear to be some 600,000 Masons, but this would include many individuals counted several times over. However, it would not include tens of thousands of Masons who have dropped out completely, like the Duke of Edinburgh. It is therefore probable that there are some 600,000 living certificated Masons in England and Wales but, if just half pay lodge dues, the number of subscribing brethren would be 300,000.

I was making these calculations when Commander Higham sent me Grand Lodge's evidence to the Church of England Working Group.[4] This included an official 'guestimate' of 320,000 paid-up Freemasons in England and Wales. In addition there are about 100,000 Masons in Scotland[5] and some 55,000 in all Ireland,[6] but there is yet another statistical problem. Many Masons pay non-dining or 'country' sub-scriptions. In other words they rarely if ever go to meetings. The average number of diners at Craft meals served in the Connaught Rooms (Britain's largest Masonic eating place) is around thirty. If this is the average throughout the British Isles, then of some 750,000 men who have sworn the oaths in Freemasonry's three Craft degrees there are some 260,000 active Masons.

If all this guessing is anywhere near correct (and if there are some 18 million males in England and Wales over the age of twenty-one), then one adult male in thirty is a Freemason. In Scotland (where there are some 2 million adult males) the ratio may be as low as one in twenty or twenty-five. In all Ireland (again, some 2 million adult males) the ratio is no more than one in forty or fifty. This reflects the Catholic ban on Masonic membership, but equally it means that the proportion of Protestants who are Masons (north and south of the border) may be as high as one in ten (some 40,000 out of 400,000 adult males).

If no one really knows how many Masons there are, we have some idea of the kind of jobs they do. In 150 obituary notices gathered from newspapers all over Britain between 1986 and 1988, I found a generation of Masons born mostly between 1900 and 1925 who held the following occupations:

Professional: six solicitors and one barrister, two doctors, two archi-tects, two army officers and one RAF officer, two bankers, the managing director of a building society, and a vicar.
Public service: two civil servants, a colonial administrator, a university administrator, a policeman, a fireman, and four teachers including a primary-school headmaster.
Local government and nationalized industries: a council waste disposal chief, an environmental health officer, a district surveyor, a health and safety officer, four other council employees, a postmaster and an electricity board manager.
Owners or directors of firms: two involved in engineering, four in haulage, nine in building and building supplies, five in car sales, three in

garages, two in seed and flower bulb sales, milling and timber. Also manufacturers of shoes, knitwear, wire and cable, tiles, paint, hats and ice-rinks.

Commercial employees: three company secretaries, a personnel officer, a factory manager, a transport manager, a marketing director, an accounts clerk, a building sales manager, a production director, a solicitor's clerk, an oil-tanker driver and a newspaper advertising salesman. Also ferry, mining, aircraft, electrical and hospital maintenance engineers; three insurance salesmen and agents for timber, football pools, leather and clothing.

Retail and High Street: four jewellers, three publicans, three iron-mongers, three butchers including the owner of a chain of shops, three grocers, two launderers and dry-cleaners, two auctioneers, three estate agents, a chemist owning several pharmacies, a coal merchant, a florist, a master-baker, a fish-and-chippie, a newsagent, a photographer, a funeral director, a hair stylist and a chiropodist.

Self-employed artisans: a scale-maker, a plumber, a plasterer, a roofer, a printer, an electrician, a window-cleaner and a naval draughtsman.

Also a property millionaire, two farmers, three local journalists, a football league administrator, a blind physiotherapist, a danceband leader, a magician, a comedian and the man who masterminded the Blackpool Lights.

From this sample we get some sense of a fraternity largely made up of mercantile, middle-class Middle England. Perhaps only people who are prominent in local life win such death notices but, even so, it seems fair to say that Freemasonry attracts many men who own their businesses, and a very high proportion of folk with goods and services to sell.

Looking at individual lodge lists, we get a similar picture. In 1986 the Borough of Hackney Lodge included eleven men in the building trade, ten publicans, nine assorted managers, nine assorted engineers, six insurance salesmen, five shopkeepers, five company directors, three bank employees, a bookmaker, a schoolmaster, a musician and the former secretary of Orient Football Club. Ironically, no lodge member appeared to be working for the London Borough of Hackney!

I acquired this list from a trusted source but, coincidentally, in 1987 Hackney Council published an inquiry into past maladministration and the possible role of Freemasonry in its affairs. I explore its findings in Chapter 26. Here I extract statistics about Masonic membership which the inquiry chief, barrister Andrew Arden, compiled as a result of the remarkable co-operation he received from Grand Lodge. From various lodge lists he established the 'occupations' of 2,534 Masons:

Finance: accountants, insurance/assurance employers or employees; bank and building society
workers   196 (7.7%)
Building: architects, surveyors, property owners,
estate agents, builders, foremen, plumbers, car-
penters, joiners   207 (8.2%)
Company directors, senior executives and contractors:
(nature of business unspecified)   303 (11.95%)
Managers, consultants, supervisors: (unspecified)   343 (13.5%)
Manufacturing: (unspecified)   44 (1.7%)
Car, sales and transport: driving instructors, chauf-
feurs, taxi operators and garage owners   102 (4%)
Air, sea and rail: train drivers, civil pilots, station
masters, a ship repairer   42 (1.65%)
*Engineers, draughtsmen, engineering salesmen and
buyers*   328 (12.9%)
Food and drink: publicans, caterers, hoteliers   111 (4.4%)
Shopkeepers and small business   160 (6.3%)
Education: teachers, lecturers, students   77 (3%)
Police   98 (3.9%)
Armed forces   48 (1.9%)
Local government   31 (1.2%)
Civil servants and diplomats   51 (2%)
Medical: doctors, dentists and a vet   34 (1.3%)
Ministers of Religion   5 (0.2%)
Agriculture   20 (0.8%)

Arden also discovered 'a film director, three musicians, two
publishers, two golfers, a footballer, six metallurgists, a piano tuner,
three sub-postmasters and a chicken-sexer'. Many of Arden's 2,534
Masons belonged to lodges outside London, but he was also given details
of fourteen lodges in and around the capital. There were eleven police
officers in one lodge. In a second most members were either in insurance,
finance and banking or in the building game. A third was manned by nine
firemen and fourteen engineers. A fourth was built on construction, for it
included builders, surveyors and painting contractors. A fifth was
founded (sparked off?) by seventeen electrical engineers. A sixth was
awash with shipping and nautical fellows, as well as policemen, publicans
and motor traders. A seventh was stuffed with the 'rag-trade': a furrier,
two ladies' outfitters, five manufacturers of ladies' wear, coats or
maternity clothes, and directors of companies trading in wholesale
trimmings, children's clothing, lingerie, gowns and textiles. Of this

lodge Arden observed: 'It is hard to think that no "common interests" are ever discussed after the lodge meeting.' The other lodges had a mix of members, though they were variously biased towards accountancy, engineering, the army, the police and the pub trade. Arden was impressed by the 'career level' of one lodge: it included twenty-one company directors, seven architects, a stockbroker, a barrister and a banker.[7]

Although this information is based on genuine Masonic documents, it is not wholly accurate, as Arden himself pointed out. Grand Lodge keeps all the application forms which Masons fill in when they join a lodge, but these are not updated as members grow older, change jobs or die. For instance, some allegedly living Borough of Hackney Lodge members joined in the 1930s. By now all these must have retired or gone to the 'Grand Lodge above'. Arden even discovered 'students' who are now over 100 years old! However, an accurate survey of jobs currently held by brethren in Ormskirk's Pilgrim Lodge emerges from a computer print-out conveniently supplied to all its members. This lists a headmaster, a policeman, a farmer, a jeweller, a printer, a draughtsman, an electrical contractor, an estate agent, a chartered surveyor, an insurance broker, an accountant, a coach firm proprietor and a soldier in the Household Cavalry. It also says twenty of the fifty-three members are retired.

Such lists show that most Masons are not royal dukes, aristocrats or captains of industry. It is certainly true that many Masons own substantial companies and are big men in their community, but many more are small shopkeepers and one-man contractors. More still are artisans or poorly paid employees. Indeed, these days a lot of Masons are unemployed, 'reduced to the lowest ebb of poverty and distress' as the first degree ritual says. Such stark truths hardly justify all those conspiracy theories about Freemasons ruling the world. If most are as humble as these lists show, why is their movement so bitterly attacked?

Look again at Ormskirk. If a man belongs to Pilgrim Lodge he has instant access to a network of contacts throughout the town. How convenient it must be for him to have a lodge list with all the members' occupations neatly printed out! If he wants to buy a house he can find a property through his Masonic brother the estate agent. He can then call on a Masonic chartered surveyor to survey it, a Masonic insurance broker to arrange a mortgage, and a Masonic builder's foreman to fix any repairs. There is nothing illegal in this network nor is any criminal offence being committed, yet it is through such connections that small-town business works. Within it are the germs of real abuse.

Pilgrim is one of eleven lodges in Ormskirk, which seems a lot for a town with only 30,000 inhabitants: there must be one Mason in every sixteen males over the age of twenty-one. In nearby Southport there are twenty-seven lodges: one Mason in every nineteen men. In Lancashire there are 920 lodges with some 50,000 members: equivalent to one Mason in every thirty men throughout the county – including Manchester and Liverpool. These 50,000 include hundreds of public servants: policemen, customs officers, tax inspectors, factory inspectors, JPs, judges, local government officers, elected councillors, even MPs. If only 1 per cent of these were susceptible to requests for corrupt favours from brother Masons, then there would be 500 Masonic crooks in the county.

This generalization may smell of injustice, for could not the same be said against any similar society? Perhaps, but there is no society similar to Freemasonry in both nature and size. Again, in the Craft's defence, it must be said that the code of mutual aid is supposed to extend only to 'laudable endeavours' and 'lawful secrets', not to 'murder, treason, felony and all other offences contrary to the laws of God and the ordinances of the realm'. Even so, the Mason's bond to any other Mason does constitute 'a sure pledge of brotherhood; . . . a column of mutual defence and support'; a duty 'to succour his weakness and relieve his necessities', to prevent if possible any injury being done to him, and to 'boldly repel the slanderer of his good name'.[8] Add these obligations together and apply them against an outsider, and that person could suffer serious damage. Whether this ever happens, readers may find out by reading the rest of this book.

Both Pilgrim in Ormskirk and the Borough of Hackney are general lodges which recruit members from many walks of life. Other lodges are restricted to a single group of professionals. There are some lodges whose members are all barristers. Others are largely composed of soldiers or naval officers or policemen. Other lodges still contain mainly solicitors, or doctors and surgeons, or estate agents, or teachers. When non-Masons working in these fields discover such lodges exist, they suspect them to be cells of mutual aid, career advancement and corruption, none of which can work to the benefit of non-members.

The greatest single proof of Freemasonry's strength in this country lies in the pages of the *Masonic Year Book*, a small black-covered paperback listing all lodges and chapters under the authority of the United Grand Lodge and Supreme Grand Chapter of England. It also lists more than 9,000 Grand Officers. Most of the names mean nothing to outsiders but from this source and other Masonic documents I have compiled a list of well over three hundred Freemasons who are prominent enough in public life to be included in *Who's Who*. Many crop up in later chapters of this book, but here it is enough to say that my unofficial 'Who's Who of Britain's Freemasons' includes forty-six lords; twenty-two past and present MPs; seventy-six serving or retired judges, QCs and other legal officials; thirty-six generals, admirals, air-marshals or other high-ranking former servicemen; fourteen retired bishops or eminent clerics; six former police chiefs; fifty-seven top businessmen, bankers and industrialists; twenty-three mostly retired 'first division' civil or public servants; and a total of more than fifty leading solicitors, surgeons, architects, regional politicians or local government officials. The apparent emphasis on retired men is misleading. It follows from the fact that men in some walks of life (notably the armed forces, the civil service and the police) cannot devote effort to achieving high Masonic rank until they have retired. With the exception of the hereditary peers, most of these men are formidable 'achievers' in their chosen careers. In all but a few cases I have no evidence to say if Freemasonry has helped them rise to the top, or helped them stay there. Whether it has the collective power to influence society at large, as anti-Masons maintain, may be answered by my chapter-by-chapter inquiry into its role in key areas of national life.

I guess that another 250 men featured in *Who's Who* are Masons. These would include more businessmen and financiers, serving civil and public servants, soldiers, judges and lawyers, medical men, politicians, police chiefs, youth movement officials, sports administrators and public entertainers. They are not listed in the *Masonic Year Book* because they do not have the time or inclination to pursue Grand Rank or they are happy to go no higher than their Craft lodges. Some may duck Grand Rank just to stay out of the *Year Book* and avoid public exposure. Thousands more Masons are men of power and influence at national or local level, but their fields of work or business are not the kind that win an entry in *Who's Who*.

Before trying to measure the power of any movement, society or organization – be it Communism, Zionism, fundamentalist Islam, the CIA, the Vatican, the Mafia, the oil cartel, the tobacco lobby or even the Mothers' Union – the writer should take one step back and ask if he/she is merely pursuing a journalistic vendetta, a self-indulgent obsession. Is he/she bending facts to fit false theories or private prejudices? This is a particularly important question for anyone investigating Freemasonry. The brotherhood has attracted the fire of conspiracy theorists for 250 years. Does it deserve it now?

One eminent Masonic scholar, a past Master of the world's premier lodge of research, suggested that I keep a sense of proportion.[9]

English Freemasonry is a mirror image of English social life as a whole, with all our snobberies and our love of 'dressing-up'. It is, if anything, 'middle class' and reflects a quite typical English pleasure in joining together with other good, average, normal chaps for entirely innocent purposes. After all, a lodge is simply a rather small, essentially *private* club in which chaps meet periodically. In my experience everyone makes for home pretty punctually at 9 P.M.

'But what about the rituals and all the secret elements?' you might ask. You'll find much the same in the Foresters, Buffaloes and similar organizations. It merely happens that the Freemasons were first in the field and have a very lengthy tradition.

The British are great traditionalists. They enjoy ceremonial. Look at the Beefeaters, the Changing of the Guard and the Lord Mayor's coach. The British also like to *belong* somewhere, especially to groups or organizations where they can encounter people with similar interests and loyalties. Hence the many 'class lodges', frequented by local government people, lawyers, doctors, the old boys of many schools and so forth. I find it difficult to believe that anyone joins them for any material benefit and Grand Lodge's very strict regulations forbid it.

Remember that English masonry is a private society, but one with a very large membership. Whether or not a man is a member is his affair so don't expect to be handed lists of lodge memberships. I would not expect to wander into Whites, Brooks or Boodles in St James's Street and be handed a list of their members. Finally there is no 'great mystery', and the 'secrets' are so innocuous that I could not be bothered to remember them.

This patrician view is echoed by men lower down England's caste system. As one northern working man put it:

There is nothing in Freemasonry which can't be found in any secret society or trade union. I by trade am a boilermaker. When I finished my apprenticeship, I was admitted to the Society. They had an oath plus a sign. I had to swear on oath that I would help all my brother boilermakers and all trade unions.

I also swore to be sober. When the swearing-in was over, I was straight away bought a pint of beer by the same people who had just told me to be sober! All oaths in secret societies have to be taken with a pinch of salt![10]

Many Masons admit they entered the Craft without premeditation or conviction. They joined simply because they felt flattered to receive an 'approach' (they like to maintain the fiction that no one is ever 'invited' to join). A Mason usually says the approach came from his father or an uncle, a schoolfriend or someone else whom he admired. Once in, he may feel like quitting but hesitates lest he embarrass his proposer or hurts his feelings. Some stay in for mercenary reasons, but most say they would be angry if they caught anyone pushing business interests or seeking career favours. Some are seduced by the religious trappings but many discover a companionship which churches no longer provide. One Mason from north-east England explained it to me this way:

> Years ago, if you belonged to a God-fearing family, it was taken for granted that you'd join the choir, the Boys' Brigade and the football team. Your whole social life revolved around the church. Now the church has no social life. Indeed, there's hardly a 'church' at all. It's not that Freemasonry is a religion, though many Masons take it as such, but it offers spiritual support which many men seek and cannot find anywhere else.

The support is also social and even sporting. There are Masonic golf and bowling clubs. In Dorset there is a darts section, in Wiltshire a Masonic caravan club. Also Masonic fund-raising is admirable in itself and may bring Masons and their families together for hundreds of good causes, as I explain in Chapter 37. In short, there would be nothing to fault and much to praise in Freemasonry if it were judged on its good works alone, but this would overlook the crucial question: is Free-masonry a corrupting force? Early in my research I came across one Mason who believes it is.

ten

A MECHANISM OF
SOCIAL CONTROL?

In *The Brotherhood* Stephen Knight asked people to write to him with more information. Many Masons responded, including one who signed himself 'Badger'. Like hundreds of other people, Badger received no reply because Stephen was already near death. In 1986 I finally tracked Badger down to his sett, but it took another three months before he would trust me with his true identity. I now know why.

Badger is a professional man with impressive qualifications. He has been a Freemason for almost thirty-five years. He used to be a manic Mason, belonging to twenty-six lodges, not just in the Craft (the first three degrees) but in many other orders. He became master of seven lodges and threw himself into Masonic labours night after night. For years he was convinced that Freemasonry was a worthy institution. As he became ever more elevated in the Masonic hierarchy he gradually came to realize it was not.

> At lodge level Freemasonry is good fun. You meet lots of people you'd never meet otherwise, and you enjoy good conversation with them over a pretty good meal. It also preaches a system of morality which can work wonders. I've known taxi drivers and scrap dealers who were reprobate characters until they came into Freemasonry. Then they seemed to improve no end.
>
> As for the ritual, you have to take it for granted. There isn't any point in saying it's a load of nonsense. If you feel that way, the only thing you can honestly do is quit. I became a very good ritualist, I was well-known for it. I could learn a whole book off by heart with no trouble. When you deliver it in open lodge it's like amateur dramatics. Indeed, I used to get criticized for being over-dramatic!
>
> There's always something new to learn in Freemasonry. It's a continuing revelation until the big moment when you serve your

year 'in the chair' as Master. Then you do another year as Immediate Past Master. After that the rot sets in. Now you've got nothing to do, you're falling off the edge. Perhaps you take on the job of secretary or treasurer, just to stay active in the lodge. I've known men do that chore for thirty years.

After I'd been master of a Craft lodge I joined other orders: the Royal Arch, Rose Croix, Knights Templars and Secret Monitor. The Monitor's ritual is based on the biblical tale of David and Jonathan – a homosexual relationship as it happens. By this time I was besotted with Freemasonry. It became my whole life. I was at it six nights a week, but it was becoming so expensive: the regalia, the subscriptions, the dining, the travel. Nowadays it costs me £45 just to attend one meeting, so I have had to resign from several orders. I can't afford it.

Being keen and active, I achieved provincial rank. I was awarded a fancy title at county level and later at national level in some degrees. Now I had contact with some very rich and influential people. At this point, I'm afraid, I became disillusioned. It dawned on me that what I had believed for years about the goodness and virtue of Freemasonry was a smokescreen to delude the masses. That's when I became disturbed about Freemasonry's real intent.

At provincial level and above people are highly indiscreet in conversation. They say imprudent things which reveal their true opinions and motives. One thing I soon realized was that Masonic promotion depends not on merit and ability but on patronage and privilege. Most promotions depend on your status in civilian life. If you are a judge or a top civil servant or you have a lot of money to dish out to charity, you are well on the way to provincial and Grand [national] rank.

I got to know one top dog very well, one of the highest-ranking Masons in the West of England. We were on first name terms. 'Jim' was extremely wealthy, having inherited a huge fortune from some aunt abroad. In our province he played a leading part in a scheme to build homes for elderly Masons and their wives or widows.

I was so impressed I paid him a private visit and said, 'What a marvellous idea to establish this old folks' home. I'm sure there are lots of elderly Masons who would like to live here, people who can't possibly afford to pay for it themselves.'

'Oh no!' he said irritably. 'We don't want any people like that! We want people who can afford to pay their full whack – preferably people who haven't any children so, when they die, they can leave all their money to us!'

I was horrified. Even back in that time the full whack would have been £120 a week, but soon I realized what else was going on. The homes were going up in an area of outstanding natural beauty. They should never have got planning permission, but it was all sorted out in one of my lodges. The chairman and two members of the local district council were in it, along with Jim and me. After one lodge meeting we were all having a drink when Jim asked, 'We've put in a planning application for this scheme. Will there be any difficulty about getting consent?'

One of the councillors replied, 'No, that's all right. It'll go through. There won't be any trouble.' How could he be so sure? The council planning committee hadn't even met to consider it!

This was typical of what I saw going on all around. Through Freemasonry I knew all sorts of useful people in my town: folk like the county treasurer and the district engineer. I was in no position to exploit such connections, but had I been a private contractor trying to fix a deal, I could have called up these top local officials and found out secret council plans in five minutes. No need for funny handshakes – those are red herrings to divert press and public. You simply use a form of words which only a Mason could know, because he's recited it so often in the ritual.

This petty corruption becomes second nature to Masons, so that in the end they cannot see how corrupt it is. I know one Mason who used to work as manager of a local water board. As soon as he retired he formed a company with other Masons to tender for pipeline work from the water authority. You can be sure he won a lot of contracts not just because he knew about water but because he was 'on the square'. Freemasonry is insider trading by another name.

I was particularly disturbed by the attitudes of top Masons. I got to know several who are high court judges. In private they talk as if ordinary people are an expendable nuisance. I've also become very friendly with Harley Street surgeons. One told me how he'd invested his exorbitant fees in all sorts of doubtful, money-making rackets. He would brag about them over dinner after the lodge. These people say appalling things about the working man. Once my provincial grand master made a ferociously anti-Labour remark in Open Lodge. I was a local Conservative official at the time but even I was shocked by his sentiments.

Freemasonry is meant to be non-political. In the lodge Masons aren't supposed to talk about politics or religion. There'd be no point in talking about religion because most Masons know nothing about it. As for politics, they don't *need* to talk about it: they're nearly all Conservatives.

I ask myself: why do so many rich and powerful men stay in Freemasonry? Why do they spend valuable time, away from their wives and families, mouthing nonsense rituals and associating with people, who can be of no real interest or importance to them? I think I know the answer.

Freemasonry is a mechanism of social control. It's a feudal pyramid, whereby people of influence in British society can mix with the ordinary bloke and lend a little lustre to his dreary life. But only certain kinds of bloke. Have you ever thought why the police are so cultivated by Freemasonry? I have met scores of policemen throughout my Masonic career, but I haven't met a single fireman or postman. There must be some firemen and postmen in Freemasonry but nowhere near as many policemen, lawyers, local government officials and businessmen. By drawing these kind of people into this network, the landed aristocracy and big business filter their values down through the social structure.

One of the first things you are taught in Freemasonry is to obey rank. There is a line in the ritual that tells how the workmen building Solomon's Temple were split into small lodges in a way 'best calculated to ensure promotion to merit, preserve due subordination and prevent confusion in the work'. Well, you can forget about merit. Freemasonry is all about due subordination.

Later, Badger sent me a list of five kings (George IV, William IV, Edward VII, Edward VIII and George VI) and over 300 aristocrats – princes and royal dukes, dukes and marquesses, earls, viscounts and barons – who have headed various Masonic orders in Britain over the past 250 years. On it he wrote,

> This illustrates that the control of Freemasonry at any time is in the hands of a very few people who conduct the organization on behalf of an elitist oligarchy. The partisans who pay to support its prodigious panoply exist only to give credence to the movement. Yet Freemasonry declares to its disciples, 'In the eyes of God, who alone is great, all men are equal'. As an emblem of hypocrisy, Freemasonry is unmatched.

Here Badger touched on something which I had found contradictory even in the first degree oath. This says the 'effective punishment' for breaching Masonic secrecy is to be branded unfit to be received into any society of men 'who prize honour and virtue above the external advantages of rank and fortune'. Yet the entire Masonic hierarchy is built on rank and fortune. Its highest offices are always held by royal dukes or by earls, while a peerage or knighthood is almost *de rigueur* even for the rank of Junior Grand Warden. The Grand Sword Bearer is usually a high-ranking officer from the armed services, so the highest Masonic rank to which any 'commoner' can hope to aspire is Senior Grand Deacon. Even this is easier achieved by someone with wealth and worldly status than by someone who has neither.

According to Badger, it is this embrace between the Craft and the aristocracy which has ensured Freemasonry's extraordinary survival and success. In his opinion the speculative lodges formed by merchants and gentry in the late 1600s and early 1700s were 'impostor lodges'. They rapidly earned the suspicion and ridicule of outsiders. The only way they could avoid being outlawed was to get nobles to front for them. This happened as early as 1721. Even in 1751 when Freemasonry split into two camps (the 'Antients' and 'Moderns'), soon both had aristocrats as Grand Master. By 1813 each was headed by a royal duke: the brothers Kent and Sussex. When Parliament passed the Unlawful Societies Act in 1799, it outlawed all organizations, 'the members of which are required to take an oath not authorized by law'. That description fitted Freemasonry perfectly. Its oaths clearly incited members criminally to disembowel men for doing nothing more than revealing Masonic secrets. Nevertheless, aristocratic Masons easily won exemption for their cult. How could royal princes, they argued, be involved in anything which was seditious or revolutionary? (See Chapter 34.)

Henceforth, under cover of Freemasonry – cloaking themselves in the clean image of the cathedral-builders – the landed nobility and the new class of international financiers formed an alliance to exploit Britain's growing imperial wealth. Indeed, Freemasonry spread rapidly throughout the empire. Just as trade followed the flag, so did Freemasonry.

Badger now regards the Masonic rituals which he used to perform with such enthusiasm as 'contrived, contorted, fatuous and fallacious'. He says that anyone reading them must be astounded that 'grown men could indulge themselves in such banality and puerility'. This helps explain why these same grown men can allow themselves to be led by a hierarchy which refuses to submit itself for election by secret ballot.

Badger is even more dismayed by the fact that a Conservative-controlled Parliament refuses to pass a law regulating Freemasonry, whereas it is very keen to pass laws controlling trade unions. 'After all, Freemasonry claims to be descended from a trade union. Through subterfuge its effect on English society is far more insidious.' Coming from a local Conservative official, these opinions are worth consideration. Badger may sound like a Marxist when he talks about Freemasonry but he is no revolutionary. On the contrary, he sees Freemasonry as the seditious force in British society: its covert ultra-reaction perpetually distorting the decisions of the State against the interests of the populace at large.

The big secret of Freemasonry seems to revolve round the movement's ultimate goal, elusive and obfuscated as that is. In this century many writers have claimed to expose that goal as world domination. Most have been discredited as fascists or anti-Semites: Nesta Webster, General Ludendorff and, of course, Adolf Hitler.[1] Volumes of 'evidence', such as the *Protocols of the Learned Elders of Zion*, have been branded forgeries. Yet it is not necessary to rely on the rantings of racist scribblers or crazed dictators. Something close to proof can be found in the texts of one of Freemasonry's own twentieth-century sages.

John Sebastian Marlow Ward was born in 1885, the son of a Church of England vicar. He was educated at Merchant Taylors' School and at Trinity Hall, Cambridge, where he read history. He became a teacher, serving as headmaster of an Anglican school in Burma before he was appointed Director of Intelligence for the Federation of British Industries in 1918. During his twelve years in that job Ward became an authority on Freemasonry. Many of his works are still sold through Masonic bookshops. Indeed, his handbooks for the Entered Apprentice, Fellow Craft and Master Mason degrees are still given to newcomers to the Craft.[2]

Ward had a magpie genius for claiming that rites he had seen performed in far-off lands were identical to those 'worked' in Freemasonry. He claimed that wherever he travelled, he had been able to communicate with primitive peoples by using Masonic signs and symbols. To him Pathan tribesmen, Mehlevi Dervishes, Hindu mystics and Australian Aboriginals all had initiation ceremonies and secret cults so similar to Freemasonry that they must all be descended from the same primordial source. He went on to assert that, because many of these cults were almost extinct, Freemasonry must be the ultimate guardian of their mysteries.

Nowadays most Masonic scholars distance themselves from Ward on the grounds that he was an occult Christian, and that Freemasonry was only his jumping-off point for even weirder beliefs. In 1935 he persuaded an Archbishop of the self-styled Church of Antioch to consecrate him as a Bishop and appoint him head of the Orthodox Catholic Church in England.[3] Ward and his wife Jessie had already established their own

'Abbey of Christ the King' in the unlikely spot of New Barnet in suburban north London. The couple were convinced that when Christ made his Messianic return – which would be very soon – Barnet would be the new Bethlehem and they would be the new Joseph and Mary.

On High Street shopping expeditions this Holy Family were a familiar sight: Ward clad in scarlet cassock, cape and biretta, Jessie dressed like a nun all in white. Alas! in 1945 the tiny community was hit by scandal. A father won damages against the Wards for enticing his sixteen-year-old daughter into their clutches. In 1946 the humiliated sect slipped abroad, taking the young girl along in disguise. In the Orthodox haven of Cyprus, 'Mar John' Ward, now elevated to the rank of Archbishop of Olivet, pursued his calling. He died peacefully in 1949.

This risible saga has not wholly discredited Ward, for the Craft has tolerated even more perverse characters such as Aleister Crowley. If Ward is an embarrassment to Freemasonry today, it is not for his religious delusions but for his account of the brotherhood's ultimate aims.[4] In *Freemasonry and the Ancient Gods* he reveals the 'Grand Ideal'. Freemasonry is 'the mightiest force in the world. All that is best in religion and nationality is united with all that is best in internationalism. Far removed from the petty struggles of the politician, with its history stretching back into the dim dawn of man, it stands calm and serene.'

Ward believed that, united, the Masons of the world possess an enormous power for good and above all for peace: 'No chauvinistic government could resist it and Masonry, tried and tested, is a far stronger and safer implement with which to attain that object than a paper league of nations.'

This vision came to nothing in 1939 when peace was shattered by the notorious anti-Mason, Adolf Hitler. As it happens, Ward's Masonic peace might have been as nasty as World War II, if his admiration for a murderous Chinese fraternity is anything to go by. In a three-volume study of the Hung Society, he praised 'the greatest and most dedicated secret society in the whole world, believed to have caused the over-throw of the old Manchu dynasty'.[5] Ward ignored these bloody activities, preferring to glorify the Hung's 'truly magnificent ritual which has striking analogies with modern Freemasonry'.

Elsewhere, Ward wrote revealingly about rank-and-file Masons: 'dumb and inarticulate brothers, often, who never hoped for Grand Lodge honours, but quietly did their duty in maintaining the grand fundamental principles of our Order'.

No leading Mason these days would be so indiscreet as to describe his humbler brothers as 'dumb and inarticulate', but Badger's testimony indicates that in Masonic high places today a similar feeling of contempt exists. Most brethren know nothing of it. No matter what scandals hit Freemasonry, they still believe the Craft stands for Brotherly Love, Relief and Truth. And yet, says Badger, in the end the truth will finally dawn on them.

Stephen Knight did not know it but, when *The Brotherhood* was published, he had Grand Lodge on the run. I know top Masons who were scared stiff he had tumbled their secret and that it was only a matter of time before he reached the heart of the matter. When he died they breathed a deep sigh of relief.

PART THREE

Freemasonry and the police

eleven

THE MANOR OF ST JAMES'S

Tourists meandering east away from London's vibrant Covent Garden piazza sometimes stray into Great Queen Street. It is only a few yards from the Opera House and Drury Lane, but this thoroughfare has no theatrical buzz, no busking musicians or performing clowns. On the contrary, passers-by may sense that any action here is taking place off the street.

The same contrast hits visitors to Egypt, as they flee from the peddlers' din and desert heat into the cool of the Great Pyramid. This is no coincidence. On the south side of Great Queen Street stands a chill stone building like a mausoleum, with no ground-floor windows. This is a mighty temple in which religious ceremonies aping those of ancient Egypt are nightly performed. Indeed, many mystic cults are invoked within its walls, in a ritual hotchpotch which some earnest disciples spend a lifetime trying to fathom.

By late afternoon the street is transformed. Hundreds of elderly men in dark suits disappear through the temple portals, each carrying a small flat case containing the garments, emblems and regalia which they need to perform rites of initiation, murder and resurrection. The temple is their Holy of Holies: Freemasons' Hall, the headquarters of the world's premier Masonic institution, the United Grand Lodge of England.

In fact, Freemasons' Hall contains nineteen temples: some grand, some plain, but one quite awe-inspiring in size and decoration. Six nights a week over a two-month cycle these chambers are rented to hundreds of London's 1,700 lodges. Here they 'work' their rituals safe from the eyes of those they call the 'profane': meaning the vast majority of men – and all women – who will never travel the brotherhood's secret path to enlightenment.

At three o'clock in the afternoon of 27 January 1986 Great Queen Street was humming with rare excitement, for the secret had leaked that one powerful fraternity was about to embrace another. Reporters and photographers hovered on the pavement outside Freemasons' Hall, hoping to spot famous faces. Some intrepid hacks in dinner jackets vanished into a catering complex next door called the Connaught Rooms, from which Masons may enter the temple directly through an interconnecting passage on the first floor. After their rituals brethren usually take a drink in the Connaught bar, where the black-tied reporters had planned to buttonhole the Masonic mighty before they took their traditional lodge dinner known as the Festive Board.

Yet the press recognized no one. No pictures hit any front pages. No public figures were exposed as closet Masons. Indeed, the occasion was a triumph for Grand Lodge. In the face of increasing hostility, it had 'consecrated' a new lodge which symbolized the long-standing (to outsiders, notorious) bonds between Freemasonry and London's Metropolitan Police.

According to its internal publicity this new lodge – the Manor of St James's, number 9179 – was founded by brethren, 'all of whom had served as Police Officers in "C" or St James's District of the Metropolitan Police. The term Manor was the colloquial expression used by police officers when referring to their own District or place of duty.'

'Manor' evokes images of 'Dixon of Dock Green', of friendly neighbourhood bobbies pounding the beat, catching masked burglars in horizontal-striped shirts with bags marked 'swag', and giving naughty boys a clip round the ear and packing them off home to Mum. The Manor of St James's is hardly that territory, for what used to be called 'C' District now consists of three historic police stations: West End Central, Vine Street and Bow Street where the legendary forebears of the Metropolitan Police, the Bow Street Runners, had first been established in the 1750s. Today this is the heart of London's West End. According to a former 'C' District commander and Manor Lodge member, all officers who serve there are united by a strong sense of brotherhood:

> It's a cauldron, a forcing-house. In 'C' district you're surrounded by vice, wealth, temptation – everything that can bring a young copper down. There's a saying in the Met, 'there's none so pure as the purified' and if you survive a tour of duty in the West End without going astray you feel you can survive anything. So when colleagues suggested we form a new lodge based on 'C' District, I thought it was a jolly good idea – a chance to keep in touch with old friends who had all been through the same cathartic experience.

The prime movers behind the new lodge persuaded seventy 'C' District veterans to join as founder members. All were already Freemasons. Fifty had been Masters of other lodges. They included some of the highest-ranking officers in the recent history of Scotland Yard:

Gilbert Kelland: Assistant Commissioner (Crime) until 1984, chief of all London's 3,000 detectives for seven years.

Peter Neivens: one-time Deputy Assistant Commissioner in charge of all public information.[1]

John Cass: retired Commander; national co-ordinator of Regional Crime Squads 1981–4; now a private security consultant.

Edgar Maybanks: retired Deputy Assistant Commissioner; formerly Commander of A8, in charge of public order in the capital. Now Chief Commandant of the Special Constabulary.

Kenneth Churchill-Coleman: serving Commander of SO13, the anti-terrorist squad.

Malcolm Campbell: serving Commander of SO11, the Criminal Intelligence Branch; until August 1988 Commander of C6, the Fraud Branch.

Almost all the other founders had reached the rank of chief inspector or above. At least a dozen had made commander. By any standard this was a formidable body of men. If a list of their names were to become public, anti-Masonic conspiracy theorists would have a field-day, especially because they would have every reason to interpret the lodge's creation as a slap in the face for the Metropolitan Commissioner at that time: Sir Kenneth Newman.

A year earlier, in April 1985, Newman had issued a stiff blue book: *The Principles of Policing and Guidance for Professional Behaviour*. This included some thoughts on Freemasonry, in response to a long-running row over the power of the Craft in the force. The text was written by Albert Laugharne, the recently retired deputy commissioner. He expressed the case against the Craft firmly but with compassion. First he referred to this police regulation: 'a member of a police force shall at all times abstain from any activity which is likely to interfere with the impartial discharge of his duties or which is likely to give rise to the impression amongst members of the public that it may so interfere'.

He then said it was all too easy for an onlooker to believe that a policeman who belongs to any group will show favours to other members of that group. 'Thus an officer must pay the most careful regard to the *impression* which others are likely to gain of his membership, as well as to what he actually *does*, however inhibiting he may find this when arranging his private life.'

Laugharne now embarked on a devastating dissection of Freemasonry which he described as having 'unique features that add to the difficulties for police officers'. First he asked rhetorically, 'What matters should an officer consider if he is thinking of becoming a freemason?'

> To begin with, he will want to weigh the advantages. If accepted as a member, he may take satisfaction from participation in a long-established institution which embraces people of many kinds from all walks of life, and which includes in its upper echelons some of the most distinguished people in the land. He may. expect too, that membership will bring social pleasure and companionship with his fellow masons, some of whom may well be his fellow police officers. With them, he may take proper pride in the charitable efforts of his lodge, and in the pursuit of the ideal of freemasonry which is 'the improvement of man both as an individual and as a member of the community'.
>
> And it is important, when considering freemasonry in the context of the police service, to remember that many officers, of different ranks, have been able to reconcile their private commitment to freemasonry with their public duty without difficulty. We should remember too, that much of the conjecture about the influence of freemasonry upon our service has not been supported by evidence. The accusers – including some police officers who criticise free-masonry – have often been wrong . . .
>
> Nevertheless, it is necessary with freemasonry, as with any institution including, of course, the police service itself, to strike a distinction between the ideal and the reality. Some of the assertions have been supportable. The activities of some freemasons have been thought, on reasonable grounds, to be motivated by self-interest and not committed to the aims of freemasonry, so adding to the suspicion that all may not be well in this very private institution. Therefore, although an officer who is a freemason may take great care to ensure that membership does not influence him in the exercise of his police powers, he may find it impossible to convince a member of the public, or a colleague who is not a freemason, that this is always so.
>
> There are a number of factors also which weigh against him. Firstly, there is the marked exclusivity of the institution and the mystery which surrounds the method by which a person is judged by freemasons to be suitable for membership of a lodge. Then there is the oddness of the initiation ceremony itself, with its strange rites which smack to some of immaturity, being reminiscent of the secret societies of boyhood. There is some oddness too, in these modern

days, about the requirement of freemasons to respect social distinctions and the status quo to such an extent as to sustain the notion that 'while some must rule, others must obey and cheerfully accept their inferior positions'.[2] And finally, and most importantly in the context of police participation, there is the freemason's solemnly sworn obligation never to reveal the secrets of the craft, including that which tells him how he can indicate his affinity to another freemason in a way that will not be discerned by onlookers.

All of these carry considerable weight. They militate against the acceptance, by colleagues and citizens alike, of an officer, who is a freemason, as a man on whose fairness it is possible to rely always, and unquestionably.

Nothing in our discussion should be taken as a criticism of freemasonry in itself. Of course, some of the factors we have looked at apply to other private and selective bodies in this group which we have in mind, but the unique combination of them in this institution does cause extreme difficulty for a police officer . . . The police officer's special dilemma is the conflict between his service declaration of impartiality, and the sworn obligation to keep the secrets of freemasonry. His declaration has its statutory obligation to avoid any activity likely to interfere with impartiality or to give the impression that it may do so; a freemason's oath holds inevitably the implication that loyalty to fellow freemasons may supersede any other loyalty.

Laugharne concluded by saying that, although it would be thought an unwarranted interference for a senior officer to instruct a policeman whether to join Freemasonry or not, nevertheless:

the discerning officer will probably consider it wise to forego the prospect of pleasure and social advantage in freemasonry so as to enjoy the unreserved regard of all those around him. It follows from this that one who is already a freemason would also be wise to ponder from time to time, whether he should continue as a freemason; that would probably be prudent in the light of the way that our force is striving, in these critical days, to present to the public a more open and wholehearted image of itself, to show a greater readiness to be invigilated and to be free of any unnecessary concealment or secrecy.

This passage can only be seen as an attempt to dissuade policemen from becoming or remaining Masons. However, it had to be hedged and ditched because Laugharne and Newman knew they had no power to stop anyone belonging to an organization which is not itself illegal. 'There is no way we can interfere with individual liberties,' Commissioner Newman later wrote to me.

Britain's top cop now hoped that any of his men who were Masons would either quit the Craft or lie low, at least until a controversy then raging over police Freemasonry had died down. He later expressed confidence that 'the advice is taking root'. In contrast, the founders of the Manor of St James's Lodge thought he was wrong to make Laugharne's views on Freemasonry official Scotland Yard policy. One high-ranking retired officer in the lodge told me that, if he had still been serving, he would have asked Newman to drop the whole section.

Somehow news broke of the existence of this new high-powered police lodge even before its first meeting. A prior notice cheekily appeared in the *Guardian* gossip column. Grand Secretary Michael Higham was soon confronted on radio with claims that it must conflict with Sir Kenneth's guidance. On the contrary, he replied, all the serving policemen in the lodge had followed that guidance: they had thought twice about belonging to Freemasonry and had decided to stay in it. Higham also claimed that the idea for the lodge had originated before Newman issued his booklet, so it could not be interpreted as a gesture against him.

If this is true, the Manor was an unusually long time in gestation. It was consecrated nine months after *The Principles of Policing* appeared. However, the anti-Masonic section of the booklet had been published seven months earlier than that: in September 1984 in the Metropolitan Police's own paper, *The Job*.

The time usually needed to found a lodge is far less than sixteen months. There are three stages in the process: the would-be founders first submit a 'petition'; Grand Lodge then issues a warrant; finally the lodge is 'consecrated'. One Mason gave me documents relating to a lodge which he had helped found in 1979, and whose name he coined. These papers prove all three stages can take as little as four months. It would later be claimed that discussions about the formation of the Manor lodge started early in 1984.[3] Yet even if it was conceived before its originators knew what Sir Kenneth's booklet would say, they had sixteen months in which to take his advice and withdraw their petition. To go ahead was an act of thoughtlessness, defiance or contempt.

By then, however, the police Masons were no longer acting alone. At its consecration the infant lodge was honoured with a prestigious line-up of Grand Officers. The ceremony was conducted by Assistant Grand Master Lord Farnham while Grand Secretary Higham performed as lodge secretary. Taking the role of Senior Warden was Sir Peter Lane, a long-serving Tory satrap and formerly chairman of the National Union of Conservative Associations. In 1986 he was also Senior Grand Warden of Grand Lodge. Every ordinary lodge's 'baptism' is blessed by such godfathers, but their attendance at this ceremony would later be interpreted as a gesture of Masonic impunity to both Scotland Yard and public opinion.

I have discussed the Manor of St James's Lodge with two high-ranking policemen who used to be active Masons but who resigned from their lodges several years ago for reasons explained in Chapter 16. The first now fills one of the highest ranks in Scotland Yard:

> The decision to set up this lodge is not just provocative. It's a disaster. Now, more than ever, the police must be seen to be impartial but these Masons just wave two fingers at the Commissioner and go ahead regardless. No wonder the public think we're all 'on the square'. That was one reason why I quit the Craft. I no longer felt membership was compatible with my duty as a policeman towards the whole community.

The other ex-Mason, a former Scotland Yard officer who is now assistant chief constable of another force, was similarly dismayed:

> The St James's lodge is a public relations catastrophe, for the Masons and the Met. Albert Laugharne was quite right. Freemasonry is open to suspicion but, as police officers, we must be above suspicion. Much of what's said about the Craft is untrue but what matters is the fear it creates. Masonry eats away the trust which should prevail throughout police work. It just doesn't sit well with our job.

A Metropolitan chief superintendent who is still an active Mason shuddered when he heard about the Manor of St James's:

> I joined my father's lodge. He was a policeman. He would be horrified at the thought of an all-police lodge. For a policeman the great joy of Freemasonry is that it takes him *out* of police company, which can be oppressive and incestuous at the best of times. I wouldn't go anywhere near an all-police lodge.

In the past fifteen years I have come to know many policemen who are Masons. During friendly verbal sparring contests about the 'rolled-up trouser brigade', they often defend the Craft on the grounds that policemen need a social outlet which enables them to get to know people in other walks of life. The very nature of their job makes it difficult for them to establish easy-going relationships with men outside the force. In the warmth of a Masonic lodge, with all its good-hearted sentiments, genuine friendships with non-policemen can blossom – but not, of course, in a lodge composed entirely of policemen.

Nowhere is distrust, fear and loathing of the Craft greater than in the police service itself. This accounts for the speed with which secret details about the Manor of St James's Lodge have repeatedly been leaked to the press. In September 1986 a non-Masonic policeman discovered a summons to attend the lodge's consecration lying around at Scotland Yard. He promptly made a copy and sent it to Fleet Street. A few days later *The People* newspaper ran a front-page story with the giant headlines:

SCANDAL OF TOP COP MASONS

Two months later a 'C' Division officer[4] climbed into a patrol car and discovered a fresh Manor summons left behind by a lodge member working at the same police station. The finder gave it to another colleague, known for his anti-Masonic views, who was appalled to see so many senior policemen's names on the lodge list. Instantly realizing its importance, he decided to pass it on before any Masons could snatch it back. He even feared that, if they found out he had made a copy and taken it out of the building, they would burgle his home to get it back. He knew I was writing this book, so he singled me out as the person who should have the document. He phoned me but I was not at home. Not having my address, he called someone who, he figured, might know where I lived.

That someone was Chief Inspector Brian Woollard who for four years had been fighting a personal crusade against Freemasonry. No one was keener to see the list than Woollard, so he made sure the 'C' Division man mailed him a copy as well as me. Only now did the full significance of the Manor of St James's lodge become clear, as Woollard guessed how and why certain things had happened to him during his long and lonely struggle against the Craft.

twelve

THE FALL AND FALL OF
BRIAN WOOLLARD

The Brian Woollard story is a classic Masonic conundrum. Read from Brian's angle, it leaves little room for doubt that he was the victim of a Masonic conspiracy. Yet a Freemason might claim it was no more than coincidence that so many Masons crossed the path of this talented policeman as he took one career tumble after another.

Brian has a most courteous style. Blue-eyed and bespectacled, he dresses impeccably, stands an erect 5 feet 10 inches, and speaks mellifluous English with what might be taken for an East Midlands accent. In fact, he is a child of the Indian Army in which his father served. Born in Sussex in 1934, he was taken to Burma as a baby and stayed in India until 1948. With this regulated, military background he could have been a 'yes man', someone who will carry out orders to the letter and always do as he is told.

Not any more. Over the past seven years Woollard has become a loner, an individualist of the kind quasi-military organizations like the police find difficult to contain. He now resembles the rebel schoolboy whom the headmaster must either expel or appoint head prefect because these are the only ways to prevent the school from being burned down. One leading member of the Manor of St James's Lodge, formerly in overall charge of Woollard, puts it this way: 'The trouble with Brian is that when you reprimand him for some offence he tells you he'll never do it again, and you believe him. Then, blow me down, if a few days later he hasn't done the same thing all over again.'

Woollard says he has never committed any offence, and so has never given any assurance 'not to do it again'. Over Freemasonry, for example, he has always reserved the right to take his fight to both press and public. Such independence of spirit is difficult for any police force to handle. It must work largely on the principle that officers do what they are told and suffer, if not in silence, then at least in private. By pressing the

Metropolitan Police's own stated policy on Freemasonry to its logical conclusion, Woollard would become in turn a thorn in the side, a stone in the shoe and a pain in the neck of all those Scotland Yard chiefs who hoped the Masonic issue would die a quiet death.

He was not always so difficult to handle. If he had been, he could not have lasted fourteen years in that most conformist police department: Special Branch. While there he was attached to the Bomb Squad and distinguished himself in pursuit of the Angry Brigade terrorists. He also served as armed personal detective to Home Secretary Roy Jenkins, and performed royal protection duties at Buckingham Palace. No known 'oddball' is assigned to these posts. What changed Woollard was a series of bruising encounters with Freemasonry.

For the first twenty-seven years of his service Brian was a model cop. He won seven commendations: two in Special Branch for his work against terrorism, five as a detective for catching robbers, burglars and rapists. In December 1980 as a detective inspector in the legendary Flying Squad he received an ecstatic annual qualification report. This grades men in twelve areas of ability such as practical application, leadership, discipline, planning, temperament and capacity for getting on with colleagues. In eleven of the twelve Woollard's chief superintendent rated him 'very good, consistently above average'. On professional ability, written work and presentation of papers he gave him the top rating: 'Outstanding, a truly exceptional officer.'

The chief then summarized the views of other senior officers who had worked with Woollard:

> A very good example to junior officers in every field of work that he does. A very hard working officer with the highest integrity. He shows keenness of mind when tackling any situation and requires minimum supervision. He holds the respect of his squad. Has a very sensible and practical approach towards his work. A thoroughly reliable officer who should go further.

With these glowing testimonials, Woollard was promoted to chief inspector and in 1981 won a place on a six-month junior command course at Bramshill Police Colllege. He emerged with flying colours and was especially applauded for his 'unquestioned loyalty to the police service'. Returning to the Metropolitan force he was posted to the Company Fraud Branch, popularly known as the Fraud Squad. It was there that he first sensed the power which Freemasonry seems to have over law enforcement in London.

He began work in a section devoted to commercial fraud. His new chief (to whom I shall give the pseudonym 'Herbert Grimm') promptly gave him an inquiry which, he explained, was extremely sensitive: it involved tape-recordings on which there was talk of policemen doing favours for non-police colleagues in a Freemasons' lodge. Woollard says that when Grimm handed him the case papers he remarked: 'I don't know which lodge you're in.' Woollard replied: 'I'm not in any lodge.' This answer seemed to surprise Grimm. He advised the new boy to be 'long-sighted' and to complete the inquiry in a week.

Woollard soon realized it could not possibly be completed so soon, for the papers revealed an intricate tale of bluff and double-bluff. The main characters were a publican who, for legal reasons, I shall call 'Pickles' and John Woolf, a self-styled boxing promoter. Woolf had told Pickles that he too could become a successful promoter if he placed £8,500 seed money in a bank account in their joint names. The publican fell for the scheme and put up the funds. The two men then jointly signed cheques made out to other names allegedly connected with the venture.

Pickles had signed away his entire £8,500 before he found out he had been tricked. He demanded his money back but Woolf gave him nothing. The publican then produced his trump card. He said he was a Freemason and belonged to a lodge with many powerful members, including senior policemen and a top customs officer. He claimed they had already done him many favours and would know how to deal with a crook like Woolf. Pretending to be intimidated, Woolf backed down and told Pickles he would give him back his money, but this was far from what he had in mind.

Woolf was a wolf in wolf's clothing. An inveterate con-man, he had only just served a four-year prison term over another bogus boxing scheme. He had no intention of returning to jail or returning the money so he had taken the precaution of tape-recording Pickles's threats of Masonic vengeance. The package which he now sent to Pickles's pub contained not money but a copy of the 'Masonic' tapes.

Woolf enclosed a note telling the publican to listen to the tapes before doing anything about the money. Pickles went to his car and played them on the stereo system. Out boomed his own voice singing the names of his police-Mason friends, and bragging of acts they had committed on his behalf. He instantly saw that, if he took Woolf to court over the money, the con-man would insist on playing the tapes. This would ruin Pickles's brother Masons and bring shame on the brotherhood as a whole. He also realized Woolf was foxy enough to make sure the story would come out in the newspapers. Indeed, the tapes were so incriminating that, even if Woolf were to suffer a conveniently fatal accident, they could win him vengeance from beyond the grave.

According to Woollard, Pickles was now reduced to a 'pale and shaken state'. He wanted to drop the affair but his wife insisted he complain to the police, despite the tapes. Indeed they could be presented as evidence of blackmail – not to 'extort money with menaces' but to retain it with menaces! £8,500 of pub profits had taken a lot of earning. Mrs Pickles was not going to let that money go without a fight.

Woollard read the tape transcript with astonishment. After half a lifetime in the police he thought he had seen and heard everything. Now it dawned on him that, if Freemasonry really worked this way, it could be both corrupt and corrupting. On the other hand, Pickles was claiming in his statements that all his talk of crooked favours by Masonic cops was bravura: just a foolish ploy to tame the vulpine Woolf. Woollard decided that the truth of all this would have to be sorted out later. The first thing to do was send the tapes to the technical laboratory to see if they were genuine, fake or tampered with in any way.

A few days later Herbert Grimm asked how he was getting on. Woollard says that when he told Grimm he had sent the tapes off for testing, Grimm had bristled.

'What on earth did you do that for?'

'Because they are evidence in this case and will certainly be challenged.'

'But don't you realize that if you produce these tapes in evidence you'll be dragging the names of innocent policemen, some of them senior officers, through the courts?'

Woollard disagreed. He pointed out that since Pickles was now claiming all his Masonic tales were fabrications, his genuine Masonic police colleagues would have nothing to fear. However, if the prosecution did not produce the tapes in court, Woolf would introduce them himself, to besmirch both Pickles and the police. The jury would immediately suspect corruption and acquit Woolf. The 'boxing promoter' would walk free and the press would have a field-day, telling lurid stories about Masonic cops suppressing vital evidence.

Woollard claims that at this point, 'Herbie Grimm went bananas! For the rest of the inquiry he subjected me to the tightest supervision. I had been in the force for twenty-seven years, but never had I been subjected to such close scrutiny.' No sooner had Woollard talked to Pickles's solicitor, for instance, or tried to see his bank accounts, than the news got back to Grimm. Even so, Woollard succeeded in one line of inquiry with perturbing results.

He found out Woolf had a criminal record and must therefore have had a Criminal Record Office file. This had mysteriously disappeared so he had to compile a new one from documents in Scotland Yard's General Registry. In the process he discovered that in 1968 Woolf had been convicted of a serious theatre ticket fraud. He had pleaded guilty but, even so, his sentence – probation – was very light. Woollard guessed that this meant Woolf had become a police informer.

Woollard then discovered that years later, in the 1970s, Woolf's mother-in-law had formally complained about what she thought was a corrupt association between Woolf and the officer who had arrested him over the ticket fraud. She said he was very friendly with Woolf and went to restaurants with him. Her allegation was investigated but came to nothing when the officer denied wrongdoing and Woolf made a statement saying there was nothing improper in the relationship.

Woollard knew nothing to the contrary. What disturbed him was that the officer concerned was none other than his current boss, Herbert Grimm: the man who had given him the Woolf–Pickles job and was now interfering at every turn. Woollard complained to his squad super-intendent that he thought it very odd of Grimm not to say right at the outset that he knew Woolf. As soon as Grimm found out that Woollard had dug up the truth, he suddenly admitted the relationship.

The two officers now distrusted each other so much that they could no longer work together. Woollard felt Grimm had put him in an intolerable position, so he asked to be transferred off the entire Fraud Branch. He left the Pickles–Woolf inquiry under Grimm's supervision. Months later he heard it had been closed with a decision that there would be 'no further action'. This neatly resolved two embarrassments for the Metropolitan Police: the fraudsman-cum-informer Woolf would not stand trial, and his tapes of Pickles's outrageous Masonic threats would never be made public.

Woollard meanwhile had been moved only to another section of the Fraud Branch: the Public Sector Corruption Squad. Here he was put in charge of an inquiry that would lead to a far worse clash with Freemasonry. It was a classic case of local government racketeering. In 1977 the London Borough of Islington had bought hundreds of decaying houses to save their occupants from the negligence, exploitation and ideological evil of private landlords. Islington did not have enough staff to repair the houses so it gave the work to two private contractors, under the supervision of outside architects.

This consortium agreed to do the job for £1.2 million, but later asked for another £750,000 to carry out unforeseen roof repairs. The council refused the extra funds so one of the firms demanded payment for its work so far, then quit. Months went by before the council realized it had paid that firm twice as much per house as was agreed in the original contract. Surveyors were instructed to investigate this over-payment of more than £100,000. On visiting the houses, they were shocked to see the work had been over-priced or done badly or not done at all. In some homes the contractor claimed to have renewed roofs, doors and windows when no such work had been performed. In one house the roof was still being repaired when it fell in on the tenants. They stayed roofless throughout the winter.

By now Islington was buzzing with tales of corruption. It emerged that the outside firm of supervising architects had wined and dined the very council officials who later agreed to the over-payments, without seeing adequate documentary proof that extra costs had really been incurred. In turn, one of these outside architects had taken an expenses-paid trip to Ireland courtesy of one of the contractors (but only, he later claimed, to talk about an entirely different job). The revelations were so shocking that the council's deputy chief executive, Bob Trickett, set up an inquiry, but this was obstructed by other senior officials. The *Evening Standard* exposed the scandal and Islington called in the Fraud Squad. Yet it was another nine months before Brian Woollard took charge, so any culprits had plenty of time to destroy the evidence.

Woollard very soon discovered that he was mucking out a filthy but deserted stable. The horse had bolted. So had the files. The detective sensed that all the employees implicated in the racket were links in an invisible chain of mutual obligation. He was encountering something worse than the usual 'them and us' obstruction which detectives expect when probing crime in a closed organization. He could not quite define the problem until the council's own investigators, blocked and sabotaged long before, told him of an additional bond. Some of the suspects were Freemasons. So were leading council executives.

At first the evidence consisted of asides by Islington employees to the council inquirers, but some chief officers (who were not suspects) later made statements to Woollard in which they admitted their Freemasonry. One very high-ranking Islington council employee who was a Mason said he had no recollection of words attributed to him at a meeting during October 1981 (which had been called to discuss the house repair scandal). One witness told the investigating detectives:

> I clearly recall this senior officer saying 'corruption is not necessarily a bad thing for the council'. I found this statement coming from a man in his position unbelievable. No one present challenged him about this comment and I therefore asked him to expand . . . I cannot remember the exact words he used but basically he said that it was his experience that so often in cases of corruption the council ended up with the best contractor for the job. I found what he was saying unbelievable but . . . formed the impression that the other

officers present acceded to this man's view, as none of them
challenged his statement.

At this stage Woollard did not believe Freemasonry held the key to the
affair, nor did he assume everyone who had benefited from the inflated
payments was a Mason. Indeed, he knew that most building contractors
in London are Irish Catholics: unlikely recruits for the Craft. He was
more perturbed when Bob Trickett, the non-Mason who had set up the
council inquiry, confided that one Mason who had worked for Islington
Borough Council for thirty-five years (and who was himself a member of
the Borough of Islington Lodge) was confidently predicting Woollard's
investigation would come to nothing. When Trickett asked him why, the
man replied: 'Because two police officers in the Fraud Branch are in the
same lodge as men in our building works department.' Both Trickett and
Woollard knew that 'building works' was the department most deeply
implicated in the scandal.

Woollard considered all his colleagues in the Fraud Branch: in the
public sector corruption squad where he now worked, and in the
commercial fraud squad which he had recently left. After his nasty
experience over Pickles and Woolf, he felt he knew one officer who must
be a Mason. And because the Pickles–Woolf file had been slammed shut
marked 'no further action', he reflected that 'NFA' might also end up on
his Islington files unless he forestalled every Masonic move.

He continued his probe believing that any further obstruction might be
Masonic-inspired. In February 1982 he formally interviewed one of
Islington Council's most senior officers. Woollard advised him not to
discuss the interview with anyone, especially another key official who
was a suspect in the inquiry and whom Woollard planned to interview in
the next few days. The man gave Woollard his word but went straight
back to Islington Town Hall where he was seen disappearing into an
office with the suspect, talking in hushed tones. That evening the suspect
locked his filing cabinet containing documents crucial to Woollard's
inquiry. He then took an unplanned but instant one-month holiday.
Woollard could not help wondering if these moves had anything to do
with the admission that both of these men were Freemasons.

On the next Monday, 15 February, Woollard was out of his office
when he was telephoned by a director of the building firm which had
received the suspect payments. When told of the call, Woollard was
surprised that the caller had asked for him by name, for neither he nor any
member of his team had ever approached the firm. He assumed the
builder was getting nervous and was anxious to know whether or not the
police were about to bring charges.

Woollard was even more intrigued when told that a second call had come in a few minutes after the builder's, from another man to whom he had never spoken. This was Richard Thomas, a senior official in the department of the Director of Public Prosecutions. Woollard guessed that Thomas was the person who would decide if there were to be any charges over Islington. He returned the call but, when Thomas said he had telephoned only to see how the case was going, Woollard did not believe him. Suspecting collusion, he told Thomas about the call from the builder. Thomas repeated that he had called spontaneously, but Woollard made it plain he thought the two calls were related. He felt sure someone had phoned Thomas after the builder had failed to get through to Woollard himself.

The Chief Inspector now had to make a decision which, if he got it wrong, would finish his career as a detective. He had become convinced that Thomas was himself a fit subject for investigation. Why had he suddenly expressed an interest in the case at the very moment when suspects were scuttling off on 'holiday' or ringing up for no logical reason?

Woollard decided he must interview Thomas face-to-face. But how to go about it? As an officer of the chief prosecuting authority for England and Wales, Thomas was not without protection. Also the relationship between the D of PP and the Metropolitan Police is extremely sensitive. If a D of PP man *were* conspiring to pervert justice it would be of great concern to Scotland Yard. Indeed, the Commissioner himself might want to consider how the matter should be handled.

If Woollard were to play it safe he would refer the request up through his Fraud Squad chiefs, but that way he might run into the very Mason detectives whom (he had been told) belonged to the same lodge as his Islington suspects. If he was then barred from approaching Thomas, he would never know if the decision had been 'straight' or dictated by Masonic vows of fraternal protection. It also crossed his mind that Thomas might be a Mason himself.

Woollard pondered for a week, then decided to interview Thomas without telling senior officers. On Wednesday 24 February he took a detective constable with him to the offices of the D of PP in Queen Anne's Gate. Calling from reception, he told Thomas they needed to speak about an urgent matter which could not be discussed on the phone. Thomas agreed but was surprised when Woollard came in and announced this would be a formal interview which his colleague would be writing down.

Woollard told Thomas he was concerned that leaks and obstruction were affecting his inquiry. He then asked what had provoked Thomas's call of 15 February. At this point Thomas asked: 'Am I being arrested?'

Woollard said: 'No. I have just come here to make inquiries.' The D of PP man then said he could not remember making any call. He checked a file which noted he had called Woollard but gave no clue why. He then said his secretary had brought the case to his attention, but in front of Woollard she could recall no such action. 'It was obvious she had no idea what he was talking about,' says Woollard. Thomas explained this away by saying she was 'a bit thick'. Unconvinced, Woollard said he thought the sequence of calls was not a coincidence. He suspected Masonic connections and that Thomas had called him at the request of the suspect contractor, or of those Islington Masons who were alleged to have been obstructing the anti-corruption probes.

According to Woollard, Thomas said he was right to be concerned about obstruction and so he would hand the inquiry to another division of the D of PP's department. As they parted Thomas asked if the interview was a political move against him by CIB2, Scotland Yard's anti-corruption squad. Woollard said no. He had acted on his own initiative. Thomas then said, 'Perhaps there was a phone call', which Woollard interpreted as an admission that someone had indeed phoned Thomas.

Woollard knew the spaghetti would now hit the fan. He went straight to Scotland Yard to tip off the Commissioner's staff officer. He was out, and the Commissioner himself was on holiday, so Woollard dictated a note for the attention of the Deputy Commissioner justifying his meeting with Thomas.

He sped back across London and told his overall boss, Fraud Branch Commander, Peter Westley, what had happened. He also told Westley for the first time about the Masonic bond between Fraud Branch officers and Islington suspects. The Commander asked Woollard if he had mentioned this Masonic angle in his note to the Deputy Commissioner. Woollard said no. Westley hurried to Scotland Yard to find out what was happening. He returned at four o'clock and asked Woollard if he felt under strain and did he wish to be placed sick. Woollard said he felt neither strained nor sick. Far from it. He wished to continue with the Islington inquiry because it had reached a critical stage and he intended to interview the principal suspects within the next week.

Suddenly Westley ordered him to 'hand over' all his inquiries. He said that, in interviewing Thomas without telling anyone in advance, he had ignored the chain of command and acted 'irrationally'. Woollard responded that he had done this solely to protect his inquiry, which had already been shot through by Freemasonry. Westley set that argument aside and spoke instead of the paramount importance of maintaining good relations with the D of PP's office, because 'we have to live with these people'. In all the circumstances (irrespective of any Masonic considerations), the non–Mason Westley must have felt he had no alternative.

Woollard walked out of Westley's office and handed over all his duties to his detective constable. The Commander had left him in no doubt that he would be moved right off the Fraud Branch, but he had no idea how far he would fall. In the next twelve months he would take a career plunge which at times was as excoriating as the fiery furnace in Dante's *Inferno* and, at others, as farcical as Alice's experiences on falling down the hole after the White Rabbit. Woollard feels it was more of a Masonic 'Black Hole', from which no light was intended to escape. Again, the outsider must judge whether to accept his perception of an all-embracing Masonic conspiracy or to plump for the 'long-arm-of-coincidence' – or perhaps to think it was a bit of both.

One decision soon taken at the Fraud Branch shows how what may have been mere coincidence might easily be taken for part of a conspiracy. This was the appointment of a Freemason to replace Woollard on the Mason-riddled Islington inquiry. In 1984 the officer concerned, Det. Chief Insp. Robert Andrews, told the *Observer* newspaper that he was no longer a Mason.[1] He also said Freemasonry 'has no bearing on my job and has not influenced me at all'. No doubt this is the case, but if Woollard's replacement had never been 'on the square', the D of PP's later decision not to prosecute anyone over the Islington scandal for lack of evidence might have been easier for Woollard and Islington's long-suffering ratepayers to stomach.

When Woollard first collided with the Craft there was no great public interest in Freemasonry. This was stimulated in 1984 by *The Brotherhood*, the publication of which coincided with the first newspaper reports about his problems. When the terminal letters 'NFA' ('no further action') were stamped on the Islington inquiry back in 1982, any Masonic network composed of men in the council, the building trade, the Fraud Branch and the Department of the Director of Public Prosecutions would not have dreamed its clandestine decision-making would ever be subject to public scrutiny.

To this day no evidence has leaked from Masonic circles to prove or disprove Woollard's most disturbing claim: that Fraud Branch officers were in the same lodge as Islington suspects. Yet evidence has emerged that on 15 May 1975 a civil engineer working for Islington Council was initiated into the Barnaby Rudge Lodge in Romford, Essex. The Master who initiated him was a detective inspector in the London (no. 9) Regional Crime Squad, one of several detectives in that lodge. Neither these policemen nor the engineer had anything to do with corrupt goings-on at Islington. All this fragment proves is that London detectives and Islington employees can indeed belong to the same lodge. If this could occur in a lodge in Romford – twelve miles from Islington – it must have occurred in several of the hundreds of lodges which meet far nearer to Islington Town Hall.

Stripped of all duties, Brian Woollard was now forced to sit doing nothing in an open-plan office, as Scotland Yard chiefs apologized to the Director of Public Prosecutions, and a senior detective investigated Woollard to find out why they were apologizing. Woollard was convinced this man was yet another Mason, a view reinforced when the man did not bother to interview Woollard himself. Meantime, D of PP official Richard Thomas was cleared. We know this from the surprising source of Lord Cornwallis, Pro Grand Master of England's Freemasons, who later revealed that the D of PP 'was satisfied that there was nothing within his office to suggest that Masonry was used to Mr Woollard's detriment'.[2] Thomas has since retired.

On 11 March 1982 Woollard was summoned before Deputy Assistant Commissioner Ron Steventon, who had overall disciplinary charge of all London's detectives. In the 1970s he had played a leading role in the war on corruption among Scotland Yard's elite squads.[3] In 1982 he took on the job of completing and closing down Operation Countryman, another massive inquiry into crookery among London detectives (see Chapter 17).

Ron Steventon was, and remains, an ardent Mason, a member of the Hertfordshire Masters Lodge. He is a Royal Arch Companion and in 1985–6 was 'Scribe Ezra' (secretary) of the Charles Edward Keyser Chapter. He also belongs to an order known as the Mark Masons. Now retired from his lofty post in Scotland Yard, in 1985–6 he was but a humble steward in the James Terry Lodge of Mark Masons.

Back in 1982 Steventon told Woollard he was being put back into uniform because he was not considered fit to be employed in a specialist department or in plain clothes. Woollard asked if anyone had made a formal complaint. Steventon said no. Woollard then asked why he had not been seen by the officer who was investigating him. That was not necessary, said Steventon, because his offence was clear: he had tried to see the Commissioner and Deputy Commissioner, by-passing the chain of command. Woollard argued that he had never sought to see the Commissioner, only his staff officer.

This drove Steventon to the heart of the matter: 'You have caused embarrassment.' He did not say how, to whom or to what. Neither man mentioned Freemasonry. Presumably Steventon meant 'embarrassment' to Scotland Yard's relations with the Director of Public Prosecutions, but Woollard thought otherwise.

Steventon told him to return to the Fraud Branch and 'wait there'. For forty days he sat in enforced idleness beside three officers who, before the uproar, had been working for him. He says he was 'stood in the corner like a naughty little boy'. His immediate boss was sympathetic. He said he could not understand how Woollard could stay so calm in such humiliating circumstances.

At last Woollard learned of his punishment: a posting to Wembley police station as a uniform chief inspector. This would be seen by all his colleagues as demotion, for when a detective is pushed into uniform without going up a rank he is taking a clear drop in status. The move was listed in 'Police Orders' which, Woollard felt, was meant to stigmatize and humiliate him before the entire force. The trouble was that, after twenty-two years as a detective, he did not have a uniform. He was told to get one overnight because next day he was being interviewed by the area's chief officer, another deputy assistant commissioner. He rushed off for a fitting and duly presented himself in blue but, as he says, wearing a uniform after twenty-two years was an 'uncomfortable exercise hardly calculated to put me at my ease' – especially when the 'uniform' DAC turned up in plain clothes.

By now some readers may feel Woollard is a whinger, if not a 'loonie'. What kind of a cop is it who moans about wearing a uniform? Isn't it the uniform which attracts men into the job in the first place? As for sitting doing nothing: he was getting paid, wasn't he? Why cry for Woollard with his petty gripes?

Woollard's gripes are worth mentioning precisely because they are petty. They are just a few of the complaints he has poured out in the past seven years, but they help tell the story of what seems to Woollard to be a long, calculated campaign to break his spirit. To him it was death by a thousand cuts.

At this point the relevance of the Manor of St James's Lodge becomes clear. Many of its members have played significant roles in the Woollard saga, although it was not until the 'Manor' list leaked out in 1986 that Woollard had documentary proof that these men were 'on the square'. Before that he was working on police gossip and the casual talk of some of the men themselves. Today he bases his claim that he was in the midst of a Masonic nexus on the fact that he was posted to Wembley when Manor Masons were especially thick on the ground there. They included three founders of the lodge:

William Gibson: Commander of Q District, including Wembley.
Ben Pountain: Chief Superintendent of Q, Gibson's Deputy.

Edgar Maybanks: He became DAC in overall charge of No. 2 area, including Wembley, shortly after Woollard's posting.

It is a singularly unfortunate coincidence that a policeman who is claiming that Freemasonry has played a major role in a bad case of public corruption is sent to a district where the line of command is solidly Masonic. Of course Masons may be so numerous in the force that Woollard would have been surrounded by them wherever he was posted. Viewed from that perspective, his Wembley posting might indeed have been mere chance. However, the fact that Maybanks, Gibson and Pountain would all later emerge in the Manor indicates that Wembley was a singularly inappropriate place to remove Woollard's obsessive suspicion that he was the victim of a Masonic plot. No other area (outside 'C' District) had so great a concentration of future Manor members.

As soon as Woollard arrived at Wembley police station he was ordered to report to Commander Gibson's office. Gibson and Pountain ruled from offices two floors above where the fallen chief inspector now had to run 'uniform administration'. Soon afterwards another new man arrived as his opposite number in charge of 'uniform operations': Chief Inspector Mike Bedwell, also a future member of the Manor.

The climate at Wembley was inhospitable. Only a few weeks earlier Woollard had been investigating major crimes. Now he was doing a clerk's job, mundane at the best of times but particularly tedious for a man who had been a detective for twenty-two years. His first annual report from Wembley catalogued a startling decline. It was written by Chief Supt. Ron Poole and his successor, Ron Plunkett, who rated the man 'unsatisfactory' or 'fair' in ten out of twelve qualities, 'good' only in written work ('poetic command of words') and 'very good' only in verbal communication.

Plunkett's wider comments were accurate but destructive. He said Woollard had arrived 'unprepared for the rigours of uniform duties and somewhat resentful of his transfer'. He had a 'good intellect, a sharp wit which is sometimes waspish, but is clearly not at ease in his present role'. He said Woollard did not know what that role was, especially when it came to checking entries in various books and registers. In short, he was 'completely unsuited to this very responsible post. He has no incentive and I consider it very unlikely that he will make any greater effort.' Plunkett then recommended Woollard be moved to 'a quiet station where he may be able to cope with all his duties'.

Woollard admits he was disoriented and unsure of his duties but his unit was very short-staffed, as even Plunkett recorded in his report. Despite this, Woollard was given even more work such as investigating complaints against the police, a job which was under the control of the Freemasons, Gibson and Pountain. This time-consuming and highly sensitive duty is the worst job in a police station: you are either fobbing off crazy people complaining that a PC has refused to get a cat down from a tree, or dressing down your colleagues. The job was even more irksome to an officer preoccupied with his own complaints against the police. Woollard was convinced he had been given this duty on top of all the others just to make sure he performed them all badly. However, it may have been just one more coincidental misfortune.

Plunkett does not belong to the Manor of St James's. He told Woollard he used to be a Mason but had quit the Craft because it was 'silly'. Again, it needs to be said that there is no way a man can stop being a Mason. He may be excluded for misconduct or not paying his dues. He may tell the lodge secretary he is resigning. Yet he is still bound to a lifetime of obligation to his brethren because of those bloodcurdling oaths which he swore on the Holy Book. If a Mason were to go to a Commissioner of Oaths, unswear his oath on the same Holy Book, and publish this fact in the local newspaper, *then* an outsider might have to accept that a man has purged himself of his Masonic bonds. As far as I know, this has never happened.

Accepting that Plunkett was no longer a Mason in spirit, I find it difficult to measure the remark which two other Wembley policemen recall that Plunkett made to a group of junior officers when he first arrived at the station in September 1982 from Scotland Yard: 'They've sent me down to get rid of that wanker Woollard.' When no one uttered a word of support for this cause, Plunkett left the room.

Woollard meantime had complained to Commander Alan Gibson that Plunkett's report on him was a travesty. During a three-hour confrontation in October 1982 Gibson accused him of having a fixation about Plunkett. He ordered him to see Scotland Yard's chief medical officer who would, if necessary, arrange for him to have a psychiatric examination and treatment.

Woollard could not help wondering if this move had anything to do with the fact that two months earlier he had sent a highly sensitive account of his case to his MP, Sir George Young. In this he had laid out the Masonic dimension and complained against named senior officers, all of whom were Masons. The only policeman whom Woollard had meant to see this document was the Metropolitan Commissioner, Sir David McNee. Young asked McNee to give Woollard a personal interview but this was refused. Young sent Woollard's account to Scotland Yard anyway, which Woollard says was against his expressed wish. Woollard had also asked the MP to ask Home Secretary William Whitelaw to set up an independent inquiry. This too was refused. Woollard was not surprised because he believed Whitelaw was yet another Mason. The now Lord Whitelaw tells me he is indeed a Freemason, but has not been active in the Craft since he became an MP in 1955. He also says this connection 'had absolutely no bearing on any actions I may have taken as far as Chief Inspector Brian Woollard was concerned'.[4]

Woollard believes that news of his various attempts to win justice must have reached Wembley not long before Commander Gibson packed him off to the chief medical officer. Already languishing in the Metropolitan Police equivalent of the Gulag Archipelago, Woollard now feared another Stalinist fate: compulsory examination by a psychiatrist in the pay of the state. This is the traditional death-knell to a policeman's career. Sure enough, the CMO questioned him on his state of mind, but gave him a 'clean bill of health'. As a result there was no trip to a psychiatrist, but Woollard saw the medical as an attempt to write him off as a 'nut' and to discredit his anti-Masonic complaints.

Of course, it may have been just another coincidence; perhaps a non-Masonic commander would also have ordered him to undergo a medical. It may also have been chance that Commander Gibson was one of the prime movers of the Manor of St James's Lodge. In January 1987 he became its Master. Indeed, Worshipful Brother Gibson is a most active Mason: twice Master of the Stone Lodge of Harrow and a founder of the Bodina Lodge in Radlett. He has even been raised to the rank of Past Grand Sword Bearer for Middlesex. By helping to found two new lodges in sixteen months he must be on the verge of national Grand Rank: a fitting tribute to his Masonic labours.

In contrast Woollard spent most of his spare time *fighting* Freemasonry. Convinced he had exhausted every internal police mechanism, he approached more MPs and finally the media. Early in 1984 his campaign surfaced in *Private Eye*, the *Observer* and other papers. In March and April he appeared on two local television shows without the permission of a senior officer. He had not sought permission because he knew it would be refused: all five officers in the chain of command above him were Freemasons!

This fact does not make them part of a Masonic conspiracy. Police forces rightly have powers to stop officers 'shooting their mouths off' to the media about sensitive criminal inquiries or controversial policies. However, Woollard was not questioning or interfering in any way with legitimate policing. He was challenging not Scotland Yard's due authority but its perversion by a private organization, stitched into the fabric of the force, which (he claimed) had smashed his career to protect its ascendancy. He was, of course, bound by the Official Secrets Act which in theory applies to everything he had learned throughout his years in the police, but it would be an outrage if a police chief invoked that Act just to stop officers publicly expressing anti-Masonic views. Freemasonry's power in Britain's police forces is still an *unofficial* secret, not an official one.

In this case Woollard knew he had no hope of getting permission. It would have had to come from some of the very Masons about whom he was complaining. Once he had shown his face on television, of course, he knew he would be disciplined. Both programmes stated he might be sacked or even lose his pension for speaking out. Sure enough, on 26 April 1984 Chief Superintendent Plunkett, acting on behalf of CIB2, served him with an instruction 'not to involve yourself in any way with the media'. Plunkett then said: 'Do you understand that this involves all the media, television, radio and press?' Woollard replied 'Yes' but added that, while he understood this instruction was designed to silence him and to prevent him causing embarrassment to the senior command of the Metropolitan Police, he had no intention of obeying it.

On 1 May 1984 he was formally interviewed by CIB2. On this occasion he knew his interrogator could not be a regular Mason: Det. Supt. Coleman was a woman. After the interview the pair found themselves waiting for the same lift. During these seconds Marie Coleman confided that she had been selected to conduct the interview *because* she was a woman, just so Woollard could *not* allege a Masonic conspiracy to prosecute him! That afternoon her boss, Det. Chief Supt. Churchill-Coleman (no relation), rejected a request from Woollard's solicitor to attend the interview. Churchill-Coleman was another future founder of the Manor.

Woollard was then ordered to appear before DAC Maybanks, another Manor founder. He advised Woollard to stay away from the media but told him that Deputy Commissioner Albert Laugharne had 'specially selected' an officer from another police force to investigate his complaint. This move did not satisfy Woollard, for it came more than two years after his original request for an independent inquiry. It was only being made now precisely because Woollard had dared to involve the media! However, in the intervening years he had complained against Commissioner McNee (for refusing to see him) and Home Secretary Whitelaw. He therefore felt any inquiry now must be independent of the entire police service and the Home Office, and answerable only to Parliament. It was manifestly invidious – and without precedent – for the chosen investigator, Assistant Chief Constable Tom Meffen of the West Midlands Police, to inquire into the conduct of a Metropolitan Commissioner and two deputy commissioners, for they far outranked him.

He was equally ill-equipped to investigate the ministerial actions of Deputy Prime Minister Whitelaw, a job which surely could be performed only by Parliament.

Woollard refused to co-operate with Meffen, whose inquiry he condemned as 'a cosmetic exercise in damage limitation to get the most senior officers I had complained against off the hook'. Meffen went ahead regardless. In April 1985 he concluded there was no evidence that Freemasonry had played a part either in the Islington Council affair or in blocking Woollard's career. This was just what Woollard had predicted. Meffen presumably knew nothing of the moves already made to start the Manor Lodge. Such knowledge might have helped him to reach another conclusion.

At the outset Meffen had assured Woollard he was wholly independent of Scotland Yard because his own West Midlands Chief Constable was responsible for his terms of reference. Yet before he had time to complete the Woollard inquiry, Meffen was under a new Chief Constable: Geoffrey Dear QPM, DL, LLB. Dear had come straight from the Metropolitan Police, where he was one of the very officers whom Woollard had named in his complaints. Thus the wholly independent outsider, Meffen, was now investigating his own boss! This was just another unfortunate coincidence, but one which increased Woollard's doubts about the impartiality of any police inquiry into his complaints.

From 1981 to 1984 Dear had been assistant commissioner in the Metropolitan Police responsible for personnel and training. In this capacity he met Woollard on 20 January 1983. Woollard says that Dear promised him his case would be reviewed and he would be granted an interview with Commissioner Newman within three weeks. Neither event happened,[5] so Woollard made a formal complaint against both Dear and Newman.

Mr Dear is not enthusiastic about inquiries into the Craft, as he made clear in a letter responding to a questionnaire which I sent to all Britain's chief constables (see Chapter 21). He refused to say if he was a Mason. Instead he found the 'over-weening interest' in this 'negative and hackneyed' subject 'rather tedious' and was disappointed that it should be 'resurrected yet again'. His private life, he said, was entirely his own concern, provided it did not adversely influence his professional standing, or that of the force, or interfere with the impartial discharge of professional duty.

Mr Dear gives no advice on Masonry to his officers because it would be 'wholly wrong to single out Freemasonry for specific advice when criticism might equally be levelled at those who belong to a large number of other organizations or institutions, whether secret or not'. Having served in five forces, he has never found a shred of evidence that police Masons 'comport themselves in such a way as to bring discredit upon themselves, their colleagues, the service or the good reputation of the force'. He has 'seen nothing which runs contrary' to the policeman's declaration of service.

I assume from this remark that Mr Dear has seen quite a lot of Freemasonry and may have studied it from within. I quote his views at length because they are diametrically opposed to those held by Scotland Yard – so long as *The Principles of Policing* remains compulsory reading for all Metropolitan recruits. Born in 1937 Geoffrey Dear is a 'high flyer', a comparatively young man who could reasonably expect to head a force bigger than the West Midlands before he retires. Although only four years younger than the present Metropolitan Commissioner, he might still aspire to that job. Were he to get it, he would presumably strike out the anti-Masonic passage in the book. I do not know for sure, because he told me he had 'no wish to prolong this correspondence'.

Woollard would labour on at Wembley for four and a half years. This brave man who had protected royalty, prime ministers and cabinet ministers, who had tracked down terrorists and armed robbers, now performed such intrepid tasks as running the charge centres at Wembley Stadium for the FA Cup Final and other events. His Masonic masters clearly believed his talents were best devoted to those twin scourges of modern sport: football hooligans and ticket touts, among whom there are believed to be few Freemasons – unless they are cops working under-cover.

Among other irritations at Wembley, Woollard suffered job sabotage to make him look incompetent. Not long after the first newspaper articles appeared about him in 1984, a box of thirty-three minor traffic case files disappeared from the process room (or administration section) over-night. As the officer in charge, Woollard had locked his door to the room but there were other ways of getting into it, and any blame going would fall on him. He reported the theft, and soon Superintendent Alan Stainsby was telling junior officers that Commander Gibson had deputed him to investigate. He was abruptly told by one long-serving constable that everyone knew the theft was part of a 'Masonic plot to discredit Woollard'. It might, of course, have been another non-Masonic coinci-dence, or a prank, but the files were never found. A few months later eight major files (breathalyser offences and traffic injuries) disappeared from the same room when they were awaiting dispatch to Scotland Yard. Luckily, Woollard had copies of them all or else he would have had more than egg on his face. Weeks later the originals miraculously reappeared.

Throughout these years Woollard's annual reports had a patronizing tone and recorded only bare improvements. Their authors admitted he would be far better employed back in the CID, but there was no chance of that. Instead, in the interests of 'career development' he should move on. In August 1986 he received a call from Chief Supt. Lionel Stapley of D 15, a department devoted to specialist training. Stapley visited him some days later. He spent much of the interview asking when Woollard intended to retire and what he intended to do then. A few weeks later Woollard saw Stapley's name on the Manor of St James's Lodge list.

In September 1986 he was posted to West Hendon station, still within the manor of Commander Gibson of the Manor Lodge. The move did not diminish his publicity drive. For two years he had been fighting on all fronts, sending sackloads of documents to MPs, judges in the House of Lords, journalists – anyone who got in touch with him. By this time he had spent some £15,000 on research, photocopying and postage, yet his campaigning had still got him nowhere. Indeed, he appeared to many media people to be going 'round the twist'. However, when the Manor Lodge list fell into his hands, some reporters changed their tune. Suddenly his seemingly manic fantasies became credible. Newspapers retold his tales of Masonic machinations and married them with names from the Manor list.

In December 1986 Woollard wrote a letter to the *Guardian* in support of John Stalker, the retiring Deputy Chief Constable of Greater Manchester, and himself no lover of Freemasonry (see Chapter 19). Referring to Stalker's struggle against false allegations of corruption and misconduct, the feisty Chief Inspector said it was time Britain's 4 million public service workers had an independent channel to investigate their complaints of injustice at work. What was needed was an Ombudsman for the Public Servant. He then juxtaposed his removal from the Islington corruption inquiry with a reference to the Manor of St James's Lodge.

His letter was published the day after Boxing Day when almost nobody read it, but the *Guardian* ran a cartoon captioned: 'If you want to know the way to join the Freemasons, ask a policeman.' This caught the attention of Radio Manchester, which interviewed Woollard. He said public servants' employment complaints will never be properly handled as long as they are investigated by the employing organizations themselves. He was pinpointing an important issue, which goes wider than the problem of Masonic mutual aid. At present employers such as the civil service, the armed forces and the police act as prosecutor, defence counsel, jury and judge in all internal complaints against themselves. Almost always they find themselves innocent. This dissatisfies the plaintiffs who feel forced to turn to the media as their last means of redress. Yet if they do 'go public' their careers will be destroyed anyway.

Woollard knew these latest acts of self-advertisement would infuriate Scotland Yard's chiefs, but someone in the hierarchy with an impish sense of humour had given him a new duty at West Hendon: liaising with the local press. This was like putting Billy Bunter in charge of the tuck shop, but he was careful not to let his private battle with the hierarchy and Freemasonry intrude. However, on 3 February 1987 three local reporters walked into his office for a news briefing just when CIB 2 called to tell him he was to be investigated for his latest media dealings. When he put the phone down, one reporter asked to know more, so the policeman gave a five-hour account of his case, turning a routine press conference into what the *Hendon Times* called 'an extraordinary event'. He won double-page spreads in the local weeklies but chastisement from his bosses. They cited his alleged undertaking to Plunkett back in 1984 not to involve himself in any way with the media. He pointed out that in the meantime he had been ordered to brief the media twice a week and could hardly be expected to ignore questions about his own case.

Woollard had manoeuvred Scotland Yard into a 'no-win situation'. His repeated public onslaughts on top officers (including Commissioners) broke standing instructions, so he could be suspended or sacked at any time. Yet if he were sacked or suspended he would cry 'Mason!' and claim this was ultimate proof that the brotherhood was running the police. Worse still, the public would believe him. Yard chiefs did not need such publicity. They also knew that, however much trouble Woollard was causing as a copper, he would cause far more as an out-of-work civilian. He would become the perfect martyred hero for newspapers pursuing their favourite pastime of 'knocking the fuzz'. As one serving senior police chief told me: 'It was better to have Woollard inside pissing out than outside pissing in.'

There was another consideration. The greatest concentration of anti-Masonic hate lies within the police itself. Freemasonry is the biggest single divisive factor in British law enforcement. Woollard's relentless, calculated campaign against the Craft had won him many admirers among London's 27,000 coppers. Frightened to support him openly, they would surely rally to his side if he were dismissed for doing no more than talking to the press.

The dilemma facing Scotland Yard was of its own making. Over generations it had failed to see any danger in the Masonic 'firm in a firm' which, unchecked, had recruited up to 20 per cent of London's bobbies, set cop against cop, and fouled relations between the force and the non-Masonic public. Woollard's belief that he was the victim of a Masonic conspiracy may be exaggerated, but he could scarcely come to any other conclusion when at every turn he encountered yet another Freemason, many of whom belonged to the same lodge.

At the top of Scotland Yard a few men sympathize with Woollard. They share his views but they have never come out in his support, either because they fear for their own careers or they feel there is too much madness in his method. It is true that discretion no longer plays any part in Woollard's valour. He long ago concluded that the only way to combat Freemasonry in an organization so riddled with the Craft is by open war – ordeal by fire.

One clue to Freemasonry's overall strength in the Metropolitan Police is the role played by known Masons in various associations of senior officers. In 1984 future Manor Master Alan Gibson represented all London commanders in negotiations with Scotland Yard and the Home Office. Likewise, Brother Ben Pountain was chairman of the London Superintendents' Association. More disabling for Woollard, in 1986 another Manor founder, Alan Turner, became secretary of the Inspectors' Branch of the Metropolitan Police Federation. Henceforth, if Woollard needed 'trade union' help against the Masons in the Manor, he would have to seek it from one of the Manor Masons.

Today Woollard recalls his final report at Bramshill College in 1982. Despite all that has befallen him and his wife Deborah, who had the bad timing to marry him four months before his sacking from the Islington inquiry, he has retained 'his unquestioned loyalty to the police service' because, he says, this applies to 'the concept of a police service of complete integrity, unhampered by a secretive sub-culture of self-interest which wants to rule the roost and crucify those who dare to challenge the extent of its infiltration'.

It now seems clear that the Manor Lodge was conceived before the publication of Commissioner Newman's *Principles* in April 1985 – and even before its anti-Masonic paragraphs appeared in *The Job* nine months earlier. Lord Cornwallis claims discussions started 'early in 1984'.[6] Yet even then Woollard had been fighting Freemasonry for two years, as Wembley brethren who helped found the lodge knew at first hand.

According to the *Daily Telegraph*, Woollard's 'anti-Masonic views undoubtedly led to Sir Kenneth Newman's advice to his men to think twice before joining the society'.[7] Perhaps his views also provoked the founding of the Manor. When he was given a clean bill of health in 1982 and could not be discredited as a 'loonie' – and especially when the media took up his case in January 1984 – it may have been felt that some central body was needed to co-ordinate the Metropolitan Masonic lobby against all comers. What better than a lodge for dear old 'C' District, where so many eminent Masonic coppers had prospered over the years? Most would have jumped at the idea, especially those who had no idea that there might have been something else behind it. But, of course, the coincidence of the Manor's rise and Woollard's fall may be nothing more than that: coincidence!

thirteen

THE MEANING OF THE MANOR

Some twelve members of the Manor of St James's Lodge have figured in the Brian Woollard affair, but what is the strength of its entire membership – and what does that tell us about the role of Freemasonry in the Metropolitan Police as a whole?

With only limited sources of information, I have discovered the ranks of seventy-two serving and retired officers (together with two 'specials' and one civilian) among the ninety-seven men who had joined the lodge by the start of 1987. Police yearbooks and newspaper files usually identify only senior officers, so my findings may exaggerate the seniority of the membership as a whole. Even so, it is clear that the Manor recruits mainly from the upper ranks of the Metropolitan Police. The seventy-two include:

> 1 assistant commissioner
> 2 deputy assistant commissioners
> 12 commanders
> 23 chief superintendents
> 10 superintendents
> 7 chief inspectors
> 12 inspectors
> 2 sergeants
> 3 constables.

An assistant commissioner has reached almost the peak of the force. There are only four ACs in the Metropolitan Police. They are outranked only by the Commissioner and his deputy. The AC and DAC ranks are unique to London and are considered equal to chief constable in any other force.

At the time the Manor list was printed, twenty-six of these seventy-two members were retired and forty-six were still serving. As I write, the retired men include the AC and DACs, nine commanders, ten chief superintendents and five superintendents. Among Manor members still in the force are three commanders, thirteen chief superintendents and five superintendents. They include recent commanders of the Fraud Squad and the Anti-Terrorist Squad (in both of which Brian Woollard used to work); and chief superintendents in Central, North, South, East and West London. Today there is barely a department of the Metropolitan Police in which the Manor does not have a member, so that when it meets in Mark Masons' Hall in St James's Street four times a year, it must be an excellent listening post for hot 'shop' gossip from all quarters. Forbidden to discuss politics and religion, its members would seem to have little to talk about except their own 'Craft': policing.

The Manor was sponsored by an existing lodge, the Prior Walter (no. 8687), whose members belong to the Order of St John. This chivalric club claims descent from the medieval Knights Hospitallers yet it was founded only in 1831. Today it is best known for the St John Ambulance Brigade and other charitable work but its 'knights' are mostly titled people, not stretcher-bearers or first aiders. The Order is not ostensibly Masonic but contains very many Masons. According to the blurb on Manor Lodge summonses, it also has a 'close affinity with the police service'.

Whether its members are now retired policemen or still serving, the Manor constitutes one of the strongest sectional interests in the force. It looks even stronger when viewed as an element within the CID. Thirty-one of the seventy-two were identifiably detectives, including the AC, six commanders and twelve chief superintendents.[1] Such figures may indicate that more than two-fifths of all the Masons in the Metropolitan Police are detectives, even though detectives constitute only one in seven of London's policemen: some 3,500 out of a total male strength of 24,000. Thus the Craft appears to be far stronger among detectives than uniformed officers, which long-time observers of London's CID would find easy to believe. It is not possible to say if men join Freemasonry as a prelude to (or in the hope of) joining the CID, or if men who are already detectives are subsequently persuaded to become Masons.

In recent years Freemasonry's strength in 'C' District has been immense. In 1981 at least six out of the twelve top jobs in 'C' were filled by Masons: all future founders of the Manor of St James's Lodge. At the top were the District Commander, Edward Stow, and Chief Superintendent Alan Gibson (who in 1982 as Commander of 'Q' District would clash with Brian Woollard). Other Masons included the detective superintendent heading Savile Row CID, the superintendent in 'Clubs Office' (which watches over West End nightspots, drinking clubs and restaurants), and the chief superintendent and superintendent at Bow Street.[2]

Several more of 'C's' 1981 top twelve are said to have been Masons but, even if only six were 'on the square', the Craft clearly dominated the district at that time. The same seems true today. Reorganization means that 'C' no longer has its own commander – indeed 'C' (like all other 'districts') no longer exists – but as recently as 1987 chief superintendents, superintendents and inspectors at each of the old 'C' stations (West End Central, Vine Street and Bow Street) were members of the Manor.

Did these men rise high in the force solely on their police skills or has the brotherhood played some part in their success? Has none ever been helped up the ladder – or saved from falling off it – by fellow-Masons? And can they all honestly claim that, in performing their duties, they have never done favours for their Masonic brothers outside the police? According to one of the highest-ranking retired officers in the Manor, the Craft played no part in his police career.

> In all my years I never allowed Freemasonry to influence my dealings with the public. I was never promoted because I was a Mason and I never backed anyone else for promotion because he was a Mason. In fact until this new lodge started I had only ever belonged to a lodge where I was the sole policeman. It was only when I turned up at the Lodge's first meeting that I realized I had worked with some officers for thirty years without even knowing they were Masons, so I assure you we never sat around in our aprons plotting the future of Scotland Yard, let alone the world.

The Manor has united in Masonic fellowship two policemen who once had a serious falling-out. In the late 1970s one future Manor member stripped another of his top detective's job and put him into uniform. This amounted to demotion, just as it did when Woollard suffered the same indignity. In this case the detective was transferred because he had taken the wife and children of an imprisoned criminal on a caravan holiday with his own wife and children. He had only the best of motives – the criminal's family were decent people and they needed a break – but his overall chief thought he had displayed very poor judgement. Imagine what the Sunday newspapers would have done with the story if they had found out! As it happens, they did not find out, and the officer went on to do very well in uniform. He was even promoted. He once told me: 'Getting out of the CID was the best thing that could have happened to me.'

As a reporter specializing in police affairs, I have been on good terms for many years with several officers who now belong to the Manor. I am now tempted to say to each of them, 'What's a nice guy like you doing in a place like this?' or, 'I thought you would never join a club that would have you as a member', but such flippancy would trivialize the threat which the lodge may pose to policing in London, a threat perceived in a lot of correspondence between public, press, police and politicians.

One week after the 'consecration' of the Manor, a citizen named D. G. Parker of Exmouth wrote to Home Secretary Douglas Hurd to ask what action he proposed to take against it. In Parker's view, the new lodge clearly contradicted the Commissioner's advice that policemen should not be Masons.

Hurd did not reply, but a Mrs C. Fitzpatrick wrote back on Home Office paper without saying what her job was. She watered down Sir Kenneth's *Principles of Policing* by stating, 'very little of the considerable amount of conjecture about the effects of freemasonry upon the police service has been supported by evidence'. Officers should consider whether Masonic obligations are really compatible with their declaration of impartiality to the public at large, but the Home Secretary felt they should make up their own minds as any attempt to ban them from the Craft would be an 'unwarranted interference with private life'.

Mr Parker was not impressed. He wrote back to Douglas Hurd in robust terms. It was hardly surprising, he said, that there was little evidence about Freemasonry and the police because 'this secret society works with great finesse', witness the 'extraordinary difficulty in getting any questions on the matter accepted for discussion in the House of Commons . . . The decent, law-abiding public have become disillusioned with the corruption and cover-ups which occur', said Parker before blasting the Home Office view that it would be an 'unwarranted interference' if policemen were banned from Freemasonry:

> It is not considered such an interference to prohibit workers at the Cheltenham Communications Centre (GCHQ) from being members of a trade union, and the trade unions are not a secret society. In this connection one may ask why freemasons are allowed to be members of the various government intelligence services when owing allegiance to a secret society as well as the Crown, and the same can be said regarding the judiciary.[3]
>
> The time is approaching when this matter will have to come into the open. There is no question of anyone wanting secrets to be divulged, and freemasons can practise their rituals as much as they wish, but a secret society cannot be allowed to use its influence

against the public interest, no matter how many of its members occupy high places.

Mr Parker's dyspeptic onslaught on the Craft got him nowhere, just another bland response from a Home Office clerk. If a member of the public only gets the 'brush-off' from the Home Secretary, members of the House of Commons fare no better, as Parker says. For six years Labour MP Austin Mitchell has fought to bring the issue of Freemasonry into the open, repeatedly petitioning Parliament on Brian Woollard's behalf.

The Manor membership list breathed new life into Mitchell's campaign. In February 1987 he wrote to Douglas Hurd saying the new lodge had been formed in clear defiance of the Commissioner. Since several of England's most senior Masons were among its honorary members, it appeared to have been given 'a particular *imprimatur*' from the movement. It even had a direct connection with Hurd's political party through its honorary member, Sir Peter Lane, former Chairman of the National Union of Conservative Associations.

On Woollard, Mitchell said he found it hard not to conclude that Masons had not only interfered with his career but had sent him to a place where he would be surrounded and constantly watched by Masons: 'This is particularly worrying because it gives real substance to Woollard's complaints about the role of the masons in his case and more generally in the police.'

Woollard himself has bludgeoned successive Home Secretaries and all the main party leaders, demanding to know where they stand on Freemasonry in the police and in society as a whole. Hotting up his campaign for an Ombudsman for the Public Servant, in 1987 he re-canvassed all the party leaders, none of whom had previously sent him more than a bland acknowledgement.

As usual, Prime Minister Margaret Thatcher's staffers thanked him for his letter which (as always) was 'receiving attention'. Woollard knew this meant that nothing would happen. Labour leader Neil Kinnock did not even reply. Whenever Woollard sent David Steel, then Liberal leader, a fresh pack of Woollardiana he received only unsigned acknowledgement slips. In March 1987 SDP leader David Owen wrote back saying, 'questions of the influence of freemasonry in the police force and the lack of redress for legitimate grievances are extremely serious ones'. He promised to talk the matter over with his Alliance colleagues. Since then Dr Owen has split from the Alliance and from most of his own party, so tackling the Masons cannot now be his highest priority![4]

Like political leaders, police chiefs find Freemasonry difficult to confront. In 1986 I wrote to all Britain's chief constables concerning the Craft. Their answers are analysed in Chapter 21, but Sir Kenneth Newman's painstaking reply deserves attention here. He said he was not and never had been a Mason. The formation of the Manor Lodge was 'admittedly a disappointment', but he felt it quite likely that 'many have not joined who might have done but for the publication of my policy'. He believed officers were taking notice of his *Principles*, which was given to all new recruits at Hendon training school. Instructors there use it as the basis of early lessons.

As he wrote this letter Sir Kenneth may not have known that one Manor member, Commander Anthony Speed, was in charge of a key part of the school. When later asked if he faced any difficulties in teaching the *Principles*, Speed pointed out that, as head of *detective* training, he 'had nothing to do with recruits and cadets'. He said Freemasonry was part of his personal life and not 'involved in my police duties'. He derided the idea that Freemasonry was a key to promotion: 'If that's the case we would be inundated with calls to join up.'[5] This answer overlooked the fact that policemen – especially detectives – have been flooding into the Craft for more than one hundred years. The rush to join the Manor proves that they still are.

Commissioner Newman told me that Freemasonry was not a divisive issue in the force. Non-Masonic officers may feel Masonic supervisors have discriminated against them in matters such as promotions, but he was confident these perceptions are now 'mistaken'. Neither he nor any of his most senior colleagues were Masons, so it could be argued that 'non-Masons have done very well in the most senior ranks'. This will 'not be lost on those who aspire to these ranks in the future'.

I am grateful for the care taken by Sir Kenneth over this reply, but I feel he did not address the fundamental question raised by the formation of the Manor Lodge: who really runs the Metropolitan Police? The *Principles* seems to have had no practical impact. Flouted by men of high rank, its anti-Masonic strictures are in disrepute. Brian Woollard thinks they were never more than a cosmetic device to appease him and his sympathizers. Sir Kenneth would deny this, but he does seem to have underestimated the impact which even the notoriety of the Manor may have on junior officers. That it flourishes without specific condemnation from Scotland Yard will also 'not be lost on those who aspire to the highest ranks'. Ambitious youngsters may decide, 'If you can't beat 'em, join 'em!'

The present Commissioner, Sir Peter Imbert, has also told me he does not see Freemasonry as a formidable element in Britain's police forces. If it were, he does not see how he could have risen to the highest ranks while some alleged Masons 'continue to strive for advancement in rank unsuccessfully'. In April 1988 he told Independent Radio News that neither he, his deputy nor his four assistant commissioners were Masons. I hate to contradict Sir Peter, but one of his assistant commissioners *is* a Mason, albeit one who has quit active membership *precisely because of its corrupting and corrosive qualities*. Even if Sir Peter counts this man as a non-Mason, he should know that another four serving or recently retired deputy assistant commissioners are staunch members of the brother-hood.

The lack of active Masons among Scotland Yard's current 'big six' proves little. Most Masons may never *want* to become assistant commis-sioner, let alone Commissioner. Not for nothing has the Craft been called 'the Mafia of the Mediocre': far better to sit out a police career in the middle and upper ranks than to risk having one's weaknesses ruthlessly exposed under the constant pressure of life at the very top. Nor would most Masons want their brother Masons to fill *all* the top jobs. They know that, if they did, Britain's police would be deprived of the much-needed leadership skills of thousands of non-Masons. Nevertheless, the presence of so many Masons in senior operational ranks such as commander and chief superintendent (which are often the most enjoy-able) may still justify the feeling that, even today, Masons are over-promoted at the expense of non-Masons.

It is also a matter for dismay that, at the end of the twentieth century, so many senior police jobs are filled by men who look for 'Truth' in the re-creation of a murder which never took place, who see no folly in submitting themselves (and others) to blindfold humiliation, who mouth boyish passwords and perform occult rituals, and who have sworn loyalty to hundreds of thousands of men they have never met – even though they have also sworn the Constable's Oath to perform their duties 'without favour or affection, malice or ill-will'.

What is even more depressing is that many of these men work at London's world-famous police headquarters: New Scotland Yard. Stephen Knight was wrong when he said the building has its own temple. We may now know why! Using the Manor as our guide to the Craft's strength in the upper ranks, we know the 'Big House' does not have a room big enough to accommodate all the inmates eligible to join. If a Scotland Yard lodge were ever formed I suggest it might be called the 'Blue Lamp', but such a creation is most unlikely after the uproar over the Manor. Of course, its founders had no reason to foresee that it would arouse so much bad publicity, or that their own names would fall so easily into hostile hands. Even so, the lodge's creation was impolitic: a public relations disaster for both Masonry and the 'Met'.

Not that the anti-Mason, Brian Woollard, has fared any better. After swapping forced labour in the Wembley 'Archipelago' for cultural exile in West Hendon, he was still dogged by the Masonic issue. On his 1987 annual qualification report his new Chief Superintendent, Alistair Kerr, wrote that he 'can allow one idea to warp his assessment'. When another officer suggested that Woollard had been the victim of a Masonic plot Kerr retorted: 'Absolute nonsense! Poppycock!'

In September 1987 Woollard was forced to stop work because of high blood pressure. His doctor diagnosed strain brought on by the long fight against Freemasonry. When the pressure subsided Woollard declared he was willing to go back to work, provided he was given an assurance that he would not be placed under the command of any officer who was a Freemason – otherwise his blood pressure would shoot back up again. No such assurance was forthcoming so he informed Commissioner Imbert that he would wait at home until the matter was examined by Judicial Review: a High Court procedure whereby he hoped to expose Freemasonry's role throughout the Metropolitan Police.

In a symbolic gesture he sent Imbert his warrant card. A few days later he received a message from West Hendon saying his warrant card was at the station. Chief Supt. Kerr then rang to say he was making arrangements for Woollard to see the chief medical officer. This sounded like 1982 all over again, so Woollard fired off another letter to Imbert: 'By the single act of returning my warrant card to the masonic fold of the Metropolitan Police you have displayed abject moral cowardice in the face of freemasonry.'

This astonishing onslaught and the accompanying publicity – Woollard had released the text to the press – would have brought any other officer instant suspension, but Woollard boycotted work for four more months before he was suspended on 8 February 1988 for 'persistent refusal to attend for duty'. It was not until 25 May that he appeared before a Scotland Yard discipline board. Through a barrister he asked for a postponement so that he could call dozens of witnesses, including Commissioners Newman and Imbert: 'To show I had acted reasonably in not going to work I had to prove that I had been persistently oppressed by Masons. I therefore needed to cross-examine my oppressors.' No postponement was granted and he was dismissed there and then. After thirty-three years he was out of a job. He promptly lodged an appeal and gave notice of a court action alleging unfair dismissal. In the meantime he would remain on full pay.

Before this hearing the Woollard saga had taken yet more serpentine twists. In February the *Independent* published a series of articles by James Dalrymple giving Woollard the biggest and best publicity he had ever received. The series also provoked bitter exchanges in the letters column.

Pro- and anti-Masons, in and out of the police, expressed outrage or enthusiasm over the articles. The outraged included Lord Cornwallis, Michael Higham and the non-Masonic President of the Royal Institute of British Architects, Rod Hackney, who was offended by an editorial implying that architects in general find both Freemasonry and corruption appealing. Two furious letters also came in from the Police Federation (the coppers' trade union) over remarks implying that it had not given Woollard full support.

As far back as 1984 the Federation had agreed to pay up to £1,500 towards his legal advice, but he never received a penny. At a meeting with Woollard and his solicitor on 9 August 1984 the Federation's deputy secretary, Patrick Johnson, stipulated that it would support Woollard's call for an inquiry, provided that '*it would not relate to matters of Freemasonry within the police etc*'. Woollard felt this was rather like asking a Jew to accept an inquiry into World War II on condition that no mention was made of the Nazi Party or the Final Solution or the Holocaust. On reviewing the entire case, his barrister concluded that the best way to proceed was to request the Home Secretary to set up an inquiry into the influence of Freemasonry in the Metropolitan Police under Section 32 of the 1964 Police Act. This opinion was sent to Pat Johnson who wrote back to Woollard on 20 June 1985, in the light of the enthusiastic press coverage which Woollard was then receiving:

I am disturbed to note increasing reference to this Organisation in a way which may be construed as indicating support for an inquiry into the effects of Freemasonry in the police service. As indicated to you during a conference at this office, it is not intended that we should be involved in such an inquiry, we are merely concerned with the single issue of natural justice. Our involvement will be reviewed at each stage and I hate to see our involvement prejudiced by injudicious impulsiveness.

From this letter it seems that, while the Federation wanted 'natural justice' for Woollard, it did not want it at the expense of Freemasonry – or, at least, not at the cost of upsetting those thousands of its own members who are 'on the square'. The thought that Freemasonry might have been what had deprived Woollard of 'natural justice' in the first place does not seem to have crossed Johnson's mind, even though he knew on excellent authority that Woollard had been greatly wronged. According to the attendance note written by the Federation's solicitor about the meeting of 9 August 1984 (referred to above), 'Pat Johnson told us that he had spoken to [Deputy Commissioner] Albert Laugharne, who takes the view that this man was very badly treated at the outset by the Metropolitan Police and, had he been more "kindly" handled, this problem would not have arisen.'

Johnson made these remarks *before* Woollard and his solicitor arrived at that meeting. It was only three and a half years later, in February 1988, when Woollard was sent a package of internal Federation papers, that he found out what Laugharne had felt. It was Laugharne, of course, who had written the brilliant dissection of Freemasonry in *The Principles of Policing*. As Deputy Commissioner he was also in charge of discipline in the entire Metropolitan Police. Yet, despite his strong sympathy for Woollard, he was unable to reverse the punishment which the Masons heading the CID had inflicted on the detective in 1984. A year later Laugharne retired, aged fifty-three, on health grounds. If *he* could spot that 'natural justice' and Freemasonry do not always march side by side, it is all the more shocking that Woollard's own 'trade union' would fund his fight for 'natural justice' only on condition that he dropped all mention of Freemasonry from his campaign.

In 1987 Home Secretary Hurd turned down Woollard's request for an inquiry into the brotherhood, so his barrister felt that now was the time for Woollard to apply to the High Court for Judicial Review. This would require more funds so Woollard again turned to the Federation. In February 1988 his solicitors submitted their first-ever bill for £900, but Federation Secretary Peter Tanner wrote back saying that it had never agreed to meet Woollard's expenditure, so he had decided that it should not pay. He added, however, that his decision could be overturned at the March meeting of the Federation's governing body, the Joint Central Committee. Just before that meeting it became clear that the committee (made up of ten constables, ten sergeants and ten inspectors) might support Woollard but at the last minute Tanner argued for the Woollard item to be withdrawn from the agenda. He felt that, as Woollard was now seeking Judicial Review, this constituted a fresh application for Federation funds. He must therefore apply all over again through the inspectors' committee of the Federation's Metropolitan branch.

This was devastating for Woollard because it meant that his request would now be considered by a board chaired by Alan Turner: a founder member of the Manor Lodge. He was not surprised when (just before the discipline hearing at which he was sacked) he received a letter from Turner saying the inspectors' board had 'decided not to recommend that you receive financial assistance for Judicial Review'. Later Woollard had to pay his entire lawyer's fees of £1,345 from his own pocket. This convinced him that Federation decision-making had been distorted by the very brotherhood he was seeking to investigate. To stop him thinking that way, all Masons on the board would have had to withdraw.

On 9 March 1988 – just before the Federation was due to consider Woollard's application for funds – Lord Cornwallis had broken the United Grand Lodge of England's long silence on the affair. His remarks were published in the *Quarterly Communication* and distributed to all subscribing Masons, including every member of the Manor Lodge, every other police Mason, and every Mason in the Police Federation. Under a bold caption CHIEF INSPECTOR WOOLLARD Cornwallis proclaimed: 'If there had been any substance in his allegations the Director of Public Prosecutions and the Metropolitan Police Commissioner would have asked Grand Lodge for assistance. They had not and it was therefore reasonable to assume that the allegations were unfounded.'

From this unlikely source, proof had at last emerged that at no point during the Fraud Branch's Islington inquiry (after Woollard's removal), or the Meffen inquiry, had anyone seriously tried to find out who was a Mason – even though the role played by Freemasonry was at the heart of Woollard's complaints. If any investigator had really wanted to discover if there was a conspiracy uniting Masons in Islington Council, in the building firms working for it, in the Fraud Branch, and in the Department of the Director of Public Prosecutions, the first thing he should have done was approach Grand Lodge to find out which suspects were Masons. Only then could anyone decide if Woollard's allegations were unfounded or well-founded.

Grand Lodge had no reason to assume that the 'allegations were unfounded' simply because it had not been asked for assistance. All it should have assumed is that no one working for the D of PP or in the upper echelons of the police had tried very hard to prove the allegations true.

In England's Masonic hierarchy, Pro Grand Master Lord Cornwallis is second only to the Duke of Kent, so his comments might well have influenced those Masons in the Police Federation with a say in whether Woollard should get funding for his anti–Masonic cause. To some folk the words of the Pro Grand Master would have the force almost of the Ten Commandments. It was as if the Supreme Architect himself had said, 'Thou Shalt Not Believe Woollard'. When Woollard found out about Cornwallis's statement, he condemned it as an outrageous interference in his case.

Cornwallis had also lamented that 'Scotland Yard does not comment on matters of police discipline', but he felt that an exception should now be made to 'dispel the suspicion which attaches to undenied allegations and here was doing as little good to Freemasonry as it did to the Metropolitan Police'. Astonishingly, four weeks later the Yard gave him just the clean bill of health he was seeking. Even better, it was endorsed by Home Secretary Douglas Hurd. On 13 April Hurd and Imbert jointly issued a statement saying there was no evidence of Masonic corruption: 'The Commissioner emphasized that there was no evidence that membership had influenced the high standards of police officers in the execution of their duties or in the internal running of their force.'

Of course Scotland Yard had no evidence of Masonic corruption: no one at the Yard had ever made any serious effort to find it. Cornwallis's remarks proved that. Hurd and Imbert had not named Woollard but, in absolving Freemasonry, they had in effect branded him a fantasist. The only beneficiary was the Craft, but this was not the first time Cornwallis had turned the Woollard controversy to Freemasonry's advantage. In September 1984 he had publicized a statement by Sir Kenneth Newman that no officers would be forced to resign because they were Masons and that promotion 'would continue to be on merit and merit alone'.[6] Four years on, the first policeman ever to be dismissed from any British police force over Freemasonry turned out to be a non-Mason: Brian Woollard.

I was with him on 9 August 1988 when he learned that his dismissal from the force had been made final. On 19 August 'Police Orders' were sent to the entire force stating baldly that he had been dismissed for being 'absent without leave from 12 October 1987 to 8 February 1988'. This was a strangely odourless way to describe the last act in Woollard's extraordinary six-year struggle against the Craft, but it ensured that there would be no mutiny demanding his reinstatement. What officers, however anti-Masonic, would rally to support a man who had been fired, at last, for not coming to work for four months? Scotland Yard had given him so much rope that, in the end, he had hanged himself.

There was life in the body yet, however, for Woollard was determined to keep up the pressure from outside the force. He would continue to fight the brotherhood in print, in court and through the House of Commons. He would not rest until the Masonic grip on the Metropolitan Police had been broken.

Scotland Yard did not try to take away Woollard's pension. It would not have succeeded had it tried, for he had paid his contributions since the 1950s and had committed no crime. In law his pension was safe. With encouragement from his long-suffering wife Deborah, he might now apply his talent with words and pictures to writing children's stories. If so, his first book could have all the nightmare quality of Maurice Sendak's *Where The Wild Things Are*: full of grotesque beasties pursuing a bold little hero. Of course, in any book by Brian, the Wild Things will probably wear aprons and delight in cutting throats, tearing out tongues and burning bowels to ashes.

Recently, three of Brian's former Wembley colleagues have also left the Metropolitan Police, but voluntarily. They are all Manor members: Brother George Wise, a former chief superintendent, is now head of security at Wembley Stadium where he hires Brothers Ben Pountain and William Gibson as part-time security advisers. Folk with suspicious minds might think this a case of 'jobs for the boys from St James's' but these Masons may well be the best men for the task. Either way, Woollard thinks he will get no offer to work at Wembley, except perhaps as a football.

fourteen

THE PHOENIX

If the Manor of St James's Lodge was formed in defiance of the anti-Masonic views of a Metropolitan Commissioner, it would not be the first time the Brotherhood has waved two fingers at the most important police chief in Britain.

Back in 1958 the new commissioner was Joseph Simpson. He was the first man ever to reach the top job after starting as an ordinary bobby. He was public-school-educated and a university graduate but, unlike his gentleman predecessors, he had done three years on the beat and had the deserved respect of most London coppers. In short, he was a policeman's policeman.

One shaft of light which Sir Joseph brought to the job was a distinct hostility to Freemasonry, or at least a dislike of its most arrogant manifestations. During his early years in office he was greatly irritated by an organization calling itself the Metropolitan Police Masonic Association. The title gave it an official air, but its founders had no authority for using the words 'Metropolitan Police'. They might have had the unofficial 'nod' from a previous commissioner, but Sir Joseph took a dim view and demanded its abolition.

The MPMA's members were not prepared to disband on the say-so of a mere commissioner – especially as earlier commissioners, such as Sir Charles Warren, had themselves been Freemasons. Rather than abolish their fraternity in a fraternity, they decided just to change its name. They also decided to keep the initials MPMA. They were determined to keep 'Masonic' in the title, and 'Association' was harmless enough, so they would have to substitute another word for either Metropolitan or Police. Some wag in the leadership had a little classical education. As this new body was going to rise from the ashes of the old, he thought, it could have no more appropriate name than 'Metropolitan *Phoenix* Masonic Association'. This would get round Sir Joseph Simpson's vexatious objections, but it would still be the MPMA and the same old bird.

Simpson died in office, from a heart attack three days after the battle of Grosvenor Square in 1968, but the Phoenix lived on. In 1971 it had 288 members. Its rulebook reveals that the inclusion of Metropolitan in its title was gratuitous and misleading for its members only needed to be 'Master Masons who are regular, serving and retired officers of *any* police force'.

The rulebook makes clear this was no Masonic lodge. Ritual was forbidden at its gatherings. Instead its objects were:

1. To introduce Master Masons of the Force who would otherwise have no opportunity of meeting as Brother Masons.
2. To promote fraternal intercourse by arranging social functions.
3. To render assistance to those who may be distressed by sickness or adversity.
4. Loyalty to Her Majesty the Queen and the Craft in general.

Aside from the genuflection to the Crown, these aims might strike an anti-Mason as a sugar-coated code of mutual aid, arousing fears in the outsider that the Phoenix was a means of achieving a kind of Masonic apartheid in the service. Could it have acted as a wedge between Masons and non-Masons, or a jungle telegraph, or a 'firm in a firm'? Its members would doubtless deny it, but the club does seem like a collective support system: ideal for help up the promotion ladder, or saving skins.

The 1971 list contains one man still serving at Scotland Yard: a deputy assistant commissioner. Another is a detective chief superintendent. Most members left the service long ago. Many held humble rank, so either the mutual aid principle never helped them gain promotion or they never sought to use it. Perhaps the Phoenix was just a social club for men with a common hobby. If so, one brother was such an enthusiast that he took the hobby with him to a Mediterranean retirement. In 1971 Brother A. J. Fookes was running a pub in Gibraltar called the Masons Arms.

The Phoenix list shows that in the early 1970s there was a network of police Masons, in lodges all over south-east England, who were doubly committed to mutual aid. Today, it seems, the Phoenix may not be the bird it was. I have been unable to find out if it is still flying. It may now be in one of its 'ashes' periods: about to burst forth in full plumage. Perhaps the Manor of St James's Lodge is it latest incarnation. As it happens, no 1971 Phoenix people show up as Manor members. Perhaps this is only because there is a fifteen-year gap between the lists, but it seems to confirm that there must be thousands of London police Masons, otherwise there would surely be names in common.

Another indicator of the Craft's strength in the force emerged when barrister Andrew Arden presented his 1987 report on the running of the London Borough of Hackney (see Chapter 26). During his research Mr Arden was assisted by Grand Secretary Michael Higham. He gave the 'profane' Arden forty-four lodge lists to help him identify Masons working for Hackney Council but, in performing this unprecedented favour, he knowingly divulged the identities of over 3,500 Masons who had no connection with Hackney and whose individual permission he did not seek.

Higham also divulged the occupations of 2,534 named Masons. Of these ninety-eight were policemen, amounting to 3.9 per cent of Arden's sample or slightly less than one Mason in every twenty-five. If this were typical of the whole country, and if (according to Commander Higham) there are between 250,000 and 500,000 Masons under Grand Lodge, then between 9,700 and 19,400 policemen in England and Wales are Freemasons. However, if my total figure of 600,000 living Master Masons, whether active or lapsed, is correct (see Chapter 9), then some 23,400 serving and retired policemen are Masons. In December 1985 there were slightly fewer than 108,000 serving male police officers in England and Wales. Even if we exclude my highest estimate and stick to the Higham figures, it would seem that between 9 and 18 per cent of all policemen may be Masons: one in eleven or one in six of all men in the English and Welsh forces. Yet, as ever, when it comes to calculating Masonic strength, huge statistical crevasses have to be vaulted. The records at Freemasons' Hall are always out-of-date because they show only the occupations declared when men become Master Masons. Should they change jobs or retire, these records stay the same. Yet even if 20 per cent of men who said they were policemen have since retired, it seems that between 8,000 and 16,000 policemen are 'on the square'. In addition, however, young policemen are being drawn into Freemasonry all the time, which may bring the total back to 20,000. There are thousands more in Scotland and Northern Ireland, where they probably form an even higher proportion of the police service, for reasons explained in Chapter 19.

Higham supplied Arden with the names and occupations of men in fourteen individual lodges. One lodge had fifty-two members, of which eleven were policemen. Another lodge contained eleven policemen out of eighty-eight members, another had five out of fifty-four. Of course these high numbers are outdone by the Manor of St James's, but the Manor is not Britain's only all-police lodge. According to the Grand Secretary of East Lancashire,[1] three lodges are composed entirely of ex-police officers: in Wales, Kent and Liverpool. The Kent lodge meets in Sittingbourne and is called the Watch and Ward. It was founded as recently as 1977, yet it has already won a place in Freemasons' Hall Museum by presenting a Masonic gavel made in the form of a police truncheon. In the early 1980s the Watch and Ward could muster only twenty-five members, but this is no proof of ill-health. Indeed, Masonic consciousness among policemen, both serving and retired, is growing stronger. The Liverpool lodge, Sovereign's Peace, was founded in 1979.

Most policemen belong to general lodges where they get to know men from other walks of life – that is one of the main benefits of Freemasonry – yet they are usually proposed by other policemen. A random sample of lodge summonses reveals that policemen are valued candidates for admission into almost any lodge.

In 1976 the Derby Allcroft Lodge of London initiated a Scotland Yard detective sergeant and a builder on the same day. It already contained several policemen, including one future member of the Manor of St James's. In 1982 the Gateway Lodge of Witney initiated a Thames Valley officer along with an electrical engineer, a British Telecom warden and an Oxfordshire fireman. These lodges contain a mix of employees, public servants and the self-employed. Whatever a Mason's job, on lodge days he must be able to stop work early enough to arrive for the meeting at three or four o'clock. Policemen can almost always manage this because they work shifts, or because senior officers are also Masons and will turn a blind eye if brothers slip off during working hours.

Thus it was that in January 1972 a thirty-two-year-old detective sergeant took a half-day off from West Hampstead police station in north London to be initiated in the Fryent Lodge alongside a Co-op produce controller. The Fryent is a general lodge but, over dinner, brethren proposed several toasts to the 'Blue Lamp', in honour of the Metropolitan Police. This may have something to do with the fact that the lodge meets at Hendon Hall Hotel, close to Hendon Police College from which it recruits some of its members.

It might be wondered how men whose work requires brain as well as brawn, a sense of truth and reality, and considerable courage, can allow themselves to be drawn into a fraternity whose ritual requires a total suspension of disbelief and a taste for the occult. The outsider might be concerned that men who must take so many crucial decisions in their careers – concerning life and death, imprisonment or liberty, kidnaps and sieges, as well as helping old ladies cross the road – can subject themselves to such a welter of gobbledegook concocted in the eighteenth century by men who were, in part, superstitious fantasists.

Let us look at the other side of the coin. Instead of caning cops all the time for rushing into the Craft, we should pause to consider why the Craft wants them in. My Masonic informant Badger explained it this way: whatever policemen may get out of Freemasonry, Freemasonry gets even more out of the police.

Why do nearly all Masonic lodges like to have a copper in their midst? Because Freemasonry is a vehicle for bringing together the various threads of a general view. It's a form of social cement, a pyramid erected on the class system. It should go without saying that the police are a vital part of that pyramid, or rather the strongest shield the status quo possesses. That is why policemen must be continually sucked into Freemasonry: to maintain the deferential structure of society and to ensure that Freemasons and Freemasonry is perpetually favoured by those who enforce the law.

Evidence appearing to support Badger's view came in a letter in the *Independent* in 1988.[2] It was from M. E. Rowe, a retired policeman with thirty years' service. In 1980, while a senior officer in the West Midlands Police:

I was approached by a local businessman I knew personally, who at that time was lobbying on behalf of a group of businessmen who were concerned with the effect of proposals in which the police and local authority were involved. I declined to discuss the matter.

This refusal was followed by the offer of membership of his Lodge. I was told that he was in a position to ensure my acceptance as a member, and he would regard it as a personal favour if I would accept his offer. I refused, saying that it was not consistent with the independence I thought was essential in my position.

However, I did indicate that in the next eighteen months I would be retiring and then I might consider his offer – I was told with some fervour that the 'offer' would not be open to me when I retired.

If policemen pursue the Craft as an amusing hobby or an antiquarian game which they leave behind at the temple, it may be as harmless as Masonic spokesmen claim. The public need to be convinced. In the meantime there is evidence to suggest that some Mason cops go on duty still mentally wearing their regalia and are not as impartial as their Constable's Oath requires.

fifteen

A CRIMINAL INTELLIGENCE

Many Masons tell stories of favours by policemen whom they have come to know through the Craft. One brother told me how his Masonic connections came in handy in unforeseen circumstances.

> A friend and I were developing an industrial heating system in our spare time. We used to do research in a workshop at the back of his house. On one occasion, while he and his wife were away on holiday, I was working there as usual when suddenly the police turned up. They'd been called to the house by a neighbour who thought I was an intruder. I promptly explained who I was and produced my key, but I had no identification on me so they weren't satisfied. They took me to the police station and told me that, unless I could prove my *bona fides*, I'd be spending the night in the cells.
>
> I was trying to think my way out of this mess when I remembered that on several Masonic occasions I'd met a chief superintendent who was based at the station. After one lodge function he had invited us back to that very station's social club where we had a few drinks. Now I found myself in this jam I naturally asked the arresting officers to let me talk to him. He came into the charge room, immediately recognized me and then took my captors into another room. A few seconds later they came out again and told me, most civilly, I was free to go.
>
> I'm sure if I hadn't been 'on the square' I would have been kept in clink all night, maybe longer. My Masonic brother, the police chief, had done me a favour: a small one perhaps, but a favour nevertheless. Freemasonry had worked like a magic wand.

Such interventions look less benign to non-Masons inside the force who see them as inextricably intertwined with Masonic manipulation of the service as a whole. Among the hundreds of letters which Stephen

Knight received from readers of *The Brotherhood*, several came from policemen who felt they had spent most of their careers battling against a masonic mafia.

John Thompson retired from the Metropolitan Police in 1970 having reached the rank of inspector. When he joined the force in the late 1940s he was aware that many senior officers were 'on the square' but like most constables he pooh-poohed the power of the Craft with what he calls 'childish flippancy'. He only became concerned in January 1953 when he was about to take the competitive examination for promotion to the rank of sergeant.

> Rumours were rife that masonic candidates had been given the questions in advance. I also heard that they were going to identify themselves as masons on their exam papers to masonic examiners. I thought these rumours were stupid nonsense but they were so rampant that they came to the attention of high-ranking officers who were then obliged to tighten up security. I sat the exam with all the other candidates and – you have guessed it! – it had to be cancelled and rearranged. As you might also guess, the inquiry which followed was inconclusive. It was generally accepted that questions had been leaked but the masonic connection remained a mystery.
>
> Throughout my career I was aware of too many incidents involving patronage and favouritism to dismiss them with the same ease as masonic policemen are always able to. Some of the incidents were so trivial that I was amazed high-ranking officers deigned to involve themselves, but some were so serious that they bordered on criminal conspiracies.
>
> As a young sergeant at Notting Hill I began to note the very effective influence of freemasonry. One night I was on duty as the station officer when at one o'clock in the morning I had to charge a man with being 'drunk and indecent'. He was a mason and was on his way home from a Ladies' Night, accompanied by his wife and others, when a constable arrested him for urinating in a shop doorway. At about 3 A.M. the chief superintendent (now Commander rank) suddenly turned up at the station. Such a visit was unknown and he had obviously been dragged from his bed. He sat around for a long time, reading and re-reading the charge, but when he realized there was nothing he could do, he left. The general consensus at the station was that this visit had masonic overtones. It seems nothing was too trivial for masonic interference.
>
> Later, as an inspector at Marylebone, I was called out by two PCs

who had arrested a nineteen-year-old youth for stealing a driving licence and using it with intent to deceive. He had managed to escape and reach his home in a block of luxury flats where his father was refusing to let the constables in to re-arrest him. When I arrived the father allowed me in and took me into his study, where photographs were prominently displayed of him in masonic dress. I noted that he had been master of his lodge and he clearly expected me to direct the PCs to forget the matter. I told him he was 'not on' and left him in no doubt he was backing a loser.

We took the son to the station. His father followed soon after, staying in the waiting room. As I was preparing the charge sheet the station sergeant told me that a Commander (now DAC rank) wished to speak to me on the phone. I had never met this man, so I told the sergeant to tell him I was not prepared to discuss the matter. You see, I had learned to face freemasonry in the force head-on without fear.

Before the father left he asked if the Commander had spoken to me. I replied he had not. He then told me they were in the same lodge and then asked me if I was 'on the square'. He had clearly assumed I was, so I had to disappoint him. As it happens, the incident did me some good. I had not hit it off with my PCs beforehand, but this broke the ice.

Masons usually claim such stories are invented by embittered non-Masons who cannot accept that their careers have failed because of their own lack of ability; instead they fantasize about malicious wrongdoing by Masonic colleagues. Thompson rejects this argument as itself a *canard*.

I admit we non-masons were resentful at our lowly rank. Yet most of us were not bitter. On the contrary, the men who were bitter were those freemasons who had expected patronage and preferment but never got it. What non-masons such as I did resent was entering a five-furlong sprint race but being forced to start at the mile and three-quarter gate.

We also resented that our masonic colleagues were likely to have their errors, omissions, inadequacies, incompetencies and indiscipline covered up, sometimes at the expense of non-masons. I concede that many masonic policemen had an aura of greater competence and many became more able because they had less pressure and could acquit themselves better on boards.

I put my hands up to being bitter in one respect. I object when masons dismiss their victims as jealous and vindictive. I am neither but what do they expect us to be? They expect us to act like the three wise monkeys: seeing no evil, speaking no evil, and hearing no evil – of freemasonry of course.

Thompson says he received at least six approaches to become a Freemason, varying from the subtle to the obvious. 'The fact that I was a known atheist did not seem to concern my would-be proposers who advised me to lie by professing a belief. I never made any attempt to become a freemason because, I hope, I did not possess the necessary hypocrisy.'

Some readers may feel that Thompson's recollections can now be dismissed because he retired in 1970, but other police correspondents bemoan present-day Masonic goings-on. Thames Valley Police was formed in 1968, through the merger of five forces in Oxfordshire, Berkshire and Buckinghamshire. Recent lodge summonses from these counties show that today Freemasonry is recruiting just as strongly among policemen in this force as it is in London. One non-Masonic sergeant knows to his cost the Brotherhood's power in Oxfordshire.

In 1983 I had some building work done on my house. When it was finished I was not entirely satisfied and paid the builder only part of his money. He put most of the faults right but I was still not completely happy and we had quite a disagreement. He then told me he was a freemason and he knew various people that I also knew, one of them being a chief superintendent.

Not long afterwards the builder had a car accident and he finished up in hospital. While he was there he received a visit from the chief superintendent who asked if there was anything he could do for him.

A few days later I was summoned to headquarters to see this chief superintendent. He 'advised' me to hurry up and sort out my dispute with the builder because his being in hospital gave him quite enough to worry about. Now whilst no threats were made, there was undoubtedly some moral pressure and I came away from headquarters feeling decidedly uneasy. The obvious difference in our ranks made it a very simple task for him to 'put the screws on'. As a result I felt bound to pay the builder the remaining money.

I find membership of this organization quite odious and not compatible with being a police officer. Incidents happen – internal politics, you understand – which defy rational explanation and can only be put down to the influence of these people. They are unknown, unseen, but seem to pull strings behind the scenes and get things done.

Even back in the 1960s John Thompson saw the beginnings of what he regards as the most sinister phenomenon involving Freemasonry and the force. He had just moved to the north London area known to the police as 'Y' Division. He soon learned that the divisional commander and his deputy were Roman Catholics but that all the other senior officers were Masons.

It was on 'Y' Division that I first noticed how former high-ranking officers – both uniform and CID – were making new careers as security or inquiry agents for solicitors, finance houses and other organizations hungry for confidential information. This has now become a huge industry and freemasonry is an important constituent in this web of intrigue. Now that more and more information is stored on computer (and its dissemination is subject to serious legal curbs under the Data Protection Act), so employers have realized that the only people who can get round the regulations are high-ranking ex-policemen – especially freemasons who are particularly well-placed to obtain confidential information with no chance of exposure, because they can get it all from their colleagues in the Brotherhood. Thoroughly illegal, of course.

Recently, police computers have been criminally abused for the purpose of keeping criminals out of Masonic employment. In 1983 the Warwickshire Grand Lodge dismissed the catering manager at its Birmingham Temple because of the way he had disciplined a member of staff. The brethren alleged that the manager, veteran Mason Derek Yeomans, had shouted at a junior employee but Yeomans says he was fired for 'telling off' his own boss at the Temple.

He took revenge on the ungrateful brethren by squealing about their criminal wrongdoings. He disclosed that one of the province's top Masons habitually checked whether applicants for senior jobs at the temple had criminal records logged on the West Midlands Police computer. According to Yeomans, this wholly illegal service was performed through a retired chief inspector, himself a leading Mason, who used to pass the applicants' names and dates of birth to an officer who worked for the local force and had access to the computer.

Such abuse of police intelligence systems is now taken very seriously by all forces, so a local superintendent was appointed to investigate the allegation. He later reported that Yeomans's only specific claim – that a certain applicant's name had been fed into the computer on a certain day – was not true. Yeomans says that the name might have been fed in on the day before or the day after but, in any case, it cannot be satisfactory when a policeman is appointed to investigate abuses of his own force's computer by another member of the same force.

Whether or not that inquiry was performed by checking computer records or searching old-fashioned criminal record files, it seems Warwickshire's Masons did call on police connections for such a service. As Provincial Grand Master Thomas Wood told the *Birmingham Post*:

> I believe that on one occasion when someone was needed for a very responsible position I was told that person had been vetted, though I am not quite sure what that meant. References are not a lot of use these days. You really have to – if you are talking about employing someone in a very responsible position – make other inquiries.

One Mason told me that his lodge always checks if any candidate for membership has a criminal record:

> That's why we've got a copper in the lodge: to check candidates out on the computer! If they have a record, their applications are withdrawn or they are blackballed – unless senior lodge members are nominating them, in which case nothing is said. Of course nowadays, if a policeman is caught using the computer for non-police purposes, he could be charged with a criminal offence himself. All this is strictly illegal, but you can be sure it goes on.

sixteen

A FIRM IN A FIRM: FREEMASONRY
AND POLICE CORRUPTION

Is a Brother off the track?
Try the Square;
Try it well on every side.
Nothing draws a craftsman back
Like the Square when well applied.
Try the Square.

Is he crooked, is he frail?
Try the Square.
Try it early, try it late;
When all other efforts fail,
Try the square to make him straight –
Try the Square.[1]

Since the Metropolitan Police was founded in 1829 there have been two complete reorganizations of its detective department. Both were provoked by massive corruption scandals leading to criminal trials exactly one hundred years apart, in 1877 and 1977. In each scandal Freemasonry played a dominant role.

Scotland Yard's first 'Detective Force' was set up in 1842. It consisted of only two inspectors and six sergeants. By 1869, 180 detectives were dealing with minor crime in outlying divisions but serious investigations in London were left to only twenty-seven officers out of 9,000. In the 1870s most of this squad was itself a criminal conspiracy in which not only were the prime culprits Freemasons; Freemasonry was what brought them together.[2]

In 1872 a confidence trickster named William Kurr was running a bogus betting operation. Like any shrewd small-time criminal with big ideas, he saw that the way to make real money was to bring policemen into the racket. Bribing detectives after you get caught is costly and uncertain. Far better to cut them in on the profits beforehand and avoid arrest altogether. The one safe place where Kurr could proposition policemen was his Masonic lodge.

At a lodge meeting in Islington Kurr made friends with just the man: Inspector John Meiklejohn. In return for £100 – nearly half his annual pay – Meiklejohn agreed to give Kurr advance warning of any police action against him or his betting racket. At first the corrupt officer kept the pay-off to himself but as the racket expanded, he involved three chief inspectors in the Detective Force whom he also knew as brother Masons.

Kurr needed bigger and better protection because he was expanding his operation with the skills of a new friend called Harry Benson. Here was a virtuoso con-man of international disrepute. In 1872, posing as a French count, he had deluded the Lord Mayor of London into giving him £1,000 for relief work in the wake of the Franco–Prussian War. He was found out and imprisoned in Newgate where he tried to burn himself to death. Instead he merely crippled himself but in 1873 he hobbled out of jail and came to know Kurr. Together they planned new scams to part mug punters from their funds.

One by one, Inspector Meiklejohn sucked his Masonic colleagues into Kurr and Benson's network. First he found out that Chief Inspector Nathaniel Druscovitch was inquiring into the swindles. He also dis-covered Druscovitch was £60 in debt and suggested Kurr might help him out. The deal was done, Kurr gave him the money and Druscovitch was neutralized. His senior chief inspector, George Clarke, was also on the swindlers' trail, but he agreed to lose the scent in return for a pay-off. A third chief inspector, William Palmer, was also bought up.

Now assured of total immunity from police zeal, Benson set up *Sport*, a news-sheet offering punters foolproof betting systems. In 1876, using the alias Hugh Montgomery, he deluded the Comtesse de Goncourt of Paris into 'investing' £10,000. He rewarded her with several non-existent winners and then requested she invest a further £30,000 with a bookmaker of his choice. At this point she had a belated spasm of suspicion. She hired a London lawyer, who reported Benson and Kurr to Scotland Yard. They were soon jailed for fifteen and ten years' hard labour respectively. Only then did they reveal the role of the bent coppers. In the subsequent investigation the Yard's chief of detectives, Supt. Frederick Williamson, was dismayed to discover that three of his four chief inspectors were corrupt, along with their uniformed seducer Meiklejohn. In 1877 all four were tried at the Old Bailey. Clarke was acquitted, but Meiklejohn, Palmer and Druscovitch were convicted and sentenced to two years' hard labour. It was a bad day for the police and hardly a distinguished one for Freemasonry with its principles of brotherly love, relief and truth.

This scandal discredited the entire Metropolitan Detective Force which was scrapped and re-formed as the Criminal Investigation Department. The CID was to have a separate career structure and higher rates of pay than the main uniform force, a distinction which was to cause grinding irritation over the next hundred years. By 1884 the new structure of twenty-four detectives at Scotland Yard and 254 in the divisions, all under the central command of a new Assistant Commissioner (Crime), appeared to be an effective answer to corruption, Masonic or otherwise.

It took a hundred years for that illusion to be pricked, although close observers of the CID had known the truth for decades. A hint of what went wrong in the meantime comes in the story of Chief Inspector Reginald Morrish, a Metropolitan officer from 1911 to 1937. Morrish worked in the CID for sixteen years, winning forty-four commendations and eighteen rewards. He also served in Scotland Yard's fraud and homicide squads. From 1943 to 1967 he was a senior instructor at Hendon Police College and wrote several textbooks. One book he did not write was an autobiography. Not long before he died, aged ninety-two, he burnt his entire police papers. His son Ivor was horrified. He wrote:

During the whole of my early life at home, including a period in which we lived at a very busy police station in south London, my father's chief topics of conversation were the police, religion, bribery and corruption (which he saw as rife at all levels in the police force) and freemasonry. The one thing which seemed to worry him most of all was the connexion which he felt existed between freemasonry and corruption, and between freemasonry and self-advancement in the force. In his view there was no room for doubt about these connexions. He used to list all the officers who were masons. He noted the dates of their promotions, whether they had jumped anyone else of equal or greater ability, and all their connexions with other officers in the force.

On many occasions he was invited to join the masons (his two brothers were members) and he used to tell numerous stories of how both police officers and criminals sought favours of him in his pursuance of the detection of crimes. They seemed to assume that – like most other 'successful' officers in the Met – he was a mason of some standing. He received masonic handshakes by the score when investigating crimes, and he was offered bribes in the form of money, goods and even the services of women, in order that he might overlook vital pieces of evidence. Of course, not all those attempting bribery were masons but, according to my father, many were.

The most common expressions used by my father in relation to work were 'he is on the take', 'he is taking backhanders', 'he is receiving the drop' and 'he is on the square' until I personally (quite wrongly?) came to equate being 'on the square' with being amenable to bribes, corruption and perjury, so often did he use these phrases in juxtaposition. Later on in life, when we discussed the position of freemasonry in the force and its connexion with corruption and self-advancement at the expense of others, it became clear that he regarded freemasonry as an evil *per se* which was to be held responsible for the larger proportion of corruption in the police force.

In 1933 or 1934 Det. Insp. Morrish had to run the Croydon Division while the divisional inspector was off sick. Looking through various registers and record books he became very suspicious of the way crimes were being recorded, so he carried out his own investigation. He concluded that the division's relatively high success rate for crime clearance was thoroughly bogus, because many crimes were being entered up as something else. A woman would have her handbag snatched, but this would be entered in the register as a case of 'Lost Property'.[3] Many other entries were far more ingenious.

After a thorough examination of every bit of routine and every crime over a period of several months, my father wrote a report on his findings and sent copies to his bosses: the divisional detective inspector and the area superintendent. As my father did not spare personalities, the facts he revealed militated strongly against both men's honesty. According to him, both were freemasons.

They met him together in private, sought at first to mollify him and then began to threaten and pressure him. He was told in no uncertain terms that, if he went on investigating the investigators, it could only lead to his own downfall. But he was adamant, and felt he had a duty to society, as well as his own integrity, to pursue the matter. He obviously had rattled his superiors who clearly warned him they would block all possible promotion for him.

I'm afraid they didn't understand what motivated him. Nothing and no one could ever browbeat him. He forthwith typed out an even fuller report which detailed all the criminal statistics he had investigated, and concluded with an account of his dealings with his superiors including their interview with him and the threats they had made. This 100 page report (which unfortunately he later burnt) he addressed to the Metropolitan Commissioner, Lord Trenchard.

Trenchard was soon paying personal visits to each station in the division, and insisted on seeing the records and documents referred to in Morrish's report. Eventually Trenchard called him up to his office but, moments before he was due to enter, Deputy Commissioner Norman Kendal tried to divert him. He suggested he need not see the Commissioner, as everything could be put right at this late stage – even his promotion – if he would only withdraw his report.

Behind this soft approach my father detected a threat that, if he didn't withdraw, he could say goodbye to any future advancement. He politely refused and insisted on seeing the Commissioner. Later, as a result of the interview and the report, changes were introduced – in the Croydon Division at least – in the methods of recording and clearing up crime, and the way statistics on crime clearance were prepared.

Very soon afterwards the two superior officers retired. My father was transferred to the training centre at Scotland Yard and began his lecturing career. About six months later, when Lord Trenchard established Hendon Police College, he told my father he was promoting him to chief inspector and making him a senior instructor. When he later met my father at the college, he insisted it was *he* and no one else who had promoted him. The message, if oblique, seemed quite clear to my father. I don't know whether Trenchard, or for that matter Kendal, was a mason or not, but my father always regarded the whole business as an indication that even the Brotherhood could be outwitted on occasions.

As evidence against Freemasonry, this account is difficult to assess. Sceptics would stress that the alleged incidents took place more than fifty years ago, might have been much exaggerated in the original telling and are recollected here by a son who might be spicing up his father's account. No documents have survived and we have no proof the 'villains' were Masons. A lawyer would dismiss it all as 'triple hearsay'. However, Ivor Morrish is a respected author of numerous teaching textbooks and a lifelong educationalist. He is unlikely to have invented so much detail. His father was a man of unquestioned integrity, an outstanding instructor, and deeply trusted by Lord Trenchard who was this century's greatest police reformer. As such, Reg Morrish's perceptions of Freemasonry should not be lightly discarded. What is more, they marry only too convincingly with the incontrovertible evidence revealed when scores of corrupt detectives were investigated in the 1970s. The full story of Metropolitan Police corruption at the time is told in *The Fall of Scotland Yard*, a book which I co-authored in 1977 with Barry Cox and John Shirley.[4] Here I isolate the Masonic aspects of the scandal.

In 1977 three Old Bailey trials revealed the tip of an iceberg of corruption in London's CID. Thirteen detectives were jailed, including two commanders, one chief superintendent and five inspectors. In the course of the investigation it emerged that most were Freemasons. The probability is that they were all 'on the square'.

One trial focused on the Flying Squad, once legendary for its detective brilliance but now notorious for having a commander, Ken Drury, who was 'on the take' (cash, gifts, entertainments and holidays) from a professional criminal and pornographer, Jimmy Humphreys. The other trials revolved around the Obscene Publications Squad. It emerged that Craft membership was a prerequisite for any detective who wanted a share of the rich pickings to be extorted from London's profiteering pornographers.

The 'Porn Squad' was at that time a unit within the CID's central office, known as C1. Getting into this team was a prestigious step up for any detective, but selection was largely in the gift of the C1 commander or the superintendent heading the squad. From 1964 until 1972 its *éminence grise* was Det. Chief Supt. Bill Moody who has a unique claim to infamy in the history of Scotland Yard. While heading one of the biggest-ever investigations into police corruption he was simultaneously collecting huge bribes from the dirty booksellers of Soho, London's notorious vice district.

Moody's extraordinary double life is revealed in *The Fall of Scotland Yard*. The essential details are that in 1977 he was convicted of conspiring to take money from pornographers over an eight-year period. Moody was convicted on sample charges, one of which involved a payment of £14,000. The trial showed that for some years he had been pocketing annual kickbacks worth £40,000. His pay-off at the Old Bailey was twelve years' imprisonment.

Bill Moody was an ardent Freemason, so ardent that he took some of his pornographer friends to his Masonic gatherings. One was Ron 'the Dustman' Davey whom he had met at another pornographer's birthday party in Trader Vic's Restaurant in the Hilton Hotel. In 1975 Davey was questioned by officers who had been appointed to investigate the porn squad's corruption. He told them he came to know Det. Sgt Cyril Jones (later sentenced to seven years in jail) through Moody's Masonic functions.

I have been to numerous of these and in fact Bill introduced me into his lodge. It has been put to me that I booked a coach on the following dates – 6.11.69 to Derry and Toms (10 people); 17.11.69 to Top Rank Suite, Croydon (12 people); 25.9.71 Regent Street. All were masonic functions at which I was a guest. Normally present were Bill Moody, Cyril Jones, 2 other police officers [whom Davey names] and our wives. I am quite sure there were many more outings.

It was part of Bill Moody's discredited defence that he had no idea Ron Davey was a pornographer. If so, he had overlooked Ron's conviction and six-month jail term in 1960 for publishing 744 improper photographs of men and 105 of women. This fact was available to Moody not simply as head of the Obscene Publications Squad; he would have read about it in the *News of the World,* for the newspaper had revealed how Davey was arrested in his darkroom with 2,486 dirty photographs. At another of his premises, police discovered 15,000 pornographic negatives and 15,000 snaps. Ron's home was an Aladdin's cave of naked lads. As the magistrate packed him off to prison, he told Davey he did not suppose anyone had ever before seen 'such a vast volume of absolute filth'.

Davey had been a pornographer for three years, after eight years working as a dustman. In 1975 when giving evidence against Bill Moody, he described himself as a 'maintenance engineer'. I have been unable to discover which of these three occupations he disclosed when applying for membership of the Craft.

Masonic activities in the dirty book trade went far beyond coach parties of pornographers, policemen and their wives living it up on the town. When Scotland Yard's anti-corruption squad went digging into the porn squad's later years, all sorts of Masonic connections emerged. One prosecution witness was Frank R. Andrews, who spent three years in the porn squad as a detective constable. When Moody recruited him in 1965, he already knew that everybody posted there immediately bought new cars or expensive houses. In short, he said, they 'sprouted wealth'.

Andrews was introduced to the system by another witness, D.C. Ernie Culver, himself later convicted of a cheque fraud. Culver explained how bribe moneys were shared out. Andrews recalled one chat with him about a forthcoming Masonic ladies' night.

He said words to the effect, 'Have you got enough money for the new dress for your wife?' I indicated that I didn't want any help but he then handed me a brown envelope and said, 'Put that towards the cost of a new dress for your wife.' I did not want the money and decided to ditch it in a nearby waste-paper bin. We attended the ladies' evening as planned. Bill Moody was there with his wife and another sergeant.

Another convicted officer was Leslie Alton, a detective inspector and a Mason. He instructed Andrews to collect the weekly bribes in packets from pornographers, then share it out among the other officers. Andrews had known Alton as a friend for many years and tried to keep an eye on him when he got drunk.

On one occasion he got drunk and said, 'Come on, let's take a walk around the West End.' I was full of trepidation. He walked into a bookshop with me and said in a loud voice, 'I am detective inspector Alton of New Scotland Yard. How much have you taken today?' He then went to the cash register, opened it and started checking the proceeds. I was embarrassed and left him in the shop. When he came out he said words to the effect, 'Discipline. That's what these people need: discipline!'

Andrews assumed that, on past form, Alton must have stuck his hand in the till and grabbed a fistful of notes. They both left the squad in 1968 but from 1970 to 1972 its overlord was Commander Wally Virgo who, I understand, was also a Freemason. Originally jailed for twelve years for corruption, Virgo was later freed because the appeal court felt the judge's summing-up had been unduly hostile.

Under Virgo the porn squad was almost entirely Masonic. When one brother, Detective Inspector Anthony Kilkerr, became a prosecution witness his colleagues came up with a disarming explanation for the £20 in pornographers' pay-off money they had stuck in his desk drawer each week. Those crisp fivers were not the fruits of corruption, one suspect told an investigator, but whip-rounds to help Kilkerr pay his Masonic initiation fees. This was a lie, of course, but the choice of lie was revealing.

Because Kilkerr would not take the money (he threw it away or left it in his desk), he was suspected of being a 'spy in the camp'. His 'Mr Clean' image so upset another detective named Peter Fisher that he told Kilkerr not to open his mouth because he was now 'involved' himself and would go down with the rest of them. If they were all caught, Fisher added, they 'could form a football team on the Isle of Wight'. This was a reference to the island's two high-security jails, but in the late 1970s convicted detectives were sent to *open* prisons in such large numbers that they could have formed their own Masonic lodges.

The porn and Flying Squad investigations were part of a massive anti-corruption drive by Sir Robert Mark. Soon after he became Commissioner in 1972 he set up a squad known as A 10 to 'rubber-heel' the entire force. By the time he retired five years later, A 10 had forced the dismissal or resignation of nearly 500 officers: 100 a year. The old regime had ousted an average of just sixteen. Most of the men sacked under Mark were detectives, among whom the concentration of Freemasons was far greater than among uniformed men. There is no way of finding out exactly how many were Masons, partly because Scotland Yard has never divulged the names of all 500.

To combat corruption Mark imposed the most thorough reform of the CID for a hundred years. In August 1975 he shuffled 300 detectives around London, in an attempt to break the dangerous custom of leaving them in one area for so many years that they tended to develop a corrupt intimacy with local criminals. In 1976 he inflicted an even less welcome reform: systematic interchange between detective and uniformed branches. No detective could expect much promotion unless he served in uniform for several years. This was devised not gratuitously to humiliate the plain-clothes men, but to destroy the closed mentality and corrupt traditions of the 'firm in a firm'.

To what extent was this 'firm in a firm' Masonic? That phrase was immortalized by Detective Sergeant John Symonds on a surreptitious tape-recording made by two *Times* reporters in 1969. The tape appeared to support the claims of a small-time thief that Symonds was extorting small sums of money from him. Symonds was suspended and charged, but he fled abroad in 1972 after a threat disguised as a tip-off from the Mason in charge of his imminent trial. This was Det. Chief Supt. Bill Moody who, while taking huge kickbacks from pornographers, had been appointed by Scotland Yard to investigate the *Times*'s allegations of relatively modest graft against lower-ranking detectives. Seven years later Symonds returned to give himself up. He was tried, convicted and given a two-year jail sentence. However he continues to proclaim his innocence, alleging (with justification) that he was offered up as a ritual sacrifice by corrupt men running the CID at that time, notably Bill Moody.

On the tape Symonds was alleged to have said:

Don't forget always to let me know straight away if you need anything because I know people everywhere. Because I'm in a little firm in a firm. Don't matter where, anywhere in London, I can get on the phone to someone I know I can trust, that talks the same as me. And if he's not the right person that can do it, he'll know the

person that can. All right? . . . That's the thing, and it can work –
well, it's worked for years, hasn't it?

Symonds was a Freemason, and his 'firm in a firm' was essentially
Masonic. Freemasonry was the security blanket – the ultimate in
comforters – for a network of crooked cops throughout the metropolis.
Their fraternal bonds reassured them that they could rely on each other's
absolute discretion. On that basis the 'firm in a firm' provided whatever
service was required. It could get criminal charges dropped against the
guilty or ensure their acquittal. It could secure the conviction of men who
did not pay bribes or who got in the way of bigger fish who were paying.
It could protect bribe-paying gangs by preventing their detection. It
could even supply the direct participation of some policemen in serious
crimes such as robbery. This standing conspiracy had several protective
layers or shells. First, everyone in it was a policeman. Second, they were all
detectives. Third, they were all corrupt. Fourth, most were Freemasons.

Within this carapace crooked cops could get away, if not with murder,
then with almost everything else. There was the classic case of Det. Sgt
Harry Challenor, a West End Central officer who planted knives,
hatchets and iron bars on dozens of innocent citizens. On one occasion he
even 'found' detonators for explosives. His undoing came in 1963 when
he framed a cluster of young men who had been demonstrating against a
visit by Queen Frederika of Greece. He claimed that pieces of brick had
been found in their pockets, presumably to throw at the Queen or at the
policemen guarding her hotel. The accused were all cleared, eventually,
because no brick dust could be traced in their pockets. Challenor himself
was now put on trial for conspiring to pervert the course of justice. Three
young constables who worked with him were convicted and jailed for
three years, but Challenor was found unfit to plead and detained in a
mental hospital at Her Majesty's pleasure.

According to a psychiatrist, he must have been 'very mad indeed' –
clinically insane – for over a year.[5] Yet throughout this time his
colleagues were apparently unaware of his lunacy. It had passed
unnoticed while, with their connivance, he planted offensive weapons on
at least twenty-six men. These same officers could not see he was crazy
even as they held down some of his victims so he could beat them up with
unimpeded brutality.

Harry Challenor was a Freemason. So were several of his very close
CID colleagues. So, too, was one recently retired high-ranking London
detective who told me how in the 1960s he was appalled by the way other
policemen used to exploit the Craft.

I became a Mason at the suggestion of an officer who is now a deputy assistant commissioner. He wanted me to join his lodge but most of the members weren't policemen. Indeed he asked a non-policeman to propose me, so that other members did not think the police were trying to take over the lodge, as sometimes happens.

I soon realized that not all police Masons were as honourable as my sponsor. At the time I was a junior detective in Scotland Yard. One day a senior colleague came in crowing that he had been selected for a place on the intermediate command course at Bramshill. I was taken aback and asked him how he did it.

He said, 'It cost me £300. I put it about in the right place.'

'You mean you bribed someone?'

'No. I took out "X" [a Commander] for a few lunches and invited him and his wife to my lodge ladies' night. I bought her a little present, paid for the meal and the drinks. And what do you know? I'm off to Bramshill next month!'

He then told me that he'd realized the Commander could get anyone from our squad on the course. Without his recommendation you didn't stand a chance. Now the Commander clearly wasn't someone you could bung fifty quid or take to a nightclub and get laid. You couldn't bribe or compromise him because he was straight. However, he was also naive so it was fairly easy to buy your way into his good books by lunching him or inviting him and his lady to your annual lodge shindig. He may have guessed what was in my colleague's mind but, even so, he felt able to accept as a fraternal Masonic gesture what in any other circumstances would have constituted an 'inducement'. You appreciate that a non-Mason would have no such opportunity.

My colleague was exceptionally unpleasant: a real crawler. Transparently obsequious, he'd do anything to get on. Most Masons are all right, so it would be unfair to damn them all because of him, but I have seen how such men manipulate Masonic connections to perpetrate acts of evil.

Some years earlier this same man worked on the same team as me. He found two villains in possession of stolen goods. They offered him a substantial bribe and he devised a way to get them out of trouble. Two fall guys were to be arrested and charged in their place. He went on holiday and our governor, a chief inspector, put me temporarily in charge of the case. However, at this stage I knew nothing of the crooked dealings which had already taken place.

I soon had to attend court because two men who had been charged with the crime were being remanded in custody. At the court one of them came up to me and said, 'You needn't think we're going to prison to save the skin of your Masonic friend' – meaning my police colleague. I asked him what he meant, and he convinced me that they had both been framed so the two villains who had committed the crime could get off.

My colleague always used Masonic phrases when speaking to anyone. He would ask people whether they were 'taught to be cautious', 'regular attenders', 'on the level' and the like. These two prisoners were not stupid and they knew from his talk that he was 'on the square', even though they were not.

I was in a quandary. I had not been involved in the arrests and I did not wish to see the wrong men go to jail. I went back to Scotland Yard and reported the affair to a senior officer: a detective superintendent who was also a Mason and whom I trusted to sort it out. When my colleague came back from holiday he admitted to the superintendent that he had framed the two men on behalf of his villainous friends, and that he had taken a bribe. The superintendent was wild, but my colleague appealed to him as a brother for help.

I dreaded what might now happen. Would my colleague be put on trial for corruption? Would I be fitted up for betraying him? Or would the trial go ahead, with the defendants squealing in open court that they had been the victims of a frame-up?

To my relief at the time, the matter *was* sorted out – but in an extraordinary way. The defendants were given a Masonic solicitor whose brother was a barrister. The solicitor persuaded them to plead guilty to the crime which they had not committed. The barrister then did a deal with the judge who let them off with a suspended sentence and a fine. That fine and all their legal fees were paid by the villains who had committed the crime! No action was taken against the crooked officer, but I was moved to another job because he said *he* could not work on the same team as me!

I asked this former detective why he had done nothing about this gross perversion of justice and why, twenty years later, he was still not prepared to be named in this account.

I cannot go public even now because, although I was only the junior officer, I was implicated in the conspiracy as deeply as anyone. I had been involved in a trial when two men pleaded guilty to crimes which, I knew at the time, they had not committed. The rest of the team were as angry as I at our colleague's actions. They were equally innocent of any criminality, but we all became 'guilty' by being caught up in the web of protection woven around a crooked Masonic brother who had appealed for help.

Remember! This happened in the 1960s when many detectives were bent. I had reported this matter once and the powers-that-be had made their decision. If I had opened my mouth again *I* might have ended up on trial on my own admissions, not the villain who put me into this mess. Besides, my only evidence against him was the word of the two defendants who later pleaded guilty and were paid off.

My informant has told me this crooked Mason's name, but I cannot name him for legal reasons. To be fair to Freemasonry, however, these horror stories have to be weighed against the fact that in the Porn Squad trials of 1977, three Crown witnesses (Kilkerr, Andrews and Culver) were themselves 'on the square'. When it came to the crunch they were ready to tell the truth, even though it would send their Masonic brothers to jail.

Similarly, the officer who spearheaded Scotland Yard's anti-corruption drive in the 1970s, Deputy Assistant Commissioner Gilbert Kelland, was a Freemason. At his right-hand was another Mason, DAC Ron Steventon, later head of A 10. Neither spared their brethren from the anti-corruption knife. This can be explained partly by the existence of two distinct Masonic traditions in the Metropolitan Police at that time. Gilbert Kelland, for example, had spent the first twenty-five years of his service in uniform. He was not a 'career detective' and he never allowed his Freemasonry to intrude into, or overlap with, his police work. In contrast Freemasonry in much of the CID had become a cover for crookery and corruption.

Towering above all such distinctions, however, is the fact that no major corruption trials would have taken place at all if it had not been for the heroic if much-hated figure of Robert Mark, who was neither a detective nor a Freemason. It was Mark who created the climate in which, for the first time in a century, corruption – Masonic or otherwise – was no longer fashionable among London detectives. It was he who gave Kelland and Steventon orders to clean up the CID.

It would be difficult to argue that Freemasonry had much beneficial effect on the Metropolitan CID between 1877 and 1977. Yet in the years since Brother Moody and his clan were purged, the Craft's reputation in the force has sunk even lower. This is partly because Masonic abuse in the 1970s propelled many honest and honourable policemen out of the Craft. One such man now holds a very high rank in Scotland Yard.

In the 1970s the old CID porn squad was so corrupt it had to be disbanded. I was assigned to the uniform squad which replaced it. We used to raid one dirty bookshop after another but, whenever I tried to fix a formal interview date with the shop owners, they would pull out their diaries and say pointedly, 'Sorry, I can't make Tuesday. It's my lodge night, you understand.'

They automatically assumed I was a Mason, which was not surprising since the crooked detectives we had replaced were all Masons. By letting me know they were 'on the square' the pornographers clearly expected me to drop my inquiries. Of course, the Masonic fix had been going on for so many years they had every expectation it would soon be 'business as usual'. I was so disgusted that I resigned from my lodge.

Another Yard officer also quit the Craft about this time. He is now ranked just below chief constable in another force:

I joined my lodge just after I had become a sergeant. I went along for a year and met some splendid people. I confess it struck me as a wonderful thing for a policeman's career, but my career was going splendidly anyway. The lodge meetings were very boring – the most infernally boring thing I have ever been involved in. Also, my job as a detective was taking such long and irregular hours that I could not get along each week to my lodge of instruction. And when I *was* free I preferred to spend time with my wife and children.

For me the crunch came when we raided a notorious West End nightclub where the hostesses were really prostitutes. I was about to charge the owners with living off immoral earnings when they appealed to me 'on the square'. They were my brother Masons and expected me to let them off. I ignored the approach and went ahead and charged them. When the case came up at the Old Bailey they were acquitted. I was appalled, but I don't think the rotten verdict had anything to do with Freemasonry.

Unfortunately, not even Scotland Yard's 'rubber-heel mob' – A 10 – was immune from Masonic manipulation. For many years I have known a London solicitor who is a Mason. In the 1970s he had a client who was also a Mason. On his behalf the solicitor made a complaint to A 10 alleging serious criminal misconduct by a detective. In due course an A 10 officer was appointed to investigate. He assured the solicitor that he had never met the detective under investigation, and that he would pursue the inquiry with the utmost zeal. Taught to be cautious, however, the

solicitor used his Masonic connections to discover more about the A 10
investigator.

> To my horror I discovered he was in the same lodge as the suspect
> detective. I promptly made another complaint to A 10 saying these
> men knew each other and that, in the circumstances, they should
> appoint another investigator. Nothing of the kind! I received a curt
> reply saying the two men did not know each other and I was
> mistaken. But I had documentation to prove they had both been
> masters of the same lodge, and must have known each other very
> well indeed.
>
> I immediately told my client about this connection and A 10's
> response. He was astonishingly philosophical. He said the investi-
> gation was now certain to be a whitewash, for no Mason would ever
> bring criminal charges against a brother Mason in the same lodge. I
> wanted to have a go at A 10 and produce my conclusive Masonic
> evidence, but my client insisted on dropping the complaint! What
> could I do? I was acting on instructions.

At this time A 10 may have been going through teething problems. No
such excuse could be made for the Complaints Investigation Bureau,
CIB 2, which replaced A 10 in the late 1970s. There are many potential
conflicts of interest when one policeman investigates another. One of
these is Freemasonry and CIB 2 must always be aware that hidden
Masonic connections might contaminate the fair investigation of
complaints. In its short existence CIB 2 has had enough Masons among
its chiefs to be aware of the very short odds that a Mason could be given
the job of investigating one of his Masonic brothers. In 1979 CIB 2 was
headed by Commander John Cass. Two years later Commander A. W.
Lampard was in charge. In 1979 CIB 2's allied disciplinary team known as
CIB 3 was headed by Chief Supt. William Gibson. Two years later he was
succeeded by Malcolm A. Ferguson. Later still, Kenneth Churchill-
Coleman took over. When the Manor of St James's Lodge list leaked out
in 1986 who should be on it but Cass, Lampard, Gibson, Ferguson and
Churchill-Coleman.

Perhaps all these men would pursue any complaint laid against a
Masonic colleague with even greater dedication than one against a non-
Mason, if only to prove that Masonic loyalties would not get in their
way. But where would a member of the Manor of St James's Lodge stand
if he were told to investigate another member? With some fifty serving
officers in the lodge, this may very likely happen (if it has not happened
already). Ideally, the investigator would refuse the job and suggest a

non-Mason do it instead. Heaven help Freemasonry if the public ever find out that a policeman under investigation belongs to the same lodge as his investigator!

A policeman who recently retired from Hampshire Constabulary wrote to me expressing his concern:

> A detective I knew was a practising mason and had been master of his lodge. He made no secret of the fact and always wore a masonic ring, tie and cufflinks. This man was, to say the least, unscrupulous in his methods and it was well known in the legal profession that he 'doctored' his evidence in court. This was confirmed to me by a barrister. This officer was the subject of several internal discipline inquiries but always appeared to escape prosecution. Senior officers seemed to be afraid of him and I always felt this was because of influential people he moved with socially.

These days internal discipline and anti-corruption units need to be seen to be above reproach and suspicion, otherwise all sorts of lobbies and pressure groups (not just disorganized anti-Masons) will cry 'White-wash!' In 1987 Scotland Yard's self-cleansing squad was put to the test again as another 'Masonic' corruption scandal broke.

Early one morning in July 1987 Detective Constable Alan Holmes shot himself dead in his back garden. Eight months later a coroner's jury confirmed that he had committed suicide, but it did not have to say why. The answer lies in a tangle of personal and work problems complicated by Holmes's Masonic bonds – not that Freemasonry was mentioned at any point during the inquest.

'Taffy' Holmes was a stocky 15-stone, broken-nosed, rugby-playing Welshman who drank to excess. He had a wife and children. He also had a mistress. He was totally devoted to the Metropolitan Police in which he had served for twenty-six years. At work he was gregarious, convivial and he would do anything for a friend. At the inquest one colleague said Taffy believed 'a problem shared is a problem solved'. Another officer felt he had 'misguided loyalties'. His perceptive father-in-law explained how it 'seemed essential to Alan that he should be liked by everybody'.

In the days before he died Holmes was under great pressure from the anti-corruption squad, CIB2, which was investigating alleged links between a detective commander and a man convicted of receiving some of the £26 million 'Brinks-MAT' gold bullion stolen in 1983. The receiver, Kenneth Noye, is also a Freemason; the commander may be one too – but it seems unlikely that the two men have ever met. Even so, CIB2 felt that Holmes (who worked on the Brinks-MAT robbery investigation) knew about such a relationship. CIB 2 may have arranged for another officer to secretly tape-record Holmes as he gossiped about corrupt acts by fellow-detectives. When Holmes learned about the alleged tape he was plunged into depression, partly because it seems these crooked officers were also Masons. He felt 'set-up' and betrayed. At the inquest one colleague (himself under no cloud) explained how, five days before he died, Holmes had returned very upset from an all-day grilling by CIB 2. He talked about another officer whom he had considered a friend but who had 'let him down and told lies about him'. He said he was going to kill that man and then kill himself. The colleague told the Coroner: 'He was very upset, but I didn't think he'd do it.'

Holmes was doubly appalled by this alleged treachery because he had only just introduced the 'traitor' into his own Masonic lodge. The treachery was even greater because that year Taffy was Lodge Master. What about the Five Points of Fellowship?: 'Breast to breast, your lawful secrets when entrusted to me as such I will keep as my own.' Lawful or not, many brothers' secrets – Holmes's included – had been betrayed.

At his funeral Taffy received full police honours. Deputy Commissioner John Dellow led dozens of Scotland Yard mourners. Holmes was eulogized as having 'a face as hard as granite but a heart as soft and vulnerable as a butterfly'. Most of the eighty wreaths came from police officers, stations and squads, but several were sent openly by Freemasons, including one large floral square-and-compasses. Another bore the inscription: 'To our brave, wonderful and worshipful master who chose death rather than dishonour his friends and workmates.'

Death may be better than revealing one's own dishonour, but killing oneself to cover up for others is taking loyalty too far – even for a Mason. In any case, what did Holmes know which could have dishonoured his friends and workmates? In a suicide note he told his wife, 'I loved the police and never did them an ounce of harm', but might not his suicide bring more dishonour on the police than telling the truth about crooked colleagues?

Taffy Holmes was Master of Lodge no. 7114. When I was first told this fact, I thought it might be part of a pattern. Lodge 7114 is another 'Manor' lodge: the Manor of Bensham. I wondered if there was a 'Manor' lodge for each of the twenty-three old divisions of the Metropolitan Police. Might they all be like the St James's: jam-packed full of fuzz? With a hundred cops in each, the full slate would be 2,300. Further researches uncovered ten more lodges in Greater London with 'Manor' in the title, but only three correspond with a Metropolitan Police district and none of them is an all-police lodge. Even the Manor of Bensham recruits from all walks of life, but it does have a strong police connection. In 1986 at least five members were past or present policemen, including retired Commander Arthur Howard, QPM: once head of C1, Scotland Yard's chief detective branch. It seems all these officers joined the Lodge while living in Croydon or serving on the local 'Z' District.

The full story behind the death of Bensham's Master may never emerge, but in March 1988 a report appeared in the *News of the World* saying he died for nothing.[6] It claimed another officer had told Holmes that a tape of his crooked colleagues' conversation existed when in fact no such recording had been made. Taffy's shame at having inadvertently betrayed his Masonic brethren was baseless. Whether or not that shame is what drove him to suicide, may the Great Architect have mercy on his soul.

seventeen

MASTER OF THE CITY

In June 1978 Detective Chief Superintendent John Simmonds – not to be confused with Detective Sergeant John Symonds who featured in the last chapter – departed from the Metropolitan Police to take on the most exciting job in his career: head of CID in the City of London Police. He might not have had the stomach for the move had he known he would spend the next five years fighting a war on corruption, a war which would drive him out of Freemasonry.

The City Police has only 830 officers but it is independent of the 27,000 strong Metropolitan force around it. It polices the historic area of Roman Londinium, which today is exceedingly rich, full of banks and a monument to Mammon. It attracts bank-robbers and pay-roll snatchers, but also white-collar con-men and fraudsters by the hundred. To be its chief detective was a challenge Simmonds greatly relished.

Yet even as he took the job there was a problem of which his boss, Commissioner Peter Marshall, was already aware. Marshall was another recruit from Scotland Yard, a Catholic and certainly not a Mason. Together the men discerned a disturbing tradition in the City CID. It was 'cosy' and inbred: the weak offspring of a tiny force which had promoted from within for generations. Simmonds was worried that its defects might include graft and corruption. Indeed, corruption had been rife in the City CID for decades. Two years before Simmonds took over, it seemed to win control. The 'Square Mile' suffered three violent robberies, each executed with an impunity which indicated that the robbers had a prior deal with the police. In May 1976 four gunmen stole £175,000 from the Fleet Street offices of the *Daily Express* newspaper. In September 1977 six men stole £270,000 from Williams and Glyn's Bank in Birchin Lane. On the last day of May 1978 a security guard was shot dead as he delivered £200,000 in wages to the *Daily Mirror*. Many men would be charged with these crimes, but none would be convicted or jailed.

Simmonds started his new job the day after the *Mirror* robbery. To distance himself from the men he was now leading (and might have to investigate) he made a resolution: he would not get sucked into any Masonic network within the force. This was a sacrifice, for he was a regular Mason, not just in his own lodge but in the social side of Scotland Yard Freemasonry as a whole. He well knew how the Craft had operated among Yard detectives, so he realized that, as soon as he took over the City CID, he would be tested to see if he was 'one of the boys'.

Masons recognize each other not just by their much-ridiculed hand-shakes but by all sorts of gestures and phrases – even by the hours they keep. What other group of men regularly quit work in mid-afternoon carrying little cases, mumbling ritual they have been trying to learn all week from little books they stuff in their pockets whenever they think someone can see them? Simmonds avoided all such traits, ignoring the Masonic signals dropped at any opportunity by the detectives under his authority. He carried this act off so well that, after a few weeks, his staff reluctantly concluded he was not 'on the square'.

Sooner or later Simmonds's ploy was bound to come unstuck. At a Masonic gathering which he did not attend, a City detective called Philip Cuthbert struck up a conversation with a man who was not a policeman. When he found out Cuthbert was in the City Police the man said, 'In that case, you must know my friend John Simmonds.' To Cuthbert's astonished disbelief, the stranger then revealed that Simmonds too was a Mason.

Next day Cuthbert popped into Simmonds's office and said, 'You've been telling *porkies*!' – Cockney rhyming slang for lies (pork pies). He chattered on, spilling out invitations to his lodge, to ladies' nights and other Craft gatherings. Simmonds swallowed hard, admitted he was 'on the square' but indicated he would prefer to keep his Freemasonry to himself. This way he hoped Cuthbert would take not offence but the hint that 'brotherly love' would not soften Simmonds's judgement over such matters as corruption. Philip Cuthbert misread these signals. Within hours Simmonds was aware that many subordinates were acting much friendlier towards him. They seemed relaxed, even relieved, now they knew the boss was 'on the level', a titbit Cuthbert had spread around the department in no time.

Only a few weeks later Cuthbert was in desperate need of a Masonic shoulder to cry on. Out of nowhere, in August 1978, an inquiry had been set up to look into statements made by criminal informers alleging certain City detectives were corrupt. Top of the list was Chief Inspector Phil Cuthbert.

This was the origin of 'Operation Countryman', a massive inquiry which at its height had eighty provincial detectives investigating their London cousins. It was ordered by Home Secretary Merlyn Rees who had accepted civil service advice that the alleged corruption went so deep and so high in both City and Metropolitan forces that only non-London policemen could investigate them to the satisfaction of public opinion. The job could not be left to the City's own discipline procedures or to the Met's Complaints Investigation Bureau. It was later alleged that Freemasonry was not only involved in the corruption which Operation Countryman was investigating, but had later caused its overall failure by sabotage.

To my knowledge, however, there was no Masonic sabotage of Countryman. Certainly many a crooked detective under suspicion was a Mason, but so was the man heading the inquiry: Dorset's Chief Constable Arthur Hambleton. His battle with Scotland Yard chiefs (Masons and non-Masons) over the direction and depth of the inquiry was fought so hard and so bitterly that clearly he never let Freemasonry or anything else weaken his determination to root out corruption.[1] As it happens, Hambleton was well aware of the way in which non-police Masons sometimes try to pressure police colleagues. When he moved to Dorset to take up his appointment as Chief Constable, he refused to join a lodge in that county until 1980 – *after* he retired.

Countryman secured its only convictions against police officers in 1982, when Phil Cuthbert was found guilty at the Old Bailey of taking up to £80,000 in bribes to secure bail, overlook past convictions and not to gather evidence against eight men who had been charged with the 1977 Williams and Glyn's robbery. He was sent to prison for three years, but back in 1978 he had no intention of going to jail and pulled every Masonic connection to obstruct the Countryman inquiry. One of them was his chief, John Simmonds.

One day that September Cuthbert asked Simmonds if he could have a quiet word 'on the square'. Simmonds knew that this meant Cuthbert wanted to tell him something as between two Masons: in total confidence and 'off the record'. The senior officer said he would be willing to listen, and agreed to meet Cuthbert in a pub a few days later. As for the chat being 'on the square', Simmonds was not prepared to treat confidentially any criminal admission which Cuthbert might make in any conversation – 'on the square' or not. Indeed, he took the precaution of notifying Commissioner Marshall of Cuthbert's approach. Marshall notified Operation Countryman and together they decided Simmonds should go to the pub 'wired-up' to tape-record the encounter.

Their three-hour conversation turned into a Cook's Tour of London crime, corruption and Freemasonry – oiled by booze and laced with obscenities. Immortalized on tape were choice remarks from a man who

was once Britain's youngest inspector but who had embraced with
enthusiasm the appalling standards of many London detectives in the
1960s and 1970s. He was holding Masonic court with a pair of legal
friends when Simmonds arrived at the rendezvous and the recording
began.

'It's my Ladies' Night, Saturday,' said Cuthbert who was reigning
Master of his lodge, the Waterloo (no. 3475).

> IRVING SHINE (a solicitor's managing clerk): Hope you've got a nice
> disco now, I don't want any more fights.
> CUTHBERT: I'm paying. I'm even treating you to your own
> ticket . . .
> PAUL DAVIS (a solicitor): Thank you.
> CUTHBERT: . . . and Laura's ticket but you can buy your own
> fucking booze.
> DAVIS: Bollocks.
> . . .
> CUTHBERT: Very short, quick speeches. I'm making one.
> . . .
> DAVIS: I must be seventy by the time I get the chair. [Become
> Master.]
> CUTHBERT: Serves you right – you got to learn the words, see!
> [Memorize the ritual.]
>
> CUTHBERT: I just want to say thank you very much for coming.
> SIMMONDS: Well, no. I think it's right that I should be here.
> CUTHBERT: May I just say, you are the first Chief Superintendent that
> has worked with me for a number of years that would have done
> it, and thanks very much, but I've got nothing to fear honestly, no
> fucking way, governor.

Cuthbert was especially revealing about 'one of the greatest unhung
villains', a senior officer whom I shall call by the pseudonym 'Georgie':

> CUTHBERT: Georgie did the *Daily Express* job, governor, and I know
> what Georgie copped on the *Daily Express* job off Chadwick. I
> know only it doesn't matter, I mean, you're new on the firm, it
> doesn't matter but I know what he did and I know who got it for
> him. I know who took it to him and I know what he give them back.
> . . .
> SIMMONDS: Well how much are we talking about on the *Express* job?
> . . .

CUTHBERT: Twenty grand [£20,000].

SIMMONDS: You told me £300 the other day.

. . .

CUTHBERT: One of the sergeants got £300. That was his share out of the twenty grand, and he got the fucking hump with it, thought it was a liberty.

. . .

[elsewhere] That was a Georgie job and he's a greedy bastard, always has been.

Of another criminal investigation:

CUTHBERT: A lot of money changed hands, governor, it's happened in the Met, it's happened in the City, it's happened in the counties, it has happened for years and years. The job is different now. I don't do fucking things like that. I'm not saying somebody doesn't get a bit of bail and a drink goes in. Fuck it. That will always happen, you will never stop it, but we don't let fucking robbers go for money. I've never let robbers go for money in my life. I never would. And if anybody has, it's not down to me.

Cuthbert also alleged that Georgie had 'had a drink' (a bribe) over the Williams and Glyn's robbery, even though he was working on the Regional Crime Squad at the time and had no direct role in the investigation.

SIMMONDS: Well, how can he have a drink out of it when he is on the Regional?

CUTHBERT: Because he was Georgie and because he worked with all of us, and, you know, he was in a position of power up there on the fucking Regional Crime Squad and covered things, same as all the blokes on the Robbery Squad had a drink out of it, going right up to the fucking top of the tree, all fucking slagging us off, it was a silly drink, wasn't a big drink, silly drink.

SIMMONDS: Yer, well, why is it people put you . . .

CUTHBERT: They're putting me in as a bad man because I did the fucking business, that's why, 'cause I had to go and do, see the people. I never met any of the villains, nobody like that. I was fucking asked to do it . . . by a senior officer.

Of the bribe over Williams and Glyn's:

SIMMONDS: What about stories of between sixty and ninety grand?

CUTHBERT: Governor, a lot of bollocks. Well, as far as I know, a lot
of bollocks . . . I didn't do fuck all. All I did was go and meet a
couple of guys and took an envelope . . . If somebody's fucking
had it, I don't know about it.

. . .

SIMMONDS: No, no. But when people turn round to me and say it's
. . . sixty grand . . .

CUTHBERT: Everybody on the Incident Room had a drink, everybody. We're talking about 50s, honestly. A soppy drink for
nothing. 'Cos they grafted and knocked themselves out . . . all
the fucking evidence we gave was bent.

Cuthbert had also served with the Robbery Squad at Scotland Yard and
said he knew the system was exactly the same over there. He claimed he
had given insurance reward money to Yard commanders who took their
share and then handed the rest to assistant commissioners, 'the fucking
top of the tree'. Simmonds gently responded, 'Yer, well, things are
slightly different today, Phil.'

In due course Simmonds's tape ensured Cuthbert and another officer
were convicted and jailed. The tape was not the only evidence. There was
also testimony from a junior officer who said Cuthbert had paid him
bribes over the Williams and Glyn's robbery and also from an underworld figure who had given Cuthbert that money on behalf of men
arrested for the crime. However, it was the tape-recording which
finished Cuthbert because it amounted to a confession that he had
participated in corruption not only over these robberies but continually in
his fifteen-year detective career.

What is the Masonic significance of the Simmonds–Cuthbert affair?
For a start, it proves that a Mason may make even the most self-
incriminating confession to another Mason on the assumption that the
confessor's lips are sealed as surely as a Catholic priest's. Second, it shows
that Freemasonry in the City Police at this time went hand in hand with
corruption, and proves yet again that Masonry rarely elevates the
conduct of its members above the norm. If anything, it debases that norm
even further. Third, before he went to meet Cuthbert, Simmonds had
decided that his duty as a citizen and a policeman over-rode the principle
of Masonic mutual aid. The Third Degree Obligation supports his
judgement, for it states that the bonds of secrecy do not apply to 'murder,
treason, felony and all other offences contrary to the laws of God and the
ordinances of the realm'.

Simmonds's integrity should therefore have been applauded by all

Masons. This did not happen. Far from receiving fraternal congratulations, he was ostracized and sent to the Masonic equivalent of
Coventry. Many Masons felt that Worshipful Brother Cuthbert had
come to him in desperation but that Brother Simmonds beguiled him
into a false sense of trust in order to betray him. As soon as it was known
in police circles that Simmonds had let Cuthbert hang himself on his own
words, fraternal warmth evaporated. He was shunned at Masonic
functions, cold-shouldered at normally convivial Craft gatherings and
boycotted by some brother officers who, only weeks before, had treated
him as a trusted member of the fraternity. At a large gathering at the
Connaught Rooms, Simmonds saw a detective he had known for twenty
years staring back and shaking his head. The man ran his index finger
across his throat from ear to ear: the first degree sign for cutting the throat
of a treacherous brother.

This was too much for Simmonds, who decided it was time to leave the
brotherhood. When he knew he would be giving evidence at Cuthbert's
pre-trial committal hearing, he resigned from his lodge so as not to cause
discord. In contrast, Cuthbert continued to attend his Waterloo Lodge, of
which he was now an esteemed Past Master. His brothers there did
nothing to oust him. He still went to its meetings long after he was
suspended from the City Police. It seems most members resolved to
stand by 'the Philly', a decision which forced two other City policemen in
the lodge to 'withdraw'. Had the elders asked them, they might have
confirmed Cuthbert had been at the heart of a corrupt network of cops
and crooks responsible for a series of violent robberies and even the
murder of an unarmed guard.

Astonishingly, it seems, no one in the Lodge wanted to know.

eighteen

A COLUMN OF MUTUAL DEFENCE

The north London suburb of Southgate basks in obscurity. It is the only place in Britain best known for its hockey team.

Southgate also has a Masonic temple, very popular with brethren from the provinces of London, Hertfordshire and Middlesex whose borders meet near there. In 1986 no less than 139 lodges, chapters and other Masonic groups performed their rituals at Southgate. They also consumed £48,000 worth of alcoholic drinks. One of the lodges deserves special attention because for some years it has had a bizarre mix of members. Whether it is typical of all Southgate lodges only their 6,000 or so brethren can tell.

On Tuesday 13 November 1979 Brother Leonard John Gibson was installed as Worshipful Master of the Waterways Lodge (no. 7913). He had achieved this distinction in very quick time, having been initiated only seven years earlier.

Just before Gibson took office, his predecessor William Sherborn intoned the qualifications essential in every Master. He must be 'of good report, true and trusty, and held in high estimation among his brethren and fellows'; he must have passed through all three degrees; he should also be 'exemplary in conduct, courteous in manner, easy of address, steady and firm in principle' and 'well-skilled' in the Ancient Charges and Landmarks of the order. The Charges were then read to Gibson, including this one: 'You are to be a peaceable Subject, and cheerfully to conform to the laws of the country in which you reside.'

Gibson assented by giving the sign of Fidelity. He then promised to 'maintain and uphold, pure and unsullied, the genuine principles and tenets of the Craft'. Duly installed as Master for the next twelve months, he was saluted by each degree in turn: Master Masons, the Fellow Craft, last the Entered Apprentices.

Worshipful Master Gibson was given the lodge warrant and complimented that 'whilst it is in your charge it will lose none of its lustre, but will be transmitted to your successor pure and unsullied, as you now receive it'. The Installing Master now offered him this guidance:

> As a pattern of excellence, consider that grand luminary the Sun, which, rising in the East, diffuses light and lustre within its circle. In like manner, Worshipful Master, it is within your province to impart light and instruction to the Brethren of your Lodge. Forcibly impress upon them the dignity and high importance of Free-masonry, seriously admonish them never to disgrace it, charge them to practise out of the Lodge those excellent precepts they are taught within it, and by virtuous, amiable and discreet conduct, prove to the world the happy and beneficial effects of our ancient and honourable Institution, so that when a man is said to be a Freemason, the world may know that he is one to whom the burdened heart may pour forth its sorrow, to whom the distressed may prefer their suit, whose hand is guided by Justice and whose heart is expanded by Benevolence.

Finally, the new Worshipful Master and his assembled brethren were exhorted 'to be faithful to our God, our country and our laws'.

These beautiful evocations all sounded fine but there was one snag. Worshipful Master Gibson was not quite right for the job. The brethren may have lauded him as a man of 'good report, true and trusty', but Gibson was a crook. Indeed, he was an underworld figure of considerable status.

Even as he became Master of the Waterways, Gibson was one of London's top 100 criminals, according to a secret booklet then being circulated in the Flying and Robbery Squads of the Metropolitan Police. The booklet was put together to help detectives identify likely robbers and contained mugshot and profile photographs of each gangster. Gibson's number (42) reflected not his criminal ranking in the 100 most wanted, just his place in the alphabet.

From his entry Gibson does not seem much of a public enemy:

> Leonard John Gibson. C.R.O. No. 49397–60, born Hertfordshire 16–3–42. 6 ft. heavy build, complexion fresh, hair light brown, eyes blue, mole on left cheek.

> Convictions for going equipped to steal, handling stolen goods, shop-breaking, etc.

However, the criminal intelligence officers who compiled it delivered their most serious observation in the last line: 'Modus Operandi [criminal speciality]. Armed Robbery.'

The existence of this document does not by itself discredit either the Waterways Lodge or Freemasonry as a whole. No lodge can be expected to have access to secret police reports on every incoming Master. Also Gibson probably did not disclose his record when he applied to join in 1971. Certainly he did not list his occupation as 'armed robber', preferring something like 'property developer', which is how he decribed himself when he became Master. It may be that he told his brethren about his criminal past but, as his first conviction went back eleven years, they might have felt he had rehabilitated himself and was now good Mason material.

Yet the Waterways Lodge cannot be so easily exonerated. By the time it elected Gibson as Master, its members included several policemen. One was Superintendent John Brian McNeil who, until 1978, had been a chief-inspector in the Flying Squad. It seems odd that, having joined the lodge five years earlier, McNeil had picked up nothing about Gibson's criminal background. He seems to have been unaware, for instance, of the 'Top 100' list circulating in Flying Squad offices. Yet, with so many serving Flying Squad detectives 'on the square', it would seem extraordinary if none of them had tipped off McNeil about his fast-moving Masonic colleague. If they really did believe Gibson was one of London's top 100 gangsters, they must have carried out surveillance on him and very probably tailed him to lodge meetings at Southgate.

Worse was to come. The first major ceremony during Gibson's year as Master was the initiation of three candidates. They were a self-employed garage proprietor; a Home Office immigration official; and a twenty-seven-year-old Metropolitan Police sergeant. The policeman, James Charles McNally, had been proposed by Superintendent McNeil. It would have been ironic if the cop had been initiated by the robber but I have been told by one Waterways member that Sgt McNally was initiated not by Worshipful Master Gibson himself but by one of his police colleagues.

After such an elevating ceremonial, it might be assumed that Entered Apprentice McNally and Worshipful Master Gibson were now on the same side, dedicated to every virtue under the Masonic Sun. Indeed Freemasonry might have so elevated Gibson's conduct since his own initiation eight years earlier, that he could have wholly rejected a life of crime. His Flying Squad top 100 rating might by now have constituted a wicked libel on a reformed character.

However, it was only too accurate. Only two weeks after presiding over the Waterways' next meeting in March, Gibson took part in what was then Britain's biggest-ever bullion robbery.

On 24 March 1980 Gibson and three other men were waiting in a layby on the A13 road in Barking, Essex, when their prey came into sight: a lorry carrying £3.4 million worth of silver to the port of Tilbury for onward shipment to East Germany. One of the gang was dressed in a police uniform, but this seems not to have been borrowed from any of the policemen in Gibson's lodge. He strode out into the road and waved the lorry into the layby to be 'checked' by two bogus Ministry of Transport officials wearing white coats and dark glasses. Suddenly they pulled out a pistol and a sawn-off shotgun and forced the bullion driver, his companion and a security guard into the back of a van. By the time they were discovered, bound up in a locked garage, their 10-ton load of 321 ingots had disappeared into another van, then hidden in a garage not far from Gibson's home.

The team were shocked by their success. At that time the price of silver was buoyant and £3.4 million worth was more than they could handle. In the next two months its value dropped by £1 million but still they could not shift it, physically or financially. By this time underworld informers had betrayed the gang's mock policeman, Michael Gervaise. He turned supergrass and informed on his colleagues, including Worshipful Master Gibson. Taken into custody in June, Gibson confessed and led Flying Squad officers to the garage where the silver was stored. Twelve ingots had disappeared (where they went is still a matter of fierce controversy), but his captors treated this as a minor infelicity. They were grateful for Gibson's help, even if his contrition rang hollow: 'When we heard about the value of the silver, we realized it was too hot to handle, and we decided to give it back.'

Gibson was remanded in custody but this caused no immediate problem for the Waterways Lodge, which had just begun its 'close season' and did not meet again till October. Unfortunately, when October came round, the Worshipful Lennie was still in Brixton, so before he could complete his year 'in the Chair' the Lodge had to elect a successor. The Waterways has installed its Masters in October ever since.

In January 1981 Gibson and the two bogus Transport officials pleaded guilty at the Old Bailey. In a staggering example of special pleading, Gibson's defence described the three men as 'amateurs'. No one on the prosecution side could reveal Gibson's prestigious ranking on the Flying Squad's top 100 list, because it amounted to mere opinion or hearsay. The trio received surprisingly light sentences of ten years each in prison.

Masonic apologists might say that Gibson was only one Freemason and 'there is always one rotten apple in every barrel'. However, as every gardener knows, one rotten apple in the barrel corrupts the lot. So it was in this fermenting tub. There was not just one Mason on the silver robbery, but three! The two 'men from the Ministry of Transport', Rudolpho Aguda and his nephew Renalto, were also 'on the square'.

Ironically, the only robber who was not a Mason was the 'policeman', Micky Gervaise. His confession caused Gibson and Rudolpho Aguda to crack and admit their role. Renalto was made of sterner stuff and refused to admit anything. When interrogated on 4 June 1980, he asked detectives to read him the two other Masons' confessions. In shocked disbelief he then asked to see his uncle. The detectives demanded he tell them why. 'I can't,' said Renalto, 'it's on the square.'

Vexed at this attempt to bring Masonic influence to bear on the investigation, one detective responded: 'Look, you can forget all about Freemasonry, because what we're talking about – the biggest robbery in this country – is totally unrelated . . . Nobody other than yourself can help you out of your present situation.'

North London's Masonic crime network stretched on and on. One man who received a controversial £135,000 reward for 'grassing' the silver bullion robbers was also a Freemason. This was a millionaire club-owner and property magnate, to whom I am legally obliged to give a pseudonym, 'Sam Lerner'. He belonged to the Bishop Ridley Lodge (no. 6196), along with several more policemen. This man was later gaoled for keeping £2 million in VAT which he had received from legitimate companies when they bought gold from him. He had thus defrauded Her Majesty's Customs and Excise, overlooking the stirring patriotic call in his Masonic initiation ceremony: 'to be exemplary in the discharge of your civil duties . . . above all, by never losing sight of the allegiance due to the Sovereign of your native land'.

One television programme included material implying that Sam Lerner was prepared to set fire to shops and bomb tenants off his land in order to get vacant possession.[1] A police detective sergeant, Peter Docherty, belonged to the same lodge. They became so friendly that Lerner gave the detective permission to shoot on his land. 'I walked round with him and I became interested in shooting,' Lerner later testified.[2] 'He obtained a shotgun which I bought and he assisted me in applying for the certificate. I purchased a number of guns through him.' This was, of course, before Lerner was in trouble over the gold fraud. To the man's credit, he withdrew from the Bishop Ridley Lodge as soon as he was charged.

Another criminal informer, supergrass Billy Young, was also a subscribing member of north London's Masonic underworld. He was the main witness against yet another member of the Craft, David Spicer. At first Spicer was convicted on Young's evidence, then cleared on appeal, so he has no criminal record. Questioned by officers from the Thames

Valley Police on 31 March 1980, Spicer admitted knowing Lennie Gibson and drinking with him in a local pub, but claimed he knew nothing of his criminal activities.

DETECTIVE INSPECTOR JOHN IRELAND: Why should you keep the company of an armed robber?

SPICER: I didn't know he was an armed robber.

DET. INSP.: You've known him for ten years, you drank with him?

SPICER: I've been to his meetings with him in the lodge. He was Master.

DET. INSP.: So in fact you were friendly with him then, and you're trying to tell us that you didn't know he was a robber?

SPICER: Yes.

DET. INSP.: I take it obviously that you're a Freemason, then?

SPICER: Yes.

DET. INSP.: And I would think that that form of following would not tolerate liars, would it?

SPICER: No.

DET. INSP.: Yet there we have an ideal example of one of their number being an armed robber and you were associating with him.

SPICER: He must have lied to get in the lodge.

There was another Masonic twist to the silver bullion robbery. It was through Freemasonry that the 'inside man' knew the main men in the conspiracy. William Parker was a transport manager for the company transporting the silver when it was stolen. He had tipped off the robbers, for which crime he was jailed for seven years. He was not a Mason but had often attended Masonic socials such as Ladies' Nights with Gibson, Lerner and the Agudas. He frolicked with these felons at Masonic temples in Southgate, Finchley and Chingford. They plied him with hospitality while he was pressured to betray his employers, and put three men's lives at risk by delivering them into the clutches of his gun-toting Masonic cronies.

Lennie Gibson came out of prison in 1986. When the Waterways Lodge met again after the summer break, he was back in attendance. He did not have to rejoin the lodge; he had never left it. During his five years away he had remained on the roll as a 'country member'. This struck other Masonic criminals as most fitting: for much of his incarceration he enjoyed the rural delights of Spring Hill Open Prison in Buckinghamshire.

In 1987 one frightened Waterways member told me: 'Gibson's name is still on the list, but what can I do about it? I'm just an ordinary brother. Of course it's a scandal, but don't tell anyone I told you. It's more than my life's worth.' Gibson himself feels he has paid his debt to society, and that the code of Brotherly Love includes mercy to a fallen brother. After all, in the third degree a Mason swears his hand, given to a Master Mason, is 'a sure pledge of brotherhood'. He swears to unite with him 'in forming a column of mutual defence and support', and to 'dispose my heart to succour his weakness and relieve his necessities'. The Waterways brethren have disposed their hearts to let Lennie Gibson remain among them.

The continuing presence in Freemasonry of men like Gibson and the Agudas causes great embarrassment to Grand Lodge which constantly expresses its concern about criminal activities in and around lodges. Grand Secretary Higham requests that any journalists with knowledge of Masonic wrongdoing should report it to him. In February 1988 on the Channel Four television programme, 'After Dark', I referred to the overlap between criminals and policemen in the Waterways Lodge. I did not, however, name the lodge. A few days later I received a letter from Commander Higham asking me to give him my information 'so that I may investigate and take appropriate action'.

I replied saying he already had the information because Grand Lodge Information Officer Ken Garrett had discussed the Waterways problem with *Observer* reporter Paul Lashmar the same week.[3] Lashmar was astonished to learn that there were not just two or three policemen in the lodge, but as many as *eight* when Gibson was Master. 'Two resigned when he was convicted,' said Garrett, 'four retired from the force while Gibson was in prison, and two resigned from the Masons when he reappeared after serving his sentence. There is only one active officer in the lodge now.' Seven months later Garrett told Lashmar that all three robbers would shortly face Grand Lodge's disciplinary system – eight years after their conviction. Worshipful Bro. Gibson says no one had bothered to tell him!

Grand Lodge is exasperated when lodges like the Waterways refuse to exclude men like Gibson. Hence, the chastising tone of a statement on 'Masonic Discipline' made by Pro Grand Master Lord Cornwallis which was distributed to all members of the Craft in March 1988:

> If an individual fails significantly in his duty to society or to his Lodge, his own conscience may compel him to drop out for a while or resign. His lodge may find his continued membership unaccept- able and exclude him. Masonic authority may take a more serious view and suspend him or even recommend his expulsion.

Cornwallis did not state that in the twenty-eight years since 1960 Grand Lodge had expelled only three convicted criminals.[4] However, he went on:

This disciplinary system has been with us for some time. I am concerned, however, that sometimes the tear of sympathy may have been too readily shed over the failings of a brother. I hope that Brethren in Lodges and others who deal with cases of Masonic discipline will bear the Craft's reputation in mind. I am not suggesting a series of exemplary sanctions: simply that we remember that the way in which we deal with unmasonic conduct reflects the value we place on the standards we profess.

Exemplary sanctions are exactly what followed. In September 1988 Grand Lodge expelled another five brethren. Four had been convicted of crimes (arson; corruption; concealing a will and obtaining property by deception; and sexual offences against small boys) while the fifth had misappropriated Lodge funds. Eventually Grand Lodge might get round to dealing with the Hammersmith Lodge (no. 2090), one of whose members, Kenneth Noye, was convicted of receiving part of the £26 million worth of gold stolen in the 1983 Brinks-MAT robbery (see Chapter 16). While he is serving fourteen years in prison his brethren are paying his lodge subscriptions. This generous gesture may reflect their belief in his continuing protestations of innocence, but it is all the more remarkable because during his trial, Det. Chief Supt. Brian Boyce, who led the Brinks-MAT investigation, claimed Noye had offered him £1 million if he could ensure Noye did not go to prison. Noye allegedly made this offer after giving Boyce a Masonic handshake. Boyce is not a Mason but says he returned the handshake, leading Noye to believe he too was 'on the square'.

Would Noye have received a friendlier response if he had been interviewed by a detective who was a Mason? And even if such an officer had rejected the bribe, would he have revealed the offer of a cool million made on the strength of a Mason's grip?

nineteen

THE ENCOMPASSING OF JOHN STALKER

MASON WITCH-HUNT ON TOP COP

MASON MAFIA FRAMED COP CHIEF

On 29 June 1986 those two deadly rivals for our Sunday morning favours, the *People* and the *News of the World*, ran almost identical stories about John Stalker, Deputy Chief Constable of the Greater Manchester Police. Four weeks earlier he had been suddenly removed from a highly sensitive inquiry into allegations of a shoot-to-kill policy by the Royal Ulster Constabulary. Why he was removed became a massive media guessing-game. Sooner or later someone was bound to blame the Freemasons.

The press had already blamed the RUC, its Special Branch, Stalker's rivals in the Manchester force, the SAS, MI5, the Northern Ireland Office, the Home Office and, of course, the British government. Each was accused of crucifying a fine bobby, yet little evidence was produced to support these claims. This may be why the newspapers hit on Freemasonry. The joy (and the danger) of a Masonic conspiracy theory is its elasticity: you can expand it to embrace any other group you care to name. Hence the *People*'s catch-all opening:

> Top cop John Stalker is the victim of a plot by Freemasons that stretches all the way from Ulster to Whitehall, according to his friends and colleagues. They are convinced that a 'get Stalker' order originated in Ulster, where he made enemies with his inquiries into an alleged police 'shoot to kill' policy. The order was taken up in Manchester . . .

The *News of the World* offered a less global but equally sinister scenario:

James Anderton, Chief Constable of Greater Manchester, is studying secret information naming eight key officers. They are all
members of the same Freemasons Lodge. Friends of Roman
Catholic Mr Stalker believe the eight were asked by their mason
colleagues in the Royal Ulster Constabulary to 'dish the dirt' on
him.

Throughout the 'Stalker Affair' I subscribed to a cuttings service which
sent me every story linking Stalker and Freemasonry printed anywhere in
Britain's press. There are 200 such cuttings, yet none contains tangible
evidence against the Craft. Even the *News of the World*'s tale of a lodge
packed with eight key officers sank without trace. The newspaper never
identified the lodge or the officers. Such stories drove East Lancashire's
Grand Lodge to hold its only press conference in fifty-seven years to deny
the existence of a 'Mason Mafia'. Instead, Manchester's Masons claimed
the witch-hunt was on *them*.

It was not that simple. Masons were active at almost every twist in
'Stalker'. Some Masonic involvement was inevitable because Masons are
numerically strong in the organizations with which Stalker was bound to
clash if he were doing his job properly. However, what the objective
researcher must try to do is work out whether these Masons were acting not
coincidentally but *in concert*: to protect each other, to protect Freemasonry or
to protect the establishments in which Masons thrive and prosper.

First I attempt a brief account of the Stalker Affair. Some of my (mostly
published) sources argue there was no conspiracy to 'get Stalker'.[1]
Others, including Stalker himself, seem to think there was one.[2] Stalker
himself identifies no conspirators, nor does he specify Masonry as one of
the conspiracy's components, but he produces evidence which (in my
opinion) points towards a conspiracy of interests, if not of individuals.

In May 1984 John Stalker was asked to lead an inquiry into three 1982
incidents in which an undercover RUC 'Mobile Support Unit' had shot
dead five suspected Republican terrorists and a seventeen-year-old boy.
All six were unarmed so questions were asked as to why they had not
been taken alive. The fear was that RUC men had committed multiple
murder. The deeper concern was that the 'murders' were not unauthorized acts by police marksmen committed in the heat of the moment, but
the product of a cold-blooded policy.

In 1984 four of the marksmen were tried for murder but were
acquitted. This distressed the families of the dead men (all Catholics) and
outraged Republican sympathizers. The two separate trials had disclosed
systematic (if badly co-ordinated) police lying. One defendant revealed
that senior Special Branch officers had told him what false story to tell,

allegedly to protect their informers (some south of the border). Stalker's job was to investigate not just the shootings but the cover stories and also the local CID's limp search for the truth, for it seemed as if RUC marksmen had been acquitted because their CID colleagues had deliberately failed to make a murder case against them.

In his own book, John Stalker tells how his Manchester team found out that, shortly before these killings, an informer had told the RUC that four of the suspects had been involved in an IRA landmine attack which killed three policemen. This incident had occurred just three weeks before the suspects' own deaths so it seemed likely that they were the victims of RUC revenge killings. Stalker asked for the intelligence file on the landmine attack, to check if the dead men had indeed been named as suspects, but RUC Special Branch (SB) repeatedly denied such a file existed. This was revealed as a lie when Stalker interviewed a very senior RUC man as a criminal suspect. He handed Stalker the thick dossier whose existence he and others had earlier denied. This was typical of the obstruction which Stalker claims to have encountered from the SB right from the start of his inquiry.

Stalker's staff were told so many lies that it seems the RUC had decided to swamp them in mendacity, but Stalker perceived enough truth to realize the CID inquiry into one triple killing was 'slipshod, and in some aspects woefully incomplete'; some RUC detectives were either 'amateur and inefficient' at murder investigation or 'they had been deliberately inept'. This approach may have been forced on them by Special Branch. In two of the incidents (in which five men were killed), SB had 'targeted the suspected terrorists, they briefed the officers, and after the shootings they removed the men, cars and guns before the CID were allowed any access to the crucial matters. They provided the cover stories, and they decided at what point the CID were to be allowed to commence the official investigation of what had occurred.' They decided what was evidence and who was an 'on-the-run terrorist'. Stalker had never experienced 'such an influence over an entire police force by one small section'. Low-ranking SB officers would tell high-ranking CID men what to do: 'the power of the Special Branch pervaded the RUC at all levels.'[3]

The Mobile Support Unit (MSU) which carried out the shootings was not part of Special Branch, but Stalker's team confirmed that senior SB men had told MSU members what false evidence to state when they went on trial. SB had also told them the monster lie that the Official Secrets Act allowed them to tell lies in court because the 'lives of an informant and others were at stake if the full story emerged'. In the most sinister incident, the 'Hayshed shooting', a seventeen-year-old named Michael

Tighe, who had no terrorist connections or criminal convictions, appears to have been killed in cold blood. He had the misfortune to be in a hayshed which may have been an IRA arms store. It seems top officers covered up this probable murder and hid evidence from a senior CID investigator. 'This is the act of a Central American assassination squad – truly a police force out of control,' says Stalker. 'The cover stories, the lies, the obstruction were insignificant when placed alongside possible state murder. I expected others to think the same. I was mistaken.'[4]

In September 1985 Stalker wrote an interim report which roasted the RUC. However, he was in an invidious position. He was obliged to submit the report to Sir John Hermon, the head of the very force he was investigating. Astonishingly, he had been appointed on Hermon's own terms, which gave Hermon the right to sit on the report until such times as he chose to pass it to Ulster's Director of Public Prosecutions – with his own comments appended.

Stalker's report was so damaging that anyone determined to protect the RUC might have thought the only way to do it was by destroying Stalker's credibility. It was shortly after (and *only* after) he had submitted his report that Manchester CID stepped up its inquiries into hoary tales about Stalker and a businessman friend named Kevin Taylor. The principal allegations had sprung from the mouth of a jailed informer named David Burton who was also *an informer for the RUC*.

RUC Special Branch in particular had so much to hide over its role in the six killings that it was bound to be 'anti-Stalker'. It was especially determined to stop him getting one piece of evidence which could help him discover what had really happened at the Hayshed. On the RUC's behalf MI5 had hidden a bugging device in the Hayshed. This was transmitting throughout the attack when RUC men killed Tighe and severely wounded another young man. Stalker needed to know if the RUC men had shouted a warning before they fired, as they had claimed in court. If not, they would be guilty of murder as well as perjury. The MI5 tape would contain the answer, yet Stalker was denied it. The SB's head, Assistant Chief Constable Trevor Forbes, told him: 'You will never be able to hear it.' A junior officer, who had been monitoring the bug as the shooting occurred, refused to divulge what was on it. Thus a mere constable was allowed by his RUC bosses to obstruct a top-level 'independent' murder inquiry, in which there was a clear public interest.[5] The inquiry would also be subject to the closest scrutiny not just by Ulster Catholics and British politicians, but by the government of the Republic and by influential Irish sympathizers in the USA.

By this time Stalker wondered if the Hayshed was an IRA arms store after all, and if the 'informant', acting as an *agent provocateur*, had planted the guns there himself. Stalker demanded access to the informant's file. This was refused. In April 1985 he asked Hermon to suspend two SB chief superintendents who had been the principal initiators of the cover-ups. Hermon refused to suspend the officers and still refused to let Stalker have the tape. Almost one year later he told Stalker the tape no longer existed. It had been destroyed. Stalker could have a transcript, but even this would require authority from Ulster's Director of Public Prosecutions or the UK Attorney-General in London.

At last, on 4 March 1986, Ulster's DPP told Hermon to hand Stalker everything on the Hayshed, including the tape transcript and all paperwork on the tape's destruction. It was only on 30 April that Stalker got his hands on a portion of this material, but even this victory was short-lived. Within weeks he was told he was 'removed forever' from the RUC inquiry, allegedly because of an inquiry in Manchester into his friendship with Kevin Taylor. It emerged that police informers who were themselves criminals had claimed there was a sinister side to the friendship. If true, Stalker had committed a serious disciplinary offence but, even if the claims were false, he was told he would never resume the RUC inquiry. Stalker was sent on instant extended leave. A few weeks later he was suspended.

He would now sit at home for twelve weeks while the allegations were investigated by the Chief Constable of West Yorkshire, Colin Sampson. Sampson was also put in charge of the RUC probe, a move which would delay the completion of both enquiries. Stalker did not wait to be judged. A week after being sent on leave, he told a packed press conference that he had committed no offence, criminal or disciplinary, and that his friendship with Kevin Taylor was wholly proper. He had still not been told what he had allegedly done wrong. The disciplinary charge merely stated that between 1971 and 1985 he had 'associated with Kevin Taylor and known criminals in a manner likely to bring discredit on the Greater Manchester Police'.

Taylor had no criminal record but his friends included a few folk on the edge of Manchester's underworld. They also included Tory MPs whom he knew in his capacity as Chairman of the Manchester Conservative Association. This had not stopped Manchester CID rummaging through his affairs, coming up with rumours that he had committed business frauds, used his yacht to smuggle drugs and, most significantly, given Stalker free holidays in Florida.

In his book on the affair,[6] television reporter Peter Taylor said the allegations against Stalker 'invariably emanated from criminals (who have a vested interest in undermining the police) and *that there was never any shred of evidence to substantiate them*' (Peter Taylor's italics). Yet some detectives regarded them as strong enough to raid Kevin Taylor's home, using a search warrant for fraud to seize photographs of Mr and Mrs Stalker attending Taylor's fiftieth birthday party in 1982 in the fleeting company of a few one-time petty crooks.

Sampson spent the summer of 1986 investigating this material, as well as claims that Stalker had made occasional private use of official cars. Meantime a pro-Stalker lobby grew up. All sorts of newspapers alleged all sorts of plots against honest John. When Sampson presented his report to Greater Manchester's Police Authority on 22 August it contained so little dirt on Stalker that many observers were convinced he had been 'set up', the victim of a vendetta, brought down not by his own failings but by a malicious whispering campaign – whipped up to protect the interests of the State, to save RUC men from jail or to advance the careers of other Manchester officers at his expense.

Sampson criticized Stalker for a 'less than excellent standard of professional performance' and advocated a further investigation by tribunal. Yet Sampson produced no evidence of wrongdoing, and admitted no one had ever claimed Stalker had committed crimes. Even the 'official car' abuse was no such thing, although Sampson persisted with it. The authority felt Stalker was cleared, told him he could return to work but suggested he be 'more circumspect in his political and criminal associations in future'. He stuck the job for four months, then announced he was quitting. The decision was forced on him because of impossible relationships with two key colleagues: Chief Constable James Anderton, and Det. Chief Supt. Peter Topping, head of CID, who had zealously investigated Stalker in the months before his suspension.

Yet even as he departed in March 1987, no one was any wiser about all those conspiracy theories. Sampson had found no evidence that the RUC or the security services had inspired the allegations. As for a Masonic connection, he did not mention it. Some anti-Masons might conclude that Sampson himself must be 'on the square' but, although he did not reply to the questionnaire on Freemasonry which I sent to every chief constable (see Chapter 21), he has told Yorkshire newspapers that he is not a Mason. As it happens, author Peter Taylor also found no evidence to support any conspiracy theory, so where does this leave those lurid tales about Masonic plots?

At its broadest the 'Mason Witch-Hunt on Top Cop' theory embraces Masons in the army, MI5, the Whitehall civil service, and the UK government. All these institutions' Masonic bonds are revealed elsewhere in this book. Here I focus on the two bodies most deeply involved in 'Stalker': the RUC and the Greater Manchester Police.

The Mason mafia theory is rooted in the idea that Masonic elements in the RUC, already shaken by the decision to hold any 'shoot-to-kill' inquiry, were incensed that the outside police chief chosen to lead it was a Catholic: John Stalker. The RUC is manned almost entirely by Protestants. Many of them are anti-Catholic, a prejudice which is no longer surprising. In twenty years of these latest 'Troubles', more than 250 RUC men have been murdered by mostly Catholic Republicans. However, if most RUC men are now deeply hostile to Catholics, they would *all* have wanted Stalker off the job, not just the Masons among them.

In any case, was Stalker's religion a factor? Probably yes. According to *Private Eye*, RUC men were soon calling Stalker that 'fucking Fenian'.[7] Stalker himself refers to an early encounter with Sir John Hermon, when the RUC Chief handed him a flattened-out cigarette packet with his mother's Irish Catholic ancestry sketched out on the plain side. It included distant cousins of whom Stalker had never heard. Hermon produced no similar packet showing Stalker's Protestant forebears through his father. Whatever this incident proves (and Hermon says it never happened), Hermon is probably not a Mason. The *Manchester Evening News* has described him as a '*reported* member of a Northern Ireland lodge'.[8] My reports indicate otherwise, but I cannot be sure because he refused to answer the Freemasonry questionnaire which I sent to every UK Chief Constable.

Even if we assume that anti-Catholic elements in the RUC had an interest in 'getting Stalker', what proof is there that Masons in the RUC – or anywhere else in Ulster – are anti-Catholic? An answer requires some study of Freemasonry throughout all of Ireland because, ironically, Ulster Freemasonry is governed from Dublin where the Grand Lodge of Ireland presides over all thirty-two counties. This is not repugnant to Ulster Protestants because Freemasonry in the South is also largely Protestant. Indeed, it may have been one of the means used by Protestants to retain disproportionate wealth and economic power in the Republic, thus counteracting their political losses arising from Ireland's independence in 1922.

Ireland's Grand Lodge is the second oldest in the world, founded in 1725, only eight years after its English counterpart. At first Catholics joined freely but they steadily withdrew after the Papacy declared its opposition in 1738. By the early nineteenth century, Irish Freemasonry was largely Protestant, but it had no strong political line: some members favoured continued union with England, others Home Rule. Throughout Ireland the Craft probably functioned as it did in the southern city of Cork:

The Craft in Cork seemed much more concerned with charitable works than with fostering a sectarian or evangelical stance amongst Protestants, even after the departure of the Catholics. Its influence and significance, then, lies entirely in the social sphere. The Craft allowed Freemasons to identify friends and enemies – those who should be helped and those who should not . . . the Craft acted for the middle and upper classes in the same manner as the Orange Order did for the lower.[9]

In his early life the Irish nationalist Daniel O'Connell was an active Mason. In 1800 aged twenty-five he became Master of Lodge 189 in Dublin and belonged to two other lodges, in Limerick and Tralee. He was a Catholic but the Papal ban was not promulgated in Ireland until 1799. At first O'Connell ignored it, then he quit. He later said that he had offered to make a public renunciation, but the Archbishop of Dublin 'deemed it unnecessary'. Many years later O'Connell said that Irish Freemasonry's only physically evil tendency was the consumption of too much drink. It therefore undermined the work of the temperance societies. However, he also declared:

> the great, the important spiritual objection is this – the profane taking in vain the awful name of the Deity – in the wanton and multiplied taking of oaths – of oaths administered on the Book of God either in mockery or derision, or with a solemnity which renders the taking of them, without any adequate motive, only the more criminal. This objection . . . is alone abundantly sufficient to prevent any serious Christian from belonging to that body.[10]

In the North, Freemasonry was also a middle-class social club but, as southern demands for Home Rule developed into a campaign for outright independence, the lodges became more like a high-grade Orange Order, staunchly committed to union with Britain. This was certainly how the Republican heroine, Maud Gonne, viewed the Craft early this century: 'Freemasonry as we Irish know it is a British Institution and has always been used politically to support the British Empire.'[11]

Masonic spokesmen in England and Ireland will point to the ban on the discussion of politics and religion as proof that the fraternity can play no part in sectarian politics. However, in 1952 in *Light Invisible* (subtitled, 'The Freemason's Answer to *Darkness Visible*') the pseudonymous Vindex wrote:

In Ireland as long as there is a danger of a backward, illiberal, and Popish state perpetrating the injustice of absorbing free protestant Britons who have no wish to be absorbed, there can be little doubt on which side the influence of Freemasons is to be felt.[12]

'Vindex' has never been disowned by the United Grand Lodge of England. His book remains the only officially recognized response to Walton Hannah's ritual exposé. Vindex's pride in Freemasonry's sectarian role in Ulster politics only confirms the shadowy power which it exerts over and within the Orange Order. The Loyal Orange Institution was formed in 1794 to defend Protestantism and the Irish constitutional connection with England. The prime mover in its creation was a wealthy farmer named James 'Buddra' Wilson. According to one Orange historian, Wilson was:

> a member of the Society of Freemasons which fully qualified him for establishing a new order of a secret character. He was already familiar with signs and passwords, and he was likewise conversant with the history of the Prince of Orange, who was himself a freemason. It is therefore clear that he knew the services which had been rendered by the ancient craft in keeping alive the principles of the Revolution and in preserving the name of Orange, many of the Freemason Lodges being called Orange Lodges.[13]

It is doubtful if King Billy (William of Orange) was a Mason but the myth that he was is pervasive among Ulster Masons. The Orange Order is avowedly Christian – unlike Freemasonry – but it shares the Craft's secret society structure. Its rituals, passwords, grips and signs are based on Freemasonry. Its initiation ceremony apes the first degree Craft ritual with rolled-up trouserlegs, the hoodwink and the poniard to the naked left breast. Two allied Protestant orders, the Purple and the Black, are also based on Freemasonry. The Sovereign Grand Master of the Royal Black Institution is James Molyneaux MP, leader of the Ulster Unionist Party at Westminster. In 1981 he addressed his followers in these sectarian terms: 'Apathy may be a luxury in which some races can indulge but you are a chosen people, a Royal priesthood, a dedicated nation, and a people claimed by God for himself.'[14]

I do not know if Mr Molyneaux is a Mason. In 1986 I sent him a questionnaire on Freemasonry. His secretary replied saying, Mr Molyneaux 'just does not have time to answer questionnaires'. One of his UUP colleagues at Westminster did reply. Cecil Walker (MP for Belfast North) told me he was a Mason, having joined in 1966. Revd Martin

Smyth (MP for Belfast South) also replied. As he has been Grand Master of the Grand Orange Lodge of Ireland since 1972, I greatly valued his explanation that he is not a Mason on religious grounds: 'As a Christian I come to the Father through Christ in prayer etc. Therefore I would have to give muted testimony to my Lord if I accepted Masonic ritual.'

Grand Master Smyth has no such anxieties about the Orange Order, for it professes faith in God through Jesus Christ. Revd Smyth is a Presbyterian Minister, so it is not surprising that he has qualms about Freemasonry. However, I do not think most Orangemen would share them. Indeed, the fragmentary evidence which I have presented here indicates that the Masonic brotherhood is a substantial behind-the-scenes force in Orange and Unionist politics. Of course, the Craft claims to be non-political but this may simply mean that, in Ulster since 1794, its politically-oriented members have simultaneously belonged to Freemasonry's neo-Masonic offshoots: the Orange, Purple and Black.

A similar outlet was devised in the southern USA during the 1860s. There Freemasons created the highly political, racist Ku Klux Klan. They devised its structure and rituals.[15] Its revival in 1915 was led by a new generation of Masons. It seems that wherever Masons have common political aims, but cannot pursue them through Freemasonry, they set up parallel public movements. These bring additional advantages. They attract a mass working-class following for the cause in question without diluting Freemasonry or its middle-class ethos. They also give the Craft a wider but secure recruiting base for its own 'non-political' activities. Only a minority of Orangemen would be socially acceptable in Ulster's Masonic lodges, but those that are may be discreetly approached and would probably be pleased to join.

In Northern Ireland's 1920 Constitution Freemasonry was awarded special status, as if in recognition of some concealed role in the Province's triumphant struggle to stay in the United Kingdom and out of the Irish Free State:

> It is hereby declared that existing enactments relating to unlawful oaths or unlawful assemblies do not apply to the meetings or proceedings of the Grand Lodge of Free and Accepted Masons of Ireland or of any lodge or society recognised by that Grand Lodge.[16]

Without such exemption the Craft would have been banned as an illegal organization like the IRA and the Fenians. Instead it was able to survive and flourish in Loyalist Ulster. Of Ireland's 45,000 Masons, at least 40,000 live in the six counties. Today there are just over 700 lodges in all Ireland. More than 560 of them – 80 per cent – are in Ulster, compared to just 143 in the Republic. Dublin has fifty-one lodges. Belfast has 162, and in suburbs and towns all around Belfast (such as Ballymacarrett, Mountpottinger, Rosetta, Holywood, Lisburn and Newtonards) hundreds more lodges meet.

Ulster's Masons include prominent businessmen, industrialists, landowners, politicians and clergymen – mainly in the Anglican Church of Ireland. There are lodges for lawyers (like the Good Counsel Lodge No. 553) and for prison officers in the Maze and Crumlin Road jails. A lot of Ulster journalists are also 'on the square', as the respected reporter Liam Clarke discovered in January 1984 when he was working for the Belfast *Sunday News*.

The newspaper's editor had agreed that Clarke could use the publication of *The Brotherhood* as the news 'peg' for an article on Freemasonry in general and in Ulster in particular. The editor was on holiday when Clarke finished the piece, which was now subjected to hold-ups and changes by other *Sunday News* staff. Clarke bowed to their advice by inserting a few remarks about Masonic charity. Then he discovered that the newspaper group's chairman, Captain Bill Henderson of Century Newspapers, was a prominent Mason and was personally vetting Clarke's article. He made several valid corrections but also struck out sentences which Clarke felt should stay in.

To sort the matter out, Clarke was told to speak to Henderson on the phone. The Captain immediately stated that he was a Mason, but then he said: 'You know there are 70,000 of those characters out there and there is no need to offend them needlessly. I am thinking of the company. That is the concern I must keep uppermost.' I asked Captain Henderson if Liam Clarke's recollection on this point was correct. The Captain told me:

> How right he is and how right I am . . . It is a fact that there are something like 70,000 Masons in our circulation area. I'm not going to stick a squib up their tail, am I, and send them up? Am I going to send up my market? . . . It doesn't matter whether you're selling ball-bearings, French letters or margarine or newspapers, you don't offend your customers. And anybody else who's dealing with his customers doesn't do anything to offend them, if he can avoid it, just to satisfy the whims of some little punk journalist.

Clarke says that Henderson congratulated him on the piece, but then suggested that the password Boaz should not be disclosed because 'it is like a thing between a man and his wife, you don't want to go publishing it'. He also said that there was nothing in Freemasonry which he felt conflicted with his own Christian sensibilities.

Clarke told Henderson, 'You're the boss' and thanked him for his time, yet after he put the phone down, he reflected how odd it was 'that the chairman of a publishing company should concern himself in an item of editorial detail, giving as his reason his fear of the influence of a secret society of which he said he was himself a member'.

Despite having agreed a text with 'the boss', Clarke found that at 8 P.M. on Saturday night his article was dropped from the Sunday paper. He was told this decision had been made on the basis of 'news values', but he could not help wondering if Masons lower down the pecking-order had decided the better part of valour was discretion.

Captain Henderson told me:

I was paying Liam Clarke to work for us. If I decided that I don't want his little offerings in our papers, right, that's my privilege. Bang! Finish story . . . The facts were not accurate. I'm not going to publish a lot of garbage about people who happen to be our customers. I would not publish articles on Freemasonry which I believed were to be send-ups of the institution and unfairly critical. Fair criticism yes, unfair criticism no.

Whatever the brethren's strength in Ulster press, business and political circles, it is even greater in the RUC. The first public hint of this came in an article in the Belfast magazine *Fortnight*, based largely on Liam Clarke's previously suppressed researches.[17] When it appeared in April 1984 Clarke was warned not to write any more about Freemasonry or he would be sacked. Not long after he quit the *Sunday News* of his own accord.

Fortnight had pointed out that in Ulster, public proof that an RUC man is a Mason may emerge only on his death, when his lodge publishes a sympathy notice in the local newspaper. Such notices in the early 1980s revealed that several deceased superintendents had been Masons. This macabre yardstick alone indicates that a large proportion of the RUC hierarchy is 'on the square'. *Fortnight* also reported that in March 1984 twenty-two RUC men from all parts of the province set up a new police lodge, named the Harp and Shamrock after the emblems displayed on the RUC coat of arms. This caused consternation among the few Catholics in the RUC who were worried about increasing Masonic membership among their Protestant colleagues and the sectarian implications.

Fortnight revealed that among the Masons at the top of the RUC is the head of its Special Branch: Assistant Chief Constable Trevor Forbes. An old boy of Dublin's Royal Masonic School, Forbes is the third Mason in recent times to head SB. Alongside Sir John Hermon, Forbes was

Stalker's sternest adversary during the Manchester man's battles to obtain the Hayshed tape material and sensitive intelligence files. I have since been informed by RUC sources that Forbes's father was murdered by the IRA in 1944.

Not every Protestant in the RUC is a Mason, as is proved by one personal tragedy which occurred during the years when John Stalker came to grief. Detective Constable Robert Patterson had been working for the RUC Fraud Squad until 1984 when he went on sick leave. He was a troubled man. He drank heavily, was violent at home and eventually agreed to undergo psychoanalysis. Although off sick, he continued to pursue police investigations from which he had been officially removed. This upset his Fraud Squad chiefs, on whose apparent behalf a detective showed up at Patterson's home and removed his police gun and a case of private papers.

Patterson now felt he was in the pincers of a Masonic conspiracy combining from two directions: several senior Fraud Squad officers were Masons; and Freemasonry had cropped up in several frauds which he had been investigating until he went sick. The frauds implicated British Army caterers, several Masons employed by the Property Services Agency, and some solicitors handling an inheritance of valuable land which mysteriously ended up in the hands of a property developer. Patterson was convinced that Masonic bonds were preventing proper investigation of all these cases, but his views were easily dismissed because of his unstable state of mind. In the words of his psychiatrist, his life had been 'completely taken over and destroyed by events at his work'.

On 28 July 1986, Patterson wrote to Chief Constable Sir John Hermon. It was a long, confused tirade against senior officers. He referred to 'serious cases of corruption with the Fraud Squad in relation to the cover-up of fraud by Freemasons'. He said he was willing to make a statement about these cases to any senior officer who was not a Mason. He closed with these remarks:

> I have been intimidated out of my career with the blunderings and negligence of my superiors, my marriage and family relationship has been destroyed . . . If I am denied an opportunity to make a full statement of complaint and denied an interview with HM Inspector of Constabulary then as a final protest I shall take my own life.

Two days later Robert Patterson was dead. His body was found on the foreshore of Belfast Lough. His legs had been bound with nylon rope, his hands tied with a pair of tights, and he had a shotgun wound to his head. The Belfast Coroner said the bonds were loosely tied and would not have greatly restrained him. The verdict was suicide.

Some of Patterson's friends were not so sure. Certainly, he had threatened to kill himself in his letter, but that was only two days earlier, and even Patterson would have known this was too short a time in which to expect a reply from his Chief Constable. Also, if he really did have evidence of any corruption among his colleagues, he might have been murdered. There was, after all, one huge problem about the 'suicide'. Patterson had a shotgun wound to his head, but the shotgun was never found: a very odd suicide indeed. One superintendent admitted that the missing weapon left 'a gap in the investigation'. The RUC searched the foreshore but failed to find it, and the tide was not strong enough at that point to have washed it away.

Doubts over the 'suicide' remain, not least because of the place where Patterson was found dead. It recalled the grotesque first degree oath sworn by all Masonic initiates until 1986. Any Mason who betrays any of the brotherhood's secrets can look forward to having his 'tongue torn out by the root, and buried in the sand of the sea at low water mark, or a cable's length from the sea, where the tide regularly ebbs and flows twice in twenty-four hours'. As one Ulsterman observed: 'If that's what they do to each other, My God! What do they do to their enemies?'

In April 1988 a former RUC officer wrote to the *Guardian* about his own encounters with the Craft.[18] He called for the enforced resignation of all Masons in Britain's police forces, 'especially in Northern Ireland where the police are thought not to be impartial because of their association with lodges'. He referred to 'colossal numbers of RUC men' in Freemasonry and all its Protestant offshoots. During his service he claimed to have noticed that Masons 'wielded enormous power in promotion selection and in all appointments to specialist branches'.

> In Northern Ireland the problem of freemasonry is about more than the benefits and privileges of masonic membership. It has much to do with the credibility and acceptability of the police in a deeply divided society. The problems of policing in the Province are exacerbated by the fact that so many RUC officers are members of lodges.

When this man's letter was published his name was withheld, but I have since spoken to him at length. He is a Catholic, which may prejudice him against Freemasonry. Yet even allowing for bias, I think his talk of the brotherhood's 'omnipotence' in the RUC rings true. He says Catholics have no hope of joining Special Branch because of 'blatant discrimination'. He also believes there is a special RUC Masonic grouping which co-ordinates this discrimination. If this is untrue, no

doubt RUC men who read this book will write to correct me. I may even
be sent a breakdown of SB strength, proving that at least a quarter of its
personnel are Catholic. Until that happens, however, I shall feel 'name
withheld' is speaking the truth.

It may now be clear that Freemasonry in Ulster is not only anti-
Catholic; it also dominates the RUC. Yet the 'MASON MAFIA FRAMED COP
CHIEF' theory demands more evidence to be convincing. For instance, it
requires some proof that RUC Masons could expect a sympathetic
hearing for any 'get Stalker' pleas they may have made to brethren across
the Irish Sea. If the Craft did lend itself to anti-Catholic ends, then police
Masons in Manchester must be almost as anti-Catholic as their Belfast
brethren. Is this so?

Today there are three forces in the old Lancashire area: Greater
Manchester, Merseyside and Lancashire itself. Until the late 1960s there
were seventeen smaller forces in the county. According to letters sent by
retired police officers to both Stephen Knight and myself, these forces'
most striking common feature was a ferocious anti-Catholicism.

One of these correspondents is himself an ardent Mason. Now in his
eighty-third year, he received me in his country cottage and confirmed all
he had said in his letters.

> I joined the Liverpool Police in 1928 as a boy of twenty-one. You
> will know well the absurd animosity occurring between Catholic
> and Protestant in that city, which of course stemmed from complete
> bigotry on each side. As I had been brought up in a village in the
> south-west of England, I was completely ignorant of this state of
> affairs. I was reared as a Protestant but, after a year in Liverpool, I
> met a young woman who was a Roman Catholic. Her faith made no
> difference to me. We married and had a son.
>
> As the years went by, I took my promotion exam and passed quite
> well, but I slowly began to realize that there existed an undercover
> movement which went very much in favour of the Freemasons and
> against the Catholic officer. It was not until some years had gone by,
> when I had been overlooked for promotion, that a retired Inspector
> told me an undercover order had been issued that I was not to receive
> any duties even as an Acting Sergeant. An extreme Protestant had
> seen my marriage certificate (which we all had to bring in for
> pension purposes) and spotted I had married a Catholic. It might not
> have mattered so much if I had been born into Catholicism, but the
> Orangeman thought I had *embraced* it. In fact I never embraced it,
> although I had no objections to attending a Catholic service with my
> family. So I was ruined for nothing.

I received eight commendations and rewards during my fourteen years in Liverpool, but I was never promoted. Instead, I sought a transfer back to the police force of my native county where I served for a further eleven years. I felt a lot happier here even though I missed the big city duties I had performed in Liverpool. Now, at last, I began to detest Freemasonry because of its injustice both in the promotion field and even worse against Catholic policemen.

When I returned here, however, I discovered my blood brother had gone into Freemasonry and wished me to do the same. I told him, from what I had seen in Liverpool, in no way was I going to ally myself with it in my police career. Later, when I retired, I did become a freemason and in time occupied the Worshipful Master's chair. I was then exalted into the Royal Arch, advancing to the Mark, Knights Templar, and Ark Mariners degrees. I have been very happy in Freemasonry and dearly love the movement.

Nevertheless, I could name many good men in Liverpool who were robbed of promotion by this stupidity, much to the shame of freemasonry. Many a competent man was ruined by the accident of his religious birth. The police lodge was then the St Johns Lodge, number 673, so when we knew someone belonged to it we could be sure he was going to be promoted. At that time Liverpool's chief constables pretty well *had* to be Masons. This wickedness went all the way up.

I was puzzled by this Mason's schizophrenia towards the Craft. As we parted he assured me that, despite everything, 'Freemasonry is one of the finest things in the world if handled properly.' Even so, be begged for anonymity, as he feared some Masonic vengeance for speaking so frankly to one of the profane.

No such cover was requested by a Catholic police officer, Louis Wooldridge, whose clashes with Freemasonry began after he had risked his life with the RAF throughout the Second World War: first as a ground staff mechanic in Singapore and Southern Africa, then through four years in Bomber Command as a rear aerial gunner. In 1944 he was awarded the DFC. In 1946 he joined the Stalybridge Borough Police Force, in what is now Greater Manchester. 'During my early service one of my colleagues expressed surprise that I had joined the police because, he said, "unless you are a Mason you have no chance of rising to sergeant and above, and none at all if you are an RC".'

This was Wooldridge's first taste of discrimination in the police. He soon left Stalybridge to join the British Transport Police and then the Fife Constabulary in Scotland, with which he served until 1976. His experience of anti-Catholic Freemasonry in those forces only reinforced his experiences in Stalybridge. After thirty years' conflict with the Craft he says:

> Until its influence is removed, especially over promotions, the police service will never achieve its true potential, due to good officers being denied promotion because they are Roman Catholics or simply because they are not members of the Masonic fraternity.

Greater Manchester Police has long since swallowed the Stalybridge force, but in doing so it may have perpetuated this anti-Catholic Freemasonry. If so, in 1986 any Masons in the GMP would probably sympathize with the desire of their brother Masons in the RUC to sink Stalker. Of course, these Catholic or pro-Catholic officers may be crying 'Mason!' merely because they were never promoted. However, we must also consider the testimony of a Protestant policeman who rose quite high in another Lancashire force. He confirms that Masons have long exercised a pernicious power over the region's police forces, way out of proportion to their numbers.

Stanley Holt joined Bolton Borough Police in 1947. He made fast progress and received two commendations for bravery. He was posted to the headquarters patrol, then to the operations room. After thirteen years' service – a short time in those days – Holt was promoted to sergeant. He came top in the inspector's qualifying examination, but when the right vacancy arose it went to another man who was a known Mason.

> I naturally felt annoyed as this man had several years' less service and had done nothing to warrant promotion except, as another officer commented, 'getting himself into debt to pay his way into freemasonry'.
>
> Some days later I had occasion to meet the new inspector in the canteen. I remarked to him that he had done extremely well to get promoted and that his sacrifices to get into freemasonry had been worthwhile. He had the courtesy to blush and say nothing. Not long afterwards my new boss, a detective superintendent, said to me, 'You have the wrong attitude in the police force and you will never be promoted to higher rank.' I had been told that this officer was also a freemason.
>
> From this time on I received open hostility from the higher ranks, including the new assistant chief constable. I served the next thirteen years in charge of CID administration, rejected at all promotion

boards. At my last promotion board the chairman said, 'I cannot understand why, with your excellent assessments and record, you have never been promoted to inspector. Can you tell me why?'

I had to reply, 'I do not know why.' If I had said, 'It is because I have spoken out against freemasonry in the police force,' I may have scuppered the last chance of promotion. As it was, I did not get promotion anyway.

By 1974 Bolton had merged first with Lancashire Constabulary then with Greater Manchester, yet Holt remained a detective sergeant. He retired after twenty-eight years' service, sorry to leave but desperate to get away from endless slights which, he felt, were inflicted because he had never kowtowed to the Craft. Assuring me he was not writing out of 'sour grapes', Holt lamented:

It was amazing from being a very popular member of the force how, with a few remarks about freemasonry, you are suddenly a leper. Even for a non-masonic officer to be friendly with me would have been akin to showing me support, though one inspector and a retired superintendent did tell me the way I was treated was a disgrace.

Freemasonry gives the police a bad name. Proportionally there are as many scoundrels in the force as out of it, and not all are freemasons. The trouble is that a freemason policeman cannot carry out his job without fear or favour because of the oaths he has taken in the satanic rites to help a brother when he transgresses.

Even where I am living now in Scotland, local folk complain they have seen a policeman helping a drunken freemason into his car after a lodge meeting. Had he not been a freemason, the policeman would have locked him up before he could spit.

None of these men's anecdotes is supported by evidence. Taken together, however, they chart a consistent pattern of conduct by a fraternity perversely strong among south Lancashire policemen for at least sixty years. I should add that none of the quoted officers knows each other. Each wrote independently to Stephen Knight or myself. By now their testimony might be dismissed as out-of-date, so we still have to assess Freemasonry's strength in Stalker's own force in the mid-1980s.

On 25 July 1986 the *Manchester Evening News* published the only major press attempt to pinpoint Freemasonry's role in the Stalker Affair. In 'The Masonic Connection' reporter James Cusick claimed that almost everyone whom Stalker had come up against was a Mason: RUC Chief

Constable Hermon, senior officers in the Manchester force, Home Office Inspectors of Constabulary, and the clerk and chairman of Manchester's Police Authority. Yet even in this double-page feature, real evidence of these men's Masonic affiliations was hard to find. Readers had to trust unidentified sources. All the named individuals were either '*reported*' Masons or '*regarded*' as such. Only one man's lodge was identified, but even this detail was denied at a singular occasion held within Manchester's Masonic Temple twelve days after the article appeared.

At a conference attended by 100 press and television reporters, East Lancashire's Provincial Grand Secretary, Colin Gregory, announced that there was no 'Masonic connection' in the Stalker affair. The *Evening News* had branded several local lodges as 'police lodges', but Gregory said each had only one or two police members and they were of low rank. 'I do not know of any senior police officers who are Masons in the Greater Manchester area.' None of the city's 129 lodges was a police lodge. As for the Manchester Ulster Lodge (a title which was mesmerizing several conspiracy theorists) it had thirty members, only one of whom was a copper. Gregory explained how the lodge had been formed by expatriate Ulstermen in 1956, but today only four or five members even had Irish names. He did not know if any were Catholics but he proudly claimed many Catholics belonged to East Lancs's 395 lodges. He seemed a little less proud when a reporter told him that Kevin Taylor, Stalker's controversial friend, was both a Catholic and a Mason (Taylor himself told me he used to belong to a Cheshire lodge before allowing his membership to lapse).

A moustached and bespectacled man in his sixties, Mr Gregory said he had spent his working life as a retailer, but his thirty years as a Mason had never brought him commercial benefit. He handled the press well but failed to satisfy reporters who wanted a figure for the number of Masons in the Greater Manchester Police. He also refused to say if any GMP officers who had crossed swords with Stalker, and whom the *News* had named as Masons, were indeed in the Craft. After all, they need not belong to a Manchester lodge. They could just as well have been members in north Cheshire or West Lancs. Gregory claimed the Data Protection Act prohibited him from divulging names. The ungrateful hacks groaned and trooped out of the Temple, while Manchester's Masons muttered oaths not to let them in again for another fifty-seven years.

The *Evening News*'s most astonishing claim had been that Police Authority Chairman Norman Briggs was a Mason of Grand Rank. This fuelled speculation that the Masons had indeed 'got' Stalker. Some readers might even have thought Briggs had *led* the conspiracy for, back

in May 1986, his agreement would have been decisive in packing the
Deputy Chief Constable off on extended leave. Was this startling new
'fact' the missing piece in the Masonic jigsaw?

Alas, no! It was the wrong Norman Briggs. The Grand Officer in
question was not Norman Briggs of the Police Authority but a Norman
D. Briggs, JP, who lived twenty miles north of Manchester, near
Blackburn. According to Provincial Grand Secretary Gregory, plain
Norman Briggs had never belonged to any East Lancs lodge.

The real Briggs had little time to issue a denial. Within days he was
dead of a heart attack. His family says it was brought on by the Freemason
tale, which literally mortified him because he was not a Mason. He was a
prominent Labour politician, and most party colleagues would have
thought less of him if they had believed he was 'on the square'. What
probably killed him, however, was the cumulative strain of 'Stalker' over
three months, not just the last 'Masonic' thrust.

For its part, the News admits it identified the wrong Norman Briggs,
but still claims the right one was a Mason. Who knows? Until Masonic
membership is a matter of public record, Mason-spotting will remain a
fallible art. Not good enough, the Freemasons' Colin Gregory told the
scribblers, 'Comment is free, but facts are sacred', quoting a legendary
editor of the Manchester Guardian. Yet if the Guardian's sister paper had
got as many facts wrong as Gregory claimed, the blame lay partly with
Manchester's Masons for failing even now to divulge the only facts
anyone wanted to know: which top Manchester cops were Masons of any
description? Gregory's fog of unknowing reinforced suspicions that
Masonic 'civil servants' have a rosy illusion about what goes on between
Masons outside the lodge. Whatever its principles, Freemasonry is open
to exploitation by many different groups, all bent on their own ends.
There is nothing in the Constitutions which says the Craft supports one
Manchester Police faction over another, or Protestant ascendancy in
Ulster, or the RUC's right to cover up the killing of unarmed suspects.
Yet groups within Freemasonry might hijack the Craft in support of all or
any of these ends.

Throughout the Stalker Affair loomed one significant figure whom
even the Evening News did not brand a Mason: Manchester's Chief
Constable, James Anderton. A combustible blend of Methodist lay-
preacher and Catholic convert, he long ago declared he is no Mason: 'I
never have been, and I never will be.' He even distributed Sir Kenneth
Newman's anti-Masonic Principles of Policing among his own force.

Responding to the questionnaire which I sent to every Chief
Constable, Mr Anderton kindly agreed to discuss Freemasonry with me
in his Manchester headquarters. I wrestle now with the difficulty of

reconciling the affable, witty and caring man whom I met with the cold, aloof and treacherous figure who emerges from John Stalker's book. I was not able to question Anderton on that book because it was not published until after our meeting. One of the tragedies of the 'Affair' is that these two able men could not (or did not) trust each other. They should have been on the same side. In our conversation Anderton confirmed he was not a Mason. Here I greatly compress his remarks.

> In my working-class Lancashire background, Freemasonry was a mystery. We wondered, 'What did it mean?' We regarded it as a kind of plague, and Freemasons as people who were not to be contacted or befriended.
> I do not like the secrecy surrounding Freemasonry, but I do not know if Masons are *unnecessarily* secret. If they are to be criticized for their sense of kinship and mutual aid, that criticism could just as well apply to Methodists and Catholics. However, Freemasonry seems to be neither fish nor fowl. If it is a serious business it may have aspects which are unacceptable, especially for a police officer. On the other hand, is it a joke? If so, what sort of a man are you to indulge in such practices, when you are meant to be a responsible person?

Anderton's doubts about Freemasonry do not drive him to conclude that it has exercised a bad influence over his force.

> I do not believe Freemasonry plays a role, or ever has played a role in the conduct of the Greater Manchester Police. I know some members of my force are Freemasons. I ask no questions. Some have volunteered to tell me privately that they are Masons, in order to assure me of their loyalty and integrity. Freemasonry has had nothing to do with force promotion, including the final promotion to superintendent rank. I have appointed many officers who are not Masons, so there are two sides to every coin.

As for John Stalker's troubles, James Anderton gave me this assurance: 'Freemasonry played no part in the Stalker Affair. It was uninfluenced by Freemasonry in any way.' Stalker himself takes a less benign view of the brethren's activities, yet even he told me that he had no firm evidence of Masonic influence at work during his difficulties.

> I have always expressed personal reservations and unease about Masonic connections in the Force and I have occasionally suspected

that some police officers benefited unfairly from their Masonic membership, but I cannot say so with certainty. I have been a policeman all my working life dealing in facts. Despite all that has happened I cannot change now.

Since neither Stalker nor Anderton, nor indeed Manchester's Masons, had any hard information about Freemasonry's strength in the GMP, I asked Mike Unger, editor of the *Manchester Evening News*, if he would publish a letter from me appealing for information on Freemasonry and/or 'Stalker'. He kindly obliged. Most of the replies were strong on opinion and weak on fact, but one 'dedicated' if 'regretfully anonymous' twenty-seven-year veteran of the Manchester force claimed that its amalgamation in 1974 with several other forces had allowed 'brothers' from Lancashire and Cheshire to reinforce the Masonic 'Mafia'. He named a recently retired high-ranking officer (not Stalker) whose 'evil influence' has caused the rift in the force today. 'The people he promoted are in power today. No wonder it was easy for them to get rid of John Stalker if he crossed their path.' The writer went on:

I know James Anderton has declared that he is not a Mason and he has stated that being a police officer and a Mason is incompatible. But what does he do about it? I hear that privately he has said two-thirds of his senior officers are masons and he would have great difficulty in enforcing a ban. So much for the crusader who has a hot line to the Almighty!

I contacted a recently retired Manchester officer, Det. Insp. John Park, whose views on Freemasonry had been quoted in the local press. In 1983 Park had won personal commendation from his chief constable for cracking a major crime ring, yet within a month he was suspended while his alleged underworld relationships were investigated – just like Stalker. After eighteen months the Director of Public Prosecutions decided to take no action, but Park's chiefs refused to reinstate him. He retired a few days later on an ill-health pension, but promptly demanded an independent inquiry into his case. He stipulated that no Masons should be on the team.

I wished to pursue a large number of complaints about police officers whom I believed to be Freemasons, so I endeavoured to ensure that the officers undertaking the inquiry were not from the 'Craft'. It took me five months to achieve this, although it was never confirmed by the police service. You may consider it unusual for an ex-detective inspector to go to such lengths, but even without 'hard-core' evidence, I am quite satisfied that within the police service there is one law for those who are members and another law for persons like myself who have no hesitation in voicing their opposition to the movement.

After plumbing so many possible sources of information, are we any nearer knowing which top Manchester cops in 'Stalker' are indeed Masons? The *Evening News* claimed that the GMP's current head of CID, Det. Chief Supt. Peter Topping, is a Mason. He never denied this but, even so, I wrote to him to ask if he is 'on the square'. He did not reply, which tempts me to conclude that he is. However, I sent my letter not long before he resumed his search for the remains of two child victims of the Moors Murderers twenty year earlier, so he was probably too busy to reply.

Topping had cropped up at many stages of 'Stalker'. Indeed, it was over Topping's astonishing search for those remains that Stalker finally felt driven to resign in mid-December 1986. Neither Anderton nor Topping had consulted him or given him advance warning. This became all the more bizarre when Stalker found himself in charge of the entire force as Anderton suddenly took an *incommunicado* three-day trip to London just before the search began. He was completely in the dark about 400 of his officers being bogged down on Saddleworth Moor, until newspapers and television companies called him up to find out what was going on. The entire probe seemed a massive public relations exercise to lift the force's image after six months' stinking press over 'Stalker'. Stalker himself found it odd that, whereas he had worked on the original Moors Murders probe, Topping had never before worked on any murder.

He had known of Stalker's friendship with the businessman Kevin Taylor for *two years* before Stalker was suspended. Nasty rumours had first surfaced only sixteen days after Stalker began his RUC inquiry in 1984.[19] Early that June a senior detective was golfing with a stranger who let drop that Stalker went to parties at Taylor's house which were also attended by criminals. The detective reported this to Topping, who was then chief of the complaints and discipline department. Topping told him to 'put it on paper', because (unknown to the golfing detective) he was already running an inquiry into underworld rumours of a corrupt relationship between Stalker and Taylor.

These seemed to take on 'flesh' about February 1985 when a professional informer, David Burton (or Bertelstein), told damaging stories about Taylor and Stalker. These later turned out to be lies. As

Burton was in jail at the time, he was probably looking for favours and anxious to please anyone in authority. If we assume that no one had suggested these fabrications to Burton (or otherwise induced him to tell tales discrediting Stalker), it would have been wholly legitimate, indeed obligatory, for the Greater Manchester Police to investigate them with vigour. At the same time, however, it would have been apparent to any detective on this job that if Taylor were to be jailed – for fraud, drugs, *anything* – Stalker would be destroyed with him.

About this time, Manchester's Drugs Intelligence Unit was told to collect information on Kevin Taylor and to send it to the head of CID Operations. This job was now filled by Peter Topping. If necessary, Topping was empowered to pass the information direct to Chief Constable Anderton without John Stalker seeing it. By now the phantom dirt was piling up so fast on Taylor that Anderton felt obliged to pass the parallel allegations against Stalker to the Home Office's regional Inspector of Constabulary, Sir Philip Myers. Sir Philip was also responsible for Stalker's role on the Ulster 'shoot-to-kill' probe. Even so, Stalker was not warned about his relationship with Taylor, or told that Taylor was being investigated, or forced to quit the RUC inquiry.

Another year went by but, despite intensive investigations, Kevin Taylor was not found to have committed any crime. Nor had any new 'mud' heaped up on Stalker who blithely attended another party at Taylor's house. When Taylor discovered Manchester CID poking into his bank accounts, he told Stalker. This was the first Stalker knew of the investigation. He promptly told Anderton he would steer clear of Taylor. Ironically, Taylor was now seeing more of Anderton than Stalker. The businessman was prominent in Manchester's social and political circles, and often ran into the Chief Constable at official functions.

Peter Topping's pursuit of Taylor was probably motivated by genuine alarm at tales of a top cop's corrupt links with an associate of minuscule criminals. It was not his fault that later the tales turned out to be bogus. When he heard about an expenses-paid holiday in Florida, he might have suspected Stalker was a north-country Ken Drury, the Masonic Commander of London's Flying Squad in the mid-1970s who holidayed abroad at the expense of pornographer Jimmy Humphreys.[20] Such a comparison would have been nonsense, of course. Drury *was* corrupt and jailed for eight years. Stalker was clean. Humphreys had a long criminal record. Taylor had no record at all. As for the Florida holiday, Stalker had paid his own way but no one in the Greater Manchester Police knew that because no one had asked Stalker.

In 'Stalker', chronology is all-important. Manchester CID turned its full investigative heat on Taylor–Stalker only after Stalker had delivered his interim report to RUC Chief, Sir John Hermon. The process leading to Stalker's suspension was activated only when Stalker had finally manoeuvred Hermon into handing over the surviving Hayshed material. Stalker was granted complete access to this crucial evidence in March 1986. He did not get his hands on any of it until 30 April. Even then the crucial papers eluded him because on 29 May, shortly before he was to fly to Belfast to get them, he was 'removed forever' from the inquiry.

By this time Manchester CID had discovered that in 1981 Taylor had used his American Express card to buy air tickets to Miami for Stalker and himself. On 7 May 1986 Taylor's home was raided and the 'Stalker' birthday party photos were seized. On 15 May Topping was told of a new golf-course conversation linking Taylor and Stalker. He promptly wrote a note which left Chief Constable Anderton with no choice but to call in Home Office Inspector Sir Philip Myers. He in turn interpreted the 'new' information as giving him no choice but to remove Stalker from the RUC inquiry. A few days later Stalker was indeed removed. Yet even at that late stage nobody had checked out David Burton's original tales. Manchester CID men had visited him four times in jail, but no one had bothered to verify anything he had said. His lies were allowed to stand unchallenged. By the time Colin Sampson took a look at them, Burton had died behind bars.

Unknown to Stalker, Burton's allegations had surfaced in February 1985, very soon after Stalker had first roused RUC Special Branch over the Hayshed tape. The most significant and best-concealed fact about Burton is that he was an informer to the RUC, and was himself tied in with terrorist-backed crime in Ulster. The suspicion therefore arises that RUC elements, who felt threatened by Stalker, may have suggested the kind of lies which Burton later told Manchester CID investigators. (The other agency who might have stoked Burton up is MI5. The Hayshed bug was planted by MI5, and Burton may have been one of its paid informers.)[21]

Ulster's Mason-dominated Special Branch certainly has the guile to use a man like Burton in this way. It did far worse during the three 'shoot-to-kill' incidents and the subsequent trials. It would also have had the motive to exploit Burton against Stalker, who made clear very early on that he condemned its goals and methods. In his September 1985 interim report (which Hermon finally passed to Ulster's Director of Public Prosecutions in February 1986) he made these savage observations:

SB has too much power. Senior SB officers feel that its covert operations should not be questioned.

SB should cease to invoke the Official Secrets Act in a way which
prevents officers from telling the truth.
SB operates as a force within a force. It should be opened up so that it
is no longer a self-perpetuating elite.
Following an 'incident' [a killing or shoot-out] officers should not be
debriefed by SB before they are interviewed by the CID.

Stalker concluded that he had found no evidence of a 'shoot-to-kill'
policy. How could he? He was still deliberately deprived of the only
possible evidence to the contrary: the Hayshed tape or its transcript. The
only other proof of 'shoot-to-kill' would have been the posthumous
testimony of the men who died because of it. There was little chance that
the officers who fired the bullets would confess to murder, and their
bosses would certainly not have committed any 'revenge killing' or
'lethal response' policy to paper.

Through March and April 1986 Stalker had stepped up his pressure to
get the Hayshed tape material. Ironically, at one point, he threatened to
quit unless he got it. The RUC Special Branch boss Trevor Forbes may
have felt he was fighting a last-ditch stand. In Manchester, CID boss
Topping thought he was closing in.

According to the Evening News, one of Stalker's team in Belfast was a
Mason: Supt. John Simons. In 1985 he became head of the Manchester
Fraud Squad while staying on the 'shoot-to-kill' team. In December 1985
Stalker asked him why his squad was investigating Taylor. Simons said he
could not help but suggested he speak to Topping who was in overall
charge. About this time Taylor contacted Simons to say he was ready for
interview and to supply all financial papers. Simons rejected the offer. The
Evening News has claimed that not only is Simons a Mason; he is in the same
lodge as Topping. Indeed they are brothers-in-law. When I spoke to Simons
about the Evening News article, he would not talk about Freemasonry.
Instead he referred me to legal action being taken against the newspaper. It
emerged that the Evening News would be apologizing for any imputation of
a conspiracy – Masonic or otherwise – involving Simons and Topping.
Their membership of Freemasonry is not in dispute.

Another possible Mason in this Byzantine maze is Sir Philip Myers, the
Home Office Inspector who played a crucial role in Stalker's RUC
appointment and his sacking. Myers is 'widely regarded as a Mason', said
the Evening News. His predecessor, James Page, and several other recent
Home Office Inspectors were definitely 'on the square'.[22] In August 1986
Myers ducked the issue when confronted at a routine meeting of
Manchester's Police Authority. Labour councillor Ken Strath asked him
about Freemasonry and was shocked by his response:

He just rubbished my questions. I started off by asking him whether he was a mason, then I asked him whether, if there was a masonic link between the police in Ireland and the local force, he would investigate it. He told me he had been asked whether he was a mason some time ago in a questionnaire, and his response was to put it in a rubbish bin. He said he would do the same to my question.[23]

Strath later accused Myers of being 'extremely rude, when you consider the responsible position that he holds. These are questions that need to be answered.' The questionnaire which Myers had put in the rubbish bin had come from Stephen Knight.

Throughout 'Stalker', Masons in key positions took key decisions. In Manchester, Belfast and the Home Office they were deeply involved in Stalker's fall. Three months later the same men did nothing to resurrect him. None of this proves they 'conspired' against him. There is no evidence that they did. By the same yardstick, however, there was never any evidence that Stalker was crooked, yet for two years empty allegations against him were allowed to lie uninvestigated, strengthened only by repetition, until the moment when he was making such an intolerable nuisance of himself in Belfast.

Might the 'dirt' on Stalker have been kept back as an insurance policy? If Stalker were to have written a tame, 'responsible' report, stating there was nothing much wrong with Ulster's SB or with the way policemen had handled themselves during the three fatal shoot-outs, the 'dirt' could then have been swept under the carpet. However, if he were to write a critical report, or display some other excess of zeal, he could always be sacked for consorting with Kevin Taylor.

The 'evidence' against Stalker was hardly any stronger in June 1986 (when he was suspended) than in March 1985 (when Burton's tales had emerged and Anderton had first notified Sir Philip Myers and the Home Office). It would have been as 'right' to pull Stalker off the RUC inquiry at the first date as it was fifteen months later. A neat opportunity arose in April 1985 when Stalker threatened to quit over the Hayshed tape. If he really was dirty, why not let him resign? That way his departure could have been portrayed as a disagreement over principle rather than a sordid matter of a top cop's venality. However, this would have left Stalker without a stain on his character. As such, he would represent a continuing threat to the power bases whom he had already criticized. The press could paint him as a good guy fighting an RUC cover-up, rather than a bent cop keeping bad company. If Stalker was not prepared to give the RUC a clean bill of health, his reputation and career would have to be destroyed.

This may be too Machiavellian a view of the world. Perhaps all concerned (including the Masons) thought Stalker's troubles, as well as his trouble-making, would get sorted out in time. What happened thereafter may have been coincidence or cock-up, not conspiracy. In any case, who needs to write Masons into this plot? The other clans involved – cops, spivs, spooks, snoops, snouts and snipers – are all chronic conspirators.

Stalker makes no claims about a Masonic conspiracy in his book, but he does relate a remarkable conversation.[24] After his reinstatement the Deputy Chief Constable asked Peter Topping about press reports that the Drugs and Fraud Squads had 'come to be members of Masonic lodges' since Topping had taken over as operational head of Manchester CID in 1984.

> He said, 'They are there on ability. I emphatically deny any wrongful influences [. . .] I would welcome any scrutiny of their activities. I choose people on their ability – nothing else – and I resent any inference that I do not.' I asked whether he would always exercise a preference for a fellow-Mason, all other things being equal. Topping replied, 'Yes, I would, and I do: and I see nothing wrong with that. In sensitive departments I need to know I can trust my officers. The ones I have chosen are all there on personal merit. I *know* without doubt I can trust them; others I only think I can trust.'

When Stalker taxed Topping about his lack of CID experience, especially of murder inquiries, Topping, who had spent the first twenty-five years of his career in uniform, said that he could have conducted a murder case if he had wanted to. 'Anyway I have been too busy with the Taylor inquiry to take on that sort of a job.'

If Stalker's recollection is correct, here Topping was almost boasting of having put brother Masons on the two squads which had targeted Kevin Taylor. Topping was properly investigating the 'Taylor' allegations and did not let Freemasonry influence his decision-making about targets. After all, Taylor was himself a Mason. The unfortunate consequence, however, of the presence of so many brethren at key stages of the Stalker affair is that obsessional anti-Masons might believe their worst fantasy had come true, even though it would still be unwarranted and un-justifiable.

In January 1988 British Attorney-General Sir Patrick Mayhew announced that, in the light of the Stalker–Sampson inquiry, Ulster's Director of Public Prosecutions had found there was evidence that RUC officers had perverted, or attempted or conspired to pervert, the course of justice during inquiries into the fatal shootings of six men in 1982.

However, having considered the 'public interest', said Mayhew, the DPP 'has concluded, with my full agreement, that it would not be proper to institute any criminal proceedings'.

This verbiage being interpreted, it seems to mean there *was* a shoot-to-kill policy; that, having applied it, some RUC men tried to cover up the consequent murders; and that the British government (in Conor Cruise O'Brien's words) 'approves and maintains the cover-up'.[25] Mayhew's statement caused uproar in the House of Commons, threatened the shaky Anglo-Irish Agreement, and outraged American politicians with an interest in Irish affairs. It also showed how, when the state requires and whatever the evidence, *asses* – including *Masonic asses* – can be saved.

twenty

PARRISH'S COUNCIL

In October 1983 Harry Lowe, Chairman of Derbyshire's Police Authority, paid his chief constable a surprise visit. The chief's staff said he was not available but Lowe told them he was willing to wait. He walked into the chief's inner office and gasped. It had been transformed into an executive suite fit for a Hollywood movie mogul or the chairman of a billion-pound corporation.

Derbyshire's police headquarters had been built only eight years earlier to the highest standards. Yet these were not good enough for serving Chief Constable Alf Parrish, whose taste ran to the most expensive desk, armchairs, lamps and wallpaper that Lowe had ever seen. He was a down-to-earth Labour councillor elected in one of Britain's poorest regions. He was also flooded with complaints about the run-down housing in which young policemen were forced to live. This conspicuous luxury appalled him. Believing he was alone, he sneaked into Parrish's chair, saw a button on the huge desk and pressed it. Just like Aladdin when he uttered 'Open Sesame!', Lowe gaped with amazement as an entire wall slid back to reveal a thickly-carpeted private lounge where Parrish was jovially entertaining guests to alcoholic drinks at the ratepayers' expense.

Lowe apologized to Parrish for disturbing his intimate beano and left, but he soon reported to the County Treasurer. 'I'd like to know how much that bloody lot cost!' he spluttered. His Labour colleagues on the authority felt the same way, so they ordered an investigation which later turned into a running national news story. When all the bills and invoices were added up, the cost proved to be a staggering £28,000, but this was only part of the public money which Parrish was wasting on personal indulgences.

The story of Alf Parrish is the Stalker Affair turned upside-down. Stalker was an honest man crucified for fictitious offences before he had a chance to speak in his own defence. Parrish was a chiseller who was given every opportunity to explain himself yet who, even when his misconduct was proved beyond reasonable doubt, retired with a full pension and a huge lump sum.

There was one other difference: Stalker was not a Mason. Parrish was. If you want to get to the top of public life in Derbyshire, Freemasonry still offers the smoothest ride up – not that anybody outside the Craft knew *how* smooth until after Parrish was exposed. It then emerged that even his appointment had been irregular. Early in 1981 the previous chief, James Fryer, had died in harness. The sudden need for a successor naturally favoured his deputy, Alf Parrish, but, even so, the vacancy was filled in haste without the proper involvement of the full Police Authority (the committee of councillors and magistrates which oversees the performance of the police force and the way it spends ratepayers' money).

The Authority should have elected a special sub-committee to choose the new chief constable. Instead, on 10 April 1981 an existing sub-committee dominated by Masons usurped this function. Its forceful chairman was Councillor Angus MacDonald Millar, an ardent Mason. A grand provincial officer of the Craft, he belonged to four more orders: Royal Arch, Mark, Knights Templars and Rose Croix. Also present were Masonic councillors, Royden Greene and Walter Marshall, who held Derbyshire's top political job: Leader of the Conservative-controlled county council. Marshall was also a member of the Royal Arch, Knights Templars and Rose Croix. Even the Home Office Inspector present was a Mason. He was James Page CBE, QPM, who had been Commissioner of the City of London Police when it was so crippled by graft that Operation Countryman had to be formed to clean it up.[1] Far fom being punished for maladministration, Page was promoted to the Home Office where he had the task of ensuring other police forces met his own standards.

The power of these four Masons far outweighed the clout of the other four sub-committee members: two more councillors – a Tory woman and a Labour man – and two male JPs. The woman was not a Mason (not a 'regular' one, anyhow) nor, it seems, were the three men. They might have chosen any of the other candidates for the job. All four had excellent credentials and later became chief constables elsewhere, and yet Brother Parrish was appointed. Of course, he might have been appointed even if the selection committee had been properly elected. After all, he was not in the same lodge as any of the men who chose him. However, he did belong to the Derwent Lodge, along with the Lord Lieutenant of the County whose duties included recommending the appointment of all the magistrates.

Appointing Parrish was not the only improper act by this sub-committee. It also urged the Home Office to approve its choice of a new deputy chief constable (also a Freemason) without advertising the vacancy. This was so irregular that the Authority later received a formal rebuke from the Home Secretary. Forced to advertise the post after all, it chose the same man anyway without interviewing any of the other candidates.

Presumably no sub-committee member knew of Parrish's extravagant tastes, but he immediately displayed so cavalier a regard for public funds that it must have been clear to any impartial observer that he was the wrong man for Chief Constable. He asked the Authority to pay his removal expenses 'in the interest of the efficiency of the force'. If he had joined Derbyshire from another force many miles away he would have deserved removal expenses, but he was a local man living only nine country miles from police HQ.

Chairman Millar was so convinced of Parrish's urgent need to move that he had already agreed to the request, a decision which the sub-committee hastily rubber-stamped. They had no need to rush: Brother Parrish did not move for another eight months, and then to a house only one and a half miles from where he was already living! The cost to the ratepayers was £3,881, including £232 to shift his house contents, £500 for carpets, £800 estate agents' fees, £800 for conveyancing and £1,300 in stamp duty. This worked out at more than £1 a yard, door to door.

Years later people asked why this decision – as well as the irregular appointment of the new deputy chief constable – had been rushed through on 6 May 1981. The answer may have been that the local elections were taking place next day. The Conservatives knew they were going to lose control of the County Council and the Police Authority. Parrish may have guessed that if Labour took over, they would reject his nonsense request for removal expenses. However, now this had been approved in principle, the expenses would have to be paid whichever party won power.

On 7 May the Conservatives were duly defeated and their Masonic leaders ousted by Labour councillors with a Puritan streak. Two and a half years later, when the Parrish affair blew up into a national scandal, no one outside Freemasonry knew how he had been appointed or had wangled his removal costs. Some newspapers portrayed the investigation into his office costs as a 'frame-up': a chief constable victimized because he had sent officers into combat against striking coal-miners whose cause was dear to Derbyshire's socialist bosses. As it happens, Parrish and the new council leader David Bookbinder were united in opposing the use of outside police forces to police the Derbyshire pits. Bookbinder had no vendetta against Parrish.

In fact, the matter was out of Bookbinder's hands. By now the County Treasurer had evidence that police accounts had been 'cooked' to pay for Parrish's tastes. A chain of police officers, from chief superintendent down to sergeant, were caught up in a spider's web of forged invoices, large bills sub-divided into small sums to avoid Police Authority scrutiny, and expenditure backdated into the previous financial year so unspent funds would not be forfeit but could be splashed on Parrish's magic wall.

The real cost was becoming clear: the armchairs had cost £600 each, the desk more than £3,300, conference table and matching drinks cabinet £1,900, wall units £8,500, and that electric partition £3,200. Worse still, all this money had been filched from the Police Housing Account and should have been spent on the dilapidated homes of young single constables. What had occurred was, in strict accounting terms, a 'planned fraud'. Parrish meantime had not only hoaxed the authority into paying him to move into a new house; he was receiving £58 a week rent allowance to live there.

In June 1984 he told the Police Committee he had no idea how much the office had cost until his deputy came up with the total. He also claimed that the high-ranking police officer who had supervised the refurbishment had never told him the overall figure. These excuses did not satisfy the committee which promptly suspended him. Parrish called a press conference, at which he talked of left-wing plots and claimed his suspension was the price he had to pay for 'not licking boots'.

At this point some of the Freemasons who had selected him in 1981 came to their brother's aid but, as Conservatives, they may also have believed his talk of left-wing plots. The former council leader Walter Marshall claimed Labour councillors wanted to get rid of Parrish so they could appoint a chief constable who would do what they wanted: 'They are not in favour of authority of any kind. Law and order does not interest them.'

The saga got better as it got worse, especially when it was revealed that Parrish's own notions of law and order included paying his chauffeur more overtime in one year than the total paid to all members of the county's traffic squads. This was because Parrish was using his official car for private visits: to a golf tournament, a race meeting, dinner parties, and to the Jaguar Warrant Holders' Dinner in London for which he also claimed overnight expenses. He even had the gall to claim trips to his London lawyers to plan his defence against the investigation into his own profligacy.

He had also arranged that on 19 September 1983 his son and daughter-in-law could stay in VIP rooms at police HQ before they flew off on holiday from East Midlands Airport next morning. It was even rumoured that the couple had been served breakfast in bed and that a police car had taken them to the airport. In the meantime their car was safely parked at police HQ. The cost had been borne by the Police Authority which only found out about it a year later. Suddenly Parrish claimed it was a mistake and offered to pay up.

Other tacky truths were emerging. The County Treasurer confirmed that £1,000 of public money was spent on fitting a burglar alarm at Parrish's home without approval. This money had been fraudulently diverted from the Crime Prevention Account where it was meant to be spent on telling the public how to deal with burglars, not on keeping burglars out of the chief's home.

At this point Parrish summoned the aid of another Mason, albeit a dead one. He claimed Neil Ashcroft, the County Clerk, had told him the authority would pay for his alarm. However, Ashcroft had just died. The alarm had been the subject of long discussion between Ashcroft and the councillors, yet he had never said he had told Parrish he could have it. As it happened, Ashcroft belonged to the same Derby lodge as Parrish's staunch supporter, Walter Marshall.

By October 1984 Parrish changed his strategy. Now he was trying to resign on grounds of ill-health. This way he would retire on full pension with a large lump sum, and he would not have to face a disciplinary tribunal. There were no corresponding advantages for the authority. Indeed, Parrish was also demanding £15,000 to cover his legal costs. Councillor Bookbinder and his colleagues realized that, if they agreed to pay them, Parrish would shout from the rooftops that this proved he had never done anything wrong.

At the authority's December meeting Parrish's Masonic supporters said he should be allowed to retire immediately, even though this would deprive him of the chance to prove his innocence, which he and they so loudly proclaimed. Labour members preferred to fight it out at a tribunal. They did not believe he was ill. First they had been told he was suffering from gastric ulcers, then exhaustion, then 'reactive depression'. In June 1985 he was said to have collapsed and was being treated in a private hospital. This coincided with another request for him to be allowed to retire on medical grounds, and for all charges against him to be withdrawn, but very soon he was out of hospital again. A solicitor hired an inquiry agent to observe Parrish convalescing. He reported that Parrish was driving around in his car (often breaking the speed limit), playing golf and working in the garden. Snaps showed him fitter and healthier than he looked in any of the old photos appearing in local papers.

In the meantime Derbyshire had no working chief constable. At last the Home Office decided the authority must retire Parrish in the interests of force efficiency, thus avoiding the issue of his health and the pending tribunal. Council leader Bookbinder saw that, if this were done, Parrish could get back all his legal costs. The Chief Inspector of Constabulary, Sir Lawrence Byford, told him Parrish would get no 'undeserved costs'. Bookbinder thought this an odd turn of phrase because, he felt, *none* of Parrish's costs was deserved.

In September 1985 Bookbinder says he told Byford and his Regional Inspector John Woodcock that some people believed 'this was just a cop-out, whereby the police were looking after their own. Parrish would get his pension, he would get his lump sum and he would get out of facing the tribunal or – as local gossip would have it – Masons were looking after Masons.'

Neither Byford nor Woodcock took these remarks well, but they confessed this was the only way the Home Secretary could sack Parrish so a new chief could be appointed. Bookbinder insisted that, if this was so, the Home Secretary should state publicly that the Police Authority had acted properly throughout and that Parrish's psychiatric condition was the reason he was going. On 25 September the Home Secretary made that statement.

Parrish was gone, but the committee had to kiss him goodbye with a £74,000 lump sum payment as well as a £16,000 a year pension. At first the pension was miscalculated but within a few hours Parrish was on the phone telling the Treasurer's Department he should be getting £700 a year more. Bookbinder was astonished: 'Mr Parrish turned out to be correct, and we were all relieved that he appeared to be making such a speedy recovery.' He had also recovered enough to know there was no point in trying to recover his costs all over again.

The battle was not over. The Authority had given up the chase, but the ratepayers had not. Two complained about the cost of Parrish's office and forced a public inquiry in 1986. Out came all the grubby details of false accounting. Parrish tried to blame the officer who had supervised the refurbishment. The lower ranks blamed each other, except for one disarmingly honest superintendent who admitted he had connived at the entire deception.

By this time a recent edition of the Derbyshire *Masonic Year Book* had fallen into Bookbinder's hands. Suddenly many mysteries of county politics began to make sense. The membership list for the Tyrian Lodge (no. 253) included two former Conservative County Council leaders, three successive County Clerks who had run the council for more than twenty years, the High Sheriff, and former Chief Constable Sir Walter

Stansfield. Clearly the lodge had dominated county affairs throughout the 1960s and 1970s. Indeed, as it had been founded in 1785 and was the oldest lodge in Derbyshire, it had probably run the county for 200 years.

Other names loomed out from other lodges: Alf Parrish, of course; several more Conservative councillors; countless magistrates, solicitors and estate agents; the Lord Lieutenant; and that celebrated landowner, the Duke of Devonshire. This slim Masonic volume amounted to a business, political, police and social directory of the entire county.

When the time came to choose a new Chief Constable, Bookbinder sat on a specially appointed sub-committee alongside Home Office Inspector John Woodcock. The council leader asked each candidate if he was a Mason and whether Freemasonry was likely to affect him in the course of duty. Bookbinder claims this raised Woodcock to a state of controlled anger, which nearly boiled over when the Labour Leader asked one candidate 'if he could be affected by grown men playing ring-a-ring-a-roses with aprons round their waists, one nipple bared and one trouser-leg rolled up'.

Despite this, Woodcock and Bookbinder agreed that the serving deputy chief constable, Alan Smith, was the right man for the job, having thoroughly earned it after eighteen difficult months as Acting Chief while Parrish was suspended. The decision was unanimous. Amid the bonhomie that followed, Bookbinder turned to Woodcock and asked if his questions about Freemasonry had upset him.

'No, not at all,' said Woodcock.

'Are you a Freemason?' asked Bookbinder.

Woodcock beamed a big smile and replied, 'Of course I am.'

Their choice, Alan Smith, was not.

There was a curious sequel to this conversation, when the two men met again in 1987. 'Still on the square?' said the council leader. 'I am not a Freemason', responded the Home Office Inspector.

Bookbinder then repeated their earlier exchange, which Woodcock did not challenge. Bookbinder therefore concluded that in the intervening two years Freemasonry must have fallen out of fashion among Britain's top cops.

twenty-one

TOUGH AT THE TOP

In 1987 I wrote to all fifty-two chief constables in the United Kingdom requesting their views on Freemasonry. I asked if they were themselves Masons, if they gave any guidance to officers about Freemasonry, whether it was a divisive issue in their forces, if it had ever been raised at Police Authority meetings, and whether members of the public had ever raised it in complaints against officers.

Not wishing to waste police time or public money, I enclosed a stamped addressed envelope with each of my individually typed letters. Despite this, twenty-eight of the fifty-two did not reply. Of the twenty-four who did, eleven refused to co-operate. I was thus rewarded with a mere thirteen full replies on which to arrive at a few conclusions: a sample of 25 per cent.

It would be tempting to conclude that the other 75 per cent are all 'on the square'. This would not be fair or true. Some may share the view of Lincolnshire's Chief Constable, S. W. Crump, who told me he was not a Mason but he did 'not propose to participate' in my 'divisive venture'. Some chiefs might be in the position in which Ian Oliver of Central Scotland found himself, when Stephen Knight made a similar approach to which Oliver did not reply. He says the inference was drawn that he must be a Mason when in fact he was not and still has no intention of becoming one. (This time he kindly sent me a detailed reply.) I also know that several police chiefs who did not reply to me have told local newspapers they are not Masons.

On the basis of the replies received, all I can say with certainty is that fifteen of Britain's fifty-two chief constables are not Freemasons. I have no proof that any of the others are Freemasons, though I guess some of them are. In Chapter 12 I quoted at length the reply of Geoffrey Dear, Chief Constable of the West Midlands. He did not say if he was a Mason, preferring to stress that his private life was his own concern, 'provided of course that it does not adversely influence my professional standing or that of the force, or interfere with the impartial discharge of professional duty. And it does none of these things.'

All the non-Masons who replied said it was not a divisive issue in their forces. Only in Derbyshire has it been raised at Police Authority meetings (after the Alf Parrish affair), and only Chief Constable George Charlton of Norfolk is aware that any member of the public has ever complained about it:

> In December 1982 a written complaint was received alleging that on an unspecified date police officers in Norwich had ignored drink/ driving offences committed by members leaving the St Giles Masonic Lodge and inferred that one of the drivers involved was a local senior police officer. When the alleged author was subsequently interviewed he disclaimed all knowledge of the complaint and, upon submission of the file, the Police Complaints Board granted formal dispensation from further inquiries.

All but two said they gave no specific guidance on Freemasonry. Only Greater Manchester and West Mercia have followed Sir Kenneth Newman in advising officers on the basis of his *Principles of Policing*. One reply pointed out that the 1964 Police Act forbids policemen from belonging to a trade union. This does not apply to Freemasonry, despite the Craft's claim to be descended from a medieval trade union and despite its continued adherence to the same principles of combination and mutual aid for which policemen are banned from joining unions today.

The only hint that Freemasonry might be hi-jacked for improper ends came in Ian Oliver's reply: 'During my sixteen years in the Metropolitan Police until 1977, it was not unknown for officers to join the Masons in the hope that it might just help their promotion prospects, but I am not aware that it ever did.' Peter Joslin of Warwickshire, another non-Mason, is even more dismissive of Freemasonry's negative potential: 'The only danger to the police service from Freemasonry seems to occur when books such as *The Brotherhood* raise doubts in the public's mind about the partiality of police officers who are Freemasons.'

Most police chiefs (Masons and non-Masons) wish the issue of Freemasonry would go away. They find it easier to blame the media for inventing a problem than to admit it exists. Many assert their officers have no interest in the subject, despite the frequent appearance of anti-Masonic letters in police journals. Many chiefs are mistaken when they claim the issue has never come up in public complaints against their forces. I have a pile of letters from citizens who have enclosed copies of formal complaints they have sent to police forces alleging Masonic wrongdoing by policemen. Many are from 'crazies' and are properly rejected, but it defies statistical odds that none has ever been found to be justified.

In the future chief constables may have to act on increasing public, press and political concern about the role of Freemasonry in the police service. Early in 1988 Home Office leaks implied Home Secretary Douglas Hurd was thinking of requiring police officers to declare their lodge membership if Freemasonry emerged as a factor in any matters in which they were involved – whether these were internal issues such as promotion and discipline or external criminal investigations. That idea came to nothing when Hurd and Commissioner Imbert concluded there was no evidence of Masonic corruption in the Metropolitan Police. (See Chapter 13.)

It is my view that Masonic membership should be declared by all police officers and that a regularly updated register of Masons serving in each force should be kept at every police station and at the headquarters of the force concerned. This register should be readily available to fellow police officers and to members of the public. If this is not a service which police forces are willing to give their paymasters, then the register should be on display in all public libraries, just like electoral rolls. There will be arguments over whether membership of other secret or quasi-secret societies, or fraternal organizations, should be declared. If a convincing case can be made that any other society is as extensive, powerful and cohesive as Freemasonry, then its members should indeed declare themselves.

If public opinion were to demand this register for policemen, it might also require other public servants to comply. It might even demand the display of entire Masonic lodge membership rolls at public libraries. This would be stoutly opposed on the grounds that it is not the 'British way' of doing things, but that is for the British people to decide. They have only recently gained access to the Land Registry. For centuries it has been considered an invasion of property owners' privacy for other people to know who really owns what in this country. However, this grossly infringed other people's right to information – especially to information which could affect themselves. The same principle applies to membership of secret, or private, mutual aid societies. Their secrecy (about both what they do and who they are) is a standing invasion of the liberty of all non-members.

The difficulty which non-Masons have always encountered over Freemasonry is epitomized in an exchange which I witnessed in the Palace of Westminster. I was present when a non-Masonic Tory MP met one of his constituents: a businessman who claimed he was the victim of a Masonic conspiracy. The businessman felt that policemen investigating the affair were dragging their feet, in order to protect Masons inside and outside the force. He wanted the MP to mention Freemasonry in a letter of complaint to the chief constable. The MP advised against it.

I don't think you should mention the Freemasons. If you want these people to do their job properly, it's best not to upset them.

PART FOUR

Masonic Activities

twenty-two

JUDGING BY RESULTS

Eighteen circuit judges, four Queen's Bench judges, three family division judges, two judges in Chancery, three Lord Justices of Appeal and one Lord of Appeal in Ordinary. This is Freemasonry's strength in the highest ranks of the judiciary today – or, rather, its minimum strength as revealed in Masonic reference books to which I have had access. Many other sources (such as provincial yearbooks and membership lists of lawyers' lodges) have eluded me, so I am forced to guess that many more judges are 'on the square'. Certainly, many recently retired judges are Masons: fifteen circuit, one Queen's Bench, two family division, one Chancery, three Lord Justices of Appeal and one Master of the Royal Court of Protection.

A recent Lord Chief Justice, the late Lord Widgery, was Past Senior Grand Warden of England. The current Chief Justice of Australia, Sir Harry Gibbs, is 'on the square'. Gibbs is also the only Australian on the judicial committee of the Privy Council. The president of the Lands Tribunal is a Mason. So is England's Chief Registrar in Bankruptcy. So was his immediate predecessor. Beyond the Royal Courts of Justice sit many more Masonic judges, from the current Recorder of Southport to an English Advocate-General in the European Community's Court of Justice. Still more barrister Masons choose to stay where real money can be made: as QCs.

So what if a lot of judges and QCs are Masons? That may say less about lawyers than that an even higher proportion went to public schools and Oxford or Cambridge: networks which are perhaps more powerful than Freemasonry. The difference is that those institutions (privileged and self-perpetuating though they are) are dedicated largely to the gaining of open educational qualifications which are essential in a lawyer. What the outsider might wonder is why many of these men, who judge the rest of us, need belong to a secret (or would-be secret) society; how can these men be trusted to find the truth in a court of law, when as Masons they swear belief in – and repeatedly enact – the mythical murder of a bogus historical figure whom they glorify as the stonemason architect of a temple built mainly of wood, even though he was neither a stonemason nor an architect!

For enlightenment on what Freemasonry means to so many esteemed dispensers of justice I wrote to Lord Templeman, a Lord of Appeal in Ordinary who sits in the House of Lords. Templeman is England's highest-ranking Mason judge. He has also taken part in a television series on the legal profession. I had hoped that someone with the independence of mind to ignore the then Lord Chancellor, Lord Hailsham's opposition to public comment by judges, might see some point in public discussion of Freemasonry. I received no reply – not that I really expected one because Templeman did not reply to Stephen Knight either. I did not approach any other senior judges because Knight had wasted many stamps on our legal hierarchy, few of whom acknowledged his letters.

Even judges who are not Masons refuse to say so. This may reflect traditional reticence about disclosing any aspect of their private lives, but a man's privacy is hardly invaded if he volunteers he is not a Mason. Perhaps non-Masonic judges feel they belong to a greater brotherhood – of judges – which takes precedence over any feelings they have about their colleagues' Masonic frolics. They may fear that 'coming out' as non-Masons would provoke retribution. One Crown Court Recorder told me, 'I'm not a Mason, but don't quote me or I may end up hanging under Blackfriars Bridge.' I reacted as if this reference to the bizarre death of the Italian banker-Mason Roberto Calvi in 1982 was a joke, but the Recorder assured me he was serious.

While researching the Craft's role in British politics, I met the Rt Hon. Sir Ian Percival QC. A former Conservative MP and Solicitor-General, Sir Ian is also a Freemason. In his chambers in the Temple (not Freemasons' Hall, but the Inn of Court) he kindly gave me an hour of his time to discuss one of the passions of his life: the Craft.

My father was a Freemason and a man of principle, for whom I felt not only love and affection, but also respect and admiration. By the time I came back from the war he was dead. I met some of his Masonic friends who asked me if I would consider joining his lodge, the Canada (I'm a seventh-generation Canadian). They told me a bit about it and I liked what I heard, so I joined and I've never regretted it.

Sir Ian's views on Freemasonry in politics are quoted in Chapter 34.

As a Crown Court Recorder, he speaks with admirable rigour on its role in the law.

> If another Mason ever sought favour from me in a trial, I'd see him in Hell first. But it's never happened. No defendant or counsel has ever tried it. If it did happen, and the defendant were found guilty, I would have to be very careful not to increase his sentence by a year, rather than let him off lightly!

Sir Ian's views reflect the formal position of Grand Lodge which, in 1984, took action against a Mason charged with stealing money from his employer. In his trial this man allowed defence counsel to mention his Masonic activities as proof of good character. He thus committed the Masonic offence of using his membership for personal advantage. He was reported to Grand Lodge which investigated and decided to 'admonish' him.[1] It alighted on this modest punishment because of 'mitigating circumstances'. A cynic might say the Masonic horse had long since bolted, for the defendant had already achieved the result he wanted: acquittal! Flaunting his Masonic virtue may have been just what swayed Masonic jurymen or even the judge into letting him off.

Sir Ian was not involved in that case. His views reflect what he sees as the essence of Freemasonry, and that rules out any attempts to interfere with justice.

> If a Freemason understood the Craft he would not try any such thing. No one gets anything out of Freemasonry, except those who are beneficiaries of charity. What you do get are principles by which to live. That's a good thing. The saddest thing is people who don't have any principles – young people who've been left to work it out for themselves. The more we live by such principles, the better lives we will have and the more we contribute to society.

I asked Sir Ian if it was mere coincidence that so many judges are Masons. Do Masons never help each other up the legal ladder?

> For judges you want men of integrity. It's no coincidence, perhaps, that Freemasons are such men because the principles of Freemasonry are ideal for public service. Masons do not go around recommending each other for advancement. It is their individual conduct which recommends them.
>
> It's the same in the police. Of course, you'll get some folk stepping out of line, masonically, but what do you need in a police

officer? Principles such as honour, probity and upholding the law.
These are identical to what is required in Freemasonry which
stresses above all, duty to God, Queen and Country! So it's natural
that good Masons make good police officers and good judges.
Indeed, I believe it would be a much better world if everyone were in
it.

Judges play a vital role within English Freemasonry: they preside over
its complex internal system of law. If a Mason objects to being 'excluded'
from his lodge for whatever reason, he may seek remedy in a Masonic
appeals court.

In 1985 members of Bournemouth's Northbourne Lodge (no. 6827)
won a glorious victory in the Dorset Masonic Darts Shield. Months later
they were ashamed to learn that one Northbourne member named
George Miller would be unable to attend the lodge for some time, as he
was now beginning six years in jail for armed robbery. The local brethren
felt his 'unmasonic conduct' warranted expulsion from Freemasonry, so
in 1986 a Grand Lodge appeals court sat to hear both sides of the matter.
As Miller could not get a day out from jail, he was allowed to state his case
in writing or through another Mason speaking on his behalf. However,
his 'jury' would not be twelve locals at Winchester Crown Court but five
Masonic notables from a panel which included Sir John Arnold (then
president of the High Court Family Division), Sir Edward Eveleigh and
Sir George Waller (both retired Lord Justices of Appeal), and the
awesomely named Sir William Stabb (a former circuit judge). Unsur-
prisingly, the five recommended the robber's expulsion.

Their decision was published in the *Quarterly Communication* which is
distributed to all lodges, presumably 'to encourage the others'.[2] Yet, if a
criminal brother is forgiven by his own lodge, he will probably not be
punished by any higher Masonic authority. This partly accounts for the
extraordinary survival of silver bullion robber, Lennie Gibson, in his
police-packed Waterways Lodge, and the enduring membership of the
other fraternal gangsters mentioned in Chapter 20 – until adverse press
comment forced Grand Lodge to act, eight years after the crime. Then
these men were all 'tried' again in a Masonic court of appeal.

One career criminal (a specialist in fraud) told me his Masonic friends
include not only senior policemen but judges whom he has met at festive
boards and ladies' nights. Judges usually prefer the company of their own
cloth in lodges restricted mainly to barristers, such as the Grays Inn (no.
4938); the Chancery Bar (no. 2456); the Midland, Oxford and South
Eastern Bar (no. 2716); the Northern Bar (no. 1610); and the Western
Circuit (no. 3154). Outside London they may mix with solicitors in

lodges such as the South Wales Jurists (no. 7092) which meets in Bridgend, halfway between Wales's main legal centres, Cardiff and Swansea. One retired Old Bailey judge, Edward Clarke, has the rare privilege of belonging to a lodge named after his celebrated grandfather, the advocate Sir Edward Clarke (no. 3601). I am told that over the years many Scotland Yard detectives have also belonged to this lodge.

Many judges who belong to lawyers' lodges also join lodges where they can relax with men of similar social standing in other walks of life. Thus, as members of the Kaisar-I-Hind Lodge (no. 1724) circuit judges Marcus Anwyl-Davies and Michael Goodman may dine at the Café Royal four times a year with Lord Belstead JP, the Conservative Leader of the House of Lords; Derek Pattinson, secretary-general of the General Synod of the Church of England; and Dr Derek Wylie, consulting anaesthetist at St Thomas's Hospital.

Circuit Judge Eric McLellan and his retired colleague Norman Brodrick belong to the all-lawyers' Western Circuit Lodge in London, and to the Phoenix Lodge (no. 257) in Portsmouth where they may dine with two Surgeon Rear-Admirals, dozens of other navy officers, doctors galore and several JPs. Recently deceased Phoenix members include a Bishop of Portsmouth and Sir Norman Skelhorn, the former Director of Public Prosecutions. Beyond the Craft, judges may also join exclusive Knights Templar and Rose Croix lodges where they can dress up in more exciting costumes and swear even more bloodcurdling oaths.

These details of a few judges' Masonic connections may seem unimportant, yet they support the view that Freemasonry bonds a cross-section of the Establishment together in a highly conservative organization. Far from fostering tolerance, Freemasonry's 'apartheid' structure may buttress the prejudices of its members. Most Mason judges may be good men with fine war records, who have spent their best years in public service, but it is wrong that judges in particular should lock themselves in so tight a social circle when they are paid to serve *all* the people, most of whose ideals, aspirations and circumstances are very different from their own. More worrying still, these judges are likely to interpret the law in ways which reflect Freemasonry's particular ethics. Most of these are unremarkable but some are reactionary in the extreme.

> Brethren, such is the nature of our Constitution, that some must of necessity rule and teach; others, of course, must learn to submit and obey, humility in each being an essential virtue.

These words are spoken in every lodge, when a new Master is installed. Non-Masonic seekers after justice sometimes fear that Freemasonry's

'Constitution' and its code of mutual aid dictate how Masonic judges interpret the laws of England, even driving them to 'bend' law in favour of brother Masons who come before them. I have many letters from people convinced that legal decisions have gone against them because of a Masonic 'fix'. Wives who have fallen out with Masonic husbands often fear divorce and custody hearings may be manipulated by a covert Masonic axis which binds judge, barristers and solicitors to the male side. Such fears may rarely be justified but, even if a case *were* rigged by Masons, the chances of proving it are almost nil.

The fear may be so great that most non-Masonic litigants dare not mention Freemasonry lest they provoke a Masonic backlash. For instance, if you dare ask a judge if he is a Mason and he says he is not, you have made a fool of yourself. If he *is* a Mason, he will deny prejudice, refuse to withdraw, and then may treat you and your lawyers with hostility throughout the case. In any event, your barrister and solicitor will try to stop you raising the subject, partly out of tactical wisdom, partly out of fear for their own careers. Of course, the only sure way to avoid male Masons is to hire a *woman* solicitor and barrister, and to demand a hearing by a *woman* judge. Of course, they may all belong to some branch of women's Freemasonry, which, unfortunately, I have not yet explored.

I know of only one case where plaintiffs succeeded in getting a case heard by a non-Mason. Ironically, they were a group of Freemasons who felt they could not get a fair trial before a brother Mason Judge. From 1985 until 1987 a bitter dispute raged over plans to sell the Royal Masonic Hospital (see Chapter 37). In favour of sale were most of England's hierarchy: Grand Lodge satraps, charity chiefs and provincial grand masters. *Against* were rank-and-file Masons, a group of doctors and some charity buffs to whom the hospital was the jewel in England's Masonic crown. For twelve months they fought a battle in Chancery against the hospital governors, to block the sale and establish terms for the election of a new board.

The rebels believed that any Mason who becomes a judge is instantly awarded Masonic Grand Rank and is then bound to support any scheme schemed by England's Masonic mighty, including selling the hospital. By the time the case reached court, they had made sure it was heard by a non-Mason, Mr Justice Warner. It ran for much of 1986, and there must have been times when Warner wished he *were* a Mason after all, so he could have been spared from hearing the most tedious of legal arguments. His thoughts may even have wandered to his favourite recreation, as declared in *Who's Who*, 'Sitting in the sun with a cool drink'.

I wrote to Mr Justice Warner to ask him how he came to hear the hospital case (known as Brooks v Richardson) and whether it established a precedent. If Masons can have a non-Masonic judge when it suits them, I inquired, surely non-Masons should have the same right? Warner saw it differently. He said the intense controversy surrounding the hospital had led the 'parties' to fear that any judge who was a Mason would already have formed his views, whereas they wanted the case to be heard by a judge who could be expected to start with an open mind.

I am told that the initial request for a judge who was not a Mason came from the Richardson [pro-sale] side. Brooks v Richardson therefore affords no 'precedent' for the kind of case you mention where there is a dispute between Masons and non-Masons.

'Nonsense!', said one Mason in the anti-sale camp. 'When I got to court I found the case was about to be heard by Mr Justice Mervyn Davies – a Freemason of Grand Rank! I told the clerk there was no way we would accept Davies, so he switched the case to Warner.'

Whichever lot of Masons first asked for a non-Masonic judge, the Royal Masonic Hospital case shows how easily they can get one. If Masons could secure a non-Mason judge on that occasion, how often have they arranged for Freemason judges to hear their pleas without their non-Masonic adversaries even knowing?

Mr Justice Warner told me he had 'personally never come across a case where it was even suggested that the fact that the judge was a Mason might affect or might have affected the result.' Four weeks later just such a case came before three of Warner's senior colleagues in the Court of Appeal. Here again a pseudonym is necessary.

In the 1970s 'Bill Rugman' was running a rapidly expanding high-street business across south-east London, when he was forced into bankruptcy by the National Westminster Bank. He claims bank officials forged a document and swore a false statement which persuaded the High Court to allow the bank to foreclose on him without a hearing.

As soon as Rugman realized what had happened, he applied for his bankruptcy to be lifted and his claims against NatWest investigated. In May 1985 he tried to present his own case at Croydon County Court but he has since sworn an affidavit saying that, as soon as the hearing began, Judge Murray-Band treated him like a hostile witness. What was meant to be a two-day hearing was over by 2.30 on day one, when the judge dismissed the application without allowing Rugman to argue his grounds for overturning the bankruptcy. Rugman says Murray-Band obstructed him and refused even to put in writing that he had refused to consult Rugman's legal sources. He has further sworn that Murray-Band's 'blatantly improper conduct is the clearest possible indication that he completely failed to carry out his function as a judge'.

I was not present during the hearing so I have no idea if Judge Murray-Band was guilty of 'blatantly improper conduct', nor do I know if he is a Freemason. However, I do know that he has never had the chance to defend himself against these allegations, because they have never been tested in any court. In his affidavit Rugman had also accused a court official of acting in a hostile manner: he twice passed his right hand across his right eye-brow as if wiping away some drops of perspiration, but ostentatiously. Moreover, he did this in the Judge's line of vision. This, thought Rugman, was the Masonic sign of Grief and Distress. According to the ritual, this has compelling significance.

> When adversity has visited our Brother, and his calamities call for our aid, we should cheerfully and liberally stretch forth the hand of kindness, to save him from sinking and to relieve his necessities.

Rugman swears that the use of this Masonic sign was 'an illegal secret appeal to the Judge to make certain I was stopped from succeeding on my Application, so that my opponent could benefit.'

Feeling he had been denied a fair hearing, Rugman took his case to the Court of Appeal where three judges ruled they could not investigate Judge Murray-Band's conduct, but that Rugman was entitled to ask the bankruptcy courts to overturn his judgment. Lord Justice Sir Francis Purchas observed, 'If only one or more of these allegations were to be substantiated they would amount to a serious miscarriage of justice and misconduct on the part of the judge.'

The Appeal Judges had already been forced to pay attention to Rugman's Masonic claims because at the outset he had applied for his Appeal to be heard by non-Masonic judges. He even cited the Royal Masonic Hospital case as a precedent. Lord Justice Purchas responded that Rugman was in some difficulty because Freemasons swear an oath not to reveal their membership.

This was an extraordinary statement coming from a Lord Justice of Appeal, for Purchas seemed to be saying that some of his colleagues would lie rather than reveal they were Masons. They would thus place their Masonic oath above their oath as a judge! As it happens, Purchas was probably incorrect. According to a 1984 Grand Lodge pamphlet, *What is Freemasonry?*, 'all members are free to acknowledge their membership and will do so in response to inquiries for respectable reasons'. Rugman's reason was overwhelmingly respectable: he was trying to reverse alleged Masonic interference with justice in a lower court.

Purchas had an excuse for his mistake – he is probably not a Mason – but one of the judges sitting with him was 'on the square': Lord Justice Sir John Stocker. We do not know if Stocker gave Purchas the correct information while they conferred, but we do know that Rugman was refused a Mason-free hearing.

It is extraordinary that Mason judges do not voluntarily withdraw from such cases. As members of a fraternity sworn to mutual aid, they clearly have an interest to declare. After all, 'justice must not only be done – it must be seen to be done.'

Bill Rugman promptly declared his intention to take his case to the Strasbourg courts: 'It seems to be the only place I will get a fair hearing.' Maybe, but he will not necessarily get a Mason-free hearing!

twenty-three

MASONIC JUSTICES

'On this island you cannot breathe, fart, piss or whistle without *them* knowing about it.' The island of which former nightclub-owner Derek Smith speaks is the Isle of Wight. *Them* are the Freemasons.

The island's sixteen Craft lodges claim 1,500 members. Wight's entire population is only 110,000 of whom some 40,000 are adult males, so one man in twenty-seven must be a Mason. If we discount unlikely Masonic recruiting material (men under twenty-five, the poor, derelicts and most inmates in Albany and Parkhurst jails) the ratio comes down to one in ten. Most are in business, local government, the police and the law, so it follows that a very large percentage of all island business goes through Masonic hands.

Certainly, Freemasons know everything about Derek Smith, who qualifies as the islander least likely to be a Mason: he is raffish, contemptuous of class distinctions and he does not suffer fools gladly. At first meeting he seemed to me rather like an end-of-the-pier arcade proprietor, so I congratulated myself when he later told me that arcades and slot machines is how he started in business. In the 1960s he was operating 400 machines on the island, as well as nine restaurants and cafés, some betting shops and two casinos. In 1968 when Britain tightened its gaming laws, he quit casinos and betting to concentrate on running nightclubs and discotheques. That is how he came nose-to-nose with the brothers.

In 1985 Derek was the owner of the Blitz discotheque in Newport which he ran with his son Nigel. Crucial to a nightspot's success is a late-night drinks licence. Without it you soon go out of business. Blitz's licence allowed the Smiths to serve drinks until 2 A.M. but the law obliged them to serve food as well. The 1964 Licensing Act states that drinks should only be incidental to the business of food and dance. The Smiths served food such as beefburgers but, like every other disco, people went there to dance, drink and make friends, not to stuff their faces with hot dogs and onions. Smith says:

> No discotheque complies strictly with the law. If they did, they would have to be able to feed everybody at the same time. One local disco can pack as many as 1,500 customers in during the tourist season, but it has only thirty eating places. The police could 'do' that place any time, and all the others on the island. It's entirely up to them who they choose to shut down.

In October 1985 eighteen police raided Blitz on suspicion that Smith was not serving food as the law demanded. They then applied for his licence to be revoked. Smith said that if he were guilty, so were all his competitors. He claimed he was the victim of 'discretionary policing'. He may be right. Nowadays chief constables perpetually cry that policing is about 'priorities'. There are so many laws, and so many crimes, that they do not have the manpower to enforce every law all the time. This leaves the choice of target in any field of crime – drug-dealing, gambling, prostitution, or after-hours drinking – to the discretion of local officers, thus giving them awesome power, which is wide open to abuse and corruption. Even if they act only in response to complaints from the public, they are still susceptible to manipulation by any groups who choose to conduct a vendetta against a particular individual or his business.

In December 1985 Smith found himself before three licensing justices, fighting for his discotheque's survival. He feared Freemasonry might have played some part in his troubles, so when the officer who led the raid, Inspector Gerald Marsh, stepped into the witness box Smith asked him directly if he was a Freemason. At first Marsh refused to answer, then (says Smith) he dropped his eyes and adopted the Masonic stance of grief and distress. Smith insisted he reply, so the Inspector said he would like to consult the police prosecutor. She told him: 'You must answer as you wish. I cannot advise you.' At last, Marsh said: 'I am.'

Smith then turned to address the three Justices of the Peace who were hearing the case:

> I am concerned at the possibility that any member of the bench hearing this case might be a Freemason, and under the terms of their obligation, would be obliged to believe the evidence of a Brother against my word . . . I am not aware that any of their worships are Freemasons but I know that Inspector Marsh is.

The JPs were flummoxed. The chairman told Smith his questioning was irrelevant, but then volunteered that he himself was not a Mason and neither was one of his fellow Justices. This was no news to Smith because one of the 'beaks' was a woman. The third remained deafeningly silent throughout.

Smith claimed he did serve meals till two in the morning. He was backed up by the chairman of the local amenities committee, Councillor Jeff Manners, who testified he had seen food served in the early hours. Despite this impeccable evidence, Smith's tactics did him no good at all: he lost his licence, was forced to shut down, and sold the premises a few months later.

Derek Smith had been battling with Isle of Wight Masons for years, especially over the widespread abuse of licensing laws by Masonic publicans. One of these had been doing roaring after-hours trade, damaging the legitimate business of a neighbouring landlord who had no Masonic protection and so had to operate within the law. Complaints to the police had no effect until Smith brought the racket to the attention of a superintendent who was a lapsed Mason and applied the law without fear or favour. One afternoon well past closing time, he drove by the pub and saw a dozen cars outside. The hostelry stood alone in a country lane, so it was obvious that heavy boozing was going on inside.

Grabbing an inspector, the superintendent raided the pub and found it was full of other publicans. The landlord claimed he was hosting a private meeting of licensees, no one was paying for their drinks, and besides they were all 'on the square'. Rejecting this Masonic approach, the inspector said: 'I don't give a fuck. You're nicked.' After taking the drinkers' names and addresses, the officers told them to leave. They were all so drunk they had to be taxied home.

The publican was fined but he kept his licence, which Derek Smith thinks was remarkably soft treatment compared with his own outright loss of licence years later. He says the power of Masonry on the island is so great that 'If you're not in it, you suffer the pain of exclusion. No one will do business with you. You are sent to Coventry.'

Smith is a rough diamond, and his blunt manner may be the cause of some of his misfortunes. Yet his case raises the possibility that Masonic bonds between police, publicans and magistrates may lead to the arbitrary application of the law, and to vendettas against anyone who dares challenge traditional ways of doing business in a small, controllable community.

There is no doubt that throughout Britain Freemasonry is very strong on 'the Bench' (the collective term for magistrates and licensing justices). In 1973 a survey in one provincial city discovered that twenty-nine out of forty-three magistrates were Masons or Rotarians. Some of the Masons' own yearbooks reveal many brethren with 'JP' after their names.

Warwickshire boasts twenty-eight JPs among Masons of provincial grand rank. Many more Masons in this heavily populated county are JPs, but the yearbook has no space to list their worldly honours. In East and West Kent the tally is twenty-six. The 1985–6 Knights Templar yearbook names sixty-one JPs as members of this Masonic order in England and Wales. Such factual morsels indicate that the true number of Mason JPs in Britain runs into hundreds. Anyone's chances of appearing before a Mason-free slate of three magistrates are almost nil – unless all of them are women.

For almost twenty-five years Ian Morton worked as an administrator in Derbyshire magistrates' courts, spending the last thirteen years as an assistant principal officer in Chesterfield. He was also a Conservative county councillor for seven years. His father had been a Mason in Scotland and Morton himself was perfect Mason material. Yet he never joined, either as a young man or when he achieved suitable worldly status. What he saw going on at the courts was more than enough to put him off joining.

> All this stuff about Masonic signals may well be true, but in my experience Masons aren't let off in court. They don't even get into court! We used to see all the police files and we could never understand why some people were prosecuted and others were not; why working-class men under thirty were breathalysed, but not professional people; why boys on 125 Yamaha bikes were done for speeding but not older men driving Rolls-Royces or Jaguars. Over many years we found out who the Freemasons were, and that's when all these decisions made sense.

Mr Morton's present wife Ray used to be married to a Mason and came to understand how the Craft justified its covert control of so much of British society. 'I was always told Freemasonry was "the benevolent Mafia" and that "we know best".' When I showed the couple a Derbyshire *Masonic Yearbook*, they identified not only a large number of JPs, but also many justices' clerks, councillors, policemen, solicitors and estate agents. This only reinforced Ian Morton's opinions which he had expressed two years earlier in a letter published in a local newspaper:

> It is high time that Freemasons were obliged to state their interests and the mere fact that they are reluctant to do so is more than adequate reason to demand that they do. Anyone in or standing for public office should be prepared to be open, as to their interests and affiliations. That is all that is being asked. If a list is successfully completed, it must be published. Anything less would be an insult.

Further evidence of how Freemasonry operates in magistrates' courts comes from the far north of England. A Justice of the Peace had read *The Brotherhood* and wrote to offer his own experiences about life on the Bench. In later conversations he asked me not to name him in this book, for obvious reasons.

> There are some sixty JPs on our bench and vacancies come up most years. They are filled on the advice of a small group of magistrates who are known as the Lord Chancellor's Advisory Committee for that area. To my surprise I was asked to go on this committee – I was the first Catholic chosen for many years.
>
> What I saw going on in the committee astonished me. For a start, no one is meant to serve on it for more than six years, but one man had been there for more than twelve. I also noticed the same two men were constantly nominating people to fill the vacancies. I was amazed at their range of acquaintances, people from all walks of professional life, and all of them thoroughly competent. They were OK in themselves. It was the way they came to our attention which was obnoxious.
>
> I soon found out that the two men who nominated them all, and the man who had served more than twelve years on the committee, were all Freemasons. Their whole operation was subtle and well-planned. Even the women they nominated turned out to be the wives of Freemasons!
>
> Although our Bench was very efficient, the Lord Chancellor's representative came to tell us that our appointments were getting out of balance. There were too many teachers and too many Conservatives. This encouraged me to use my power of veto. All you have to do to stop the appointment of a new JP is to say you object. No one may ask you why – you simply say so. Whenever the two Masons pushed their luck by putting up too many of their friends I would say, 'I cannot support this nomination.' They got the message after a while and cut down on their offers.
>
> I'm off the Committee now, having served my maximum six years, but the other fellow is still on it! One of my colleagues suggested our whole selection procedure should be made public, but this did not go down very well and was rejected. Certain people must have thought their way of doing business would have been exposed at last!

The Coroner's court is another place where Masons often preside. This merely reflects Masonic dominance in the professions from which coroners are selected: the law and medicine. Until recently Gloucester's District Coroner was the Freemason Russell Jessop. In 1978 this solicitor was Grand Registrar: England's fifth highest Mason that year. For ten years he was also Grand Secretary of Gloucestershire, overseeing sixty-seven lodges with some 5,000 members. He is also a 30th degree member of the Ancient and Accepted Rite. His St Thomas's Chapter colleagues revere him as Grand Elected Knight Kadosh and Knight of the Black and White Eagle.

In 1983 Jessop presided over a controversial inquest. That July a nineteen-year-old motorcyclist named Mark Bilney had died from multiple injuries after colliding with a police constable and crashing into an oncoming car. At the inquest PC Peter Rowlands testified that he had 'walked crisply' into the road and used his torch to signal Bilney to stop, but that Bilney accelerated straight at him. Rowlands claimed he was hit and spun round, but made 'no action at all to add to a collision'. He said that Bilney's action was 'not far short of a suicide attempt'.

Death by misadventure, recorded Coroner Jessop. However, three eye-witnesses had given him a different description of the tragedy. They said that Rowlands had appeared from behind a police car and jumped into Bilney's path. Far from deliberately driving at the policeman, Bilney had slowed to avoid him but Rowlands ran at him, waving his torch and shouting 'Stop'. An eighteen-year-old girl, named Jane Manning, saw what happened:

> The police officer ran into the road. Mark was nearly on top of him. The police officer was facing Mark. His right arm was held out with the torch in it and I heard him say 'Stop'. Mark had to swerve to avoid the officer. There was not time for Mark to pull to a stop. I saw him swing his right arm forward and hit Mark on the right side of his face or shoulder. Mark seemed stunned. His bike went off into a car that was behind us . . .

Mark died in the road from multiple injuries. His mother is convinced that when she saw his body in hospital, there was a mark on his right cheek: 'It was a circular indentation and had not broken the skin.' When the pathologist was later asked by a journalist if he had recorded this indentation, he refused to discuss his report because it was 'confidential to the Coroner'.

Following complaints by the dead boy's parents, the Director of Public Prosecutions investigated the incident but decided there was insufficient evidence to support criminal proceedings against PC Rowlands. Later Mr and Mrs Bilney were denied legal aid for a private prosecution against the police. However, the Bilneys' grievance is against not only the police but also Coroner Jessop for the way he handled the inquest. They claim he accepted only the police version of what happened and played down all evidence conflicting with it. Mr and Mrs Bilney wanted him investigated but the D of PP has no jurisdiction over coroners' courts, nor could they get legal aid to fight his 'misadventure' verdict.

Jessop served as Gloucester's Coroner for twenty-four years, a reign topped and tailed by controversy. When he was appointed in 1960 twenty-three doctors objected. They felt the post should have gone to the acting Coroner, whose father and grandfather had held it for the previous fifty years, but Jessop was confirmed. The post, after all, was not hereditary. Yet when he retired in 1984 Jessop expected the job to go to his deputy: a partner in Jessop's own firm of solicitors. When another solicitor was chosen instead, Jessop called it a slur on his own man.

In a letter to the *Gloucester Citizen*, he said he found it difficult to understand how a coroner could supply the best possible public service when he had no experience of the job. He thus overlooked the circumstances of his own appointment back in 1960. Jessop had to call on all his experience when he convened the Mark Bilney inquest. He managed it all on his own, without the aid of a jury. It took years for Mark's parents to realize how odd this was. According to the law governing inquests, a coroner shall proceed to summon a jury if there is reason to suspect 'that the death occurred while the deceased was in police custody, or resulted from an injury caused by a police officer in the purported execution of his duty'.[1]

Several witnesses say in their statements (available to Jessop before the inquest) that Mark Bilney crashed because of the actions of a police officer purportedly doing his duty. This is clear even from PC Rowlands's statement. He denied deliberately hitting Bilney with the torch (which, incidentally, was not produced in evidence) but the collision was clearly caused when, doing his job as he saw fit, he walked out on the road into the path of the advancing motor-cyclist. He himself said,

> I felt I had no time to react before I felt a strong blow to my right arm just below my elbow. I remember it spun me round but I don't recall whether I fell or stumbled. I don't know whether it was the deceased or the motor-cycle that collided with my arm, but the collision wrenched the torch from my hand. I did not see the torch again.

This version, alongside the accounts of other witnesses, would seem to demand that Jessop summon a jury. Yet he did not do so.

In 1963 Jessop himself had been on trial, over an accident which occurred when he was travelling home from Cardiff. In order to overtake a vehicle he drove his car onto the opposite side of the highway. This caused a head-on collision and the death of two people. Charged with dangerous driving, he pleaded not guilty but was convicted, fined £100 and disqualified from driving for three years. The killings had occurred in another Coroner's territory. Otherwise, surely, Coroner Jessop would have been compelled to stand down.

twenty-four

THE COTTON INHERITANCE

Many of Britain's most prominent solicitors are Freemasons. They all appear in *Who's Who*, yet none of their entries contains any reference to the Craft.

Sir Desmond Heap, President of the Law Society 1972–3. Solicitor to the Corporation of London for twenty-six years and England's greatest expert on town and country planning law.

Sir Edmund Liggins, President of the Law Society 1975–6. An eminent Warwickshire solicitor.

Sir David Napley, President of the Law Society 1976–7. England's leading defence solicitor. A lapsed Mason.

Sir John Stebbings, President of the Law Society 1979. Member of a Derbyshire lodge (deceased December 1988).

David Sumberg MP, partner in a Manchester firm, member of a Staffordshire lodge.

Bert Millichip, Chairman of the Football Association, senior partner in the family firm in West Bromwich, where he is active in Staffordshire Freemasonry.

Other prominent Masonic solicitors include Julius Hermer, Lord Mayor of Cardiff 1987–8; John Evans, for twenty years Official Solicitor to the Supreme Court of Judicature; and Colonel George Kelway, High Court Registrar for Pembroke and Carmarthen from 1940 to 1962.

These folk are not household names. They do not match singers, sportsmen or soap opera stars in public recognition. Yet they are the backbone of Britain, men of status and respect in the regions where they have built their careers, and nationally influential in the legal profession. Most are Masons of Grand Rank and all are citizens above reproach.

In contrast, rank-and-file Masonic solicitors are regarded as pillagers and looters by many anti-Masons. Stephen Knight's post-*Brotherhood* files were full of letters alleging all manner of conspiracies against the profession. I too have received dozens of complaints from the understandably distressed, as well as the near-paranoid and the clinically insane. Most of these correspondents suffer from the same problem: they have no evidence that Freemasonry has played any part in their troubles. They write in not to provide evidence but to ask for it.

Their allegations are a shocking litany of businesses destroyed, bankruptcies precipitated, investments mishandled, trust funds defrauded, trials rigged and murders covered up. The writers all claim Masonic solicitors have conspired with a permutation of Masonic bank managers, estate agents, business rivals, policemen, judges – and even Masonic relatives. They usually send stacks of documents, often illegible, stretching back many years. Each tragic tale has dozens of characters with an apparently bottomless capacity for evil. Some 'victims' are themselves solicitors, driven out of business by Masonic competitors, or so it is claimed. Even if 95 per cent of this stuff is fantasy, the rest shows there are a lot of wicked people in the world, be they Masons or not.

Freemasons did play a large role in one miserable story of an old Lancashire lady who came to sign a new will only days before she died. In 1980 Mrs Esther Cotton aged ninety-two was sick with cancer. She was living alone at home, taking tablets to kill the pain and slow the cancer's growth. On 9 December her doctor discovered she was suffering not just from cancer but from bruises to her face and legs, black eyes and cuts, broken ribs and collapsed vertebrae. He promptly put her in Ormskirk General Hospital where she complained of leg and neck pains. Her ankles were swollen and the cancer had completely destroyed her right breast. Tests also showed she was very deaf and suffering from severe heart trouble and anaemia. Two days later she was sinking fast: noisy at times but very drowsy in between. By 12 December, despite fairly heavy sedation, she was in constant pain.

On this same day Mrs Cotton was the subject of frenzied attention which was far from medical. Shortly after midday a solicitor named Gordon Brown appeared at her bedside insisting she sign a new will. He was not her regular solicitor but was acting on instructions from her son, Ernest. Because of the noise and bustle in the ward, Brown asked that the dying woman be moved to a private room where, witnessed by two hospital administrators, she scrawled a mark where she was meant to sign her name.

Within hours her condition rapidly worsened. Her face turned grey, she suffered a relapse, and had to be treated for congestive cardiac failure. Her condition further deteriorated. On 17 December she slipped into a coma and died. Her funeral was attended by her son Ernest and her daughter, Mrs Juneth Pilkington.

Juneth had been visiting her mother twice daily but the first she knew of the will was on 29 December when a copy came through the letterbox. She thought it strange that her mother had never told her about this will but stranger still that she could have made it at all. In hospital her condition had been so bad that she could say almost nothing, could recognize no one and, says Juneth, had quite lost her mental faculties.

As Juneth read through the will (in which she and her brother were named as executors) she was stunned. It said she would get just one-quarter of the value of her mother's house. Each of four grandchildren would get a mere £100, but the rest of the estate would go to her brother Ernest, 'for his own use and benefit absolutely'. The estate was no pittance. It was worth some £60,000, much of it tied up in the family business, a motor coach firm. Yet only five months before she signed this 'hospital will', Mrs Cotton had signed another with a very different message: she was going to leave each grandchild £1,000, but everything else was to be split between her son and daughter 'in equal shares absolutely'.

What shocked Juneth was not the loss of so much money, but the clandestine way in which the new will had been concocted. The solicitor Gordon Brown had never acted for her mother before, whereas her solicitor for the past thirty years was not consulted. Indeed, no one had even told him she was ill.

In the period between these wills the future of the coach firm had caused great family bitterness. The trouble went back to 1948 when old Mr Cotton had died without a will. The business had been held in trust ever since, with shares divided between Mrs Cotton and the children. Juneth refused to sell her shares to Ernest, who ran the business and wanted total ownership. The 'hospital will' did not give him that – it could not take away the shares Juneth already had – but it gave him his mother's 50 per cent share, and thus majority control for the first time.

Juneth herself had been very ill during her mother's last days at home but she had called in to see her on 4 December, when she found her squatting on a settee in an incoherent state. Juneth called the doctor but does not know if he saw Mrs Cotton before 9 December when he sent her to hospital. However, she is sure that on 4 December the old lady was not suffering from cuts, bruises, broken ribs or collapsed vertebrae.

Years later Juneth gained access to previously withheld hospital notes and discovered that on 6 December someone had called the hospital to report that Mrs Cotton's back had 'caved in' and she was covered in bruises because of several falls. Juneth also learned that on 8 December Mr Brown, acting on her brother's instructions, had twice visited Mrs Cotton so that she could dictate a new will. Neither he nor a colleague could have noticed her caved-in back, or they would have realized she was in no condition to make a will. Instead, Gordon Brown took down the details and later had them typed on to the appropriate form. On 12 December, by which time Mrs Cotton was in hospital, she signed her new will. Two hospital employees initialled a few handwritten words saying the contents had been read over to her, 'she appearing perfectly to understand the same'.

Re-reading the will with care, Juneth felt her mother could have had no idea what she was signing. Her signature was illegible, and unlike her normal signature as it appeared on the earlier will. The E (for Esther) was vaguely recognizable, but the A (for Annie) was like an M. In place of 'Cotton', there were a few gnarled loops with no 't's or an 'n'.

Juneth did not dispute that her mother made that scrawl but felt that maybe her hand had been held, but what was extraordinary about the will was that it contained two gross errors. Mrs Cotton's 'dwellinghouse' is described as '22 Brighouse Close, Ormskirk', whereas she lived at number 33. Even more astonishing, the document is made out in the wrong name: 'Hester Annie Cotton', not Esther Annie Cotton. At no time in her life had Esther ever been called Hester.

Would anyone in his or her right mind voluntarily sign a will made out in the wrong name and address? Can such a will be valid?

In succeeding months and years Juneth tried to find out if her mother could possibly have known what she was doing. In 1981 her doctor wrote that, on 9 December 1980: 'my patient appeared to be in agony and under a great deal of distress. I therefore did not think it appropriate to assess her mental capacity. I immediately arranged her urgent admission into hospital.'

On 10 December a hospital physician (whom Brown had approached) wrote, 'She is in a fit mental state to sign a will.' Later he explained that on 12 December he thought her capable of understanding and signing a will, and could appreciate the extent of her property, the persons who should be considered, and the way her estate should be divided.

If so, how did she not protest that her new will made a hash of her own name and address? The opinion also clashes with Juneth's experience on 10 December when her mother failed to recognize her and two other familiar visitors. Next day she did not recognize her grandchild. The day after, she again failed to recognize Juneth, *only one hour before she signed the new will.*

Just before that happened, one hospital witness had read the will out very loud to Mrs Cotton. While doing this, he stopped to ask a doctor about her condition but was told she understood what she was doing. The witness later recalled that she was wearing a hearing aid, but I did not check to see if it was working properly, as I had no reason to suspect that it wasn't. When I spoke to Mrs Cotton I did so in a loud voice, bending over the patient. Mrs Cotton did not make any comment regarding mistakes in her name and the address of her property. I asked the patient if she understood what I had read out and if she agreed with it. As far as I can recollect Mrs Cotton did not make any comments. Mrs Cotton appeared to be an elderly, ill lady.

Juneth's solicitors sent all available hospital records and statements to a consultant physician in Liverpool. In his Opinion he stated, Mrs Cotton had been very ill for six weeks before she died. When she signed the will, her mind may have been clouded by pain from widespread cancerous growth; impairment of metabolic and cardiovascular functions through cancer, and toxic absorption; lack of natural sleep; effects of drugs against pain and for sedation; and difficulty in communication and resulting frustration due to advanced deafness. He went on:

> It is indeed quite possible that Mrs Cotton may have given the appearance of not only hearing, but also understanding the contents of the will, as read to her. It is, however, more doubtful whether her cerebral functions were sufficiently unimpaired for her to express her own viewpoints on the contents of the will and to use her independent judgement . . . I am inclined to believe that only an extraordinary effort on her part would have enabled her to rise above her suffering in order to concentrate her mind on the task presented to her by the solicitor on December 12th 1980.

No independent evidence exists to show that Mrs Cotton had ever wanted to make a new will. In a letter to Juneth's solicitors, Gordon Brown said that Ernest Cotton had told him to visit his mother and take instructions. He cannot comment now because he died in 1984, yet the question remains: for whom was Brown really acting? Even if Mrs Cotton were *compos mentis*, she would not have known Brown from Adam. Her son only brought him into her ninety-two-year life at her last gasp. So what was the relationship between Cotton and Brown?

They were both Freemasons – both members of Ormskirk's Pilgrim Lodge (no. 6207). In 1946 Cotton's father had been one of its founders. Ernest was Master in 1962 and later achieved the mighty provincial rank of Senior Grand Deacon. He was a big wheel in West Lancashire Freemasonry, whereas Brown had only just been initiated. When Brown drew up the 'hospital will' he was still a mere Fellow Craft. Just three weeks later he was raised to the third degree and became a Master Mason. The gap in the two men's Masonic status was immense, notwithstanding that, in the wider world, Brown was a prosperous solicitor while Cotton ran a modest coach firm. When Cotton asked him to make a will for his mother, it was an offer Brown could not refuse. The job had even been arranged in the lodge. On 3 December 1980, as some brothers stood drinking at the bar in Ormskirk Masonic Hall, Cotton walked over to Brown and was heard saying, he 'had a little job for him'.

Such deals may go on all the time in Ormskirk, which has many Masons. The mid-Lancs town has a population of 27,000, of which about 10,000 are men over twenty-one. The Masonic Hall in Park Road caters for eleven lodges with some 700 members. Even if many of them live in other communities nearby, it seems one Ormskirk man in twenty is 'on the square'. The town's most powerful lodge is Ormskirk Priory (no. 4007). At six o'clock on the fourth Wednesday of each month from September to April, its members slip into the hall to perform rituals, quaff a gin and tonic and sup at the festive board.

This lodge showed its power one morning in July 1985 by bringing the town to a halt for the funeral of one of its most revered members. By nine o'clock Ormskirk was paralysed by traffic. Everyone was late for work and shops could not open because the assistants had not arrived. Tradesmen, office staff and shoppers sat in their cars and fumed because, without warning, the main carpark had been closed to the public so mourners would have only a short walk to the parish church.

The dead man, Howard Ballance, had been a pillar of the community since World War II. A dentist, he had been a councillor for town and county for thirty-eight years. He was chairman of Lancashire Police Authority for three years, and was still a JP and chairman of the Magistrates' Bench when called to the 'Grand Lodge Above'.

Nobody begrudged Ballance a good funeral, but giving his mourners sole use of the carpark sent the town wild. The Chamber of Trade was furious and rang the police to complain. The cops said the council had told them to do it. The Chamber's president blasted the council's 'Kremlin-like attitude' of 'we are equal, but some are more equal than others'. The council blamed the idea on the police, but said that, anyway, 'it was a sensible way out of what could have been a ticklish problem'. The *problem* may have been how to appease Lodge no. 4007, whose members included several more councillors, and Ormskirk's ten other lodges. In all they could call on a total of fifteen of the town's fifty-five JPs and quite a few brethren among the local police.

One policeman belonged to Pilgrim Lodge with Ernest Cotton and his solicitor. Other members were factory owners, engineers, builders, shopkeepers, estate agents, an accountant, a printer, a farmer and an instrument technician named Derek Pilkington. He was Juneth's husband, and it was her brother Ernest who had nominated him in 1978 at old Mrs Cotton's insistence.

Derek was raised to Master Mason in October 1979 and regularly attended lodge meetings until November 1980 when the family was in dispute over the future of the coach business. Until this was sorted out Derek decided to 'withdraw', thus avoiding a row with his brother-in-law and complying with Freemasonry's Antient Charge that, 'no private piques or quarrels must be brought within the door of the lodge'.

However, the Pilkingtons did complain to a lodge elder about what they felt was Cotton's 'unmasonic' behaviour. They said he had put undue pressure on his mother to sign a will to his own advantage and the near disinheritance of his sister. He had also damaged the interests of a brother Mason (Derek Pilkington), breaking the Masonic commandment of brotherly love. The elder was upset and rang Ormskirk's top Mason (another JP) for advice. The Pilkingtons hoped this call would result in a pledge of Masonic justice, but they received none. Far from getting help from Freemasonry, they were soon ostracized by it. In Juneth's words:

> We very soon gathered that our past Freemason friends and their wives no longer desired our company. After learning the good points of Freemasonry, and believing in its foundations, and having enjoyed so much the company of the brethren and their families, this sudden treatment came as a shock. We were obviously being treated with the alternate treatment to murder, as laid down in the rituals. Instead of having our throats cut across, we were branded as 'wilfully perjured individuals, void of all moral worth and totally unfit to be received into this worshipful lodge'.

Derek was promptly struck off the lodge stewards' list, perhaps in retribution for branding Ernest Cotton's conduct 'unmasonic', perhaps because he had stayed away from three meetings rather than clash with his brother-in-law. It was on the advice of her mother's doctor that Juneth decided to fight the 'hospital will' but she ran into widespread obstruction. She wanted to see insurance papers for the coach firm of which she had long been a partner. Swinton Insurance's local manager, George Parr, refused to let her have them. He said she was 'on dangerous ground' and added, 'my firm has not got enough money to fight this'. He did not explain these remarks but Juneth thinks he was referring to the 'secret and silent power of Freemasonry'. He may not have been a Mason but he was in Rotary: 'Many Rotarians are Masons and it seems clear that if Parr was to help me in my troubles he would be working against the interests of his close professional colleagues.' When Parr died in 1983 many Masons attended his funeral, including two bank managers who had refused to give Juneth details of the family firm's accounts. Pilgrim Lodge kept its funds in one of those banks.

Meantime, Derek had been the victim of a forgery which could only have been perpetrated by a Mason. According to the constitutions every lodge member should receive a Grand Lodge certificate as soon as he is registered as a third degree Mason. Derek's certificate arrived twenty-three months late: on 28 August 1981 in a dirty crumpled envelope dropped through the letterbox at dinnertime. He complained to the Provincial Grand Secretary, who wrote back saying Pilgrim Lodge had kept the certificate in order to present it to him in person. When he did not turn up, it was sent on by registered post.

That letter contained two errors, fed to the writer by some Pilgrim Lodge member. Derek had attended all its meetings for a full twelve months after he became a Master Mason: ample time for him to receive the certificate in person. As for 'registered post', he had never signed for the document because it had been stuffed through the door when no one was at home.

Derek got in touch with the local acting Post Master who referred to the registered mail receipt book. This contained a signature in Derek's name which showed he had received the letter on 26 August 1981: a full two days before it landed on the doormat. The official admitted the signature looked new and stood out from the page, but said it must have been made on that date.

If so, it had not been made by Derek because he and Juneth were on holiday in France on 26 August, and did not return until two days later. No one else had been at home to sign on his behalf or in his name. Besides, the letter bore no registration slip. The Pilkingtons called in the police. A CID man confirmed that the signature looked 'fresh' yet nothing came of his inquiries, even though the suspects were obvious. The forgery could have been perpetrated only by a high-ranking Post Office official with access to the registered mail pen, or with such a person's co-operation.

This may sound trivial, but it proves Freemasonry can pervert even the Royal Mail. If it interferes with registered letters, what else does it contaminate? The incident also shows how far some Masons will go to cover up a breach of their own rules. First forge the signature, then lie to the Provincial Grand Secretary (a former policeman!), then get him to regurgitate the lie to the victim, even though he too is a Mason.

Handing out certificates on time and in the correct manner is the job of a lodge secretary. In 1981 the secretary of Pilgrim Lodge was Ernest Cotton. In November that year Derek sent a cheque to cover his annual subscriptions and £10 for Masonic charities. He also enclosed a note which he asked the Master to read in open lodge to the assembled brethren:

> Please accept my apologies for my non-attendance at Pilgrim Lodge. Being unable to attend has been a bitter disappointment to me, but, as you know, there is a brother in the Lodge with whom I am at variance over matters which have caused deep distress for almost two years to my wife and myself.
> I regret so few of my Brothers feel able to discuss my problems with me or are prepared to listen . . . However, when the time comes, the Great Architect of the Universe will surely as always be on the side of righteousness.

The letter was not read out and Derek never got a reply, only retribution. In 1983 he lost his job. The manager who sacked him was also in the brotherhood. Freemasons are exhorted to give a brother work, not deprive him of it, yet Derek's dismissal was unfair and unnecessary, as he later proved to an industrial tribunal which found wholly in his favour.

In January 1984 the Masonic solicitor Gordon Brown died aged little more than fifty. His funeral was attended by many Pilgrim brethren, but not by Ernest Cotton. Some Pilgrim men felt Brown's health had declined largely because he had spent three years trying to defend the indefensible 'hospital will'. The Pilkingtons are convinced its 'mistakes' were deliberate.

For instance, the will says Juneth Pilkington is to get one-quarter of the value of Mrs Cotton's 'dwellinghouse' but then gives the wrong address. This might have been a mistake, but it could have been a deliberate ploy to cut her out of the inheritance altogether. As it is worded, she would have received one-quarter of a property which her mother never owned – in other words, nothing at all.

The Pilkingtons also say the mistake over Mrs Cotton's name is a Masonic sign. Falsely named 'Hester Annie', not 'Esther Annie', her initials become H.A. These also stand for Hiram Abiff, the 'architect' of the Temple of Solomon. Then 'Widow' is inserted, a word which did not appear in the earlier will. However, if this is a 'Masonic' will, 'Widow' is there to show that Ernest is the 'Widow's Son'. In Masonic ritual Hiram Abiff is the 'Widow's Son', a phrase Masons use to identify themselves to other Masons.

Derek Pilkington has often complained to top Masonic officials, but they refuse to get involved, saying his dispute with Cotton is a legal matter in which Freemasonry cannot interfere. He retorts that Masonic lawyers have interfered from the start, first by drawing up a 'Masonic will' and then by ensuring no other lawyer in town dare fight it. When he complained to Freemasons' Hall in London, Commander Michael Higham wrote to suggest he consult another lawyer 'in another town'.[1]

This is just what the Pilkingtons did, when they eventually found a non-Masonic solicitor in Manchester. In 1987 they were about to fight the will in court, when Ernest Cotton's side made a last-minute offer: half the value of the mother's house and £4,500 for Juneth's share in the business. This came to £18,000 out of an estate worth some £60,000. Her barrister urged her strongly to accept, to avoid a legal contest which would exhaust the estate and leave her with nothing.

As a result the will's glaring mistakes (or Masonic signs) were never tested, nor was the legality of Mrs Cotton's signature nor the issue of her mental state. Instead, a highly suspect will – perhaps made under duress – was laundered and legitimized by the legal process itself. Now the law took its own cut. Juneth had to pay costs of £9,000: half her entire share of the estate.

Cotton meantime had been Master of Pilgrim Lodge a second time. He has now been awarded the lofty rank of Past Provincial Grand Warden, an honour which goes only to men who embody what the Antient Charges call 'the benign influence of masonry, as all true masons have done from the beginning of the world, and will do to the end of time'. A former town councillor, Cotton has even had a road named after him.

In contrast, Derek Pilkington has been 'excluded' from Pilgrim for non-payment of dues but, as he told officials, he could not attend until the anti-Masonic deeds of other members had been remedied. His unfair dismissal by another Mason and subsequent unemployment were two more reasons why he could not pay £35 a year. Yet his brethren resolved that it was Pilkington, and no one else, who was 'void of all moral worth and totally unfit to be received into this worshipful Lodge or any other warranted Lodge or society of men, who prize honour and virtue above the external advantages of rank and fortune'.

For many years Worshipful Brother Cotton ran a funeral business from the same premises as the family coach firm. A decade later, on the shelves of the unlocked and deserted garage, a plastic bag was discovered. It contained the remains of a named individual incinerated at Thornton Crematorium on 15 November 1974. Out of respect for this man and his family I shall not name him here. However, his crematorium reference number was C9856. Perhaps he too was a Freemason. Even if he was not, his ashes deserved rather better care from a Masonic undertaker.

twenty-five

MASONIC LIGHT IN TOWN HALLS

In June 1987 Derbyshire County Council issued a new employment application form. In one section it stated:

> The Council believes it is essential to maintain public confidence in the fair and impartial way in which it conducts its business affairs and that membership of a Masonic Lodge by an employee could seriously undermine that confidence.
>
> (a) Are you a member of a Masonic Lodge? YES/NO
>
> (b) If the answer is 'yes' would you be willing to reconsider the question of your continued membership of the organization before a final offer of appointment was made? YES/NO

The council leader, David Bookbinder, warned that if Freemasons did not agree to give up Masonic membership they risked not being appointed to 'sensitive' posts which involved handling council contracts. The council's experience during the Alf Parrish affair justified a robust approach (see Chapter 20), but singling out Masons might raise an issue of civil liberties, especially as the same form states that all applicants for council jobs 'receive equal treatment in employment regardless of their age, sex, marital status, disability, sexual orientation, race, creed, colour, ethnic or national origin' Bookbinder responds, 'Because of Freemasonry's undue influence here in the recent past we merely ask, "Are you a Freemason and, if so, are you prepared to leave the order?" We take the secrecy out of it and I think that is healthy'.

In 1988 in neighbouring East Staffordshire, a Labour move to force councillors and officers to declare Masonic membership was parried by a Tory motion demanding parallel disclosure by members of trade unions, the Co-op, Militant Tendency, CND, Amnesty International and

Greenpeace. The point was well made but, even so, Freemasonry flummoxes the libertarian because it is itself discriminatory – and not just against women. Despite unrelenting denials, it discriminates perpetually against the 96 per cent or so of all men who are not Masons. That much is written into its Constitutions, in which a Mason is charged 'to prefer a poor brother that is a good man and true before any other poor people in the same circumstances'.[1]

Mention Freemasonry in any local council chamber and watch democracy explode. Since *The Brotherhood* was published in 1984, the Craft has been angrily debated in more than 100 authorities, including some of Britain's biggest cities (Birmingham, Manchester, Leeds, Bradford, Bristol, Nottingham, Plymouth, Reading), eleven counties (Lancashire, Cheshire, West Yorkshire, Cumbria, Derbyshire, Staffordshire, Essex, Cambridge, Hampshire, Devon, Cornwall) and ten London boroughs.

Such debates are characterized by posturing on both sides. The anti-Masons, usually left-wing Labour or Liberal (SLD) councillors, are driven by a gut feeling that Freemasonry is the preserve of their Conservative or right-wing Labour opponents. Yet they rarely have evidence that other councillors are Masons, or proof that Masonry has ever perverted council decision-making.

Freemasons and their defenders are just as dissembling. In accord with the Antient Charges they try to 'divert the discourse' by eulogizing Masonic charity, attacking pressure groups favoured by anti-Masons, and claiming any move against Freemasonry invades the privacy and liberty of everyone else.

When all this cant has been decanted, anti-Masons usually demand that councillors and senior officers declare Masonic membership on a register of interests kept at the town or county hall. Labour and Alliance-ruled councils tend to pass such motions, but Tory councils throw them out. In 1987 a Liberal councillor in Slough proposed that his fellow councillors declare their membership and not stand for re-election or 'resign from the Masons forthwith'. A Tory came back with the standard libertarian response: 'We live in a free country and as long as people are within the law then it is up to them if they want to be Masons.' Slough opted for voluntary declaration, but this may have little effect. In nearby Reading in 1988, four out of fifteen Tory councillors had declared themselves in accord with a ruling by the town's Labour-controlled council. This was an admirable response, but usually few Masons 'come out' because no real penalty can be applied if they do not. On some councils they might get banned from committees, but the fact that they have been democratically elected gives them an absolute right to their council seat. No sanction can force them to 'own up'.

Typically futile was the 1985 resolution by the London Borough of Enfield that all councillors should declare membership of societies such as the Masons. Two years later the *Enfield Gazette* discovered only twenty out of twenty-eight Labour councillors had filled in the confidential form, just one admitting he was 'on the square'. Of thirty-eight Tories only fourteen complied, none of whom was a Mason. Yet the newspaper claimed at least ten Tory councillors were in the Craft.[2] Labour councillors said they suspected Enfield was run by Masons but one Tory who publicly admitted he was a member retorted: 'There is no reason why Masonry should clash with council business. But I can't tell you anything about it.'

Such evasive dismissals reduce socialists to maniacal frustration. Trying to pin something on Freemasons is like cutting soup with a knife. Yet left-of-centre folk feel their hostility to the Craft is justified when its defenders speak almost as members of the Conservative Party:

> If you really want to see idiots at work, then attend a few political rallies, such as those perpetuated by Messrs Scargill and co. (Anonymous letter in *Enfield Advertiser*, June 1987)

> Your boots are getting bigger and bigger. It is not the Conservative Group on Bradford Council you are damaging, it is democracy. If you carry on abusing your power central government will take it away. (Cllr Ronnie Farley, leader of Conservatives on Bradford Council, October 1986)

> Groups such as the Militant Tendency are much more dangerous than the Freemasons. (Tony Mazey, Conservative, Calderhead Council, December 1986)

> It is not masonry which has brought this country to its knees with strikes, riots and violence. This witch-hunt is being conducted by the same termites who have been gnawing away at the pillars and institutions of British Society, our backbone, and strength in a relentless effort to bring about its collapse. Thank heavens we have a government which knows a bit about pest control. (R. R. Redmore, a non-Mason, Bristol *Evening Post*, July 1987)

This last letter was written during a furious controversy on Bristol Council over a move for compulsory Masonic declaration. The proposer was Labour councillor Vernon Hicks, who is adamant that he and his family had been on the receiving end of a Masonic hate-campaign for many months. Minority leader Sir Bob Wall said that his Tory group would probably 'tell them to get stuffed'. Even so, the council voted to set up a new register on the basis of detailed questions – for council officers as well as elected members. In theory, at least, Bristolians will now be able to see which of their leaders are 'on the square'. Many will rush to look, if another letter to the *Evening Post* is any guide.[3] This was from a former employee and 'friend of some Masons': 'I did not find them all honest and law-abiding, in fact quite the opposite. Unless perjury, drunken driving and purloining other people's property is normal procedure – plus hatred of unions.'

'Letters to the Editor' columns may be unreliable gauges of public opinion, but whenever Britain's town, city and county halls reverberate to rows about the Craft, scribes spit blood on the pages of local rags. Sometimes the editors join in. In July 1986 the Labour-controlled Manchester Council banned Masons from using the town hall for their functions. At this time the city's Masons were being blamed for John Stalker's downfall, but Oldham's *Evening Chronicle* rushed to their defence:

> They may have secret ceremonies and special handshakes, but they are not in the business of subverting the state and democracy. For that you need to go into smoky back rooms, where left-wing cabals set out to infiltrate the Labour Party, oust those whom they do not like, and then ride to their dictatorial power on the backs of the deluded electorate.[4]

Two *Manchester Evening News* letters spat out similar views:

> It appears that lesbians, gays, ethnic minorities can, and are, encouraged to use council premises with the statement that 'they also pay rates'. I would think that Freemasons pay rates . . . more than others if in business.

> Anyone who seriously believes that Freemasonry poses a dangerous threat to democracy should seriously think of having his/her head examined. The only threat to democracy comes from those who control Manchester City Council.[5]

At this time High Peak Council in Derbyshire was discussing whether to check on the Masonic connections of all companies to which it awarded contracts. Cllr Jane Inglefield protested that if this scheme went ahead the council should also find out who were Roman Catholics. She later explained she was not attacking Catholics but saw Labour's attack on Freemasonry as the thin end of the wedge: 'From what we hear, religious freedom is not given a lot of encouragement in left-dominated countries such as Russia and Poland.'

Another defence of Freemasonry works on the principle that 'my enemy's enemy is my friend'. In 1986 Alan Cornelius wrote to the London *Standard* pointing out that Freemasonry was persecuted by Hitler and Franco, and is now attacked by anti-Semites, communists, fascists and the Labour left. He went on: 'Any organization reviled by such groups is an irresistible attraction. How do I go about joining?'[6]

Cornelius would have relished a 1987 *London Daily News* article by socialist Ken Livingstone, in which he denounced the 'corruption' he had found on joining the London Labour Party in 1969: 'Half the members of some Labour councils in the same Masonic lodge, scratching each other's backs and filling their own pockets.'[7]

Readers anticipated juicy revelations, but Livingstone offered none. This matched his 1981 response to a letter from Stephen Knight asking for information about Freemasonry in local government and County Hall, where 'Red Ken' then reigned as leader of the Greater London Council. The politician said he had 'no knowledge of Freemasons at the GLC but that there is a lodge'. He thus missed a golden opportunity to tell Knight of all the Masonic back-scratching and pocket-filling he later claimed to know about.

All this huffing and puffing is no substitute for evidence, which local government conspiracy theorists rarely produce. This might be taken to prove Britain's town halls are free of Masonic wrong-doing, yet this too would be an illusion. On the rare occasions when councillors and reporters have used their investigative *nous*, they have proved the Craft's extraordinary influence.

The seaside resort of Worthing in Sussex is best known as the destination on a first-class ticket in the pocket of a very charitable gentleman who found a babe in a handbag in the cloakroom at Victoria Station. In *The Importance of Being Earnest* Oscar Wilde does not say if Ernest Worthing's benefactor was a Freemason. In Wilde's day there was but one lodge in Worthing. Today there are fourteen and, if anyone wants to be mayor, membership is near enough a necessity.

In 1986 few Worthing folk understood how a hearse driver named Mike Parkin could suddenly become mayor when he had only recently been elected on to the council. Certainly he belonged to the ruling Tory group, but so did several long-serving councillors who had been passed over. Reporter Mike Montgomery touched on the mystery in a *Worthing*

Gazette article headlined, 'Carve-Up or Coincidence?'[8] He revealed that not only was Parkin a Mason; so too were three out of six members on the committee which chose him. Two others, Liberal non-Masons, were so outraged that they walked out accusing the Tories of 'procedural skulduggery'.

Montgomery discovered Parkin was the sixth male Tory mayor out of the past seven who was 'on the square'. The only recent non-Masonic mayors had been three women and a Liberal. One loser because of this cosy nexus is another Tory councillor, John Cotton. Most observers thought he would be mayor in 1986 but, as he told the *Gazette*, 'I don't know why I was not put forward. I have been asked at least six times if I wanted to be a Mason but have always declined. This has given me food for thought.'

Cotton missed out again in 1987. The new mayor was yet another Mason: Eric McDonald, a former policeman turned accountant. Like undertaker Parkin, McDonald is a past master of Worthing's oldest lodge, the aptly named Lodge of Friendship. Of course, both men reject suggestions that *Masonic* friendship helped them don the chain of office, but do a mere 800 Masons deserve to monopolize Worthing's civic honours when its total population is 90,000? Apparently not, for in 1988 the non-Mason John Cotton finally became Mayor.

The same question could be asked in North Wales where Masons have an octopus grip on local government. One exasperated hotelier wrote to me claiming he was being forced out of business by the 'Mason Mafia' in Llandudno, which he calls 'Masonville'. He has since quit. Thirty-five miles away in Ruthin there are so many Masons that in 1983 democracy almost broke down. In July Glyndwyr District Council resolved to buy a church hall for community use, yet five months later it had still not done so. Several non-Masonic councillors suspected this was because the local Gabriel Goodman Lodge (no. 4533) wanted the hall for ritual purposes. If true, this would have been against the public interest because many Glyndwyr councillors are Masons and might have exploited inside information for fraternal advantage. Suspicions hardened with rumours that the council's offer had been 'gazumped' by a bid from the lodge.

The affair came to a head at a council meeting when the legal officer stated that, in these circumstances, elected members and full-time officers ought to declare their Masonic affiliation and withdraw. First to walk out were the chief executive and a councillor who belonged to another lodge, the Denbigh Castle (no. 4916). Other Masons followed, including the chief technical officer and three more councillors. Another councillor stayed after insisting he had resigned from the Craft. Membership of the Church in Wales (vendors of the hall) caused yet another to withdraw, along with the treasurer and the chief administrator. Six more councillors had already left, for reasons they did not disclose. By the time the debate began, there were barely enough councillors to form a quorum.

Only now did the truth come out. Despite a previous denial, the Gabriel Goodman Lodge had made a written offer for the hall. At £12,000 this was a persuasive £2,000 more than the council bid. It never became clear why the council had not closed the deal before the lodge slipped in with its offer, nor did any councillor or officer admit belonging to Gabriel Goodman. Even so, in Welsh Wales suspicions still linger that a direct link was unnecessary. The local inter-lodge grapevine would have done the trick instead.

Embarrassed by bad publicity and chastened by village support for the council bid, the lodge withdrew. This triumph for local democracy was achieved only because of exposures by a few determined councillors and the *Denbighshire Free Press*.[9]

Elsewhere, Masonic 'insider dealing' has succeeded because no one outside the Craft found out what was going on until too late. For instance, the 1972 Local Government Act reduced the status of the Lancashire town of Blackburn from county borough to urban district council. During the change-over the delightful medieval pele tower at Turton, previously available for a variety of public functions, was leased to local Masons for their exclusive use. Citizens were astonished to discover the brethren had secured so long a lease that it would be almost impossible to get them out. It took five years before the tower again became available to the general public.

The villagers of St Agnes, Cornwall, were not even this lucky. A few years ago they also had the chance to acquire a hall, which had been built as a grand entrance to British Legion premises. The Legion could not afford to finish the project, so the hall was put on sale. It looked ideal for the villagers who had no hall of their own. They held a public meeting to decide whether to buy but, when it came to a vote, most people present voted against.

The defeated enthusiasts could not understand why such a popular scheme had been lost, but they later found out that local Masons had gone to the meeting to vote it down. Shortly afterwards the Masons themselves bought the place for a mere £3,000, but not for use as a Masonic Temple. They just wanted the land *around* the British Legion hall as a carpark for their existing temple next door. Meantime the villagers looked on in dismay as the Masons rented the hall to a wholesale paper supplier who uses it to store thousands of toilet rolls. As one appalled villager put it, 'We've been wiping the shit off our faces ever since.'

Such unreported scandals occur literally from one end of Britain to another: 800 miles north of Cornwall, in 1986, the Orkney Islands Council policy and resources committee decided to exempt Freemasons' halls in the North and South Isles from paying any local rates. Councillor J. R. T. Robertson later asked how many councillors were members of this 'wonderful organization' and if they should not have declared their interest when the decision was made.

Chief executive Ron Gilbert explained that Masonic halls had paid only 50 per cent rates for several years, but the fall in population was making it difficult for the brethren to pay even this amount. There was no logic in Gilbert's answer. If the population was falling, there was no reason why the few folk remaining should bear the even greater burden of rate-free Masonics. As one letter to the *Orcadian* pointed out: 'Cllr Robertson does not seem to have received an answer to his very pertinent question.'

In Yorkshire, Freemasonry has been a by-word for racketeering ever since the Pontefract architect John Poulson scooped up contract after contract in the 1960s by corrupting local and national politicians.[10] However, Mr Poulson rejects the idea that Freemasonry ever helped him in his career. In 1987 he told me that he never used Masonic activities for business advantage: 'I was an enthusiastic loyal member of my lodge [De Lacy, no. 4643] for many years. I found Masonry fascinating and I gave myself enthusiastically to its service. I can only say I did not use Masonry to further my business interest.'

Journalists who spent years researching Poulson and his empire felt that, on the contrary, the Craft was of 'great use to him in his business-seeking activities'.[11] He attended lodge meetings not just with his solicitor but also with Sir Bernard Kenyon (the powerful Clerk of Yorkshire West Riding Council who later chaired one of Poulson's companies), the Secretary of Leeds Regional Hospital Board, and Bradford's City Architect. It happens that Bradford, Leeds and the West Riding were three councils from which Poulson extracted huge, lucrative contracts. He also picked up nearly £1,000,000 in fees for building two Leeds hospitals.

Poulson's right-hand man and 'public relations' fixer was T. Dan Smith, the most powerful politician this century to emerge from the city of Newcastle. For hustling on Poulson's behalf Smith was sent to jail for six years in 1974. He was not a Mason but found his Masonic handshakes could open doors that would have stayed shut if he had been considered a non-Mason. In a television interview in 1988 he told me, 'There may be some Masons who join for the highest of motives. If there are, it hasn't been my good fortune to meet them. All the ones I have met joined simply and explicitly for commercial gain, and most have been un-

ashamed in admitting that the advantage was in getting good contracts'.[12] By himself exploiting corrupt Masons Smith was able to buy a
£6.5 million housing contract from the London Borough of Wandsworth
for just a few thousand pounds in bribes.

Smith contradicts his one-time paymaster by claiming Freemasonry
played a big part in their success. He says Poulson told him he had
become a Mason to get business from the many authorities controlled in
the 1960s by Labour councillors who were also Masons. As a prominent
Tory, Poulson did not need Freemasonry to win business from Conservative councils! According to Dan Smith, the system is the same,
whichever party is in power.

> The only areas of corruption in local government are over contracts,
> supplies, professional services and building. And these are the areas
> where Masonic pressures are applied. You know the process: a
> building site comes up for planning permission. If an application
> comes in from the developer, and the Masonic people know
> beforehand, then they meet beforehand, discuss it beforehand and
> take the decision beforehand.

I reminded Smith that a large proportion of council building contracts are
given to Catholic non-Masonic building firms. 'But they haven't got the
iron discipline,' he said. 'It's like the party whip in Parliament. It's
difficult for Conservative MPs to defy the whip, though some do. The
Masonic structure is just as disciplined, whether Masons admit it or not.
Wherever it is necessary for Masonic influence to be applied at a decisive
point – be it commercial, political, in the provision of local authority
services or not – then that influence is an evil influence, because it can
operate across the political board, the professional divide, and across the
contractual divide.'

The Poulson–Smith tale may seem a little dated now, and Smith might
be accused of special pleading, but Bradford's *1 in 12* Publications
Collective (a group of unemployed young people) recently exposed even
more intricate fraternal dealings. In 1986 one of its investigations was
printed in the *Leeds Other Paper*. It was a probe into Masonic scheming
over council plans to drive a by-pass through the suburb of Headingley
into Leeds city centre.[13] In 1966 twelve local lodges formed the 'Shire
Oak Property Company' to buy five acres of land in Headingley for
£30,806. To build a stretch of the by-pass Leeds Council had already
resolved to buy half the land, but only did so in 1971 when it paid Shire
Oak £23,500. The lodges had planned to develop on the other two and a
half acres which previously had no road access but which would become
prime building land as soon as the by-pass was built.

Five more years went by. The council had still not built the road, partly because of intense local opposition, yet the Shire Oak Masons were not dismayed. In 1976 they applied for planning permission to build on their two and a half acres, but at this point their plans collapsed. The Labour government announced that there would be far less money for road improvements. The county council had to cut spending by £30 million and the Headingley by-pass was shelved. In 1977 a report recommended that nothing be done until at least 1982. By then Shire Oak was in voluntary liquidation.

The trouble was that, without the by-pass, no vehicles could get on the Shire Oak land. On one side stood Headingley Castle, on the other a house of nuns known as the Little Sisters of Mercy. The Little Sisters spurned the advances of the 'Big Brothers' and would not let them build a road across their grounds. This left the Masons with land which nobody could reach and nobody wanted to buy. In 1982 the Sisters relented, but only if the land were sold to a non-Masonic housing association to build sheltered homes. With only one possible buyer the Freemasons were forced to accept £42,000 for land which would have been worth £120,000 on an open market. If the by-pass had ever been built, it would have been worth far, far more.

After deducting the liquidation costs, Shire Oak shareholders made a notional profit: they received 83p for each 50p share. However, since they had bought the land nearly twenty inflationary years before, the 'profit' was in fact a heavy loss. They would have done far better investing their money in a building society.

The significance of this story is not that even Masons get burned sometimes; it is that when those twelve lodges got together in 1966 to buy the land, they had every reason to believe they were going to make a killing. Personal investors in Shire Oak included:

John Astle JP, a Leeds city councillor on the transport and traffic committees (200 shares).

Irwin Bellow JP, councillor and Leader of Leeds City Council 1975–9. Created Lord Bellwin in 1979 by Margaret Thatcher to become Minister of State for local government in the Department of the Environment (100 shares).

Donald Bradley, councillor on the finance and planning committee (200 shares).

Allan Bretherick, councillor and Lord Mayor of Leeds.

Harold Jowitt, councillor on the finance and planning committee.

Donald Wolstenholme JP, another councillor.

Peter White and his wife, both councillors. Mr White (60 shares) was
also political agent for Sir Keith Joseph (MP for Leeds North-East,
1956–87).
Alfred Vickers, councillor (80 shares).

A further 100 shares were held by the husband of another councillor.
Other shareholders prominent in Yorkshire's then West Riding included
two deputy lieutenants: Bernard Lyons JP and Joseph Hiley, Conservative MP for Pudsey for fifteen years and a Lord Mayor of Leeds.

Another curious twist is that Shire Oak had lent money to the Leeds
Masonic Hall Company, whose shareholders included three more
councillors, one of whom was another Tory MP: Sir Donald (later Lord)
Kaberry of Adel, who held Leeds North-West from 1951 to 1983. His
constituency included the very Headingley area which faced destruction
if the by-pass were ever built. When angry locals complained in 1972, the
Yorkshire Evening Post reported that Kaberry told them: 'I'll keep an eye
on those road plans.' Two months later the newspaper revealed that work
would start on the road in 1975.

As individuals, none of Shire Oak's eminent Yorkshiremen can be
shown to have besmirched their honour by using knowledge gained
through public office for personal gain, yet the concentration of so many
local politicians in a company set up to benefit from a local government
decision ought to disturb anyone who expects elected representatives to
act for the good of all the people. Listed Shire Oak shareholders alive
today claim they cannot remember why the land was bought. The local
past Grand Master has even forgotten he was a shareholder.

Today, Leeds is a Labour-controlled council which requires councillors, employees and even head teachers to declare Masonic membership.
In 1987 it banned the Masonic Knights Templar from meeting in a local
high school. In neighbouring Bradford, Kirklees and Calderdale similar
measures are in force. West Yorkshire's Fire Authority requires firemen
to admit if they carry a Masonic square-and-compasses alongside their
axe. This may smack of McCarthyism, but the Shire Oak affair seems to
justify it. Local Masons have brought fear and loathing on themselves.

In most of England, however, anti-Masons are less resolute than in
Yorkshire. The Essex resort of Southend seems to be controlled by
Masons, yet the citizens are too apathetic or scared to overthrow them.
The Masonic hall houses forty-three Craft lodges, twenty-three Royal
Arch chapters and many side orders. This town of 50,000 adult males
contains 3,000 Masons who dominate not only the traditional Masonic
power bases but also new growth industries. Essex Radio, formed in
1982, has no less than nine Grand Provincial Officers among its
shareholders, including a Past Essex Grand Master.

One of Southend's most eminent Masons is William Muckley, worshipful past master of Crowstone Lodge (no. 3298). He spent most of his adult life working for Southend Council. For more than ten years he controlled the town's council house allocations, a position of immense patronage, if abused.

In 1982 Muckley's private life was in flux. He had left his wife and moved in with a deputy headmistress named Christine Holliday. She had just been allocated a council house by the very department which Muckley headed as assistant director of housing. Even odder, the marital home where Mrs Holliday had left her husband was not in Southend so it is not clear why Southend had any responsibility to rehouse her.

Christine was allowed to live in the council house only while the sitting tenants spent a year in Wales but, when they returned and she moved out, mail kept pouring through the door addressed to a William Muckley. The tenants concluded that Southend's housing mogul must have lived there with Mrs H. for quite a while.

Paul Foot of the *Daily Mirror* asked Muckley for an explanation, but the handsome six-foot-four-inch official told him he had never lived with Mrs Holliday so he had no idea about the mail. Unconvinced, Foot stated in print that Muckley used to spend his nights there with Mrs Holliday. He also revealed that when Mrs H. moved out, Southend Housing Department quickly awarded her a brand new housing association flat, where again she and Muckley were nocturnally conjoined.

Later the couple bought their own house and married, but before this happened Muckley had to get a divorce from his first wife. Mrs Joan Muckley did not want to move from her marital home, but the divorce settlement required it to be sold and the proceeds divided. This would have meant Mrs Muckley had nowhere to live, a problem which would obviously delay the settlement.

It may have been coincidence, but while Muckley was still married to Joan, Southend Housing Department nominated her for a housing association flat under her maiden name of Thoroughgood. Her nomination form was signed by none other than her husband: assistant housing director William Muckley. Challenged again by Paul Foot, Muckley said he signed hundreds of letters every day but had not noticed his own former address on the form. When the housing association director found out that Joan Thoroughgood was really Joan Muckley, he protested to the town clerk. The hapless Mrs Muckley was struck off the list, but no action was taken against her adulterous husband.

Muckley's professionalism had been questioned long before his own complex housing arrangements became public knowledge. In 1978 he was on the examination board of the Institute of Housing. In this capacity he made an approach to a twenty-six-year-old trainee named Mrs Jane Saxby who was about to sit the Institute's exam. Suggesting she take notes, he asked her if she had studied such unusual areas as underleasing and distress. Jane was suspicious because she knew he had access to the exam questions as a member of the board. 'I glanced at the paper he was reading from. I could see it was laid out exactly the same way as a question paper, although it was not an official question paper.'

Jane felt that if Muckley was telling her the questions in advance, it would be improper for her to take the exam. She was furious because she wanted to pass on her own merits. She went to see the Institute's secretary, Denis Crouch, who read her notes of Muckley's hot tips and confirmed that they referred to the forthcoming question areas. He also told her she could not sit the exam. Shortly afterwards Muckley resigned from the board. He told the *Southend Standard* that he did not see eye-to-eye with the Institute. Crouch also downplayed the affair when asked for a comment. He said Muckley had been guilty of 'no more than a minor indiscretion which anyone might have committed'.

This scarcely matched what Crouch told Jane Saxby: 'Prompt action has been taken . . . to ensure there can be no recurrence of the situation you have reported, and appropriate disciplinary measures have been imposed.' The only loser turned out to be Jane herself. She had to wait another year before she could take the exam. Meantime Muckley prospered. He was promoted to the job of town housing boss and given the new title of Chief Housing Officer.

Muckley was made redundant in 1985, ostensibly because Southend had too many chief officers and he was near retirement. It is unclear if the council had been shamed into ousting him by Paul Foot's revelations. These certainly did not impress the folk in Crowstone Lodge who installed him as Master only days after his masterly housing arrangements had been exposed in the *Daily Mirror*.

Paul Foot now switched his attentions to one of Southend's other Masons. In 1985, Councillor Geoffrey Baum was a member of the planning committee which recommended that, in future, anyone wanting to turn a semi-detached house into an old people's home should be refused planning permission.

Months later just such a scheme came before the town planning officers. They advised refusal but a sub-committee recommended approval by yet another committee with the final say. Councillor Baum sat on this too, a fact which might have embarrassed a lesser man because he owned the semi-detached in question. Challenged by Foot he retorted: 'This is an exceptionally large property. It's not like any other semi-detached house in the town. Every case should be treated on its merits.'

Baum said he would declare his interest when the scheme was discussed, an act befitting an Essex Grand Chapter Mason. Following Foot's *exposé*, his scheme was turned down. Today Southend's grandest Freemason is still living in its grandest semi.

Freemasonry is so strong in towns like Southend that the song 'Oh, I Do Like to Be Beside the Seaside' deserves to be included in books of Masonic music. On England's South Coast the neighbouring resorts of Bournemouth and Poole contain thirty-two lodges, and it sometimes seems that, even on this sunset strip, Masonic apron-strings are pulled.

Back in 1972 Arthur Lloyd-Allen was Conservative leader of Poole Council and chairman of its policy and resources committee. However, he did not usually attend a subordinate highways committee so it was a surprise when he turned up at a meeting of that committee and pressed for a wide new road to be built through the outlying rural district of Merley. Such a road was vital, he said, because Poole was short of homes. Served by a new road, Merley would be just the place to build the right kind of houses.

Another Conservative, Councillor Edna Adams, smelled a rat. This doughty lady, who later became sheriff and mayor of Poole and who still serves on Poole and Dorset councils, felt Lloyd-Allen was concealing an interest. She did not know what it was until she went to London and searched files at Companies House in which she found irrefutable evidence: Lloyd-Allen was a director of a firm called Broadstone Developments, along with a prominent local building contractor named Harry Palmer. Evidently the company aim was the exploitation of the very area through which Lloyd-Allen had been pressing for the new road to be built. Mrs Adams instantly realized that this road would greatly enhance the value of land which Broadstone Developments already owned. Yet Lloyd-Allen had never declared his interest to the committee.

Mrs Adams wrote to the Town Clerk reporting her discovery. She pointed out that Lloyd-Allen should have acted within established local government guidelines, not least because he was also a magistrate. The Town Clerk showed the letter to Lloyd-Allen who demanded that Mrs Adams withdraw it and give an amount to charity. She refused, so Lloyd-Allen put her though a twelve-day libel action at the High Court in 1977. The jury found in Mrs Adams's favour. Lloyd-Allen was required to pay all her court costs. Even so, she was still £1,500 out-of-pocket when it was all over.

Lloyd-Allen could well afford to pay, for the jury verdict did not stop the road getting built. Sure enough, the acres owned by Broadstone Developments became prime building land, enhancing Lloyd-Allen's substantial fortune. It so happens that in 1975 he and his partner Harry Palmer founded a new Masonic Lodge, the Broadstone (no. 8641). Other founders included the financial director of Palmer's own firm, H. J. Palmer Ltd. Cynics now wonder whether they named the lodge after the locality of Broadstone of the company.

Poole is overshadowed by its big neighbour, Bournemouth, where everything is done on a grander scale. For generations this town relied on seven miles of golden sands and its Winter Gardens Pavilion to attract holiday-makers, but sunshine and discos in Mediterranean fleshpots had eaten away at the resort's appeal. By 1980 Bournemouth resembled a dowager in moth-eaten gladrags, down-at-heel and very short of funds.

At this moment some town council members came up with an idea which, they claimed, would reverse the resort's decline. What Bournemouth needed was an international conference centre to thrust it into the twenty-first century. It would earn millions of pounds of revenue from multi-national corporations holding business jamborees. TV companies would rush to hire its arenas for showbiz spectaculars and dance competitions. It would also be ideal for political party conferences. Continual media coverage would keep Bournemouth in the news and attract thousands more holiday-makers to its traditional delights.

The council as a whole approved the idea, but now the real battle began. Where would the centre be built, who was going to build it, how much would it cost, and where was the money coming from?

The first problem was that there was no space big enough for the project. The town centre was all built up, while the beach front to the east and west was hemmed in by cliffs on which hotels and apartment blocks already occupied all habitable land. At last it was resolved that the only suitable site lay on the West Cliff, but even this required the demolition of twenty hotels. Some ratepayers felt this was a shocking start to a scheme aimed at attracting *more* visitors to the town, especially as the land occupied by the doomed hotels would cost £6 million. This was a sizeable chunk of the £16 million which the council had approved for the entire scheme, which now paraded under the grand title of 'the Bournemouth International Centre'.

The choice of architect-contractors was equally restricted. Dozens of conference centres have been built across Britain in the past decade. Nearly all have been built by one firm: Module Two. In open competition Module Two predictably won the Bournemouth job, much to the chagrin of many councillors and citizens who felt the proposals of its rivals were more suited to the town's needs.

Finance now became paramount, for neither Bournemouth nor Module Two had any money to bankroll the scheme. The council turned to merchant bankers Morgan Grenfell for funding. By the time the centre was completed it had cost £25 million, leaving Bournemouth's citizens £9 million more out-of-pocket than the elected representatives had led them to expect. The centre was also a completely different shape. Module Two had won with a proposal for an oval structure, but built a stark rectangular block.

The huge excess was made up largely of over-runs by contractors. Heating and ventilation equipment was installed for a breathtaking £2.4 million by an Anglo-Dutch company, ADEC. For this much ratepayers might have expected a summer temperature of less than 100 degrees Fahrenheit in the centre's swimming-pool restaurant, but 100 degrees was what they got. The contract had been awarded to ADEC on the assumption that it held exclusive patents on the system chosen by Module Two. It turned out that the firm had no such patents. All it did was assemble bits and pieces made in Britain by British companies. Worse still, ADEC went into liquidation owing sub-contractors over £1 million on the Bournemouth job alone. These firms are suing Bournemouth for the full amount. The council's only defence is that, since it paid ADEC the full £2.4 million, it cannot be held liable for ADEC's debts.

The cost over-run and the heating fiasco might both be forgivable if the Bournemouth International Centre had soon yielded profits to help pay off its huge capital debt, but it has yielded only runaway debts. In the financial year 1985–6 it lost £1.2 million. In 1986–7 the council finagled this down to £861,000 by including profits earned by the Winter Gardens Pavilion. Meanwhile the council has reduced the capital debt only by selling off 200 acres, previously earmarked for housing and sports fields. Far from adding to Bournemouth's civic amenities, the centre has reduced them substantially. To cut the debt further, the council has sold some heavily mortgaged properties. Today the mortgage interest on these properties still runs at some £175,000 a year, but this pay-out is not listed on the centre's deficit sheet, which clearly it should be.

It is doubtful if the centre has brought the town any benefit. Nothing could deter visitors more effectively than television pictures of security checks at Tory Party conferences. For weeks beforehand Bournemouth is invaded by Special Branch officers and anti-terrorist squads on the alert for guns, bombs and booby-traps. During the conferences hundreds of police search bags, hotels and motor cars, while traffic jams ensure the entire West Cliff area is 'off-limits' to anyone wanting a quiet holiday. Does the conference bring any revenue to the town? Some hotel-owners benefit, but Bournemouth's Tory-controlled council lets national political parties use the centre for absolutely nothing!

What has all this got to do with Freemasonry? Simply this: if it had not been for the presence of Freemasons on Bournemouth Council the centre might not have been approved and the townsfolk would never have suffered the resulting financial catastrophe.

In 1981 Councillor Margaret Hogarth was sitting on both Bournemouth and Dorset Councils. She was a popular member of the borough Conservative group, to which she had been elected since 1969. She was due to be mayor the following year.

Mrs Hogarth carefully studied the economics of the centre and knew it would be a disaster. The sums did not add up. In February 1981 she asked for a special council meeting at which she tried to block the decision. The public turned up in droves, including members of many residents' associations opposing the scheme.

> I was doing quite well in getting it deferred for further study [says Mrs Hogarth], indeed, I think I gave the best speech I had ever made, when up stood another Conservative councillor who, I knew, used to attend a local Masonic lodge. I knew he was an enthusiast for the scheme, but I was astonished when he suddenly cried: 'I call on the Great Architect of the Universe to support me at this hour.'
>
> I knew instantly what this man meant. My former husband was a Freemason so I was well aware that 'T.G.A.O.T.U.' is how Masons describe God. The chap was summoning all his brother Masons to support the Module Two scheme. Sure enough, they did. I lost by four votes, the centre was built, and this town has been asset-stripped to pay for it.

Soon after the meeting Mrs Hogarth visited Bournemouth's most senior Mason to complain about this public misuse of Craft membership. He sympathized but said he was powerless to do anything about it. Henceforth she was the victim of a concerted Masonic onslaught because of her opposition to the scheme.

There is no evidence that Module Two is a Masonic firm or that its directors knowingly exploited a Masonic political axis to win the Bournemouth contract. Yet within weeks of speaking out against the Module Two scheme, Mrs Hogarth was dropped as a Tory candidate in the county elections, even though she was a sitting member. Her replacement was Gordon Anstee, a 31st degree member and Grand Inspector Inquisitor Commander of the Rose Croix Masonic order, in which he belongs to three prestigious chapters.

Still a member of Bournemouth council, Mrs Hogarth found that her outspoken opposition to the Centre had isolated her within the Tory group. Realizing its supporters would no longer back her for mayor, she left the group and sat as an independent. Today she sits on the committee responsible for the centre's finances: 'The only thing that makes a profit there is the carpark.'

Margaret Hogarth wonders if her problems with Freemasonry really began back in 1979 when she was on a slate of three candidates in a Bournemouth election. There is a convention that all publicity material should display all three names with equal prominence. Mrs Hogarth discovered that the other two candidates were putting out publicity omitting her name altogether. This prompted her to distribute personal cards with her name alone. She won by a landslide but one of her Conservative colleagues was defeated. At an angry inquest in a private house a few days later, he swore vengeance. Mrs Hogarth says that he threatened to make sure she would never get any responsibilities on the council and he would get her out of the Conservative Party.

The constituency chairman was also present. As the meeting reached a bitter climax he suddenly said to the loser, 'We were taught to be cautious, weren't we?' and the two men gave each other a Masonic handshake. Mrs Hogarth knew that the expression, 'taught to be cautious', was a direct quote from the second degree ritual, and she could not help noticing the handshake. Another Mason who witnessed the incident was astonished at the flouting of Masonic secrecy: 'I've never seen such a thing done outside the lodge.' Subsequent protests to Masonic elders failed to bring any rebuke for the offenders. Instead, Margaret was given a rocket by local Tory bosses for distributing those canvassing cards.

Her Masonic adversary did not oust her from the Conservative Party; instead she left when she saw the Masonic writing on the wall. Since 1979, however, that man has done very well. He was re-elected to the council and even became mayor of Bournemouth, a post which Masons have made sure Mrs Hogarth will never attain.

In 1987 in Torbay, Devon, the council rejected a plan for a new Sainsbury's superstore by just one vote. A few days later at an additional council meeting two Conservatives changed their minds and voted in favour, so the scheme could go ahead after all. Both men were Freemasons, so rumours were soon flying that they had changed their minds on Masonic orders. The pair said these tales were 'totally untrue' and 'unsubstantiated'. They had simply changed their minds on looking into the scheme more deeply. The local *Herald Express* promptly published a letter from a high-ranking Mason, containing this message to the general public: 'You have nothing to fear from us . . . Relax, we are on your side. Our civic duty comes before any allegiance to Free-masonry.'[14]

These sentiments might ring hollow to some readers, especially when they consider the words of one Conservative councillor who wrote asking me to remove a true story from this book for fear of fraternal vengeance: 'The local Masons are waiting for me to make a false move and they are gunning for me.'

This might sound like the politics of paranoia but in fact it is the reasonable fear of a sane person. How outrageous – and dismaying – that democractically elected politicians in Britain at the end of the twentieth century feel forced to curb their tongues lest they upset a secretive and still, in many ways, secret society!

twenty-six

LONDON BELONGS TO THEM

Nowhere in Britain has the battle over Freemasonry been fought more bitterly than on London's local councils. It is not always Labour versus Conservative; the roughest fights have broken out between rival factions within the Labour parties which have ruled most inner London boroughs for most of this century.

For generations Freemasonry was not an issue in London's town halls. Nobody dared raise it because of one stark truth: the power-brokers in both main parties were Masons and usually belonged to the same lodge. Many lodges were created especially so elected councillors and full-time officials could socialize together off-duty. The lodges were often named after the boroughs themselves, but now many have lost their municipal connection. Today it would be wrong to conclude, simply because a lodge bears the name of your London borough, that a nest of knuckle-crunchers is diverting the entire council budget into the pockets of brother Masons.

Even so, some lodges are still active town hall fraternities. One such is the Wandsworth Borough Council Lodge (no. 2979). Founded in 1903, this survived a 1970 corruption scandal which revealed long-standing Masonic bonds between Labour leader Sydney Sporle and Ronald Ash, his Conservative opposite number. Ash was not implicated in any crime but Sporle was later jailed for six years for corruption in the first of the 'Poulson' trials.[1]

Undaunted, the lodge continued to bridge Wandsworth's party divide, as an underground newspaper *Lower Down* proved in October 1976 when it surreptitiously photographed numerous male personages arriving at a Masonic suite in Clapham Junction, clad in dinner jackets, bow-ties and carrying regalia cases. That evening they were installing the new lodge master.

Included in their number were Norman B. White, the Chief Executive; Cllr Dennis Mallam, Leader of the Tory Minority; Cllr Maurice Heaster, Tory Whip; Tory Cllr Michael Chartres; ex-Mayor, Cllr Jimmy Hill; ex-council solicitor Harry Sargent; plus a number of other Council officers and local notables.

Freemasonry attempts to be a secret society. Members of Masonic Lodges are sworn to give primary allegiance to their Masonic brethren, and to keep secret all the doings of their order. Is it right that officers and elected members of our Council, whose first duty should surely be to the public, should belong to an organization that requires this of them?

There are a number of ex-employees of the Council who received the cold shoulder from their colleagues for refusing to join the Lodge; they are only too ready to identify those who are 'on the square', and tell some hair-raising stories of what 'they' get up to. And they don't mean performing silly rites and ceremonies or rolling on the carpet in silly aprons. They allude to much more sinister goings-on. The implication is that the Freemasons constitute a significant, mainly non-elected power elite within our Corporation.

Powerful stuff! Yet *Lower Down* never published the low-down because it shut down soon afterwards. At the time I was making a television programme about Freemasonry, so I tried to find these folk who were 'only too ready' to tell 'hair-raising stories'. None materialized, but in 1980 another broadsheet, *Hard Times*, published the summons for a 1979 meeting of the same lodge. This carried the names of two Tory councillors, seven former Tory and Labour councillors, and the directors of the technical services and development departments. It also revealed that the Lodge of Instruction (a rehearsal class where Masons practise rituals and go through their lines) met at the Tooting Conservative Club, a fact which caused its Labour members no obvious embarrassment.

In the 1980s Wandsworth has consistently returned a Conservative majority, but it seems Freemasonry's power within it has probably diminished. Across the Thames, one Mason-dominated Tory group has certainly taken a drubbing.

In 1984, when the Borough of Brent was Conservative-controlled, a letter was sent out through the town hall post-room addressed to 'Brother W. R. Moody'. Post office staff could not locate this fellow, so they stamped the letter 'undelivered' and returned it to the town hall. A mail-clerk spotted the title 'Brother' on the envelope, assumed it was a fraternal socialist communication and sent it to the office of Labour group leader, Martin Coleman.

Imagine Coleman's surprise when he opened the letter and found a notice headed *Anselm Lodge No. 7685*. It was written by Conservative Councillor Eric McDonald. As lodge charity steward, McDonald was seeking sponsors for Masonic teams running the London Marathon 'in the name of the Provincial Grand Master'. His letter named other lodge members who had already pledged support: the Tory group secretary and finance committee chairman, the deputy leader, the former leader, the chairman of the development committee, the district building surveyor, the senior education awards assistant and the former chief architect.

Coleman used this windfall to demand that all councillors who were Masons should declare that fact. If they did not, and were later caught out, they could be banned from serving on council committees. He argued that lodges whose members include councillors, officers and local builders 'give rise to suspicion that decisions on jobs and contracts are being taken away from the public eye'. Therefore the public 'have a right to know whether a member is a Freemason'. Brent's Tory leader claimed this stank of Nazi German discrimination against Masons and was based on nothing more than a 'vague vision unsubstantiated by any factual evidence'. His arguments failed to convince Labour and Liberal councillors who voted for compulsory declaration. Within two years Brent's register of interests contained admissions from fourteen Tory councillors out of thirty that they were 'on the square'.

In the mid-1980s similar moves tried in other boroughs but only in Brent were Masons forced to own up. Elsewhere anti-Masonic spleen yielded no action, largely because no one produced any *evidence* proving Masonry was to blame for the corruption, inefficiency and waste which had plagued London local government for decades. One man who spotted this logical cavity and decided to call the anti-Masons' bluff was Grand Secretary Michael Higham.

In September 1985 the Borough of Hackney acted on persistent tales that the council was in the grip of corrupt Masonic employees and crooked Masonic contractors. In short, Hackney was rumoured to be a Masonic honeypot. The borough's socialist leaders hired a non-Masonic barrister named Andrew Arden to head an inquiry into 'the extent of Freemasonry within the authority and its effects on the operations of the council'. An expert in local government law, Arden was given six months to do the job but he soon realized that, if Freemasonry was all he was to investigate, there was not enough work for six days, let alone six months. This was because Hackney had no *evidence* whatsoever against the brotherhood, only (as Arden later reported) 'loose slander' and paranoid allegations against defenceless individuals whipped up in the town hall's prevailing 'climate of gloom'. There was reason to believe some officials, even whole departments, had acted corruptly. There was no evidence that any of the culprits were Masons.

After four months Arden persuaded Hackney to widen his terms so that he could look into 'such other abuses' as his team discovered and to recommend ways of eliminating them. This turned the spotlight off Freemasonry and on to maladministration as a whole. The inquiry budget rose from £50,000 to £250,000, including £500 a day for Arden himself. In return he would produce an organizational blueprint for Hackney and all Labour authorities trying to regenerate impoverished inner city areas in the face of financial cuts and ideological hostility from the Tory government and internecine bickering from the left. When Arden submitted his final report in March 1987, he proved there was nothing socialist about running a Labour council into the ground.

This conclusion may have been foreseen by the Hackney branch of the town hall union, NALGO, which boycotted Arden. It claimed his expanded terms of reference were a sneaky way of conducting a 'dubious overhaul of council procedures' and bashing the union in the process. Cynics might say that NALGO was all in favour of attacks on Freemasons, but did not want any inquiry into the poor performance of its own members.

NALGO's boycott contrasted ill with the action of Grand Secretary Higham who had already approached Arden, offering to co-operate. When Arden asked for help in identifying Freemasons on Hackney Council Higham agreed. He is also a qualified barrister, so it was under the quasi-Masonic trust which barristers operate among themselves that he told his staff to give Arden any information he wanted from Grand Lodge records.[2]

Arden duly handed over the names of 500 senior Hackney employees and 500 contractors who carried out work for the council. These were checked against the roll of some half a million brethren at Freemasons' Hall. Such 'historic co-operation'[3] would have backfired on Higham if it had shown members of the Craft were up to their neck in corruption, as was likely in a 'rotten borough' like Hackney. However, the news was good. Arden discovered only thirty Masons on a council payroll of 8,000. Not a single Mason was caught with his hand in the till, and no one who was considered corrupt was found to be 'on the square'. In short: there was no Masonic conspiracy within Hackney Council.

However, Arden did not exactly 'clear' Freemasonry as he pieced together a frightening mosaic of what it was like to work for a council weighed down by 'widespread malaise'. Hackney's greatest resource was its staff, yet how did it 'get so little performance out of the commitment of so many?' Employees were trampled underfoot by 'confrontational' industrial relations. The working environment was 'positively cruel. The sheer human waste is outrageous.'[4] Decision-making was in perpetual motion. Arguments about what was to be done, how and by whom, went on for ever.

At the same time, bad money management prevailed in most areas: from house building to highway repairs to buying photocopiers and cars. Strict accounting fell into disrepute. In some departments the 'sheer want of documentation' was a matter of policy: if you don't keep records or write anything down, the wicked Tory government cannot prove anything against the council or strip it of more public funds. Alas! This ideological purity encouraged thievery and corruption: if you do not keep precise records of work done by contractors, you cannot challenge their accounts. Some firms exploited this negligence by submitting grossly inflated bills. First Hackney would refuse to pay. Then it was *forced* to pay because it had no records to dispute the bills.

Arden listed kickbacks and freebies taken by Hackney staff from contractors and suppliers seeking more council business. Out of an annual £100 million budget, millions were lost through inefficiency, the corrupt payment of crooked contractors' bills and the purchase of computers nobody knew how to use. Meanwhile long-suffering council tenants had to wait months for basic repairs to their ramshackle homes.

Where did Freemasonry fit in this tragi-comical saga? Arden found that no Hackney staff implicated in the building rackets were Masons. Indeed, it was a Mason who had first exposed the rackets. As for 168 firms of contractors who had done work for Hackney, 31 per cent had a 'Masonic connection', but Arden felt this only reflected Freemasonry's strength in the building industry as a whole. Of firms suspected of making excessive claims 28 per cent were Masonic, a statistic which might be made to prove Masonic builders are marginally *less* dishonest than non-Masonic!

Arden made only one serious charge against Hackney's Masons, but it was damning. From the 1970s until the early 1980s the council's central core of five was solidly Masonic: the chief executive, the deputy chief executive and director of personnel, the borough solicitor, the head of computer and audit, and the head of building works. None was guilty of corruption or active misconduct, yet 'they did not succeed as a force for good or for progress'. Their overall standard of performance 'permitted serious abuse'. They held the top jobs during a most troubled era, so they must be held responsible for the chaos, corruption and disorder beneath them. In a roundabout way Arden was saying, these men were lords of misrule. Their inertia allowed the lunatics to take over the asylum.

When he sent a copy of his report to Grand Lodge, Commander

Higham responded by saying he could accept Freemasonry may not have acted as a force for betterment, but this was as much a criticism of Hackney as of Freemasonry: 'If standards of supervision are low, it takes an outstanding man . . . to start improving them.'

This was also true of Freemasons' Hall. In seven years Higham had wrought astonishing changes to a rigid institution. He had dragged it grumbling into the twentieth century. A few years earlier his pact with Arden would have been unthinkable, but it was a triumph for the Commander when, despite complete access to Masonic records, Arden discovered no evidence against the Craft. Higham's paymasters, the Board of General Purposes, may have felt less happy when they saw Arden's final recommendations:

> Councillors and council employees should be obliged to declare their Masonic membership and lodges.
> Freemasonry may be incompatible with membership of certain council committees and with certain council posts. Contractors should be required to declare their Masonic connections.

Higham complained that to suggest Freemasonry may be incompatible with public service was 'at variance with Arden's findings' and reflected 'unsubstantiated prejudice'. He may have felt the same about one Arden quip: 'It is not believed that there is any basis in the rumour that Freemasons whip donkeys, give poisoned sweets to schoolchildren, or drink boiled nail-clippings.'

Higham was right to feel wronged, but the lack of a clear connection between Freemasonry and corruption was not surprising. Arden had started work four years after Chief Inspector Woollard had smelled Masonic rats in Hackney and Islington's dealings with private building firms. Woollard's removal from the Public Sector Corruption Squad stopped him proving a case (see Chapter 12). If there had ever been evidence of corruption, Masonic or otherwise, it was 'lost' during those four years. Hackney's 'sheer want of documentation' might have been the work of socialist visionaries; it smacked rather more of guilty men destroying evidence.

Next door in Labour-controlled Newham no one needed to pay a lawyer £500 a day to prove a Masonic nexus. In 1977 a summons headed *Borough of Newham Lodge No. 8027* had fallen into the hands of some young Labour councillors. They were shocked to see the lodge included senior Labour and opposition councillors, and senior employees. In 1980 a full roll of seventy-five members leaked out. It named seven Labour councillors, nine council officers, four lower-ranking council employees, a supplier of 'one-arm bandit' fruit machines, and a fellow who happened to be the heaviest man in England.[5] Non-Masons were perturbed by the influence which these lodge members collectively wielded in council affairs. They were also alarmed at Masonic links between councillors on committees which oversaw big-spending departments and those same departments' full-time directors. Newham housing was the concern of ten lodge members, including Councillors Bill Watts JP and Peter Billups (chairman and deputy chairman of the town planning and housing committee), John Turner and Brian Platt (director and deputy director of housing), George Tovey JP and Brian Rom (head and deputy head of housing improvements) and another three employees.

For some years the housing department had bemused non-Masonic councillors with its allocation decisions. In 1979 £12,000 had just been spent on a house in Prince Regent Lane when a divorcee moved in. On the surface Mrs Ivy Willis seemed deserving: she was single, with two sons (one sub-normal, the other incontinent) and an unmarried pregnant daughter. Yet she already had a three-bedroom council house and swept into this far larger home without going through the council's normal procedures. She was not on its transfer list, had never applied in writing and, if she had ever applied verbally, there was no record of it. When she first occupied Prince Regent Lane the house had not been formally offered to her. She had got it solely on the say-so of housing chairman, Councillor Bill Watts. She had told him that she needed to take delivery of new furniture which she had ordered but which the shop could no longer store itself.

Poverty and deprivation are so widespread in Newham that hundreds of local families were far worse off than the Willises. In 1979 there were 8,000 homeless people in the borough. They had nowhere to put *any* furniture but, of course, they did not have any. More significantly, they did not have a Masonic connection. Ivy's connection was Lou Fox of the Newham Lodge. Brother Lou was an ex-Labour councillor who had served on the town planning and housing committee. He could not apply for Prince Regent Lane himself because he was the named tenant of another council house occupied by his wife and family but, when Ivy moved in, Lou moved in too. The next lodge summons gave the Prince Regent Lane love-nest as Lou Fox's home address.

Lou had been a councillor in the ruling Labour group along with the housing chairman, Worshipful Brother Bill Watts. The pair drank in a pub where Ivy worked as a barmaid. Another Labour councillor, Fred Jones, took a dim view of this cosy Masonic axis. He was particularly upset because a family in his electoral ward had been hoping to move into

the house in Prince Regent Lane. They were in far worse straits than the
Willis–Fox 'family' and, unlike the Willises, had put their request in
writing. Cllr Jones was already pressing their claim to Prince Regent Lane
when Bill Watts gave Ivy the all-clear to move in. The director of housing
at this time was the Lodge's Master-elect, Brother John Turner.

In December 1979 the *Newham Recorder* printed the Prince Regent Lane
story, with questions from Fred Jones about expensive central heating
gear installed to replace an adequate existing system. The following week
the disappointed applicants wrote to the paper saying they and their
children had to sleep in damp rooms with soaking wet walls. They also
had no heating because the gas fires were unusable. A second letter
claimed that a family living in a condemned house had caught two rats in
their only bedroom. When local citizens took to the streets to protest, one
boy was photographed carrying a placard, 'WOULD IT HELP IF I WAS A
FREEMASON'S SON?'

In 1981 Chairman Watts was confronted on BBC Radio's 'Checkpoint'
programme about his intervention over Prince Regent Lane. He claimed
Lou Fox's name had not been mentioned when he made his personal
decision to rehouse Mrs Willis. All Watts knew was that her husband 'had
buggered off and gone'. The house was 'just for this woman and her
children'. Then, said Watts, 'all hell breaks loose with people saying I've
done it because it was Lou Fox, who's a friend of mine, and that again is
absolute balls. I go to bed at night and sleep with an absolute sound
conscience.'

In 1981 'Checkpoint' featured another odd decision which was closer
to Watts himself. This involved the housing of Mrs Marie Brown, a
housing improvements officer who worked right next to Watts's office
and often drove him round the borough. Newham banned its employees
from being housed in any council accommodation except its least
desirable tower blocks. Despite this rule, Marie was given a flat in a
charming house, described in council literature as 'restored to a very high
standard' and 'one of the best examples of Victorian architecture in the
area'. There was an even better reason why Marie should not have been
given this home. She already had another in rural Essex, in the grounds of
a mansion owned by Newham's newly retired head of housing improvements, George Tovey. He enjoyed the double distinction of being
Marie's recent boss and a member of Newham Lodge.

When 'Checkpoint' doorstepped Marie Brown and Brother Tovey by
the rolling lawns and swimming pool that separate their homes, neither
had anything to say. Marie slammed her door and Tovey said he had
retired. 'Checkpoint' then accosted Bill Watts. He claimed not to know
about his own council's written policy banning the housing of its

employees in anything but tower blocks. When 'Checkpoint' referred to suggestions that he knew Marie 'rather too well' Watts blustered: 'Nonsense. I've got a wife at home. We go out socially on occasions with her and her husband. I mean, if someone's suggesting there's any bottling going on or something, well they want to forget it, I can tell you.'

According to Eric Partridge's *Dictionary of Slang*, the verb to 'bottle' means to 'coit with a woman'. In 1978 I had interviewed Bill Watts on television for the 'London Programme'. He told me:

> You mustn't come into Freemasonry expecting to get anything out of it except fellowship and goodwill for each other. I mean you're not supposed to, it's made quite clear that you mustn't expect to make any pecuniary gains or business gains at all. And there is nothing that you get out except what you put in.

Watts said one of Freemasonry's charms was that it gave men an excuse to get away from 'the wife'. He also told me that when it came to appointing men to council jobs, he would always want the best man for the job, even if he were not a Mason – but if two men of similar abilities applied for the same job, he would favour the Mason. Three years later 'Checkpoint' (in the person of Roger Cook) confronted Watts about the choice of Newham Lodge Brother Brian Rom as deputy head of housing improvements. Watts countered any hints of impropriety with the tale of what happened when the job of deputy housing director came up. He said that one favourite was a Mason, but 'I couldn't stand the bloke. As far as I was concerned, as chairman of housing, no way was he going to be deputy director of housing. But to hear some people talk, you've only got to say "I'm a Freemason", it's "Oh, that's it! The job's yours!" I mean, absolute nonsense and balderdash.'

'Checkpoint' reminded Watts that this job went instead to yet another Mason, Brian Platt. 'He is now, yes,' admitted Watts, 'he's a junior member of Freemasonry, but it wasn't because he was a Freemason.' In fact Platt was initiated into the lodge in 1976, three years *before* Brother Bill backed him for the job.

Watts is a Past Master of Newham Lodge which he helped found in 1975. He was initiated twelve years earlier in the Borough of Finsbury (no. 3901), another town hall lodge.[6] Watts says, 'Nearly every borough's got a lodge', and he should know, for both he and Peter Billups used to work for Mason-run Hackney while serving as elected councillors in next-door Newham. Such cosy arrangements spilled over into the world of sport, for Newham Lodge is intimately bound up with West Ham United Supporters Club. It even holds its meetings in its Club House in Castle Street 'by special dispensation' from Grand Lodge.[7]

West Ham supporters are notorious for their 'Inter-City' mob of designer hooligans. It is unlikely that any of these louts belong to Newham Lodge, even though the supporters' chairman for many years was Cllr Tom Jenkinson: chairman of highways and works and Past Master of Newham Lodge. When Scottish footballer Ray Stewart joined West Ham in 1979, his girlfriend Caroline Bell was pining for him back in Perth. The council soon found her a job in the housing department, and then a council-owned home. This was no coincidence, as she giggled to a *Daily Mirror* sleuth: 'I met someone through the club who knew about a job that was going. I was taken in on a temporary basis, but now I work full-time. There were a few strings pulled, actually.'[8]

The most serious allegation against the lodge concerns the council's 'sale' of the Woodlands Community Centre to a publican named Edward Smith. The deal had many curious features:

1. In 1977 the centre was badly damaged by fire and then repaired for £20,000. It was heavily in debt so Newham decided to sell it. Housing Chairman Bill Watts was to consider suitable offers, in consultation with his staff.
2. The property was advertised only in the *Morning Advertiser*, the newspaper for publicans and the licensed trade. It was later discovered that the sale and consumption of alcohol on the premises was prohibited.
3. Four offers were received for the freehold. The second highest bid was £38,000, just £2,000 less than a £40,000 bid from Edward Smith, licensee of the Dartmouth Arms. In November 1978 Smith's bid was accepted. He renamed the Centre the 'King Edward Club' – after himself.
4. Smith was well known to Bill Watts and his Masonic brethren. The Newham Lodge of Instruction met each Wednesday at the Dartmouth Arms. Now the lodge's general purposes committee transferred its meetings to the King Edward Club.
5. Two years after 'buying' the premises Smith had still not paid the £40,000, because the booze ban had not been lifted. However, he had been selling alcohol at the club ever since moving in. Despite this profitable business he paid no rent and only paid the rates fifteen months in arrears.
6. In March 1981 a reporter for the *Daily Mirror*'s Paul Foot rang the club. A man responding to the name of Edward Smith told him: 'Look, I'll tell you something, mister. You print what you like. And if you print anything, your feet won't hit the dust, mister. I'll take you people for a few quid.'

7. The same month the slight but terrier-like Cllr Fred Jones was working in his café when two men came to see him. One told him to 'lay off the King Edward', as his 'interest' was 'upsetting a lot of people'. He claimed Jones had been shooting his mouth off 'on the telly', because he 'had a grudge' against some people 'in the council'. Only at the end of the chat did the man admit to a name: Clancy. One John Clancy was then bar manager at the Dartmouth Arms and the King Edward, both sometimes known as Clancy's.

8. In December 1981, Newham Council finally received £40,000 for the King Edward Club, but it got nothing for Smith's free use of the premises over the previous two years.

Meantime, Brother Watts had come in for more stick from the local press. Week in, week out the *Newham Recorder* was running stories of housing department cock-ups, but the newspaper said it was impossible to get hold of Chairman Bill Watts to check the facts. Reporters left messages on telephone answering machines at his home and office but he never called back.[9] In contrast, his Masonic brothers could easily get hold of him. As Newham Lodge Secretary he had put his office answer-phone number on all fraternal circulars.

When 'Checkpoint' reminded him that this number was for the use of local people who needed to report urgent housing problems, Watts said it was for incoming calls only, so his Masonics did not cost ratepayers a penny. Sipping a pint of beer at the King Edward Club, he complained that all these half-truths and innuendoes about Freemasonry 'just get on your wick'. Soon afterwards he resigned as chairman of housing, blaming the press for its anti-Masonic attacks. In 1982 he was 'deselected' by his party, so he stood as an independent in the next borough election and lost. His successor as housing chairman was the indefatigable Fred Jones. In 1985 Jones became council leader, a job he still holds. He feels Freemasonry is a chronic threat to local democracy.

There is good reason for concern about the Masonic influence in the borough. If a councillor makes a solemn declaration to serve the electorate even-handedly, but also takes a more solemn oath (on pain of fearful penalties) to prefer a fellow-Mason to another in all his dealings, many people will see that it is irreconcilable, and ultimately favouring the Mason against the non-Mason.

It must also be of concern that Newham Borough Lodge comprises (among others) council members and officers, when the Local Government Association has adopted a Code of Conduct pointing out the dangers of fraternizing between members and officers of the same authority. There can be little closer familiarity than taking part in Masonic ceremonies where councillors and officers partially disrobe each other, and attend intimate social functions together.

The presence of Masons in positions of power may not in itself be an insidious and corrupting influence, but Freemasonry's secretive nature, and examples of anomalous treatment involving other Masons or their friends, add credence to the belief that it is potentially corrupting.

Fred Jones once said he was 'not of a mind to sit back and see my people screwed up'. Without his determination the Newham Lodge might still be running the borough as a kind of Masonic republic.

The biggest screw-up in Newham Council's history occurred in 1968 when the twenty-two storey Ronan Point residential tower block collapsed, killing five people. It was merely coincidence that Ronan Point had been built in Freemason's Road, that Councillor Harry Ronan (after whom the tower had been named) was a Freemason, and that the Borough Architect in charge during its erection had also been 'on the square'.

twenty-seven

EVERY BREATH YOU TAKE

Watlington is a town of only 2,000 souls on the south Oxfordshire plain. Robert Hilton used to be Chairman of its tiny Ratepayers' Association. A retired London local government officer and former JP, he owns a small farm on the town's outskirts in Hill Road. At the beginning of 1983 some folk living closer into Watlington on the same road started to complain about music coming from a pub called the Carriers Arms. Being self-employed and having some free time during the day, Robert Hilton offered to represent his distressed neighbours when the Carriers' drink licence came up for renewal.

This act of public-spiritedness would bring him no end of trouble because the man who had just bought the Carriers, John Watman, was passionate about live music. A semi-professional bass-guitarist, he had bought the pub in 1982 for the express purpose of making it the best music venue in the region. 'As a businessman', says Watman, 'I was always on the lookout for a good proposition. As a musician I was always looking for venues where I could present and play music. And I needed somewhere to live. The Carriers Arms in Watlington seemed to fit the bill perfectly.'

Born in London in 1944, Watman had served a toolmaking apprentice-ship and worked in the plastics industry before setting up his own engineering firm with a dozen employees. He combined business with pleasure in a venture called the 'Oxon Sound Studio' where entertainers such as Val Doonican, the Wurzels and Jimmy Savile used to record. He launched a record label, Roxon Records, and the Roxon Roadshow, a company of country artists who played at top nightspots and made many radio and television appearances. The Roadshow mounted concerts for the Stoke Mandeville Hospital, raising £250,000 in all, much of it from an outdoor show attended by the Prince of Wales.

By 1982 Watman was having so much fun with music that he decided to buy the Carriers Arms. To raise the money he sold his engineering firm to two employees, but they could not afford the factory lease on which he still owed £38,000, so his bank lent him £100,000 to buy the pub freehold at £142,000. The risk seemed worth taking. Watman had often played at the Carriers and knew its potential. As soon as he moved in he was putting on different music each night: traditional and modern jazz, rhythm and blues, country and middle-of-the-road. The mix was so successful that 1983 looked like being a great year. Watman sees his life in terms of certain songs he has performed over many years. Kris Kristofferson's 'For the Good Times' sums up his feelings while the Carriers boomed.

> It was a dream come true, but it was a dream that gradually disintegrated as I entered a world where I had very little control over my own destiny. It became a living nightmare in which I was to lose every material thing I possessed. My health would be affected and my personal relationships would crack under the strain. This sounds like a Victorian melodrama, but it all happened in the 1980s.

Watman's big problem was the Carriers' drinks licence. A pub's licence to serve alcohol must be renewed every year. So must its music licence, if it has one. Drink had been served at the pub for 200 years and music had been played there for decades. However, Watman's ambitious music programme upset some local residents. By January 1983 police were paying frequent visits to the pub, responding to mostly anonymous protests. John was sure his music was no louder than the previous landlord's but he wanted no trouble. He fitted £3,000 worth of sound-proofing but some locals continued to complain.

When the drinks licence came up for renewal in February 1983 several Hill Road residents registered opposition. So did Tom Butcher, chairman of the parish council, who alleged 'an unbelievable high level of musical noise', yet he had no authority to appear. His fellow councillors swiftly demanded to know why he had objected in the council's name but without its permission. He explained that he had become involved 'with certain people' in Hill Road.

Leading the Hill Road opposition was Robert Hilton. Watman could not understand why Hilton had become involved when he lived a quarter of a mile away and could not have been disturbed by any pub noise. Hilton, of course, was objecting not for himself but as chairman of the Ratepayers' Association, but Watman took it personally.

His licence was renewed anyway. The magistrates dismissed the noise complaints as irrelevant to the issue of whether Watman was a 'fit and proper person' to run a pub. They may also have been impressed by several townsmen who spoke forcefully on his behalf. Undeterred, the objectors promptly raised a petition against Watman's music licence, which was due for renewal two weeks later. They could muster only twenty-four signatures. Watman's friends retorted with a petition in his favour signed by 160 Watlington residents, but now anonymous telephone callers told him 'friends in high places' were making sure he would lose his music licence. He very soon learned that this time the parish council would be objecting officially, despite a letter from Watman costing all his efforts to sound-proof the premises.

He now sought the support of other Watlington traders, among them his old friend Gerald Hollis, a transporter who used to supply lorries free for John's charity concerts. According to Watman, Hollis said he could not sign the petition because he was in the local Freemasons' lodge along with Robert Hilton. Watman alleges that greengrocer Terry Varley said the same. This started a train of thought in Watman's head which would eventually become an anti-Masonic obsession. Before asking Hollis and Varley to sign his petition, Watman had been wholly unaware of Freemasonry. He had no concept of what it was, and no animosity towards any individual Mason. He did not even know Watlington had a lodge. Henceforth, however, he could not help wondering what kind of fraternity could turn men who had formerly been his friends into adversaries.

When I first met Watman in 1986 I was concerned that he might not have an accurate recollection of these men's remarks, especially as he could produce no proof that any of the trio in question were indeed Masons. I even wondered if he had invented the entire tale, but I was reassured when I acquired a Freemasons' Directory for Oxfordshire which named all the members of the Icknield Way Lodge (no. 8292). This showed that Worshipful Bro. Hilton had been its Master in 1977 when Bro. Varley had been Almoner. A few years later Bro. Hollis had become Charity Steward. I showed Watman the Directory. It was the first Masonic document he had ever seen. After careful study he identified three more Past Masters of Icknield Way Lodge among his neighbours in Hill Road.

Back in February 1983 the music licence had been a matter for South Oxfordshire Council. Its own tests proved that, contrary to all Hill Road protests, his music was not at 'nuisance level'. He therefore retained his licence, after offering to put on live music only four nights a week. This good neighbourliness won him no friends. The police kept coming back: once over noise complaints – when the only music came from an unamplified acoustic guitar – often over claims of after-hours drinking. These always proved false, indeed they were slanderous, but the police

would not say who had made them so John had no one to sue. The same
applied to numerous allegations about under-age drinkers, when almost
all his customers ranged from twenty-year-olds to pensioners. In ten
months the pub was descended on forty times by Thames Valley officers,
yet they never caught anyone drinking under age.

Their visits were now so frequent that Watman felt he was the victim of
a vendetta. When he obtained a supper licence, enabling him to serve food
and drink in his restaurant until the early hours, the police trooped in
again. They interrogated customers and ruined their evening. Watman
made an official complaint but nothing happened. 'Why are you
harassing us?' demanded one diner. They mumbled a few words, so he
said, 'If you don't get out, I'll ring your superior to find out what's going
on.' As he picked up the phone they left.

Watman felt that his distinctive American black Ford Mercury was also
receiving special attention. He was often stopped on suspicion of
drinking but not charged. Despite this constabulary zeal, he found
'there's never a copper around when you need one'. He was especially
worried about a violent criminal whom he had refused to serve. One
night John told him to leave the pub but he would not go, even when John
called the Thame police. He started throwing punches so John phoned
again for immediate assistance. As the thug was carted out by friends he
shouted, 'The next time I see you, you're dead.' When it was all over the
police arrived.

A few days later the pub was burgled. John went for help but the same
criminal jumped out from the shadows and gave him a beating, cracking
his cheekbone and ribs. It was September 1983 and John now felt he was
in a predicament which no publican can afford: the police were
investigating every petty complaint against him but at the same time, he
felt, they had withdrawn all protection for him or his property. Worse
was to come:

> A friend warned me that the police were planning a drugs raid on the
> Carriers. I just laughed, but my friend insisted it was true. I told him
> I did not take drugs and never had them on the premises. The police
> could check all they wanted but, as on all their other visits, they
> would be wasting their time.

Even so Watman decided to shut down before any raid could take place.
He went to Thame police station to report he was closing the Carriers
until he could find a buyer. He told officers where he would be staying
and said he would visit every few days to make sure the alarms were
working. He then put the pub on sale for £155,000. This was £13,000
more than he had paid a year earlier, but he had installed the sound-

proofing and had greatly increased the takings. His estate agent felt sure he would get a buyer at that price – until he rang John with bad news.

Rumours were being spread around Watlington that the police were going to oppose the Carriers' licence. Would-be buyers soon lost interest because a pub without a licence is worth no more than a house. How do you fight rumours of this kind? I only knew that anonymous calls I had received in the past threatening opposition to my licences had always proved right. These people didn't want me as a publican but now it seemed they didn't want me to sell either.

It was now December 1983. One freezing evening John made a routine visit to the pub and discovered a burglary. He called the police and showed them some valuable goods which had been shifted to the back door, apparently so the thieves could remove them promptly on a return visit. He went to a friend's pub and had a few drinks, then plucked up the courage to go back to the Carriers late that night in the hope of catching the thieves. This time, however, the police had acted on his information and were themselves waiting to ambush the thieves. When the hapless Watman arrived, they bundled him into a police van alongside a growling dog. At Thame a breathalyser showed he was over the limit. He was allowed to leave, but when he asked for the key to his car boot (in which he had locked his other keys) the police refused to give it to him. He was left stranded on the street with nowhere to stay and no money. He had to break into his own factory nearby to avoid freezing to death. He was later fined and banned from driving for eighteen months.

In February 1984 the police added their objections to Watman's drinks licence on the grounds that the Carriers had been shut for four months. This struck him as ridiculous because a licence states only the hours during which a pub is allowed to be open, not the hours it *must* be open. Furthermore, they knew that the Carriers was shut only until he could find a buyer. Worse followed. On the day of the hearing the police announced five surprise witnesses. Watman's barrister argued that these should not be heard as there had been no advance warning. The magistrates agreed and only allowed evidence which the defence already knew about. This consisted of two officers' inaccurate accounts of break-ins at the pub and Watman's security measures. One of them admitted that Watman had taken all reasonable precautions. Even so, he lost his licence on the grounds that the pub should have stayed open to provide a service and that storing liquor on unoccupied premises incited burglary and posed a danger. Self-evidently this decision could only delay the day when the pub would finally re-open. It thus further deprived Watlington's citizens of that very service they allegedly needed. The magistrates clearly felt that the town's alcoholic dependency could not be slaked by five other pubs within 200 yards of the Carriers Arms. For Watman himself the decision was a catastrophe. It knocked one-third off the Carriers' value. Watman was bereft.

> I had entered the court owning a pub and left it owning no more than a house. The song says, 'There's nothing so lonesome, morbid and drear, as to stand in the bar of a pub with no beer.' Don't you believe it! You try standing in a pub with no licence!

Watman's life fell apart. He owed Barclays Bank, Norwich Union and Ushers Brewery more than £170,000. His entire future depended on a flourishing pub, but this was now gone. With interest rapidly mounting, he was forced to sell the Carriers for £112,000 – £30,000 less than he paid for it. This settled most of his bank debt, but he could find no buyer for the factory. In 1984 he was forced into bankruptcy. Norwich Union took the factory but did not sell it for two years, and only then for £60,000. By then it claimed interest, and legal charges had boosted Watman's debt from £38,000 to £78,000, so he still owed £18,000.

As he handed the Official Receiver his last one-pound premium bond (a gift from his mother when he was a child), the most appropriate song he could think of was 'There Goes My Everything' until he remembered 'I Who Have Nothing'. Watman had nothing: no money, no credit, no home, no car, no job and no idea why all this had happened to him.

He talked the whole affair over with his friend Brian Bonner, a retired policeman who was clerk of the local courts. By now he knew that Bonner was a Mason in the same Icknield Way Lodge as thirty other Watlington residents, but Bonner shocked him by revealing that several local policemen were also Masons, including Inspector Ron Duncan of Thame police station. In 1980 Duncan had been Master of St Mary's Lodge (no. 1763) which meets at Thame Masonic Hall, as does the Icknield Way Lodge of Watlington. Coincidentally, Duncan was in charge of the officers who had come to the Carriers over the noise complaints and had himself paid formal visits to the pub. He had also turned up in court when the magistrates decided to take away the Carriers' drinks licence: he was one of the five surprise witnesses against Watman who were not allowed to testify.

It goes without saying that Inspector Duncan had always acted in accordance with his public duty and his oath as a constable (to serve 'without favour or affection, malice or ill-will'), but Watman's state of mind was such that he saw conspiracy where he had no proof of such a thing. Merely because almost everyone he came up against – objectors, ratepayers' leaders, parish councillors and policemen – happened to be Masons who all happened to meet at the same Masonic hall (and in most cases knew each other very well) did not prove a conspiracy. Nevertheless, such a series of coincidences is likely to provoke a man who already feels 'got at' to focus his bitterness on a particular building and on all those who meet there.

Naturally Icknield Way's Robert Hilton takes a different view: 'I can understand a man feeling aggrieved if he feels that justice hasn't been done, but it is no way my responsibility or that of other people that I know . . . This Freemason's side of it is blown out of all proportion. It's a silly little lodge, a local lodge. I don't think there's that many in it. I don't know where or why the connection came about. None of my friends have had anything to do with Mr Watman or his problems.'

The connection had come about because Hilton's own lodge brother, Brian Bonner, had planted it in Watman's brain. He then stoked him up further by telling him he should be aware of a planning application which had gone before South Oxfordshire Council one month before he lost his licence. Watman acquired the relevant papers and saw that a field behind the Carriers was to be developed as a recreation ground. This would require new parking places and changing rooms. On the grapevine he learned of further plans to erect an office block behind the pub. He also saw that the application had been submitted by Beechwood Estates, the company which had just bought the Carriers for £30,000 less than he had paid. John realized that, so long as he had owned the Carriers, he would have been an obstacle to such a scheme. Now he was out, Beechwood could do almost anything they liked.

But why, thought Watman, did Watlington need a new recreation ground when it already had one? He read the papers again and saw that Beechwood also owned the town's present ground which, it claimed, it wanted to return to agricultural use. This struck Watman as odd until he gained one more piece of information. For the past twenty-one years the parish council had leased the ground from Beechwood at a peppercorn rent. To keep it, all the council had to do was renew the lease by September 1983. According to council minutes, this was not done 'due to a technical default'. Suddenly, it seemed, Watlington would have nowhere for its townsfolk to play.

The councillors must have realized that, as soon as this news leaked out, they would face a mass of seething Watlingtonians, from lusty footballers to dog-walking pensioners, furious at the loss of the town's main open space. Another site would have to be found very soon. This duty fell mainly on the new chairman of the recreation committee:

Councillor Robert Hilton of the Icknield Way Lodge. This selfless pillar of society now faced a very difficult task because all the suitable land around Watlington was owned by Beechwood Estates, yet the only land which it was offering was the field behind the Carriers Arms.

Beechwood is owned by Lord Macclesfield and run by his two sons. None of these men are Freemasons. In 1986 Beechwood revealed new plans for the old recreation ground. No longer did it seek to bring it back into agricultural use. It wanted to drive a road right through it and build 350 houses on surrounding land. At a parish council meeting Robert Hilton summed up 'the advantages or not' of a fifty-year lease on the field behind the Carriers. According to the *Watlington Times*, he said negotiations had been going on for over two years and the town 'should not lose any chance of obtaining a recreation ground on good terms.'[1]

The council submitted the scheme to a town referendum. Chairman Eric Newman (another Icknield Way Lodge member) strongly recommended a 'yes' vote but got a resounding 'no'. Now the tables were turned. The scheme's most vocal opponent, Norman Greaves, knew nothing about Freemasons or Freemasonry. He slammed the retailers, estate agents and landowners who stood to gain from more housing: 'Fortunately, they are a small minority, albeit very vocal.' He asked how the council could have so misjudged the town's feelings and pilloried its failure to renew the old recreation ground lease.

The referendum result ensured that, for a few years at least, one small town had held off the developers. Watlington had been saved from suburban sprawl. At the time of writing its townsfolk are still using the old recreation ground. Robert Hilton and Eric Newman resigned from the parish council in November 1986. Norman Greaves – no anti-Mason – observes, 'It happens that those people with Masonic connections are off the council. We're all "Green Yuppies" now.'

John Watman meantime has got nowhere. He made many complaints against Thames Valley Police alleging conspiracy, harassment and mistreatment, but a twenty-month inquiry by Hampshire Police found insufficient evidence to justify criminal prosecution or disciplinary action. Watman took his anti-Masonic allegations to Grand Secretary Michael Higham, who made inquiries and wrote a painstaking reply. He said both Terence Varley (the greengrocer) and Gerald Hollis (the transport contractor) independently stated that they refused to sign Watman's petition because they objected to the noise and nuisance caused by his pub entertainment.

They deny that any mention of Freemasonry was made to you, and more specifically, refute entirely your allegation that they said they did not wish to upset their lodge.

Enquiries have also been made of senior members of Icknield Way Lodge and I can confirm that at no time has your name or matters concerning your Public House, ever been raised as a point of discussion in Lodge business.

I have no reason to doubt the veracity of the statements of these men.

In the circumstances, although recognizing the strength of your belief that Masonic influence has been brought to bear on your life, I can only say that the fact that some of those involved in the difficulties you have faced are Freemasons is purely coincidental.[2]

No doubt Commander Higham was accurately reporting what he had been told. However, Watman had no idea that Robert Hilton was a Mason – and no knowledge that a Watlington Lodge existed – until Varley and Hollis had told him so. Similarly, they would have had no reason to disclose these facts except in conversations about the campaign against Watman's music licence. Furthermore, Watman had never claimed his name or pub had been raised 'in Lodge business'. What concerned him was what might have gone on *outside* the lodge. It probably was 'pure coincidence' that 'some of those involved' were Masons, but Watman was trying to make sense of a long series of coincidences which caused him to feel perpetually surrounded and spied on. By now a psychoanalyst might have diagnosed some form of paranoia. Some hint of this might lie in the fact that Watman feels his current predicament is summed up in one song by Police (the group, not the force): 'Every breath you take, every step you make, I'll be watching you.'

John Watman is typical of hundreds of people in small communities all over Britain who feel, rightly or wrongly, that local Masons have interfered with their business and ruined their livelihoods. In big cities Masonic influence is less tangible but, as it is almost impossible to discover who the Masons are in towns like London, Birmingham and Glasgow, it is equally impossible to assess their true power. The suspicion that Masons abuse their connections would be less rampant, of course, if complete and up-to-date lodge lists could be scrutinized at public libraries. Even better, were the fraternity itself to display such information voluntarily, its individual members would be far better protected from becoming the victims of any unjustifiable conspiracy theory, such as that which still haunts several members of the Icknield Way Lodge.

twenty-eight

A MASONIC EDUCATION

There are more than 150 old boys' lodges in Britain, each founded on a public or grammar school. Against Masonic tradition these openly canvass for members, although one Watford Grammar school-leaver was surprised at a recent old boys' dinner: in the midst of this non-Masonic reunion up sprang the chairman to propose a toast with members of the Old Fullerian Lodge (no. 4698). Had the youngster scrutinized the school magazine, he would have known he too could join the fraternity just by contacting its secretary (home address supplied). No god-fearing old boy would be turned away, nor are such lodges restricted to old boys. Teachers have long been allowed to join and at least one such lodge 'welcomes any candidates who have close associations' with former pupils. This could mean their workmates, drinking companions, garage mechanics or milkmen. Many public school lodges have thrown membership wide open to keep the lodge going. In contrast, the Adeste Lodge (no. 5445) for old boys of Whitgift School, Croydon, preferred to 'surrender its warrant' and close down rather than dilute its connection with the old school.

In 1979 Haileybury's school magazine published a letter headlined *Freemasonry* from the secretary of its old boys' lodge (no. 3912). 'Anyone wishing to become a mason' could join if he was either 'educated at or connected with' the school; 'attainment of 21 years of age and belief in a Supreme Being are the only other qualifications'. This disgusted one non-Masonic reader who complained to John Stubbs, then Grand Secretary of Grand Lodge. Stubbs brushed the man aside by saying he did not think that 'in a closed community magazine such as this any exception could or should be taken to a letter of this kind'.

The most prestigious old boys' lodges link up through the Public School Lodges Council which holds annual festivals in historic piles such as Haileybury and Marlborough. There is also a Public Schools Installed

Masters' Lodge (no. 9077). Some schools muster Royal Arch and even Rose Croix chapters with prominent men at their head. In 1979 the Old Wykehamist Rose Croix Chapter had the Viscount Gough as its 'Most Worshipful Sovereign', while the Recorder of the Eton and Harrow was His Honour Judge Verney.

The Masonic bug has bitten deep into higher education. Lodges named after Trinity College, Cambridge, and Trinity, Dublin, meet in London. So do lodges called Trinity College and its 'daughter', Trinity College Jubilee. In 1984 Trinity College Lodge initiated a quantity surveyor, a structural engineer and the director of a construction firm. When they meet with forty like-minded brethren, it would seem that scholarship plays a smaller part in their conversation than the ins-and-outs of the building trade.

Several university lodges meet in the capital (Durham, Edinburgh, City University, and London) while many colleges have their own lodges: Imperial, Goldsmiths, Guildhall School of Music and most teaching hospitals (see Chapter 29). Many London polytechnics and training colleges have lodges, and more university lodges meet in Durham, Cardiff, Sheffield, Birmingham, Aston, Manchester and Nottingham. In Cirencester there is a Royal Agricultural College Lodge. In 1980 its Almoner was a local landowner, the Earl of Ducie.

Members' lists for these lodges (indeed, *all* lodges) are difficult to come by, but it seems that less than half the brethren are academics. Most are administrators, technicians, porters and other staff. Few are students, if only because no man can become a Mason before he is twenty-one, except Masons' sons ('Lewises') who may join at eighteen. However, some university lodges actively recruit undergraduates who are the sons of Freemasons. This is true of Cambridge's Isaac Newton Lodge (no. 859) and Oxford's Apollo (no. 357), the most celebrated university lodge of all. Traditionally the Apollo has had a huge membership: more than 400 in 1974. In 1976 it initiated seventeen men when most Oxfordshire lodges took in three or less. By 1983 membership had fallen to 280, but this is still far greater than most British lodges. The decline may reflect increased anti-Masonry among the 'educated classes' or just increased fees driving older members to resign.

The Apollo has some distinguished members – former Grand Secretary Sir John Stubbs (initiated in 1930) and Sir Lionel Brett, a one-time colonial judge – but most have not scooped up any of life's glittering prizes: no one notable in the arts, sciences, politics, the church, or indeed education. The Apollo's academic members seem as obscure as the college porters. It seems most brethren today are yeomen, small-town accountants and village Hampdens, rather than great 'achievers'.

What a far cry from 1875 when the Apollo raised Oscar Wilde! His father, Sir William, was Master of Dublin's Shakespeare Lodge, but perhaps young Oscar found a particular thrill in donning an apron, waving wands, and performing occult rituals in all-male company. Of all England's lodges only the Apollo demands the wearing of white ties, tails, white waistcoats, knee breeches and buckled shoes.

School, college and university lodges may be seen as extensions of the 'old boy network', with Masonry's virtues and vices added on. Most men join to keep in touch with their *alma mater*, but British socialists will think these lodges as pernicious as the public school system itself. Less doctrinaire folk may feel they are the harmless resort of 'consenting male adults in private', with little or no impact on the rest of society.

That cannot be said when Freemasonry affects education itself. It is a common complaint that senior teaching jobs go to incompetent or second-rate men because they are Masons, while better teachers of both sexes are rejected because they are non-Masons. Such allegations are difficult to prove or disprove. One distinguished teacher writes that when he was a public school housemaster he was strongly pressured to become a Mason.

> I could not see how such a step could benefit me, and I eventually declined because I refused to enter into something quite so indefinite and secret. Yet I have often wondered to what extent my career prospects might have been affected. Now as a prep-school head responsible for keeping his school full, I wonder whether member-ship of the Brotherhood might influence recruitment.

Britain's state education system is blighted by Freemasonry, if letters I have received from teachers are to be believed. One letter came from a retired Nottingham primary school head, Maurice Hemstock, who has since died.

> Before the war I was on the local committee of the National Union of Teachers. Our secretary, Cyril Jackson, was a friend of mine, about twelve years older. He joined the Masons and was soon on the ladder to promotion. In Nottingham there were two ways to promotion: (a) grease certain Labour aldermen (b) become a Mason. The Masons were clever. They dragged in Labour councillors, Conservatives and so on. One Labour alderman, an ex-engine driver named Joe Baldwin, was very important on the education committee, although he had no education at all. He was also a Freemason. Cyril confided in me that he would be getting the next headship, but he didn't get it. So one day when he was giving me a

lift home, he asked me to wait in his Austin, whilst he went in to complain to Brother Joe Baldwin. Cyril was there twenty minutes, and he got the next headship at Bulwell Hall Junior School.

In the 1930s we had only one assistant to the Director of Education. His name was Peat. He was a Mason and there were three more on our staff. On Friday afternoons once each month, they arrived at school in black tie and dinner jackets and left at three o'clock to go to their lodge meeting. Their classes were divided up between the rest of us so that we had a class of forty plus half of another (often of a different age). After the war the meetings took place at night so this practice stopped.

Some years after the war I walked into the Grosvenor pub, Mansfield Road, and met two other teachers. 'Are you putting in for the Peveril School headship?' one asked. 'Of course I am,' I replied. He said, 'Don't bother, Stanley Ward has got it.' This was impossible, as the applications were not due in until two weeks later, but I was told he had already held a party to celebrate. He had even asked staff to go with him to the new headship. Mr Ward was confirmed in that job three weeks later. I needn't say that he was the Freemasons' organist. The Deputy Director had been Master of the teacher's lodge [Semper Fratres, no. 4467]. Mr Hutchinson, the Chief Clerk, was a Mason, the Inspector of Schools Mr Wall was a Mason, and so the dreary list goes on.

Another letter came from a man who taught in further education for many years. He became head of a large engineering department before retiring in 1978. He admits that the situation today may not be as bad as it was in his day, but he suspects it is.

Freemasonry has become a scourge and disease in jobs in the public service. It reigns supreme in Manchester where, when I was working, the Chief Education Officer, all senior education officials and most if not all Headmasters and college principals were Masons. I was one of the few non-Masons in a senior post. They did their best to make life awkward for me. All the top brass were Masons, including two successive incompetent Principals who worked, together with Freemason lecturers in my department, to by-pass me. Discipline was therefore dreadful.

My appointment was a mistake. The brothers had fixed it for one of their number, but a very determined woman, Dr Kathleen Ollerenshaw who was very famous in educational circles, attended the appointments committee unexpectedly. With her present, fiddles became impossible so I got the job. They never forgave me.

I could have become a Mason but I have always regarded the movement as childish, evil and sinister. What has happened in public life is that the message has got around that the way to be successful and get senior posts is to become a Freemason, so that the most unscrupulous candidates use the movement as a ladder to success. It is alarming that these people now control large sections of our educational system.

I taught in five colleges and encountered the movement all over the country. One example of its strength is that many years ago a Mason Director of Education for Gloucestershire stonewalled and defeated a Board of Governors who were investigating a Mason headmaster.

This man claims Freemasonry is getting even stronger as men rush to join. In north-west England, where he still lives, 'it is almost mandatory to join, if one is to enjoy any status in the community'. There are, he says, three standards of service in this part of Britain:

1.' Freemason to Freemason: nothing is too much trouble. All obstacles will be removed. Scruples count for nothing.
2. Freemason to non-Freemason: the non-Freemason must take what is left. If the interests of another Freemason clash with those of the non-Freemason then the Freemason must be given priority.
3. Non-Freemason to non-Freemason: what one would expect. Cases judged on their merits. But the non-Freemason sector is not very strong and has little influence.

Masonic defenders will claim these letters reek of sour grapes. Many years on, it is impossible to prove whether the events they describe ever happened. Yet, as unco-ordinated tales from different parts of the country, they marry together in a believable way. Such perceptions convinced Leeds City Council in 1984 to require all its 8,000 education employees to declare if they were Masons. 'A witch-hunt', Masons might cry, but a few months later some London Masons were casting the nastiest spells on a man who had never done them any harm. For the purposes of this book I give him a pseudonym, 'Kumar Patel'. After extensive unemployment, he now has a full-time job at last. I have had to change one more name but all the rest are genuine, so that no one can doubt it really happened.

In February 1985 Kumar was jumping with joy. Born in the West Indies this handsome man had just been offered a wonderful job: Chief Education Officer of the Commonwealth Institute. He had won this prestigious Foreign Office appointment in rigorous open competition. It was the top job in his field and he was outstandingly qualified. He saw it as a unique chance to work for the good of all races, to travel the world and to put his education theories into practice throughout the Common-wealth. Astonishingly, he was the first black person ever to fill the post.

Patel could not contain himself. In the education department of the London Borough of Waltham Forest, where he worked as a youth and community officer, he told his colleagues his good news. He naïvely assumed they would all share his pleasure. How little he knew of human nature. The jealousy of petty-minded men was about to destroy his career.

On 5 February Patel wrote a letter of resignation to his ultimate boss, senior education officer Richard Gan, giving the usual three months' notice. However, he made the mistake of stating that he was leaving to take the Commonwealth Institute job. A few days later Gan asked Patel's line manager, 'Henry Tribe',[1] if he had heard he was leaving. 'Yes,' said Tribe, 'I am glad he has got such a good appointment.' Gan seemed upset and replied, 'I'm glad he's going but very sorry he's going to such a good job.'

Gan had known nothing of Patel's plans because Patel had named referees more suitable for this particular job. Even so, Commonwealth Institute Director James Porter telephoned Tribe who told him Patel was an excellent employee. Porter explained the call was a formality, as Patel had already won the job.

Now Patel noticed that Gan had turned cold and hostile towards him. He brought one meeting to an end by telling Patel, 'I will hound you out of your new job – your prestigious job.' Patel was appalled but the threat became reality on Monday 18 March when Gan told him he had been accused of fiddling his expenses. Gan suspended Patel and ordered him to clear his desk. At a disciplinary hearing on 2 April he was suspended for four weeks, just until his resignation took effect and the council would no longer have to pay him anyway.

The charges were baseless. Patel had been framed. He was in deep trouble and did not know where to turn. The letter formally suspending him allowed only ten days for an appeal, but six had already passed because it had got stuck in the post over the Easter break. Worse still, he could not contact his union representative who was away at a conference. Patel re-read the letter and was relieved to see it alleged only 'irregular-ities', not dishonesty. He felt the trouble was not as bad as it had at first seemed. Also Gan had told him that the official council line would be that Patel was on leave. Nothing was to be said about suspension.

To his horror, that same day a letter arrived from a Commonwealth

Institute official saying he understood Patel had been suspended without pay. Patel visited the official to explain that the council had decided to dispute expenses which he had been claiming, on a 'custom and practice' basis, for more than four years. These were subsistence and car mileage rates for night visits to youth and community centres which were all less than six miles away. He added that all his claims had been approved by his boss and authorized by the Audit department. Despite this, he got the message that because of the suspension, the Institute had no wish to employ him.

On 19 April the Institute wrote to say no final decision would be made without him having the chance to put his case to its director, James Porter. A few days later Porter gave him no such opportunity before he told him the job offer was withdrawn. In a letter Porter said he understood the 'incorrect claims' had been 'admitted or substantiated'. Had he given Patel a chance to speak, he would have realized Patel was denying all 'incorrect claims' and that none had been substantiated.

Patel faced ruin. He had no job and less than a reputation. He asked Waltham Forest if he could withdraw his resignation but was answered with a flat 'No'. He and his wife had to sell their house (they could not keep up the mortgage) and move into a friend's flat. Yet Patel was so sure the Institute would see he had been framed, and reinstate him, that he did not claim unemployment benefit for two months.

Down, but not out, Patel vowed to find out who had inspired the bogus charges, and who had poisoned the Commonwealth Institute against him. On his own initiative, without help from his union, he launched an industrial tribunal case against Waltham Forest alleging racial discrimination. Through sympathizers still working for the council, he learned that two white employees, guilty of far worse offences, had been treated far less brutally. A man had been reinstated after striking a black youth in his charge, and a woman who had claimed excess expenses was just given a warning and told to pay the money back, but she kept her job.

When Patel's case came before the tribunal in 1986, the adjudicators drew two distinctions between these folk and Patel: they were white and he was black; they were guilty but he had done no wrong. In evidence the council auditor was forced to admit that Patel's claims were valid after all. He also admitted he had never checked what was 'custom and practice' in the youth and community department. The tribunal decided the worst Patel had done was use two cars on separate occasions for work. Waltham Forest said he could only use the car he was buying on a council loan but, by using the other car, he had not cost the council one extra penny. The tribunal said he 'had been treated very, very harshly' and found the council guilty of discriminating against him, in breach of the Race Relations Act.

Waltham Forest lost the case mainly because of the actions of two employees: Richard Gan and Neil Hobday JP, who was a youth and community officer like Patel. The tribunal was 'quite unable to accept most of Mr Gan's evidence. His recollections of events suffered from convenient amnesia', while his attitude towards Patel appeared to be 'vindictive'. Gan testified that he had never told Patel, 'I will hound you out of your new job – your prestigious job,' but the tribunal believed another witness to whom Gan admitted the remark but said he had been quoted out of context. He thus conceded that he had said it.

On Hobday, they accepted the view of one witness that he would not be 'very partial to working with a black colleague . . . The fact that he [Patel] was black would have registered most acutely with Hobday.' The tribunal concluded that 'the degree of malice and vindictiveness' shown to Patel could not have been motivated only by 'dislike, jealousy and envy. The only inference we could draw was that the additional dimension was racial.'

The first person at the Commonwealth Institute who had heard of Patel's suspension was Dr Moses Idem. He told the tribunal how, on his own initiative, he rang Waltham Forest to speak to Patel's boss, Henry Tribe. Hobday answered instead and told him Patel had been suspended for irregularities in his travel claims. A day or two later Hobday twice rang back to say he might lose his job for telling Idem what had happened to Patel. Hobday said that, if he were ever confronted, he would deny giving him the information.

Sure enough, at the tribunal Hobday testified on oath that he had told no one at the Institute of Patel's predicament. He had simply told Idem that Patel was on leave. The tribunal reported, 'we do not believe Mr Hobday's evidence'. Even Waltham Forest decided that Hobday had to answer a case of 'gross misconduct'.

What has all this got to do with Freemasonry? Over many months some of Hobday's youth and community colleagues had noticed he was spending a lot of time with Gan. Fraternization between different ranks in local government is discouraged and usually resented. Gan was two tiers above Hobday, so their friendship made difficulties for Henry Tribe, who was in charge of Hobday and Patel but was answerable to Gan.

Eventually, onlookers realized that Hobday and Gan were drawn together by Freemasonry. Their tête-à-têtes were often dedicated to Masonic business: they were overheard talking about a City of London lodge, and about a function at Sion College (a one-time Anglican theological school on the Thames Embankment which is now home to many lodges). In 1986 the council's own inquiry into the Patel affair required that all witnesses be asked if they were Masons. Hobday and

Gan declined to answer, as did Gan's solicitor. This seemed unnecessarily clandestine on Hobday's part for he had previously talked openly about his Freemasonry. Years before he had told a colleague that he joined the Craft in Solihull and that his father had also been 'on the square'.

Gan's fraternal bonds did not become clear until a Middlesex Masonic Yearbook came into my hands. This showed that in November 1984 he had been installed as Worshipful Master of the Robert Mitchell Lodge (no. 2956). He was also First Assistant Sojourner in the Strawberry Hill Royal Arch Chapter, and Marshal in the Undivided Trinity Chapter of the Rose Croix. All these clusters meet at Freemasonry's Twickenham premises, in the Borough of Hounslow where Gan began his meteoric rise in local government.

Several observers, including Patel, believe Masonry has protected Gan and Hobday. Why else should the committee of inquiry, set up by the Labour-run council to consider the tribunal findings, claim that court had got its facts wrong? The committee said there was no evidence that Gan or anyone else had acted with a racial motive, but it did say Gan accepted his 'hounding' remarks 'could be perceived as a threat' to Patel. It also reported that the man who prepared the council's tribunal case had felt hampered by 'lack of co-operation . . . specifically from Mr Gan'.

The committee found no evidence that the probe into Patel's expenses was started other than on the impartial initiative of council auditors. In that case, was it mere coincidence that Patel's 'irregularities' were brought to Gan's attention only three days after he had threatened to hound Patel out of his new job? How odd too that, despite union protests, Gan himself conducted the discipline hearing and suspended Patel. Gan, it seems, was determined to be Patel's judge, jury and prosecutor. A few weeks later he told the Commonwealth Institute there was no evidence that Patel's colleagues were claiming car mileage on the same basis as Patel. The tribunal had found it 'difficult to believe' Gan could have been so unaware of custom and practice. But then, Gan had never discussed the matter with Patel's immediate boss, Henry Tribe, who had approved his expenses and everyone else's in the department.

The committee reported that Gan and Hobday should have been suspended as soon as Waltham Forest received the tribunal findings. After all, Gan had suspended Patel instantly without pay, but Gan suffered no such fate because of 'scepticism about the decision and because an appeal was being considered'. As it turned out, the council withdrew its appeal but claimed this was 'not in any way an acceptance of the tribunal's findings'. This was mere bluster because it later paid Patel not only maximum damages of £8,000 to settle the tribunal judgement, but also substantial damages to avoid legal proceedings'. This second payment can only be interpreted as an admission that Patel had been wronged and ruined by Waltham Forest employees.

What price did the main offenders pay? Gan had niftily applied to be head of schools in another London borough, Kingston. He got the job on 20 June 1986: the day the tribunal published its report. Kingston's personnel committee had no idea he had been condemned by any tribunal until *after* they had appointed him. Gan did not tell them. Now Kingston had to explain its humiliation, so in 1987 it held its own inquiry which, like Waltham Forest's, rejected the tribunal findings. Now at last Gan took up his new job. He told a local paper: 'I am delighted that I have been able to clear my name unequivocally.' He claimed both councils' inquiries were 'independent', despite the fact that both were pre-occupied with covering up their own mistakes. As for the only truly independent inquiry, the industrial tribunal, Gan claimed that, as a mere witness, he had been unable to defend himself. All along, however, his supporters knew he 'was blameless and that the truth would out in the end'.

Whatever suffering Gan had endured, he had endured it in the comfort of his home where he had sat on full pay for six months. This contrasted grotesquely with how Gan had suspended Patel without a penny. When the *Surrey Comet* asked for his comments, Patel responded:

> The appointment of Brother Gan, a convicted racist, a man who has been established as an arrant liar with great facility for vindictiveness, envy and jealousy is disgraceful. Mr Gan is a morally deformed character and consequently is unfitted for such a position. It seems it's now up to the parents of Kingston to do something about this aberration.[2]

The Rt Hon. Norman Lamont, Kingston's Conservative MP and a minister in Mrs Thatcher's government, said: 'I'm very concerned at the council's decision and surprised. I simply cannot see how a group of councillors can overturn a view taken by a court of law.' Immigrant groups and the Kingston branch of the National Union of Teachers said they had seen nothing to diminish their grave concern at Gan's appointment, but they now had to work with him to educate Kingston's children. Gan had stressed how he too had come to Britain as a refugee child from Poland and was committed to helping all immigrants. Yet some Kingston folk cannot understand *why* their council went so far out of their way to defend him. They sense he must have had something extra going for him, some hidden force.

Neil Hobday has fared almost as well. He was suspended for nine months and then reinstated, but he had been on full pay throughout – unlike Kumar Patel who, of course, had been suspended without pay. At the end of 1987 Hobday quit the council. This came as a surprise to his former colleagues until it was learned that he had been paid £16,000 as a redundancy pay-off. Even more surprising, he was still a JP even though a court of law had found him guilty of racial discrimination. After protests from Mrs Patel, the Lord Chancellor's Department stood him down for a while but (just like Waltham Forest) reinstated him, for reasons which it later gave her in writing:

> Mr Hobday was not a respondent to the proceedings before the Industrial Tribunal and was unable to defend himself . . . He has since been able to give his full account of the matter . . . to the Committee [responsible for his appointment] who, after the most careful consideration, have accepted his version. To do otherwise . . . would have required clear corroboration of the very serious allegation. Mr Hobday has been on the bench since 1977 and is held in high regard.

When Waltham Forest dropped its inquiry into Hobday's alleged 'gross misconduct', the Lord Chancellor's Department felt it was only fair to reinstate him as a JP: 'Had both sides of the matter been professionally argued, and then decided in a proper judicial manner, the outcome would have been more readily appreciated.'

This betrays breathtaking double standards. The department was spurning the tribunal verdict, 'proper' and 'judicial' though it was, because a local council had dropped a *non-judicial* inquiry for fear of exposing its own dirty linen. How many other men, condemned of racism in a British court, are allowed to sit in judgement in another? How can non-whites who come before Hobday JP have any faith in British justice? The answer is, they won't know he is Hobday, for no defendant has the right to know a magistrate's name.

Magistrates' courts are thick with Masons, as I showed in Chapter 23. In *The Brotherhood* Stephen Knight quoted a Mason in a senior post in the Lord Chancellor's department who said that many of his work colleagues were 'on the square'. When the book appeared Lord Chancellor Hailsham wrote to several newspapers denying that his patronage office was staffed by Masons, but how did he know? He said he himself was not a Mason, so how could he tell? Presumably the Department does not oblige its staff to declare Masonic membership. If it does, that rule should be extended to other public bodies. If not, he was making his claim without valid supporting evidence.

Lord Hailsham's repeated, and sometimes unsolicited, defence of Freemasons puzzled me from the moment I began my researches until 1988 when I acquired a book listing all Grand Lodge's former officers. This revealed that in 1927 Hailsham's father, the first Viscount Hailsham, was appointed Past Junior Grand Warden. This means he was one of England's leading Freemasons.[3] An eminent Conservative politician, the Viscount preceded his son as Lord Chancellor. It seems likely, therefore, that the present Lord Hailsham regards Masons as citizens above suspicion, if only out of regard for his father. It would have been Hailsham, acting on subordinates' advice, who ultimately cleared Neil Hobday.

Brother Hobday has many qualities. He is dedicated to the public service. For ten years he was full-time camp commandant of Gilwell Park, the Scout Association's training centre. By chance an anonymous correspondent wrote to me claiming that Freemasonry plays a major role in both scouting and the professional youth service, the two fields in which Neil Hobday has spent most of his working life. My informant said the Red Scarf Lodge (no. 8448), which meets in the City of London, is 'especially for people who took part in the famous Scout "Gang Shows" under Ralph Reader'. He also said Gilwell Park is often used for Masonic gatherings. This seems unlikely but from another source I learned that the Essex Scout lodge, Venturer (no. 7897), meets nearby at Chingford. Every year, on the evening before the Scouts' Gilwell Re-union, lodges associated with youth work used to hold a joint meeting at Freemasons' Hall. They may still do so. If so, there would be representatives from many Scout lodges but also from four Boys' Brigade lodges, each of which includes the Brigade motto 'Sure and Stedfast' in its name.

Rudyard Kipling, whose *Jungle Book* stories provided so much of scouting's inspiration, was a staunch Freemason. He was initiated in Lahore, India, in 1886 in a lodge which included Catholic, Hindu, Muslim, Sikh and Jewish brethren. Back in England he wrote a poem recalling his 'Mother Lodge', and the integration which it alone offered in the race-, class- and caste-bound structure of British India:

> Outside – "Sergeant! Sir! Salute! Salaam!"
> Inside – "Brother," an' it doesn't do no 'arm.
> We met upon the Level an' we parted on the Square,
> An' I was Junior Deacon in my Mother Lodge out there!

'I wish that I might see them, My Brethren black and brown,' wrote Kipling. When I read this poem to Kumar Patel, he responded, 'I wish

Rudyard Kipling had joined a lodge in Waltham Forest. I could have used a good poem about Masonic racial discrimination at the industrial tribunal!'

For all its claims of multi-faith and multi-racial tolerance, Freemasonry underwrites apartheid in South Africa. England's United Grand Lodge has more than 275 lodges in the Republic, Scotland has 156 and Ireland 56. All these lodges are for Whites Only or, as Masonic historians put it, 'those of European descent'. Even in the USA, with its tens of thousands of lodges, it seems only one lodge is integrated, in New Jersey. Elsewhere America's black brothers belong to 'irregular', all-black 'Prince Hall' lodges. In most other countries Freemasonry seems to be integrated, but even in Britain many lodges are self-segregating. For 200 years most Jewish Masons have been initiated in all-Jewish lodges: partly out of choice, partly because of discrimination. Now non-whites are following suit. Half the members of the Pearl of Africa Lodge (no. 9052) are Asians of East African descent.

In Waltham Forest the Patel Affair had one last racist twist. In 1985 the Council introduced a register of interests which required 250 male employees handling outside contract work to declare 'membership of the Freemasons and other secret organizations'. Less than 60 per cent returned the forms, and only one man stated he was a Mason. Far from extinguishing the issue, this response led to demands for the Masonic declaration to be required of men in other areas of council work, including education, because of 'questions raised about it in connection with attitudes on racism and sexism'.

Not long after, three black Labour councillors were outraged by the council's whitewash inquiry into the Patel affair. Two were sacked from senior posts for opposing the prevailing Labour view, so all three resigned other party posts in solidarity. They said they 'were not prepared to accept the view of an all-white committee, sitting in secret, overturning the decision of a properly-constituted court which sat in public'.

Inadvertently, these men had given a classic definition of a Masonic fix.

twenty-nine

WHAT'S UP, DOC?

Just mention 'Freemasonry in the medical profession' and fearful images bubble up in the minds of the paranoid. I have letters from several people, apparently on the outer edges of sanity, who claim Masonic doctors have poisoned them, murdered their parents, or covered up Masonic murders by writing false diagnoses on death certificates. I have discounted these tales as lunatic ravings or the work of agents-provocateurs testing Stephen Knight's gullibility or mine. I am still left with several accounts which, after careful scrutiny and consideration, seem worth airing.

A non-Masonic general practitioner who has worked in Liverpool since the mid-1970s writes:

> When I first came here medicine in this city was very inbred and very Masonic. I obtained a consultant appointment in a leading teaching hospital. Everyone thereafter assumed that I was a Mason and the Craft was spoken of freely in my presence. I found this mildly amusing and became an avid Mason-spotter. About 1981 word clearly got back to the organization that I was not of their number. Since that time I have received four overtures from very senior figures in the local Masonic establishment. I find it amusing that they seem so keen to enlist me: I have no intention of joining and am presumably seen as an embarrassment by virtue of being 'profane'.
>
> I would add that Masonic influence within medicine does not seem to be used in a manner deleterious to patients or profession.

A young doctor's mother, writing from the Channel Isle of Guernsey, takes a less benign view:

> I have been very worried about Freemasonry for various reasons, but most about its possible influence on my son's medical career, and I have not known where to turn for advice or any sort of assurance.

Shortly after qualifying as a doctor, my son married the daughter of a fairly eminent consultant gynaecologist who is a Mason. He strongly advised my son to join the Masons, 'as it would help your career'. The marriage broke up after a while, which made my daughter-in-law's family very bitter. She passed on a message from her father that he 'would see that he would get no further in his career'.

Up to this point the young man had done very well in his examinations. A qualified physician, he wanted to become a surgeon and had already passed part one of the FRCS exams first time. This is unusual, as part one is considered harder to pass than the second and final part, which is usually a formality. However, the son was to fail part two four times and was forced to give up hope of becoming a surgeon. He is now happily settled as a GP, yet the worry remains that his former father-in-law somehow put the Masonic influence on the Royal College of Surgeons (which has many Masonic Fellows) to make sure he would fail.

His mother was not leaping to the conclusion that her son had definitely been 'fixed' by Freemasons. She says 'If I *knew* the whole thing was only coincidence and that there was no undue or unfair influence whatsoever in this matter I would not be the slightest bit worried.' There is, of course, no way that the Royal College is ever going to admit the possibility that its exam procedures are anything but wholly objective. It seems, therefore, that neither mother nor son will ever know the truth.

Masonic yearbooks billow with the names of doctors and surgeons. Just two of Surrey's most prestigious lodges, the St George's (no. 370) and the Surrey (no. 416), together boast some nineteen Past Masters who are medical men, including thirteen surgeons. Almost all London teaching hospitals have their own lodges, including Bart's, St Mary's, St Thomas's, King's College, the London and the Westminster. One doctor within Guy's hospital listed seven senior surgeons and physicians whom he claimed '*ran*' Guys. He also relayed this tale:

Sir Rowan Boland was Dean of the Medical School from 1945 until shortly before his death in 1970. A prestigious new hospital block was named after him. Sprung from an old Highland family which had always kept the Catholic faith, he was forced to renounce his religion and enter the Craft on becoming a Guy's house physician in 1934. Through his Masonic connections he then rose swiftly to the highest position in the hospital.

I have been unable to prove the truth of this story. I must also allow for an excess of zeal in my informant who hopes to have 'the satisfaction of seeing the demise and complete extinction of this utterly corrupt and evil movement'.

Undoubtedly his anti-Masonry will be reinforced when he learns there is a Masonic aspect to a present-day medical *cause célèbre*. In July 1986 fourteen villagers from the far north of Scotland travelled to London to give evidence to the General Medical Council against their GP, John Forbes-Proctor. The 'Melness Martyrs' (as they came to be known) considered him a chronic boozer, and had stomached enough of his intoxicated prescriptions. Drink is the occupational disease of doctors, but in most of Britain discontented patients can go to another GP for treatment. In 400 square miles around the Kyle of Tongue, the forty-six-year-old Forbes-Proctor was the *only* doctor. If any of the 500 inhabitants did not want his treatment, they would get no treatment at all. They might drive thirty or forty miles to see another GP, and then be turned away because of a no-poaching deal between local physicians. If forced to choose between death and 'Dr Dram', some Tongue residents would have chosen death.

To avoid that fate, the villagers trekked 750 miles south to tell the GMC's Professional Conduct Committee of ten occasions when Dr Dram attended patients while under the influence of drink. Once he mistook a fit man for his sick brother and congratulated him on a miraculous recovery. Another time a fellow nicknamed Red Pete knocked himself unconscious in a tavern. While examining prostrate Pete (who fell over so often, said Forbes-Proctor, it was usual to ignore him), the doctor consumed a whisky offered by the house. To Dr Dram whisky was itself a medicine which he prescribed for many ailments and frequently supervised the dose. Not everyone approved, nor did they see the joke in his favourite prescription: a 'leather injection' (a kick up the backside) for alleged hypochondriacs and malingerers.

The plaintiffs wanted Forbes-Proctor struck off the GMC list, but the committee was unimpressed. GMC President Sir John Walton announced that, under cross-examination, a strong *prima facie* case did not reach the standard of criminal evidence: proof beyond reasonable doubt. In fact the witnesses had been overwhelmed by the ferocity of the cross-examination. Crofting folk are not used to the wiles of whizz-bang London lawyers hired by the Medical Defence Union. Forbes-Proctor was fighting for his professional livelihood so he deserved the best defence, but what shocked observers was that the 'prosecutor' did not *re-examine* the witnesses to re-establish their credibility. It was as if the case against Dr Dram was being put forward half-heartedly. For procedural reasons some of the strongest witnesses were excluded, including one holidaymaker who claimed that a gash in his daughter's head had been erratically and painfully stitched by the doctor when he was the worse for drink.

On the GMC steps a stocky, bearded Forbes-Proctor posed triumphant in a fine kilt, enhancing his eccentric image. This kilt irked the pants off everyone else from Tongue, for Forbes-Proctor is not a Scotsman but an immigrant from England. The real Scots shuffled back to the Highlands in defeat, dreading what would now happen if they or their relatives fell sick. They vowed to stick together. One-third of the families on Dr Dram's register requested a transfer, but the Highland Health Board turned them down. Forbes-Proctor could have told them they would get nowhere, for he hung a sign in his surgery saying: 'If you want a second opinion, ask MacTavish.' MacTavish was his dog, who often took lunch in the surgery itself.

In five years as many as 100 complaints had been made about MacTavish's owner, but the Health Board rejected them all as trivial, unjustified or out of time (six weeks after the event). In response to prompt complaints, the board sent out intimidatory warnings about defamation. Whatever his captive patients flung at him, they could get no satisfaction. They were stuck with Forbes-Proctor until he died – or they did.

Some brave locals decided to do a little research into the man's background. They found he had an equally colourful and convivial reputation in Peterlee, England, where he had lasted five years, and in Lagan near Inverness where he had achieved notoriety for treating a girl's burned breast in a hotel bar with a slab of butter meant for the sandwiches. It also emerged that Dr Dram was 'on the square' and he had let it be known before the GMC hearing that he had 'friends in high places' who would see him right. After that event he said: 'It didn't bother me from the start. I spoke to the GMC beforehand and I knew I was in the clear.' He indicated Freemasonry had been the mechanism.

By this time a local landowner of impeccable pedigree had decided to call a square a square. Lt-Colonel John Moncrieff, with 24,000 acres and thirty years in the Black Watch to his credit, blasted Forbes-Proctor for his 'bastard tartan' and went for the Masonic jugular. He lambasted the Highland Health Board for being packed with Freemasons and for erecting a 'legal and masonic smokescreen': 'Whose side is the Board on? It should be protecting patients, not doctors.' He despatched letters to the board attacking one official for doing a 'marvellous job in keeping Forbes-Proctor in Tongue and we all know that this is because they are both Freemasons'.

In 1987 not even the Masons could save Dr Dram, when he drove 200 miles to a vintage car rally in Forfar. While there he drank too much and was observed, by police, acting in an inebriate manner. As he drove off, traffic patrolmen followed and brought him to a halt. In December he was fined £150 and banned from driving for one year. This meant he could no longer transport himself around his huge parish. At the same time yet another patient complained he had injected her with a painkiller one year after its 'use-by' date had expired. Forbes-Proctor realized that he could no longer go on, and resigned at last.

The true role played by Freemasonry in this affair may never be known. However, in January 1988 the Craft's local Grand Secretary broke cover in a newspaper letters column by asking Moncrieff to send him the names of all the village Masons who, the Colonel had said, backed Dr Dram. The Secretary said he had 'no personal knowledge of any Masons in the Tongue area'. Moncrieff could have named several men but if he did so, he realized he might be entrapped in a libel action. As no lodge meets in Tongue itself, he could have responded that by the time brethren have travelled thirty miles to the nearest lodge, they would be in their aprons but out of Tongue.

thirty

SQUARING THE SQUARE MILE

In *The Brotherhood* Stephen Knight described a 1982 meeting of the most prestigious lodge in the City of London: the Guildhall (no. 3116). Knight revealed that almost every Lord Mayor who is a Mason (and that means almost every Lord Mayor) becomes Master of Guildhall. This exposure so upset Grand Lodge that it has since claimed, 'many of the persons Knight categorically states to have been present at the meeting . . . were absent'.

In fact, Knight *categorically* asserted the presence of only four people: the Master, Master Elect, Senior Warden and Chaplain. As the Master Elect was to be ceremoniously 'installed' in the Chair that night, it would have been a very poor 'do' if these four brethren did not show up. Knight said another ten men were invested in office that evening. Whether they attended or not, all ten were Guildhall Lodge officers in 1982–3. A summons to the meeting lists all their names and ranks.

The Masonic upper echelon is very touchy about the City of London. I felt this at first-hand when I wrote to Sir Peter Gadsden, Lord Mayor of London 1979–80 and Guildhall Lodge Master 1980–81. During his year as mayor I had attended a dinner which he hosted for members of another network: the college at which we had both studied (though at different times). He had kindly laid on the Mansion House for the occasion, and the diners paid for the privilege of being his guests. I thought this clubbable bond might have encouraged him to tell me about Free-masonry's role in the City, in Australia (where he has substantial interests) and in the business community at large.

I misjudged the man. In a terse reply he said: 'Freemasonry has no role in the City of London or in the business community.' He added that if I needed 'further information' I should contact Commander Higham (with whom I was already in contact). Sir Peter's own 'information' – that Freemasonry has no role in the City or business – was no information at all, so I wrote back. I pointed out that the ratio of Masons to non-Masons among men in England is about one to twenty, yet among male Lord Mayors of London this century the ratio was reversed, at some twenty to one. I added:

> If my rough estimates are anywhere near correct but if, as you say, Freemasonry has no role in the City of London, we have discovered an extraordinary statistical freak. The odds against so many Lord Mayors being Freemasons by chance would appear to be many thousands to one. There must be another explanation.

Whatever the explanation, this Past Senior Grand Deacon chose not to answer a question which any non-Mason might reasonably ask. One of at least sixty-four Guildhall Lodge Lord Mayors since 1905, he is deluding himself if he believes Freemasonry has no role in the City. No doubt he has achieved his career success on his own merits, for this 'self-employed Mining Consultant' (as he describes himself on lodge application forms) is a mineral expert of the first rank. While digging deep in search of titanium, zirconium and hafnium, he has also plumbed the mysteries of Freemasonry. He is a Past Master of Mount Moriah Lodge (no. 34). Just to be invited into so ancient a club, founded in 1754, requires excellent connections. In 1967 he joined his school lodge, the Old Wrekinian (no. 5481), becoming Master in 1975; then the City of London Installed Masters (no. 8220), the Guildhall, and the Barbican (no. 8494). For years an honorary member of Farringdon Without (no. 1745), named after the City Ward which he had represented as an alderman since 1971, he became a full member just before he was paraded through the City as its new Lord Mayor.

Sir Peter belongs to many other City institutions with Masonic bonds. He is an honorary liveryman of the Worshipful Company of Plaisterers whose lodge meets in Plaisterers' Hall – one of at least twenty-one City Livery company lodges. He has been Master of the Cripplegate Ward Club. Like most City Wards, Cripplegate has a lodge. He is a governor of St Bartholomew's Hospital and a Knight of the Venerable Order of St John of Jerusalem, both of which have their own lodges. Sir Peter also sits on the committees of the City of London and City Livery clubs, at both of which dozens more lodges meet. In short, the very density of Masonic activity in the City makes a nonsense of his assertion that the brotherhood has no role there. In truth, the 'Square mile' has been squared, and encompassed, many times over by the men in lamb-skin aprons.

All the City's great commercial and financial pillars are also pillars of Freemasonry. Take Lloyd's, probably still the world's premier insurance market. One underwriting member is Sir Peter Gadsden, but he plays no part in running the place. That is the job of a committee composed of full-time insiders: a self-electing élite of underwriters and brokers. From 1982 until 1985 one committee member was the most successful underwriter of modern times: Ian Posgate. He made so much money for the 'names' who invested with him that they called him 'Goldfinger'. In 1982 his syndicates were handling £150-million-worth of premiums: almost 10 per cent of Lloyd's total market, and 25 per cent of all marine business.

Posgate's success had been upsetting rivals for years. Like them he went to public school, but he was always an outsider in this patrician club. A self-made man, he told author Godfrey Hodgson: 'Lloyd's has a second-generation problem.'[1] All his competitors had inherited their cosseted positions from their fathers, but he was earning an incredible £1 million a year on his own merits. That fell apart in 1984 when a scandal broke over the massive Howden syndicates for which he was a lead underwriter. He had nothing to do with the worst affair (the 'disappearance' of £55 million of investors' funds) but Lloyd's discipline committee found him guilty of planning to buy a Swiss bank and receiving a Pissarro painting intended as a bribe. The new ruling council tried to expel him, but a judge toned this down to a six-month suspension. Many eminent people, for whom he had earned fortunes, backed his attempts to return but in 1986 the council declared he was not a 'fit and proper person' to start underwriting again. Ousted at last, 'Goldfinger' was now melted down.

Many Lloyd's folk share Posgate's view that he was shut out for doing nothing more than a lot of less talented members do all the time. What he lacked was their special brand of reinsurance. He was not a Freemason. Over lunch at a self-service café in the Barbican, Goldfinger himself told me a remarkable story.

> I was first approached to become a Freemason in 1966 when I already had something of a reputation at Lloyd's as an underwriter. The approach came from Kenneth McNeill who was deputy chairman of Lloyd's and Sheriff of the City of London. Then my own boss, Frank Davey, asked me to join. When he died I handed all his Masonic paraphernalia to Tom McNeill, because they were both members of the same lodge, Lutine.
>
> My wife is a Catholic, so naturally I discussed these approaches with her. It was partly because of the Catholic Church's opposition to Freemasonry that I didn't join. But in the early 1970s I received an altogether more formal approach. It came from a man who was simultaneously a director of a merchant bank, a director of Lloyd's

and the Lord Lieutenant of his county. This was the heavy artillery. He impressed on me that it would be good for my career, but again I turned the offer down.

Years later when I was suspended from Lloyd's, this same man came up to me and said: 'You see, Ian, if you had accepted my offer all those years ago, none of this would have happened. Everything could have been sorted out.' I was in no doubt that he was referring to his Masonic approach.

Freemasonry's power over Lloyd's can scarcely be over-estimated. Its seat is the Lutine Lodge (no. 3049), founded in 1904. Posgate claims that, from the first moment he stepped into Lloyd's, 'there has never *not* been a Lutine Lodge member on the committee. At any time either the chairman or deputy chairman belongs to Lutine. Some people say that as many as half the committee may belong. Nothing can happen at Lloyd's without the Lutine Lodge knowing about it.' Posgate does not claim he was 'framed'. He does claim that Lutine members look after each other. If he had accepted the whispering Lord Lieutenant's suggestion, he might still be earning a million a year as Lloyd's top underwriter.

Only once has the Masonic axis at Lloyd's been openly attacked: in a row over a 1981 robbery in Los Angeles when $2.7-million-worth of diamonds were stolen from a jewellery store. The diamonds were insured with forty-one syndicates at Lloyd's which refused to bear the loss. The diamonds' owner, Moshe Tubero, was shocked to discover he was now being bilked as well as robbed, so he instructed London solicitor Brian Chase Grey to try and get the pay-out to which he was entitled. Chase Grey had no alternative but to sue all 12,000 syndicate 'names' (investors). In November 1984 the case was about to be heard in the Royal Courts of Justice by Master Robert Turner, but at the very last minute it was switched to the Senior Master, John R. Bickford Smith.[2] He blocked the action for reasons which outraged Tubero's London solicitor, Brian Chase Grey. He later appealed Bickford Smith's decision but another judge upheld it. Even so, in December 1985 Labour MP Brian Sedgemore (a scourge of City corruption) used the House of Commons to attack Bickford Smith for taking the case in the first place:

J. R. Bickford Smith, for reasons that nobody can understand, grabbed it for himself and insisted that he should deal with it . . . Counsel said to him, 'Do you really feel you can deal with this case, because one of the defendants is called J. Bickford-Smith?' J. R. Bickford Smith does not have a hyphen in his name, but J. Bickford-Smith does. Master Bickford Smith lied to counsel. Yes, he lied. He said, 'You will not find another master in this corridor, nor a single judge in this building, who is not a Lloyd's underwriter.' This statement was manifestly untrue because all the masters are not Lloyd's underwriters.

Sedgemore alleged that, with or without a hyphen, the Bickford Smiths were cousins. The implication was that the Senior Master's conduct aroused suspicions of an extended family interest in the case. The MP then pointed to a closer bond than blood. He stated that Master Bickford Smith's best friend, another Master 'just down the corridor', was a Lloyd's underwriter and a defendant in the case. Sedgemore then seized on a Masonic connection:

> Master J. R. Bickford Smith – who happens to be a member of the Athlumney Freemasons Lodge, and there appear to be other Freemasons in this case (we have a curious combination of Freemasonry and the power of Lloyd's) – actually makes orders which are outside the rule book for which he is personally responsible. When the Lord Chancellor looks into this case, he will find a viper's nest.

This speech was made at three o'clock in the morning. In the cold light of a winter's day further explanation was needed, notably from Bickford Smith. He told *The Times* he had 'no recollection of any point on a relationship having been raised'. When the diamond merchant's solicitor, Brian Chase Grey, read the quote he was appalled. He distinctly remembered walking into the Law Courts a year earlier to see clerks scurrying from Master to Master, and to be told that the case was being switched to Bickford Smith seconds before it was to start. This had infuriated Chase Grey. He felt even more perturbed when he recalled glimpsing a 'J. Bickford-Smith' among the 12,000 investors. He instructed his barrister to bring this possible clash of interests to the Master's attention. Far from taking the point that family relationships obliged him to withdraw, Bickford Smith made this astonishing challenge: 'You will not find another master in this corridor, nor a single judge in this building, who is not a Lloyd's underwriter.'

Chase Grey instantly guessed that there must be dozens of judges in the Law Courts who are not Lloyd's underwriters – these days you need to be a lot wealthier than many judges to become a 'name' – but he assumed that, nevertheless, Bickford Smith wanted him to believe that all judges qualified to hear the case were probable defendants, therefore he had no hope of an impartial hearing so he should shut up. He then felt that

Bickford Smith acted with a heavy bias against him and his American client. However, Chase Grey could not force a change of judge because he still had no proof that the Bickford Smiths were related. That came one year later when a genealogist tracked down the precise blood tie.

When Lord Chancellor Hailsham and Attorney-General Sir Michael Havers read Sedgemore's remarks, they were outraged. Nothing so upsets England's law officers as attacks on a judge's integrity. Sedgemore had demanded a Lord Chancellor's inquiry but Hailsham waited almost a year before replying, and only then through the odd device of a written Commons answer by Havers to a question from a government back-bencher. The answer should have been given directly to Sedgemore, as the Speaker later confirmed when he ruled that the Attorney-General had abused parliamentary privilege. Havers had also used that privilege unjustly to attack Chase Grey (though not by name) with a ferocity that made even the brute-tongued Sedgemore look a softie. Extraordinary though it seems, Chase Grey had not been interviewed for this 'inquiry'.

First Havers implied that the Los Angeles robbery had never taken place, and the claim was a fraud. He then said that, far from grabbing the case, Bickford Smith had taken it at the defendants' request, 'in view of his knowledge of United States law'. Chase Grey read this with astonishment, for this was the first he had heard of such a move. He later protested that any bearing which American law had on the case should have been decided on expert evidence, 'not Master Bickford Smith's personal interpretation'.

Havers also stated that, when Bickford-Smith the defendant was first mentioned, the Master 'has a clear recollection to the effect that he explained that the underwriter was probably a cousin of his'. Chase Grey saw this as more deception, for Bickford Smith had previously told *The Times* 'he did not remember any counsel in the case telling him that one of the defendants had the same name'. Furthermore, in September 1985 Tubero's American lawyer had received a letter from the Lord Chancellor's department saying, 'You assume that it is Master Bickford Smith himself, or one of his relations, who belongs to Lloyd's Syndicate 127/128. *This need not be so* [my italics]. Bickford Smith is an unusual but not unique surname in this country.'

Chase Grey reasoned that if Master Bickford Smith had admitted he was the defendant's cousin during the hearing, this would have been stated in the Lord Chancellor's letter to America, which was surely sent after consultations with Bickford Smith. Chase Grey felt this sleight-of-hand proved some folk had changed their stories, perhaps so that Havers could dismiss any sinister interpretation of the Bickford Smiths' relationship. Had the Master admitted this during the original hearing, Chase

Grey would have *insisted* he withdraw. Reading the admission two years after, he felt big fish must be hooked on the end of big lies.

Havers claimed Bickford Smith had never said there was not 'a single judge in this building who is not a Lloyd's underwriter'. The allegation was 'fantasy or fabrication'. As Bickford Smith was not an underwriter himself, said Havers, he was 'living disproof of the assertion'. Chase Grey says he knew that Bickford Smith's remark was not true even when he made it, but that the Senior Master was relying on the near impossibility of establishing who is or is not a member of Lloyd's. Chase Grey had managed to get lists of the 12,000 defence 'names' only after the lead underwriters had tried to suppress them.

Havers also attacked Chase Grey and his clients by quoting Bickford Smith's view that they had abused the process by suing in both Britain and America. In fact, claimants have the right to start proceedings wherever they have a claim. Bickford Smith had over-ruled that right, then dismissed a second action by claiming Chase Grey had made 'a crude attempt' to obtain money 'by trick wording' at the expense of a US bank which had a share in the claim. This was a slander on Chase Grey who had written to the bank's lawyers asking them to join in the London action. They wrote to decline, as Chase Grey had explained to Bickford Smith who ignored the point.

Havers made much of the fact that Chase Grey did not appeal the last of Bickford Smith's judgements in the affair. He also tried to debunk Sedgemore's 'Masonic conspiracy' by mouthing a testimonial from Hailsham: 'So far as is known to the Lord Chancellor, Freemasonry is a perfectly lawful organization and in any case, apart from the Senior Master, none of the persons involved in the proceedings appear to be Freemasons.'

Chase Grey studied Havers's attack before writing to defend himself and his clients on every point. First, the diamond robbery *had* taken place. Even the defendants' on-the-spot assessors reported there was no reason to believe it was anything other than a genuine crime. Second, in America, the underwriters eventually had paid $2 million to settle the claim. As soon as he knew of this triumph, Chase Grey dropped all English proceedings. That was also why he did not appeal. Third, by not referring to the $2 million pay-out, Havers had given the false impression that the claimant was a crook and Chase Grey was his knowing accomplice.

Chase Grey ended his letter saying: 'The distortion of facts and miasma of untruths which have beset these actions have been multiplied by your Answer to the House of Commons.' Eighteen months later neither Havers nor Hailsham had replied. Havers told Sedgemore he would reply 'shortly' to Chase Grey, but never did. In May 1987 Chase Grey wrote to Hailsham: 'As you well know, the main purpose of your inquiry was to suppress evidence of a major conspiracy to pervert the course of justice and to deceive the House of Commons.' Hailsham never replied.

Hailsham had earlier felt obliged to state he is not a Mason. He also explained that, though a name at Lloyd's, he was not in any syndicates sued by Chase Grey. No doubt John Bickford Smith, 32nd degree Sublime Prince of the Royal Secret in the Rose Croix and Deputy Great Sword Bearer of the Masonic Knights Templar, feels he acted impeccably throughout this affair. In 1987 he retired.

There is far more to the City than Lloyd's, lawyers and Lord Mayors. The biggest City business is probably banking. Here again Freemasonry is rampant. Lodges are centred on the Bank of England (no. 263), Lloyds Bank (Black Horse of Lombard Street, no. 4155) and National Westminster (no. 3647). It was from within the Midland Bank that I gained some real insight into the Craft's role in banking. My source had already been a Mason for some years when he was asked to join Midland Bank's lodge, the Holden (no. 2946). Some years ago he went as a guest and found himself alongside four senior officials in the Midland Bank Trust Company: the then managing director, general manager, chairman of the investment committee and a regional director. Others present included a director of Midland Montague merchant bank and other Midland moguls.

My source could not decide if these men had become powers in the bank because they were already Masons, or if Masonry had co-opted them once they had achieved power. He chose not to join the lodge because by then he felt the Craft was spiritually flawed. When this became known to his Masonic colleagues, his career collapsed. He was denied promotion and told his services were no longer required. He now reflects, 'The lodge seemed composed entirely of senior managers. I spotted no low-level staff, no messengers or maintenance men – and of course no women. If the lodge does have any say over who gets on in the bank, its existence certainly can't do women bankers any good.' 'Would any Masonic presence in the bank reduce the quality of its service to customers?' I asked. 'Surely, if Masons lived up to their principles, it might improve it?' My now *former* banker shook his head and jested, 'You know why the Midland calls itself the Listening Bank? That's because it daren't speak in case its tongue gets torn out by the root.'

Freemasonry's strength in the London HQs of England's clearing banks is more than matched in the regions. One northern lodge secretary wrote saying it was nonsense to believe bank managers join Free-

masonry for business: 'To illustrate that point let me tell you that every
bank manager in our town is a Mason, so how do you think they can get
any advantage from any of our members? In fact when they send me their
cards, they all ask to be seated together!' This story, far from proving
bankers do not join Freemasonry for business, raised more serious
questions:

1. What specific talents do Masonic bankers alone possess to justify their
   monopoly of managers' jobs in any community?
2. Bank managers may not be in Freemasonry to get *new* business, but if
   every other manager in town is 'on the square', a non–Mason may feel
   he must join, to ensure he does not *lose* business.
3. If these fellows often meet at Masonic functions, where they gossip
   the night away over bottles of wine, how can their non–Masonic
   customers hope to keep their personal and business finances secret?

A non-Mason wrote to explain how the Masonic grip in banking is just
as strong overseas, and how 'demoralizing and demotivating' it is to
work as a senior manager in a British bank in Africa:

When I took over the job, I was asked by my outgoing colleague to
hand the financial records of his Masonic lodge to another colleague
who was to succeed him as treasurer. They were open and included a
subscription list. I unashamedly studied the names and was horrified
to find I was virtually the only executive in Head Office who was not
a member – with the exception of the managing director who had
got his job through his family, not Freemasonry. He was frequently
scathing in his comments about the organization – quite unaware
that he was surrounded by secret members.

I was in a first-hand position to observe their activities and was
mesmerised by their blatant self-promotion. I saw people totally
unqualified for responsible posts being promoted beyond their
ability, to the chagrin and bewilderment of officials who had every
right to expect the posts themselves. In the peculiarly school-like
methods of assessing bank staff ability, I saw the appallingly sub-
standard work of brotherhood members receive all the plaudits
while the sterling efforts of more worthwhile staff went unre-
marked. When promotion openings arose, their names were far
ahead. Independent assessments of two of these executives, before
they came to the territory, stated they had already been promoted
greatly in excess of their ability. Both are now making a frightful
mess of their appointments and losing shareholders' funds.

In one instance the Italian managing director of a company complained to me that one of our branch managers had refused to increase his overdraft or give him foreign exchange facilities. Foreign exchange was in short supply in this country and rationed on a national priority basis. I was also well aware that he used his increased overdraft to purchase foreign exchange illicitly on the black market which he smuggled back to his native Italy.

He was a member of the brotherhood, and I knew he assumed that I also belonged – an illusion which I did nothing to dispel. I was aware that he valued his membership chiefly for the engineering contracts which were awarded to his business from the mining company which was the chief source of wealth in the area. The masonic brethren in the mine saw to it that his tenders were successful. He was astonished when I said I could not agree to increased facilities for his company. However, I knew him quite well and let him appeal to the ultimate authority – the general manager's assistant for advances. I added that he was a fellow Mason and that he was to be sure to give him the proper handshake! I introduced them and left them together. He called at my office on the way out, wreathed in smiles, giving a thumbs-up sign to indicate total success. His borrowings are now at unprecedented levels and are in the 'doubtful' category – meaning they will inevitably be written off and deducted from the shareholders' funds. In the meantime, many worthy applications have been turned down – incuding one for the importation of ethical drugs for the hospital.

This letter's author cannot be named because he is still working for the bank. If he is telling the truth, Freemasonry cannot only make and break careers; some Masons will even betray their employers by diverting company funds to crooked brethren. The commercial survival of a company, even a nation, could thus be subverted by Masonic 'insider-trading'.

In the City, insider-trading is the crime *par excellence*. Exploiting information for financial gain is the 'name of the game', and the fine line between 'inside' and 'outside' knowledge vexes many a stock-and-share trafficker who wants to stay out of jail. I am told there is at least one lodge for members of the Stock Exchange: the Verity (no. 2739). Before 'Big Bang' this included both brokers and jobbers, a distinction which no longer exists. Doubtless all lodge members exercise super-human restraint, lest they utter a word which might help brother Masons make money. They surely remember their initiation pledge about wanting to join Freemasonry 'uninfluenced by mercenary or other unworthy motives', but they may feel more bound by a 'sincere wish to render themselves more extensively serviceable to their fellow-creatures'. The outsider might surmise that a Mason could become no more serviceable to his fellow-Masons than by tipping them off about where to get the fastest return on investments.

Masonic spokesmen cite such pledges to show no true Mason would ever seek a financial or career advantage through the Craft. This must be nonsense when a lodge is based entirely on one commercial institution, be it Lloyd's of London or Lloyds Bank. There is an inevitable overlap between the social life of the lodge and the commercial concerns of the business on which it has been erected. Documents have come to me concerning what seems the oldest company lodge. For more than 250 years the Union Lodge (no. 52) has met in Norwich. It is closely involved with Norwich's biggest company, Norwich Union Insurance, although it may be that the lodge name has a different origin (there are eight other Union lodges in England). On the first Tuesday of every month from October to April Union brethren troop straight from work to the Norwich Masonic Hall in St Giles Street, with their aprons hidden neatly in their briefcases.

In 1959–60 the Union Lodge's Master was Worshipful Brother Basil Robarts, who was also the General Manager and Actuary of Norwich Union Life Insurance Society. On 13 December 1960 Mr B. O. Rolph, a top official in the firm, wrote to a senior employee in the London office on Norwich Union's headed stationery:

Dear Bro.——
On the 3rd January next Bro. Tom Barton is being installed as Master of Union Lodge and I am wondering whether it would be convenient for you to come down to visit us at Head Office on that day. What I have in mind is that you could then stay the night and attend Union Lodge as my guest. We have no particular points which need discussing but I feel that a visit from you once a year at least is helpful in general, discussing arrangements regarding the running of the London Board, etc. I hope you will be able to come and on your advising me I will let you have a formal invitation and also put in hand the reservation of accommodation for the night, if required . . .
    With kind regards.
    Yours sincerely . . .

Mr Rolph was himself a Past Master of Union Lodge, so his letter was a command from the hierarchy of both company and company lodge. He makes little distinction between them: the lodge seems to be the natural extension of Norwich Union – or perhaps Norwich Union is an extension of the lodge. Whichever, in the 1960s Freemasonry was so woven into the company fabric that careers may have hung by a Masonic thread. This might no longer be true, yet at the top of Norwich Union today sits one of Britain's highest-ranking Masons: the 7th Marquess Townshend (past Senior Grand Warden) has been vice-chairman of NU Life since 1973, NU Fire since 1975 and NU Holdings since 1981. As heir to the legendary seventeenth-century agriculturalist, 'Turnip' Townshend, and one of Norfolk's richest landowners, the Marquess would probably have penetrated the NU boardroom if he had never become a Mason. In contrast, many employees grubbing away at full-time jobs may have had no choice. Joining the Lodge may still be the best insurance they can take out – better even than a Norwich Union policy.

thirty-one

THE REGIMENTAL SQUARE

No British institution, not even the police, is more steeped in Free-masonry than the army. England's first recorded initiate, Elias Ashmole, was a captain in Lord Ashley's Royalist regiment when he joined a Warrington lodge in 1646. In his diary he says his fellow-initiate that day was Colonel Henry Mainwaring, who was a Parliamentarian. He was also Ashmole's father-in-law. Ashmole had been captured by the Roundheads, but also by a Roundhead's daughter and by Freemasonry. He changed sides and returned to London a Roundhead himself. It seems likely that he became a Mason to appease his captors, even to save his own skin.

On this evidence Masonic lodges may have been cells of sedition from their earliest recorded days. So much for the Antient Charges that oblige a Mason 'cheerfully to conform to the laws of the country' and 'not to be concerned in plots or conspiracies against government'. However, a Mason also promises 'patiently to submit to the decisions of the Supreme Legislature', so it seems he still has the choice: to back Parliament or the Crown!

In later centuries Field Marshals Wellington, Roberts, Wolseley, Kitchener, French, Haig, Alexander and Auchinleck all belonged to the fraternity, along with thousands of humbler soldiers who fought for king, queen and country. If trade followed the flag, so did Freemasonry. Indeed, the formation of a lodge seems to have happened as soon as British soldiers or sailors claimed some corner of a foreign field for the empire. Many lodges travelled with their regiments. From 1776 to 1812 the garrison town of Dover played host to regimental lodges hailing from Lancashire, Middlesex, Devon, Stafford and Cornwall. When the regiments moved on, so did the lodges – in one case, to the West Indies.

Today the Grand Lodge of England recognizes no 'ambulatory' lodges, yet two British regiments still hold travelling warrants from the

Grand Lodge of Ireland. It seems extraordinary that the 4th/7th Royal Dragoon Guards and the Worcestershire & Sherwood Foresters allow their soldiers to join lodges controlled by a foreign authority, especially one based in Dublin. This might be justified on antiquarian grounds but the same cannot be said of eleven English lodges in Germany, most of whose members are soldiers in the British Army of the Rhine. These lodges come under the ultimate authority of the United Grand Lodges of Germany which (as explained in the Introduction) has twice since the war been headed by ex-Nazi Grand Masters.

Dozens of London lodges have military origins: the Bloomsbury Rifles, City of London National Guard, City of London Rifles, Hertfordshire Imperial Yeomanry, Household Brigade, Kensington Battalion, London Irish Rifles, London Scottish Rifles, London Rifle Brigade, Middlesex Imperial Yeomanry, National Artillery, Paddington Rifles, Royal Engineers, Second Middlesex Artillery, Third Middlesex Artillery, United Artists Rifles, Victoria Rifles, and the Warrant Officers. Today only a few of these lodges' members have served in the army. Most are too young to have done National Service.

Some lodges still recruit only military personnel, such as Hertfordshire Regiment Lodge (no. 4537). Its membership consists of officers and men from all three services. Recent masters have included privates, aircraftsmen, sergeants, a flight sergeant, lieutenants and majors. In 1986 its stewards (the men who pour the drinks) were a major, a gunner, a warrant officer and a signalman. The St Barbara Lodge (no. 8724) of Staines, Middlesex, is an all-army lodge founded in 1976. It makes no distinction between officers and other ranks. Its Past Masters range from colonels to corporals, all of whom seem to have been serving in the army when installed. The Fort Royal Lodge (no. 4565) of Worcester is less democratic: officers only.

In recent years the United Grand Lodge hierarchy has included seven retired Major-Generals (the late Sir Allan Adair, Sir Leonard Atkinson, Sir Stuart Greeves, Sir Ralph Hone, Dennis Beckett, Rudolph Green and Andrew MacLellan) and two Lieutenant-Generals (Sir Robert Drew and Sir Alexander Drummond). What role Masonry played in their careers is difficult to gauge. Three of the most distinguished generals of modern times are unaware of any negative Masonic activities in the army. First, Sir John Hackett, a courageous warrior in World War II who became Commander-in-Chief, British Army of the Rhine, and a distinguished academic:

I am not, and have never been, a Freemason though my father, who died in Western Australia in 1916, was a Grand Master and I still

have somewhere his Masonic jewel. I know virtually nothing about
Masonry and do not have the slightest evidence of the influence that
membership of the Order may have had upon military careers. You
may find this difficult to credit, but I cannot think of any officer in
my whole acquaintance, during thirty-five years of service, who *was*
a Mason.

I asked Sir John if he had ever seen officers promoted far above their
abilities for inexplicable reasons:

The answer to that must be yes, particularly into the very highest
appointments. It had never occurred to me, however, and I can
honestly say I have never heard it suggested, that Masonic patronage
played any part in this. It is much more the case that the very highest
appointments demand qualities which are not very widely spread
and it is probably inevitable that men should find their way into
them who are not in every respect up to the demands made upon
them . . . If I had any close friend among military men who was, to
my certain knowledge, a Mason I suppose I could ask him about
this, but the simple fact is that I do not know of any.

A similar view is held by General Sir Harry Tuzo, one-time Gurkha
Commander, GOC Northern Ireland, and deputy Supreme Allied
Commander, Europe:

I am not a Freemason and know little or nothing of the Craft. I
know that I must have met military Freemasons during forty years
in the army but I certainly cannot identify them at this range . . . I
am afraid I simply do not believe that Masons receive preferential
treatment in some regiments. The promotion system depends, in
the junior ranks, on time and passing exams. After the rank of Major
it depends on a selection system which is based in the Military
Secretary's Branch in MOD. It is, I suppose, possible to imagine
that the branch might, at a given moment, contain a few Masons but
even their advocacy would have to overcome the great care and
fairness exercised by Selection Boards drawn from officers outside
MS branch. I personally do not believe that a more equitable system
could be devised . . . I have certainly seen officers promoted above
their ability, but I have never connected this with Freemasonry. It is
more a matter of human fallibility and faulty judgement.

Sir Harry does not give Masonry a wholly clean bill of health:

From the little I know of Masonic virtues, I would not say that they equate with military ones. So far as is possible, the Army is run on team work and mutual loyalty. These demand openness and a complete understanding in all ranks of the objectives to be attained. There is no room for secrecy or whispering in corridors.

I also asked the opinion of General Sir Anthony Farrar-Hockley, former Commander-in-Chief Allied Forces, Northern Europe, and a respected military historian. He too feels the system of promotion by boards, based on annual reports, is so carefully structured that 'the army would have to be riddled with Masons to ensure their preferences through this system'. He believes this is not so. Indeed: 'I have more often heard people say that favouritism is shown by one Roman Catholic to another than by membership of the Masonic order!' Sir Anthony expressed one very serious reservation: 'I am not a Mason, and even if I had been invited to become one, should not have accepted. I do not believe that membership of any society of that sort, however innocent, is compatible with holding office under the Crown.'

A brigadier wrote to condemn Masonry on principle and experience:

I was open-minded on the subject of Masonry in the Services until 1938 when a new rank – Platoon Sergeant Major – was created to overcome the shortage of junior officers in preparation for the approaching war. In my regiment three NCOs were promoted. They were all inefficient and quite unsuitable, and they all failed. They were also all Freemasons. From then on, I took a very jaundiced view of the possible unfortunate effects of Freemasonry in the Services. It's a side of service life which is very difficult to research, as one comes in contact with 'towers of silence'.

I sent the brigadier a lodge list for the Aldershot Army and Navy Lodge (no. 1971), some forty of whose members were army officers. He pointed out that none had risen higher than colonel:

The Aldershot–Camberley–Fleet area is where a lot of 'below par' officers are put out to grass. Most are incapable of establishing second careers, so they supplement their pensions by getting jobs as 'Retired Officers Re-employed', or RETREADS, in the many local military establishments such as Sandhurst and the Staff College. They probably use this lodge as a means of retaining social contacts.

What RETREADS do in their spare time has little effect on the rest of us.

Greater concern surrounds the use by Freemasons of one publicly-owned military building in central London: the Duke of York's Headquarters in King's Road, Chelsea. Here twenty-six lodges meet, including the Army & Navy, National Artillery and Victoria Rifles. They contain few serving army officers, but there is greater overlap with the part-time Territorials, whose national HQ is in the Duke of York's HQ. It is also home for the TA's most glamorous regiment: the 21st Special Air Services, which supports the regular 22nd SAS in acts of derring-do and counter-terrorism at home and abroad. It was the 22nd which broke the 1981 siege of the Iran Embassy with ruthless precision. Based in Hereford, the soldiers of the 22nd are too busy training to have much time for Freemasonry, but the 21st is different. One lodge which meets at the Duke of York's is the Rosemary (no. 2851), which (I am told) includes a number of men in the 21st. One non-Mason in the 21st takes a dim view of the brotherhood's power over the regiment.

During my service in the regular army, I fought in several secret wars overseas in which Britain had no public involvement but in which our government had a political and strategic interest. As an SAS officer, I killed more 'enemy' soldiers and terrorists than any British servicemen has had a chance to kill openly since Malaya and Korea.

When I came out of the army I joined the 21st (Territorial) SAS as a reservist. There is a rule that even if you were an officer in the 22nd, in the 21st you go back down the ranks. At first this did not worry me, as I was doing well in my civilian career and wasn't interested in military status. I became less philosophical when I saw how poorly led the regiment was. Very few of the officers have served as full-time soldiers. They have worked their way into the officer cadre without firing a shot in action. Meantime those of us who know how the *real* SAS fights, languish in the ranks. This sounds arrogant, but we feel like British 'tommies' during World War I: 'Lions led by Donkeys.'

After some years without promotion, I found out what was holding me down: I wasn't a Freemason. The Masons have got it sewn up: not just in the 21st but in the rest of the TA. They promote each other over non-Masons, to the detriment of the defence of the realm. If we were talking about the Catering Corps this wouldn't much matter, but when it comes to the SAS you cannot afford to have incompetent or inexperienced men in charge. Highly trained soldiers' lives are at stake. Whether you're in London or Timbuctoo, when you go in to break a siege, release hostages and kill terrorists, you must be sure the people in command know what they're doing and are up to the job. I do not feel that way about the 21st and I think it's a scandal. Sooner or later military or civilian dead will pay the price for a promotion system based not on ability but on Free-masonry.

What can non-Masonic colonels do to curb the Masonic presence in their regiments? Nothing at all, if the memoirs of former Grand Secretary Sir James Stubbs are any guide.[1] In 1979 the Certo Cito Lodge (no. 8925) was founded especially for the Army Corps in which Stubbs had served:

Almost every corps in the Army and a good many regiments too had a lodge connected with them: yet Royal Signals did not, and efforts over many years seemed to come up against the perpetual brick wall of a minute, many years old, in which a number of long since dead-and-gone Colonels Commandant had recorded their opposition. Having nothing to lose by incurring the displeasure of the current Corps Committee and feeling pretty certain that Brigadier Fair-weather . . . and Colonel Dicker [two senior Masons] . . . were quite a match for the committee if there was still opposition rather than inertia I pressed on.

Stubbs then gathered together Signals personnel, past and present, to plan the lodge's formation. At the 'consecration' the role of Senior Grand Warden was performed by a former Signals major: Earl Kitchener of Khartoum, a Mason like his great-grandfather of 'Your Country Needs You' fame. It was 'a great evening' and the lodge has since met not only in London but at Catterick, Richmond and Blandford (presumably, near Signal Corps Barracks). Stubbs's account shows how Masons ignore even formal army hostility to a new lodge. The same contemp-tuous approach was displayed in 1986 when the Manor of St James's Lodge was founded in conflict with Scotland Yard policy. If Freemasons can defeat even official military and police opposition with such ease, no wonder they treat the public's animosity with disdain.

The Royal Navy has less of a Masonic tradition than the army. Many noted sailors have been Masons, but probably not Lord Nelson who is claimed as a brother on very weak evidence. Admiral Jellicoe, Com-mander of the Fleet in World War I and later Chief of Naval Staff, became a Mason in 1922 aged sixty-three, when Governor-General of New Zealand. He promptly became that country's Grand Master, which proves again that Freemasonry's leaders value a man's public status (and the glory it reflects on the Craft) more than his knowledge of, or devotion to, Freemasonry. One recent sailor who despises the brother-hood is Rear-Admiral David Kirke: 'I consider the Craft to be a dangerous, malicious and malignant Mafia, exerting an evil effect in our society. It needs to be denounced, exposed and preferably eradicated. I find it utterly disgusting.'

Among today's Grand Officers there is one Admiral: Surgeon Rear-Admiral John Holford. The oldest lodge in Portsmouth, the Phoenix (no. 257), boasts two more Surgeon Rear-Admirals: William Forrest and Edward Cadman, both retired directors of Naval Dental Services and both trained at Guy's Hospital. The lodge contains four more naval surgeons but does not appear to admit 'other ranks' (see also Chapter 22). However, Freemasonry can blur social distinctions, according to one former officer who asked me not to name him:

In 1937 our ship was docked in Aden when the Governor's car appeared alongside, with two Naval Officers inside. A Leading Stoker got in and shook hands. As the car moved away, the blinds were pulled down! You will be aware that social distinctions were very rigid in those days, but there was only one Lodge in Aden, so RN Rules had to come second to Masonic Rules. This probably would not have arisen in UK ports or other outposts of the Empire where there were separate lodges based on class and occupation: one for dockyard foremen, another for the better-educated service personnel, and yet another for P&O stewards, among whom Freemasons could always be found.

These class distinctions sound appalling nowadays, but the Navy was riddled with them forty years ago, which is what made Freemasonry's role even more extraordinary. As an officer I had my own servant, who was a stoker of more than twenty years' service. Once he told me, 'Sir, there are only two things that over-rule RN discipline: (1) Freemasons and (2) Arse'. I hope you know what that refers to!

The most famous sailor in Freemasonry today is Grand Secretary Commander Higham RN, whom I have often quoted in this book. Here I give a fragment of his Masonic career, which he seems to have built largely round service lodges. He belongs to Navy Lodge (no. 2612) and to the Masonic Knights Templar and Knights of St John. In 1986 'Eminent Knight Commander' Higham bore the title: 'Preceptor and Prior of the Connaught Army & Navy Preceptory and Priory, No. 172.'

His brother knights include a major-general, a brigadier, two lieuten-ant commanders, an RAF squadron leader, a clutch of colonels, majors and captains, and retired police commander Jim Nevill QPM. Nevill also belongs to the Manor of St James's Lodge of past and present policemen. In September 1986 this Preceptory installed a regular army major, currently serving in the Royal Electrical and Mechanical Engineers, as a Knight Templar.

Many years earlier Michael Higham joined a most influential chapter in the Rose Croix: the United Studholme (no. 67). This boasted no less than eight naval commanders, a general, a brigadier and many other officers. In the 1974 Rose Croix Yearbook Higham was listed as a mere lieutenant. Just four years later he had risen to commander, but by then he was out of the Navy and working full-time as deputy Grand Secretary.

There are four high-ranking Royal Air Force men in Grand Lodge: Air Marshals Sir Victor Groom and Sir Donald Hall, Air Vice-Marshal Sir Bernard Chacksfield and Air Commodore Sir Peter Vanneck, who was also Lord Mayor of London and is now a Euro-MP. There are at least four RAF lodges: Ad Astra (no. 3808) and Pathfinder (no. 7255) which meet in London, Daedalus (no. 3843) for RAF Cranwell, and Hermes (no. 6861) for RAF Manby.

I have received no letters alleging Masonic malpractice in the RAF but four people – unknown to each other – have written to complain of Freemasonry's role in civil aviation. Two are pilots (one formerly with British Airways, the other with British Caledonian) who allege their careers were sabotaged by Masons. They have no firm proof that any of the 'saboteurs' are Masons, so it would be unjust to publish their claims unless supporting evidence emerges in the future. The Lodge of Aviation (no. 7210) is said to include many senior British Airways staff.

As with other areas of alleged Masonic back-scratching, it is difficult to pin the career advance of Masons in the forces on their Craft connections. However, fraternal literature shows us what military Masons themselves regard as true Masonic conduct and helps us understand what Brotherly Love really means.

One role model is Lord Moira, an Anglo-Irish soldier who at twenty-four was an adjutant-general on the king's side in the War of American Independence. He became Governor-General and Commander-in-Chief in India for nine years. He was also Masonic Grand Master of Scotland and Acting Grand Master of England. One Masonic historian[2] tells how the Earl was working one day on papers in the library of his country house when a woman forced her way in to see him. Her son had just been drawn for military service: 'I cannot help you,' was the Earl's rejoinder; 'if your son has been regularly balloted for and drawn in the Militia, he must serve.' The woman then told the Earl how her father, three brothers and husband had all died in action. Her son now supported the entire family. If he were sent to fight, the family would be destitute. When she named her husband, Isaac Wardroper, Moira remembered him from their days together in the 63rd Foot Regiment. She then produced a vellum certificate and some insignia. Moira examined the documents and told her:

> 'Your husband, it appears, was a Mason. Of that I am satisfied. He belonged, unquestionably, to a Military Lodge . . . For you it is well. Go with a light heart. So good a son had best remain where he is. He will not be torn from you. I require no thanks. I.can listen to nothing further; go and have no fears for the future.'
>
> A substitute for Stephen Wardroper [the son] was procured – who provided him? Who sought him? Who paid for him? And who, before the week's end, sent a £10 note by post to the Mason's widow? The poor woman accurately conjectured, and so without a doubt will the reader.

This tale may tell Masons that Moira was a wonderful chap, to help a poor Mason's widow so. Non-Masons may draw a nastier conclusion: he would have happily despatched her son to war – which, with his family's luck, would have meant certain slaughter – if his father had not been 'on the square'. The patriotic sacrifice of his five male relatives would have counted for nothing. All that mattered to Moira was that Masonic certificate. For young Stephen it was the difference between life and death.

A similar tale of Masonic preferment is told in that Masonic classic, *Preston's Illustrations of Freemasonry*.[3]

> A Scottish gentleman in the Prussian service was taken prisoner at the battle of Lutzen, and was conveyed to Prague along with 400 of his companions-in-arms. As soon as it was known that he was a Mason, he was released from confinement; he was invited to the tables of the most distinguished citizens, and requested to consider himself as a Freemason, and not as a prisoner of war. About three months after the engagement, an exchange of prisoners took place, and the Scottish officer was presented by the Fraternity with a purse of sixty ducats to defray the expenses of his journey.

It is therefore considered laudable among Masons that brethren should be spared the deprivation of military captivity inflicted on their non-Masonic comrades-in-arms. Another tale from Preston illustrates how Masonic sailors share this perverse morality:[4]

The Mason is a citizen of the world; and in whatever clime misfortune may overtake him, should he meet with Brothers, his relief is certain. In this particular Masonry is respected even by pirates, who are a terror to every other order of men; and I rejoice that it is in my power to record a triumphant and well-authenticated illustration of the fact. At a meeting of the Leith and Canongate Lodge on Thursday evening, March 5th 1829, a visitor, who was the captain of a ship, stated, that, when sailing in the South American seas, he was boarded by pirates, whose numbers were so over-powering as to render all resistance unavailing. The captain and several of the crew were treated with rudeness, and were about to be placed in irons while the plunder of the ship went on.

In this situation, when supplication and entreaty were dis-regarded, the captain, as a dernier resort, made the mystic sign 'which none but Craftsmen ever knew'. The commander of the piratical crew immediately returned the sign and gave orders to stop proceedings. He grasped his newly-discovered brother by the hand with all the familiarity of an old acquaintance, and swore he should sustain no injury. Mutual acts of kindness then passed between them; every article that had been seized was restored to its place, and the two ships parted company with three hearty cheers.

There is an unintended hilarity to this story. The idea that any pirate chief would dare order his crew to give back their loot is risible in the extreme. This would seem the surest way to provoke a mutiny and win yourself a Masonic funeral. Whether or not the tale is true, many Masons want to believe it is true, for it symbolizes true Freemasonry at work. You may be in the direst straits, but a brother Mason will always help you out.

An even more grotesque tale is told in one of J. S. M. Ward's books.[5]

In 1917 I was on a steamer going through the Red Sea and noticed an Arab dhow evidently in difficulties. The Arabs were shouting and gesticulating wildly to us, and I said to the Captain (a brother Mason with whom I was very friendly): 'Captain, won't you stop?'

'Stop,' he almost yelled, 'no fear. I've mails on board, and in any case it may be a trap, there's a war on. Catch me delaying my boat for any —— niggers.'

Seeing the Captain was annoyed, I cleared out (we had been on the bridge), and fetching my glasses watched the Arabs from the deck. Truth to tell, I felt sorry for the —— niggers, for the dhow was obviously sinking. Suddenly one of the Arabs ran to the bow of his boat and began to make the Scotch sign of Grief and Distress quite correctly. I could hardly believe my eyes, but there was no doubt about it.

I rushed up the steps of the bridge and said, 'Captain, you are a Mason. Look what that Arab's doing.' So saying, I pushed my glasses into his hand. 'By God,' he replied, 'that's done it. I shall have to stop now,' which he did and we took the lot off. Half an hour afterwards that dhow sank.

Now how was it they knew that sign, for they weren't Masons as we understand the word?

Today's Masonic revisionists may claim all these stories are bunkum, even though they appear in books by Masonic historians which are still sold in Masonic shops. Yet the romantic ideal of a Masonic *internationale* was put into practice during World War I in a bizarre way. Every Freemason serving in the British forces could apply for a special Masonic pass known as a 'Service Certificate'. Each English lodge could issue certificates identical to the one issued by a Bradford lodge, the King Edward VII (no. 3442) – 'under the jurisdiction of the Grand Lodge of England' – to Brother E. Vincent Heaton. It was signed by the Lodge Master and Secretary on 9 September 1914. The inscription reads:

> The above-named Lodge presents and vouches for the Brother to whom this card is issued as a worthy Master Mason, and so commends him for brotherly care and lawful aid to any Mason who may find him in distress or need – incident to his service as a British sailor (soldier) – with the assurance that any courtesies so extended will be deeply appreciated, and reciprocated should the occasion arise.

The pass is printed in five languages. English, French and Italian were spoken by the Allies, but German and Turkish were spoken by the enemy Axis powers. This pass, therefore, was an attempt by the highest Masonic authority to procure special treatment for Masons, not just from French and Italian comrades but *from the enemy*. It is grotesque that the Masonic brotherhood which included Field Marshals Kitchener, French, Haig and Joffre – who despatched millions of soldiers to their deaths – should have tried to soften the war just for its own members. Even to conceive this passport was a betrayal of the millions of Britons who spilt their blood in that war but who did not belong to the Craft. The certificate bears a note: 'This card is not available for use within the United Kingdom and MUST BE RETURNED to the Secretary of the Lodge as soon as possible after Peace has been declared.'

No wonder! If any non-Mason had got his hands on it during the war, Brother Heaton might have been lynched. In fact, Heaton was discharged from army service in 1917. He returned his card to the lodge and took a job as company secretary of a Bradford textile firm. He later became Lodge Master, boss of the firm, a JP and deputy lord mayor. It is not known if his Masonic Service Certificate did him any good, but thousands of these documents were issued during the war. For example, one was handed to a T. C. W. Molony of Aldershot's Army & Navy Lodge.[6] The St Andrews Lodge (no. 1046) of Farnham, Surrey, had spare passports, already signed by the Master, ready for the next member sent off to the front.[7] Another such pass was on display in the Grand Lodge Museum the last time I was there.

Freemasons' Hall is dedicated to the 3,533 English Masons known to have died in World War I. Their sacrifice was supreme, but no greater than the sacrifice of a million other Britons who could not call on the Masonic *internationale* for protection. Yet in retrospect it seems that the 'Service Certificate' might have increased the dangers facing a Masonic prisoner-of-war, rather than diminished them. When General Ludendorff published his *Destruction of Freemasonry Through Revelation of its Secrets*, his hatred of Freemasonry in the German army was so great that he included a photograph of a military field lodge meeting on the Somme. If any British Tommy bearing a Masonic passport had fallen into Ludendorff's hands, it would have become a passport only to a firing squad.

thirty-two

YOUR MASONIC PUBLIC SERVANT

Late one night in February 1987 fire officer David Grove swigged a last drink at the lodge Festive Board, bade farewell to his brethren and walked out of the Masonic Hall in Llanelli, west Wales. Filled with good fellowship, this Ammanford station chief climbed in his car and drove off home. He was in for an unbrotherly shock. Not all the local Dyfed-Powys policemen were with him at the lodge that night. Some were on duty. They saw him careering along the streets and brought him to a halt. He was thrust into a patrol car and driven to the police station. He now did exactly what many non-Masons think Masons always do when arrested. He grabbed the right hand of Sergeant Glyn Hughes and applied an inebriated Masonic grip. Twisting the officer's finger Grove told him: 'I will not forget this.' Hughes was 'absolutely digusted with his behaviour' and spurned the gesture.

Undeterred, Grove then asked if the police surgeon was a Freemason, before stumbling down the corridor with his trouser-leg rolled up as a further advertisement of Masonic membership. All these efforts came to nothing. Grove was found to have more than twice the legal amount of alcohol in his blood. Indeed he was so drunk he could neither stand nor dial a phone number. When the case came to court, he was banned from driving for eighteen months and fined £125. Fraternal to the end, he showed no bitterness towards the coppers who had testified against him. Indeed, he followed one out of court shouting: 'I want to shake that man's hand.'[1]

Like Falstaff, Grove had mistaken his erection. Freemasonry is not meant to be a passport to break the law. Grand Lodge would condemn his conduct as an abuse of the Craft, but such abuses often occur. Grove's mistake was not playing the Masonic card but playing it too soon, too blatantly and probably to a non-Mason. Had he asked for a quiet word with a senior officer whom he knew to be a Mason, he might have got away with it.

A non-Masonic fire chief wrote to Stephen Knight claiming Freemasonry plays a significant part in fire service promotions. He produced no evidence but he is now one of Britain's top firemen (a fire inspector in the Home Office), so he cannot be dismissed as a thwarted careerist trafficking in 'sour grapes'. Some support for his claim emerged from the Hackney survey into 2,500 Freemasons' occupations: one London lodge contained ten firemen, including two chiefs and one deputy (see Chapter 9).

Most firemen work for local councils, but 2 per cent of Masons in the Hackney survey were state employees. If this were true of all Masons under the Grand Lodge of England, there would be between 5,000 and 10,000 Masons in the civil service, which seems rather low. Recent lodge summonses from across the country show public servants are still being initiated into the Craft in substantial numbers. A Home Office immigration official was initiated into the Waterways Lodge, the mother lodge also of gangsters and policemen. Other lodges have recruited Customs officers and British Telecom engineers (before the telephone network was privatized).

I have no evidence to suggest that these particular men would use or abuse Freemasonry in their working lives. However, one lapsed Scottish Mason showed how easy it is to use Masonic phraseology to get confidential information out of public bodies. He needed the ex-directory telephone numbers of two former associates who had taken every precaution to hide their present whereabouts from him. One was a former mistress who had disappeared from his home late one night with all his property. The other was a businessman who had registered a false address on all company records.

On 12 November 1983 the Mason wrote to British Telecom's London headquarters in these terms:

Dear Sir,
Please be assured that I am on the level and am looking for a square deal.

I require two addresses and telephone numbers. The locations are either in West London or Middlesex or Preston; somewhere in these areas.

The names are D. J. S—— (male) and I. or A. L—— (female).
Thank you.
Yours, in distress . . .

The Mason signed and typed his name at the bottom of the letter. The phrases 'on the level', 'square deal' and 'in distress' would be instantly picked up by any Mason. A week later he received a reply from the chairman's office, dated 18 November, saying that 'arrangements are being made for the matter to be looked into'. On 28 November a British Telecom employee called to give him both people's addresses and telephone numbers. The Mason comments: 'You will readily appreciate that any common criminal wishing to harm these people could have obtained their addresses, in their cases highly secret information, by pretending to be a Freemason. That information was released with the approval of the head office of a major nationalized company.'

The Mason conveyed this information to Commander Higham on 1 December 1984. He received no reply, which is hardly surprising since his letter was full of anti-Masonic remarks. Before signing himself 'Yours fraternally', the Scotsman had cast a last swipe: 'Let us hope that the Great Architect of the Universe gives you insight and persuades you to tackle rogue Freemasonry before it destroys democracy in this country.'

In contrast, another Mason who is a high-ranking Inland Revenue official told me (over lunch in his Pall Mall club) that no other Mason had ever asked for or received fraternal assistance from him over tax problems or other Inland Revenue matters. He has identified only one other Mason in the department, and their relationship has not involved Masonic mutual aid, back-scratching or 'fast-track' career advance for either of them. However, a recently retired Ministry of Defence employee complains about the Craft's 'clandestine operations' in the Meteorological Office. He does not claim Masons tamper with the weather forecasts – or the weather – but he does attack Masonic preferment.

> The Met Office, where I worked for thirty years, has a high percentage of Freemasons because of the large overseas commitment in remote locations, where the local lodge has to recruit all reasonable 'whites' to have any hope of keeping itself going. Thus some meteorologists are Masons who, had they stayed in Britain, would not normally be considered for membership.
>
> Masons can easily sway Met Office administration through the system of Annual Confidential Reports (ACRs). Despite the 'clean-up' of the early 1970s, when Job Assessment Reports (JARs) were introduced, the system remains a Masons' Charter, enabling individuals to be damned by faint praise or derogatory remarks from a high-ranking officer, without the victims' knowledge. As usual, the Masonic system does not give the laurels of promotion to the technically able, but to its own kind. As in my own case, it is reasonably simple for a person to be 'detrained' and denied certain rights by the pressures of Masons in higher office.

It is difficult to evaluate these claims, which are linked to the weatherman's belief that he was retired early because of a false 'reduced efficiency' accusation, brought 'directly as a result of masonic activity'. 'Reduced efficiency' is a euphemism for saying someone is no longer any good at his job. I have no way of knowing if this man was efficient or not, or if Freemasons pushed him out. It may be that, even if all or none of his bosses were Masons, he was retired early for incompetence. On the other hand, he may be correct in claiming he was the victim of a Masonic fix.

Stronger evidence comes from a retired British ambassador who worked in both the Colonial and Foreign Offices for forty years.

I saw Freemasonry at work in the diplomatic service over at least thirty-five years. In the old Colonial Office I felt its impact most strongly in 1953 when I was working as an assistant district commissioner in Africa. The province to which I was sent was full of diehard, paternalist, anti-Independence colonial officers who were mostly Freemasons. They did their worst to stop me fulfilling my appointed task of updating local government in preparation for Independence. I only overcame their opposition by threatening to expose them to my non-Masonic bosses.

In the Diplomatic Service Freemasonry is pretty strong among the administrative (A stream) grades. My most traumatic experience came in a Commonwealth country when I was serving as Head of Chancery. Our High Commissioner was a notorious head-cruncher and a bully, proud of his ability to wreck careers. He and his deputy were both Freemasons. The deputy was afraid that because the Commissioner and I had both studied at the same university college we would combine against him. This certainly wasn't the case, but that is how many Freemasons' minds work. They think members of every other fraternity conspire just like they do.

The deputy set out to make trouble and he succeeded. The proof came when the High Commissioner told me I was inadequate in my job, and he would ensure I never attained any of the highest diplomatic posts. I happened to be wearing my breast pocket handkerchief in the same Masonic way as he was wearing his that day (protruding in a straight line, parallel with the top of the pocket). This irritated him profoundly, for he suddenly took the handkerchief out of my pocket, crumpled it and stuck it back. On my return to London, the officer responsible for personnel told me I had been 'fixed' by the High Commissioner, but the service would do its best for me, which indeed it did as my subsequent career shows.

I served as an ambassador in South America some years before the Falklands War. Dr David Owen is quite right in saying that 'we got it right' during an earlier crisis with Argentina in 1978. The record clearly shows what steps were taken to avert war that year. Had the same steps been taken in 1982 we should not now be paying £3 million per day to protect the Falkland Islands which, in the long run, is a quite useless exercise. One of the principal actors in 1982 was a British defence attaché accredited to a South American capital. I could never understand how such a 'dummkopf' could be assigned to such a sensitive post. Yet he was, and he remained there for several months after the outbreak of hostilities. The subsequent White Paper proved he was one of two people directly responsible. The other man has since been promoted. The explanation which best covers the facts is that both men are Masons and have been protected by the Brotherhood. The British taxpayer bears the burden.

My final posting was as High Commissioner in a country which was a Masonic hotbed. The last Governor General had been a very senior Mason, as was the country's last British Cabinet secretary. The many former colonial officers maintained there since Independence on the payroll of Britain's Overseas Development Administration include a high proportion of Masons. While there I encountered constant obstruction from parts of the British community and was excluded from the usual social and non-official activities. I concluded that a Masonic 'ring' was in operation.

From time to time I was asked if I was a Mason – the implication being that if I wasn't, I ought to be. On several occasions Freemasons attached to the High Commission sought special privileges because they were Masons. Once a communications expert, who had been seconded from GCHQ Cheltenham, wanted to visit a Masonic lodge in the country's second city several hundred miles away. There was an official High Commissioner's residence nearby. This man had the nerve to ask me if he could stay in it for the duration of his trip. He had no official business in that town. He was only going for a Masonic knees-up. I told him that I found his request extraordinary and he would have to find his own accommodation.

The ambassador recommends a series of measures to counter the power of Freemasonry which he sees as 'a palpable danger to the realm'. I list his ideas in the Conclusion to this book. His greatest concern is the triumph of mediocrity in the Civil Service which may be brought about by Masonic mutual advancement. The danger of public corruption is no less palpable. In 1988 national newspapers reported guilty verdicts in a series of Old Bailey trials, and the judge's remark that corruption in a big-spending government department was 'rife from top to bottom'. However, they failed to tell readers that many of the rackets were hatched and executed under the cover of a Masonic Lodge.

The Property Services Agency has an annual budget of £1 billion and employs 26,000 staff. It manages and maintains more than 8,000 public buildings, including Buckingham Palace and the Tower of London. Recently the PSA became so steeped in corruption that many senior staff considered gifts of cash, luxury kitchens, fine clothes and exclusive club memberships as their rightful 'perks'. In return they made sure that the builders bribing them won juicy government contracts, even though their bids were grossly inflated. One deal diverted £3-million-worth of maintenance work on Hampton Court Palace to contractors handing out free holidays. The extra cost of such racketeering was paid ultimately by the long-suffering taxpayer. In six successive trials a total of nineteen public officials and contractors were convicted of fraud. Four belonged to the same Masonic lodge.

Three PSA employees and one contractor had turned 'Queen's Evidence', a fitting act for men who made fortunes out of royal palaces. The key witness was Maurice Hearn, a builder who was also a Mason. In 1967 he joined the Queenswood Lodge (no. 4718), which now meets at London's Freemasons' Hall. The Queenswood had long been a hive of men in the building trade, but by the early 1980s it had become a honeypot for both contractors and civil servants. One contractor was sixty-year-old Hearn who now says the only way to get work from the PSA was 'by bribing the civil servants and by ringing [inflating] the contracts'. Hearn invited another builder named King to a lodge Ladies' Night. He brought along a PSA technical officer, Eric Wenborn. King introduced Wenborn to Hearn who encouraged him to join the lodge. He was initiated in 1981, and King joined a few months later. The contractors now had the civil servant just where they wanted him.

By October 1983 Wenborn was flying off to Las Vegas, all expenses paid by a crooked Queenswood brother. The *News of the World* exposed how company boss King sent high-class prostitutes to his hotel room, although Wenborn claims he never used their services. Throughout 1983 they paid £1,000 a month into a Jersey bank account he had opened in his wife's name. In 1984 he was off on another 'freebie', to Miami. This time his mistress went too. She also benefited from £33,000-worth of bribes, with which Wenborn bought her a flat in south London. Other crooked money went on lavish furnishings for his own home and an £8,000 car.

In June 1988 Wenborn pleaded guilty to five charges of corruption and conspiracy to obtain bribes. He was jailed for two years. His downfall had two main causes. First, he was grossly underpaid. He had joined the Civil Service aged sixteen, yet, forty years on, he was earning only £8,000 a year: a pittance in respect of his huge financial responsibilities and minuscule compared to the bribes which contractors were likely to offer. Second, he had worked incorruptibly for thirty-five years *until he joined Freemasonry*. He must have been a weak man, a plum ripe for picking but, instead of being suffused with Freemasonry's pretensions of civic virtue, he became contaminated by the greed of his cynical lodge brothers. Yet Masons will still rebut claims that their fraternity is corrupt and corrupting by citing ritual passages such as this:

> Our order, being founded on the purest principles of piety and virtue, should teach us to measure our actions by the rules of rectitude, square our conduct by the principles of morality and guide our conversation, aye, even our very thoughts, within the compass of propriety. Hence we learn to be meek, humble and resigned; to moderate those passions, the excess of which deforms and disorders the very soul; to be faithful to our God, our country and our laws.[2]

Masonic interplay between officials who hand out government contracts and the businessmen who get them is not restricted to the Property Services Agency. It extends deep into the Ministry of Defence and its procurement executive, which employs 30,000 people and has an annual budget of £8 billion.

By the early 1980s one of Britain's most successful private arms firms was QED Design and Development of north-west Kent. The secret of its success was a special relationship with the Ministry of Defence and regiments like the SAS, for which it designed specialist weapons such as night sights, stun-grenades and booby-traps. The firm's co-director Frank Turner also built up a flourishing trade overseas which occupied so much of his time that day-to-day liaison with the Ministry was left to QED's general manager, Peter Webb.

Early in 1984 Turner had just returned from a trip abroad when he walked into QED's factory and noticed a civil servant named John Spellar sitting in the boardroom surrounded by company documents. Webb later revealed that Spellar had been writing a report which would allow QED to claim for 'Post-design Services' (maintaining design drawings on the Ministry's behalf). This report was then typed up as if it came from QED and then submitted to the very MOD department for which Spellar worked. When the department cleared the claim, QED was paid £10,000 out of Ministry funds.

This was the maximum allowable payment, which Turner knew was far more than QED's due, for the firm was doing little if any post-design work at the time. He was also outraged that Spellar should be doing this work for QED, which it should have done for itself. He became even more suspicious when he discovered that Webb had told two employees, Christine Shaw and Irene Farrell, to remove all references to Spellar from the visitors' book and the telephone log. Mrs Shaw clearly remembers the incident.

> Mr Webb came down to the reception area and said that, from now on, we were not to enter Mr Spellar's name in the telephone book. Webb asked if Spellar's name was in there already. We said yes, and he blanked it out. He told us that in future we were to write any notes of calls that came in from Spellar on loose, plain pieces of paper. He also said that from now on we were not to say anything about Spellar's name in the visitors' book. He didn't want it to be shown that Spellar had visited or been in touch with the company.

Webb told Turner that, in the course of this clandestine affair, Spellar had been given a second-hand Commodore computer. It was later claimed that he bought it for some £20. Even so, Turner thought it odd that a civil servant should get so involved with a company doing business with his own Ministry. He also recalled that Peter Webb was an ardent Mason who often attended Masonic functions with his brother Mason, John Spellar. The procurement man belongs to the Lodge of United Friendship (no. 6284) which meets in Gravesend's Masonic Hall. So does the High Cross Royal Arch Chapter (no. 4149) to which Webb belongs. Turner was not sure if Webb was a typical Mason – he was always boasting about rubbing shoulders with top brethren, including the Duke of Kent – but he thought Webb's attempts to hide Spellar's visits to QED did not match the standard of conduct which Freemasonry claims to instil. Turner also feared that, if the Spellar–Webb relationship were corrupt, the firm itself would be indicted for bribery, so he reported the affair to the Ministry of Defence.

MOD police took almost two years to investigate, but in July 1987 Turner received a letter which confirmed that irregularities had occurred. Det. Superintendent K. G. Taylor told him that although there was not enough evidence to take court action against QED's Peter Webb, there was enough to take internal action against Spellar, who had been suspended. Months later Turner inquired again, provoking a letter from Deputy Chief Constable Norman Chapple, saying there was 'insufficient independent evidence to justify criminal proceedings'. Spellar had been 'the subject of internal discipline within the Ministry and it would be inappropriate of me to provide further details of this'.

Turner was mystified. He accepted that Chapple had honestly interpreted the evidence before him, but he could not help wondering if Freemasonry had cast its long shadow over the inquiry. Many MOD policemen are Masons, because most of them are recruited from two Masonic crucibles: the civil police and the regular army. In 1987 the all-police Manor of St James's Lodge welcomed a former Metropolitan officer who now works for the MOD.

Frank Turner had another reason for suspecting Freemasonry. In 1985 he had fallen out so badly with his QED partner, Gordon Harrold, that they could no longer work together. Neither would agree to be 'bought out' by the other, so Turner won a High Court order allowing him to put the company into liquidation. Peter Webb sided with Harrold, so he devised a scheme to frame Turner. On 27 February 1985 Turner's home was raided by a Kent police squad, led by Sergeant Nigel Harrison, who was friendly with Webb and had lunched with him the previous day. Turner was wrongly accused of keeping weapons at home which were not covered by his firearms licence. However, Harrison told him he would not be checking QED's firearms register (in which the guns could have been legally signed out to Turner) for one week.

Turner suspected he was being 'set up' so he tape-recorded a meeting with Webb, when the Mason admitted this was blackmail: unless Turner dropped his plan to close QED, Webb would tell Harrison that Turner had asked him to make a back-dated entry in the gun register, so he could get off the firearms charges. In another conversation Webb told Turner that, if he gave in, he would arrange for a very senior officer to let him off with just 'a bollocking'. Turner assumed Webb was referring to one of many senior policemen he boasted of knowing through Freemasonry.

Turner refused to be blackmailed, so Webb told his police friends. Turner was charged with attempting to pervert the course of justice, which carries a penalty of seven years in prison. In July 1986 he went on trial at Maidstone Crown Court but, when his defence produced the 'blackmail' tape, the prosecution case collapsed. He was cleared on all charges except a technicality over an antique gun, and given an absolute discharge. In December 1987, two days before a Channel Four television programme exposing this scandal was to be broadcast, Kent Police finally charged Webb with perjury.[3] In June 1988 he pleaded guilty and was jailed for one month, with a further three months in jail suspended.

Because both the Ministry of Defence and Kent Constabulary were taking so long to inquire into his complaints, Turner felt he might be up against a wider Masonic alliance embracing Webb, the police and the

MOD. This was why, months before his own trial, he asked me to investigate. I was unable to prove such an alliance, but I did obtain evidence proving that Masons other than Spellar worked in MOD procurement. Today, Service in Unity Lodge (no. 7843) meets in Freemasons' Hall but it used to gather at the Kingsley Hotel. At first glance it seems just another armed forces lodge. Between 1972 and 1982 its Masters included an RAF flight lieutenant, two wing commanders, two retired REME lieutenant-colonels and a major. In 1974 two serving RAF officers were initiated on the same night.

My knowledge is derived from a discarded lodge file bought from a north London junk shop. The perturbing side of the lodge emerged only when this file disgorged a cluster of business cards. These revealed that some lodge members worked in the defence supply industry, including the secretary and Past Master, W. Osborne-Smith. Indeed the file may have been thrown out following his death. In the late 1970s he was employed by the Military Projects Division of a firm called Industrial Service Outlets. In October 1979 he seconded the Masonic candidacy of William Acton, a thirty-six-year-old electrical engineer working for the Ministry of Defence in Chertsey. The only MOD establishment in that area is the Royal Armaments Research and Development Establishment, formerly known as the Military Vehicle Examination Establishment, and before that as the Fighting Vehicle RDE. This is a division of the Procurement Executive. Acton's proposer was an RAF Wing Commander named J. D. Pattinson. A few years later, one of Acton's business cards showed that he had left the Ministry to work as a Military Sales Engineer for Westair, a contractor which relies heavily on MQD patronage.

Other cards came from men employed by Lucas Defence Systems, Honeywell (Aircraft & Military Markets division), Microwave Pathfinder, Electrothermal Engineering, and Pylon Developments. Nothing on the cards says these men are Masons. They may simply have met Osborne-Smith and exchanged cards during normal business. Yet this would not explain why he kept the cards in a file devoted to Masonic business. I have confirmed that one of the card-givers was a Mason in another lodge, so perhaps all of them were 'on the square'.

Even more worrying, the file contains a confidential MOD contract report, marked 'specimen'. This shows how Ministry staff, working for the contracts branch in St Christopher House, are meant to record day-to-day developments on military purchases. The report concerns a £30,000 deal. 'Specimen' it may be, but Britain's security chiefs might twitch a little at the presence of an internal MOD document in a Masonic lodge file maintained by someone working for the defence supply industry.

If we rely solely on Service in Unity's own documents, it is clear that defence industry salesmen, serving soldiers and civil servants in MOD's biggest-spending department all belonged to the same lodge at the same time. Even the most sympathetic explanation cannot allay fears that such fraternization is not in the public interest. It justifies suspicions that government and democracy may be subverted through the Craft. The British have long been taught to trust in an incorruptible civil service. This trust is now revealed as folly, for it is clear that Masonic apron strings may be pulled in any area of state activity. Maybe no Service in Unity Lodge member has ever dispensed or secured government contracts through Freemasonry, yet the public cannot ignore the possibility that such a nexus might become a cell of defence industry corruption in the future or that one of Britain's 9,000 other lodges has achieved that status already.

This must have been obvious to Whitehall mandarins for decades, but most of them seem to view the world differently from the citizens who pay their wages. They may consider Masonic racketeering over government contracts a small price to pay for the 'anchor' effect which the Craft has had on British society for 250 years. This might also explain the government's remarkably relaxed reaction to Stephen Knight's most sensational claim: that Russia's KGB could have infiltrated English Freemasonry. Perhaps the state knew something that he did not.

thirty-three

SPOOKS IN APRONS

In *The Brotherhood* Stephen Knight asserted that KGB agents could have joined Freemasonry to infiltrate British society, and in particular the security services. In support he cited a document written by a retired high-ranking diplomat, whom he dubbed the 'Chinaman' because he happened to be an expert on China. It is inconceivable, says Chinaman, that so conservative a force as British Freemasonry could be consciously suborned by Soviet Russia, yet 'dangers arise from numerous possibilities for covert exploitation of a movement which is almost co-terminous with "the Establishment".'[1]

This is fine as a theory. Any KGB hack would view Freemasonry as useful 'cover' in Britain, for he would probably know it was one tool used by Brother Alexander Kerensky and his colleagues to make Russia's first Bolshevik Revolution in February 1917. The October Revolutionaries outlawed the Craft as a 'most dishonest and infamous swindle of the proletariat by the radically inclined section of the middle classes'.[2] In contrast, few of England's 'regular' Masons have ever been radically inclined. Most are conservative, as any communist infiltrating the Craft would soon discover. The sight of apron-clad members of Britain's middle and artisan classes – or the sound of their opinions in the bar – would make him realize the impossibility of Marxist mass-conversion, and convince him to start the Revolution elsewhere. As Grand Librarian John Hamill has observed, most Freemasons treated Knight's KGB infiltration theory 'with hilarity'.[3]

The problem with the 'KGB penetration' theory is that we have no proof any penetration has ever occurred. Doubtless some unidentified traitors have joined Freemasonry, but this would be no great achievement. It is the 'club' most male Britons find easiest to join – provided they have a white skin, a dark suit and the colour of money – and mouthing a belief in God would not strain a dedicated communist agent. For their part, Masons are usually under great pressure to recruit. Many lodges are desperately short of active members, and the Craft is a kind of pyramid sales racket. If you want grand rank (and you are not an aristocrat or a High Court judge), one way to impress the hierarchy is to help found a new lodge. Today more than thirty new lodges are formed in England and Wales every year. Each demands a fresh clutch of initiates. In accord with Dr Oliver's golden rule, brethren are taught to 'Be very cautious whom you recommend as a candidate for Membership; one false step on this point may be fatal . . . If you have a good Lodge keep it select. Great numbers are not always beneficial.'[4] Yet even this would not exclude the smooth-tongued Oxbridge graduates traditionally recruited by Britain's security services – and by Moscow. Such men have always been welcomed into Freemasonry, as Chapter 28 shows. It would be no surprise if a few KGB agents have been among them, but they could have joined many other British institutions – the Royal and Ancient Golf Club, the Garrick, the House of Commons – with greater espionage returns.

Bereft of Masons among Britain's known traitors, Knight tried to justify his theory by citing the *alleged* spy, Sir Roger Hollis, MI5's director-general from 1956 to 1965. Knight claimed Hollis almost certainly joined a Shanghai Lodge while working in China in the 1930s. Knight said proof was impossible because inter-war membership of Shanghai lodges is a 'closely guarded' Grand Lodge secret. Grand Lodge says this is 'nonsense' and asserts that Hollis was certainly not a Mason.[5] It has the records, so I must accept its word. There is also still no incontrovertible firm proof that Sir Roger was ever a spy. Indeed, he was acquitted in a recent TV 'trial'.[6]

Even so, Freemasonry might have been the British Establishment's 'soft underbelly' precisely because, until very recently, it has been above suspicion. As Chinaman explains, when he joined the Foreign Service he was obliged to sign the Official Secrets Act and swear he was not, and had never been, a member of certain listed extreme left- and right-wing organizations. And yet:

> I was never required even orally to state whether I was or had ever been a member of any secret society whether of the Masonic type or not. This is less surprising given the social respectability of Freemasonry and the assumption by both members and non-members alike that it could not possibly come to represent in any way a threat to the established order.[7]

When *The Brotherhood* appeared, Knight's KGB allegations won huge newspaper coverage. Publication coincided with uproar over the government's ban on trade unions at Britain's electronic spy centre, GCHQ

Cheltenham. Some folk demanded a ban on Freemasonry at GCHQ because they felt Knight's book proved the Craft was a bigger threat to national security than the unions. On 26 January 1984 Conservative MP Patrick McNair-Wilson wrote to Prime Minister Margaret Thatcher, asking if Masonic membership is taken into account when vetting members of the security services, and whether Knight's grave charges justified a full inquiry. He would also welcome her 'assurance that no threat either has, or does exist, as a result of membership of this secret society'. On 13 February Mrs Thatcher replied that, 'while it would not be right for me to give details of positive vetting procedures, I can tell you that there is no information that the KGB have sought to use Free-masonry in any way'.

Mrs Thatcher's answer appears to confirm that members of MI5, MI6 and other intelligence agencies are not banned from joining Freemasonry, and may not even be asked if they belong. As for her remark about the KGB, I assume she did not rely on a promise from the KGB itself but may have consulted two leading Masons in her party: her then deputy Prime Minister and Leader of the House of Lords, Viscount William Whitelaw, and the former Solicitor-General Sir Ian Percival. They would both have told her of the Craft's obedience to 'our God, our country and our laws'. The security services' response would also have reassured her. Steeped in their own Masonic-type culture (clubbish, covert, secretive), many MI5 men would have derided the idea – especially if they were Masons themselves.

The theory that KGB agents within Britain's security services might have joined Freemasonry is double-edged, for it seems these services have themselves long regarded the Craft as a positive, if unofficial, screening aid. In *Spycatcher* MI5's former assistant director, Peter Wright, describes the laughable vetting procedure he went through in the mid-1950s during an interview with MI5's personnel director, John Marriott.

'Just wanted to have a chat – a few personal details, that sort of thing', he said, giving me a distinctive Masonic handshake. I realized then why my father who was also a Mason [and a wartime Naval Intelligence officer] had obliquely raised joining the brotherhood when I first discussed with him working for MI5 full-time.

'Need to make sure you're not a Communist, you understand.'

He said it as if such a thing were impossible in MI5 . . . But apart from this interview I was not subject to any other vetting. Indeed, although this was the period when MI5 were laying down strict vetting programmes throughout Whitehall, it was not until the mid-1960s that any systematic vetting was brought into MI5 at all.[8]

Probably some loyal security servicemen have joined the Craft as additional proof of their patriotism. To Freemasonry's credit, if it really is the 'mechanism of social control' which Badger describes in Chapter 10, then Masonic glue may well have helped bond 'young MI5 recruits of generally poor calibre' (Wright's description) into a mildly cohesive counter-espionage organization. I suspect that most government 'spooks' who join Freemasonry do so for the same reasons as other men: to extend their circle of friends, to advance their careers and for mutual aid. If they really are as 'poor calibre' as Wright suggests, they would have even more need to reinsure their careers through Freemasonry against the slings and arrows of any boss who realizes they are not up to the job.

By chance, another book published by Granada/Grafton in 1984 claimed Freemasonry was open to KGB infiltration. *Doors of the Mind* was written by Michael Bentine – comedian, clairvoyant and paranormal researcher who has two claims to credibility in this area. He is a self-proclaimed pro-Mason;[9] and during World War II he worked in British Intelligence – in MI9 which helped allied servicemen shot down over Europe to evade capture and return to Britain.

Bentine sees a 'danger that Freemasonry in the democracies will be infiltrated by Soviet so-called sleeper agents'. Such men, who might work in trade, diplomacy or journalism, could easily infiltrate a Masonic Lodge and 'mingle freely with many brethren whose professional background could be of use to the Soviets'. He describes how KGB agents, masquerading as refugees, could come to the West and join professional lodges whose members work in government military contracting, and where 'mutual trust between the Brethren would invite an easy flow of information'.

> I have talked over this scenario with a number of top security men who also happen to be Masons. I was alarmed to find that my conjectures (based on information I had gleaned from old friends in wartime intelligence) are correct and that there is a blind spot in international security organizations in this area.[10]

Despite the combined claims of Bentine, Knight and Chinaman, I sense that this 'KGB infiltration' view of British Freemasonry is a distraction: not invalid, but far less significant than the greater truth that stolid Whitehall bureaucrats have joined Freemasonry in far greater numbers than any spies. Such mandarins may be mediocre, even incompetent, but they are the people who keep the ship of state afloat. If a few of them corruptly feather their nests by feeding juicy contracts to

Masonic friends in private industry, so be it. These men may not be the backbone of the civil service, but they constitute several ribs.

Knight went more dangerously off-course with a second KGB theory: that Italy's P2 Masonic Lodge conspiracy was a KGB plot.[11] He was fed this idea by someone whom he described as 'an impeccable source within British Intelligence', but his strongest *evidence* appears to have been the perverse fact that of all Italy's leading political parties, 'only the Communist Party had no links with P2' and so could exploit the P2 scandal with impunity. 'From the beginning,' he continued, 'Lodge P2 was a KGB-sponsored programme aimed at destabilizing Italy, weakening NATO's southern flank, sweeping the Communists into power in Italy, and sending resultant shock waves throughout the western world.'

Even when *The Brotherhood* first appeared, this seemed an unlikely story. Five years later it is clear that Knight's 'impeccable source' had filled him with disinformation. To understand this government spook's motives we have to explore the P2 story from several angles, but first a brief summary of P2.[12]

In March 1981 two Milan magistrates were investigating the fake kidnapping in 1979 of a swindling Sicilian-born international banker, Michele Sindona. They were also probing his role as financial adviser to the Vatican and his links with the Mafia. They discovered that, while hiding in Palermo, he had travelled 600 miles north to Arezzo to visit a textile manufacturer named Licio Gelli. They promptly ordered a search of Gelli's premises. On 17 March finance policemen discovered 962 Italian names on lists kept in his office safe and a suitcase. The names belonged to members of a Masonic Lodge named Propaganda Massonica, also known as P2. Gelli was its Venerable Master.

What astonished the investigators was that the names on the lists amounted to a state within a state. They included forty-three MPs (among them three cabinet ministers), forty-three generals and eight admirals (including the current heads of all the armed forces), security service bosses, hundreds of public servants and diplomats, the police chiefs of Italy's four biggest cities, industrialists and financiers, television stars and twenty-four journalists, including the editor and publisher of *Corriere della Sera*. Sindona was a member. So was another controversial banker, Roberto Calvi, who would later be found hanging under London's Blackfriars Bridge.

But who was Gelli? In succeeding months the magistrates discovered that this seeming small-town industrialist was a fascist war criminal who had opportunistically betrayed his colleagues as soon as he realized Germany was going to lose the war. A few years later his past caught up with him, so he fled to Argentina and made valuable political friends such as General Perón. In the mid-1960s he returned to Italy and was appointed Argentina's honorary consul. He soon had connections everywhere. He had no problems doing textile business in Eastern Europe, but he also popped up in Rome's right-wing circles. He even had friends in America's Republican Party, through whom he was invited to President Reagan's 1981 inauguration. He was masterly at collecting influential people. He manipulated them to aggrandize himself. At times his motive seemed to be financial, at others ideological, but what *was* his ideology? What mystified the Milan magistrates – and other people on his trail – was, who did he really work for? For Italy's secret services, for America's CIA or Russia's KGB?

The KGB theory was always the least likely. There was little evidence to support it, whereas there was overwhelming proof of Gelli's continuous involvement with fascism for more than forty years. Significantly, the 'P2–KGB plot' fantasy resembles a parallel propaganda myth which fooled many other journalists at the time: that the 1981 assassination attempt on Pope John Paul II was a Bulgarian plot.[13] 'Western intelligence experts are now generally agreed that the attempted killing was inspired by the KGB,' wrote Stephen Knight. If Western intelligence experts really believed that, the West was (and is) in deep trouble.

It has now been shown that this theory was concocted by two Americans: a former CIA operative named Paul Henze and a right-wing journalist named Michael Ledeen. Ledeen had previously known a rising Italian businessman, Francesco Pazienza, who had links with SISMI: Italian Military Intelligence.[15] However, Pazienza rejects the 'Bulgarian plot' theory and claims he is himself the victim of black propaganda, falsely branded as a P2 member and as Gelli's nominated successor. He is a Mason, but says he has never met Gelli. In 1988 he was sentenced to ten years in prison over the 1980 bombing of Bologna railway station, but he has now been cleared on appeal.

At a future date I hope to portray the political, military and commercial rackets which P2 members have continued to perpetrate years after P2 was officially dissolved. Here I show how the reactionary forces, in Italy and America, which created P2 are tied in with British intelligence and British Freemasonry. Many of my comments are based on evidence gathered by an Italian Parliamentary Inquiry into P2.[16] Its 1984 report was never published in English. Indeed, it has rarely been mentioned in the British or American media, even though its contents have worldwide significance. The report also helps explain why – and on what basis – British intelligence misled Stephen Knight into believing P2 was a KGB plot. To understand P2, however, we must have some idea of the history of Freemasonry in Italy.

The brotherhood has had a controversial history ever since it first reached Italy in the early 1730s (see Chapter 8), but its political ascendancy was ended in 1925 when it was outlawed by the fascist dictator Benito Mussolini. Twenty years later it was legalized again, but only after the US Office of Strategic Services (the forerunner of the CIA) had pressured Italy's weak and impoverished government. The OSS planned to use Freemasonry just as it used the Mafia: to prop up a sickly democracy threatened by Soviet-inspired destabilization and the prospect of a communist election victory.[17]

The OSS/CIA backed Italy's strongest Masonic faction, the Grand Orient, which today has some 15,000 members. From 1961 until 1970 its Grand Master was Giordano Gamberini who (whether for the CIA or his own ends) sought to influence Italian elections by canvassing for candidates who were Freemasons and giving them money.[18] At the same time he was desperate to win recognition from the United Grand Lodge of England, which most 'regular' Masons in the world regard as the sole source of legitimacy.[19] If England could be persuaded to recognize the Grand Orient, all other regular Grand Lodges would follow suit. England had always refused, largely because of Italian Freemasonry's historic involvement in politics. This offends the Basic Principles on which England's Grand Lodge decides whether to recognize any other. Principle 7 states: 'The discussion of politics and religion within the Lodge shall be strictly prohibited.'[20] By meddling in politics Gamberini was breaching this principle, so the Grand Lodge of England should have shunned him like the plague. Instead it acted as if in total favour – or blissful ignorance – of his political game.

In the 1960s Grand Lodge was more distracted by the fact that the Grand Orient (also known as 'Palazzo Giustiniani') was one of two Italian Grand Lodges clamouring for recognition. There was also the Palazzo del Gesù, with some 5,000 members. James Stubbs, then England's Grand Secretary, described the dilemma in his 1985 autobiography, *Freemasonry in my Life*:

It was . . . well-known in Italy that we were not prepared to plump for one, leaving the other out, or even to recognize them both; eventually the moment came when at least the cracks were papered over and the Palazzo Giustiniani seemed to be in control. We felt justified in recognizing Italy.[21]

★

The man who had master-minded the unification of the Grand Orient
and Palazzo del Gesù, paving the way for recognition by England, was
none other than the subsequently notorious Licio Gelli.[22] He had entered
Freemasonry only in 1965, yet he was instantly recommended to Grand
Master Gamberini as someone 'able to make a great contribution to the
institution in terms of recruiting qualified people';[23] in other words, to
draw into Masonry men dedicated to right-wing goals. If we remember
the OSS's fierce anti-communist intent in resurrecting Freemasonry after
World War II, and Gamberini's 1960s electioneering, it is clear that the
political meddling of modern Italian Freemasonry did not start with Licio
Gelli. He merely increased its effectiveness.

In 1970 a Florentine doctor named Lino Salvini became Grand Master.
This freed Gamberini to act as the Grand Orient's roving ambassador in
the search for international recognition. At the same time he sought to
develop Propaganda Massonica Lodge (P2) as a nexus for the Italian
Right to seize control of Italian society, if ever the need arose. The lodge
had been founded in 1877 to meet the needs of provincial Masons living
temporarily in Rome and thus unable to attend their home lodges. In time
it evolved into a 'reserved' or secret lodge whose members were known
only to the Grand Secretary.

In the mid-1960s P2 had only fourteen members, but in 1970 Salvini
asked Gelli to 'restructure' the lodge. Suddenly numbers soared. Within a
decade it had 400 members, a few years later almost 1,000. Gelli has
received all the credit and blame for this achievement, but Gamberini
supervised many of the initiation ceremonies which Gelli performed in
P2's Excelsior Hotel headquarters. Grand Master Salvini was just as
involved. In December 1971 he told P2 members that henceforth they
could pursue their 'profane' (worldly) aims under the cover of their
concealed order:

> If until now it has not been possible to meet at our places of work,
> with this restructuring we shall have the possibility and pleasure of
> more frequent meetings, to discuss not only the various problems of
> a social and economic order which interest our brothers, but also
> those regarding the whole of society.[24]

The minutes of one P2 meeting in the early 1970s reveal what kind of
society appealed to Gelli, Salvini and Gamberini. Gelli wrote that
members discussed

> the political and economic situation of Italy, the threat of the Italian
> Communist Party, in accord with clericalism, aiming at the

conquest of power, the lack of power in the forces of law and order, the spread of immorality, indiscipline and all the worst aspects of morality and of civic virtue . . . relationships with the Italian state.[25]

In a note to absent members Gelli added:

Many have asked . . . how we should behave if one morning we awoke to find the clerico-Communists had seized power, whether it would be best to resign ourselves to passive aquiescence, or to take on well-defined positions – and if so, on the basis of what emergency plan.

In other words, P2 was a secret cell for the preparation of a right-wing coup like those which engulfed Greece in 1967 and Chile in 1973 (in Chile's case, to overthrow President Allende, who was a communist Freemason of an 'irregular' Masonic order)[26]. Gelli hosted frequent P2 meetings where the politics of destabilization and subversion were discussed by police chiefs, army generals, security service bosses and appeal court judges. He knew this was not orthodox Freemasonry: 'Philosophy has been banished, but we felt we had to do this in order to tackle only solid and concrete arguments affecting national life.'[27]

During these years Grand Master Salvini knew exactly what Gelli was doing, indeed he had told him to do it. The same year that P2 'banished philosophy' with Salvini's blessing, Salvini himself was blessed by the Grand Lodge of England. In September 1972 Great Queen Street declared it was 'convinced that the time is ripe and conditions are favourable' for recognizing the Grand Orient.[28] After 200 years Italian Freemasonry was respectable, but if England really did believe in 'no politics', the time could not have been less 'ripe'. Italy's Masonic bosses were in their most aggressive political mood since Mazzini and Garibaldi a century before, but whereas their efforts to bring about Italian unification had been a cause of which most politically aware Victorians could approve, the brutal politics of fascist subversion embraced by Gelli and his backers had no redeeming features.

The 1970s were some of the blackest years in the history of modern Italy. The state was torn apart by left- and right-wing terror, but many of the horrific acts originally blamed on the Left (from the Red Brigades to the Communist Party) turned out to be acts of black propaganda by the extreme Right. These included the 'Italicus' train bombing in 1974, in which twelve people were killed, and the 1980 Bologna Station massacre in which eighty-five died. In both events P2 had a guiding control. The most demoralizing crime of all was the 1978 kidnapping of Christian

Democrat chairman Aldo Moro, in which five bodyguards were killed. This elder statesman was the one leader capable of achieving the 'Historic Compromise': finally bringing the Communist Party into a coalition government on the understanding that it renounced any intention of overthrowing Italy's democratic system.

To the men of P2, this was the ultimate betrayal. Also, if the 'communist threat' really did cease to exist, the extreme Right would lose most of its political appeal. There is no doubt that it was the Far Left which kidnapped Moro and killed him two months later, leaving his body in a car dumped on a busy Rome street: fifty-nine Red Brigades terrorists were later convicted of the assassination. Yet Moro's family and friends still ask why the government refused to negotiate his release, and why the security services acted so incompetently in their attempts to find him.[29] In 1981 the Red Brigades seized a far less important Christian Democrat politician, Ciro Cirillo, yet SISMI chief (and P2 member) General Musumeci dealt with a jailed Naples underworld boss, Raffaele Cutolo, to win Cirillo's release.[30] When Aldo Moro was kidnapped, the security services refused to deal with anybody. Their conduct is the most disturbing aspect of the Moro affair. It was as if his death served their interests and P2's. In effect the security services *were* P2, but this emerged only years later.

Throughout these tragic times, orthodox Italian Freemasons were appalled at P2's activities. Despite the lodge's cloak of secrecy, they attacked its political activities as a gross breach of Freemasonry's avowed principles. In 1974 Grand Orient Masters from all over Italy met in Naples, demanding P2 be 'demolished', yet in 1975 Salvini and Gamberini did the opposite. They turned P2 into a lodge with a wholly secret membership and defiantly elevated Gelli from lodge secretary to Venerable Master.

The duplicity continued. In July 1976 the Grand Orient formally suspended P2, but Salvini secretly authorized it to carry on. At a meeting in Rome in September a 'democratic' Mason named Francesco Siniscalchi asked Salvini to answer a series of questions on Gelli and P2. Siniscalchi added that if a 'profane' (non-Masonic) magistrate ever asked him what he knew about Masonic wrongdoing he would have to tell the truth. Salvini not only refused to answer the questions; he expelled Siniscalchi and other 'democratic' Masons from the Grand Orient as traitors for daring to confront him.

Siniscalchi realized that this body which England had recently recognized as its Italian equivalent was a perversion of true Freemasonry. He was especially pained by England's complacency for, in 1954, while an engineering student at Marconi College, he had often visited

Chelmsford's Good Fellowship Lodge (no. 276). In December 1976 he gave Rome judges a dossier exposing numerous illegalities by Gelli and his P2 clan. It was this dossier, and other discoveries by Siniscalchi, which first exposed the P2 conspiracy to 'profane' eyes. Five years later, when finance police raided Gelli's office, they already had a good idea from Siniscalchi what they might find.

In 1987 I wrote to Grand Secretary Ernesto Zampieri and asked why the Grand Orient had not reinstated its expelled brother Siniscalchi and honoured him for the sterling service which he had done Italian Freemasonry by exposing the evil of P2. Zampieri's reply made no reference to Siniscalchi but stated: 'We can assure you that our organs of Justice do act with a great sense of responsibility for the safeguard of our institution.' This presumably means Siniscalchi will not be reinstated, probably because the Grand Orient feels he has done it no good whatsoever. Like many Masons who practise the movement's finest principles, Siniscalchi has been ostracized by his Masonic bosses who, no doubt, would have preferred him to keep his mouth shut.

In September 1981 the Grand Lodge of England felt obliged to explain where it stood to its own bemused members, 'in view of the very wide publicity attracted by the so-called P2 Lodge'.[31] It said it had recognized the Grand Orient in 1972 when satisfied that it accepted Principle no. 7 banning discussion of politics and religion. Now, Grand Lodge said, it 'had been informed' that the Grand Orient had suspended P2 in 1976 and had authorized no Masonic activity by P2 since then. Licio Gelli had also been suspended, and the Grand Orient had recently reaffirmed adherence to the Principles of Recognition, including no. 7. Grand Lodge would keep the matter under review, but in the meantime did not intend to take action.

Had Grand Lodge 'been informed' of the real truth it would have *had* to take action, even to withdraw recognition, but its 1981 statement contained many untruths. P2 was not a 'so-called' lodge. It had been a legitimate lodge for almost a century. Furthermore, its suspension in 1976 had been a sham for, as we have seen, Grand Master Salvini promptly authorized it to carry on. In 1977 he instructed Gelli to continue 'perfecting the Masonic vocation' of P2 members:

> You will answer only to me for what you do to this end, promoting and encouraging those activities which you think of use and interest to Masonry. I am sure that you will conduct the task with the fearless spirit you showed when faced by the treacherous attacks of the traitors of the institution.[32]

'Traitors' is a reference to the torch-bearers of true Freemasonry, Siniscalchi and his allies.

Grand Master Salvini resigned in 1978, but his successor General Ennio Battelli continued to accept all Gelli's recruits as legitimate Freemasons. In 1980 the Grand Orient was still accepting lump sum payments from Licio Gelli as P2 members' dues. Battelli also supplied Gelli with blank Grand Orient membership cards. In autumn 1981, when P2 had at last been officially dissolved and Gelli suspended, the Grand Orient transferred P2's members to other lodges: an act which proved the P2 shutdown was a cosmetic device. In reality, the lodge's reactionary ethos was now spread like a virus throughout the Grand Orient.

Salvini had been forced to resign because of intense American Masonic dissatisfaction over his relationship with Gelli. Yet the new Grand Master, General Ennio Battelli, brought even greater shame on the movement. It turned out that Gelli had paid for Battelli's Masonic election campaign and then gave him regular pay-offs in succeeding years. The general would later be charged with criminal involvement in the Bologna Station massacre.

When England's Grand Lodge goes silent about a Masonic controversy the nearest thing to a leak may be found in the magazine *Masonic Square*. In March 1987 it published an article on Italian Freemasonry which referred to the 'bogus P2 lodge, a spurious body not affiliated in any way to the Grand Orient'.[33] Was this untruth published through ignorance or had the writer been fed disinformation to delude England's Masonic faithful? Either way, the writer also claimed that the Grand Orient 'enjoys the warmest relations' with the Grand Lodges of England, Ireland and Scotland.

Perhaps these 'warmest relations' have blinded England's Grand Lodge to the need to discover and disseminate the truth about Italian Freemasonry. To spread the myth that P2 was a perversion, rather than the logical climax, of the Grand Orient tradition would obviously suit the Grand Orient. In the early 1980s not only England's Masonic masses but also much of the Western press were hoodwinked into thinking P2 was not part of Freemasonry at all. This was necessary if a second act of deception – blaming the P2 scandal on the KGB – could be achieved without tainting the Grand Orient or the Grand Lodge of England. This may explain why British intelligence sought to mislead Stephen Knight in 1983.

To discover the source of this deception we must study that part of the Italian Parliamentary Report which deals with the role played by Italian intelligence in the P2 affair. Italy has three secret services: SISDE (internal security), SISMI (external intelligence) and CESIS (which liaises between the first two). The investigating MPs were disturbed by the fact that these services seem to have stopped gathering information about Licio Gelli in about 1950, just when he deserved intensified scrutiny.

From 1945 to 1950 the secret services had shown great interest in Gelli, especially in his war service as a lieutenant in a parachute regiment, and as a fascist liaison officer with the German SS in the province of Pistoia. In 1944, when it became clear that the Germans would be defeated, Gelli contacted local communist partisans. Secret service files show he gave them advance warning of intended arrests and ferried them food and arms. When the Allies liberated the region, he co-operated with American counter-intelligence, while simultaneously holding a letter of recommendation (a free pass) from the local communist partisan chief.

This mostly favourable account of Gelli's war came from Gelli himself. The full story shows he had been a fascist since 1936, fighting for Franco in Spain. During World War II he rounded up anti-fascist fellow-countrymen and British prisoners. He caused the arrest of a partisan priest and was involved in the execution of four deserters. His 1944 support for the partisans was no humanitarian gesture but opportunism to save his skin. 'Whilst still wearing a German uniform,' says the Parliamentary Report, 'he put himself at the disposal of the Communist partisans, in a constant and equivocal balance between the two sides, which allows us to understand completely the subtlety of the man.'[34]

In 1945 local magistrates saw right through Gelli. They sentenced him (in his absence) to thirty months' imprisonment for kidnapping and robbery, and ordered his arrest for war-crimes. This came to nothing because of a good word from the same partisan chief. In 1947 the Ministry of Interior still had him under 'careful surveillance', but about this time he fled to Argentina, and was eventually removed from the Ministry's list of suspects in 1950.

That year a report was lodged in the secret service files which painted a different picture. It claimed that Gelli was an agent of Cominform (the Communist Eastern bloc) and that he disguised his activities by posing as a manufacturer, trader and bookseller. It also said that during this period he joined three right-wing political parties, but only to gain a respectable cover and to get the passport he desperately needed for his covert activities. When the Italian Parliamentary team looked into Gelli they decided that this 'Cominform Report' was a masterpiece of disinformation, hidden in the files until such times as Gelli might have to be disowned.

The MPs interpreted it this way because if its tales had been true, the security services would surely have conducted deep and continuing inquiries into Gelli. Yet no significant reports appear in their Gelli files for

the next twenty-nine years. The MPs were shocked by this omission:
'Just when the secret services should be increasing their interest in Gelli,
they suddenly lose it . . . The Cominform report, far from marking the
end of information-gathering about the man, should have increased it.'[35]
Even as late as the mid-1970s, the only agencies gathering information on
Gelli were the finance police and the anti-terrorist squad. They saw him
as a fomenter and organizer of right-wing subversion. Meanwhile the
secret services did almost nothing. In 1978 when SISMI was finally forced
to investigate Italian Freemasonry, it produced a woolly philosophical
analysis which said far less about P2 than even the press had revealed at
the time. It also seemed more concerned about the motives of Masonry's
critics (including the Communist Party) than checking if what they said
was true.

The Italian MPs concluded 'that Gelli himself must belong to the secret
services, since this is the only logical explanation for the cover they gave
Gelli, both in a passive way (not gathering information on him) and an
active one (not providing information about him to political authorities
who requested it)'. The Cominform Report was stuck in his file just
when he joined the secret services as 'a sort of insurance policy', to give
them the power of blackmail over a brilliantly manipulative individual,
who might well change sides again. They hid the 'Red' Gelli file away for
a rainy day. The heavens finally opened in 1981 when P2 cascaded into
Italy's biggest postwar scandal. To limit the damage to themselves and
Italy's Right, the secret services revealed the Cominform Report. It was
declassified by SISMI just two weeks after Gelli's P2 lists were
discovered. His distant communist past enabled them to paint P2 as a
KGB plot. SISMI declared:

> Gelli could have become an agent of the Eastern bloc in the
> immediate postwar period in exchange for his later salvation. He
> could have been 'frozen' according to a methodology typical of the
> secret services, and could have been gradually made to penetrate the
> sensitive sectors and been kept 'on tap' for exploitation on more
> propitious occasions.[36]

The Parliamentarians said this analysis might be correct, but it would
have rung truer if SISMI had written it *before* the discovery of the P2 lists,
not after. The Cominform Report had been in SISMI's 'Gelli' files for
thirty years. Why did it wait so long to act? The MPs concluded that,
while Gelli *might* have been an Eastern bloc agent, he was nevertheless
controlled by Italy's secret services. Until 1981 they had protected him
with a wall of silence. 'The real reason' for their actions 'must be sought

not in Gelli's presumed control over the security services but just the opposite: the control they have over him'.[37] Far from being the 'Burrattinaio' (Puppet-master), manipulating people and events for his own ends, Gelli was the marionette of others far more powerful than himself.

The secret services had another reason for unloading the Cominform Report when they did. The Gelli raid had humiliated them all, for all their chiefs were on the P2 lists: General Grassini (SISDE), General Santovito (SISMI), General Musumeci (head of SISMI security and control) and Prefect Pelosi (CESIS). They must have assumed their membership would never be revealed, nor would it have been without the extraordinary determination of Colonel Bianchi who carried out the raid. When he found the lists, he received an intimidating phone call from his boss, General Giannini, the finance police commander. He warned Bianchi to be careful about what he was doing because 'all the leaders' were on the lists. When questioned by the Parliamentary team, Giannini was unable to explain how he knew who was on the lists. It turned out, of course, that he also was a P2 member.[38]

The role of SISMI's boss, General Giuseppe Santovito, is especially significant. His involvement with Gelli shows once again that in Italy Freemasonry, politics and spying go hand in hand. It may be that Santovito was duped into joining P2 but this would be an act of extraordinary naïveté on the part of a military intelligence chief. He was also involved with American counter-intelligence. This was only to be expected, as Italy's secret services were created by the OSS/CIA after World War II, and have remained essentially local intelligence-gathering operations for the USA ever since.[39]

Santovito was also well known to Britain's secret services, sometimes visiting London to meet his counterparts in MI5 and MI6. During 1981, for example, he lunched with British intelligence chiefs at Cunningham's Restaurant in Curzon Street, a few steps from MI5 headquarters. The connections between British intelligence and leading members of P2 have never been exposed, but they existed. Bearing in mind the Masonic presence which Peter Wright encountered in MI5, and the brotherhood's strength in the armed forces and the Ministry of Defence, the possibility of Masonic links between the security services of Britain, Italy and other countries cannot be ruled out.

Only now does it become clear why Stephen Knight's 'impeccable source' in British intelligence misled him into embracing the 'P2–KGB plot' theory. This would have been the only way General Santovito could have explained away his own exposure in the P2 scandal to his British counterparts. The Cominform Report of 1950 would have given him a plausible excuse. By the end of 1981 the scandal had forced Santovito to quit, but there was a continuing need to shield NATO and the Western alliance from the public realization that all the security bosses of a member state were involved in a plot to overthrow that state's democracy. It was far less damaging for them to claim they had been unwittingly sucked into P2 by 'KGB agent' Licio Gelli, with his bogus ultra-patriotic Italian sentiments, than to admit that he and they had been running a huge conspiracy against the popular will.

Neither England's Grand Lodge nor any leading English Masons could have had any knowledge of a P2 plot – KGB or fascist – to subvert Italy. If Grand Lodge *had* known, it would not have displayed such naïvety in its relations with Italian Freemasonry over the past twenty years. Only total ignorance could have allowed its leaders to stumble into the heart of the conspiracy in 1973.

Early that year Grand Secretary James Stubbs and Board President Jeremy Pemberton[40] paid the first formal visit to Italy since Grand Lodge had recognized the Grand Orient. Engulfed in Italian hospitality, the pair were escorted by Grand Master Lino Salvini – who was at that very time conspiring with Gelli over P2. On a visit to Florence the Englishmen were guests of honour at a lush reception at the mansion of Allessandro del Bene. Presumably they were unaware that Signor del Bene was the 'Godfather of Florence' and that his malignant influence ran throughout Italy.[41] Outwardly a respectable import–export merchant, 'with all the appearance of a peaceful Florentine gentleman',[42] del Bene financed Salvini's successful campaign for Grand Master in 1970. He also sponsored Gelli's mercurial rise in Freemasonry and was one of P2's most ardent members. A leading international arms dealer, he joined in Gelli's attempts to buy extra Exocets for Argentina during the 1982 Falklands War. His name also cropped up during inquiries into the Bologna bombing. In Monte Carlo he set up P2's daughter lodge – mainly as a cover for gun-running and subversion. It was also a bolt-hole when the P2 scandal broke, and it was in Monte Carlo that he died in 1984.

In 1973 the Grand Orient magazine, *Revista Massonica*, featured photographs of Stubbs and Pemberton in del Bene's home, and Stubbs dining alongside Lino Salvini. The Englishmen's unwitting frolic with Tuscany's crooked Masonic 'Mafia' had a historic justice about it. P2's sponsors were fêting them in Florence because it was the seat of Italy's first Masonic lodge, founded in 1732 by Charles Sackville, Earl of Middlesex. And just like P2, the old English lodge at Florence had been full of spies, con-men and political intriguers.[43] As P2 seems (in some respects) to have been modelled on this fraternity, its history is worth telling here.

The lodge had flourished under the benign neglect of Grand Duke Gian Gastone, the last Medici. Early eighteenth-century Florence tolerated a large English community. Many were there for trade, recreation or the purchase of art. Others were on a paramount affair of state. Their job was to collect intelligence about the Stuart Pretender, James III, and his sons, who were sheltering in Rome under the protection of Pope Clement XII. No British spymaster could safely reside in Rome, but in Florence information could be gathered from paid agents and travellers returning from the Holy City. James II had been overthrown more than forty years earlier, but the Jacobite threat to Protestant England was real. The 1745 rebellion still lay ahead. Sir Robert Walpole and his Foreign Secretary, the Duke of Newcastle, paid handsomely for information about the Pretender's moves and intentions.

If this Florence lodge was a prototype P2, then its prototype Licio Gelli was Baron Philip von Stosch – a German-born archaeologist with British nationality. At first he had spied on the Jacobites in Rome itself, but he had to flee in 1731, fearing assassination. Just like Gelli, Stosch was later suspected of spying for both sides.

The 'intelligencer' simply shifted his base to Florence and joined the new lodge. He maintained a spacious home in the aptly-named Via dei Malcontenti, mostly paid for by his espionage activities. It was frequented by many Italian members of the lodge, whom ardent Catholics branded 'impious enemies of our Holy Religion'.[44] According to one Masonic writer, Stosch 'belonged to that class of men of letters who thrive by intrigues and the doing of dirty work'.[45] His brazen anti-Papal plotting and the 'heathenish talk'[46] of the lodge's Italian members are what ultimately drove Pope Clement XII to issue his Bull In Eminenti. This claimed Freemasonry endangered the soul, told Catholics not to become Masons, and ordered Inquisitors to put Catholic Masons on trial for heresy (see Chapter 8).

Although Florence was not under the Pope's political control, its Grand Duke recognized the religious authority of the Inquisition so Florence's Freemasons promptly shut up shop. 'If ever it be possible to feel satisfaction at the extinction of a Masonic lodge', says one Masonic writer,[47] 'in this instance we can indulge in that feeling . . . When the brethren discovered that the plant they had imported to Italian soil was not suited to the climate . . . they wisely preferred to uproot it.'

This action did not mollify the Holy Office which was determined to consume its first Masonic victim. In May 1739 a poet and satirist named Tomasso Crudeli, who belonged to the Florence lodge, was arrested and jailed. At his trial the Chief Inquisitor threatened Crudeli with perpetual imprisonment unless he betrayed the Masonic goings-on in Stosch's house. Crudeli said he had no idea that Freemasons held meetings there, but this was not what the Inquisitor wanted to hear. Crudeli was convicted of heresy, but as he had already been locked up for a year and a half, he was sentenced to house arrest, and regained full liberty a few months later. His punishment could have been worse but, even so, he is hailed as Masonry's first martyr to Catholicism.

The notorious Baron Stosch had simply carried on as before. The English lodge had been dissolved but many of its members continued to gather at his house. In 1739 the Papal Nuncio forced Grand Duke Francis to expel him but Britain's diplomatic resident, Horace Mann, arranged for the expulsion to be suspended, originally for a week and then indefinitely. Stosch lived in Florence for another eighteen years before expiring of natural causes. He was on England's spy payroll until the day he died.

His protector, Horace Mann, was a kinsman of Britain's Prime Minister, Sir Robert Walpole. Mann needed to keep Stosch in Florence because he knew how valuable he was to the government which paid both their salaries. Mann, 'while still very young as a diplomat, was far from pleased at the thought of losing a serviceable villain, skilled in espionage, counter-espionage, and the similar indispensable but dirty jobs of high politics with which no gentleman could soil his own hands.'[48] Thus 250 years ago, Freemasonry was recognized as an ideal tool for espionage and political intrigue. The English lodge at Florence may have been founded without the authority of England's Grand Lodge, but one of its members was Robert, the 2nd Earl Raymond. He returned to London and became Grand Master of all England in 1739. He had probably been initiated in Florence, so the 'Lodge of Spies' must have had some official recognition or else its child would not have been considered fit to be made the grandest Mason of all.

Horace Mann remained Britain's diplomatic resident in Florence until his death in 1786. There is no proof that he was a Mason, although one reputable modern Masonic writer claims he was,[49] but he is a hero to Italian Masons. In the early 1970s Grand Secretary James Stubbs paid a second official visit to Florence to 'consecrate' an English-speaking lodge named 'Sir Horace Mann 1732'. The name might have been chosen on sentimental grounds, to honour one of Florence's greatest English friends, but in Masonic terms it must have seemed like a 'green light' for skulduggery. To the power-brokers of Italian Freemasonry – Salvini, del Bene and Gelli – this handshake with the most notorious lodge in English Masonic history must have seemed like support for their own subversive activities. Their P2 lodge could now be seen as continuing a legitimate Masonic tradition in which politics, espionage, even meddling against the Papacy, were all 'OK' by the world's premier Grand Lodge. Unfortunately, no one at Great Queen Street – certainly not James Stubbs – appreciated the symbolism. In 1976 he did it again: 'consecrating' a Royal Arch chapter in Florence in the name of the 'Martyr' Mason, Tommaso Crudeli, the most famous Italian member of the 'Lodge of Spies'.

In June 1982 Masonic symbolism and reality united to tragic effect when P2 member Roberto Calvi was found strung up under Blackfriars Bridge, less than a mile from London's Freemasons' Hall. The death is still unsolved, despite two inquests, continuing inquiries by Calvi's family and several excellent books investigating his problems and possible motives for his murder.[50] In this book I do not exhume the entire Calvi affair or claim to solve the mystery of his death, but there are several Masonic aspects which deserve scrutiny.

At the time of his death Calvi was chairman of Banco Ambrosiano, Italy's largest private bank. He had fled to England because the Bank of Italy in Rome wanted to question him about $1,400 million which he had loaned to overseas-based companies but which had since disappeared in an apparent fraud. The Vatican Bank and its head Cardinal Marcinkus were implicated.[51] So were Michele Sindona, the Sicilian-born banker with Mafia connections, and Licio Gelli, both of P2. Among those trying to sort out Calvi's problems were his employee Francesco Pazienza (the young Freemason with links to Italian military intelligence), and Armando Corona, who had just become Grand Master of the Grand Orient. A former President of Sardinia, Corona had given up politics to devote himself to cleansing the order, which had suffered three scandalous Grand Masters in succession. Yet Corona too was touched by scandal. He was a friend of millionaire playboy Flavio Carboni: the man who had procured Calvi's false passport, accompanied him on his secret flight to London, and was with him just a few hours before he died. Carboni was not a Mason, but Corona knew him as a fellow-Sardinian. As Banco Ambrosiano's problems mounted, Corona met Calvi five times to try and sort out the debts.

Five weeks after Calvi's death an inquest jury in London decided that the banker had committed suicide. The verdict was jeered by Italian reporters, and overturned in June 1983 by a second jury which recorded an open verdict: Calvi might have killed himself or he might have been killed by others. Jury foreman Bruce Kitchen continued to study the case in his own time, consuming the vast literature pouring out about the Italian background to Calvi's problems. Four months after the inquest he told The Times: 'I believe that had we known what we know now, a majority of the jurors would have returned a verdict of murder.'[52]

The 'suicide' had always seemed doubtful. Would a man who barely knew London walk five miles across town in the middle of the night, load his pockets with 12lb of bricks, climb on to scaffolding which was almost invisible from Blackfriars Bridge itself, tie a rope round his neck and hang himself? If he had wanted to kill himself, he could have done it many times over with the twenty-eight types of drugs he had in his suitcase. Or, since he could not swim, he might just as easily have flung himself into the Thames from a bridge nearer Chelsea where he was staying.

It seems more likely that Calvi was murdered, by being hanged from the scaffolding − or by strangulation, poisonous inhalation or drug injection a few minutes earlier. He could then have been tied on the scaffolding, probably by men in a boat, at about 2 A.M. (his time of death) when the tidal river's level would have been just below where his head was found, slumped, six hours later.

Calvi may have felt depressed enough to kill himself, but he also knew *he* had not stolen all $1,400 million himself and may have believed that some creditors might eventually get their money back. By 1988 some of the funds had been recovered.[53] In 1982, however, many people could have wanted him dead: not just creditors but debtors, fraudsters, employees, Vatican bankers, Mafiosi, even Masons. If, during his time in London, he did decide to return to Rome and talk to the Bank of Italy investigators, many of his associates would have felt threatened.

Who really killed Calvi − or had him killed − is still a mystery, but some people feel that the way he died was rich in Masonic symbolism. Here are some of the interpretations which have been read into the death − by Masons just as much as non-Masons.

The place of death, Blackfriars Bridge, was resonant of P2's emblem. On the rare occasions that any P2 members performed rituals, they were meant to wear black cassocks like Dominican friars.

The Bridge is only a few hundred yards from the Temple. Now one of the Four Inns of Court to which all England's barristers belong, in Medieval times it was the home of the English wing of the Knights Templar, Christendom's avenging warriors. The Knights were suppressed and their leaders executed in 1312, but today a Masonic re-creation has many members in England and Italy [see Chapter 7]. The Knights took their name from the Temple of Solomon, on which Freemasonry's central myth is based. Some Masonic fantasists have claimed the Freemasons are the secret continuation of the original Templars, otherwise known as the 'murdered magicians'.[54]

The noose round Calvi's throat recalls the cabletow round the candidate's neck during Freemasonry's first degree ceremony. As the hoodwink or blindfold is removed from his eyes the initiate is told, 'the dangers you have escaped are those of stabbing [from the poignard or dagger thrust against his naked left breast] and strangling . . . there was likewise this cabletow with a running noose about your neck which would have rendered any attempt at retreat fatal'.

The traditional First Degree oath contains the penalty of having one's tongue torn out and 'buried in the sand of the sea at low water mark, or a cable's length from the shore, where the tide ebbs and flows twice in twenty-four hours . . .' All this, and having one's throat cut across, awaits the Freemason who betrays his brothers' secrets. Calvi was not buried, of course, but he was found hanged where the tide ebbs and flows.

The coarse bricks and stones found on Calvi's body recall how Freemasons are taught that when a man enters the Craft he is like a rough, uncut stone and is progressively hewn into a 'Perfect Ashlar'. The newcomer learns that the Rough Ashlar 'represents man in his infant or primitive state' until his mind becomes cultivated 'and he is thereby rendered a fit member of civilized society'. In contrast the Perfect Ashlar (a smooth cubic block) 'represents man in the decline of years, after a regular well-spent life in acts of piety and virtue'. Of course, the bricks may have been on Calvi's body to weigh him down and ensure strangulation, but they may have symbolized the murderer's belief that he was not a fit member of civilized society.

If Calvi really was murdered, the act would have required several conspirators. Suspicion has inevitably fallen on the two Italians who accompanied him to London: Flavio Carboni and Sylvano Vittor. Both left Calvi shortly before his death, albeit at different times, yet no evidence connects either with his death. We therefore have to consider two networks with London connections which both had an interest in Calvi. The Mafia is one. As recent criminal trials have proved, several Italian Mafia families are active in London and maintain a continuing presence.[55] They are only too capable of committing murders, especially symbolic ones.[56]

The other network is Freemasonry. No evidence links any British Masons with a plot to kill Calvi. However, his 'protector' Carboni did contact one Mason while he was in London with Calvi. His long-time girlfriend in Italy had an English uncle named William Morris, a former local government officer living in Heston. Carboni asked Morris to help him find a flat, but the day Calvi died, Carboni lost interest. He told Morris to forget the idea and then flew to Rome via Edinburgh, not the most convenient routing.

Calvi himself had been to London before on several occasions. His British friends included Peter de Savary, the millionaire businessman who in 1983 became widely known for his bid to win yachting's Americas Cup. Two years earlier in London Calvi had signed a deal with de Savary, in which his Banco Ambrosiano Overseas bought 20 per cent of de Savary's Artoc Bank. Calvi saw this as a way of injecting large amounts of Arab cash into his flagging financial empire. De Savary appeared to have access to such money, but the deal never went that far.

I have written twice to Peter de Savary, asking about his links with Calvi. According to Calvi, they were not purely financial. He used to say that he had visited a Masonic lodge in London, of which de Savary was the Treasurer, and that a member of England's royal family also belonged to the lodge. As only two living 'Royals' are active in Freemasonry – the Duke of Kent and his brother, Prince Michael – the only Craft lodge Calvi might have been talking about would be the Royal Alpha (no. 16) to which they both belong. He might have meant the Navy Lodge (no. 2612) to which both George VI and Prince Philip used to belong. This would seem appropriate for a yachtsman like de Savary, but is it really possible that the fallen Italian banker ever attended either lodge? I assume not but, because I have received no reply from Mr de Savary, I do not know.

Some journalists have pointed out that the City of London Police, in whose bailiwick Calvi's body was found (and which therefore investigated his death) is steeped in Freemasonry. This was demonstrated, only one month later, in the corruption trial of Det. Chief Insp. Phil Cuthbert (see Chapter 17). It would be unfair to claim the force's grossly premature commitment to the 'suicide' theory was a Masonic cover-up. All that emerges from studying the Masonic aspects of Calvi's life and death is a depressing realization: the ring of suspects for his probable murder should be widened to include not just his Italian enemies but members of many British institutions affected by his financial problems and by the P2 conspiracy as a whole.

Calvi was one of many P2 members to die a strange death. In 1979 Mino Pecorelli, a journalist, was shot dead through the mouth after publishing damaging information about Gelli's perfidious past. In 1986 Michele Sindona died after allegedly poisoning himself with a cup of coffee laced with potassium cyanide. He had just started a life sentence for murder.

In 1987 Licio Gelli returned voluntarily to Italy, after escaping from a

Swiss jail in 1983 and fleeing to Uruguay. He is now facing trial for fraudulent bankruptcy over the collapse of Calvi's Banco Ambrosiano. He has already been sentenced to ten years' imprisonment for conspiring to protect the perpetrators of the Bologna Station massacre but due to a technicality this sentence is unenforceable. Gelli claims that he returned to receive open-heart surgery. In the meantime he is avoiding the kind of heart surgery made with small, rapidly-propelled metal objects – and refusing all cups of coffee made by anyone but himself.

thirty-four

THE TORY PARTY IN APRONS?

In June 1988 Mrs Thatcher rewarded one of the Conservative Party's most dedicated servants. In the Queen's Birthday Honours Neil Westbrook CBE FRICS MA was awarded a knighthood for public and political services, performed largely in Manchester where he was once Lord Mayor. He had served on the council and in senior regional party jobs for more than twenty years. Now in his seventies, he is still on the Conservatives' national Board of Finance. A chartered surveyor, Mr Westbrook is chairman and managing director of Trafford Park Estates, one of Britain's biggest property companies. Naturally, his knighthood was greeted with eulogies and plaudits in local newspapers, yet none of them mentioned another side of his life. Neil Westbrook is one of Lancashire's highest-ranking Freemasons.

Very early in my research my Masonic mole 'Badger', Past Master of seven lodges, told me, 'Freemasonry is a mechanism of social control' and the Conservative Party is one of the main beneficiaries (see Chapter 10). The evidence I accumulated in the next three years proved how right Badger was, but it was only when I learned one of Freemasonry's best-kept secrets that I gained a necessary grasp of the brotherhood's modern political history.

When the 'war to end all wars' ended in 1918, the class war began again at home. Shell-shocked survivors of the trenches returned not to a 'fit country for heroes to live in' but to a land of unemployment, hunger marches and industrial unrest. Even police forces went on strike. At first the enemy confronting Britain's ruling classes was not bloody Bolshevik revolution but socialist reconstruction of society through the ballot box. In the general election of December 1923 the Labour Party won 191 seats. Ramsay MacDonald formed Britain's first socialist government but this fell within a year because Labour MPs were greatly outnumbered by Conservatives and Liberals combined. In the October 1924 election the party lost forty seats and was replaced by a Tory government with a massive majority. For the next four years a bitter working class had no effective Parliamentary voice.

The struggle took a non-Parliamentary turn with the 1926 general strike. Its outcome was a humiliating defeat for organized labour but this only strained Parliamentary democracy even further. Forced back down the pits for less than they were earning before, many miners joined the Communist Party which doubled its membership in a few months. Some reactionaries feared that, if this trend were to continue, there was a chance that Britain's royal family would go the same way as their Russian cousins, slaughtered eight years before. One man who naturally hoped they would not was Edward, Prince of Wales. A means must be found, he vowed, to draw Labour into the middle ground of British politics. He knew just the organization to do it: Freemasonry.

The future King Edward VIII had been Senior Warden of England's Grand Lodge in 1922 and Provincial Grand Master of Surrey since 1924. He was therefore familiar with the Craft's first Antient Charge, that 'masonry is the centre of union between good men and true, and the happy means of conciliating friendship amongst those who must otherwise have remained at a perpetual distance'. If Labour MPs and local councillors could be encouraged to don the apron, class war might be mollified into consensus. The second Charge, that a Mason 'is never to be concerned in plots and conspiracies against the peace and welfare of the nation', would further ensure that any socialist joining the British brotherhood would shed his revolutionary zeal.

Yet in the late 1920s the Prince was disturbed to learn that rising Labour politicians who applied to join lodges were being blackballed and excluded. Such action not only went against Masonic principles; if it continued, the Craft would stand condemned as the Tory Party in Aprons. By shutting out the leaders of Britain's most dynamic political movement, Freemasonry might lose all control over the nation's future. A future Labour government might even make it illegal, as Mussolini had made it in Italy as recently as 1925. Edward consulted some of Parliament's leading brethren. He had a lot to choose from. At this time some seventy members of the House of Lords were active Masons: including three other royal princes, at least four dukes, two marquesses, fifteen earls, ten viscounts and thirty-four barons. In the House of Commons sat a further seven Grand Officers.

The time had come, the Prince advised, to create a Parliamentary lodge in which to initiate Labour MPs: not just those whom the Craft had already rebuffed but any other would-be Masons. The Prince felt such a lodge should be run with a perpetual bias in Labour's favour. For instance, if a choice had to be made over who should fill any office –

including Master – a Labour man should always be given the job. Also the lodge should have a name reflecting its spirit and intention. The founders chose 'New Welcome'. It was consecrated towards the end of 1929 and given the roll number 5139. The Prince's initiative had come only just in time. In the May 1929 election Labour had won 287 seats. It lacked an overall majority but for the first time there were more Labour MPs than Conservative.

For the next two years Ramsay MacDonald led a Labour government which was increasingly torn between helping its impoverished supporters and balancing the national budget. In 1931 the Cabinet split over a plan to cut wages and unemployment benefits. The trade unions and most Labour MPs felt this was a betrayal of the party's working-class vote. MacDonald resigned as Prime Minister but promptly formed a National Government of Conservatives, Liberals and his few Labour allies. In the October election this alliance won 558 seats, while Labour took only forty-six. The 'national interest' had triumphed. Socialism had been beaten back. It took fourteen more years and another world war before Labour won again.

I do not know if Freemasonry played any role in Labour's troubles or in the formation of the National Government. Some anti-Masons might espy a Masonic conspiracy but the split was so public, and over so fundamental an issue, that no one has ever needed to blame the Craft. It so happens, however, that the continuity of national governments for the rest of the 1930s (even after MacDonald lost his seat in 1935) accorded perfectly with the brotherhood's second Charge, that a Mason must 'uphold, on every occasion, the interest of the community, and zealously promote the prosperity of his own country'.

Freemasonry certainly played a big role in what was left of the Labour Party, particularly in Clement Attlee's election as leader in 1935. According to Hugh Dalton (the future Chancellor of the Exchequer) both Attlee and his rival Arthur Greenwood were Masons.[1] Dalton says that a Masonic caucus of MPs and Transport Union officials backed Greenwood in the leadership ballot. He came third, so in the run-off the Masons switched their votes to Brother Attlee. This ensured his victory over the non-Mason, Herbert Morrison. Attlee was still leader when the party won the 1945 election. He was Prime Minister for six years and continued as leader until 1955, when poor Morrison again came second to Hugh Gaitskell. Neither Gaitskell nor any subsequent Labour leader seems to have been a Mason, but if the Craft did play the role attributed to it in 1935, it might have influenced equally momentous British political decisions this century – despite its claim never to interfere in politics.

The New Welcome Lodge has been one of British politics' longest and best-kept secrets. Persistent rumours that a lodge existed somewhere in Parliament have been laughed off until now because of false tales that it meets within the Palace of Westminster. In fact it meets five times a year at Freemasons' Hall. One Past Master is the highly respected Tory back-bencher, Neil Thorne. A chartered surveyor by profession, he sports a monocle, not out of affectation but because of an eye-wound sustained in military service. This 'verray parfit gentil knight' is the last man to inspire fears of a Masonic political conspiracy. He was initiated in the lodge for City of London School old boys and he joined New Welcome after being elected MP for Ilford South in 1979.

When I met Neil Thorne in 1986 he stressed Freemasonry's social and charitable activities. He said that of New Welcome's sixty members, only about twenty are past or present MPs. The others are assorted Parliamentary staffers. The current Master was a policeman who had worked in the lobby for many years. At the time Thorne was nursing one Labour MP through New Welcome. He would not say which one, nor would he identify any other MPs in the lodge. He felt that if he named Labour members their chances of re-selection would be damaged, but he did say that some recent New Welcome initiates have been Catholics.

Thorne says the main reason why Masons keep their membership secret is that, if they went round proclaiming it, they might be accused of touting for business. Some commercially-minded brothers used to frame their membership certificates and stick them on their shop or office walls. This is now forbidden because it was open to abuse as a form of advertising. Masonic secrecy, says Thorne, is not motivated, therefore, by clandestinity but by a sense that the reverse – pushy openness – might arouse even greater suspicions about Masonic abuse. He says there is nothing illicit about the Craft. Indeed, he stresses one part in the Masonic speech which he most likes to perform – the Installation Address to all brethren when a new Master takes office – in which a Mason is reminded 'to be faithful to our God, our country and our laws'.

The current *Masonic Yearbook* identifies twenty-seven members of the House of Lords as Grand Officers, but the only current MPs listed are Neil Thorne and former health minister, Sir Gerard Vaughan. Four ex-MPs are Grand Officers: Sir Charles Taylor (Eastbourne 1935–74), Sir Ian Percival (Southport 1959–87), the former Solicitor-General, Sir Ted Leather (North Somerset 1950–64) and Niall Macdermot (Lewisham and Derby North between 1957 and 1970). Another Masonic high-flier is Euro-MP Sir Peter Vanneck, Lord Mayor of London 1977–8. All are Conservatives, except for Macdermot who was Labour. Other former Tory MPs who are Masons include Sir John Langford-Holt (Shrewsbury 1945–83), Sir Donald (now Baron) Kaberry (Leeds NW 1950–83), Baron

Harmar-Nicholls (Peterborough 1950–74), Joseph Hiley (Pudsey 1959–74), Sir Edward Brown (Bath 1964–79) and Michael Fidler (Bury & Ratcliffe 1970–74).

Dr Sir Gerard Vaughan has been MP for various parts of Reading since 1970. I wrote to him in 1986 asking about Freemasonry but he did not reply. The Reading *Evening Post* had better luck:

> I'm quite a way up in it. I'm a prominent Mason with a low profile. I have always regarded it as something like Rotary. I have never seen any abuses and have never been asked if I am a Mason or told anyone. It's never been something particularly to mention to people or to conceal.[2]

Vaughan said he joined because two people who had helped him were Masons and 'they were very, very nice people'. Sir Ian Percival joined for similar reasons (see Chapter 22). He believes that Masons make good police officers and good judges. 'Indeed, I believe it would be a much better world if everyone were in it.'

Sir Ian has an impish sense of humour and a disarming lack of pomposity – he once wind-surfed in the Thames next to Parliament in front of a crowd of press photographers and promptly sank. Yet, if pricked about the Craft, he can become very serious. After another Tory MP had expressed his dislike of Freemasonry, Sir Ian told him he had got it all wrong. The other man restated his objections, so Sir Ian cast his eyes up around the Palace of Westminster and said: 'Well, when all this has crumbled, Freemasonry will still be going strong.'

When I met Sir Ian in his barrister's chambers, he was still MP for Southport. I said I knew that his predecessor, the late Roger Hesketh, was also a Mason. Now that the Lancashire seaside town had been represented by brethren for more than thirty years, was it fair to say Southport was a Masonic rotten borough? Not at all, he assured me.

> I had never been to Southport until four days before I was selected as its prospective MP. It's true Roger Hesketh is a Freemason – indeed, he was married to the daughter of the 11th Earl of Scarborough [the Duke of Kent's predecessor as Grand Master] – but at the time neither of us had any idea the other was a Mason. If I'd said to Roger, 'I'm a Mason too,' that would have been curtains! Nobody on the selection board knew I was a Mason.
>
> People always put the worst interpretation on things. The truth is that, rather than trading on Freemasonry, most of us prefer to forgo any possible advantage. I would find it offensive if any

Masonic constituent were to ask a favour, like being put at the front
of the council housing list, or getting preferment for a job. No one
has ever come to my Southport 'surgery' and stated he was a Mason.
The town has many lodges (though I didn't find out until years after
I became its MP), so it's no coincidence that I know quite a few
Masons there. They may confide in me, yes, but ask favours? No.

One of the nice things about Freemasonry is that there *isn't* this
patronage thing. I think if I were wrong, I would have noticed it by
now. Over all these years I don't think I have had one case of a
Mason asking me a favour. Well, maybe one, but he's a man I would
have expected to consult me anyway.

Sir Ian told me he did not often attend the New Welcome Lodge
because it meets on a Friday, the day he had to travel north to Southport.
He also had other Masonic duties. He still belongs to his mother lodge,
Canada (no. 3527), and a Southport lodge, the County Palatine (no. 2505).
He also serves on Grand Lodge's Board of General Purposes. Sir Ian is
one of only twelve past and present MPs listed thus far, so who might the
New Welcome's other political members possibly be?

Today the United Grand Lodge has twenty-seven officers in the House
of Lords, compared with about seventy in 1929. Most declare a party
affiliation, but few involve themselves in day-to-day politics. An
exception is John Ganzoni, 2nd Lord Belstead, who belongs to the
exclusive Kaisar-i-Hind Lodge (no. 1724). In 1988 he became Leader of
the House of Lords in succession to Viscount Whitelaw, who had also
been Mrs Thatcher's deputy prime minister. Whitelaw has long been
accused of being a Mason by Chief Inspector Brian Woollard who feels he
did not get a fair hearing in 1982 over his earliest complaints about
Masonic interference with his Metropolitan Police career (see Chapter
12). Woollard had addressed those complaints to Whitelaw who was then
Home Secretary responsible for the policing of London. As no journalist
seemed ever to have asked Lord Whitelaw about Freemasonry, I did so
myself in 1988. I received a most helpful reply.

I am in fact a Freemason and was a member of a Scottish lodge many
years ago. I have never been an active Freemason since I entered the
House of Commons in 1955. Needless to say, my connection has
absolutely no bearing on any actions I may have taken as far as Chief
Inspector Woollard was concerned . . . As Home Secretary I
certainly could not have interfered in any individual police officer's
career.

With the benefit of this kind of reply, I can state that the two latest Leaders of the House of Lords are both Masons. This is some achievement for a fraternity whose influence is generally believed to be on the wane. Information on the Craft in the House of Commons is more elusive, so in 1986 I sent a questionnaire to every male MP, except Percival and Thorne whose views I already knew. My letter contained eight questions:

1. Are you a Freemason?
2. If yes, when and why did you join?
3. If yes, have you lapsed or withdrawn?
4. If not, have you any objections to becoming one?
5. If not, have you ever been approached to join?
6. Should MPs be obliged to disclose membership in the same way as they register financial or economic interests?
7. Should councillors, judges, policemen, civil servants and local government officers? (Yes/No to each)
8. Do you have any other comments, for instance on the role of Freemasonry in British society today?

At this time only twenty-six out of 650 MPs were women, so I sent the questionnaire to 622 men, enclosing a stamped, addressed envelope in which they could return their answers. Two hundred and seventy-eight did so. By adding in Percival and Thorne, I now had the views of 280 male MPs: 44.9 per cent of the total. I have no idea what the remaining 344 did with my envelopes or stamps. Perhaps they sent them to charity. After all, Richard Page MP told me that only 'Receipt of a cheque for £100 made out to St Francis hospice will secure this information'. Alas! My research budget did not stretch that far.

Robert Hayward (not a Mason) found 'it difficult to understand why there should be this apparent neurosis about an overwhelmingly honest and charitable organization'. Richard Holt's entire response was 'I abhor Communism'. John Powley was 'not prepared to answer this letter'. John Cope saw 'no reason to contribute to my work' but did tell me, 'any club or society of any size will have in it some people who misuse it. Any club or society can provide a member with extra contacts which can be used or misused – socially, politically or at work.' John Corrie, the famed anti-abortionist from Cunninghame North, told me: 'This is none of your business.' In the 1987 election he lost his seat.

All the above 'refuseniks' were Conservative MPs. So were several more who felt my questionnaire had a McCarthyite tinge. Sir Keith (now Lord) Joseph suspected that it would 'be used – I do *not* write "intended" –

to smear people because they are members of a perfectly legal organization'. Jerry Hayes was more forthright:

> I must say I regard with considerable distaste circulars to anyone,
> not just public office holders, asking personal questions. To be
> frank, whether I am a Freemason, a Roman Catholic, a homosexual,
> or have a deep and meaningful relationship with my Pekingese, are
> all purely matters for me and me alone. As Members of Parliament,
> all of us expect to some extent our private life to be on show.
> However, you must be aware that in many countries where detailed
> files are kept on the personal habits of individuals, the slippery slope
> to McCarthyism begins.

In all, forty Conservatives returned the forms blank or said they never
fill in questionnaires. Four Labour members did not fill them in either.
James Molyneaux, Leader of the Ulster Unionists, had more pressing
calls on his time but at least his secretary replied. Nothing at all was heard
from Labour Leader Neil Kinnock or Social Democrat David Owen.
Both Robert Maclennan, stand-in leader of the SDP's merger faction, and
David Steel, his then co-leader of the Social and Liberal Democratic
Alliance, said they do not fill in questionnaires. Mr Steel added that he is
not a Mason. In this respect he differs from his father (see Chapter 2).

I did not write to Mrs Thatcher. As a woman she cannot belong to
regular Freemasonry, and I did not think it appropriate to ask if her
husband was 'on the square'. That might have verged on McCarthyism.
In 1988 Labour MP Max Madden picked up a rumour that Mrs Thatcher
was a member of a Masonic organization, the Eastern Star, but when he
tried to ask her a Parliamentary question, it was blocked in the tabling
office because it might cause 'annoyance'. I understand Mrs Thatcher is
not and never has been an Eastern Star member.

Excluding forty-three replies 'rejecting' my questionnaire, I had 237
respondents (38 per cent of all male MPs) to some or all of the questions.
Nine said they were Masons; 228 said they were not. Just under half (133)
revealed an objection to joining, although in some cases this was only
'lack of time'. Forty-eight (21 per cent) of the non-Masons said they had
been approached to join Freemasonry but had refused. Twenty-seven of
these were Conservatives (24 per cent of all the Tories who replied) but a
surprising fifteen were Labour MPs (16 per cent of all Labour respondents). Six belonged to other parties.

One hundred and ninety-two members answered question 6, on
whether MPs should be obliged to declare membership of Freemasonry.
These included eighty-five Labour MPs, of whom eighty-one (95 per

cent) said they should. Their strength of feeling was perhaps predictable but, surprisingly, twenty out of eighty-seven Tories (23 per cent) felt the same way. Overall, 113 MPs or 58.9 per cent of respondents believed Masonic MPs should come out of the closet. An even higher proportion (60.3 per cent) felt councillors, judges, policemen, senior civil servants and local government officers should be obliged to disclose Masonic membership.

When I began this exercise I expected that Labour MPs would be opposed to Freemasonry and that Tories would be uncritical or supportive. When I analysed the answers, I was surprised by the ferocity of Labour's near unanimous hostility to the Craft, but astonished that almost a quarter of Tories felt the same way. This means that Freemasonry is a hotter issue – generating far stronger feelings – than any party boss has so far realized.

Tory MPs who are not Masons but who are broadly sympathetic with Freemasonry expressed these views:

> I do not see it in any sinister or secretive light. From my experience and contact, it is basically benevolent and harmless. (Jim Lester)

> I have never encountered any suggestion, let alone evidence, that in the constituencies I have represented for thirty-six years that Freemasonry plays a significant or improper role in British society. I would not hesitate to denounce *improper* influence being brought to bear if evidence was placed before me. (Sir Bernard Braine, Father of the House)

> People's private lives are their own affair and should not be subject to the whims of 'Big Brother'. That is a precious freedom. Whilst I have no interest in Freemasonry, I do not object to other people's membership. It is for the leaders of Freemasonry to ensure that its bond is not abused. (James Couchman)

> Far too much silly fuss is made about a harmless, indeed honourable organization. The critics would be better employed conducting their lives as usefully as most Freemasons! (Sir Anthony Grant)

> There is nothing unlawful or, as far as I can see, improper about being a Freemason. We do not require public disclosure of an individual's beliefs, religious practices etc, and I hope we never shall in a free society. (Sir Eldon Griffiths)

Freemasonry seems to get a disproportionate amount of attention. Why not a survey of membership of the Rotary Club or the MCC? (Michael Latham)

I do not believe that they are a sinister organization, which are worth your time, or anyone else's to investigate. My personal view is that they are no different from any other association, such as Rotarians, Lions, Kiwanis, Elks, Buffalos, Oddfellows etc. Therefore I see no reason to 'get up-tight' about anyone in any named activity who happens to be a Freemason. (Sir David Price)

I don't understand why there is such a fuss about Freemasonry. If people wish to belong to secret societies, that is their own business. (John Whitfield)

I do not wish to join Freemasonry and I shall *not* do so, but I don't believe that any special obligations should be placed upon those persons that do – such as declaring membership – any more than such obligations should be placed upon those who are members of other 'closed' organizations including certain minority political parties. As long as any organization is entirely legal and exists for purposes consistent with our unwritten constitution, no special requirements are necessary. There is still some honour in public life. (An MP who requested anonymity)

Some Tories explained why they had never become Masons. Two Catholics, Sir Patrick Wall and the now late Sir John Biggs-Davison, said they were forbidden by the Pope from joining. Sir John explained: 'I have no wish to enter a secret society contrary to the laws of the Church.' Julian Critchley feels it is 'just not my scene'. Jeremy Hanley's father was a Mason but, when he was approached to join, 'it was not something I felt committed to, nor did I think I needed such member-ship as part of my life'. He thinks there has been corruption in some cases, but 'there are many reasons why bias might be present in a decision-making situation – politics, sexual reasons, family, colour, school, religion etc. – I find Freemasonry no more "threatening" than any other organization or connection'. Even so, he feels judges should be obliged to disclose Masonic membership. Sir Ian Lloyd said that although he had never been asked, he would object to becoming a Mason because of 'possible conflicts of interest and loyalty in the public domain'.

William Powell, a barrister, said he had read *The Brotherhood* by

Stephen Knight and felt it exaggerated the danger of Freemasonry, although

> I do not exclude the possibility/even probability that membership has been used to secure influence, promotion etc. where it should not have so done. But you must avoid equating Masonry with such abuses. My own feeling is that it is mostly irrelevant and sometimes ridiculous. You must avoid the temptation of libelling by general- ising. I know of judges who are Masons. I would take a good deal of convincing that any of them had misused their position through Masonry.

Three recent government whips were critical of Freemasonry. Richard Ryder feels Masonic membership should be like Rotary or the Lions: 'I see no reason for secrecy.' The Hon. Archie Hamilton believes 'their claim to be beneficial to the community. However, secrecy can produce paranoia among outsiders and can be counter-productive.' He therefore feels that MPs and the public servants listed in question 7 should disclose membership. So does one high-ranking member of Mrs Thatcher's 1988 government. In confidence he wrote:

> I have never been certain whether to take Freemasonry seriously or not. On balance I think not. To the extent that I am prepared to take it seriously, I am not sure that I would regard either its initial purposes or its present-day activities either helpful or constructive, so far as society at large is concerned.

David Atkinson is sure they are a 'good' organization, 'but why the need for secrecy? And all the childish "mumbo-jumbo". It does not help their cause!' Sir Paul Hawkins and Andrew Bowden both said they would not join any organization that will not tell you the rules *before* you join. Den Dover was more critical: 'I consider it is a disruptive and unproductive movement, except in fund-raising.' Cecil Franks declined to join because of 'unresolved and questionable "secret" influences'. Robert Key feels it is 'anti-Christian, anti-social' and although it does good work, this is 'negated by the furtiveness which surrounds it'. Michael Mates feels that it 'divides loyalties'.

Sharper criticism came from Labour MPs. Tony Lloyd says: 'At best Freemasonry is childish, at worst a potential perverter of decisions.' Michael Martin feels it is a separate religion (despite its denials) and that, in Scottish factories where he has worked, Masons discriminate in each other's favour. However, another Scot, Martin O'Neill, says that north of the border there are many working-class lodges without the 'insidious influence of the police, legal and business lodges found elsewhere'. He does not believe MPs and public servants should be forced to declare membership because of the 'danger of McCarthyism'. In contrast, former Home Secretary Merlyn Rees feels it should be declared: 'I expect most freemasons are ordinary decent chaps, but "it" is so often a means of advancement.'

Some Labour MPs are even more hostile. A Mason once told Robin Corbett he should join the Craft because it would help his business. Not surprisingly, Corbett feels it must be against the public interest to have this restrictive 'old pals' league' operating among councillors, judges and policemen. John Evans says 'all secret societies tend toward corruption, both of the individual and society'. Ted Leadbitter feels Freemasonry should take every possible initiative to say 'what it is, what it does, what privileges and favours membership bestows. It should be open and accountable'. Hugh MacCartney says: 'There are still too many people in influential positions who consider it their duty to protect their own at the expense and to the detriment of others.'

Most Labour MPs object to Masonry because they are opposed to all secret societies. Alan MacKay says it should be subject to a Freedom of Information Act. Stan Thorne senses, 'its tentacles stretch far and wide and who knows just where and when, and in what circumstances, they operate?' Martin Flannery says it is sexist, racialist and completely anti-democratic: 'It should be illegal.' Robert Parry observed that: 'Stephen Knight's book exposed the danger of Freemasonry in a free society, and he may have died through it.'

All members of Northern Ireland's SDLP and Wales's Plaid Cymru want MPs and public servants to declare Masonic membership. My sole Scottish Nationalist respondent, Gordon Wilson, stated he was not a Mason. Most Liberals are opposed to Freemasonry, but they do not support compulsory declaration. Michael Meadowcroft, who lost his seat in 1987, feels 'insidious secret organizations are not conducive to a healthy, open, liberal society'. He says he greeted an approach to join with 'spontaneous, wild laughter'. Masonry 'needs to be marginalized by promoting counter values of openness, visible dependability and forth-rightness', but he is against a legal ban, because 'banning one secret society catalyses two more into existence'. Liberal elder statesman Richard Wainwright feels that only Ministers of the Crown and those involved in the administration of justice, including JPs, should be compelled to declare Masonic affiliations.

Another non-Mason is Ulster Unionist MP Martyn Smyth, Pres-byterian Minister and Grand Master of the Grand Orange Lodge of

Ireland. Despite strong links between the Orange Order and Free-masonry, Revd Smyth has profound religious objections to Freemasonry (see Chapter 19). Yet he does not believe Masons in public life should be forced to disclose membership, believing that 'general awareness provides a defence against improper influence'.

Of the seven MPs who told me they are Masons, one is an Ulster Unionist: Cecil Walker, MP for Belfast North, who joined the Craft in 1966. Five more are Conservative:

> Sir William Clark, now MP for Croydon South since 1974, has sat in Parliament almost uninterrupted since 1959. Born in 1917, he became a Mason in 1948. He is an accountant and company director.
>
> Anthony Nelson, MP for Chichester since 1974. A merchant banker, he joined Freemasonry in 1969 at the age of twenty-one. He was attracted by the principles of fraternity and the charitable activities: 'It is wholly charitable and commendable. It is sad that ignorance breeds suspicion among some non-Masons.'
>
> Peter Rost, MP for Erewash since 1983 and for Derbyshire SE 1970–83. Born in 1930, he became a Mason in 1960 on his father-in-law's recommendation. An investment adviser, he 'has had no personal experience of any financial or other benefit, privilege or career promotion through Freemasonry – only social enjoyment, like belonging to any other club or social group with mutual interests.'
>
> Tony Baldry, MP for Banbury since 1983. Born in 1950, he is a barrister, publisher and company director. 'I am not aware of any scintilla of a suggestion that MPs who are Freemasons have ever acted as such for their own benefit or against the public good. I think the burden of proof falls on others to show why the groups you list in para. 7 should disclose membership of Freemasonry. I am unaware of any suggestion that any judge has ever used his membership of Freemasonry contrary to the public good.'

The last self-declared Tory Mason also told me he had withdrawn from the order: Sir Anthony Kershaw, MP for Stroud from 1955 until 1987. He was recruited at Oxford University in the 1930s by his tutor. He says he left the Craft at no particular time, so presumably he just faded himself out. He still respects it as 'a charitable and business association, like Rotary'.

The only other 'brother' to reply is also the only one hostile to the fraternity: Stephen Ross, Liberal MP for the Isle of Wight from 1974 until he retired in 1987. He joined Masonry in 1959 but resigned after twelve months because he 'found the ceremonies and general structure unnatural and hypocritical'.

Of Mrs Thatcher's 1988 Cabinet only Kenneth Clarke and John Major completed the questionnaire. Neither is a Mason. Major (who was not in the Cabinet when I wrote to him) stated that all MPs and public servants listed in my question 7 should be obliged to disclose Masonic membership. Nigel Lawson, Douglas Hurd and Malcolm Rifkind did not complete the form but volunteered they are not 'on the square'.

Secretary of the Environment Nicholas Ridley said he was 'not prepared to answer my questions'. Perhaps this has something to do with the fact that his elder brother, the 4th Viscount Ridley, is a leading Freemason. Their ancestor, the first Viscount, was Grand Master of Northumberland for eighteen years. In April 1988 Nicholas Ridley's Ministry introduced a strict legal ban on local authorities imposing their own bans on doing business with companies which have Masonic connections.[3]

Foreign Secretary Sir Geoffrey Howe told me he does not answer questionnaires, but a further ten Cabinet members did not reply: Kenneth Baker, Paul Channon, Norman Fowler, Tom King, John MacGregor, John Moore, Cecil Parkinson, John Wakeham, Peter Walker and George Younger.

Overall, the responses show that Freemasonry causes anxiety among a large proportion of MPs. My 'sample' was only 38 per cent of all male members, but most professional opinion pollsters would be overjoyed with so large a 'sample'. It must be significant that 60 per cent of the respondents believe that key public servants should be obliged to disclose Masonic membership and 58.9 per cent believe MPs should do the same. This majority reflects almost universal disquiet about Freemasonry among Labour MPs, but the Parliamentary balance is tipped because 23 per cent of Conservatives have similar fears.

Such concern has never been reported by Britain's Parliamentary press. Its silence may have something to do with the fact that a second lodge operates in the Palace of Westminster. Thirty-eight years before MPs had their own New Welcome Lodge, the press lobby had set up the Gallery Lodge (no. 1928). Its most eminent member was Sir Alfred Robbins who, as President of the Board of General Purposes 1913–31, was Freemasonry's 'Prime Minister'. He had been initiated in the Gallery in 1888 when he had just become London correspondent for the *Birmingham Daily Post*. He became its Master in 1901, but remained a member of the Westminster press gallery until 1923.

On Robbins's retirement that year, the 'nearly' Prime Minister Austen

Chamberlain told the *Birmingham Post* their correspondent had 'enjoyed in a quite unusual degree the friendship and confidence of men of all political parties, and has shared more secrets than fall to the lot of most men. And in forty years of journalism he has never broken a confidence, written an unfair sentence, or made a personal enemy.' From this Sir Alfred sounds like a perfect Mason, but such compliments from a top politician makes one wonder whether he can have been a perfect journalist!

The Craft's role in British journalism is not explored in this book because I have little information about it. Some reporters have told me that when they started their careers on small-town newspapers they soon discovered their editors were Masons. These men were so stitched in with the local Masonic establishment that no comments hostile to the Craft, or even court reports about the crimes of individual Masons, were ever published. This kind of claim requires a higher level of proof than my sources have been able to supply. Similarly, I have no evidence to support claims that members of the Gallery Lodge have done reporting favours for their Masonic brothers in the House of Commons.

If they ever have, it would be almost impossible to prove such favours had anything to do with Freemasonry. The entire lobby system – of unattributable leaks, unreportable briefings and ministerial whispers – is so corrosive and damaging to open government that it does not need Freemasonry to corrupt it. It is corrupt by definition. MPs and hacks hover round each other so incestuously – each craving the other's favours – that a degenerate sub-Masonic culture permeates their entire dealings. This probably outweighs any mutual aid which may be practised by MPs and journalists who happen to be members of the Craft.

I have still not answered a fundamental question: is Freemasonry today the very Tory Party in Aprons which the New Welcome Lodge was founded to prevent? Is the Craft's active political membership now so one-sidedly Conservative that all its protestations of political non-involvement are self-delusion?

Of thirty-six Masons whom I have identified in the House of Lords, twenty-three are Conservatives, eight are 'Independents' (which usually means unaffiliated Tories), two are Social Democrats, one is Labour, one Liberal and one undeclared. In the House of Commons there are five self-declared Masons: four Conservative and one Ulster Unionist. As only 116 male Tories out of 379 (30.6 per cent) answered my questionnaire there are probably another dozen Masons on the Tory benches. One is certainly David Sumberg, MP for Bury South, a past Master of Smith-Child Lodge (no. 2064) in Stoke-on-Trent; another was Stefan Terlezki, MP for Cardiff West 1983–7, who belongs to Dinas Llandaf

Lodge (no. 8512). Yet another is Gary Waller, MP for Keighley, who was initiated in Brighouse's Clifton Lodge (no. 7112). There must also be a few closet Masons in the Parliamentary Labour Party, but as all Labour MPs who did reply (47.4 per cent of the entire PLP) volunteered they are not 'on the square', it seems the Craft is even more 'Tory' now than it was in the 1920s.

A party is not just its MPs, of course, but a mass movement throughout the land. Freemasonry may still be strong in some local Labour parties, trade unions and the Co-operative movement (see Chapter 26). Indeed, recent attempts by the Scottish Co-op to force disclosure of Masonic membership were blocked by the movement's own Masons. Even so, Labour's Masonic element is minuscule compared to the Tories'.

The current chairman of English Freemasonry's finance committee is Sir Peter Lane. He was formerly Chairman of the National Union of Conservative Associations and is now its vice president. Earlier Masonic NUCA chairmen have included the late Sir Herbert Redfearn (a prominent West Yorkshire Tory) and Sir Edward Brown. Tory politics in cities such as Leeds and Westminster, and counties including Cheshire, Worcestershire and Essex, have all been dominated by local brethren. Grand Lodge may argue that the party activities of individual Masons have nothing to do with their 'Masonics', and that any Masons who discuss politics in the lodge are breaching Masonic law. However, the prevailing Tory ethos of the Craft today can only lay it open to attack from other parties: not just ridicule on the hustings but legislative onslaught from Parliament itself. For my part, I think legislation concerning Freemasonry is not only likely in the next decade. It is also necessary, but not for political reasons. In the conclusion to this book I make a few suggestions.

PART FIVE

Masonic Troubles

thirty-five

PLAIN TALES OF THE LODGE

In February 1985 a Freemason wrote to Stephen Knight lamenting the decline of his lodge. He offered to reveal more, but Stephen was so ill that they never met. In 1986 I wrote to the man and explained my interest. We met at a pub where he talked of his disillusion. His story was outrageous but he produced authentic Masonic papers confirming much of what he said. I then gathered evidence from non-Masonic sources which corroborated his claims and convinced me his other tales were true. The material is so strong that if I named the 'villains' they would not sue for libel but, to avoid reprisals, my informant wishes to remain anonymous. This means I cannot name the men who might strike back or the lodge to which they belong. I shall call the man 'George' and say he is a retired sales representative living in the north of the country. This is his story.

I became a Freemason in the late 1950s, and was installed as Master fifteen years later. Ours was an old boys' lodge – we had all been to the same grammar school – but there came a time when we weren't able to recruit enough genuine old boys. After a lot of agonizing we threw the membership open. This was the beginning of the end. I'm not a snob – ours wasn't a school you could be very snobby about. It's just that we no longer had a way of measuring the candidates or any solid excuse for keeping people out.

First, I'll give you an example of the kind of person who *didn't* want to join. One of our Past Masters was a prominent local undertaker. He took his son into the business and he desperately wanted him in Freemasonry too. The son would have none of it. No matter what pressure his father applied, he refused to join. This so upset the father that he fired him from the family firm. The boy wasn't going to stand for this. He fought the dismissal in various court cases, but he lost every time. Of course, the one thing he couldn't mention was Freemasonry. He had no way of proving this was the real reason why his dad had sacked him. Anyway, the court officials might have been Masons themselves. It would have killed his claim stone dead. Masons, of course, are told that their own families should come first!

I have to admit that, although the father had been to the same school as myself, he was a rogue: an 'ambulance chaser'. He had a deal going with a policeman who was also a member of our lodge. This copper worked as a Coroner's officer, and whenever someone died and needed a decent burial, he would call up our brother-Mason in the funeral parlour. The undertaker would then rush round to the mortuary or the home of the grieving family and Boaz!: he had another funeral to arrange. Death is big business, of course, so he could afford to give the Coroner's officer £50 for every corpse. It was all done 'on the square'.

Eventually someone found out about this arrangement and reported the policeman to his chief. Our man was suddenly transferred to outdoor PC Plod duties. His earnings plunged because he no longer had any bodies to 'sell'. One night in our lodge bar he was talking with our worshipful brother, the undertaker. The next we knew, he had left the police and was working for our colleague as a pall-bearer.

I never found Freemasonry any help in my business, but I think it's fair to say that three-quarters of people use it as a way of developing business or getting on. It's also a boon when you're retired, especially if you move to somewhere like Devon where otherwise people won't talk to you for years.

It also brings unexpected benefits, as I discovered when visiting a friend's lodge. We were having dinner at the festive board when the chief Customs officer at the local airport stood up and made a speech. He said: 'Now you all know me. If any of you have trouble with any of my lads, just call for me and I'll sort it out.' I was astonished. I thought Customs men weren't corrupt. Maybe he didn't mean he would turn a blind eye to smuggling, but it still sounded like an offer to interfere with the course of justice.

I was appalled at the hypocrisy of Freemasonry. It claims to welcome men of all races, colours and creeds, yet whenever someone in our lodge suggested asking a West Indian or a Pakistani if they'd like to join, the majority would retort: 'He's black, isn't he? Oh we can't have anyone like that!' There are a few blacks in Freemasonry in England, but they tend to join 'ghetto' lodges where practically everyone is non-white. So much for Brotherly Love.

There are two other prime Masonic virtues, Relief and Truth, but Relief – or Charity – isn't our strong point either. At our Masonic Hall some years ago a man was going through his initiation ceremony when he had a heart attack and died. Some weeks later his widow asked if the lodge could assist her financially, as she had heard Freemasonry was a charitable organization. She was astonished to receive a reply saying she wasn't entitled to any charity, because her husband had collapsed *before* taking the Obligation so he had never become a Freemason.

Such heartlessness contrasts with an astonishing laxity over the criminality of brother Masons. You probably know what a Tyler is. He's the guard who sits outside the lodge room while the ritual is in progress to stop strangers from getting in and seeing what goes on. Most Tylers serve a number of lodges. They're usually poorly off, so £12 a meeting and a meal is quite a good deal for them. Well, one night our Tyler was caught 'importuning' at the local public toilet. It was one of those underground toilets, and the 'gay' problem got so bad that they had to shut it down and cement it over. Our Tyler was convicted and sent to prison for two years, but he was never expelled from Freemasonry.

Our lodge policeman (the same one who later became the pall-bearer) used to check to see if any would-be members had criminal records. About ten years ago it was made a crime for policemen to check criminal records on police computers for private purposes. Doing a check on behalf of the lodge obviously had no official justification, but nothing would ever happen to a copper who does this, because in this country Freemasonry and the police are so intertwined.

This officer came up trumps one day when the membership committee considered the application of a local doctor. Apparently the man had gone on holiday and given a friend permission to use his front garden and driveway to repair second-hand cars. You can imagine what it was like for the house-proud residents of a leafy suburban avenue to have their high summer tranquillity ruined by a lot of paint-burners, spray-guns, discarded tyres, blaring radios and foul-mouthed mechanics. Even worse, the cars turned out to be stolen!

The neighbours took legal action. Our copper told us that the doctor would soon be up in court and there would probably be some bad publicity in the local newspapers. Several members of the committee, including myself, felt this doctor wasn't a man we wanted in the lodge, but at this stage nothing had been proved against him.

Every candidate to join a lodge must have two backers: a proposer and a seconder. They may take it as a personal insult if their candidate is rejected. In this case the proposer wrong-footed us by arranging for the doctor to be balloted for and initiated on the same night. This meant that even as we were deciding whether to let him in, he was outside expecting to be admitted. The ballot is secret. Every lodge member is handed a white ball which he may discreetly drop in either the 'Yea' or 'Nay' drawer within a ballot box. If the 'Nay' drawer is found to contain more than one ball, a candidate is automatically barred. Well, this doctor was 'blackballed' by seven members. His proposer went crazy. He threatened that he and his blood brother would walk out of the lodge that night, otherwise he could never look the doctor in the face again. He demanded another vote, but this time round there were still five balls in the 'Nay' drawer. At this point all visitors [Masons from other lodges] were asked to leave.

The proposer was now homicidal and repeated his threat. Seeing he was determined to have his way, but wishing to save the lodge, five of the original blackballers promptly resigned. The other two – including myself – refused to vote. On the next round: Surprise! Surprise! There were no 'Nay' balls. The doctor was admitted and duly initiated. A few days later his case came up, he was convicted and given a conditional discharge. That fact would have been enough for the committee to have stopped his name being put to the vote, but of course it wasn't available to us at the time. We realized this was the reason why the whole process had been rushed through in just one evening. What a poor show!

I soon resigned, but was then the victim of an extraordinary freezing-out process. Men I had known for decades, at school and in Freemasonry, would cut me dead. I was 'sent to Coventry'. I became a non-person. It spilled over on to my wife. She found that other Masons' wives whom she had met at ladies' nights and other social occasions for twenty years would stare right through her or cross the road to avoid contact. Rather than punish the proposer for his monstrous manipulation, vote-rigging and histrionics, the brethren had closed ranks and ostracized their former colleagues who had tried to maintain Masonic standards. No doubt they had vowed to cast me in the role of a 'wilfully perjured individual, devoid of all moral worth, and totally unfit to be received into this worshipful Lodge', as it says in the first degree. Of course, I hadn't betrayed any Masonic secret but I had dared to stand up to a bully. I suppose I should be thankful I wasn't found swinging under Blackfriars Bridge.

You may think all this fuss over repairing a few stolen cars in a residential street is too 'petty bourgeois' for belief, but this doctor was dangerous. He used to treat private patients for obesity, but was later struck off by the General Medical Council for giving them the wrong drugs. They say you can never get a doctor struck off unless another doctor testifies against him, which means almost never. In this case other doctors did give evidence, so he must have been doing something pretty bad.

I checked with the GMC, which kindly sent me its Professional Conduct Committee's judgement on the man. This confirmed George's story. Indeed, the full truth was far worse. The doctor had been found guilty of giving patients amphetamine, thyroid extract and other drugs repeatedly and over long periods, without properly examining them, without checking their medical history and without consulting their general practitioners. He never told the GPs what drugs he had given the patients or in what dosages.

The facts in a second charge were 'not proved': that he had issued medical certificates to a woman stating she was suffering from glandular fever, 'whereas you should have known that it was more probable . . . she was suffering from the adverse effects of drugs supplied by you'. He told the woman's GP he hadn't seen her for three months when he had given her drugs only two weeks before. The committee was 'appalled', found the doctor guilty of serious professional misconduct and, after an unsuccessful appeal, erased him from the GMC Register. What impact did this grubby affair have on the lodge? George made further inquiries.

In fairness to the doctor, I must say he immediately offered to resign but the secretary told him that, if he went on the non-dining list and laid low for a while, the cloud would soon blow over. This way he would not have to quit. The brethren displayed this spirit of 'forgiveness' only because the lodge had lost so many members in the row over his admission that they couldn't afford to lose any more. They needed his fees!

thirty-six

FALLING MASONRY

'One of the greatest projects that Freemasonry in the United Kingdom has seen.'

Thus spake the chairman of the Central London Masonic Centre in 1978, the year the brotherhood bought Clerkenwell's eighteenth-century courthouse and began its transformation into a Masonic shrine. To men who claim descent from England's cathedral-builders it seemed only fitting to buy a beautiful but run-down pile in the heart of London and make it good again. By the 1970s it was also an economic necessity. Many London lodges were alarmed at the increasing cost of meeting and eating on non-Masonic premises: in banqueting rooms, hotels and pubs. There was no more room at Freemasons' Hall, so when the courthouse came up for sale it seemed an ideal place to conduct both ritual and recreation.

The building was bought for £500,000. It was estimated that a further £500,000 would be needed for refurbishment and fittings. The money would be raised by 300 lodges each putting up an unsecured investment or 'Debenture' of £3,000, which would leave £100,000 in the kitty as working capital. Things did not work out this way. By June 1980 only 225 lodges were using the centre, and they were £91,000 behind on contributions. This would not have mattered if reconstruction had cost no more than £500,000, but it cost more than twice as much, and interest was still accruing. The builders were owed £777,000 and the bank £140,000. There was no way of paying them off, so each lodge had to kiss £3,000 goodbye. They were not pleased, so they set up a debenture holders' committee to 'investigate certain complaints and alleged irregularities'. Their report was devastating.[1]

We have been informed that no professional building survey was carried out prior to the purchasing of the freehold. Structural

problems were discovered . . . by the builders, whose estimated
figure was £640,000 but which had been considerably increased to
over £1 million.

There was no written contract for the job. The project manager was
given no terms of responsibility and no limits of discretion. As a 'listed
building' the courthouse was entitled to a public grant worth up to half
the cost of reconstruction. No correct application was made so no grant
was given. The directors then hoped to save the project by raising a
£500,000 loan against the building's increased value.

At the beginning of this venture we were told that the building had
value in excess of £1 million. The recent valuation puts a value of
£500,000 . . . This naturally had an effect on the Directors' plans.[2]

No doubt it did. Having spent a millon pounds, they were told the
place was worth no more than they had originally paid for it because of
'its very specialized use'. There is no market for second-hand Masonic
Temples! Meantime the centre lost £93,000 in one year's trading,
including 'a very large loss' on catering. The restaurant had to be closed
and outside caterers brought in, yet the brethren continued to moan
about the food and the price of drinks. Overall, reported the committee,
'administration is obviously lacking'. The centre could be kept going
only if lodges handed over even more money.

It should be noted that the original idea of the centre was well-
conceived, but was under-capitalized and operated by enthusiastic
amateurs . . . It should have been obvious a scheme of this
magnitude must of necessity be operated as a strict business
operation, and Masons must not expect to get 'Masonry on the
cheap'.

A desperate package was devised. In return for the lost £3,000 each
lodge would get one £1 company share, and would pay a £1,000 levy. A
further £350,000 would be raised by issuing £25 bonds to lodge members.
Meantime the builders agreed to accept £500,000 by March 1981, wait
three years for the rest, and charge no more interest. The package
worked. Most debts have now been paid and the centre trades at a profit.
Four hundred lodges and chapters meet there and brethren no longer
complain about the food. One question remains. How could a fraternity
whose name, symbols and rituals honour the finest traditions of the
master builder lose so much money on one construction job?

Financial mismanagement is one of Masonry's chronic problems, especially at lodge level where amateurism and incompetence often go hand-in-hand. In 1986 one treasurer made this appeal to the members of his lodge:

V Dear Bro.,
I took over the treasurership in June, and having studied the books, I am appalled. There are no entries in either the cash book or ledger since 1983. All records since then are on sheets of paper, often undated, and only occasionally match the amount banked. No accounts were presented for 1984/85 and the 1985/86 dues slips were not sent out at all. As a result the Lodge has debts of £450. Please pay your own dues as soon as possible.

This lodge's problems seem to have been caused by laziness, but sometimes the trouble is more serious. From 1960 to 1988 only twelve Masons were expelled from the Craft by the Grand Lodge of England.[3] Two had committed Masonic disciplinary offences:

1961 – W Bro. S. of Transvaal, South Africa. Joined a quasi-Masonic order and refused to resign.
1964 – Bro. L. of West Lancashire. A Fellow Craft (second degree) Mason attended meetings in the third degree.

Three others had stolen Masonic funds:

1979 – Bro. G. of Natal, South Africa. Treasurer, misappropriated lodge funds and committed forgery.
1988 – W Bro. M. of Cheshire. Misappropriated funds from the Gorsey Hay Masonic hostel.
1988 – A brother in Nigeria. Misappropriated lodge funds.

If this were Freemasonry's full 'criminal record' since 1960, it would be remarkably good for a movement which claims between 250,000 and 500,000 members. Yet it seems most Masons caught with their hands in the fraternal till resign before anyone complains to Grand Lodge. Others are 'excluded' by their lodge and do not appeal, in which case Grand Lodge does not feel obliged to 'expel' them. Most crimes do not result in expulsions. For instance, none followed the 1987 conviction of two Sussex Masons for illegally selling alcohol at Crawley Masonic Hall. The licence for the hall, where four lodges meet, permitted drink to be sold only to Masons, but for eighteen months non-Masons boozed away. One defendant, Paul Abbott, was a Past Master of Worth Lodge (no. 7496). He claimed the entire hall committee knew what was going on. Even after the police raid (led by the hall secretary), one committee member used it for his own wedding reception. Many non-Masons, including the blessed bride, downed champagne with no thought for the law. Abbott and his co-defendant John Byrd claimed they were victims of an internal Masonic feud.

Far worse offences occurred at Gillingham Masonic Club in Kent. From 1984 to 1986 treasurer Bernard Morris stole £21,000 by forging signatures on club cheques. In 1988 he was sent to prison for two years, but blame must fall on the Masons who had given him the job. Morris had once been a pillar of society, a Justice of the Peace, but in 1984 he was given a two-year suspended sentence on sixteen counts of theft from a building society. In 1985 he was bankrupted with debts of £198,000. His brother Masons may have thought they were doing him a favour by paying him £1,000 a year to look after the club accounts, but they were putting him in a position where he faced irresistible temptation.

Masons are reluctant to unleash the full force of law against an offending brother. Their dilemma is clear from a letter which I received from the son of the late Sir George Evetts, Master of Ewell Lodge (no. 1851) some fifty years ago.

In 1932 I persuaded my father to buy me a motor-cycle. He quibbled for days as to paying £35 instead of £30 which he considered ample, and kept on lecturing me 'on the value of money'. Eventually he gave in and I thanked him. The sequel came in 1941 when I was serving as an officer in the RNVR.

One Saturday afternoon Father was driving with Mother to Croydon for a very important Lodge meeting. On the outskirts of the town the bombs began to fall and she begged him to abandon the trip. He refused and stated the meeting was very important and he *must* attend. When I came home on leave in 1942 Mother told me of this incident and said,

'The blessed Masons are more important than any of us. I will now tell you that ten years ago, three weeks after Father argued about an extra £5 for your motor-bike, the telephone rang. It was the Master of the Lodge telling Father that the Treasurer had left his wife and taken the Lodge's funds of £1,300 – plus a lady friend! Father offered between £600 and £800 as his share towards making up the loss. I told him he should not give his hard-earned money to protect a rogue. His reply was to sulk in his study and say, "You do not understand. As a well-to-do brother, I am honour-bound to replace so much, so that we do not prosecute." '

Keeping the brotherhood out of court is still a Masonic virtue. In 1986 I met a man who had hinted in a letter at odd events in his own Masonic experience. He was a bachelor, a former army officer, living in a delightful English holiday spot. After talking to him on the telephone, I expected to meet a well-to-do Colonel Blimp in his sixties, basking in comfortable retirement. When I arrived at his home I found a broken man in a tiny flat on a vandalized council estate. We talked about his family, his distinguished war record, his long service as a JP, and the fine seaside hotel he had owned and run until 1977. Naturally I wanted to know what had brought him to this sorry pass. In explaining, he said he did not mind me telling his story in this book but he asked me to change his name. I therefore call him 'Edgar'.

About 1972 Edgar was slandered by two brothers at a Masonic function in a prestigious local yacht club. They had told two other Masons and a woman neighbour who was a guest, that he was grossly neglecting his widowed mother, and that he owed them £10,000 but was claiming he could not pay it back because he had cancer. None of this was true but, as three witnesses had told him of these remarks, Edgar felt he must sue for slander. He instructed his solicitor to issue a writ. However, the solicitor was an ardent Mason in both Craft and Royal Arch.

Some weeks later an elderly man came into Edgar's hotel and asked to see him. He introduced himself as Major-General Allan Adair, but his full title was Sir Allan Adair GCVO, CB, DSO, MC, DL, JP. Sir Allan (who died in 1988) was not only a distinguished retired soldier and a war hero. At this time he was also deputy Grand Master of United Grand Lodge: the third highest Mason in England. He engaged Edgar in conversation and then broached the subject of the forthcoming court case. Edgar was astonished that he knew anything about it, but Adair explained that Edgar's solicitor had told him. Edgar was shocked, for this meant his solicitor had committed a gross breach of confidence. Adair did not seem to be concerned about that, but he pleaded with Edgar to drop the case because it would 'bring Freemasonry into disrepute'.

Adair asked Edgar how many people would believe what the two men had said. 'Nobody who knows me,' Edgar replied. 'Then forget it,' suggested Adair. Edgar retorted that Freemasonry had already been brought into disrepute by the admission of his two slanderers, both of whom were convicts. He knew this because he was chairman of a nearby prison visitors' board. Prison sources had revealed that the pair were among five local villains with long records who were all Masons. Edgar was shocked. He knew several of them had sought initiation in local lodges but had been blackballed.

He made further inquiries and found out they had all sneaked into the

Craft by boarding a ferry from Weymouth to France, where they were rushed through all three degree rituals in one weekend. They had become 'bucket-shop' Masons in a lodge of the Grand Loge Nationale Française, which is recognized by the Grand Lodge of England. At this time anyone could do this if he knew a friendly Mason with French connections and was prepared to pay for his travel. The deal cost around £100. Back in England these new 'Master Masons' could attend any local lodge as a guest and later as joining members in their own right.

When Edgar recounted this seedy saga, he says Adair told him that Grand Lodge knew what was going on in France but could do nothing about it. Eventually Edgar agreed to drop the slander action, largely because he had been a career soldier like Adair. The Major-General (a Grenadier Guardsman, on and off, for nearly sixty years) had pulled rank on Edgar – emotionally at least.

Having heard this extraordinary but credible tale, I was still no wiser as to why Edgar was now destitute and stuck in this council flat. That too was due to the intervention of his brother Mason, the solicitor. In 1977 Edgar had sold his hotel for £70,000, intending to live off the income and rent a spacious flat. For a few years things went well, until his solicitor introduced him to another Mason, a smooth-talking charmer who worked in the City of London. He offered to invest Edgar's £70,000, an offer which the old soldier assumed was honourable. Alas, the City slicker was a swindler. He stole Edgar's money (and many other people's), fled the country and now lives in style on Spain's Costa del Crime. Edgar was ruined. He moved out of his rented flat and threw himself on the mercy of the State.

By the time I had heard this awful story, I was beguiled by the victim and very angry on his behalf. I offered to pursue the fraudster and invoke the power of the press (such as it is) to bring him to justice. Edgar might even get some money back. Yet Edgar did not want to cause trouble. Legal counsel in London had advised there would be more chance of getting the money back if there were no publicity. This seemed to me a ludicrous proposition but the soldier would not be moved. Not long ago Edgar sent me a letter.

Only one piece of bad news: I will never see any of my money again and as far as I am concerned it is now a dead letter. Now the good news. An old friend made overtures to a retired officers' organiz-ation on my behalf. I was immediately offered help which leaves me with no financial worries AT ALL. I am not now one of the filthy rich, but a modest outlook is ensured. I am even promised a place in an officers' retirement home. I have been to see it and it really does resemble a top flight London club, set in glorious countryside.

Even the Freemasons seem to be chipping in with some financial help. I have always been, and remain, a fairly staunch Mason, which does not prevent me from recognizing and deploring abuse where it occurs. The stories I told you are true and accurate, but they could happen anywhere. Every organization I have been connected with – Masonry, Rotary, the Magistracy – has had its sins and omissions ever since time 'immoral'! Best wishes, Edgar.

A less forgiving view is taken by another Mason JP who claims that in the late 1970s £35,000 a year was evaporating within Leicester's Freemasons' Hall. In 1978 David Morris of St Martin's Lodge (no. 3431) noticed some brethren had stopped attending because of the soaring price of meals. He checked the hall's accounts and deduced that ingredients were costed at 69 per cent of each meal's total price: when brethren paid £4.90 for a meal, they were being charged £3.38 for the ingredients. When Morris bought the same ingredients in local shops they came to only £1.20 a portion, so he realized that each diner was being overcharged by £2.18. At that time the hall was serving 22,000 meals a year, so up to £47,000 was disappearing. It was certainly not reappearing as a surplus in the Hall accounts, for in 1977–8 'Catering' made a profit of only £1,330.

Morris consulted colleagues and then raised his findings with the hall chairman, Tom Stops (Leicestershire's deputy Grand Master). He asked Morris to write a detailed letter, which Stops promptly gave to the hall treasurer, Geoffrey Jackson. Morris was appalled: by alerting Jackson so early, Stops made an effective inquiry very difficult. Jackson was naturally perturbed, for Morris's figures implied someone had their hands in the Masonic till. He was rattled by one Morris phrase: 'serious implications.' As Jackson had signed the cheques to pay for all food ordered by the chef, did Morris mean *he* was seriously implicated? Jackson rebuked Morris for going behind his back. He said his accounts were in order and had been approved by internal Masonic auditors.

Morris was a Mason of only ten years' standing, a mere assistant lodge secretary, but in the 'profane' world he was a Bachelor of Science and a chartered surveyor, much of whose work was estimating the true cost of materials. His anxieties were shared by an accountant named Bagshaw. Together they sought a convincing explanation from the hall committee. It gave them none, approved the suspect accounts and demanded that any future complaints should be raised not by Morris but by senior lodge officials.

Ignoring Masonic lines of command, Morris increased the pressure. He consulted two brother Masons who lectured in catering at a local college. They calculated the disputed meal's ingredients cost £1.69 a head.

This was more than Morris's £1.20, but enough to indicate a yearly discrepancy of £37,000. When Treasurer Jackson disgorged his figures, even these showed £10,000 was disappearing. After one year's pressure Morris and Bagshaw met Leicestershire's Grand Master. He expressed total confidence in the staff and said it was most unlikely anything was wrong. He did not want an inquiry because it would cause resignations and disrupt catering, but he asked if anyone was suspected. The pair replied that without an inquiry it was impossible to say why there was a discrepancy. They then invoked the 'Public Interest', suggesting their complaints might form the basis of criminal proceedings. This was such a bombshell that next day the Provincial Grand Secretary asked the men's lodge to 'deal with them as a matter of the utmost urgency'. However, far from silencing the trouble-makers, the lodge said there 'appears to be a prima facie' case and passed the buck back up.

Now one of Britain's leading caterers, Brother Robert Smith (catering boss of the National Exhibition Centre), costed a meal which he had just eaten at the Masonic Hall. He found the price 'way out', noted his colleagues had also complained, and said 'it is quite apparent to me there is no catering policy and the chef gives a price off his head'. He also reported that the fried scampi was 'very poor quality crumbed'.

A committee was set up to 'look into the catering' but, when it assessed the meals, it did not cost like for like. It substituted 'Jumbo' scampi – at over £1 a head – for the 'very poor quality crumbed' scampi consumed and condemned by the expert Smith. It also insisted Smith and the other catering experts cost a meal including this 'Jumbo' scampi, even though it had only just swum into the freezer. Such devices procured a report which 'completely refuted' Morris and Bagshaw's 'assertions'. Thus spake the Provincial Grand Master who told the rebellious duo:

> The Committee unanimously concludes there was no substance in your complaints, the food served was first-class in quality and was not in any way unreasonable in price, all food was properly checked in and properly booked out to Lodges, there was no evidence of improper invoicing of food or wines and no evidence of any defalcation or inefficiency . . . I hope you will now feel able forthwith to withdraw your allegations which have caused much unnecessary worry to many. Yours fraternally, Gayton Taylor.

Refusing to bow down, the pair said they could not comment until they had seen the entire report. They also asked how the three eminent caterers' original costings had been dismissed. In response, the PGM ordered every Leicester lodge secretary to read out a statement whitewashing the accounts which, he said, had been 'kept meticulously'. He also took the

> gravest possible view of people starting 'hares' of this nature, and emphasizes that the results of this inquiry should be a lesson to everyone who is prone to instigate assertions of this kind. It could not only be prejudicial to goodwill in the Province but verging on non-masonic conduct, and this is most reprehensible.

Morris and Bagshaw knew this statement was itself unjust and therefore un-Masonic. Far from being 'kept meticulously', the hall's books contained no records linking food purchases with the content of meals sold, so to claim there was no evidence of defalcation or theft was highly misleading. The only reasonable assumption was that there had been a Masonic cover-up.

In 1980 they brought the matter to the attention of Grand Secretary Michael Higham. He saw no reason to interfere with the Provincial Grand Master's jurisdiction. Morris resigned from his lodge in disgust in 1983 but, on learning that the discrepancy was continuing, he notified Leicestershire Police of possible fraud. Such a complaint from a JP demanded action. A senior detective looked into it, but a few weeks later Morris received a letter saying no action was being taken because 'the Freemasons' organization have conducted inquiries and made no complaint to the police about irregularities'. The Inland Revenue proved more forthcoming. Its high-powered investigation branch, the Special Office, wrote to Morris to say his suspicions were 'well founded', but the tax men could do nothing because there had been no loss of revenue.

The public image of Leicester's Masons was thus preserved. They may have been defrauded of £200,000 but, by ensuring there was no criminal trial, they avoided falling 'into disrepute'. Yet the questions remain. What *did* happen to the large purchases of food stated on the receipts? Did it all exist and, if so, was it all delivered to Freemasons' Hall? Clearly there was a large excess which was never consumed on the premises and, in any case, why was all the food being bought in London when wholesalers in Leicester itself were just as cheap? What was going on will never be known because no one – except Brothers Morris and Bagshaw – ever really wanted to find out.

thirty-seven

CHARITY BEGINS AT HOME

Is Freemasonry now 'in great measure directed to charitable purposes', as the Unlawful Societies Act claimed – rightly or wrongly – in 1799? Yes, if photo-spreads in many local newspapers are to be believed. Their less-informed readers might assume that giving money away is *all* the Masons do, for their good works are trumpeted as loudly as those of every other do-gooding club and fraternity in Britain's complex social web. Today when Masons go a-fund-raising, press cameras are never far away.

In Abergavenny an elderly Mason is snapped knitting a ten-foot length of scarf to raise money for an old folks' home. In Oxfordshire a Masonic Hall serves as a day-time drop-in centre for Age Concern. Shropshire Masons give a £2,000 electro-therapy machine to a cottage hospital. Yorkshire Masonic charities support a spastics' workshop and sailing clubs for the disabled. In Solihull the Muscular Dystrophy Group and two local nursing homes share a £2,000 fraternal hand-out. A Leeds lodge hands over £100 to a hospice fund. Huddersfield Masons give £4,060 to a bodyscanner appeal while Wiltshire brethren hand £8,000 to another. Nottingham Masons fund Guide Dogs for the Blind, the Salvation Army, a local brass band (to buy new instruments), physically-handicapped Brownies, a housing project for homeless youngsters, the Zeebrugge ferry disaster fund and several local medical appeals. Masons in South Wales give £1,100 to the principality's Trust for Sick Children for a cardiac unit. In Cornwall they buy a new ambulance for a Leonard Cheshire Home. In Lancashire they put up £500 to purchase laser equipment for eye surgery. In Aberdeen a Masonic cheque goes to a Church home for mentally-handicapped boys and girls. Masons on Merseyside support seaside holidays for deprived children. In Blackpool they buy an insulin pump to help diabetics.

In February 1988 Gloucestershire Masons hold a Grand Ball, where frolicking brethren and their families give cheques worth £18,500 to Save the Children and local charities. 'We are particularly pleased to be able to mark the occasion with substantial donations,' says the Provincial Grand Master, 'helping others being one of the main principles of our activities.'[1] In Lancashire a local lodge 'throws a lifeline' to a Pennine mountain rescue team with a £250 donation: 'We are most grateful to the Freemasons for their gift. If all our responses were as positive, our future would be assured.' Not far off in Teesdale the brethren give £100 to the Guard-a-Grannie campaign, to fit spy-holes and chain-locks to old folks' front doors.

In the later 1980s hundreds of stories about Masonic charity appeared in Britain's local press, usually adorned by photos of four or five people thrusting blown-up cheques into the camera lens. The tribe that for so long hid its face from man – and woman – is now publicizing itself with stunts as brash as those of any betting shop, building society or superstore. In June 1987 the *Kent Evening Post* explained why.

BUILDING A NEW IMAGE

Masons have been told to build a new image and 'go public' on some of their good works. That's why the cameras were there to record this cheque hand over at the special care baby unit in All Saints Hospital, Chatham. Howard Mark, worshipful master of the Peace and Unity Lodge in Gillingham, is shown giving Dr Tony Ducker £250 for a baby breather alarm.

Mr Mark explained: 'We've had a directive from above to let the world know what's going on. In the past we've done lots for local charities, but many have been under the misapprehension that all our money goes back into Masonic funds. It's simply not the case, and we're under orders in a way to bring things to light.'[2]

In 1988 a bashful tale appeared in the *Aldershot News and Mail*: 'Hospice receives gift from a Mr X.' A photo of a (physically) huge cheque for £1,000 from Ash and Ash Vale Masons had a coy caption about the Craft's charity usually going 'unpublicized due to strict anonymity. However, the *News* was invited to photograph the ceremony provided names were not mentioned.' These days anything· positive about Freemasonry gets good coverage, and beaming brethren are usually only too happy to be named.[3]

When people hustle publicity for their acts of giving, fair comment on their less attractive deeds is often stifled, which may be just what the donors intend. History is littered with the lives of public benefactors who, in other respects, were tyrants, rogues and thieves. Even that Masonic hero, the Earl of Moira, whose generosity was legendary and whose tear-jerking charity towards a brother Mason's widow is recounted in Chapter 31, died owing far more money than he ever gave away. A brother Mason, Sir Walter Scott, dug a fit grave for his one-time friend in 1826:

> Poor old honour and glory is dead – once Lord Moira, latterly Lord Hastings. He was a man of very considerable talents but had an overmastering degree of vanity of the grandest kind . . . He died, having the credit, or having had the credit, to leave more debt than any man since Caesar's time. £1,200,000 is said to be the least.[4]

Commitment to any worthy cause should never be derided, yet scores of groups do work as good as the Freemasons, without sharing their urge to dress up in aprons and perform bizarre rituals. 'Community Action' is the name which the *Yorkshire Evening Post* gives to a weekly column on the charity efforts of local Rotary, Round Table and Lions groups. Some of their members are also Masons who presumably have a sense of service to the entire community. Yet if helping non-Masons were a Mason's *main* aim, he could do it just as well *outside* the lodge. The brotherhood's external charity is irrelevant to any assessment of its other aspects.

Also, as Christian theologians have observed, the more Masons emphasize their *giving*, the more they appear guilty of the Pelagian heresy: that good works rather than faith in Christ is the path to eternal life. As the Church of England Working Group put it, charity 'is not to be equated with Christianity. The Christian faith sees its charitable giving as a response to the love of God in Christ (not just a response to human need) and as an integral part of the mission of God in the world. "Buying your way into Heaven" is impossible.'[5]

Of course, non-Christian Masons do not have to worry about this problem but all brethren are taught the undiluted Pelagian idea that 'by square conduct, level steps and upright intentions we hope to ascend to those immortal mansions whence all goodness emanates'.[6] A Mason's 'working tools' – square, level and plumb rule – all 'teach us to bear in mind, and act according to, the laws of our Divine Creator, that, when we shall be summoned from this sub-lunary abode, we may ascend to the Grand Lodge above, where the world's Great Architect lives and reigns forever'.[7]

Whether Masonic generosity to non-Masonic charities springs from human kindness, the urge to book seats in heaven or a PR strategy to 'buy off' public opinion, a lot of 'under the moon' giving goes on. Just as local lodges hand out money to local causes, so England's Grand Charity gives nationwide. In 1986–7 it disbursed £504,000 for 'non-Masonic charitable purposes'.

In recent years the beneficiaries have included the Royal Marsden Hospital and the Liverpool School of Tropical Medicine (£100,000 each); the universities of Oxford (£45,000 for research into premature brain disease), Cambridge (£250,000 for a professorship of Clinical Gerontology), Nottingham and Wales (£175,000 and £100,000 respectively for research into Health Care of the Elderly); the Mental Health Foundation (£250,000); and more than seventy hospices across the country (a total of £250,000).

Jokers have mused if this list, biased towards the old, the dying, the brain-diseased and the mentally ill, proves yet again that Masons only 'look after their own'. When Cambridge explained that its new Professor of Gerontology would be trying to understand 'the effects of human ageing and find ways to prevent them', one newspaper exclaimed: 'So the Freemasons are now in pursuit of immortality.'[8] Such sarcasm may have encouraged the Grand Charity in 1988 to give £250,000 to a younger cause: the Great Ormond Street Hospital for Sick Children.

On close examination it emerges that many non-Masonic charities supported by Masonic donations in recent years have strong Masonic connections. The St David's Foundation, a hospice in Newport, gets regular donations from the Grand Charity. The hospice president, Sir Maynard Jenour, is a prominent Freemason. In 1980 Grand Lodge gave £300,000 to the Royal National Lifeboat Institution to build a lifeboat. *The Duchess of Kent* was duly launched in 1982 by the Duchess of Kent. It was no coincidence that the RNLI President is England's Grand Master, the Duke of Kent. Of course, the Craft might have paid for a boat anyway. Masons have been giving large sums for lifeboats for 100 years. Also the Duchess of Kent is a woman of near-saintly goodness, worthy of far more than a lifeboat in her name. Yet as one Masonic MP told me, one reason why the RNLI has received so much money was that 'we like to keep even our external donations in-house'. Grand Secretary Higham also remembers the Grand Master's 'almost mischievous pleasure' in giving the lifeboat on behalf of Grand Lodge to himself as President of the RNLI.[9]

Other non-Masonic organizations with Masonic bonds include the St John Ambulance Brigade, the Boys' Brigade, the Scout Association, the Police Dependants' Trust and several ex-servicemen's societies. These are among 175 causes which received small donations (£500 to £1,000 each) in 1986–7.[10] Grand Charity also helped disaster victims abroad, giving £30,000 to alleviate 'distress' caused by earthquakes in El Salvador, Ecuador and Chile. However, the money was sent to those countries' Grand Lodges, so it is legitimate to ask if these 'donations for non-Masonic charitable purposes' really did end up with non-Masons.

If all the Charity's 1986 hand-outs to 'non-Masonic' causes are added together, at £504,000 they come to just £1 a head for every Mason in England and Wales. Even if we accept the lowest estimate of 250,000 active Masons on Grand Lodge's books (an average of thirty-three in each lodge, or less than half the membership of most provincial lodges), the Charity is giving only £2 per head per year to non-Masonic causes. Each Mason may give another £2 or £3 to local 'profane' charities through his lodge, so the movement probably gives a total of £5 a head to non-Masons. This scarcely proves the Craft is 'in great measure' a charitable organization. It also compares ill with the efforts of just one of the brotherhood's self-styled 'victims', John Watman, who raised £250,000 for charity from country-and-western concerts (see Chapter 27). Nor does it look good against the hundreds of pounds which each active Mason spends on lodge dues, costume, regalia, and wining and dining at the Festive Board every year.

Recently, clerical eyebrows have been furrowed by Masonic bequests to decaying Anglican piles. Anti-Masonic priests wondered why, just as the Church Working Group embarked on its inquiry into Freemasonry and Christianity, the brotherhood gave well-publicized sums to cathedral restoration funds. In 1986 forty Wiltshire lodges gave £3,850 to help save the spire of Salisbury Cathedral. This was topped up by £5,000 from Grand Charity which gave the same amount to five more cathedrals. Were these payments made 'out of concern for the country's architectural heritage' as the Charity stated, 'to mark Freemasonry's links with its operative forebears',[11] or to blunt any criticism arising in the course of the inquiry?

Grand Charity could respond that it had been giving to cathedrals for years, so nothing sinister should be read into these latest gifts. In 1987 some Anglican Masons turned the criticism on the Church as another six cathedrals each pocketed £5,000 from Masonic funds. When the Working Group's anti-Masonic views were published, one *Daily Telegraph* reader felt it was hypocritical of the Church to take the money: 'Will the Synod now be returning this whence it came?'[12] Yes it should, said the anti-Masonic Revd Peter Greenslade of Looe in Cornwall. In 1988 he greeted Truro Cathedral's acceptance of a Masonic gift of £3,535 with 'horror and dismay', especially now the Church's own team had branded some Masonic rituals 'blasphemous'.[13]

Greenslade might have demanded the demolition of the entire cathedral if he had known that its very foundation stone had been laid in 1880 by the Prince of Wales in his Grand Master's apron, scattering corn and pouring wine in a wholly Masonic ceremony. This was preceded by the longest Masonic procession ever seen in Cornwall, with brethren

parading in full costume and waving silk lodge banners. *The Times* said
the occasion was conducted 'with mystic ceremony, and with a pomp
and glitter almost barbaric in its splendour'. In his address the Prince
spoke not of Jesus Christ or the Holy Trinity, but of this 'temple' erected
for the 'glory of the Grand Architect of the Universe'.[14]

Where does Grand Charity get all the money which it gives away?
Most comes from a general fund, worth over £5 million by 1986. That
year it had an income of £1,476,000: dividends and interest on investments
(£242,000), 'sundry receipts and contributions' (£226,000), a payment
from Grand Lodge (£88,000), gifts from lodges (£484,000) and income
from a Festival (£435,000).[15] Every year a festival is held by a different
'province' when all its lodges raise extra-large sums. In 1987 Northumberland raised £1,554,000, which Grand Charity shared with the brotherhood's wholly internal benevolent funds.

In 1986 the Charity gave £641,000 to needy Masonic 'petitioners' or
their families. Yet the Charity also *receives* huge sums. The biggest was a
bequest now worth nearly £5 million from a Midlands industrialist named
Harry Ellard. He died in 1983 but the 'Ellard Fund' surfaced only in 1986
when it gave £72,000 to Help the Aged to buy six minibuses. A year later
the fate of the remaining £4.7 million had still to be decided, but an old
people's 'Harry Ellard Home' is now planned. Perhaps Ellard should
have left some of this money to the forty employees who lost their jobs
when his engineering firm shut down on his death, but most of those
were non-Masons.

There are three other national Masonic charities for England and
Wales. The Benevolent Institution cares for elderly Masons and their
dependants. It maintains fifteen residential homes in England and Wales,
housing nearly 1,000 people and costing £5.8 million a year to maintain. It
distributes annuities totalling £370,000 to another 1,700 recipients, who
can be Masons or their 'wives, widows, spinster daughters and spinster
sisters'.

The Trust for Girls and Boys exists for 'the relief of poverty and the
advancement of education', mainly for the children, adopted children and
step-children of Masons. The Royal Masonic School for Girls comes
under its wing. This well-equipped college for day and boarding pupils
has been on its present site in Bushey, Hertfordshire, since 1934. It has
excellent relations with the local community and seems now to avoid the
'ghetto' mentality which its narrow recruitment base used to inculcate.
The problem is not that most of the girls depend on charity, but that they
receive it only because a male relative happens to have belonged to a
fraternity which they, as women, can never join. Ironically, the School
for Boys never achieved the same firm financial footing. Its closure in

1977 provoked fratricidal rancour and recrimination. Now the Trust pays for the sons of impoverished Masons to go to other independent schools. Like Grand Charity, the Trust benefits from provincial Masonic festivals. In 1986 South Wales raised £3,483,000 for the education of 'Masonic' boys and girls.

I have received letters from former pupils of the Masonic schools. Some state they are grateful for the education, and that Freemasonry has been a benign force in their lives, but one young woman feels the girls' school had a 'heavy and oppressive' atmosphere. She recalls the 'sense of evil' which overcame a coachload of her classmates after they had visited the Grand Temple. Today a born-again Christian, she may now be over-dramatizing her revulsion, yet she is fair-minded enough to say the Masons had 'got us out of a pickle' by providing this schooling after her father had suffered a mental breakdown and could no longer work. Another Old Masonian, the actor Anthony Andrews, describes the boys' school as having been 'run on public school lines, but it wasn't like any public school you would know. I hated it, but they did try to give us a good education.'[16]

Being on the receiving end of Masonic charity can be painful, as another young woman explains:

My father, who loved his Masonic life, died in the 1960s when my sister and I were both very young. Within a few months the Lodge tried to persuade my mother to send us to the Royal Masonic School as boarders. She explained that she did not wish to send us away, but she was persuaded to take us on a visit to the school and was sent the forms to sign.

I remember the misery my sister and I felt as we were shown round, the real fear that constant persuasion would wear down our mother's resolve. The Lodge then offered a sum of money so we could study as 'outboarders' at a local independent day school. This was not solicited by my mother, but gratefully accepted as our financial position was very bad. The most we ever got was £200 a year but it was a help.

However, the manner of giving us this charity was positively Dickensian. First we were visited at home by the Lodge Almoner and his wife. We were questioned in detail and the wife inspected every room of our flat, including my bedroom. I was only seven and I resented this deeply. All subsequent Almoners visited us and I never ceased to feel 'inspected'.

Every year my mother had to go to the Trust's HQ in London to give full details of her financial position. This was fair enough but the worst aspect for me was that, every year of my schooling from seven to eighteen, the Masons sent a form that I had to ask my head teacher to fill in. This covered academic achievement but also conduct, punctuality etc. I was a child who enjoyed school and was very academic but I have often wondered what would have happened if I had not been bright, or if the shock of my father's death had caused behavioural problems. Certainly the thought of what would happen to this precious money, if I got into trouble or did not do well, played on my mind.

Worse still, the head invariably passed the questionnaire on to my form teacher, so that all my form teachers knew I was the recipient of charity. Not all teachers are models of tact and I found this extremely humiliating. My mother explained this to the various Almoners, but they still insisted on these questionnaires. When I finished school and prepared to go to university, I refused to take any more money. The Almoner wrote and promised there would be no more questionnaires if I would let him know how I was getting on. I agreed and received £150 a year, which saved me from spending my summers working in a food factory.

I hope you will see that I *do* believe the Lodge meant well, but I feel very strongly that any help it wished to give us should have been given freely. As it was, I felt like property – an investment. The Almoner often informed my mother that my successive university examination results were published in the Lodge papers. I am sure this was intended kindly, to give me a glow of pride. In actual fact, it made me feel like a racehorse, or a tin mine being written up in an investors' report.

I got shot of the Masons ten years ago and no longer feel any animosity towards them, but in my younger years I felt subservient and rather ashamed.

In Scotland each donation for the education of a Mason's child is described in the *Quarterly Communication* of that country's Grand Lodge. In December 1981 it published a list of twenty-five students, aged between thirteen and twenty-two, who had each received 'Board of Benevolence' donations of £140. It gave each youngster's name, age, school or university and subject of study, and also the father's name and lodge. Nineteen of the fathers were dead, but six were still living. This document would normally be seen only by Scottish Freemasons but, even so, it seems humiliating to distribute these intimate details to at least 50,000 men, some of whom must live in the same town or community as the students themselves.

Ask any English Mason for the biggest single example of his brotherhood's charity and he will probably cite the Royal Masonic Hospital. For over fifty years the 250-bed 'RMH' in Hammersmith, London, has been caring for the Masonic sick and their dependants, charging them only what they can pay. If they are in financial straits a Samaritan Fund exists to meet some or all of the bills. In the past fifteen years many Masons and Masons' widows have bequeathed the hospital a total of more than £10 million in their wills. Today it claims to be Europe's largest and best-equipped private hospital, but its survival owes little to the Craft's upper crust whose efforts to shut it down provoked the worst split in English Masonry for 200 years.

The trouble began in 1984 when the Foundation for the Aged and the Sick, which controlled most of the hospital's purse-strings, set up an inquiry into how medical care for Masons could best be provided. Chaired by High Court Judge Sir Maurice Drake, the committee made recommendations which astonished the Craft.

> The Hospital should be sold 'on the most favourable terms which can be obtained'. The proceeds should be added to its existing capital assets and put in a Fund to help needy Masons and their families. This will enable patients to be treated in private hospitals or private beds near their homes where they can easily be visited by friends and relatives.[17]

The 'sale' case was carefully argued. Running the hospital was taking 'too large a share' of charity funds. This was unfair to Masons living far away in, say, Newcastle, Plymouth or Llandudno, who found it neither practical nor economic to be treated at the RMH. If they had no money for private medicine, how could their families afford to visit them in London? Besides, by the mid-1980s there were many private clinics in Britain, as well as private beds in National Health hospitals, so the new fund could buy care for Masons much nearer home. 'Drake' predicted that by 1987, if legacies stayed at the same level while medical costs continued to grow, the RMH would be losing £2–4 million a year. A Masonic MP simplified the case for me by saying: 'It no longer makes sense for us to run a hospital. That's not what Freemasonry's about.'

On the contrary, argued many 'rank-and-file' brethren: running a hospital is precisely what Freemasonry is and ought to be about, especially now Mrs Thatcher has brought the Victorian values of self-help, mutual aid and charity back into fashion.

The task of selling the hospital fell to the chairman of its board of management, Michael Richardson. When not wearing an apron

Richardson is managing director of merchant bankers N. M. Rothschild.
Yet even he could not just go ahead and sell. He had to get the agreement
of the hospital's 300,000 'Governors'. They had each paid a modest £5.25
for this title, but they could all vote on any plan to sell. In most other areas
of Masonic decision-making the ordinary Mason has no say. Over the
years this powerlessness had created a sense of frustration which would
now overwhelm Richardson. His misfortune was that he personified
everything about Grand Lodge which many 'grassroots' Masons resent:
wealth, power, connections and the City of London. He was also seen as a
'front-man' for the aristocrats who had given him the job. They
dominate Grand Lodge's committees and are still held responsible for
that earlier 'betrayal' of Masonic charity: closing and selling the School
for Boys in 1977.

'No-sale' fundamentalists now read a conspiracy into Richardson's
selection as chairman back in 1982. His predecessor had been Lord
Porritt, an eminent surgeon who had supervised an £11 million refit of the
entire hospital. The fact that a merchant banker, rather than a medical
man, had taken over from the saintly Porritt was now seen as proof that
the scheme to sell the place had been hatched two years *before* the
'independent' Drake Committee made the same recommendation.
Hospital loyalists wondered if Richardson had been chosen because
'privatization' was a Rothschild speciality. Around this time the bank
handled a succession of government share issues: Brit Oil, Amersham
International, the Royal Ordnance Factories and, by 1985, British Gas.
Could flogging off England's 'family silver' be the prelude to 'asset-
stripping' England's Masons?

Sale opponents also thought it odd that if this man was such a City
wizard, how was it that under his stewardship a hospital which had made
a small profit in 1982 was making a £387,000 loss by 1984? In any event its
books had not been audited for two years. Average daily bed-occupancy
had been falling long before he took charge, but by 1984 it was down to
50 per cent. The 'no-sale' brethren felt it was a trend which Richardson
should have reversed.

The Drake Report revealed that a firm named American Medical
International had approached Richardson to buy the hospital. In
November 1984 AMI was so sure the deal would go through that it
arranged a press conference to announce its new acquisition. It must have
been led to believe the governors would obediently rubber-stamp
Richardson's plan to sell the place for £20.2 million, but at a meeting in
Freemasons' Hall they committed a rare act of insubordination and voted
it down.

The suspicions of hospital loyalists were not diminished when it became known that the man appointed as its chief executive in 1982 had previously worked for AMI.

Sale opponents then discovered that the hospital was insured for £45 million: more than twice the amount for which Richardson was ready to sell. He pointed out that £45 million was what it would cost to rebuild the hospital, not its current worth. The objectors countered by showing that fourteen hospital-owned houses and a 199-room nurses' home, worth £2.4 million in all, were valued in the RMH books at a mere £350,000.

Richardson's most embarrassing moment came when the 'rebels' discovered he had never paid the necessary £5.25 to become a governor of the hospital. According to its constitution, this made his chairmanship illegal. To get round this offence he could have been reappointed as a trustee, then chosen as chairman, but he would have had no vote.

In October 1985 Richardson and his board revived the sale plan, but now they changed the rules to put it to a postal vote, which they hoped would produce a pro-sale majority. The anti-sale campaign was spearheaded by a Harley Street doctor named Gordon Kells. This fiery Irish Catholic published colourfully-phrased circulars but they reached only some electors. He delivered stacks to Freemasons' Hall, asking for them to be sent to 1,700 London lodge secretaries whose addresses he had no way of knowing. Grand Secretary Michael Higham refused to oblige, telling Kells to collect his paperwork 'when convenient'.

In contrast, Richardson was able to send six tons of pro-sale papers to all lodge secretaries with the full co-operation of the London Grand Rank Association and provincial grand lodges. He called on top Masons to deliver the 75 per cent majority he needed to sell the hospital: 'Any help that you, as Provincial Grand Master, are able to give the Board of Management would be deeply appreciated.' Some PGMs interpreted this as a commandment from the Great Architect himself. They printed their own circulars, in effect ordering their brethren to vote for sale. Great Queen Street also prodded the masses into line. In December 1985 pro-Grand Master Lord Cornwallis told Grand Lodge and (through the *Daily Telegraph*) the brotherhood at large that the board 'should be trusted' and 'urged members' to support it.

The anti-sale brigade retorted: how can anyone support a board which has an illegal chairman? They pointed out that Grand Lodge had no jurisdiction over the hospital, so its intervention was also illegal. They countered predictions of huge losses by revealing that fee-paying patients (Masons and non-Masons) owed £1 million in unpaid fees. These were still 'collectable', so the hospital had really made a profit. The peppery Kells tiraded: 'The time has arrived when the feudal-minded hierarchy of

Great Queen Street must realize they are dealing with responsible men, and not with a group of recalcitrant schoolboys.'

Even so, the hierarchy's pressure persuaded 65 per cent of voters to back the sale. This caused the no-sale camp, led by a financial consultant named Douglas Brooks, to drag Richardson and his board into the High Court and accuse them of trampling on the constitution. The Court confirmed that Richardson was not qualified to be chairman (he did not pay his £5.25 governor's fee until September 1986) and the postal vote was null and void. The judge ordered a constitutional revision, after which 300,000 governors would elect a new board to decide the hospital's fate.

In the hearing Brooks had claimed the board falsified the 1984-5 accounts so that the hospital appeared to lose £600,000 when its cash assets had really risen by £1 million. He held it to blame for the missing million pounds in fees. Meantime counsel nitpicked over the constitution and the terms of the election. Three successive actions cost £200,000, which the board had to pay because Brooks proved they were not complying with earlier court orders. It settled these costs from funds made up of donations scraped together by brethren all over the country for poor Masons' medical care. They had no idea it would be used to line lawyers' pockets. By the end of this affair, the hierarchy had spent huge sums of charity money to persuade Masons to sell a hospital for whose continued survival they had given the money in the first place!

Mr Justice Warner, the non-Mason who had the chore of hearing the dispute (see Chapter 22), coaxed both sides into agreeing election terms. In December 1986 voters would choose twenty-one out of 100 candidates. Most were no-hope independents. The only real choice was whether to back a slate of 'Board of Management' candidates favouring sale or a 'Brooks' slate who were against it. Each candidate's loyalties were stated on a five-page ballot form to be sent to all voters by lodge secretaries. The Electoral Reform Society was hired to count, to ensure no one could claim the vote had been rigged. By this time Brotherly Love was in short supply.

Except for brief campaign statements, the judge banned all electioneering, but suddenly Masons – and even the 'profane' press – were bombarded with anti-sale propaganda. One publication called *Third Rising* ran an editorial headed: 'All that is necessary for Evil to triumph is for good men to do nothing.' Other captions read, 'Souls for Sale' and 'Drinking clubs or Hospitals'. Grand Secretary Higham was so shocked that he sent every brother a circular condemning *Third Rising* as 'highly coloured and inaccurate'. This had the unforeseen consequence of telling thousands of Masons who had never seen the broadsheet (and were never likely to) that there were brethren who dared to claim 'those responsible for the government of the Craft do not have the good of Freemasonry at heart'. Far from sinking *Third Rising*, Higham's attack endowed it with a Robin Hood glamour, even credibility.

In February 1987 the result showed that, although only 30,000 governors had voted, most had brushed off the hierarchy's pressure and voted to keep the hospital. The winning board consisted of sixteen no-sale brethren, two pro-sale and three independents. Every member of the old board was thrown out, including Michael Richardson who came a humiliating twenty-ninth and vanished from the scene. Triumphant no-sale rebels took charge, appointing supporters to the hospital's full-time posts previously occupied by men regarded as too close to Richardson.

'This is the biggest rebellion against the Brotherhood's bosses since they cast Christ out of the Ritual 150 years ago,' said one overjoyed brother. The integrity of Grand Lodge itself was under fire.

> What it fears more than anything else is a peasants' revolt. Our lords and masters realized some time back that they had wholly misread the rank-and-file, but they couldn't back down over the hospital because they would have lost face. Now it will never be sold so they'll pretend to support it, but they don't know what's coming next. We may press for the Rituals to be Christianized again, like they are in Sweden. The hospital vote could mark the start of a Masonic revolution, nothing less.

Grand Secretary Higham reacted with outward calm: 'This has been a dispute within a family, not a rift.'[18] Perhaps so, but his Masonic 'family' was so riven with hate that observers wondered if he meant something like the Mafia 'families' of Sicily, New York, Philadelphia or Chicago.

Throughout the row the Duke of Kent as RMH President had quietly sided with the grandees of Grand Lodge. In October 1985 a board circular stated he had 'indicated his support' for the sick fund which could be set up if the RMH were sold. Perhaps he was unaware of the words of a previous Grand Master, the Duke of Connaught, when he laid the foundation stone in 1932: 'We pray God this Hospital may deserve to prosper by becoming a place of Concord, for good men and for the promotion of Harmony and Brotherly Love, until time shall be no more.'

Throughout these bitter years Connaught must have turned and turned again in his royal mausoleum. In September Viscount Chelsea, President of the Foundation of the Aged and the Sick, told a gathering of Provincial Grand Masters that if the hospital tried to remain open, the foundation would 'starve it of funds'. When the 'no-sale' camp won power they successfully demanded the hospital be given back its former independent status, to ensure that Chelsea no longer had control over any of its funds.

The new board assured the brotherhood of 'a warm welcome from our staff, all of whom live up to the Hospital's motto – WE CARE'. New specialist surgical and cancer therapy units would be installed. The run-down nursing school would be reopened and Britain's first independent medical school would be established, with places reserved for the children of Masons. To cater for brethren outside London, plans were laid for new Masonic hospitals all over the country.

Just when it seemed Brotherly Love would heal fraternal wounds, the victors began carving each other up. Sixteen of the board had won on the 'Douglas Brooks' ticket, but Brooks himself was not elected chairman. A bitter campaign had been launched against him and against Dr Paul MacLoughlin, who had become a Mason only because he had been asked to set up the RMH's private medical school. The physician was astonished when he and his school were being damned along with Douglas Brooks. Indeed, the main excuse for ousting Brooks were his links with MacLoughlin, who had been in financial difficulties over earlier attempts at launching a medical school. The doctor claims his problems were engineered by other folk acting with malice. He produces convincing arguments and documentation to support his case.

MacLoughlin, a tall ex-SAS man, was bemused by the role of Dr Gordon Kells, the pro-hospital campaigner who had proposed him for initiation into Amity Lodge (no. 172) in 1985. Kells himself had been initiated in 1981, the year he was cleared of manslaughter at the Old Bailey. He had unfortunately given an overdose of anaesthetic to a Mr Leslie Holt, who had come to his clinic to have a few warts removed from his feet.

Kells rented rooms from MacLoughlin in the Harley Street property which he had leased from the Crown. The men had known each other since they were medical students. Thirty years later it was Kells who propelled MacLoughlin not only into Amity Lodge but also into the RMH. By 1987 they had so fallen out they were threatening to sue each other for libel. Meantime both MacLoughlin and Brooks fell victim to anonymous character-assassinating circulars. In May 1988 a rowdy meeting of hospital governors voted Kells onto the board. Brooks felt the meeting was controlled by a 'rent-a-mob'. Some brothers described it as 'a shocking advertisement for Freemasonry' – others as a 'triumph for democracy'.

This was all too much for the man best known for saving the hospital.

In June Douglas Brooks resigned from the board and wrote a stinging letter to the chairman.

> I no longer wish to feel that my reputation and good name continue to be besmirched by an association with such a body, many of whose members in Board and Committee meetings continue to display a total disregard for those basic Masonic precepts of Truth, Honour and Virtue.

This fratricidal feud was a sorry end to a brilliant campaign, but to the moguls in Great Queen Street it may have seemed a 'consummation devoutly to be wished'. With their Masonic enemies split, it may be many years before another issue threatens their authority. Who was right and who was wrong over the hospital will not be clear for several years until it can be seen if the place really can pay its way or raise enough money through legacies and donations to break even.

One group of people who have not been impressed by the practical application of Brotherly Love, Relief and Truth are the hospital's 500 staff. They have been demoralized by five years' non-stop Masonic bickering. Some surgeons have quit in disgust, taking their fee-paying patients elsewhere, and the Nursing School has collapsed. As one nursing sister told a brother, 'even the bloody Americans couldn't have treated us worse than you Masons'.

thirty-eight

THE DESTRUCTION
OF ARTHUR EDMONDS

In 1976 Arthur Edmonds was working for a small tour company named Cruise Drive Tours Ltd. For several weeks each year he escorted groups of passengers on cruise ships. His wife Joyce went too, to 'look after the ladies'. Arthur was a Freemason, Master of Temple Porchway Lodge (no. 7209). On many cruises Masons identify each other and hold Masonic gatherings. No formal Masonic business can be conducted – no on-board rituals – but a convivial time is had by men with a common interest. In such a meeting someone suggested that a party of Masons, wives, widows and friends should go on a cruise together the following year. Arthur volunteered to organize the trip, for his firm had already made a block booking on a Mediterranean cruise that September. Back on shore he asked his many Masonic friends if they would like to join the party.

Arthur knew that Masons are forbidden to use Freemasonry for personal profit. He therefore persuaded his company to allow all profits from the Masonic booking to go to the Royal Masonic Hospital. The cruise was a resounding success and the Masons aboard were doubly satisfied: they benefited from a special discount which Arthur had negotiated, and he gave the hospital the entire 'profits' of £1,406.

He now had a grander idea: to charter an entire cruise ship and fill it with Masons. He explained the project to a high-ranking Masonic friend, Clarence Smart. Arthur could arrange a thirteen-day voyage to Madeira and the Canaries, and get a 10 per cent fare reduction for all the passengers. He would give 5 per cent of all fares, plus all profits, to Masonic causes. In this case the cause would be the Central London Masonic Centre, of which Smart was Chairman and which desperately needed money (see Chapter 36). According to the rules of English Freemasonry, this would constitute an 'appeal to the brethren', so it would have to be sanctioned by Grand Lodge. That was why in March

1977 Clarry Smart, a Grand Rank Mason, went to see Grand Secretary James Stubbs. According to Edmonds, Smart placed 'every facet of the exercise' before Stubbs, who granted 'permission to proceed'. With this green light, Arthur's firm chartered the *Black Watch* from Olsen Lines for £95,000. Britain's first Masonic cruise would soon set sail.

Arthur booked entertainers for the cruise. He printed special ticket covers and envelopes, bought gifts for the ladies, arranged for fresh orchids to be given them in Madeira and left nothing to chance. 'All we needed now was 360 passengers!' He sent letters to all London's lodge secretaries, requesting them to read out details of the cruise in open lodge. Most of the letters ended up in the waste-paper basket, so Arthur and Clarry received only twenty bookings. To save the project – and Cruise Drive Tours which now faced heavy losses – they decided to place a small advertisement in the *Sunday Telegraph*. This generated 8,000 replies and the cruise was a sell-out. It embarked in November 1977 and raised £14,229 for charity, including all Cruise Drive's notional profit of £7,000; £9,000 went to the London Masonic Centre, the rest to agreed Masonic charities.

Letters of thanks and congratulations flooded in from people who went on the cruise and others who had heard about it. Masonic widows wrote glowing testimonials about the fun they had, and their feelings of safety and well-being in such a company. For people unable to book on that cruise, Arthur chartered another for January 1978. This time the entire proceeds would go to the Royal Masonic Hospital. An advertisement was placed in the *Daily Express*, with words approved by the Hospital Appeals Secretary and (said Clarry Smart) by Grand Secretary Stubbs. This time the *Black Watch* was again sold out, so another 150 passengers had to be booked on a sister ship. These voyages raised £10,810 for charity, and neither Arthur nor his company took a penny.

No sooner had he returned than some West Lancashire lodges asked him to organize a cruise for the Royal Masonic Benevolent Institution as part of the province's RMBI festival, while other Masons demanded another hospital cruise. Arthur duly chartered two more ships and thus committed his firm to risking £400,000 of its assets for Masonic causes, with no prospect of profit. He was therefore surprised when Grand Secretary Stubbs summoned him to Great Queen Street to discuss his cruise advertisements.

When Arthur arrived at Freemasons' Hall on 3 April he was thrust into a 'kangaroo court'. James Stubbs was not alone. He introduced the Grand Registrar by saying he was present to advise on legal matters relating to the cruises. Had Arthur known 'legal matters' were involved he would have brought his own lawyers, but Stubbs had not had the courtesy to warn him. 'I was to learn that Grand Lodge is a law unto itself,' says Arthur. 'Against all the teachings of Freemasonry, it has little respect for natural Justice.'

The Grand Registrar insisted that where Arthur's cruise adverts had stated, 'Proceeds will be donated to the Royal Masonic Hospital', that meant *all* monies received by Cruise Drive Tours would be donated – not just 5 per cent of ticket sales plus profits. He told Edmonds that he would be called to account to Grand Lodge for the 'missing money'.

> I was dumb-founded! Surely, anyone but a fool would realize that the cost of chartering an ocean-going liner, with the overheads of staff, offices, postage and advertising, would amount to hundreds of thousands of pounds. In any case, it was clearly stated in the cruise brochures that 5 per cent of the ticket sales would be donated to the charities, so no ambiguity could possibly arise. I explained all these points but they were completely ignored.
>
> Stubbs then said he had received a number of complaints from Masons about the advert, and showed me a very thin file of letters. I responded by showing him a very fat file of letters, all congratulating me and urging me to continue with the cruises. This argument too was ignored.

Edmonds pleaded that the relevant Grand Officers, in the hospital and the London Masonic Centre, had authorized these appeals, as had the *Grand Secretary himself*. The Grand Inquisitors rejected this defence, disallowed any evidence from Edmonds and threatened him with expulsion from Freemasonry. He says he 'stormed out, accusing them of conducting a Star Chamber inquisition unworthy of the good name and traditions of Freemasonry'. Stubbs himself considered that Edmonds had now been formally warned not to place any more cruise advertisements and Edmonds was sent a letter to that effect in June 1978. Stubbs assumed that was the end of Masonic cruising, but Edmonds did not get that impression.

Bloody but unbowed, Arthur carried on organizing the two latest cruises. These yielded £8,587 for the Benevolent Institution, £7,097 for the hospital and £2,948 for other charities. In one year Arthur had raised a total of £45,000 for Masonic causes. His thanks from Grand Lodge's rulers was unrelenting hostility. Without being allowed any chance to defend himself, he understood that he stood accused of two offences.

First, he was conducting an 'unauthorized appeal'. His defence would have been that Grand Secretary Stubbs had himself given permission for each cruise to take place under the title 'Grand Masonic Cruise'. Clarry Smart claimed he had obtained his permission back in March 1977. Why was Stubbs denying this, and why was he stopping Edmonds from presenting his case to Grand Lodge's inner council, the Board of General Purposes?

Edmonds feels the answer lies in the Book of Constitutions. Under 'unauthorized appeals' this states: 'It is irregular for any appeal to be made to the Craft in general to support particular objects, causes or movements, without the sanction of the Most Worshipful The Grand Master.' Edmonds now wondered whether the Grand Master, the Duke of Kent, had ever been consulted about the cruises. Edmonds himself could not consult him, for another rule 'forbids any Brother, whatever his rank, to write or communicate with the MW the Grand Master except through the Grand Secretary'.

> Was it not reasonable for we mere Masons, on receiving the permission of the Grand Secretary, to assume that he had obtained the necessary permission from the Grand Master, since we were forbidden from so doing?

Edmonds's second 'offence' was that he had used Freemasonry for commercial advantage. This was nonsense. His firm was not paying him more money, indeed he was working far harder for nothing. So were Cruise Drive's non-Masonic staff, who were putting in a sixteen-hour day for no extra pay. Nor did the firm profit. Outside auditors reported it was *losing* money on the cruises. This was also noticed by the Inland Revenue, who queried why its overall profit margin was so low.

By now Arthur was committed to more Masonic cruises. His company signed £900,000 worth of contracts for two public and two Masonic cruises for 1979. An April Masonic cruise was filled without any advertising. It raised £6,593 for the Benevolent Institution and £637 for other charities. Meantime Arthur and his sympathizers pressed Grand Secretary Stubbs for a resolution of the problem, but their letters went unanswered. Instead Stubbs dropped a bombshell in the newsletter which Grand Lodge sends to every English Mason four times a year. On 14 March 1979 Grand Lodge approved a *Quarterly Communication* saying that recent advertisements about so-called 'Masonic Cruises' did not have official approval or sanction and describing the cruises as 'commercial ventures.' This, says Edmonds, was a travesty of the truth.

The *Communication* made no mention of the vast sums given to charities, nor of the fact that the company was donating all net profits to the charities, nor of the cruises' popularity. As usual, Grand Lodge rubber-stamped the document and adjourned for lunch.

This *Communication* was now sent to every Mason in England and Wales, so its impact was bound to be devastating – as its authors surely knew. Edmonds claims he had no warning, and therefore no chance to avoid binding contracts. Even if a cruise now sailed empty, his firm would have to pay up. An October cruise was not affected because it was already sold out, raising £7,720 for the hospital, but Edmonds had also chartered a three-week Masonic cruise to Africa for April 1980. When the *Communication* was read out in all lodges, bookings dried up and cancellations poured in. One week £70,000 had to be returned to Masons all over the country. Edmonds had to reschedule the cruise, throw it open to the public and spend an extra £67,000 on advertising. Contract penalties imposed by the shipping line took Cruise Drive's losses to £250,000, just because of what was said in the *Communication*. The ship was allowed to sail only because Edmonds (now a Cruise Drive director) voluntarily paid over all his personal savings, and a co-director sold his home.

Edmonds was not just under attack from Grand Lodge. He was also the victim of the very charities he had done so much to help. In May 1979 the Benevolent Institution returned a cheque for the £6,953 which he had raised on the April 1979 cruise. Institution secretary Noel Grout explained that he had 'been instructed not to accept this cheque', but did not say by whom. In September 1979 Grout wrote to another Grand Officer saying, 'our records are unable to discover that this Organization has ever received direct from the Masonic Cruises a donation of £8,587.47 which you speak of. No receipt has been issued for that sum or to the Organization.'

This was misleading. On 28 September 1978 a receipt for that precise sum had been issued by the Institution at the Liverpool offices for the West Lancs Festival. In a 1980 letter Grout admitted the Institution had received the sum through a lodge in St Helens, but said he had no reason to apologize to Edmonds 'as no misleading statement had been made'. He then uttered the fantasy that 'the Organizers of the Cruises also make a profit'. The man who received this letter sent a copy to Edmonds, who was able to explain that the organizers made *no* profit. At the same time Edmonds wondered how many letters containing the same distortion had been sent to other Masons who believed it.

Edmonds received even shoddier treatment from Raymond Harrison, a Grand Officer who was Appeals Secretary at the Royal Masonic

Hospital. He had sent Edmonds effusive letters thanking him for the money he had raised and enclosing receipts.

Thank you . . . for so very kindly sending your cheque of £1,320 . . . I am sure you know how greatly I appreciate all you are doing to help this Institution . . . I have made arrangements to set up a special file at the Hospital recording the work you do and the handsome donations you anticipate being able to forward us. (19 September 1977)

I am sure you would wish to know that I have had the pleasure of speaking with three or four of the Masonic passengers on board this cruise ship, all of whom have given me glowing accounts and confirm that everything was to their entire satisfaction . . . With very kindest fraternal regards and best wishes. (21 October 1977)

It is with true gratitude I write to thank you most sincerely for the cheque of £9,256.31 from Cruise Drive Tours Ltd . . . through your efforts we have now benefited to the extent of approximately £11,000. (2 February 1978)

This morning I received a cheque for the handsome sum of £7,097 from W Bro. Clarence Smart, presented to him by your company (undoubtedly your good self) during the last cruise . . . Such continued and generous support is most gratifying and very truly appreciated. (23 November 1978)

In 1979 Harrison's effusive tone abruptly changed. He refused to accept £7,220 raised on a Masonic cruise, so Edmonds took the trouble of sending every penny back to the passengers. In May 1981 Harrison wrote to one perturbed brother,

With regard to your enquiry concerning Cruise Drive Tours Ltd, I am afraid I am unable to confirm or otherwise the amount you state which had been contributed through this Company to Masonic Charities . . . Cruise Drive Tours, as I am sure you are aware, is an entirely private Company in no way connected with the Craft.

Edmonds was heartbroken when he read this letter. After gushing unction for so long, Harrison could not now admit that the hospital had taken one penny from the cruises, even though he himself had signed receipts to Cruise Drive Tours for more than £17,000. His phrasing left

Edmonds vulnerable to rumours that he had pocketed money which had really gone to the hospital. The strain of fighting such innuendoes had already broken him.

> The work and the worry took its toll on my health. In March 1980 I was so ill I had to resign from the Company which I had spent many years building up. I was 58 years old, out of a job and had very little money. My fellow director – a brother Mason – fared even worse: he lost his job, his savings and his home.
>
> Due to the vicious rumours circulating from Masonic lodges, I had also lost the trust of my friends in the travel trade. Shipping company directors, many of whom are themselves Freemasons, would not even let me charter a ship for public cruises. So much for Masonic Brotherly Love.
>
> Cruise Drive Tours went into liquidation in July 1980. The Official Receiver felt obliged to call in the Metropolitan Fraud Squad because many Masons had written to him saying they had been informed that the Masonic charities had received no money. Of course, when the police looked at the books they found nothing whatsoever wrong.
>
> Grand Lodge was less willing to face the truth. Grand Secretary Stubbs had retired and collected a knighthood, so I applied to his successor Michael Higham for a fair hearing by the Board of General Purposes. I finally appeared before a Sub-Committee in November 1980, but I was not allowed to call witnesses. However, to prove Grand Secretary Stubbs had approved the advertisements I needed to call Stubbs himself and Clarry Smart. Without them, my case was brushed aside for 'lack of evidence'. I then produced evidence of other people's Masonic advertising which was wholly commercial and brought no charitable benefit whatsoever, but I was told 'not to spoil my case by giving too wide an interpretation of the word "commercial"'.

Smart wrote a letter in Edmonds's defence, which was later admitted as evidence.

> I clearly recollect informing Bro. Stubbs about the Grand Masonic Cruises, and that I would be arranging Classes of Instruction on Board . . . I further recollect that at one meeting with Bro. Stubbs when Bro. Edmonds was in attendance, following I understand a complaint from Bro. Stubbs regarding advertising in the National Press, which I think was late in 1978, it was then agreed that National

Press advertising could continue until April 1979, particularly since Bro. Edmonds was committed to certain cruises and literature had already been prepared.

At last, on 1 June 1981, Edmonds received a letter from Grand Secretary Higham containing this statement:

I can categorically say that no evidence has been produced to me or the Board of General Purposes that any of the funds destined for the charity have been misapplied. Without an auditor's statement I cannot go further, but I think what I have said in this paragraph should help to put your position into perspective.

In fact Edmonds had given Higham an auditor's certificate, issued by a chartered accountant, saying Cruise Drive had been operating the Masonic cruises without net profit. This had been accepted by the Inland Revenue but was ignored by Freemasonry's Board of General Purposes.

Arthur now asked for his name to be cleared in the place where it had been besmirched: Grand Lodge's *Quarterly Communication*. He asked for a statement to be published saying he had not made any unauthorized appeal, that all net profits had been donated to Masonic charity, and that the charities had received all monies due to them. This was refused. Ruined by Masonic whispers, Arthur ruefully recalled the instruction to all Masons 'to support a Brother in all of his laudable undertakings, and to support his character in his absence, as in his presence'. In Arthur's case this command had been flouted by men in Freemasonry's highest circles. So had the Fifth Antient Charge which says that 'None shall discover envy at the prosperity of a Brother nor supplant him, nor put him out of work if he be capable to finish the same.'

Out of work to this day, Edmonds is a doubly tragic figure. In 1963 he was charged with deception and fraud in a business which had nothing to do with travel. The case papers showed that the crimes had been perpetrated by others, yet his barrister strongly advised him to plead guilty, and he was sentenced to three years in jail. When Edmonds later attended his own bankruptcy hearing, the Registrar declared in open court that he had been the innocent victim of a 'forced conviction'. However, because he had pleaded guilty on a QC's instructions, he must go back to jail.

The prison governor was so sure Edmonds was innocent that he allowed him out every day to study business management at a nearby university. When he was freed, his wife set up Cruise Drive Tours and he worked for her. Only when he was discharged from bankruptcy could he become a Cruise Drive director. That was the year Grand Lodge dropped its bombshell and blew his life apart for a second time.

All along Freemasonry had known of Arthur's record. He had been initiated in Temple Porchway Lodge in Croydon in 1958, but while in prison he was 'excluded' because he had no money to pay his dues. In 1970 Grand Officer Clarence Smart invited him to rejoin and he became Master in five years. During the cruises row, neither Stubbs nor any other inquisitor had said his criminal record was the real reason they wanted the cruises stopped. If it was (but no one dared say) this would have been a rare outburst of civic conscience by Grand Lodge. As we have shown many times, Grand Lodge knows of far worse criminals among England's Masons – bank robbers, receivers of stolen gold and crooked cops – yet it has not expelled them. From 1960 to March 1988 it expelled only three Masons for criminal offences which led to imprisonment, and only two for lesser crimes.

In any case, if anyone deserved a second chance, it was Edmonds: the man who raised more than £60,000 for Masonic charities but was ruined by Freemasonry for his pains. It is understandable that his bitterness against Grand Lodge knows no limits.

In Freemasonry today Brotherly Love, Relief and Truth has been replaced by envy, hypocrisy and lies. A Freemason's word of honour which was once regarded as sacrosanct, and something to be relied upon, now has no moral worth whatsoever. If the trend is continued, the Craft must eventually founder on the very rocks which our forebears strove so valiantly to avoid.

Another issue arises from this story. How does Grand Lodge define a 'commercial undertaking'? As we have seen Edmonds never sought to make money out of the cruises, yet many Masons profit from Freemasonry without getting roasted by Grand Lodge. One example is Toye, Kenning and Spencer, the regalia shop facing Freemasons' Hall in London. Masons make their living from this business. Non-Masons can have no objection to that, but they might like to know how this commercial undertaking can be acceptable to Grand Lodge when the cruises were not.

Grand Lodge turns a blind eye to a great many Masonic money-makers. These advertisements have all appeared in *Masonic Square*, a magazine which itself makes a profit:

STAY COOL Don't pay those outrageous prices for your FESTIVAL

GIFTS. The Specialists are at your service in a newer bigger way. HODGHTON WHOLESALE. (June 1979)

A. R. FABB Bros Ltd. Masonic Regalia for all degrees. Hand embroidered in the traditional manner. (December 1986)

OPPORTUNITIES FOR RETIRED GENTLEMEN to represent a Bonafide Gift Company who already supply many lodges. Some business ability, telephone, but no travelling required. Applications to M. Josephs (Gift Department). (March 1978)

INVEST SECURELY and HELP YOUR CHARITY! Retired Past Master and owner of villa development in Menorca . . . offers at large discount to Brethren plots of land from £2,000 and architect-designed villas from under £8,000 **and will pay £100 to any Masonic Charity on exchange of contracts. Be clever and buy now** before Spain enters the Common Market and prices really take off! (March 1979)

Our existing 25 lodges are very satisfied with the SQUARE DEAL they get from PARK COURT HOTEL. If your lodge is looking for a new temple please contact—— (June 1980)

It's experience that counts at the Café Royal . . . For further information please contact The Masonic Banqueting Manager. (June 1983)

ABANO TERME [An Italian Health Spa]
Only 20 miles from Venice lies Abano Terme – the world's largest thermal zone. LA RESIDENCE, BRISTOL BUJA and ARISTO MOLINO Hotels. The Proprietors of these three hotels are brothers, free-masons, they shall be pleased to offer brothers and their relatives special prices, if you do not use credit cards. (June 1987)

And right next door to Freemasons' Hall stands Freemasonry's most famous eating house:

The home of 1,000 lodges and chapters. The Connaught Rooms is unique . . . (December 1980)

Masonic Square is published by Lewis Masonic, a firm which generates some of its huge sales by exploiting that persecution complex which is exclusively Masonic:

MASTER MASON/WORSHIPFUL MASTER APRON CASE To hold Apron flat.
The ideal case for brethren who wish to carry their apron with them
and use their case for everyday purposes. A lift-up concealment tray
hides regalia from view and papers and everyday articles can be held
on top. You can open the case without fear of revealing your regalia.
(September 1986)

Lewis Masonic is part of a bigger concern, the Ian Allan Group. This
connection came in handy back in 1978.

Masonic Visit to Australia. In connection with the opening of the
new Sydney Freemasons' Hall in October 1978 a special tour is being
arranged by Masonic Square, in conjunction with Ian Allan Travel,
for freemasons, their wives and friends . . . the total cost of the tour
. . . will be from £900.

Was this advertisement cleared by Grand Lodge? Did Ian Allan Travel
make money out of the voyage? Even if not, how did it differ from the
cruises then being run by Arthur Edmonds? If his efforts were a
'commercial undertaking', was not this one too?
    In 1979, Grand Secretary Stubbs and his deputy Michael Higham
visited Lewis's premises. *Masonic Square* photographed them alongside
its editor and the boss, Ian Allan, himself a Mason. Any reader might
imagine this constituted an official endorsement of the firm's myriad
paraphernalia:

ALADDIN'S CAVE or SOLOMON'S TEMPLE? Our showroom has been
likened to both. From lapel pins to regalia cases – Hymn cards to
Encyclopaedias. If it's masonic then it must be LEWIS MASONIC.

In 1985 Sir James Stubbs's autobiography appeared. The publisher was
Lewis Masonic. I have not found out which charity, if any, benefited
from the sales.

thirty-nine

THE LADIES – GOD BLESS THEM!

> From youth up to age, Our love they engage,
> We're proud to defend and caress them:
> Twill e'er be our boast, To honour the toast
> The Ladies for ever – God bless them![1]

Once a year every lodge holds a 'Ladies' Night': a dinner-dance to which brethren invite friends, prospective Masons, Masons from other lodges and all their wives or women friends. From these occasions outsiders return to the 'profane' world with tales of sycophantic speechifying, tedious toasts to Masonic potentates and endless encounters with salesmen, contractors and people who do something at the town hall. If the talk is not about cars, it is usually about foreign holidays.

The evening is dedicated to 'The Ladies, Those nearest and dearest to us', who have suffered yet another year of male absenteeism. A ladies' night is not just an excuse for a knees-up. It is a bribe, a guilt-ridden gift to every 'Masonic widow', especially those who feel the Craft is a standing offence because it excludes them solely because they are women. One old Masonic ditty shows wives have been complaining about this for 200 years.

> The ladies claim right to come into our light,
> Since the apron they say is their bearing:
> Can they subject their will, can they keep their tongues still,
> And let talking be chang'd into hearing?
>
> This difficult task is the least we can ask,
> To secure us on sundry occasions;
> When with this they comply, our utmost we'll try
> To raise lodges for lady Freemasons.

Till this can be done, must each Brother be mum,
Though the fair one should wheedle and teaze on;
Be just, true and kind; but still bear in mind,
At all times, that you are a Freemason.[2]

Since this sexist diatribe was written, women's Masonic organizations have been created – there are now even co-Masonic lodges – but these have few members and no formal connection with Freemasonry as practised by the Grand Lodges of England, Ireland, Scotland or any other 'regular' order. Even today most male Masons walk out with their briefcases so many times a year, assuming their wives will never know what they actually *do* in the lodge. If interrogated, they are duty-bound to 'divert the discourse'. Hence the need for a ladies' night to bridge a marital chasm which, many wives claim, is vast. One woman sent me this short essay entitled *Life With a Masonic Husband*.

It is important for any prospective Masonic wife to appreciate that her needs (both emotional and financial) will always come second to those of the Lodge, although ideally she will be made to feel special and 'protected'. Masonic activities are never disclosed, no matter how close the couple, and any inquiries are met with a wall of silence. Masons pride themselves on loyalty to their oath.

Membership of a lodge is recognized in the home by the familiar briefcase containing books, apron and other paraphernalia, together with the white gloves which must be kept laundered to pristine whiteness at all times.

Wives are expected to patiently put up with their husbands' absence at regular meetings and these always take precedence over everything else. There are no exceptions. By way of illustration: a long overnight flight back from sunnier climes and a tiring drive home was insufficient to deter an immediate departure for the regular lodge meeting.

When the husband returns from the lodge, usually long after the wife has gone to bed, he may be seen beaming with self-satisfaction. He 'glows' as if he has discovered some deep mystery of life or the Hereafter, which 'profane' mortals – especially women – could never know or comprehend. This glow is not convertible into physical energy.

The Ladies' Evening is meant to offer small compensation for regular absences during the year. We are wined, dined and serenaded in a most gallant manner. A gift is invariably presented to each lady during the course of the evening.

As a man progresses through his lodge he is invited, and feels duty-bound to join, other related lodges. This means more absence and further annual expense. Membership of any lodge is expensive, and there are always collections for the Masonic charities and appeals for the needs of the home lodge. In all respects Masons support each other – an admirable trait – but this is often to the detriment of non-Masons. In all matters ranks are closed in the Brotherhood.

A happy marriage can be knocked off course by the Craft, as another disillusioned spouse confesses:

> Freemasonry is a wedge between man and wife. Marriage is all about sharing – doing things together – whereas Freemasonry is secrecy, bogus knowledge jealously guarded, and ridiculous all-male rituals. I love my husband deeply but I am hurt that he needs this gobbledy-gook. He thinks I don't know what he gets up to, but I know the rituals inside out, because he always leaves his little books around. They are easy to understand, once you know what the initials stand for: 't.c.a.' means 'throat cut across' and 't.t.o. by the r.' means 'tongue torn out by the root'. The sad thing is, when you know what it all means, you cannot believe that your husband, who is otherwise sane and logical, can seriously utter such drivel.

Not all women share this sense of the ridiculous. Some see nothing but good in Freemasonry. A classic defence of the Craft came in one woman's attack on Stephen Knight:

> Freemasons are a caring and compassionate body of people who look after children, widows, the sick and the elderly, all of whom have no influence with anybody. These people, of whom I am one, are only able to repay by expressing their gratitude and refuting unjust criticism.
>
> My father was a Mason for a few years before his death when I was six years old. My mother was homeless and practically penniless, but the Freemasons gave me a secure and stable background. They offered me a place at their school, where I remained for nine years, receiving an excellent education and every care for my health. My college fees were also paid. I sincerely believe that the many Freemasons I have met are only interested in making the world a better place for people who need help, and I would ask you to weigh up my experience against allegations and insinuations which cannot be substantiated.

In researching this book I have received many letters from women, yet
this is the only one written in Freemasonry's defence. Another Mason's
daughter recalls not high morals but low farce:

> My father belonged to two lodges, but he was never Master of
> either. He found it difficult to commit the working to memory and
> was told he did not take the ceremonies seriously enough. He was
> apt to laugh at the wrong moments. It was just as well that he was
> never in the Chair. The expense would probably have ruined us,
> because the Worshipful Master has to bear the cost of the annual
> Ladies' Night.
>
> My father used to attend a Lodge of Instruction on Sunday
> mornings. He would promise to be home by mid-day, but it was
> usually four or five in the afternoon before he returned, always the
> worse for drink and in an aggressive mood. His companions in the
> lodge were all heavy drinkers.

Understandably, this woman chose not to marry a Mason! In 1986
drink drove 'Mrs H.B.' to write to a Southampton newspaper:[3]

> My husband was recently initiated into a masonic lodge; leaving
> home at 6 P.M. on the evening of his initiation. Readers may be
> interested to hear that he did not return until 6 A.M. the following
> morning in a completely drunken condition.

Mrs H.B. realized that not all Masons are drunks but, in view of this
experience, she was 'a little sceptical' about Freemasonry's moral code.
She may be relieved to know that in 1981 the Duke of Kent recognized the
damage Masonic boozing can do:

> The social side of lodge meetings has always formed an important
> part of the occasion and I should not want this to disappear, but
> hospitality these days does not come cheaply and there is no absolute
> necessity for lavish wining and dining after every meeting . . . I am
> anxious that brethren who may well be of limited means should not
> feel obliged to strain their family budgets in order to keep up an
> unnecessarily high level of conviviality.[4]

The Duke gave this advice five years before Mrs H.B.'s husband got
plastered. Perhaps Southampton lodges were too blotto to heed it.
'Conviviality' is not the only problem, according to one very well-
informed wife in the North of England:

I come from a Masonic family. Both my grandfathers were Masons, my father is a Mason and my mother is a lady Mason. Brought up in such an atmosphere, I naturally accepted my husband's wish to enter the Craft. He was initiated into one of England's oldest lodges whose members regard themselves as Masonic aristocrats and have an uncompromising view of the Craft. Their attitude to the 'profane', and women in particular, is entrenched in the nineteenth century. Other local lodges have a more flexible approach, and women are far more involved. Scarcely a week goes by without some mixed entertainment. Some lodges even organize their meetings so the Ladies can join the Brethren towards the close of the 'Festive Board'.

Yet old habits die hard. One recent Christmas we went to sing carols at the Masonic Hall, organized by one of the friendlier lodges. Many brethren in my husband's lodge were already there, but when we ladies arrived they walked out. Whatever the lodge, there is still no discussing lodge affairs or rituals in mixed company. The conversation is skilfully steered to other topics.

Some Masons take their all-male mania with them to the grave. When Wiltshire Freemason Herbert Northover died in 1980 his widow discovered he had ruled there should be no female mourners at his church service. 'I simply can't understand it,' she said.

We were blissfully happy for forty-five years and Herbert never mentioned anything like this to me. I could understand him not wanting me to go to the crematorium, but the church service ban . . . I just don't know. I can't attend, can I? It was my loving husband's dying wish that I didn't. It has upset me greatly and it came as a great shock when the will was read.

Mrs Northover said the ban might have been because her husband was a Mason: 'It is male-dominated, but he could have been trying to save me from extra distress.'[5]

Nowadays there is no provision for Masonic funerals, so perhaps Mr Northover was acting with exaggerated protectiveness towards his wife. Masons describe death as going to 'the Grand Lodge Above' where presumably there are no women at all. Down on earth times are slowly changing, as one Essex wife describes:

I know many Masons rehearse their rituals with their wives. Some even admit the Craft must drag itself into the twentieth century and recognize that a modern wife demands fewer male bastions. We have friends in a Dutch lodge who were amazed to learn I was totally excluded from my husband's Masonic life. When we stayed with them on a Masonic visit, we went to a lodge meeting where the men paraded before us in their aprons and regalia. My husband was most embarrassed and clearly wished I wasn't there, but he could do nothing about it. That is the only time I have ever seen him in his full kit!

His total silence about his Masonic life has been a constant irritant to me. I am fortunate because I have a career and a family to occupy me, but I have heard many women complain that their husbands are being consumed by Freemasonry. It's a 'domino' situation: men make friends in other lodges, so they visit those lodges. They are then invited to visit further afield and so on. They may also visit Provincial Lodge, and when their year as Master is over, they are asked to join an all-Master lodge. If a man joins many side degrees, which have their own super-structures, he may be busy on Masonics five nights a week, thirty weeks a year.

For some women a husband's year of office can prove a stimulating event. I recall one couple especially. The wife basked in reflected glory when her husband was Master. It would be true to say the year was not his but hers.

For many others Masonry can mean widowhood or, at best, purdah: being brought out and displayed at various social functions. In some instances Masonry contributes to marital breakdown. Of course, nobody really knows why a marriage fails, except the people directly concerned. Certainly a 'Masonic Widow' leads a very lonely, isolated existence, I spent my twentieth wedding anniversary alone while my husband was at the lodge. It rankles, and there are times when a wife feels enough is enough.

Some women shout 'Enough!' as soon as their husbands join. One wife sent this complaint to the United Grand Lodge of England from the Commonwealth island where her husband was then working:

I wish to place on record that my husband is being initiated into the Mason movement against my own and my family's wishes, and this is causing us great distress. I understood this was an open organization and that, as the family was involved, a person was invited to join in a formal way, with a committee member being invited into the home to discuss it with the wife. This was not done and I am of the opinion the matter was hidden because my feelings on this subject were known.

Last year at a beach bar your organizer, 'Mr X', asked me what I thought of my 'old man becoming a Mason'. I looked at my husband who winked and laughed, so it was passed off as a joke. 'Mr X' then said my husband and I should discuss the matter, 'as the wife was involved'. As we walked away, my husband again laughed it off and said 'X' had been drinking.

The matter was never mentioned again and I completely forgot about it until my husband said he was going to a lodge meeting – the degrading ceremony with noose and blindfold – which lasted until the early hours and resulted in nightmares. I pleaded with him to stop but within two weeks he went again for a 6.30 meeting and didn't come back until 1 A.M. so drunk he did not remember where he had been, and driving the car. On both occasions I asked him to inform the lodge of my objections but I do not know if this was done. Apparently it does not matter! I cannot consider this is a respectable place or good for my husband, and he is always very drunk and this is not good for his job.

As Christians we can never accept the worshipping of pagan Gods – Jahbulon (or the great Architect) – and my husband was under the impression it was Christian. He has since read *The Brotherhood* but seems to be lost in all the archaic ritual, and the talk of the other men, and is no longer as open and honest as he was, in fact people have noticed a change. I pray to God that he will not go through with this.

I have no objection to my husband joining an *open* club or drinking in moderation and giving money to general charities in which he believes, but not to be asked for donations for a select few . . . We are not a rich family, but average, although my husband might give that impression as he spends easily.

I do not know what reply, if any, this wife received. Whatever comfort she was offered worse times may lie ahead, according to this Masonic wife in New Zealand:

After we had been married ten years my husband casually mentioned that his father wanted him to become a Mason. I didn't know what he meant, and he didn't know either, except that in the family there was a special apron from a Scottish ancestor, and it was like going to Church. In our district most people know who the Masons are, and scoff at them because of their knocks and secret handshakes.

For several weeks men would visit our house and talk with my husband. We were invited to the homes of two elderly couples. The ladies would chat to me while the men went to another room. One day two men came and asked if I would allow my husband to become a Mason. That was ludicrous as there was no way I could refuse him – unless I wanted a divorce! I said he was old enough to make up his own mind. They made much of their charity to the community, their integrity and 'Christianity'. Because of rumours about racism and anti-Catholicism I asked if Maoris or Catholics were able to be members. They said 'Yes'. I then asked, could women join? 'No'. Why not? 'It's a man's organization.'

Eventually came the Initiation evening, with all those jokes from non-Masons about 'clean underwear', 'riding the white goat', 'prancing around in aprons', and being voted out by 'black balls'. His Mum and Dad came several hundred miles for the occasion. My father-in-law showed me the special Scottish apron – the pride and glory of the family! He went with my husband to the initiation, and I took his mother to the Ladies' Night that followed.

When lodge Masters are installed, there are huge functions with visitors from different lodges. I used to be asked to provide food, serve and clean up. I provided food a couple of times but I certainly didn't serve or clean up. My husband would come home very late and very drunk from these functions.

We haven't ever received any favours because of my husband's membership. He doesn't even get visits when in hospital, probably because of my 'anti-attitude'. I don't mix with Masons or their wives, who are always running round them like little ants. They seem proud of their husbands' status, and even grow flowers in lodge colours to decorate the hall for installations. One man said his installation as Master was more important than his wedding!

It is impossible to say how much of New Zealand's corruption is caused by Freemasonry, because there is so much corruption here in all walks of life. There are rumours that a 'Mason's handshake' is an Open Sesame! and a form of protection, but I don't think that is exclusive to Masons.

I am not a 'feminist', but it always surprises me that the extreme feminist core have not yet attacked Freemasonry. I am a very independent woman and I do not have any time for the Brotherhood!

Some wives regard their husbands' nightly preoccupation with Freemasonry as a kind of adultery. Others claim the brotherhood condones real infidelity and may even encourage it. One abandoned wife in southern England makes just this point:

I am intrigued by the emphasis which Masons purport to put on duty to wife and family. To break Masonic 'vows' is subject theoretically to terrible penalties, but to break other vows, binding in law and in the sight of God, appears not to be regarded as serious.

My husband was invited several times to join a lodge. At no time did any member of the committee come to our home and ask me if I approved. He finally joined after a colleague told him in my presence how much Masonry had done for him, and how he had become a much better person because of it. My husband seemed attracted by this aspect until he heard that a man in his firm, notorious for many disagreeable acts, had been accepted in the same lodge. He was rather concerned, but reflected that this man might also become a better person in due course.

My husband was now nearly fifty years old. Shortly after his initiation he started an affair with someone twenty-four years his junior, even younger than his own son. He left home to live with her, neglecting his own family and grandchildren. Because of his newly-taken Masonic vows, he was worried about what his Freemason colleagues would think of him breaking his marriage vows. He was told 'it was a matter for the individual's conscience' and was not reminded of the Masonic teaching that a man's first duty is to his wife and family. I found this hypocritical – almost tantamount to saying that lying and cheating are alright, as long as it is not to another Freemason. I have also been told their view is that extra-marital affairs are alright as long as they are not with another Mason's wife!

That is a reasonable reaction to the third degree 'Obligation' in which a Master Mason swears to 'most strictly respect the chastity of those nearest and dearest to him, in the persons of his wife, his sister and his child'. There is no parallel requirement to respect the chastity of any other man's wife, sister or child. When I first read this oath, I was struck by its similarity to the oath taken by members of the Sicilian Mafia and its North American offspring, the 'Cosa Nostra'. Joe Valachi, the first American Mafioso to break *Omerta* (the Mafia's code of silence), told a Senate sub-committee in 1963 how, on joining a Mafia 'family', he swore not to violate the wife, sisters or daughters of another member. A recent Mafia squealer, Jimmy Fratianno, told me his oath (when translated) said, 'You mustn't fool with another member's wife or girlfriend.'[6] In Mafia and Masonry this rule exists partly to prevent discord, even 'fratricide', over women but the similarity in their oaths makes one wonder if both organizations have a common ancestry. This deserted woman draws no parallels with the 'Mob', but she does find the Masonic oath two-faced.

It seems to set two standards for moral behaviour, which I find very strange and contradictory to their general teachings. My husband and I are not legally separated and there is no acrimony between us. He attends the lodge regularly and I think he derives comfort from the Masonic association because his actions have been condoned, so to speak, by a 'higher authority' than Christianity and the laws of marriage. So much for Freemasonry making my husband a better person!

A Surrey wife blames Freemasonry for much of her marital trouble:

In 1977 my husband felt a great need to become a Mason. We had not long moved house, and I could not see where the £40 joining fee would come from, when there was so much we needed. Nor could I understand his desire to pursue another 'hobby' on top of two very time-consuming ones which already took him from home a good deal. Added to this, he worked shift hours. Anyhow, I respected his wishes and he joined.

We lived in a rural area where a car is a necessity. He told me that if I wanted a car, I'd have to work for it. We had a young son at the time which meant a job was not going to be easy, and in any event I would need a car to do it. I was also keen to study music, as I'd always been a keen piano-player. My husband objected because 'You won't be able to do all the things you should be doing at home.' He also said, 'You only want to get among those young students.' As his happiness was threatened, I gave up the idea.

As time went on I was told I would have to work more to help with increased bills. I was already teaching piano at home and out all weathers doing market research surveys. I tried to work during school hours and my husband's work hours, a feat which tied me up in knots and was very tiring. I found I was working more and contributing all I'd got in earnings and strength to the home, but I was sharing it with a man who disappeared at every turn, and then dictated how we'd spend our weekends on his activities. I made thousands of loaves of sandwiches for the hockey club, and held hundreds of pints while sweaty morris-men danced, yet now *I* was paying for *him* to leave me regularly to go out in evening dress to this or that dinner. Sometimes I was alone at home for eleven consecutive evenings, desperate for company and affection, and only too appreciative of my piano and its solace.

There is a limit to the pleasure a piano can give a woman, so there came a point when understandably my head was turned. Another man was offering the affection I needed, and the proof that I was a normal woman. This relationship could go nowhere, but it did make me realize that my marriage was in a very bad state. One of us had to go! In 1983 my husband moved to a male friend's house and I agreed to be divorced.

Just two and a half months after our separation, my husband went to a ladies' night with another woman. He told me that he had to take her because he had the duty of making a speech on the ladies' behalf. I felt this was inappropriate in his situation, and a public show of his lack of respect for me. Also the tickets for his party must have cost £100, which I could have used to pay a household bill.

One day, when we met over our son, I told him exactly what I thought about Masons. He said, 'I hope you never get lost at sea.' I took this to be a reference to Freemasonry's support for the lifeboat charity. Yet here was I, unable to pay my gas and electricity bills! My son was more likely to die of hypothermia at home than by drowning at sea. We tried to revive the marriage. We spent weekends away together, but then I discovered he'd gone back to his girlfriend. Why, I asked. 'You did it, so why shouldn't I?'

By this time he was Mason-mad. One week he was booked to spend four successive nights on Masonic activities. On one of these nights he had committed himself to three different meetings, so he had to tear round making apologies. This shows how obsessed he'd become with the brotherhood.

The divorce went through, and we were due to go to court over our finances. Naturally I feared a court packed with Masons who would decide in his favour. We eventually sorted things out, but he is paying very little towards our son's maintenance. There must be other families wrecked by the intrusion of Freemasonry. I shall always hold it partly responsible for the absence of a constant Dad in my son's life.

It would seem there was much wrong with this marriage which had nothing to do with Freemasonry. Given the frequency of divorce these days, it would be unfair to blame every divorce in which the husband was a Mason upon his Freemasonry. In this case, it may have been the hockey or the morris-dancing, or everything added together. Yet Freemasonry seems to have taken more time than anything else – if the man was out 'Masoning' eleven nights in a row. Another 'Masonic Widow' tells a similar story:

After twenty-seven years of happy married life serious arguments began when my husband, a respected doctor (who was also a talented musician and artist), was asked if he would become a brother – an invitation which he welcomed with open arms. I was already prejudiced by my father's experience, working for the old LNER railway. He was invited to join the 'company' lodge with a hint that promotion would come his way. After he refused to join, he never got promotion.

I understood my husband's need for a social life away from medical matters and there was an obvious attraction in a 'men only club', just as many women enjoy gatherings of their own sex. Yet now I somehow lost respect for him as he embarked on what a friend called 'an ego trip'. I didn't like to think of him in the 'apron', white gloves etc., going through the spurious mumbo-jumbo rituals, and learning the florid, over-blown prose necessary to fulfil his duties. His easy acceptance of secrecy was hurtful. We could always discuss my activities, but his nights had to be cloaked in secrecy. As for the Ladies' Nights, they always seemed faintly ludicrous, full of false bonhomie and endless 'wine-taking'.

In closing, I must be honest. In 1982 my husband fell in love with a younger woman, and we are now divorced. She happily accompanies him to all Masonic social events. Perhaps I should have been more charitable, but I still feel in my bones that he is worth something better, and it was wrong for him. There's a lesson to be learnt from this, no doubt.

Another divorcee in Lancashire clearly blames the institution of Freemasonry, not just her wayward spouse:

My husband has been a Freemason for sixteen years, the last ten being most unhappy due to his involvement with the group and its secrecy. Whilst I am aware that many brethren are good people, I feel that a large number are willing to condone behaviour amongst their group which to people outside their sect would be considered unethical and abhorrent.

Contrary to the popular belief that home and family take precedence over the lodge, this wasn't so in our case. My husband is at present heavily involved with an ex-waitress from the lodge. This association has been known to the brethren for some time but was previously denied. Now it is an open secret. My husband petitioned for divorce on the grounds of my unreasonable behaviour, but my behaviour was caused by his involvement with Masonry. I feel I have become paranoid because most lodge members condoned this situation, even to the point of accepting the girlfriend at the Ladies' Night long before we were divorced.

Another divorcee in a south coast port views the Craft with equal contempt.

My husband 'Leonard' was a police officer in the Special Branch and a Freemason. He was a member of two lodges and often blamed his Masonic commitments for being short of money. At first I believed Masonry would be an opportunity for him to mix in reliable company, so I contributed more of my earnings to the family budget than I would have otherwise hoped. Masonic meetings were explanations given for various absences from home. I knew my husband was a flirt but, as a Masonic 'widow', I wouldn't consider asking questions.

1976 was our silver wedding anniversary. It was also the year 'Leonard' suggested we make up a foursome with a Mason friend 'Harry' and his wife 'Jane'. We all used to go out for dinner, and attended Masonic and police functions together. The men met almost daily for drinking sessions and seemed great buddies. Several times I overheard 'Leonard' inviting 'Harry' to join him for a 'good session' on cross-channel ferry trips which he was making on duty for the Special Branch.

'Harry' owned his own company and often travelled north on business. On these occasions my husband would visit 'Jane'. He eventually told me they were having an adulterous association, which she also admitted to me. I phoned a retired chief inspector whom I had met at a Ladies' Night when he was lodge Master. I asked him if adultery was acceptable in the lodges. He said, 'Not if it involved another Mason's wife!', and then quoted the Mason's oath to respect the chastity of brother Masons' wives and daughters.

This woman took revenge by 'shopping' her spouse to Grand Lodge.

Our divorce took a very long time to go through. There was immense unpleasantness over money. I became so angry that in 1983 I sent the United Grand Lodge of England a copy of my divorce order. This stated that my husband had been having an association with a brother Mason's wife, whom I had named as a co-respondent. The Grand Secretary's office sent me an acknowledgement saying 'the contents have been noted'.

I believe that, as a result, my husband was obliged to withdraw from the Masons. In a divorce affidavit he said that I had written 'to an organization he had belonged to for many years acquainting them of his adultery and thereby forcing his resignation'. He also said, 'This is totally malicious and without merit.'

If 'Leonard' was thrown out for breaking a Masonic commandment, his wife believes that for the previous ten years Masonic policemen had shielded him from the punishment which his worst acts deserved. She says he repeatedly drove his car blind drunk, a crime she reported several times to his senior officer. Once he clouted someone who happened to walk into the police station, an assault witnessed by another policeman. He also had an affair with a ferry employee from the Republic of Ireland.

Despite the fact that candidates for Special Branch are said to be thoroughly vetted for security purposes (as are their families and in-laws), my husband and another Special Branch Mason were known to be associating with two women who worked for the ferry company. In 1980 I wrote to their inspector, asking how the authorities vet mistresses with addresses in Dublin. I received no reply. Freemasonry must be the reason why, more than once, my husband escaped disciplinary action in the police. The Special Branch are supposed to be our protectors. What a shambles!

Revulsion may overcome the wives of low- and high-ranking Masons alike. Today there are 750 lodges overseas under the United Grand Lodge of England. These are organized into 'Districts', each headed by a Grand Master. The wife of a District Grand Master in one Commonwealth state told me of her deep disillusion:

Throughout thirty years' marriage to a Mason I have never pried into the organization's workings. I believe it to be vaguely religious but a sensation of something wrong and sinister has prevented me from taking any part in the social activities to which Masons' wives are invited. Whatever we learn about the Freemasons, I am left feeling there is something very ugly just a bit beyond the point where the explanations stop. Maybe this is pure fantasy but the feeling persists. Despite scorning female intuition as one of the world's worst instincts, it comes back so persistently that I am convinced it is true.

Lots of English colonials join the upcountry lodges where it tends to be like an all-male club, with drinking that goes on to the early hours and (I'm told) jokes of various shades of blue are the order of the day. Don't think I'm a prude. I enjoy jokes myself, but these elderly men exchanging whispered smut and then shouting with laughter somehow lacks the dignity that grey hair should bring.

As far as marriage is concerned, I must try to be fair. We aren't rich in any sense, but we are accepted in the highest social circles. I was first upset that my husband would spend money on the Masonic movement before he would spend on the family. On one classic occasion I asked him how he could possibly pay Masonic bar bills when children's school fees remained unpaid. His reply was that Masonic debts were 'debts of honour'. I was horrified but the school fees stayed unpaid until the Masonic bills were settled.

My husband has become more and more embroiled in the Masonic world, while our marriage has not been a physical success. He very rarely forgoes a Masonic meeting in favour of a family commitment. I have grown to resent Freemasonry mainly because he escapes all responsibility by saying, 'I'm going to a meeting.' Sometimes he comes home next morning. I have no control over this situation, either in a moral or a physical sense. At the same time he tells me the Masonic rules, like the well-known fable that Masonry must never come before the family. It has always come before ours!

Another woman who blames Freemasonry for the collapse of her marriage describes the calamity in terms of psychological, even spiritual, possession.

I cannot pretend to know how this fraternity operates, for the whole operation is shrouded in mystery and suspense. All I am able to say is that seemingly normal family life suddenly becomes disrupted when fraternities claim their stake, and the victim is alienated from the hearth.

I would not say that everything in my married life sailed along to perfection, or that I was not in some way to blame for a marriage that ended 'on the rocks'. Yet I feel convinced that we would have gone on to better understanding but for the intrusion of Freemasonry.

Men who enter into fraternities are not necessarily criminals, although some may be. More often they are escapists from reality. Some are of high calibre and background, who expect everything in life to measure up to their desire. Yet they are unable to face disappointment, or cope with the rough and tumble that afflicts us all from time to time.

It is by this route that they subject themselves to a mystical movement which, in the first instance, flatters their egos by inviting them to join. It then spells protection, backing and support. It offers to put their wrongs to right and shield them from adversity. Never do they consider the price they may have to pay. Life thereafter, protected though it may be, would appear to rob them of their individuality, and their countenance becomes as marble.

THE REMEDY

In this book, wherever possible, I have laid out first-hand evidence, not third-hand rumour. I have tried to provide sober deduction, not exaggeration. I have resisted embracing conspiracy theories until the point where the evidence has become overwhelming. It should go without saying that anyone investigating a secret society – or even just a 'private' one, as Grand Lodge now characterizes Freemasonry – will almost always find evidence hard to come by. Therefore 'rumour and speculation', though unsatisfactory, become legitimate. If the investigator 'exaggerates' what little evidence he or she gets, the 'private society' should hold itself most to blame. Freemasonry and paranoia were made for each other – they deserve each other – but this does not mean that all who question the Craft are 'paranoid', 'obsessed', or any of the other dismissive adjectives which trip off Masonic tongues. Freemasonry gives rise to genuine public concern, which Masons ignore at their peril.

What action should be taken? I suggest it should be more than would appeal to the Tory MP who says, 'if people wish to belong to secret societies, that is their own business', but probably less than required by the Labour man who feels it 'should be illegal'. Most MPs who completed my 1986 questionnaire said that councillors, local government officers, civil servants, policemen, judges and MPs should all be required to disclose Masonic membership. Even so, only 30 per cent of male MPs answered these questions. The only proper way to test political opinion would be to put a 'disclosure' bill to the vote. There is no chance that the present government would sponsor it, so an MP should introduce a private member's bill and a free vote should follow.

This bill should also give the public access to full and up-to-date membership lists of all Masonic lodges. As I suggested in Chapter 21, these should be available at reference libraries in the localities where the lodges meet, and at town and county halls. Thus in Bromyard one Craft lodge list would be open for inspection, in Truro six, in Cambridge eleven, in Sunderland twenty-nine, in Croydon eighty-nine, in Manchester 129, in the City of London some 200, and in Greater London another 1,450 – including all the lodges which meet in Great Queen Street. This degree of 'publication' might also be required of all other Masonic bodies: from the Royal Arch right the way through to the 'Soc Ros'.

The list of any lodge affiliated to a particular workplace, or recruiting mainly from within a specific organization, should be open for scrutiny by everyone who works at that place or in that organization. Thus the list for a town hall lodge, such as the Borough of Newham, should be available at Newham Town Hall; the Holden Lodge list at Midland Bank; the London Hospital Lodge list at the London Hospital; the list for the Union Lodge of Norwich should be given on demand to any employee of Norwich Union; the Lutine, Lloyd's and Fidentia lodge lists should be viewable at Lloyd's of London; likewise lists for all military lodges (including the 21st Territorial SAS) at regimental HQs; lists for barristers' and judges' lodges should be displayed in the Inns of Court, at the Bar Council and the High Court; and the Manor of St James's list at New Scotland Yard, and at Bow Street, Vine Street and West End Central police stations.

Most Masons would argue against these measures. They would say that, although they have nothing to hide, why should their lists be publicly available if the same is not required of the MCC, the Athenaeum, the Labour Party, the Transport and General Workers' Union, the Royal and Ancient Golf Club, the Manchester Unity of Oddfellows, the Ancient Order of Foresters, the Sons of Temperance, the Druids, Rotary, the Round Table, the Elks, the Royal Antediluvian Order of Buffalos, the Lions, the Kiwanis, the Baker Street Irregulars, the Sovereign and Military Order of Malta, the Catholic Police Guild, BUPA, the AA, the Women's Institute, the Mothers' Union or the subscription department of *Reader's Digest*?

The answer is simple. It is for Masons to demonstrate that any other organization has *all* these features of Freemasonry:

1. A code of mutual aid, sworn by all members, to assist each other *beyond* the aid they swear to perform for *all* other people in society.
2. Oaths (however watered-down in recent years) which threaten that some physical, economic or social penalty – or negative moral judgement – will be applied to those who reveal the organization's secrets.
3. Rituals which make use of blindfolds, nooses, daggers or similar menacing objects or disorienting devices.

4. · Secret passwords, signs, grips or handshakes.
5. Widespread public concern about the organization's activities or those of its members.

I know of no golf club which has any of these features, and no political party, trade union, friendly society, insurance company, businessmen's club, social group, or mainstream religious fraternity which has more than two. If it can be shown that any other group manifests all these elements, it should be subject to the same curbs as may be imposed on Freemasonry. Some Masons claim that three Catholic organizations – the Knights of Columbus, the Catenians and Opus Dei – are quasi-Masonic. If their rituals and oaths do resemble Freemasonry's, if genuine texts can be produced to prove it, and if there is widespread public concern, they too should be subject to any obligations imposed on the Craft.

If Masons have nothing to hide, none of this should cause them great disquiet. Just as their secretiveness breeds paranoia among the 'profane', so a new openness would help dispel it. If the Craft is primarily a charitable organization, a movement of moral regeneration or just a load of men pursuing an arcane hobby, they have nothing to fear. Personal anxieties could be accommodated. Maybe they would not want home addresses disclosed. However, all voters' addresses are already on view at public libraries on electoral rolls. At Companies House the home addresses of all company directors are available to anyone who pays a small fee. As it happens, Freemasons' home addresses might not be required, provided every lodge discloses the full names of all members.

Today's MPs should bear in mind that any law to curb Freemasonry will face widespread evasion, as the history of the 1799 Unlawful Societies Act shows. Brought in 'for the more effectual Suppression of Societies established for Seditious and Treasonable Purposes', this was passed when there were fears of French plots to overthrow the government of Great Britain and to achieve Irish independence. The Act claimed that societies such as United Englishmen, United Scotsmen, United Britons and United Irishmen were plotting seditious ends, and that their members swore oaths and secret vows, used secret signs and operated a cell-like structure across the country. However, a blanket ban on such organizations would also have banned Freemasonry, which shared all these offending characteristics. To gain exemption, England's rival Grand Lodges (the 'Moderns' and the 'Ancients') jointly lobbied politicians with a skill which would do credit to today's ruthless 'political action committees' in the USA. Their respective leaders, the Earl of Moira and the Duke of Atholl, pressured Prime Minister William Pitt.

According to 1799 Grand Lodge minutes, the Masonic delegation reported that Pitt

> expressed his good opinion of the Society and said he was willing to recommend any Clause to prevent the New Act from affecting the Society, provided that the Name of the Society could be prevented from being made use of as a Cover by evilly disposed persons for Seditious purposes.[1]

The pressure worked. Pitt duly introduced a clause stating the Act did not apply to 'Lodges of Free Masons, the meetings whereof have been in great measure directed to charitable purposes'. Pitt must have been beguiled by the smooth-talking aristocrats, particularly Moira. According to one Masonic historian, Moira's 'timely intervention had saved Freemasonry from extinction'.[2]

Presumably Moira and Atholl had told Pitt that no British Masonic lodge was likely to contain plotters bent on 'overturning the laws, constitution and government, and every existing establishment, civil and ecclesiastical' in Great Britain or Ireland.[3] Yet even 'regular' Freemasonry (as opposed to the truly seditious continental variety) had harboured traitors. Many American Revolutionaries were 'regular' Masons, notably George Washington, Ben Franklin and Admiral John Paul Jones who had been initiated in Scotland. One Boston lodge, St Andrew's, was full of rebels, including Paul Revere, General Joseph Warren, John Hancock and John Rowe. It was Rowe who inspired the Boston Tea Party which, according to one of the 'Indian' raiders who belonged to the lodge, was planned within St Andrew's itself.[4]

The American Revolution had begun only twenty-four years before the Unlawful Societies Act became law. It is extremely unlikely that Pitt had any idea of Freemasonry's strength among the Revolutionaries – for sure Moira would not have told him! – but, had he known, he would have had good reason to suspect that the Craft might again be 'made use of as a Cover by evilly disposed persons for Seditious purposes'. He would also have had excellent grounds for believing that not all brethren subscribed to their second Antient Charge: 'A mason is a peaceable subject to the civil powers, wherever he resides or works, and is never to be concerned in plots and conspiracies against the peace and welfare of the nation.' Of course, even if Pitt had known about the Masonics of Washington and his brother rebels, he may not have pressed the point because the Craft's leading petitioner, the Earl of Moira, had himself been a hero on England's side in the Revolutionary wars. He would also have been 'snowballed' by Moira's revelation that no less than six of George III's sons were 'on the square', for how could a fraternity boasting 'so many of His Majesty's illustrious Family' possibly be seditious?[5]

Nevertheless, the Act did impose major restrictions on Freemasonry. The 'names and descriptions' of all members of each lodge had to be registered with the local clerk of the peace. By the time the Act was repealed in 1967, it had long been widely ignored. Many lodges did not make returns. One pre-1967 lodge secretary told me: 'I never bothered, and many other secretaries never knew the law existed. Besides, who was going to make you do it? In our town most law enforcers – the Clerk of the Peace, half the JPs and the police chief – were all in our lodge!'

Even more restrictive, the 1799 Act had exempted only meetings of 'regular Lodges of Free Masons held *before* the passing of this Act' (my italics). For some years the Masonic orders subverted this clause by reissuing the warrants of dormant or dead lodges, thus back-dating the foundation of many new lodges. Not only were these Freemasons breaking the criminal law; their stealth and deceit show they knew their actions were illegal.

On the rolls of United Grand Lodge today there are fewer than 300 lodges which were founded before 1799, yet by 1967 another 6,000 had been 'consecrated'. A broad view of the 1799 Act might have encouraged Masons to feel the exemption applied to any future lodges formed under both Modern and Antient Grand Lodges (united in 1813) and two more Grand Lodges in Scotland. The terms of another Act in 1817 may have supported that view. However, neither Act legalized other Masonic Orders such as the Knights Templar (which had barely got going by 1799), the Rose Croix (founded in 1845), the Mark (organized about the same time), the Red Cross of Constantine (whose earliest lodge was founded in 1865) and the Societas Rosicruciana in Anglia (founded in 1866). All these orders are self-governing and have never come under the authority of the various Grand Lodges, which regulate only the Craft and Royal Arch degrees, so they could never have been exempted from the ban on other societies imposed by the 1799 Act.

The illegality of the Masonic Knights Templar is confirmed by the fact that their Grand Master, Lord Rancliffe, 'was personally concerned with the bill in the Lords' and neglected the Order thereafter.[6] Masonic historians differ over whether the revival of the Masonic Templars some years later indicates that 'any question of illegality was over' or whether it suggests 'the authorities were turning a blind eye'.[7] My own view is that all these 'higher' or 'side' degrees (from Knights Templar onwards) met illegally for more than a century until 1967. Nobody would have dared enforce the 1799 Act (even had they known about it) because many magistrates, judges and policemen belonged to these same degrees.

Through such vested interests, Masonic law-breaking has been constantly connived at by the forces of law and order.

Today, any Parliamentary moves requiring public disclosure by Masons should be matched by legislation creating an Ombudsman for the public servant and the police, as advocated by Brian Woollard (see Chapter 13). This is necessary to prevent the kind of career abuse which 4 million other state employees may suffer at the hands of Masons or, indeed, non-Masons. There must be many Masons in public service who feel that they too have had a raw deal at work. In future they should have a means of redress against anti-Masonic prejudice, especially if they are to be obliged to disclose Masonic membership.

The former British ambassador featured in Chapter 32 has further suggestions.

> It should not be too difficult to procure from civil and public servants who belong to secret societies some written declaration and assurances about their activities. I also suggest that something should be done about the confidential personal reporting system. It seems that any officer who believes he may be the subject of victimization through the reporting system (as I was) should be entitled to state that the reporting officer is a Mason and that this should be taken into account in assessing the report. Ideally, in my view, Masons should be excluded from the reporting process, but that is too much to hope for.
>
> I also suggest that the numerous voluntary organizations and charities which serve this country and have been one of its great strengths, should be required by law to keep an indication of any secret society membership by its officers. Members of any society – or indeed contributors to a charity – should, as a matter of routine, be able to obtain a statement of its officers' affiliations. This is not an unreasonable request, but a simple reassurance that the society is being run for the benefit of all members and not primarily for Masons perpetuating themselves in office.
>
> In the present diminished and dangerous situation of our country, a very real danger exists from organizations such as the Brotherhood – partly through infiltration, partly from the disillusionment and frustration which arises when our meritocratic system is deliberately and consistently distorted.

In the House of Commons in June 1988 Labour MP Dale Campbell-Savours introduced a bill to compel police recruits to swear they would not join any organization such as Freemasonry. He also demanded that officers who are already Masons should resign from their lodges or leave the police. On first reading the bill was passed by 117 votes to sixteen, but it had no chance of becoming law because of shortage of Parliamentary time.

If any future bill along these lines looks as if it might become law, it will encounter fierce lobbying just like the 1799 bill. It will also infuriate Masonic cops. If it ever reached the statute book, it could provoke their mass resignation from the force. This might be no bad thing, but it seems unlikely that policemen could be banned from joining Freemasonry unless this private, voluntary organization is itself made illegal. In the present political climate (of near perpetual Conservative rule) there is no chance of this happening, nor am I yet convinced that it *should* happen.

However, because an action is otherwise legal, it does not mean that public servants have an inalienable right to perform it. In many respects the civil liberties of public servants are already severely curtailed. Millions of public servants (including the police) sign the Official Secrets Act which curbs their right to discuss, publish or otherwise disseminate information which they may learn in the course of their work. Also no civil servant, member of the armed forces or policeman may stand as a candidate in local or national elections without first resigning his or her employment. Since 1984 no employees of GCHQ may belong to a trade union. The armed forces and the police have long been deprived of that right, just as they have surrendered their civil liberty to withdraw their labour and go on strike. Thus, imposing a similar curb on policemen in respect of Freemasonry has undeniable precedents. They would retain the right to become or remain a Mason, but they would lose the right to remain a copper. This same rule might be imposed on other public servants.

All this is for Parliament and public to decide. In the meantime Dale Campbell-Savours says: 'If Freemasonry were to shed itself of its secrecy, its exclusiveness and its oath of allegiance, I would have no objection to police officers being members.'

If it were to do all that, it would no longer be Freemasonry!

The need to impose outside curbs on Freemasonry does not mean that the brotherhood is wholly unwilling or unfit to reform itself. On the contrary, it shows signs of a genuine wish to get rid of dishonourable elements. For instance, since writing my chapters on Brian Woollard I have met several more members of the Manor of St James's Lodge. As might be expected, they argue that the press has wilfully misinterpreted their lodge's aims (mainly fellowship and charity, for which it has raised impressive sums), but they also express concern about excessive 'tears of sympathy' dropped elsewhere for brethren who have been convicted of serious crime. Former Deputy Assistant Commissioner Peter Neivens (an honorary Manor member) feels such men should be excluded from Freemasonry and never taken back, even though the usual sense of justice in this country is that a man who has served time in prison has discharged his debt to society. 'As far as Freemasonry is concerned he has let us down beyond redemption and there should be no road back, but that is my individual opinion.' As for lodges which have allowed major criminals to remain members for years after conviction: 'If that were proven to me, then if the authority rested with me, I would seriously think of disbanding that lodge.'

If this policy were to be rigorously applied throughout Britain, not only would Freemasonry be far healthier: its opponents would have far less meat to feed on. Yet it must be doubted if the hierarchy as a whole would want to apply such discipline. As things now stand, Grand Lodge only acts against lodges like the Waterways many years after they have become a haven for criminals, and only then after embarrassing media exposure. It is therefore no wonder that in the meantime other lodges like the Queenswood contain cells of public corruption and the entire institution of Freemasonry is brought into disrepute as a result.

Of course, the merits of an institution as vast as Freemasonry do not turn on the vice or virtue of individual Masons. It does not change its essence because one Grand Officer, his Honour Judge Joseph Butler-Sloss, was exposed in the *News of the World* in July 1988 as a regular patron of Nairobi prostitutes while serving as a High Court judge in Kenya.[8] The private quirks of prominent men who happen to be Masons should not be held against the Brotherhood. As Masons themselves have frequently told me, that would be like condemning Christianity because quite a few vicars over the years have been caught molesting choirboys.

As I write these final pages in December 1988 I am still being sent evidence of Freemasonry's reluctance to punish those who transgress its own moral code. The material comes not from outsiders but from men who are themselves staunch Masons. One such source is Leonard Acklam, a well-to-do self-made Yorkshire businessman who has fought for seven years to win redress for a Masonic Grand Officer's outrageous attempt to interfere with justice. A Mason for thirty-three years, a Past Master of Brighouse Lodge (no. 1301) and a thirtieth degree member of the Rose Croix, Acklam is worth a hearing.

In 1979 he was owed £10,000 by a firm for whom he had done some contract plumbing, so he asked a solicitor to recover the money. The solicitor was also a Mason, but not in Acklam's lodge. Some two years passed but this solicitor had still not recovered the money. Whenever Acklam asked what was going on the solicitor would fob him off, so eventally Acklam rang Leeds Crown Court himself to find out what had happened. To his shock and dismay he was told his case had been thrown out one year earlier because his solicitor had not attended a crucial hearing with the registrar and the defence.

> When I realized that my solicitor had lied and lied to me I turned to another solicitor. Through this man (a non-Mason) I threatened to report my first solicitor to the Law Society and sue him for negligence. At this point he became very worried and turned for help to powerful Masons in his own lodge, the Clifton (no. 7112).
>   Shortly after this I was visited by one of these men, Sir Herbert Redfearn. He told me that if I sued his lodge brother I would 'lose a lot of friends'. I told him that I would do whatever I had to do. A few weeks later Redfearn came to me again and said I should 'look on it in a true Masonic manner and forget it. After all, you can afford it.' He was not only interfering with my legal action against the solicitor. He was also telling me to forget about £10,000!

Acklam's new solicitor was able to recover the £10,000 from the debtor, so Acklam decided not to sue the first one after all. However he did seek Masonic action against Redfearn, so in 1981 he sent a letter of complaint to the local Yorkshire West Riding grand secretary. This did not go down at all well, for Redfearn was not just a Grand Officer of English Freemasonry. He was a leading industrialist, a deputy lieutenant of the county, a knight of the realm, a one-time chairman of the National Union of Conservative Associations and the local Tory king-maker (future Tory MP Gary Waller was initiated in his lodge in 1971). He was also photographed at Conservative party occasions alongside Prime Minister Margaret Thatcher. It was extremely unlikely, therefore, that any Yorkshire Masonic body would dare condemn him.

Acklam waited in vain for provincial action to be taken against Redfearn, and against other Masons over separate irregularities. After four years he turned to Grand Secretary Higham in London. He put his case so forcefully that he spurred Higham into sending a letter to the West Riding secretary. By mistake this was put in the wrong envelope and sent to Acklam himself, who was much intrigued by its contents:

> Bro Acklam is persistent and he may have a case. He won't go away until he's had his say and if what he has to say has substance 'we' should do something about it. [9]

Higham recommended that his West Riding counterpart should find an 'acceptably independent' brother to investigate Acklam's complaints. Acklam had omitted Redfearn's name from all his missives to Higham in order to discover the Grand Secretary's view of the offence, irrespective of the rank of the perpetrator. In July 1986 Higham made this request:

> As I understand it, you believe a senior Freemason put pressure upon you to act to your detriment. If this indeed happened, it would be quite improper and the matter must be investigated. Yet you appear reluctant to name that other person; if the matter is ever to be resolved you must name him, so that inquiries can be made.[10]

Acklam was relieved because at last a leading Mason had admitted the impropriety of what he claimed had been done. Yet he was also dismayed because, although he had never named Redfearn to Higham, he had named him in his written complaint to the West Riding grand secretary back in 1981, which had led to no inquiry whatsoever. Redfearn had never challenged Acklam's account, even when Acklam put it in a letter to Redfearn himself. Redfearn merely wrote that the government of Freemasonry was by 'benevolent autocracy' and that if it 'ever becomes democratic it will cease to have attraction'. He then implied that Acklam should not publicize his complaint because 'the leaders of the Craft have quite sufficient complications at the present time attempting to deal with subversive elements from outside'.

In 1988 a High Court judge conducted an internal Masonic inquiry into Acklam's other allegations, but not into the Sir Herbert Redfearn matter because a Grand Lodge employee had advised Acklam not to mention it in his written submission. Looking back, he feels he was wrong-footed by this advice but it was just one of many incidents which drove him to contact me in 1988. In earlier years he had written to many other folk including the Grand Master, the Duke of Kent, whom he asked what right a high-ranking Mason had to 'put me under Masonic blackmail'. He also wrote to Sir Kenneth Newman, when he was Commissioner of the Metropolitan Police.

> The purpose of this letter is simply to confirm what you already know. There are corrupt people in the order, and the person who put me under Masonic blackmail is a very big man in very big circles. That is why no one DARES to do anything about him. But please be assured that we have little insignificant men like me who are trying like hell to clean the order up. It is not the rank-and-file who are 'using the order' but the men who have attained high rank . . . We 'Good Freemasons' want them out.

Redfearn died only a few weeks after Acklam gave me his name, so I was unable to ask him for his side of the story. As for Grand Secretary Higham, after reading all the papers very carefully, I feel he has done what he can to make a provincial Grand Lodge do its duty. Even so, I feel Acklam has been treated in a very odd way. He is not alone. I have a 1988 letter from another longstanding Mason in the south of England, a past Master of four lodges and a provincial grand officer. He raises another string of damaging allegations:

> The amount of crawling that is necessary to obtain Masonic promotion is unbelievable, and when I protested about a crook being appointed to one of the highest offices in my province, I was told, 'But look what he has done for charity.' The fact that the money he donated was stolen (directly or indirectly) from his share-holders did not seem to matter and my protest to the Provincial Grand Secretary was the matter for some laughter.

I invited this man to tell me more. On the telephone he revealed that the crook in question had been convicted at the Old Bailey and yet his Masonic career had soared. We arranged to meet in November 1988 but, a few hours before the appointed time, he rang to say Grand Lodge had instructed him not to see me until it had carried out an investigation. Since the man first complained about this affair more than ten years ago, it is difficult to see how anything Grand Lodge does now can affect the issue. However, I await the results of its inquiry with interest and look forward to including them in any book I may write to follow this one.

English Freemasons naturally boast that the royal family and Freemasonry have been intertwined for more than 200 years, for this gives both them and their brotherhood a highly honourable façade. They tend not to point out that crookery and the Craft have also run into each other over the centuries. In 1777 the Rev William Dodd, first Grand Chaplain of the Grand Lodge of England, was convicted of forging a bond for £4,200 in the name of his patron, the Earl of Chesterfield. For this crime he was hanged in public, allegedly the last forger in England to suffer this fate. In those days Grand Lodge was quicker than it is today to get rid of the crooks and racketeers in its midst: it expelled Grand Chaplain Dodd five months before he swung at Tyburn.

It was of Dr Dodd that his friend Samuel Johnson made the immortal statement, 'When a man knows he is to be hanged in a fortnight, it concentrates his mind wonderfully.' Today English Freemasonry has longer than a fortnight to contemplate its condition but, if it does not reform itself soon, more and more scandals will emerge, and more books will be written exposing them.

In the First Degree ritual the Worshipful Master tells the newly initiated Mason that 'no institution can boast a more solid foundation than that on which Freemasonry rests – the practice of every moral and social virtue'. If that claim rings hollow these days Masons might rapidly restore their collective reputation if they also 'remember that wherever we are, and whatever we do, He is with us, and His all-seeing eye observes us'.

'He', of course, is the 'Grand Geometrician of the Universe'.

NOTES

FOREWORD

1. William Preston, *Illustrations of Freemasonry*: Book I, Section VII. All citations in these notes refer to an edition 'with copious notes and additions by the Revd G. Oliver DD', London 1822 (as reprinted in New York, 1855).
2. August Wolfstieg, *Bibliographie der freimaurischen Literatur*, cited by Alec Mellor, *Our Separated Brethren, the Freemasons* (Harrap, London 1964).
3. William J. Whalen, Preface to *Christianity and American Freemasonry* (Bruce, Milwaukee 1958; Our Sunday Visitor, Inc., Huntingdon, Indiana 1987).
4. *Horace Walpole's Correspondence*, Yale Edition, Oxford & Yale 1955.
5. Freemasonry has been called a 'Mafia' in many letters from members of the public to Stephen Knight and myself. 'The Mafia of the Mediocre?' was the billing on the front cover of the *Listener* on 24 April 1980 for an article by the late Revd Robert Foxcroft, 'Brotherhood of Man'.
6. Evidence on Compatibility submitted by United Grand Lodge of England (UGLE) to Church of England Working Group, April 1986.
7. Until recently Freemasons themselves often used this phrase to describe their fraternity, e.g. as cited by the non-Mason Foxcroft, op. cit.
8. Grand Secretary Higham in 'Freemasonry – from Craft to Tolerance', talk at St Margaret Patten's Church, 1 October 1985.
9. Junior Warden's words closing the lodge in the Second Degree (Taylor's Working).

INTRODUCTION

1. *Masonic Square*, September 1986.
2. *Evening Standard*, Diary 1988.
3. Peter Rhodes, *Wolverhampton Express and Star*, 16 May 1988.

4. 'The Freemasons', Griffin Productions, Director Monique Hayat, broadcast on 6 May 1988.
5. The song was first published in Dr James Anderson's *Constitutions of the Freemasons*, 1723, and attributed to Matthew Birkhead. The verses are still printed in Masonic yearbooks, e.g. Oxfordshire.
6. Richard Cobb, Times Diary, *The Times*, 12 April 1988.
7. Levin, 'A star chamber in the land of the Free?', *The Times*, 27 March 1984; 'Hidden hand of conspiracy', 21 April 1988.
8. Victor Epstein, letter to *The Times*, 2 April 1984.
9. See Ellic Howe, 'The Collapse of Freemasonry in Nazi Germany 1933–35', vol. 95 (1982) of *Ars Quatuor Coronatorum* (Transactions of Quatuor Coronati Lodge) – hereafter *AQC*.
10. My remarks on post-war German Freemasonry are based partly on Theo Marti, *Des Hérésies Maçonniques à l'Histoire de la LUF*, Lielens, Brussels 1978. Professor Marti, a Swiss, was past President of the Universal League of Freemasons, an order not recognised by 'regular' grand lodges such as the United Grand Lodges of Germany. He might therefore be considered hostile to that body, but he supported his case against the Masons named in my text with authentic original documentation.
11. My account of the Brown-Frommholz affair is based on conversations with Major Harvey Brown, and Marti, op. cit.
12. Marti, op. cit.
13. Walton Hannah, *Darkness Visible*, Augustine Publishing Co., Chulmleigh, Devon 1952, paperback edition 1984. *Christian by Degrees* (also Augustine) 1954, paperback 1984.
14. On Morgan see Whalen, op. cit. In *The*

Antimasonic Party in the United States (University Press of Kentucky 1983), William P. Vaughn seeks to refute the anti-Masonic version of the Morgan 'murder' story, as traditionally told in *Morgan's Freemasonry Exposed and Explained*, New York 1825, and in *Letters on the Masonic Institution* by John Quincy Adams, Boston 1847. Adams, a dedicated anti-Mason, was President of the United States 1825–29.

15. On Markov see Gilbert Kelland, *Crime in London*, The Bodley Head, London 1986.

16. Summarized from Knight, *The Brotherhood*, Granada/Grafton, London 1984. He based that account on his own *Jack the Ripper, the Final Solution*, Panther (now Grafton) 1977.

17. *Jack the Ripper, the Final Solution* enjoyed huge sales in the UK and abroad. It also provoked Masons in several countries to write angry letters to Stephen Knight.

18. Letter to a British MP, 30 January 1984.

19. My remarks are based partly on conversations with Dr Peter Fenwick, Consultant Neuropsychiatrist of the Maudsley Hospital, who treated Stephen Knight's epilepsy and cancer. Dr Fenwick kindly spoke to me on the written authority of Stephen's family. He is not a Freemason.

20. E.g. rituals of the Third Degree in Craft Freemasonry and the Masonic Knights Templar.

21. UGLE Evidence 1986, op. cit.

22. *AQC*, vol. 99 (1986).

CHAPTER ONE

1. Taken from the Second Degree ritual in which an Entered Apprentice is raised to the rank of Fellow-Craft.

2. Canon Richard Tydeman in an address, 'Freemasonry and the Church'.

3. UGLE Quarterly Communication, March 1988.

4. E.g. Joseph Fort Newton, *The Builders*, Macoy, Richmond, Virginia 1914, revised 1951.

5. Act 37, H VIII.

6. See A. L. Miller, *Notes on the Early History of the Lodge, Aberdeen*, University Press, Aberdeen.

7. According to Ashmole's diary entry for 14 October 1646, cited in most Masonic histories and encyclopaedias.

8. Explanation of the First Degree Tracing Board, as printed in many printed versions of the ritual, and in Hannah, *Darkness Visible*.

9. Preston op. cit., Book I, Section VII.

10. E.g. Fred L. Pick and G. Norman Knight, Chapter 1 of *The Pocket History of Freemasonry*, Muller, London 1953, revised 1983.

11. See UGLE Quarterly Communication, May 1986.

12. Revd Andy Arbuthnot, *Should a Christian be a freemason?*, The London Healing Mission, 1988.

13. In response to C of E Working Group Report, UGLE 24 June 1987.

14. Higham on *Call Nick Ross*, BBC Radio 4, 3 May 1988.

15. Higham at Freemason's Hall press conference, 5 May 1988.

16. Higham: 'Now what is Freemasonry? It is for most of us a spare time activity, but above all it is FUN'; in talk at St Margaret Patten's Church, 1 October 1985, 'From Craft to Tolerance'.

17. The 'Buchanan' manuscript is also held by Grand Lodge.

18. *Constitutions of the Antient Fraternity of Free and Accepted Masons* under the UGLE, Freemasons' Hall, London.

19. 'Registration Form L', as currently issued by UGLE.

20. Pick and Knight, op. cit.

21. *Coil's Masonic Encyclopedia*, Macoy, New York 1961.

22. C. N. Batham, letter published in *Masonic Square*, March 1985.

23. W. R. Tigerdine, letter, as 22 above.

24. *Third Rising*, Hospital Governors' Association, October 1986. The title refers to a stage in Masonic proceedings (following the ritual) when matters of general interest may be discussed.

25. In a letter to all Governors of the Royal Masonic Hospital, 7 November 1986.

26. UGLE Quarterly Communication, December 1986.

27. UGLE Board of General Purposes, 'Report on the Penalties in the Obligations', May 1986.

28. As 27 above.

CHAPTER TWO

1. Song VI in Preston, op. cit.

2. Free Presbyterian Synod 1987, quoted in *The Tablet*, 30 May 1987.

3. *Aberdeen Evening Express*, 4 March 1987.

4. *Glasgow Herald*, 29 April 1987.

5. *Aberdeen Evening Express*, 8 April 1987.

6. Quoted in James Dewar, *The Unlocked Secret*, William Kimber, London 1966.

7. R. A. R. Wells, in *AQC*, vol. 97 (1984).

8. See list of Gothic Constitutions, Coil op. cit.

9. A few arguably Christian phrases survived even after 1816, notably the Third Degree reference to the 'bright Morning Star', a phrase from The Revelation xxii, 16, which is generally taken to refer to Jesus Christ. Some Jewish lodges replace this phrase with 'Him whose Divine Word'. See Harry Carr, *The Freemason at Work*, Lewis Masonic, Shepperton, 1986. For an alternative interpretation see my Chapter Seven.

10. Grand Secretary Higham in his talk 'From Craft to Tolerance'.

11. In this Chapter I have quoted the rewording of Anderson printed in modern editions of the UGLE's Book of Constitutions. In 1723 Anderson himself wrote 'Masonry becomes the Center of Union, and the Means of conciliating true Friendship among Persons that must have remain'd at a perpetual Distance'.

12. Revd Neville Barker-Cryer, ending his paper 'The De-Christianizing of the Craft', *AQC*, vol. 97 (1984).

13. Alphonse Cerza, *Anti-Masonry*, Missouri Lodge of Research 1962.

14. Address to Grand Lodge at Annual Investiture, 25 April 1984.

15. *Freemasonry and Religion*, UGLE 1985.

16. Cited by Whalen, op. cit.

17. This rave review appeared in *10,000 Famous Freemasons* by William R. Denslow, Missouri Lodge of Research, Macoy 1957–1961.

18. *The Builders*, op. cit.

19. As above.

20. Ward, *Freemasonry, Its Aims and Ideals*, Rider 1923.

21. Cockburn, *Freemasonry, What, Whence, Why, Whither*, Masonic Record, London. Cited in Hannah, *Darkness Visible*.

22. Wilmshurst, *The Masonic Initiation*, Lund Humphries, London 1924.

23. 'Vindex', *Light Invisible*, Regency Press 1952, Britons Publishing Company, London 1964.

24. *Freemasons' Chronicle*, 2 January 1954, cited in Hannah, *Christian By Degrees*.

25. John Hamill, *AQC* paper delivered in 1988.

26. Printed in UGLE Quarterly Communication, April 1984.

27. Vindex, op. cit.

28. For a masonic funeral service see Preston, op. cit. For an ordinary Masonic church service see Hannah, *Darkness Visible*.

29. Mervyn Stockwood, *Chanctonbury Ring*, Hodder & Stoughton, London 1982.

30. *Daily Telegraph*, 2 January 1967, cited in *AQC*, vol. 95 (1982).

31. Fisher, letter quoted in *Chanctonbury Ring*.

32. Cerza, op. cit.

33. Dr S. Vacher, *AQC*, vol. 83 (1970).

CHAPTER THREE

1. Marius Lepage in *Le Symbolisme*, October 1953, quoted in Hannah, *Christian By Degrees*.

2. The Working Group referred to Hannah's *Darkness Visible* and *Christian By Degrees*, the Methodist Report of 1985, *The Brotherhood* by Knight, and *Freemasonry – A Way of Salvation?* by Revd John Lawrence, Grove Books 1982. In 1988 Kingsway Books published another book by Lawrence: *Freemasonry – a Religion?*.

3. Hannah, *Darkness Visible*.

4. UGLE, February 1986.

5. The Group was chaired by Dr Margaret Hewitt, Reader in Social Institutions, Exeter University. The other woman was Dr Christina Baxter, registrar at a theological college. The second Mason was Robert Hart, a medical doctor and microbiologist. The Group was completed by three non-Masonic reverends: John Broadhurst, James Duxbury and David Holloway.

6. According to the 'Five Points of Fellowship', see page 41.

7. Para 69, *Freemasonry and Christianity, are they Compatible?*, Church House Publishing, London 1987.

8. As 7 above, para 71.

9. *Freemasonry and Religion*, UGLE.

10. *Freemasonry and Christianity*, Church House, para 110.

11. As 10 above, para 122.

12. Notes on the C of E Working Group report, UGLE 24 June 1987.

13. UGLE Report on the Synod debate, 21 July 1987.

14. Martin Reynolds, *Church Times*, 3 July 1987.

CHAPTER FOUR

1. In an unpublished letter to *The Times*, 16 July 1986, reproduced in UGLE evidence to C of E Working Group.

2. In *The Brotherhood* Stephen Knight was mistaken when he wrote that the Rose Croix claims ascendancy over the Craft.

3. Each Royal Arch Chapter is attached to a Craft Lodge of the same name. The

1987–88 Masonic Yearbook lists 7,532 lodges in England and Wales but only 2,836 chapters, which have somewhat smaller memberships than lodges.

4. According to a version published by Special Services, Walsall, 1986.
5. Methodist Church inquiry report, 1985.
6. *Reading Evening Post*, 14 October 1987.
7. Letter to *Reading Evening Post*, 5 November 1987.
8. E.g. version cited in note 4.
9. As in the Aldersgate working, Hannah, *Darkness Visible*.
10. As 9 above.
11. *Freemasonry and Christianity*, para 89.
12. Notes on C of E Working Group report, UGLE 24 June 1987.
13. Heydon's address to Grand Chapter, 14 November 1984.
14. The outcome of the Committee's discussion was the present ritual, in which 'three Principals' represent Freemasonry's three original Grand Masters. The routine opens with all three standing, and balancing a Bible on their intertwined upturned left palms. Each says a few phrases in turn, starting 'We three do meet and agree . . . in love and unity . . . the sacred word to keep . . .' They then each chant JAH, BUL and ON – the names of God in their respective languages. By chanting in quick succession, however, they collectively chant the Sacred Word JAHBULON, without any one uttering the entire 'Name which no man might pronounce'. Now imagine, for example, a policeman, a judge and an MP – with their hands and feet locked in three simultaneous triangles – doing this together.
15. In the Old Testament the plural Baalim is used to describe the Gods of all gentiles. OED, Oxford University Press.
16. Tydeman's address to Grand Chapter, 13 November 1985.
17. Dyer's address to Grand Chapter, 12 February 1986.
18. Letter to Grand Officers and Scribes E, November 1984.
19. Bishop Richard Pococke LL D FRS, *A Description of the East*, 1743–45, *Travels in Egypt*, 1755.
20. *Description de l'Egypte*. Vol. 5 of a 20-volume folio published in Paris over decades during the reigns of Napoleon I and Louis XVIII.
21. Lepsius, *Discoveries in Egypt and Ethiopia*, 1842–45.
22. For insights into On-Heliopolis see *The Book of the Dead*, many editions including E. A. Wallis Budge, Medici Society 1913; Peter Tomkins, *The Magic of Obelisks*, Harper & Row, New York 1981; George Hart, *A Dictionary of Egyptian Gods and Goddesses*, Routledge & Kegan Paul, London 1986.
23. Antient Charge 4, 'Behaviour in Presence of Strangers, not Masons'.
24. Emulation Working. Current editions of Taylor's Working also contain this Explanation. (In England craft ritual is 'worked' in many variations, a result of the brotherhood's oral tradition.)
25. Notes on C of E Working Group report, UGLE.
26. Pike, *The Holy Triad*, Washington 1873.
27. *Freemasonry and the Ancient Gods*, Simkin, Marshall, London 1921.
28. Hall, *The Lost Keys of Freemasonry*, Macoy, 1923 and 1976.
29. The 'broad lunatic fringe' in this respect includes Anderson and Preston.
30. Near the end of his life J. S. M. Ward behaved most oddly (see Chapter 10). The writings of other Masonic authors (e.g. Manly Hall) indicate a slim hold on reality.

CHAPTER FIVE
1. Hannah, op. cit.
2. Notes on C of E Working Group report, UGLE.
3. At least sixteen serving and retired bishops were Freemasons around 1956, according to the *Masonic Year Book Historical Supplement*, UGLE 1969.
4. UGLE evidence to the C of E Working Group.
5. Albert Mackey, *The Symbolism of Freemasonry*, Powner, Chicago, reprinted 1975.
6. Robert Burns, as quoted in Mackey, op. cit.
7. C. N. Batham, In Memoriam notice for George Draffen, *AQC*, vol. 98 (1985).
8. Grand Lodge of Scotland Yearbook, Edinburgh 1986.
9. In unpublished letter to *The Times*, 16 July 1986, reproduced in UGLE evidence to C of E Working Group.
10. First Degree ritual, as published in ritual books and Hannah, *Darkness Visible*.
11. As 10 above.
12. UGLE evidence to the C of E Working Group.
13. Mackey, op. cit.
14. Hannah, *Christian By Degrees*.

15. *Freemasonry and Christianity*, Church House, para 91.
16. Notes on C of E Working Group report, UGLE.
17. Wilmshurst, *The Masonic Initiation*, op. cit.
18. Unpublished letter to *The Times*.
19. Hannah, *Christian By Degrees*.
20. UGLE Notes on C of E Working Group report.
21. As 20 above.
22. See *A Concise Index* to *AQC*, vols 1–80 (London 1971) and later volumes.
23. Cited in Pick and Knight, *The Freemasons' Pocket Reference Book*, Muller 1955, revised 1983.

CHAPTER SIX
1. Quoted in McCormick, *Christ, the Christian and Freemasonry*, W. J. McCormick, Great Joy Publications, Belfast.
2. On obelisks see Tompkins, op. cit.; Erik Iversen, *Obelisks in Exile* (two vols.) Copenhagen, 1968, 1971. John A. Weisse, *The Obelisk and Freemasonry*, Bouton, New York 1880.
3. From E. A. Wallis-Budge's notes on Ra/ Re, included in Medici Society reprint of *The Book of the Dead*, University Books, Secaucus, New Jersey 1960.
4. On Osiris, Ra/Re and other Egyptian gods see Wallis-Budge, op. cit.; Hart, op. cit.
5. Pliny in *Natural History*.
6. See Mackey, op. cit.; J. S. M. Ward, *Freemasonry and the Ancient Gods* and *Who Was Hiram Abiff?*, Lewis Masonic.
7. Hart, op. cit.
8. See Tomkins op. cit., especially chapters 17 and 18, with quotations from Hargrave Jennings, *Phallicism* and *Obelisks*.
9. Weisse, op. cit.
10. *The Book of the Dead*, op. cit.; also Tompkins op. cit., chapter 16.
11. William Bankes, the obelisk's buyer who also paid for its transportation, may not have been a Mason.
12. Weisse, op. cit.
13. Preston, *Illustrations of Freemasonry*.
14. The Acacia also symbolizes Masonic re-birth in general – see Mackey, op. cit. and others.
15. *Masonic Square*, March 1978.

CHAPTER SEVEN
1. *Voice* (Full Gospel Business Men's Fellowship International magazine), European edition No. 2.84.
2. *Freemasonry and Christianity*, Appendix 10.
3. On page 49 of the UGLE's evidence to C of E Working Group, the current holder of Pike's office (in the USA) is quoted as confirming that 'his records show Pike did not make the "Lucifer" statement and assumes it was invented by A. C. de la Rive' (the French authoress concerned).
4. The Rose Croix's formal title is the 'Ancient and Accepted Rite for England and Wales'. Scotland and Ireland have their own organizations.
5. R. A. Gilbert in *The Golden Dawn, Twilight of the Magicians*, Aquarian Press, Wellingborough 1983. My account also relies on Ellic Howe, *The Magicians of the Golden Dawn*, Routledge & Kegan Paul, 1972.
6. Sussex Masonic *Year Book and Directory*.
7. Version published in Gilbert, op. cit.
8. Aleister Crowley, *Confessions* (Ed. Symonds and Grant), Routledge & Kegan Paul, 1979.
9. As 8 above, Chapter 72.
10. Crowley, *Magick* (Ed. Symonds and Grant), Routledge & Kegan Paul, 1973, pp. 296 and 172.
11. See *AQC, Concise Index*, op. cit., like Yarker, William Wynn Westcott often lectured to the lodge.
12. Pentagram, August 1964.
13. *Masonic Square*, September 1984.
14. Ellic Howe, 'The rite of Memphis in France and England, 1838–70', *AQC*, vol. 92 (1979).
15. J. S. Hawkins, *Gothic Architecture*, 1813, quoted in OED.
16. Ward, *Freemasonry and the Ancient Gods*, Chapter 8: 'The Vesica Piscis in the Craft'.
17. Emulation Working, as quoted in Hannah, *Darkness Visible*.
18. Harry Carr, *The Freemasons at Work*, Lewis Masonic 1976, Explanation of 'The point within a circle'.
19. See previous notes citing books on Egyptian gods and works by Hargrave Jennings (a Victorian Freemason).
20. Grand Lodge of Scotland Year Book, Edinburgh 1986.
21. *AQC*, vol. 97 (1984); and Carr op. cit.
22. This account of the Masonic Knights Templar ritual comes from Hannah, *Christian By Degrees*. It has never been challenged as inaccurate by the order's authorities.
23. *Freemasonry and Religion*, UGLE pamphlet 1987.

24. *Daily Mirror*, 28 April 1973.

CHAPTER EIGHT

1. Alec Mellor, *AQC*, vol. 89 (1976), 'The Roman Catholic Church and the Craft'.
2. See Whalen, op. cit.
3. As quoted in the German Bishops' statement, 12 May 1980.
4. *L'Osservatore Romano*, 'Irreconcilability between Christian faith and Freemasonry', 11 March 1985.
5. Cardinal John Heenan, *Not the Whole Truth*, 1971.
6. See Chapters Eleven to Twenty-one (on the police) and Chapter Thirty-one.
7. Carr, op. cit.
8. Mellor, *Our Separated Brethren, The Freemasons*, Maison Mame, Paris 1961; Harrap 1964. *La Franc-Maçonnerie a l'heure du Choix*, 1963. See also Mellor, *AQC*, vol. 89.
9. Letter to Cardinal John Krol of Philadelphia, 18 July 1974.
10. 'Catholics and Freemasonry', Episcopal Conference of England and Wales, November 1974.
11. Carr, op. cit.
12. Mellor, *AQC*, vol. 89.
13. As quoted in *New Liberty* magazine.
14. Letter to the *National Catholic Reporter*, 10 April 1981.
15. Decree of Holy Office, 31 May 1911.

CHAPTER NINE

1. Higham gave this estimate in his talk, 'From Craft to Tolerance', at St Margaret Patten's Church, 1 October 1985.
2. According to Higham at Freemasons' Hall press conference, 5 May 1988.
3. In Arabic-speaking countries non-Masons call the local Masonic temple 'El Beit es-Sheitan', literally 'the House of the Devil'.
4. UGLE evidence to the C of E Working Group.
5. Marcus Humphrey of Dinnet, Grand Worshipful Master Mason of Scotland, quoted in *Aberdeen Evening Express*, 8 April 1987.
6. According to K. W. Henderson, *Masonic World Guide*, Lewis Masonic 1984.
7. More of Arden's Hackney findings appear in Chapter Twenty-six.
8. Third degree ritual, see Hannah, *Darkness Visible*.
9. In a letter dated 9 June 1986.
10. In a letter dated 18 August 1988.

CHAPTER TEN

1. Nesta Webster's best read books were *World Revolution, The Plot against Civilization*, London 1921, and *Secret Societies and Subversive Movements*, 1924. Erich Ludendorff's most notorious effort was *Destruction of Freemasonry through Revelation of their Secrets*, Munich 1927, Hitler makes three references to Freemasonry in *Mein Kampf*.
2. Ward's handbooks are published and sold by Lewis Masonic, Shepperton. For other books by Ward, see Chapter 4, note 27 and Chapter 6, note 6.
3. Peter Anson, *Bishops at Large*, Faber and Faber, London.
4. That Ward *is* an embarrassment to modern Masons emerges from John Hamill's 1988 *AQC* paper, 'The Sins of our Masonic Fathers . . .'
5. Ward (with W. G. Sterling), *The Hung Society*, Lewis Masonic.

CHAPTER ELEVEN

1. Neivens is an honorary member of the lodge.
2. From the Installing Master's address to the brethren after the new Master has been installed.
3. In a letter from Pro Grand Master Lord Cornwallis to the *Independent*, 20 February 1988.
4. By 1986 the old Metropolitan Police 'districts' had been renamed 'divisions'.

CHAPTER TWELVE

1. *Observer*, 25 March 1984.
2. Quoted in UGLE Quarterly Communication, 9 March 1988.
3. See *The Fall of Scotland Yard* by Barry Cox, John Shirley and Martin Short, Penguin 1977.
4. Letter from Viscount Whitelaw to the author, 5 May 1988.
5. I.e. until the far later appointment of Meffen.
6. In his letter to the *Independent*, 20 February 1988.
7. *Daily Telegraph*, 15 April 85.

CHAPTER THIRTEEN

1. Every policeman starts his career in uniform. About one in seven becomes a detective. Nowadays detectives do not necessarily stay in the CID, as was the custom until the mid-1970s. This interchange has caused me to list as detectives some men who have spent most of their

careers in uniform. Similarly I have counted some long standing detectives as 'uniform' because they returned to uniform late in their careers. My resulting 'statistics' are not scientific but, nevertheless, I believe they are informative.

2. Source: *Police and Constabulary Almanac 1981*, R. Hazell.
3. On Freemasonry in GCHQ and other sections of Britain's security services see Chapters 32 and 33.
4. On British politicians and Freemasonry see Chapter 34.
5. Quoted in *Edgware Times* article by Brandon Malinsky, 21 April 1988.
6. Quoted in UGLE Quarterly Communication, 12 December 1984.

CHAPTER FOURTEEN
1. During the 'Stalker' press conference, 6 August 1986.
2. *Independent*, 18 February 1988.

CHAPTER SIXTEEN
1. Masonic poem by David Barker, quoted in *A Treasury of Masonic Thought*, Robert Hale, London 1981.
2. This story was told briefly by Stephen K night in *The Brotherhood*. I expand on it here to make a different point. For a full account see George Dilnot, *The Trial of the Detectives*, Geoffrey Bless 1928.
3. If an article was listed as 'lost', rather than stolen, no crime would appear to have been committed. Morrish's experience resembles that of Det. Con. Ron Walker of the Kent Constabulary who alleged in 1986 that some colleagues had been rigging the force's crime 'clear-up' rate by persuading convicted prisoners to confess to crimes which they had not committed.
4. Penguin, 1977.
5. See the James Report (Home Office appointed Inquiry into the Challenor Affair), HMSO 1965. Mary Grigg, *Challenor Case*, Penguin 1965. For a more sympathetic view of Challenor, see Gilbert Kelland, op. cit.
6. *News of the World*, 20 March 1988.

CHAPTER SEVENTEEN
1. Hambleton's main onslaught on the Metropolitan Police came in *World In Action*, 20 July 1981.

CHAPTER EIGHTEEN
1. *World In Action*, Granada Television, 3 November 1986.

2. Evidence given by Docherty at gun-licence hearing, Wood Green Crown Court, May 1983.
3. *Observer*, 21 February 1988.
4. UGLE's own figures, given by Higham at Freemasons' Hall press conference, 5 May 1988. Cornwallis made his remarks in the UGLE Quarterly Communication, 9 March 1988.

CHAPTER NINETEEN
1. Peter Taylor, *Stalker, The Search for the Truth*, Faber 1987.
2. John Stalker, *Stalker*, Harrap 1988.
3. Stalker, op. cit.
4. Stalker, op. cit.
5. Stalker, op. cit.
6. Taylor, op. cit.
7. *Private Eye*, 1986.
8. *Manchester Evening News*, 25 July 1986.
9. Ian d'Alton, *Protestant Society and Politics in Cork, 1812–1844*, Cork University Press 1980.
10. Letter of 19 April 1837 to *The Pilot*, Dublin, as quoted in Cerza op. cit.
11. Maude Gonne MacBride, *A Servant of the Queen: Reminiscences*, 1938.
12. Vindex, op. cit.
13. *Orangeism*, vol. 1, quoted in McCormick, op. cit.
14. Quoted in McCormick, op. cit.
15. On the Ku Klux Klan and Freemasonry, see Whalen, *Christianity and American Freemasonry*.
16. The Government of Ireland Act 1920, article 65 section 1.
17. *Fortnight*, April 1984.
18. *Guardian*, 19 April 1988.
19. According to Peter Taylor, op. cit.
20. On Drury and Humphreys see *The Fall of Scotland Yard*.
21. Para 396 of the Sampson report, as quoted in Stalker, op. cit.
22. On Page see Chapter Twenty, and Knight, *The Brotherhood*.
23. As quoted in the *Daily Telegraph*, 9 August 1986.
24. Stalker, op. cit.
25. *The Times*, 27 January 1988.

CHAPTER TWENTY
1. On City of London Police see Chapter 17. It is important to state that members of the late Mr Page's family made strong representations to Grafton Books about what they felt was an unfair and inaccurate portrayal of Page in *The Brotherhood*.

CHAPTER TWENTY-TWO

1. UGLE Quarterly Communication, August 1984.
2. UGLE Quarterly Communication, September 1986.

CHAPTER TWENTY-THREE

1. Section 13 (2) of the Coroners (Amendment) Act 1926, as amended by the Administration of Justice Act 1982 section 62.

CHAPTER TWENTY-FOUR

1. In a letter to Derek Pilkington dated 3 January 1985.

CHAPTER TWENTY-FIVE

1. Antient Charge 6, 'Behaviour towards a strange brother'.
2. *Enfield Gazette*, 4 May 1987.
3. *Bristol Evening Post*, 3 August 1987.
4. Editorial in *Oldham Evening Chronicle*, 31 July 1986.
5. 'Once Proud Mancunian', 5 August, and R. H. B. Gatley, 7 August 1986, *Manchester Evening News*.
6. Cornelius letter in *Standard*, 28 May 1986.
7. *Daily News*, 5 March 1987.
8. *Worthing Gazette*, 27 March 1986.
9. *Denbigh Free Press* articles, 7 and 21 December 1983, 1, 8, 15, 22 February and 7 March 1984.
10. *The Orcadian*, 27 March 1986.
11. *After Dark*, 19 February 1988.
12. See Ray Fitzwalter and David Taylor, *Web of Corruption*, Granada, 1981. Martin Tompkinson and Michael Gillard, *Nothing to Declare*, John Calder, London 1980. Also *The Salmon Report* (Royal Commission on Standards of Conduct in Public Life), HMSO 1976.
13. *Leeds Other Paper*, 12 December 1986.
14. *Herald Express*, 2 October 1987.

CHAPTER TWENTY-SIX

1. See Knight, *The Brotherhood*; Fitzwalter and Taylor, op. cit.; Gillard and Tompkinson, op. cit.
2. Revealed by Arden at Hackney Town Hall press conference, 7 April 1987. See also Chapter 10.
3. As detailed in Arden's *Final Report* to Hackney, March 1987.
4. As 3 above.
5. George MacAree. According to the *Guiness Book of Records* 1974 he then weighed 38½ stone.
6. In 1965 the Borough of Finsbury was absorbed into Hackney. In its 1986 evidence to the Church of England Working Group, UGLE attacked Stephen Knight for 'slack research' in listing lodges named after London boroughs which ceased to exist when the GLC was formed in 1965. However, some have retained a local government membership, as the remarks of Bill Watts confirm.
7. As stated on Newham Lodge summons to a meeting on 18 September 1980.
8. *Daily Mirror*, 28 May 1980.
9. *Newham Recorder*, 27 March 1980.

CHAPTER TWENTY-SEVEN

1. *Watlington Times*, 26 March 1986.
2. Letter to John Watman, 5 January 1987.

CHAPTER TWENTY-EIGHT

1. 'Tribe' is another pseudonym.
2. *Surrey Comet*, 27 February 1987.

CHAPTER THIRTY

1. Godfrey Hodgson, *Lloyd's of London, a Reputation at Risk*, Allen Lane 1984, Penguin 1986.
2. A Master is a junior judge.

CHAPTER THIRTY-ONE

1. Sir James Stubbs, *Freemasonry in My Life*, Lewis Masonic 1985.
2. R. F. Gould, *Military Lodges (1732–1899)*, Gale and Polden 1900.
3. Editor's note (by Dr George Oliver) in Preston, op. cit.
4. As 3 above, taken from the *Stirling Journal*.
5. Ward, *Freemasonry and the Ancient Gods*.
6. Reproduced in *AQC*, vol. 83 (1970).
7. Reproduced in the St Andrews's Lodge (No. 1046) history, *The Story of 100 Years*, 1965.

CHAPTER THIRTY-TWO

1. From the Installation Address, delivered annually in every lodge when the new lodge Master is installed in the chair.
2. 'Gunning for Government', made by Twenty-Twenty Television for the *Dispatches* series, broadcast 4 December 1987. Producers Claudia Milne and Martin Short.

CHAPTER THIRTY-THREE

1. *The Brotherhood*, Chapter Ten.
2. Resolution adopted at the Fourth Congress of the Communist International, quoted in Cerza, op. cit.

3. John Hamill, *The Craft*, Crucible (Aquarian), 1986.
4. This advice appears on the meetings summonses of many lodges.
5. UGLE evidence to Church of England Working Group. Annex K.
6. 'The trial of Sir Roger Hollis', London Weekend Television, 3 April 1988.
7. Knight, *The Brotherhood*.
8. Peter Wright, *Spycatcher*, Heinemann (Viking in USA) 1987.
9. Michael Bentine, *Doors of the Mind*, Granada 1981, also Grafton Omnibus edition 1987.
10. As 9 above.
11. Knight, *The Brotherhood*.
12. Books in English touching on P2 include Larry Gurwin, *The Calvi Affair*, MacMillan 1983; Rupert Cornwell, *God's Banker*, Gollancz 1983; David Yallop, *In God's Name*, Cape 1984; John Haycraft, *Italian Labyrinth*, Secker and Warburg 1985.
13. See *The Rise and Fall of the Bulgarian Connection* by Edward Herman and Frank Brodhead, Sheridan Square Publications, New York 1986.
14. As 13 above.
15. SISMI stands for Servizio Informazione e Sicurezza Militare.
16. *Relazione della Commissione Parlamentare d'Inchiesta sulla Loggia Massonica P2*, President: Deputy Tina Anselmi, Rome 1984. Hereafter called the Italian Parliamentary Report (IPR).
17. On the Mafia and OSS see Martin Short, *Crime Inc.*, Methuen 1984.
18. See *In Nome Della Loggia*, Gianni Rossi and Francesco Lombrassa, Napoleone 1981.
19. Freemasonry world-wide divides into main camps. The larger considers itself 'regular'. This includes the grand lodges of England, Ireland, Scotland, all Commonwealth states, all 49 grand lodges in the USA, and others in most countries where Freemasonry is tolerated. The smaller camp includes the Grand Orients of France, Belgium and affiliates in many other states. 'Regular' Freemasonry shuns Grand Orient Freemasonry mainly on the grounds that the latter is godless, anti-clerical and political.
20. From 'The Basic Principles of Recognition', listed in the *Constitutions*, UGLE.
21. Stubbs, op. cit.
22. Italian Parliamentary Report, page 12.
23. IPR, page 12.
24. IPR, Salvini quote page 16.
25. IPR, Gelli quote page 16.
26. See note 19.
27. IPR, Gelli quote page 18.
28. UGLE Quarterly Communication, September 1972.
29. Herman and Brodhead, op. cit.
30. As 29 above.
31. UGLE Quarterly Communication, September 1981.
32. IPR, Salvini to Gelli quote page 24.
33. *Masonic Square*, March 1987.
34. IPR, page 72.
35. IPR, page 70.
36. IPR, page 68.
37. IPR, page 76.
38. IPR, page 33.
39. Herman and Brodhead, op. cit.
40. I.e. President of Grand Lodge's Board of General Purposes.
41. Article in *Panorama* magazine, 16 April 1984.
42. As 41 above.
43. My main sources here are J. H. Lepper, 'the Earl of Middlesex and the English Lodge in Florence', *AQC*, vol. 58 (1945); and Mellor, *Our Separated Brethren*.
44. Lepper, op. cit., page 14.
45. As 44 above, page 12.
46. As 44 above, page.
47. As 44 above, page 27.
48. Lepper himself, in *AQC*, page 36.
49. Mellor, *Our Separated Brethren*.
50. See Gurwin, Cornwell op. cit.
51. The Vatican Bank's true title is the 'Instituto per le Opere di Religione'.
52. *The Times*, 1 October 1983.
53. The full story of the Banco Ambrosiano affair is told in Charles Raw's forthcoming book for Collins.
54. There are only too many florid books on the original Knights Templar. For a sober account read Peter Partner, *The Murdered Magicians*, Oxford University Press, 1982, Crucible (Thorsons), 1987.
55. See Martin Short, *Time Out*, 18–25 March 1987.
56. See Martin Short, *Crime Inc.*

CHAPTER THIRTY-FOUR

1. Hugh Dalton, *The Fateful Years*, Muller.
2. *Reading Evening Post*, 14 July 1986.

CHAPTER THIRTY-SIX

1. Secretary J. E. Laughton's report to the DHC, 22 December 1980.
2. As 1 above.
3. Source Commander Higham, letter to the author, 4 October 1988.

CHAPTER THIRTY-SEVEN

1. *Gloucester Citizen*, 2 February 1988.
2. *Kent Evening Post*, 18 June 1987.
3. *Aldershot News and Mail*, 22 March 1988.
4. Quoted in *AQC*, vol. 93 (1980).
5. *Freemasonry and Christianity*, Church House, para 98.
6. Second Degree ritual, quoted in above, para 100.
7. Third Degree ritual, ditto.
8. *The Times Higher Education Supplement*.
9. Higham, *From Craft to Tolerance*, 1 October 1985.
10. *Masonic Year Book* 1987–88, pp. 743–746.
11. UGLE, Quarterly Communication, 9 March 1988.
12. W. L. Wilson, *Daily Telegraph*, 22 June 1987.
13. In a letter to *Church Times*.
14. Quoted in *Masonic Square*, September 1980.
15. *Masonic Year Book* 1987–88, pp. 747–749.
16. *Sunday Express Magazine*, 1 February 1987.
17. The Drake Report.
18. The *Guardian*, 11 February 1987.

CHAPTER THIRTY-NINE

1. Verse from song sung at Ladies' Nights, by A. Ploughman 1833.

2. Song XXI in Preston, op. cit.
3. *Southern Evening Echo*, 26 November 1986.
4. UGLE Quarterly Communication, April 1981.
5. *Sunday Mirror*, 5 October 1980.
6. See *Crime Inc.*

CONCLUSION

1. Cited in *AQC*, vol. 93 (1980), page 47.
2. J. M. Hamill, 'The Earl of Moira', *AQC*, vol. 93, page 34.
3. Preamble to the 1799 Act.
4. Coil's *Encyclopedia*, op. cit. In contrast, Alphonse Cerza denied the role of the St Andrew's Lodge in *AQC*, vol. 98 (1985).
5. Moira in address to Grand Lodge, 3 June 1800, *AQC*, vol. 93.
6. According to A. C. F. Jackson in *AQC*, vol. 93.
7. Harry Mendoza responding to Jackson, in *AQC*, vol. 93, following Mendoza's paper, 'the Articles of Union and the Orders of Chivalry'.
8. *News of the World*, 17 July 1988.
9. Letter from Higham, 25 October 1985.
10. Letter from Higham, 11 July 1986.

INDEX